WORDPERFECT®

COMPLETE TUTORIAL

9

Mary Alice Eisch

Larsen, Wisconsin

VISIT US ON THE INTERNET
www.swep.com
www.thomson.com

South-Western
EDUCATIONAL PUBLISHING
Thomson Learning™

Cincinnati • Albany, NY • Belmont, CA • Bonn • Boston • Detroit • Johannesburg • London • Madrid
Melbourne • Mexico City • New York • Paris • Singapore • Tokyo • Toronto • Washington

Team Leader:	Karen Schmohe
Managing Editor:	Carol Volz
Project Manager:	Anne Noschang
Consulting Editor:	Judith Voiers
Cover and Internal Design:	Grannan Graphic Design, Ltd.
Cover Illustration:	Grannan Graphic Design, Ltd.
Art/Design Coordinator:	Mike Broussard
Manufacturing Coordinator:	Carol Chase
Production Services:	Electro-Publishing

Open a Window to the Future!

How to Use This Book

What makes a good applications text? Sound pedagogy and the most current, complete materials. That is what you will find in the new *WordPerfect® 9 Complete Tutorial*. Not only will you find a colorful, inviting layout, but also many features to enhance learning.

SCANS (Secretary's Commission on Achieving Necessary Skills)–The U.S. Department of Labor has identified the school-to-careers competencies. The five workplace competencies (resources, interpersonal skills, information, systems, and technology) and foundation skills (basic skills, thinking skills, and personal qualities) are identified in the exercises throughout the text. More information on SCANS can be found on the *Electronic Instructor*.

Step-by-Step–The Step-by-Step exercises guide you to mastery of the software.

Notes–These boxes provide necessary information to assist you in completing the exercises.

Objectives– Objectives are listed at the beginning of each lesson, along with a suggested time for completion of the lesson. This allows you to look ahead to what you will be learning and to pace your work.

Enhanced Screen Shots–Screen shots come to life on each page with color and depth.

Tips–These boxes provide enrichment information about WordPerfect features.

Internet–Internet terminology and useful Internet information is provided in these boxes located throughout the text.

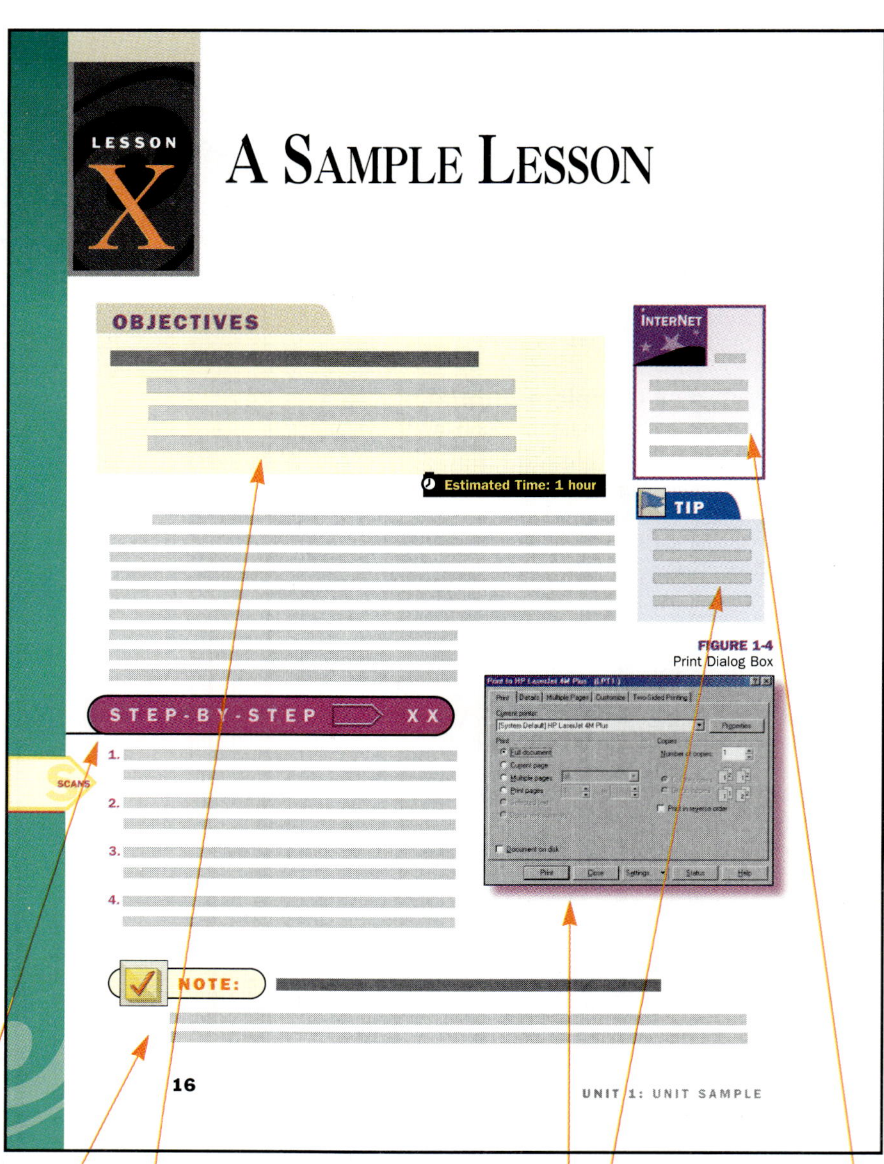

How to Use This Book

Summary–At the end of each lesson you will find a summary to prepare you to complete the end-of-lesson activities.

Review Questions– Review material at the end of each lesson and each unit enables you to prepare for assessment of the content presented.

Lesson Projects– End-of-lesson hands-on application of what has been learned in the lesson allows you to actually apply the techniques covered.

Critical Thinking Activity–Each lesson gives you an opportunity to apply creative analysis to situations presented.

Command Summary– At the end of each unit, a command summary is provided for quick reference.

End-of-Unit Applications–End-of-unit hands-on application of concepts learned in the unit provides opportunity for a comprehensive review.

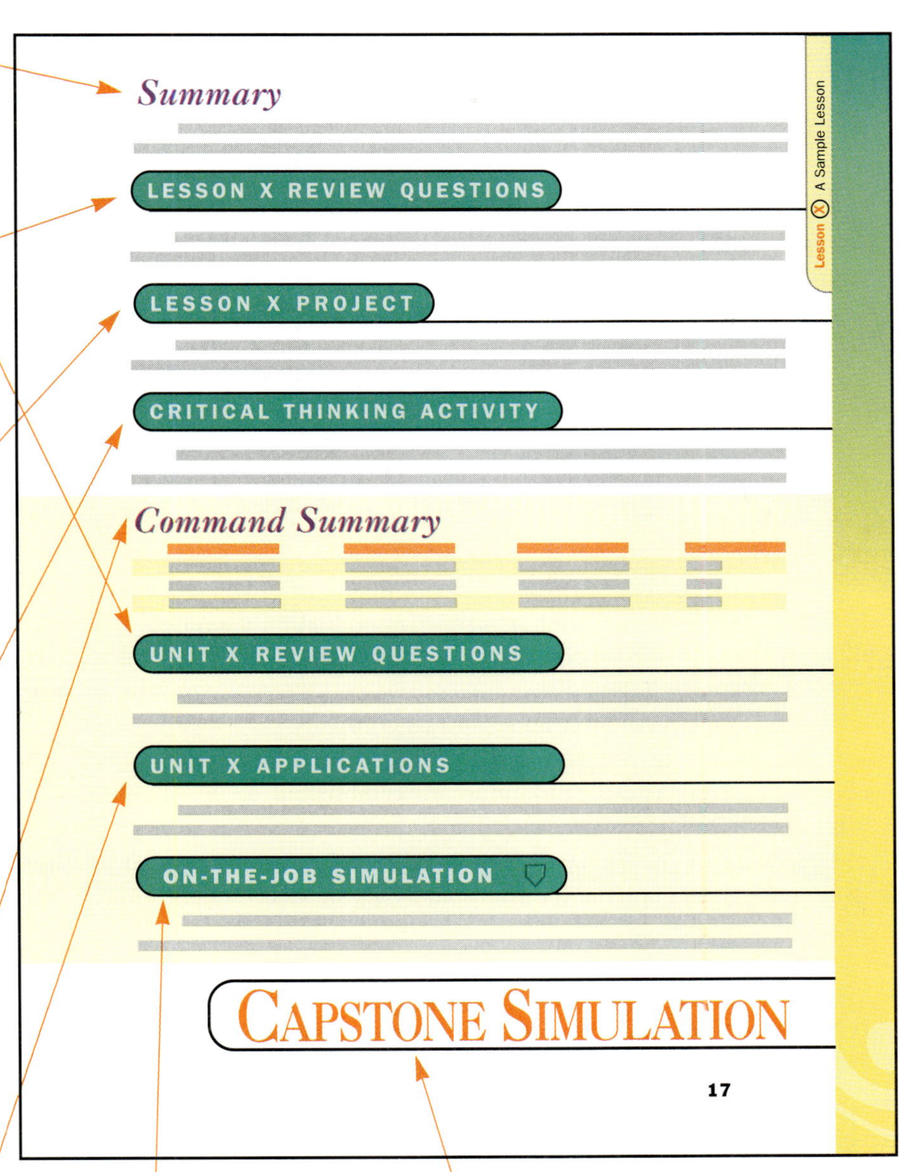

On-the-Job Simulation–A realistic simulation runs throughout the text at the end of each unit, reinforcing the material covered in the unit.

Capstone Simulation–Another simulation appears at the end of the text, to be completed after all the lessons have been covered, to give you an opportunity to apply all of the skills you have learned and see them come together in one application.

PREFACE

To the User

Congratulations on choosing to learn how to use WordPerfect® 9. This comprehensive office productivity program provides one-stop shopping for people needing to develop computer skills for the office. Learning materials for the wide variety of available features are included in this text.

Organization of the Text

Take a few minutes to page through this text. It is divided into units and lessons. Each unit begins with a listing of the lessons in the unit and the estimated time for completion of that unit.

The lessons contain explanatory material about WordPerfect features and tools, along with short step-by-step exercises designed to provide practice using those tools. Each lesson begins with an introduction and list of objectives for the lesson. Each lesson ends with review questions, a hands-on project or two, and a critical thinking activity.

End-of-unit materials include a command summary listing tools learned in the unit, a set of questions to reinforce learning, a series of application exercises, and one or two simulation jobs. The applications review skills acquired in the unit. The on-the-job simulation runs throughout the text, with jobs at the end of each unit. These jobs provide additional review as documents are prepared for Singing Wheels Tours, a local charter and tour bus company.

Together, the lesson and unit activities meet WordPerfect Certification Exam guidelines at the Expert User level. These guidelines are established to ensure thorough preparation for the use of WordPerfect in today's office workplace.

Following the lessons is a comprehensive Capstone Simulation requiring the use of WordPerfect skills to make arrangements for a seminar. This simulation may be included as part of a course or taught as a separate course.

At the back of the text is a set of Quick Reference cards containing an alphabetical listing of all WordPerfect features learned in the text, together with information about how to choose those features from WordPerfect menus or how to access the features from the keyboard.

It is important to proceed through the lessons in order, reading the information provided in the paragraphs carefully to get background information for each of the WordPerfect tools. The Step-by-Step exercises that provide practice in the use of the tools are printed in a different font face and have numbered steps leading through the use of the feature. It is helpful to read completely through an exercise before beginning it, to get a general idea of the purpose of the exercise and then work through the steps methodically.

A suggested time for completion of the lesson is provided at the beginning of each lesson. The actual completion time may vary depending on the following variables:

- previous experience with computers and Windows

- previous experience with WordPerfect

- the learning setting—an independent or instructor-led classroom

Other Resources

A set of prerecorded documents saves keying time in the exercises. These documents are saved in what's referred to in the text as the **datafile** folder. When a prerecorded file is needed, instructions will clearly specify that the file is in the **datafile** folder. (These files are available on the *Electronic Instructor* CD-ROM or in the text/data disk package, ISBN 0-538-69245-6.) Determine the location of the **datafile** files before beginning the lessons.

A Progress Record is located in the opening pages of the text. It lists each document printed in the exercises so the instructor can check off completion of the lessons.

Appendices A through G provide important introductory materials to be covered before beginning Lesson 1.

- Appendix A introduces computer hardware (the equipment).

- Appendix B introduces the WordPerfect working window, starting and exiting from WordPerfect, as well as the basics of creating and saving text.

- Appendix C introduces file management using Windows. File management using WordPerfect is included in the lessons.

- Appendix D introduces the intricacies of using a mouse.

- Appendix G provides important information about the Windows environment.

- A separate Activities Workbook may be purchased. This workbook contains additional hands-on activities grouped by lesson.

The *Electronic Instructor* provides support for the instructor. It contains a variety of instructional materials such as lesson plans for the instructor and learners, tests, prerecorded **datafile** files, solution files, SCANS materials, and much more. Packaged with the *Electronic Instructor* is the printed instructor's manual, which contains hard copy of the solutions as well as answers to the lesson and unit review questions. A separate CD-ROM contains a testing package that generates printed tests to evaluate learner progress.

Welcome to the wonderful world of WordPerfect. You are about to begin an exciting journey through a wealth of tools designed to improve your efficiency and productivity.

Acknowledgments

Special thanks to Judy Voiers, consulting editor on this project, for her friendship, guidance, and inspiration on this project and to Anne Noschang for holding it all together. As always, much appreciation to my family—Achim, Sara, Peter, Bea, and Chester—as well as the little ones who have joined the family—Jacob, Lucas, Afton, and Julia. They keep us young and bring us much joy.

Mary Alice Eisch

TABLE OF CONTENTS

UNIT 1 — GETTING STARTED

UNIT 2 — WORDPERFECT® BASICS

WHAT'S NEW IN WORDPERFECT 9

The WordPerfect 9 software includes the following new features:

- The Power Bar has been replaced with a series of context-sensitive Property Bars to provide the tools needed for the current application.

- The Status Bar has been replaced with the Application Bar which shows, in addition to the usual Status Bar information, the names of all open documents.

- A large number of context-sensitive Toolbars have been added.

- QuickTasks, templates, and Coaches have been combined into a feature called PerfectExpert projects that WordPerfect remembers from one use to another.

- The PerfectExpert panel provides button access to designing and formatting tools.

- The Address Book allows you to enter business and home information about your contacts.

- HTML support has been improved to help with the preparation of Web documents.

- A drawing layer has been added that enables you to draw graphics directly into your text, group the objects, and specify the order of the graphics layers.

- TextArt can be displayed in either 2-D or 3-D format.

- The Bullets & Numbering feature contains full Outline flexibility.

- The Prompt-As-You-Go feature helps you with spelling and grammatical errors and provides help with finding the correct word (thesaurus).

- QuickWords allows you to automate the insertion of frequently used, formatted text.

- The Tables tool includes features that make it easy to split cells and columns and add formatting to your tables as well as skew rows or columns.

- Changes to features such as fonts, columns, borders, tables, and lines can be previewed before they are applied with Real Time Preview.

- More than 100 new shapes are included for drawing objects.

- Block Make It Fit™ enables you to expand or condense text to fit in a defined space.

- Print Preview helps you check document layout before printing.

- Speed Links can be added that enable users to jump to a different part of a document or to a new document.

- Five new navigational controls enable users to browse efficiently in documents of all sizes.

- The Clipart Scrapbook contains tens of thousands of graphics images organized by category.

START-UP CHECKLIST

STANDARD EDITION

Hardware

Minimum Configuration

- ✓ PC using 486 processor operating at 66 MHz
- ✓ 16 MB RAM
- ✓ Hard disk with at least 100 MB free disk space
- ✓ CD-ROM Drive
- ✓ VGA monitor with graphics adaptor
- ✓ Mouse or tablet
- ✓ Printer

Recommended Configuration—same as above except:

- ✓ PC using 486 or Pentium processor operating at 66 MHz (faster preferred)
- ✓ 32 MB RAM
- ✓ 295 MB hard disk space for typical install

Software

- ✓ Microsoft Windows 95, 98, or Windows NT 4.0
- ✓ WordPerfect Office 2000 Standard Edition

VOICE-POWERED AND PROFESSIONAL EDITIONS

Hardware*†‡

Minimum Configuration

- ✓ PC with 133 MHz Pentium processor
- ✓ 48 MB RAM for Windows 95, 64 MB RAM for Windows 98 and Windows NT 4.0
- ✓ 260 MB of hard disk space
- ✓ CD-ROM drive
- ✓ VGA monitor
- ✓ 16-bit sound card or built-in audio output
- ✓ Speaker for sound output
- ✓ Mouse or tablet

Recommended Configuration—same as above except:

- ✓ PC with 200 MHz Pentium processor
- ✓ 380 MB of hard disk space for typical install

Software

- ✓ Microsoft Windows 95, 98, or Windows NT 4.0
- ✓ WordPerfect Office 2000 Voice-Powered Edition

* Contact Dragon Systems or visit **www.naturallyspeaking.com** for an up-to-date list of supported hardware.

† Laptop users may require additional hardware

‡ Owners of portables and IBM-MWave-equipped systems should contact Dragon Systems for compatibility information

PROGRESS RECORD

Name ____

UNIT 1 GETTING STARTED

Lesson		Printed[1]	Score	Date Completed	Instructor
Lesson 1	education 1-2	. . . .	_____	_____________	_____________
	matter proj1a	. . . .	_____	_____________	_____________
	matter proj1b	. . . .	_____	_____________	_____________
	Lesson 1 Quiz	. . . .	_____	_____________	_____________
Lesson 2	foreign 2-7	. . . .	_____	_____________	
	working 2-10	. . . .	_____	_____________	
	nasa proj2	3 pages	_____	_____________	_____________
	Lesson 2 Quiz	. . . .	_____	_____________	_____________
Lesson 3	appearance 3-3	. . . .	_____	_____________	
	appearance 3-4	. . . .	_____	_____________	
	foreign 3-6	. . . .	_____	_____________	
	music 3-8	. . . .	_____	_____________	
	gifts 3-10	. . . .	_____	_____________	
	sasoot 3-11	letter & env.	_____	_____________	
	skeleton proj3	. . . .	_____	_____________	_____________
	Lesson 3 Quiz	. . . .	_____	_____________	_____________
Lesson 4	gifts 4-3	. . . .	_____	_____________	
	seasons 4-4	. . . .	_____	_____________	
	gifts proj4b	. . . .	_____	_____________	_____________
	Lesson 4 Quiz	. . . .	_____	_____________	
	quality u1ap1a	. . . .	_____	_____________	
	quality u1ap1b	. . . .	_____	_____________	
	gifts u1ap2	. . . .	_____	_____________	
	canada u1ap3	. . . .	_____	_____________	
	schedule job1	. . . .	_____	_____________	
	schedule job2	. . . .	_____	_____________	_____________
	Unit 1 Quiz	. . . .	_____	_____________	_____________
	Unit 1 Production Test	. . . .	_____	_____________	_____________

[1]All printed exercises are one page unless otherwise indicated.

		Printed	Score	Date Completed	Instructor
Lesson 9	record 9-2	. . . .	______	______________	
	record 9-3	. . . .	______	______________	
	record 9-4	. . . .	______	______________	
	record 9-5	. . . .	______	______________	
	salad 9-7	. . . .	______	______________	
	hostas 9-8	. . . .	______	______________	
	record 9-9	. . . .	______	______________	
	Mildred 9-10	. . . .	______	______________	
	cheese proj9	. . . .	______	______________	______________
	Lesson 9 Quiz	. . . .	______	______________	______________
Lesson 10	pcug 10-1	. . . .	______	______________	
	pcug 10-2	. . . .	______	______________	
	wind 10-7	2 pages	______	______________	
	wind 10-8	title page	______	______________	
	gifts 10-10	. . . .	______	______________	
	wind 10-11	last page	______	______________	
	footnote 10-12	. . . .	______	______________	
	footnote 10-13	. . . .	______	______________	
	wind 10-15	4 pages	______	______________	
	pc proj10a	2 pages	______	______________	
	pc proj10b	page 2	______	______________	______________
	Lesson 10 Quiz	. . . .	______	______________	______________
Lesson 11	gifts 11-3	. . . .	______	______________	
	char 11-5	. . . .	______	______________	
	pc 11-9	3 pages	______	______________	
	pc 11-10	3 pages	______	______________	
	pcug 11-13	. . . .	______	______________	
	nasa proj11a	3 pages	______	______________	
	nasa proj11b	3 pages	______	______________	______________
	Lesson 11 Quiz	. . . .	______	______________	______________
Lesson 12	pc proj12	3 pages	______	______________	
	Lesson 12 Quiz	. . . .	______	______________	______________
	sasoot u3ap1	2 pages	______	______________	
	lighthouses u3ap2	3 pages	______	______________	
	boxes u3ap3	. . . .	______	______________	
	mall job6	2 pages	______	______________	
	coach job7	2 pages	______	______________	
	Unit 3 Quiz	. . . .	______	______________	______________
	Unit 3 Production Test	. . . .	______	______________	______________

		Printed	Score	Date Completed	Instructor
Lesson 16	berry 16-5	letter & env.	_____	_______________	
	fax 16-8				
	sasoot proj16	2 pages	_____	_______________	_______________
	Lesson 16 Quiz	. . . .	_____	_______________	_______________
	sasoot u4ap1	2 pages	_____	_______________	
	fax form u4ap2	. . . .	_____	_______________	
	release u4ap3	. . . .	_____	_______________	
	online u4ap4	. . . .	_____	_______________	
	schedule job8	. . . .	_____	_______________	
	coach job9	2 pages	_____	_______________	_______________
	coach job10	2 pages	_____	_______________	_______________
	Unit 4 Quiz	. . . .	_____	_______________	_______________
	Unit 4 Production Test	. . . .	_____	_______________	_______________

UNIT 5

MERGE TOOLS

		Printed	Score	Date Completed	Instructor
Lesson 17	micro 17-5	3 letters	_____	_______________	
	micro 17-7	letters 2 & 4	_____	_______________	
	micro 17-8	1 envelope	_____	_______________	
	micro 17-9b	2 letters	_____	_______________	
	referral 17-11	2 referrals	_____	_______________	
	im spec proj17d	3 let. & env.	_____	_______________	_______________
	Lesson 17 Quiz	. . . .	_____	_______________	_______________
Lesson 18	flowers 18-4	. . . .	_____	_______________	
	flowers 18-7	3 let. & env.	_____	_______________	
	accounts 18-8	. . . .	_____	_______________	
	ziepke 18-11	4 letters	_____	_______________	
	reference 18-12	2 pages	_____	_______________	
	interest 18-14	4 letters	_____	_______________	
	ziepke proj18	letters 2 & 4	_____	_______________	
	Lesson 18 Quiz	. . . .	_____	_______________	_______________
Lesson 19	sort 19-3	. . . .	_____	_______________	
	sort 19-5	. . . .	_____	_______________	
	flower list 19-6	2 pages	_____	_______________	
	table 19-10	. . . .	_____	_______________	
	small 19-12	. . . .	_____	_______________	
	im spec proj19c	. . . .	_____	_______________	_______________
	Lesson 19 Quiz	. . . .	_____	_______________	_______________

UNIT 6 — GRAPHICS TOOLS

		Printed	**Score**	**Date Completed**	**Instructor**
Lesson 23	lines 23-2	. . . .	_____	_______________	
	lines 23-3	. . . .	_____	_______________	
	lines 23-4	. . . .	_____	_______________	
	footer 23-5	. . . .	_____	_______________	
	borders 23-6	. . . .	_____	_______________	
	borders 23-8	2 pages	_____	_______________	
	borders 23-10	. . . .	_____	_______________	
	borders 23-11	2 pages	_____	_______________	
	borders 23-12	. . . .	_____	_______________	
	borders 23-13	. . . .	_____	_______________	
	lighthouses proj23a	title page	_____	_______________	
	proj 23b	. . . .	_____	_______________	
	proj 23c	. . . .	_____	_______________	_____________
	Lesson 23 Quiz	. . . .	_____	_______________	_____________
Lesson 24	days 24-1	. . . .	_____	_______________	
	wind 24-5	. . . .	_____	_______________	
	redline 24-6	. . . .	_____	_______________	
	redline 24-7	. . . .	_____	_______________	
	nasa 24-9	2 pages	_____	_______________	
	formula proj24a	. . . .	_____	_______________	
	cheese proj24b	. . . .	_____	_______________	
	nasa proj24c1	. . . .	_____	_______________	
	nasa proj24c2	. . . .	_____	_______________	_____________
	Lesson 24 Quiz	. . . .	_____	_______________	_____________
	beach u6ap1	. . . .	_____	_______________	
	greeting u6ap2	. . . .	_____	_______________	
	tovar u6ap3	. . . .	_____	_______________	
	lighthouses u6ap4	3 pages	_____	_______________	
	new england job16	. . . .	_____	_______________	
	coach job17	2 pages	_____	_______________	
	job18	. . . .	_____	_______________	_____________
	Unit 6 Quiz	. . . .	_____	_______________	_____________
	Unit 6 Production Test	. . . .	_____	_______________	_____________

MORE POWER TOOLS

GETTING STARTED

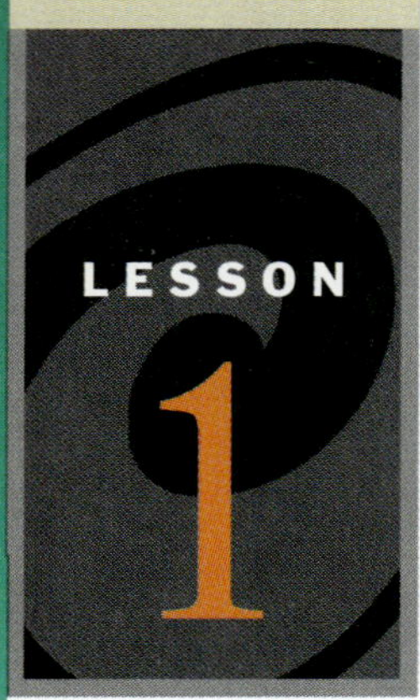

INTRODUCTION TO WORDPERFECT®

You are about to embark on the process of learning to use WordPerfect® 9 to create, save, and modify files (also known as documents). In addition, you will learn many ways to make your work easier, as well as ways to create attractive documents.

The first thing you need is to be good at starting the program, creating text, saving a file, and closing that file. You need to know how to open a file that has been saved, make changes to that file, and then save it again, either with the same name or with a different name.

Before You Begin

If you have never before used a computer, study Appendix A now to get information about the sophisticated piece of equipment you are using.

In addition, if this is your first experience with WordPerfect for Windows, it is imperative that you study the following appendices:

- Appendix B introduces you to the Windows environment and the WordPerfect working window. It includes Step-by-Step exercises to help you learn how to start and exit from WordPerfect and how to create and save text.

- Appendix C is an introduction to file management. Read it. You'll learn more about file management in some of your lessons.

- Appendix D introduces you to the intricacies of using a mouse.

- Appendix G introduces the Windows environment. If you have not had an introduction to the operating system under which WordPerfect 9 runs, read it.

Assuming you are familiar with the material in the appendices, you can begin by starting WordPerfect and creating a document.

Starting WordPerfect

Beginning at the Windows desktop, start WordPerfect using either a shortcut on the desktop or the Start menu. Your instructor may have some special instructions for starting WordPerfect on your computer.

When the WordPerfect window is showing, compare it with Figure B-2 in Appendix B to see if it looks approximately the same. You should see the Title Bar, Menu Bar, Toolbar, Property Bar, Application Bar, vertical scroll bar, and the insertion point at the guidelines in the upper left corner. The Application Bar should report that you are on *Pg 1*, at *Ln 1"* and *Pos 1"*. When your window looks like the window in Figure B-2, you are ready to begin.

Creating Text

Now let's practice creating a document. Follow the steps in the Step-by-Step exercise carefully.

S TEP-BY-STEP ⟹ 1.1

1. Key the paragraph illustrated in Figure 1-1. If you misspell or make an error keying a word, WordPerfect will probably underline the word in red. Don't worry about errors! Do NOT press **Enter** at the ends of the lines.

   Just let your text *wrap* to the next line if it doesn't fit on the line above.

2. When you reach the end of the paragraph, press **Enter** twice and continue reading to learn how to save your first document.

NOTE: **Keep in mind two important things when keying text:**

- When you key text in paragraphs, press **Enter** only at the end of the paragraph or when you purposely want to go to a new line. Allowing the text to wrap to the next line is a very important part of working with computers. If you press **Enter** at the ends of lines within paragraphs, you will cause yourself a great deal of trouble when you try to edit your documents.

- Space twice on the space bar following the punctuation that comes at the end of a sentence. If you are keying work that will be published using desktop publishing or some other electronic method, one space following ending punctuation is preferred. For office work, two spaces are used for readability.

Perhaps more than ever before, American public education is an issue of national concern. Major studies have focused on the weaknesses in our education system. These studies cite statistics that appear to reflect a degeneration of teacher and student performance as well as apathy on the part of parents.

Saving a Document

When you have created a document, the first step is to proofread your work. Then you should save it before printing it. If you are going to continue to work with the document, you may keep it open. Otherwise, you will close the document.

You learned to save a document in Appendix B. This involves giving the document a name and selecting the disk or folder where the document is to be saved. All of this takes place in the Save File dialog box.

When you open the Save File dialog box, the *File name* text box contains **.wpd* which is selected, or displayed in reverse video.

It is best to begin by specifying the location for the document. Then provide the name for the document. Let's save this document on your disk in Drive A. (If your instructor specifies a different location, you will have to make the appropriate adjustments to this Step-by-Step exercise and all of the Step-by-Step exercises that follow.)

For this training, each of your document names will have either three or four parts, with each part separated from the others by a space. The parts will always appear in the same order. You will be asked to include the following:

- A word that briefly describes the subject of the document.

- A set of numbers that identify the lesson and Step-by-Step exercise.

- Two or three letters that represent your initials (shown as *xxx* in the Step-by-Step exercises).

- WordPerfect's default setting adds the *.wpd* extension to all documents saved in WordPerfect 9 format. Usually that extension does not show with the document name, but it is assumed because when the *File name* text box contains **.wpd,* all of your documents will be listed.

Except for very rare instances, the names of the files will always be given to you in the Step-by-Step exercises.

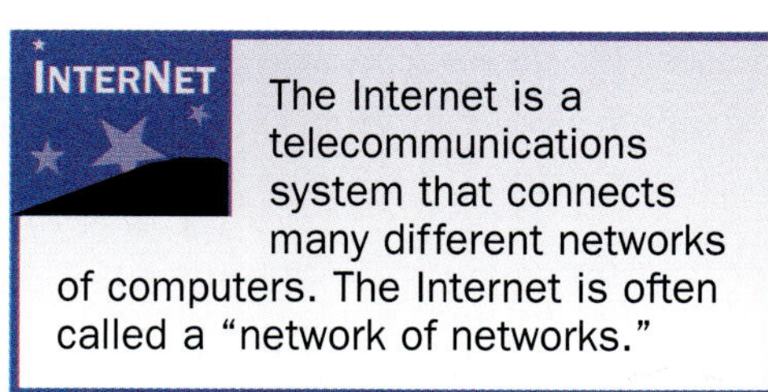

STEP-BY-STEP 1.2

1. Open the **File** menu and choose **Save**. The Save File dialog box will open, looking somewhat like Figure 1-2.

2. In the *Save in* text box near the top of the dialog box, look for *3¹/₂ Floppy (A:)*. If it doesn't already show there, click the arrow at the right end of the text box and select it from the list. (You might need to use the scroll bar.)

3. At the bottom of the box, in the *File name* text box, key **education 1-2 xxx**, replacing the *xxx* with your initials.

4. When everything is appropriately set, press **Enter** or click the **Save** button at the right of the dialog box.

5. Keep the paragraph in the window as you read on.

FIGURE 1-2
Save File Dialog Box

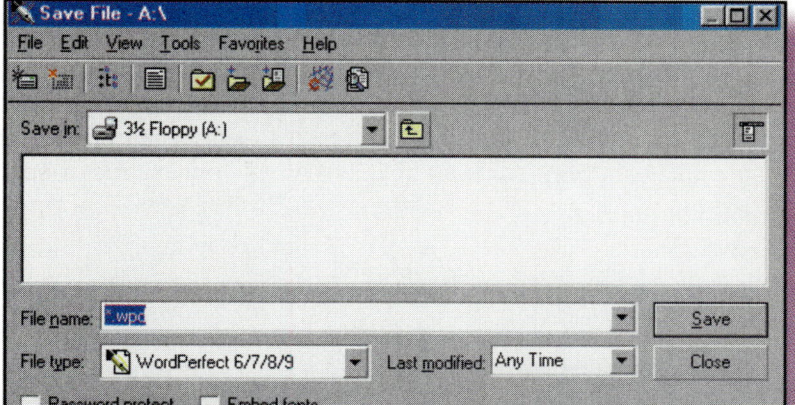

Viewing a Document

When working in WordPerfect 9, you may work in one of three views. These views are described in the following list.

- Draft view   shows the text almost exactly as it will appear when printed. Headers, footers, watermarks, footnotes, and margin spaces do NOT show.

- Page view   shows the text exactly as it will appear when printed. Items such as headers, footers, and watermarks appear as they will on the printed page, and the margin spaces are also displayed in Page view. For now, don't worry if you're not familiar with headers, footers, or watermarks.

- Two Pages view shows the document as it appears in Page view, except two small consecutive pages are displayed side by side in the same document window.

The view you choose for your work depends on what you are doing. If you are formatting headers (information that is repeated at the top of each page) or footers (information that is repeated at the bottom of each page), you will probably want to work in Page view so you can see how the headers or footers appear on the page. Draft view responds more quickly as you move through your document, because time is not required to display headers, footers, and other document parts that appear in Page view. In addition, in Draft view you don't have to look at the bottom and top margin spaces of your pages.

Two Pages view is most useful for checking the layout of your documents before printing. The text is so small in Two Pages view that it would be virtually impossible for you to actually edit normally unless you were working with very large letters.

Zoom

If you need more options regarding how you view your documents, you can use Zoom. Zoom can be chosen from the View menu or from the Toolbar. The Zoom button  on the Toolbar gives you a list of zoom choices from which to select. Choosing Zoom from the View menu opens a dialog box that looks like Figure 1-3. As you can see, the normal viewing percentage is 100 percent, although you can zoom from 25 to 400 percent if you choose Other at the bottom of the right column.

Now that you know about a variety of ways to look at your documents, let's practice some of them.

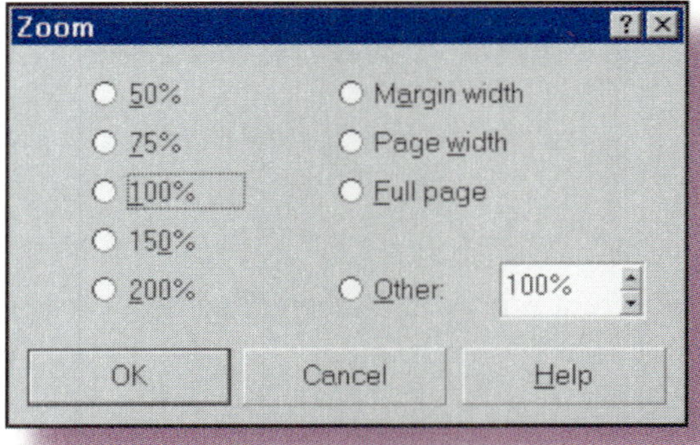

S TEP-BY-STEP 1.3

1. With **education 1-2 xxx** showing in the window, press **Ctrl+Home** to make sure your insertion point is at the top of the document. Can you see about an inch of white space (the top margin) above the top margin guideline? If so, you are in Page view.

2. Open the **View** menu and choose **Draft** to go to Draft view. The top margin should disappear. (Ctrl+F5 also selects Draft view.)

3. Open the **View** menu and choose **Two Pages**. Now you should be able to see side-by-side pages of the document.

4. Open the **View** menu and return to **Page** view. (Alt+F5 also selects Page view.)

5. Click the **Zoom** button on the Toolbar and choose **200%**. Then return to **Zoom** and choose **Full Page**.

6. Finally, use **Zoom** to return to **100%**.

Printing a Document

It is usually a good idea to have a full-page view of your document before printing. You can achieve this by choosing Full Page from the Zoom dialog box or the drop-down menu. Another option is choosing Print Preview from the File menu. Print Preview shows your document without margin guidelines. When you view the whole page, you can see how the text fits on the page. Viewing this paragraph was less interesting than if you were viewing a letter or a heavily formatted document. In future Step-by-Step exercises, you'll see how a longer or fancier document looks using Two Pages view. How you are viewing a document will not affect the way the document looks when it is printed.

Printing in WordPerfect is simple. As with just about anything else you do in WordPerfect, there are a number of ways to print. The method you will probably use the most is to print the full document currently showing in the window.

Print can be chosen from the File menu, the Toolbar, or the Application Bar. On the default Toolbar, the Print button is the fourth button. Whether you choose File, Print, or you click the Print button on the Toolbar or Application Bar, a Print dialog box that looks like Figure 1-4 appears. (You can also choose Print by pressing Ctrl+P.)

Look at the dialog box. At the top you'll see tabs for various print options. Be sure the *Print* tab is chosen. Next you'll see the printer driver for the currently selected printer. If you are working with several printers, you may click the arrow button in the dialog box to change to a different printer before sending the document to be printed.

At the left in the dialog box are buttons enabling you to choose how many of your pages are to be printed. *Full document* is the default setting. When you choose the Print button, your entire document is sent to the printer. This dialog box provides a number of other options. You'll learn about them in a later lesson. For now, let's print the full document.

FIGURE 1-4
Print Dialog Box

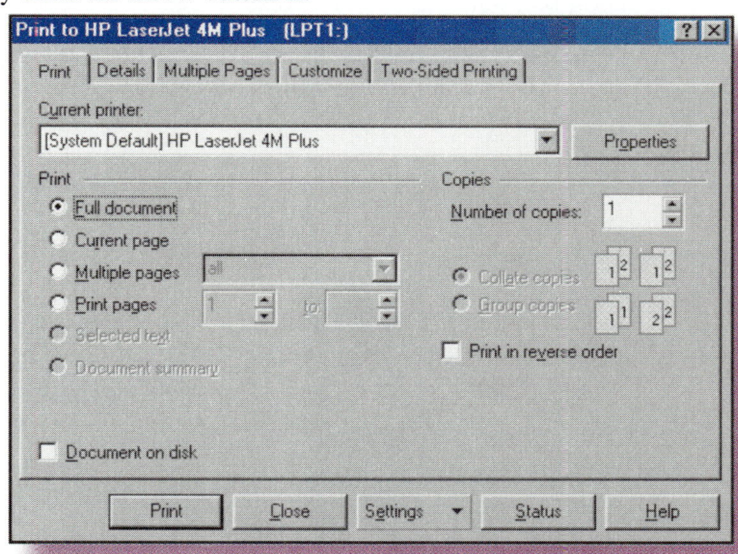

STEP-BY-STEP 1.4

1. With **education 1-2 xxx** still showing in the window, choose **File**, **Print**, or click the **Print** button on the Toolbar or on the Application Bar.

2. Compare your dialog box with the one illustrated in Figure 1-4. Your dialog box may show a different printer driver.

(continued on next page)

3. Make sure the printer described at the top of the box matches the printer to which you are connected. You may need to check with your instructor regarding what you need to know about classroom printers.

4. Finally, when everything is ready, click the **Print** button near the bottom of the dialog box (or press Enter because the Print button is selected).

5. Close your document without saving it again. Then retrieve your printed copy from the printer. Congratulations! You have your first document to take home and put on the refrigerator!

Opening a Document

After a document has been saved and closed, you may open it and edit it. You will learn about editing in Lesson 2. Open can be chosen from the File menu or by clicking the second button on the default Toolbar. (The icon on the Open button looks like a small yellow file folder.) When you make either of those choices, the Open File dialog box will appear, looking much like the Save File dialog box—it displays your disk drives or folders and a list of the files saved in each. You can also display the Open File dialog box by pressing Ctrl+O.

In the next Step-by-Step exercise we'll open the document you just saved and printed and add your name to it. Then we'll learn about Save As so you can save the document with a different name.

STEP-BY-STEP 1.5

1. Open the **File** menu and choose **Open**, or click the **Open** button on the Toolbar.

2. Look at the Open File dialog box. In the *Look in* section at the top, you need to see *3¹/₂ Floppy (A:)* because that is where your work is stored. If a different drive or folder appears, click the down arrow and use the scroll bar, if necessary, so you can select *3¹/₂ Floppy (A:)*.

3. Look in the large white box in the center. Does your **education 1-2 xxx** document appear?
   a. Yes? Click the icon to the left of the document to select the document.
   b. No? Look at the *File name* text box at the bottom. If it shows *.wpd, double

click to select *.wpd and change it to *.* (the asterisks represent all files with all extensions). Press **Enter**. Does the file appear now? Click to select the **education** file.

4. With the desired file highlighted, open the file using one of these three methods. Then keep the file open as you read on.
   a. Point to the file and double click to open the file.
   b. Press **Enter** to open the file.
   c. Click the **Open** button at the bottom right of the dialog box.

With the old document appearing in the window, we'll make a change to the document. Then we'll give it a new name and save it again.

STEP-BY-STEP ▷ 1.6

1. With your insertion point at the top of the document, key your entire name and then press **Enter** three times. (The paragraph is pushed down on the page when you press Enter.)

2. Open the **File** menu and choose **Save As** to display the Save As dialog box. WordPerfect should remember the name of the current file (displayed in the *File name* box near the bottom of the dialog box) and the location of the current file (in the *Save in* box near the top of the dialog box).

3. Click to the right of the *2* in the document name. Backspace once to delete the *2* and replace it with **6**.

4. Click the **Save** button at the bottom right of the window. The document will be saved in the same location but with a different name.

5. Open the **File** menu and choose **Close**. Your document should be closed without any prompts because you had already saved it.

Summary

Congratulations! You've completed your first lesson! In this lesson you learned a number of important things. You learned that:

- Word wrap puts words that don't fit on one line onto the next line.

- You must use the Save File dialog box to name and save files.

- You close documents using the File menu.

- You can view a document in Draft, Page, Two Pages view, or with Print Preview.

- To open a document, you must identify the document and the location of the document.

- Your printer description must match the printer you're using before you print.

- If you close a document that has been modified, WordPerfect will ask if you would like to save it again.

- You can save a document with a different name using Save As.

The skills learned in this lesson will be used many times throughout your training. If you have any questions about anything covered in this lesson, ask your instructor to help you with it before you go on to Lesson 2. Before you do that, however, it is time to review your skills with the Lesson 1 Project.

At the end of each lesson is a short project to review the skills learned in the lesson. As you complete each of the projects, work carefully and thoughtfully. See how much you can do on your own—without having to look back in the lessons for help.

TRUE/FALSE

Circle the T if the statement is true. Circle the F if it is false.

T   F   1. When you are keying text, you do not need to press Enter at the end of each line because your text will automatically wrap to the next line.

T   F   2. To save a document for the first time, you must first name your document and then open the Save File dialog box.

T   F   3. When working in WordPerfect 9, you may work in one of four views.

T   F   4. You can choose Zoom from the View menu or press the Zoom button on the Toolbar.

T   F   5. How you view a document will affect the way a document looks when it is printed.

T   F   6. The icon on the Open button looks like an opening file folder.

WRITTEN QUESTIONS

Write your answers to the following questions.

7. When you start WordPerfect, name at least four features you see in your window.

8. What does the Application Bar indicate as your position when you start WordPerfect?

9. To what location have you been instructed to save your documents?

10. What are the four ways you can choose Print?

LESSON 1 PROJECT

SCANS

1. Key the paragraph in Figure 1-5. Remember to let the text wrap at the ends of the lines.

2. At the end of the paragraph, press **Enter** two times. This leaves a double space between the paragraph and any text that might follow it.

3. When you finish, save the document as **matter proj1a xxx**.

4. Print your paragraph.

5. Close the document.

Everything in the universe is made up of matter. This includes all living things, from amebas to whales, from the smallest bacteria to giant sequoias. Matter is anything that occupies space and has mass. Mass is the quantity of matter held by an object. The pull of gravity on the mass of an object gives the object weight.

6. Beginning in a new document window, open **matter proj1a xxx**.

7. Key your name at the top and press **Enter** four times to separate your name from the paragraph.

8. Use **Save As** to save the document again, this time as **matter proj1b xxx**.

9. Print the new version of the document and close it.

CRITICAL THINKING ACTIVITY

You are beginning to realize how useful WordPerfect is going to be to you in many ways, especially in completing your school assignments for all your other courses. Think about how you will start naming the documents you will be preparing and make a list of possible names you will give them. Make sure you develop a system that will be easy for you to use and remember.

MOVING THE INSERTION POINT AND CORRECTING TEXT

OBJECTIVES

Upon completion of this lesson, you will be able to:

- Move the insertion point using several methods.
- Delete text using several methods.
- Insert text into existing documents.
- Insert the Path and Filename code into your documents.
- Use Typeover to replace old text with new text.
- Select text for deletion.
- Use Undo and Redo.
- Use the Reveal Codes feature to help you with editing.

Estimated Time: 1½ hours

Editing in WordPerfect is accomplished by moving the insertion point, using the Backspace and Delete keys in a combination of ways, and inserting new material. In this lesson you will learn how to do simple editing, and you'll have several little Step-by-Step exercises for practice.

Don't try to learn everything at once. Read the material carefully. Work through the Step-by-Step exercises. Make a note of the fact that Lesson 2 is a place you can return to for review later when some of these features may have more meaning. To get the feel of the various keys and features as you study this lesson, you should have some text showing in the window. We'll use a practice document that has been prepared and saved in the student **datafile** folder for you. To open this file, you must know where the data files are saved and how to access them. Your instructor may need to help you open this first file from the student **datafile** folder.

S TEP-BY-STEP 2.1

1. Open the **File** menu and choose **Open**.

2. Check the *Look in* text box to see if the student **datafile** folder is displayed. If it is not, click the arrow beside the text box and move to the folder containing the data files.

3. Locate the file named **nasa** and open the file, using one of the methods you learned in Lesson 1.

4. When the document appears in your window, open the **File** menu and choose **Save As**.

5. Change the name of the file to **nasa 2-1 xxx**, where *xxx* represents your own initials. For example, if your name is Sara Anne Stewdent, the file name will be **nasa 2-1 sas**. Choose **Save** or press **Enter**.

6. Open the **View** menu and choose **Two Pages** to see how a multiple-page document looks in Two Pages view.

7. Change back to **Page** view, and keep the document in the window as you read on.

Moving the Insertion Point

In order to edit your documents, you need to move the insertion point to the point of correction. WordPerfect offers you a number of ways to move the insertion point in your document. You can move the insertion point with the keys on the keyboard, or you can move the insertion point with the mouse. Let's look at both methods.

Using the Keyboard

THE ARROW KEYS

The up, down, right, and left arrow keys on your keyboard can be used to move the insertion point a line or a space at a time. If Num Lock is turned off, the Number Pad keys 8 and 2 move your insertion point up and down a line at a time. Number Pad keys 4 and 6 move your insertion point left and right a space at a time.

In the set of keys beside Enter and Backspace are four more keys useful for moving the insertion point.

- **Page Up** moves your insertion point backward through your text a full window at a time.

- **Page Down** moves your insertion point forward through your text a full window at a time.

- **Home** moves your insertion point to the beginning of the line on which it is currently located.

- **End** moves your insertion point to the end of the line.

In addition to these single keystrokes for moving the insertion point, a number of keystroke combinations can be used to move from one place on a page of type to another place. Figure 2-1 lists a number of these combinations. The plus between the keystrokes indicates that the first key is held while the other is pressed. For example, with Ctrl+Home, you hold Ctrl while you press Home. This combination always takes your insertion point to the beginning of the document.

1. Press **Ctrl+End** to move your insertion point to the end of the document. Look at the *Pg* indicator on the Application Bar. It should report that you are on page 3 of the document.

2. Press **Ctrl+G** and key **3** in the *Page number* text box. Click **OK**. Your insertion point should be moved to the top of the third page.

3. Change to **Two Pages** view and go to the end of the document with **Ctrl+End**.

4. Press **Alt+Page Up** twice to return to the beginning of the document.

5. Return to **Page** view and practice all of the keystrokes in Figure 2-1.

6. When you are comfortable with these keystrokes, move the insertion point to the beginning of page 1 and read on.

FIGURE 2-1
Keystrokes for Moving the Insertion Point

End	moves to the end of the line		Ctrl+→	moves one word to the right
Home	moves to the beginning of the line		Ctrl+←	moves one word to the left
Page Up	moves to the top of the window		Ctrl+↑	moves up one paragraph
			Ctrl+↓	moves down one paragraph
Page Down	moves to the bottom of the window		Alt+Page Up	moves to the first line on the previous page
Ctrl+Home	moves to the beginning of the document		Alt+Page Down	moves to the first line on the next page
Ctrl+End	moves to the end of the document		Ctrl+G	Go To enables you to move to a specific page.

Using the Mouse

Click to Position. You can position the insertion point by positioning it and clicking the left mouse button. If the desired location doesn't show in the window, you can use the scroll bars to move forward or backward in the document to find the location. Then point and click to position the insertion point.

Scroll Bars. Look at the vertical scroll bar at the right of your window. It has an arrow at the top and an arrow at the bottom. Between the arrows is a box that indicates how far through a document you are. When the box is at the bottom of the bar, you are looking at the bottom of the document—regardless of the length of the document. When the box is at the top of the bar, you are looking at the top of the document. (A horizontal scroll bar is available, if needed. Sometimes it needs to be chosen to be displayed.)

When you move around in a document using the keyboard or the *Browse by...* buttons, the insertion point goes along. When you use the scroll bar and Autoscroll, the insertion point remains in its original position until you click to reposition it.

1 4

Autoscroll. The Autoscroll tool enables you to use your mouse to scroll rapidly through your text. This tool is chosen from the Toolbar, and it remains active until you click into your document. You can control the speed of scrolling with Autoscroll. The closer the Autoscroll icon is to the center of the window, the slower it will scroll. The closer the icon is to the top or bottom of the window, the faster it will scroll.

Browse Buttons. The three buttons at the bottom of the scroll bar enable you to browse through your document using one of eight different criteria—tables, footnotes, comments, page, etc. The default is page. You should see the tiny page image on that middle button now.

Reposition Arrows. At the right of the WordPerfect 9 default Toolbar are two blue arrows used for repositioning the insertion point. The blue arrow pointing to the left will move your insertion point to its former position. If you click it a second time, it will move the insertion point to the position before that one. The arrow pointing to the right moves the insertion point to the next position. Depending on the size of your screen, those blue arrows might not be showing in your window because the Toolbar contains too many buttons. If they don't show, a tiny scroll bar at the right of the Toolbar should take you to them.

Let's try all of these tools and move through your document with the mouse.

S TEP-BY-STEP ▷ 2.3

1. With the insertion point at the top of your document, point to the scroll box and drag it to the bottom of the bar. You should see the white space at the bottom of page 3.

2. Touch the right arrow key on the keyboard. You will be returned to the top of the document because the insertion point remained at that point when you used the scroll bar.

3. Click below the scroll box as many times as necessary until you can see the white space at the bottom of the document again. Note that each time you click, you are seeing the next consecutive windowful of information. Note the page breaks.

4. Look at the Application Bar. It should report that your insertion point is still at the beginning of the document. Click above the box as many times as necessary to return to the beginning of the document.

5. Click the **Autoscroll** button on the Toolbar. Your mouse pointer will look much like the icon on the button. Without clicking in the document, experiment with fast scrolling (pointer near the top or bottom of the window) and slow scrolling (pointer near the middle of the window). Click at the end of the side heading *Insulin Infusion Pump*. Look at the Application Bar. It should now report that you are about 7" from the top of page 2.

6. Point to the button between the two buttons with double arrows at the bottom of the vertical scroll bar. The Quick Tip should tell you that you are browsing by *page*. Click the button as many times as necessary to return to *Browse by page*, looking at the Quick Tip for each choice.

7. Click the double arrow pointing up to return to the first page. Note that the insertion point moved along and is now positioned at the beginning of the page.

(continued on next page)

8. Click the double arrow pointing down twice to move the insertion point to the end of the text in the document.

9. Locate the reposition arrows on the Toolbar. Click the arrow pointing to the left. Your insertion point should be moved to its previous position. Click that same arrow to move to the next previous position. Now click the right arrow to return to the position where you just were.

10. Practice moving around in the document using the scroll bar, Autoscroll, the browse buttons, and the reposition arrows. Then keep the document open as you read on.

When using the mouse to position the insertion point at the beginning of a line, MAKE SURE THE INSERTION POINT LOOKS LIKE A LARGE "I" BEFORE YOU CLICK. If a crossbar tool appears, WordPerfect will think you want to adjust the margin. If a fat white arrow is pointing to the right, clicking will tell WordPerfect to select the entire sentence. When selected, the sentence will be displayed in reverse video (white letters on a black background). If that happens, click in that black area to deselect the line and try again.

Inserting Text

It is very easy to insert letters, spaces, and words into text that has already been keyed. To do this, simply position the insertion point at the point immediately following the location for the added material and key the new text. Let's try it. (Are you remembering to read all the way through each Step-by-Step exercise before beginning it?)

STEP-BY-STEP ⟹ 2.4

1. With **nasa 2-1 xxx** showing in the window, use **Save As** to save your file as **nasa 2-4 xxx**, remembering to replace *xxx* with your initials.

2. Check to be sure the word *Typeover* isn't showing in the Application Bar. If it is, turn it off by pressing the **Insert** key.

3. Position the insertion point at the end of the word *Administration* in the first line of the first paragraph of the document.

4. Space once and key **(NASA)**. Include the parentheses. Check the spacing around the added text.

5. Position your insertion point between the word *disasters* and the period at the end of the *Weather Forecasting* paragraph. Space once and key **such as hurricanes**. Check the spacing around the added text.

6. Save the document again with the same name. Keep it open while you learn to delete text.

1 6

Deleting Text

Text can be deleted with either the Backspace key or the Delete key. Figure 2-2 lists the delete keystrokes and how they may be used in WordPerfect.

FIGURE 2-2
Delete Keystrokes

Backspace removes text to the left of the insertion point, one character or space at a time. Hold down this key to delete several characters quickly. The text to the right of the insertion point will shift to the left to close up the space as you press the Backspace key.

Del and **Delete** are used to delete characters following the insertion point. Again, if you hold the key down, characters will be deleted as they scroll in from the right.

Ctrl+Backspace deletes the word in which the insertion point is located. If you hold the Ctrl key and press Backspace several times, you will delete several consecutive words.

Ctrl+Delete deletes from the insertion point to the end of the line.

STEP-BY-STEP 2.5

1. Working with the document you have in your window, try each of the four delete methods listed in Figure 2-2.

2. Watch what happens as you use each method of deletion. Don't worry about destroying the document.

3. When you finish, open the **File** menu and choose **Close**. Do NOT save the changes to the document.

TIP

If you do something you didn't really mean to do, you can undo it with Ctrl+Z. You must do this immediately.

Now that you know how to insert and delete text, let's make corrections to a document that was keyed and saved with lots of errors. As you will see when the document is open, WordPerfect underlines in red words that might be misspelled. A quick way of correcting those underlined words is available. Because you are learning to insert and delete text, however, you should make the corrections to this paragraph manually. (When each word is correctly spelled, the red line will disappear.)

S TEP-BY-STEP ▷ 2.6

1. Beginning in a new document window, go to the student **datafile** folder and open the document named **foreign**. Use **Save As** to save the file with your documents using **foreign 2-6 xxx** as the name, substituting your initials for *xxx* in the file name.

2. Comparing the document in your window with the copy in Figure 2-3, manually correct the spelling in the words that are displayed in bold.

3. When you finish, keep the document open in the window and read on.

FIGURE 2-3
Text for Step-by-Step 2.6

An **increasing** number of American companies are doing **business** with overseas **companies**. **Most** Americans are at a **disadvantage** in foreign business **negotiations** because we are ignorant of **their cultural differences** and **value systems**. In many cases, **foreign** business people have all the power **because** they have studied our **culture** and our language.

Path and Filename Code

WordPerfect provides an easy way for you to identify your documents. You can tell the program to insert the file path and file name with the insertion of a simple code. Let's add the code to the document that's open in the window.

S TEP-BY-STEP ▷ 2.7

1. Use **Save As** and the procedure in this step to save the file as **foreign 2-7 xxx**, remembering as always to replace *xxx* with your initials. (The Save As procedure listed in Steps a-c saves much unnecessary keying.)

  a. In the *File name* box near the bottom of the Save File dialog box, click the insertion point next to the character to be changed—in this case, the *6*.

  b. Delete the number with either **Backspace** or **Delete**—depending on the location of your insertion point.

  c. Then key **7** in its place. Click **Save**.

2. Move the insertion point to the end of the document and press **Enter** twice.

3. Open the **Insert** menu and choose **Other**. In the cascading menu, choose **Path and Filename**.

4. Look at the information that was added to your document. Note that it was added at the location of the insertion point.

5. Print your file. Then close it, saving it again as you close.

Typeover

While it isn't exactly a delete function, *Typeover* is used to key new text over existing text. You can turn Typeover on by pressing Ins, or Insert. (That may seem backwards, but remember that the Insert mode is the default in WordPerfect.) When you press Insert, the word *Typeover* appears just to the right of center on the Application Bar at the bottom of the window.

When you've made your correction and press Insert again, you return to the Insert mode and the word *Insert* reappears at the bottom of the window. Don't leave Typeover on when you are formatting your documents. Typeover may give you some results that are quite different from what you expect. Let's try a quick practice with Typeover.

S TEP-BY-STEP ⇒ 2.8

1. Key the following sentence:

The dog jumped over the moon and the cat laughed.

2. Position the insertion point to the left of the *d* in *dog*. Press **Insert** and key **cow**.

3. Move the insertion point to the *c* in *cat* and key **dog**. Press **Insert** to return to Insert mode.

4. Close the practice Step-by-Step exercise without saving it.

Select

Text can also be deleted by first *blocking,* or *selecting,* it. When text is selected, it shows in reverse video (white on a black background). WordPerfect provides several ways to select text. Once text is selected, you can delete it with either the Delete or Backspace key.

You can select text with the keyboard or mouse in the following ways:

■ Position the insertion point at one end of the text to select, press F8, and use the arrow keys to extend the selection to the desired ending point.

■ Click to position the insertion point at the beginning of the text to be selected. Hold the Shift key while you click at the end of the selection.

■ Position the mouse pointer at the beginning of the text to select, depress and hold the left mouse button, and drag the pointer to the end of the desired text.

If you make a mistake in selecting text and you still have the mouse button pressed, you can move the pointer around until the correct text is selected. If you have already released the button with the incorrect text selected, you can deselect the text by clicking the left mouse button and beginning again.

The following QuickSelect options are available with the mouse:

■ **Word**. Select a word by pointing to it and double clicking.

■ **Sentence**. Select a sentence by pointing to it and triple clicking.

■ **Sentence**. Point in the left margin opposite the sentence and click once.

- **Paragraph**. Select a paragraph by pointing to it and quadruple clicking.

- **Paragraph**. Point in the left margin opposite the paragraph and click twice.

S TEP-BY-STEP 2.9

1. Open **education 1-2 xxx**. Point to the word *American* in the first line. Double click to select it.

2. Click once to deselect the word.

3. Point to the word *American* again and double click to select it. Press either **Backspace** or **Delete** to delete the word.

4. For practice, point to the last sentence and triple click to select that sentence. Click to deselect it. Then triple click to select it again and delete it.

5. Finally, point anywhere in the paragraph and quadruple click to select it. Deselect it by clicking once.

6. Close the document without saving it.

Undo and Redo

WordPerfect helps you fix certain kinds of mistakes you might make.

Undo (from the Edit menu, the Toolbar, or Ctrl+Z). You can reverse the last change you made to your document by choosing Undo from the Edit menu or by pressing Ctrl+Z. For example, if you have deleted text from your document and moved the insertion point to a different location, you can use Undo to put the text back in the original location. Undo must be used immediately.

Redo (from the Edit menu, the Toolbar, or Ctrl+Shift+Z). You can reverse the last Undo action by choosing Redo. To see a "history" of your edits using Undo and Redo, choose Undo/Redo History from the Edit menu. WordPerfect will display a list of up to 300 edits in a document. You can reverse several revisions at a time.

Although it is normally not recommended because of the amount of disk space it might take, you can choose to save Undo/Redo items with your documents. To do so, open the Edit menu, choose Undo/Redo History, choose Options, and click the check box. You will have plenty of opportunities to practice Undo and Redo.

- As you key the paragraphs in Step-by-Step exercise 2.10, you may notice that some words are underlined in red and that some of your errors are automatically corrected. Two WordPerfect features that you'll learn about later are responsible for this. Don't worry about it for now.

STEP-BY-STEP ▷ 2.10

1. Key the paragraphs illustrated in Figure 2-4. Press **Enter** twice following the first paragraph.

2. Choose **Save** from the **File** menu.

3. Save the document as **working 2-10 xxx**, replacing *xxx* with your initials.

4. Press **Enter** twice at the bottom of the document. Then open the **Insert** menu and choose **Other**. Choose **Path and Filename** to identify your file.

5. Choose **Save** from the **File** menu to save the document again.

6. Print the document. Then keep it open for the next Step-by-Step exercise.

FIGURE 2-4
Text for Step-by-Step 2.10

```
When you key a document on the computer, key carefully so you don't
make many mistakes.  Most people can "feel" a mistake when they make
it.  Learn to press the Backspace key by touch to correct your errors
as you proceed.

Develop the habit of proofreading all of your work while it is showing
in the window.  At the same time, you might also decide to do some
editing.  Use the skills you learned in this section to move around in
your work quickly and efficiently.
```

Now let's practice using different methods of deleting text and putting the deleted text back into your document. Follow along carefully.

The Internet is not a single network, but a super network made up of thousands of smaller networks.

STEP-BY-STEP ▷ 2.11

1. Point to the word *proofreading* in the first line of the second paragraph. Double click to select it and press **Delete** or **Backspace** to delete it.

2. Press **Ctrl+Z** (Undo). The text will be replaced. Press **Ctrl+Shift+Z** (Redo). The text will be removed again. Replace it once more with **Ctrl+Z**.

3. Press **Enter** six times after the word *proofreading*. Remove those six lines by clicking **Undo** on the Toolbar.

4. Replace the six lines by clicking **Redo** on the Toolbar.

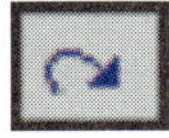

(continued on next page)

5. Use the mouse to select the six blank lines and delete them. Then open the **Edit** menu and choose **Undo** to replace the lines. Use **Redo** from the **Edit** menu to remove the lines a final time.

6. Use the mouse to select any three words in the paragraph. Delete them. Use any method of Undo to replace the words in the paragraph.

7. Click once to position the insertion point in any word of the paragraph. Watch the window as you press **Ctrl+Backspace** twice to delete that word and the following one. (This is a method of deletion you used earlier in the lesson.)

8. Practice a little more on these paragraphs. Then close the document without saving. It is probably a mess, anyhow.

Reveal Codes

Hidden behind the characters of any word processing text are codes for bold, tab changes, center, temporary margins, etc. In WordPerfect you can see the entire text, including the codes, with the Reveal Codes feature. *Codes* are revealed by pressing Alt+F3 or by choosing Reveal Codes from the View menu. When your codes are revealed, the window is split with a gray section at the bottom, as illustrated in Figure 2-5.

The text at the top is separated from the text at the bottom with a double line. The text below the line contains formatting codes, with the codes in boxes that look like buttons.

When you move the insertion point in your document (in the top portion of the window), the insertion point moves in the Reveal Codes view of the document. The insertion point in Reveal Codes is a small red box. Let's work with Reveal Codes.

FIGURE 2-5
Document with Codes Revealed

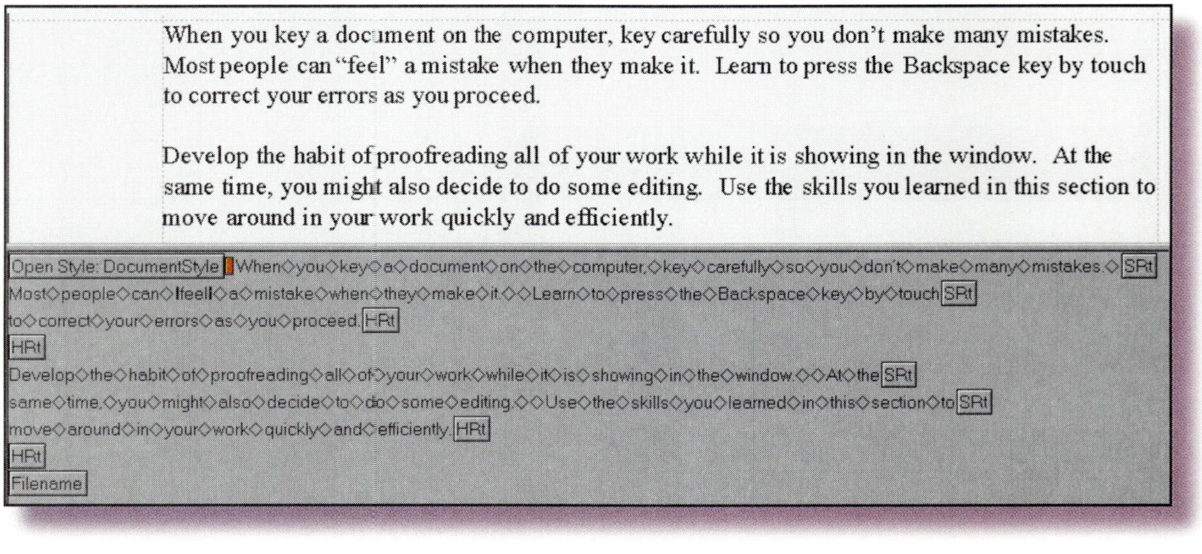

STEP-BY-STEP ⟩ 2.12

1. Open **working 2-10 xxx** again. With the insertion point at the top of the document, choose **Reveal Codes** from the **View** menu, or press **Alt+F3** to reveal your codes.

2. Look at the text in Reveal Codes. The document code [Open Style: DocumentStyle] appears at the beginning of each document. Notice that a diamond character appears between each of the words of text, representing the spaces you keyed.

3. Use → to move the insertion point a few characters to the right. Watch the insertion point in both windows as you do this.

4. Look at the [SRt] codes at the ends of the lines. These are the returns that WordPerfect puts at the end of each line when text is wrapped to the next line. These are called *soft returns.*

5. Look at the two *Hard Return* [HRt] codes between the two paragraphs. A Hard Return code is put into your text each time you press **Enter**.

6. Using the form in Appendix E, begin a list of the codes you've seen in your documents. (So far you have seen only the [Open Style: DocumentStyle], [Filename], [SRt], and [HRt] codes.)

7. Close the Reveal Codes window by choosing **Reveal Codes** from the **View** menu or by pressing **Alt+F3**. Then close the document. If you are asked about saving it again, choose **No**.

You can also reveal your codes by pointing to the tiny button at the bottom of the scroll bar and dragging the top of the Reveal Codes window to the desired position. That two-headed arrow can also be used to size the Reveal Codes window after Reveal Codes is displayed.

Because the use of Reveal Codes is so important to the editing of your documents, you will be using this feature regularly. Most of the codes are easy to figure out. While you don't need to memorize the codes, you should make a conscious effort to learn to work with them.

Summary

In this lesson you learned the important skills of moving through your document and editing it. For example, you learned that:

■ There are a number of different ways to move the insertion point from one location to another in your document.

■ The Path and Filename code identifies a document and its location on your disk.

■ You can use QuickSelect options to select chunks of text of varying sizes.

■ Text can be deleted using a variety of methods.

■ You can insert text by positioning the insertion point and keying.

- You can replace text by using Typeover.

- Reveal Codes helps you to see how your document is formatted.

LESSON 2 REVIEW QUESTIONS

MULTIPLE CHOICE

Circle the best answer to each of the following statements.

1. To move your insertion point to the end of the document, press
   - **A.** End.
   - **B.** Page Down.
   - **C.** Ctrl+End.
   - **D.** Ctrl+Alt.

2. You can delete from the insertion point to the end of the line with the _______ keystroke combination.
   - **A.** Ctrl+Backspace
   - **B.** Ctrl+Delete
   - **C.** Ctrl+End
   - **D.** Ctrl+Alt

3. The Delete key deletes _________ at the insertion point.
   - **A.** characters
   - **B.** words
   - **C.** sentences
   - **D.** lines

4. The QuickSelect option allows you to select a sentence by pointing to it and
   - **A.** double clicking.
   - **B.** triple clicking.
   - **C.** quadruple clicking.
   - **D.** clicking once.

5. You can reverse the last change you made to a document by choosing _______ from the Edit menu.
   - **A.** Undo
   - **B.** Redo
   - **C.** Undelete
   - **D.** Reverse

MATCHING

Write the letter of the term or phrase from Column 2 that best matches the description in Column 1.

Column 1

____ **6.** Used to reverse a change made with Undo.

____ **7.** Used to key new text over existing text.

____ **8.** Used when text shows in reverse video.

____ **9.** Used to see the entire text, including the codes.

____ **10.** Used by pressing Ctrl+Z.

Column 2

A. Typeover

B. Undo

C. Restore

D. Reveal Codes

E. Redo

F. Insert

G. Select

H. Path and Filename Code

LESSON 2 PROJECT

Let's review some of the skills you learned in Lesson 2. We'll work with a document you used in this lesson.

1. Open **nasa 2-4 xxx**. Use **Save As** to save the file as **nasa proj2 xxx**.

2. Press **Ctrl+End** to move the insertion point to the end of the document. Press **Enter**, if necessary, to add blank lines so you can position your insertion point a double space below the last line of text.

3. Insert the Path and Filename code.

4. Select and delete the paragraph that tells about MRI equipment.

5. Select and delete the side heading for the paragraph you just deleted.

6. Click **Undo** on the Toolbar twice to put the side heading and the paragraph back into your document.

7. Move to the section about *Scratch-Resistant Glasses*. Delete the words *visibility-reducing* in the last line of the sentence. At the end of the sentence, add the words **that reduce visibility for the wearer.**

8. Move to the section about *Flame-Resistant Materials*. In the second line of the second paragraph, insert the word **have** between the words *cable* and *spread*.

9. Save the document again with the same name. (You can do this by simply clicking the Save button on the Toolbar.)

10. Print the document and close it.

CRITICAL THINKING ACTIVITY

You have just come into class and turned on your computer. As soon as you start WordPerfect, you open a document that you worked on yesterday and begin keying new material to add to the first paragraph.

Instead of the new text being added, you see that it is replacing the old text. Determine what is causing this problem and what you can do about it.

TEXT ENHANCEMENT

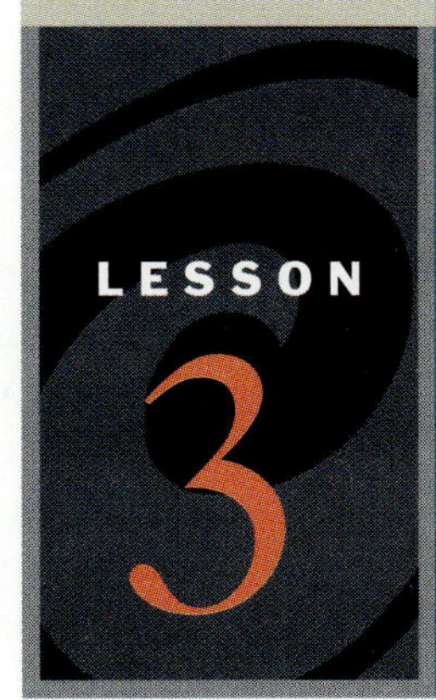

Often when you are creating a document, you need a way to make a word or two, or fifteen, stand out from the remainder of the text. You must be careful when you do this so that you don't have so many words "standing out" that the formatting is distracting and the text is difficult to read. With that warning in mind, let's look at some of the ways you can enhance the words in your documents to give them emphasis.

Caps Lock, Underline, Bold, and Italic

Caps Lock, Underline, Bold, and Italic are tools you'll use in your work to add interest to your documents. Except for Caps Lock, these formatting tools can be chosen in a variety of ways. In the section below you'll learn only one method—one that is easy to remember. You'll learn about some of the alternate methods shortly. Don't worry about them for now.

All of these formatting tools must be turned on at the beginning of the text to be formatted. After you have keyed the text, the format must be turned off—usually the same way it was turned on.

Caps Lock. Find the Caps Lock key on your keyboard. The Caps Lock key, as well as the AB button on the Application Bar may be used to tell WordPerfect you want all letters keyed to be capitals. On most keyboards, a light tells you when you have Caps Lock turned on. The AB button also appears to be depressed when Caps Lock is on. Caps Lock affects only alphabetic keys. It doesn't enable you to key symbols, such as $, #, or %. The use of Caps Lock does NOT put any codes in your documents.

Underline. An easy way to turn Underline on is to hold the Ctrl key while you press U. When you have Underline on, your text will be underlined as you key it. To stop underlining, press Ctrl+U again. The Underline code is [Und].

Bold. Press Ctrl+B for bold. When Bold is turned on, any text you key will show in bold. Bold is turned off the same way you turned it on—by pressing Ctrl+B. The Bold code is [Bold].

Italic. Italic can be turned on and off with Ctrl+I. Any text you key while Italic is turned on will appear in italic. The code for italic is [Italc].

S TEP-BY-STEP ⟹ 3.1

1. Press the **Caps Lock** key and key your name. Don't worry if a red underline appears. Press **Caps Lock** again to turn it off, and press **Enter** two times.

2. Save your Step-by-Step exercise as **appearance 3-1 xxx**.

3. Key your name again in all lowercase letters. Choose **Reveal Codes** from the **View** menu and note that there is no code for capital letters.

4. Press **Enter** twice. (Keep your codes revealed so you can see them as you add to this document.)

5. Press **Ctrl+U** to turn on Underline. Key your name using "initial caps" (that's a capital letter at the beginning of each "word" in your name). Press **Ctrl+U** again to turn off Underline. Look at the Underline codes that surround the Underlined text. Press **Enter** twice.

6. Press **Ctrl+B** to turn on Bold. Key the words **WordPerfect Word Processing**. Notice that the words show in bold in your document. Press **Ctrl+B** to turn off Bold again. Look at the Bold codes and press **Enter** twice.

7. Press **Ctrl+I** to turn on Italic. Key your name one more time and turn Italic off. Press **Enter** two more times. Key your name one final time so you can compare the normal text with the text formatted with **Italic**, **Bold**, and **Underline**. Press **Enter** twice.

8. Save the file. Keep it in the window for the next Step-by-Step exercise.

As you can see, it is very easy to format characters as you key them by using what are known as *keyboard shortcuts*. Now let's look at another place where you can make changes to the appearance of your text.

Fonts

One way to change the appearance of text in WordPerfect is by changing the font face or the font size. If you have never before worked with fonts or if your knowledge of fonts is sketchy, Appendix F provides you with terminology and information important to the use of fonts. Please study that appendix before leaving Lesson 3.

2 8

The default font for WordPerfect 9 is 12-pt. Times New Roman. However, a wide variety of both serif and sans serif fonts are available through Windows, WordPerfect, and through your printer driver. You can change fonts in the following ways:

- Open the Format menu and choose Font to open the Font dialog box.

- Select the font from the Property Bar drop-down menu. As you browse through this list, WordPerfect provides a preview of each font. The Real Time Preview feature also gives you a look at your document formatted with any font before you make the font choice.

- Press F9 to open the Font dialog box. The appearance of each font is previewed here, too.

- Choose recently used fonts from the QuickFonts list.

Let's explore fonts.

S TEP-BY-STEP ⟹ 3.2

1. With **appearance 3-1 xxx** showing in the window, use **Save As** to save the file as **appearance 3-2 xxx**.

2. Press **Ctrl+End** to be sure your insertion point is at the bottom of your document.

3. Look at the Font Face button on the Property Bar. It is probably the first button. What is the name of the font that is listed? Look at the next button. What font size is chosen?

4. Open the **Format** menu and choose **Font**. It's at the top of the menu. The Font dialog box should open, looking much like Figure 3-1.

5. Look at the font face listed in the *Font Face* portion of the dialog box. Is it Times New Roman, or is your computer set for a different font?

6. Does the selected font size match the size on the Property Bar button? It is probably set at 12 pt., but something different might be chosen.

7. Without making any changes, click **OK** and key a sentence naming the font face and font size using the following sample: **The current font is 12-pt. Times New Roman.** Press **Enter** twice.

8. Open the Font dialog box again. This time do it by pressing **F9**. The font faces are listed alphabetically. Scroll through the list of font faces until you find *Arial*. Click to highlight **Arial** and change the font size to **20 pt**.

9. Look at the following parts of the dialog box:
   a. The preview area at the bottom of the dialog box. It should show a sample of Arial Regular 20-pt. type.
   b. The Appearance section where you can choose Bold, Italic, Underline, and a number of other attributes.
   c. The other features, such as color, in the right section of the dialog box.

10. Click **OK** to close the dialog box.

11. Key another sentence identifying the new font face and size. (If you have forgotten what you chose, look at the Property Bar buttons.)

12. Press **Enter** twice. Save the file and keep it open for your next Step-by-Step exercise.

(continued on next page)

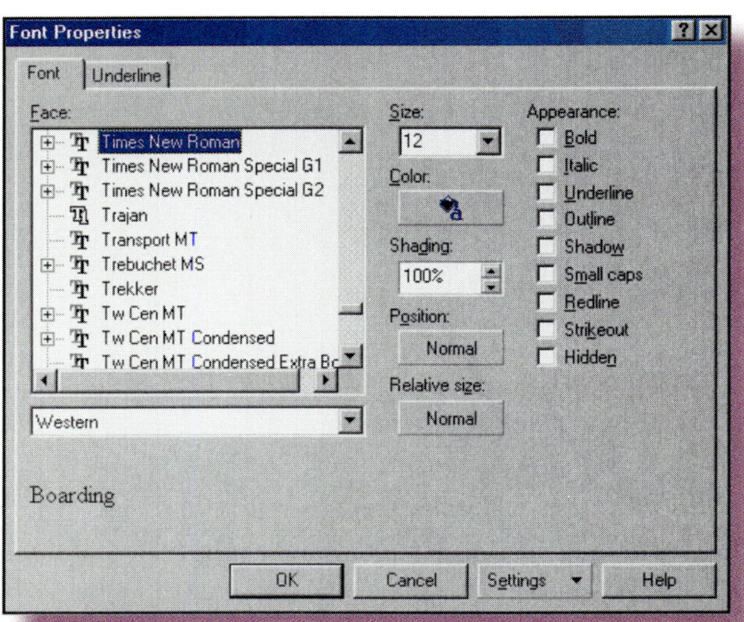

QuickFonts

The QuickFonts button on the default Property Bar compiles a list of the most recent font faces and sizes that you have used. As you use more fonts, the oldest will "fall off" from the bottom of the list. QuickFonts saves you time in going back to frequently used font faces and sizes. Let's see how easy it is to use QuickFonts.

S TEP-BY-STEP ⟩ 3.3

1. With **appearance 3-2 xxx** showing in the window, use **Save As** to save the file as **appearance 3-3 xxx**.

2. With your insertion point a double space below the second sentence you keyed in Step-by-Step exercise 3.2, click the **QuickFonts** button on the Property Bar. (If your Property Bar has been edited and the QuickFonts button has been removed, you will not be able to do Steps 2–4 of this Step-by-Step exercise.)

3. Find *Times New Roman 12* (not italic) in the drop-down list and select it.

4. Key your name one more time and press **Enter** three times.

5. Look at all of the codes in your document. Add them to the list you are keeping in Appendix E.

6. Add the Path and Filename code to the bottom of your document. Then print it.

7. Close the file, saving it one more time.

3 0

Formatting Codes

Formatting codes fall into two categories—open codes and paired codes. Open codes are codes that appear in the document at the beginning of the text to be formatted. With open codes, the format continues in effect until another code is entered to change that particular format.

Paired codes "enclose" the text they format. Bold, Underline, and Italic are paired codes. If you delete one of the pair, both codes will be removed, and the text will return to a normal format.

The Step-by-Step exercise you just printed was fine to introduce changes in appearance. But the examples were not quite what you would have in a normal document. Let's key a short paragraph using your new knowledge.

S TEP-BY-STEP ⟹ 3.4

1. Beginning in a new document window, key the paragraph illustrated in Figure 3-2. Use **Caps Lock**, **Bold**, **Italic**, and **Underline**, as shown. Substitute the name of your school for the name in the paragraph.

2. When you finish keying, save the document as **appearance 3-4 xxx**. Then press **Enter** twice and insert the Path and Filename code.

3. Press **Ctrl+Home** to return to the beginning of the document. Reveal your codes.

4. Look at the [Bold] codes, the [Italc] codes, and the [Und] codes. Do you see any [HRt] codes? The only [HRt] codes should be at the end of the paragraph.

5. Turn off Reveal Codes.

6. Position the insertion point at the end of the paragraph. Press **Enter** twice so the insertion point is halfway between the paragraph and the Path and Filename code.

7. Press **F9** to open the Font dialog box. In the Appearance section, choose **Bold**, **Underline**, and **Italic**. Click **OK** to close the dialog box.

8. Key the name of your school.

9. Finally, print your document and close it, saving it again with the same name.

FIGURE 3-2
Text for Step-by-Step 3.4

WINCHESTER BUSINESS COLLEGE provides all kinds of classes on computers for eager students. One of the popular areas of training is **word processing** training since **word processing** is widely used in the *Fox River Valley* area. This is a course using the **WordPerfect** **9** word processing program. Students find that **WordPerfect** is <u>easy to learn</u> and <u>easy to use</u>.

So far, you know that you can use keyboard shortcuts for Bold, Italic, and Underline and that you can make those choices from the Font dialog box. These attributes can also be chosen from the Property Bar. Figure 3-3 illustrates the buttons for these choices. To use the Property Bar buttons, simply click the Bold button to turn on Bold. Click it again to turn off Bold. Use the same procedure for Italic and Underline. We'll use these buttons in your next Step-by-Step exercise.

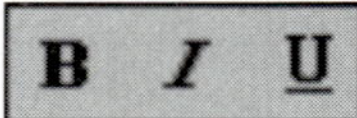

FIGURE 3-3
Property Bar Bold, Italic, and Underline Buttons

Applying Attributes to Selected Text

As you've worked with Bold, Underline, and Italic, you've been instructed to turn the attribute on, key the text, and turn the format off. It is possible to format something that has already been keyed without having to delete the text and rekey it. To do so, you must first select the text.

In Lesson 2 you learned several ways of selecting text for the purpose of deleting that text. Deleting is only one of many things you can do with selected text. Let's practice adding appearance attributes to selected text.

S TEP-BY-STEP ➲ 3.5

SCANS

1. Open **foreign 2-7 xxx**. Use **Save As** to save the file as **foreign 3-5 xxx**.

2. Click to position the insertion point in the word *American* in the first line. Then click the **Bold** button on the Property Bar to bold the word. Bold the word *Americans* in the second line using the same procedure.

3. Position the insertion point in the word *companies* and click the **Italic** button to italicize the word. Repeat the procedure for the other occurrence of *companies*.

4. Point to the last sentence of the paragraph and triple click to select it. Click the **Underline** button on the Property Bar to add underline to that sentence.

5. Use the mouse to drag across the words *cultural differences*. Add both **Bold** and **Italic** to the selected text. Repeat the procedure with *value systems*.

6. Click the **Save** button on the Toolbar (the third button from the left), but keep the document open for the next Step-by-Step exercise.

Convert Case

Occasionally, you'll key something in lowercase that should be in uppercase. Or you'll key something in uppercase that should be in lowercase. It is time-consuming to delete and rekey the text correctly. WordPerfect offers you a feature called *Convert Case* that enables you to change the case of selected text.

Convert Case is chosen from the Edit menu. Let's practice on our little practice document. (It already is jammed full of special effects!)

STEP-BY-STEP 3.6

1. With **foreign 3-5 xxx** open in the window, use **Save As** to save the file as **foreign 3-6 xxx**.

2. Drag across the words *foreign business people* to select them.

3. Open the **Edit** menu. Choose **Convert Case** and then **UPPERCASE**.

4. Select the word *American* in the first line. Return to **Convert Case** and choose **UPPERCASE** for the word at the insertion point.

5. Do the same for *Americans* in the second line.

6. Position the insertion point in the word *FOREIGN* that is in uppercase letters and press **Ctrl+K**.

7. Select the word *AMERICAN* n the first line. Go to **Convert Case** and choose **Initial Capitals**. Do the same with *AMERICANS* in the second line.

8. Print the practice document Then close it, saving it again with the same name. (Are you remembering to put your initials in the *xxx* locations?)

Note that to change the appearance of text with bold or italic, you didn't need to select the text. You only needed to position the insertion point in the word. With Convert Case you don't need to select the text if you use the keyboard shortcut (Ctrl+K). If you use the Edit menu, the text must be selected.

Also, in the sentence that you underlined, you triple clicked to select the sentence. That included the period at the end of the sentence. Normally the ending punctuation isn't underlined. To select the sentence and NOT the period before applying the underline, you would need to use the mouse to drag across the words in the sentence to select them—up to the period. Then apply the underline attribute. You can practice more with that at your leisure.

Center and Flush Right

As you learned in the previous sections, text can be enhanced with character formatting such as bold or italic. The location of the words on the page can also make a difference in how text is perceived. For example, centering text or aligning it at the right margin makes some kinds of text stand out from the other text on the page.

Center. You can automatically center a line of text between the margins by pressing Shift+F7 or by opening the Format menu, choosing Line, and then choosing Center. You can give the command before you key the text, or you can position the insertion point at the beginning of the line to be centered and give the command. Press Enter to end centering.

Flush Right. To make a short line end even with the right margin (*flush right*), press Alt+F7 or open the Format menu, choose Line, and then choose Flush Right. If you give the command before you key the text, it will "back up" from the right margin as you key. If you give the command after the text has been keyed, the insertion point must be at the left of the text to be formatted with Flush Right. Press Enter to end flush right.

As if you needed to know more ways of giving these commands, you might find it easier to choose them from the QuickMenu (point to the text and right click).

STEP-BY-STEP 3.7

1. Press **Shift+F7** and key your full name. End by pressing **Enter**. Is your name centered between the guidelines?

2. Beginning at the left margin, key your name again. Press **Enter**.

3. Position the insertion point at the beginning of the first letter of the name at the left margin. Press **Shift+F7** to center the name again. Press **Ctrl+End** to go to the end of the "document."

4. Press **Alt+F7** and key today's date. Press **Enter**. Does the date end at the guideline for the right margin?

5. Key the date beginning at the left margin. Position the insertion point at the left of the date and press **Alt+F7** to move the date to the right margin.

6. Look at the Center and Flush Right codes in Reveal Codes. Add them to your list. Then close the document without saving it.

Now let's use your new skills with Center and Flush Right on a real Step-by-Step exercise. Work quickly and efficiently. Then we'll practice printing from the disk rather than from the window.

STEP-BY-STEP 3.8

1. Center the title of the Step-by-Step exercise in Figure 3-4 on page 35. Format the title with bold and all capital letters. Press **Enter** three times after the title. (This is a *triple* space. You will be using triple spaces often.)

2. Key the name of the character at the left. Then give the command for Flush Right and key the name of the actor or actress.

3. Insert the Path and Filename code a double space below the last line of the Step-by-Step exercise. NOTHING WILL SHOW because your document does not yet have a name.

4. Save the document as **music 3-8 xxx** and close it.

5. Open the **File** menu and choose **Open**. Click once to highlight the file named **music 3-8 xxx**. In the Open File dialog box, open the **File** menu and choose **Print**. Close the Open File dialog box.

Users of the Internet include schools, government agencies, businesses, libraries, colleges and universities, military bases, and more. Every year, in addition, more and more people can access the Internet from their homes.

```
                              CAST

Professor Harold Hill                           Charlie Stowe
Marian Paroo                                     Sally Martin
Mrs. Paroo                                      Lindsey Chang
Winthrop Paroo                                  Phil Holverson
Mayor Shinn                                      Jeff Rodriguez
Eulalie Mackeckine Shinn                         Doris Derkson
Tommy Washburn                                  James Timanez
Zeneeta Shinn                                 Brianna Boscobel
```

Dot Leaders

Dot leaders can easily be added to material that is formatted with Flush Right. Simply press Alt+F7 twice (instead of only once) before keying the text at the right. The result will be a document that looks like this small section of the Step-by-Step exercise above.

Professor Harold Hill . . . . .Charlie Stowe
Marian Paroo. . . . . .Sally Martin

You can also add dot leaders to text that has already been keyed. Reveal your codes and align the insertion point at the beginning of the text following the Flush Right command. Press Alt+F7 and watch the dot leaders appear. Let's try dot leaders.

STEP-BY-STEP ▷ 3.9

1. Key **Marian Paroo** at the left margin. Press **Alt+F7** twice and key **Sally Martin**. See the leaders? Press **Enter** twice.

2. Key **Marian Paroo** at the left margin again. Press **Alt+F7** and key **Sally Martin**.

3. Position the insertion point just to the left of *Sally* and press **Alt+F7** again. Voila!

4. Close your practice without saving.

Dot leaders are very useful in drawing your attention from one side of the page to another. They are often used in financial statements and in programs like the one in Step-by-Step exercise 3.8.

Tabs

The Tab key is located next to the letter *Q*. It is normally used to indent the first line of a paragraph. WordPerfect's tabs are preset at each half inch. These tab stops can easily be changed. You'll learn to do that in a later lesson.

ALWAYS use the Tab key instead of the space bar to indent lines from the left margin so each paragraph is indented an even amount of space. Sometimes you may need to press the Tab key several times to move the insertion point to where you want it to be.

The Tab key can also be used to tab to the left. To do so, you must hold the Shift key while you press Tab. That's why the Tab key often has an arrow pointing to the left along with the arrow pointing to the right.

Let's create a short four-paragraph document. Each of the paragraphs should be indented with Tab.

1. Key the four short paragraphs illustrated in Figure 3-5. At the beginning of each paragraph, press **Tab** once and begin keying. Key each paragraph continuously. Press **Enter** twice between paragraphs.

2. When you finish the last paragraph, press **Enter** twice.

3. Proofread carefully and correct any errors that you detect. Save your document as **gifts 3-10 xxx**.

4. Insert the Path and Filename code a double space below the final paragraph.

5. Print your file and close it, saving it again as you close it.

FIGURE 3-5
Text for Step-by-Step 3.10

```
     Regardless of the country where you are presenting a gift to a
host or business associate, there are some general guidelines
regarding international gift giving.

     Flowers are acceptable in most cultures, but in many countries you
should avoid red roses because they signify romantic interest.  Also,
in most European countries, white flowers and chrysanthemums are given
only for condolences or sympathy.  Avoid giving an even number of
flowers, and unwrap the flowers before presenting them to the
recipient.

     Chocolates or gifts of candy are usually appropriate.  Be careful
not to give candy manufactured in a rival country.

     Gifts with company logos are usually acceptable, providing the
logo is small and unobtrusive.  In some countries, caps and T-shirts
with logos are considered souvenirs, not gifts.
```

Now let's create a letter that uses Tab. The letter is longer than one page. When you are about two-thirds of the way through the letter, a line will appear across the window that separates page 1 from page 2. (This line is called a *soft page break*.) If you are working in Page view, you will also see the bottom margin space on the first page and the top margin space on the second page. Don't worry about the location of the page break or a second page heading. We'll return to this letter later and fix it.

The first thing we'll do in this document is give it a 2" top margin. We'll do this by adding extra space at the top of the letter with the Enter key. You can watch the *Ln* indicator in the Application Bar so you know when you've pressed Enter enough times. This is called "giving your document a 2" top margin." You'll be doing it often!

Then we'll use Tab to move the date to a location near the center. The same procedure will be used to position the closing lines of the letter.

STEP-BY-STEP 3.11

1. Prepare the letter in Figure 3-6 on page 38. Press **Enter** until the *Ln* indicator says approximately *2"* to give your letter a 2" top margin.

2. Press **Tab** as many times as necessary to move the insertion point to **Pos 4"** and key the current date. Spell out the date; e.g., **July 1, 200x**. Follow the date with a quadruple space (press **Enter** four times).

3. Key the mailing address and the greeting at the left margin.

4. Use **Center** and **Bold** for the subject line.

5. Use **Tab** to indent each line of the display matter in the body of the letter. (If QuickCorrect causes the *T* of *Time difference* to appear as a capital letter, use **Backspace** to delete the *T* and change it to lowercase. It may take two tries.)

6. At the end of the letter, tab to **Pos 4"** for the complimentary closing. Press **Enter** four times after the closing and key your name, again at **Pos 4"**.

7. Save the letter as **sasoot 3-11 xxx**. Press **Enter** two more times below the enclosure notation and insert the Path and Filename code at the left margin.

8. Open the **View** menu and choose **Two Pages** so you can see the entire document at once. Then proofread the letter carefully and print it.

9. Whoops! The list in the letter should have been in bold. Select the entire list and give the Bold command to change the items to bold.

10. Print the letter and save the letter again. Keep it open for the next Step-by-Step exercise.

(continued on next page)

(Current Date)

Mr. Antonio Larsen
Suite 334
789 Embassy Drive
Sasoot 3G76H
GRAPHIA

Dear Mr. Larsen:

Subject: International Awareness

We are aware that there has been an increase in the amount of trade between businesses in your country and ours. We are launching a project to learn more about some of the differences and similarities between our homelands.

Our project will begin with some geographic basics that will provide our company's administrative assistants with information needed for international communications and to arrange for international travel. Some of the topics about which we'd like information are listed below:

    time difference
    currency used
    exchange rate
    telephone prefix
    climate
    language spoken
    type of government
    location of international airport
    housing opportunities
    cultural practices affecting trade
    major products of your country

Your name and address were provided by a mutual friend who has traveled to Graphia. He was certain you would be willing to pass this request on to someone who could provide some answers to help us with our project.

Also, if you have any brochures describing your country, please send them. A map of Graphia, as well as a map of Sasoot or any of your other major cities, would be wonderful! Information of this type is extremely valuable in visualizing a place never visited. I am enclosing a brochure about our city that you may share with your coworkers.

Thank you for your help with this endeavor.

                Sincerely,

                (Your Name)

Enclosure

Envelope

Since you're not likely to hand deliver this letter to Sasoot, you need an envelope in which to mail it. WordPerfect has made the preparation of envelopes easy, providing you have a printer that will print envelopes. Most ink jet and laser printers will print envelopes if you hand-feed them. For one envelope at a time, that shouldn't be too bad.

To create an envelope, simply choose the Envelope feature from the Format menu. WordPerfect will do the rest of the work for you. We'll try it in a Step-by-Step exercise. Before you begin the Step-by-Step exercise, check with your instructor to see if you can print envelopes on the classroom printer. Your instructor may wish to give you special instructions.

STEP-BY-STEP 3.12

1. With **sasoot 3-11 xxx** showing in the window, open the **Format** menu and choose **Envelope**. You'll see that WordPerfect picked up the mailing address from the letter and inserted it on the envelope.

2. Click in the return addresses location and key your own name and return address.

3. Look at the envelope tools on the Property Bar (see Figure 3-7). Click the **Return Address** button. Note that the item on the bottom is the Address Book. You'll learn about that later.

4. Click the **Mailing Address** button. That, too, refers to the Address Book.

FIGURE 3-7
Envelope Buttons on the Property Bar

5. Click the **Bar Code** button. This envelope can't have a POSTNET bar code because it doesn't have a standard 5- or 9-digit ZIP code. Close the dialog box.

6. Click the **Envelope Positions** button. You can specify the exact location of your return address and mailing address using this dialog box. Normally the default location is fine.

7. Click the final envelope button. This drop-down menu gives you a choice of standard envelope sizes. You can also go to the Page Format dialog box to set up your own envelope size if a special size is needed.

8. With your insertion point on the envelope, choose print. In the Print dialog box, specify **Current page** to tell WordPerfect to print the envelope only. Your printer may prompt you when it is ready to print the envelope. You may do one of the following to print the envelope:
   a. Insert a regular envelope.
   b. Cut a piece of paper to measure 9.5" x 4" and feed that into your printer in place of the envelope.
   c. Turn your letter over and print the "envelope" on the back of the page.

9. After printing, close your document without saving it again.

Summary

As you learned in this lesson, WordPerfect makes it easy for you to enhance your text in a number of ways. You learned that:

- You can use attributes such as Caps Lock, Bold, Underline, and Italic to make sections of text stand out from the rest of the document.

- A wide variety of font faces and sizes are readily available.

- Some formatting codes come in pairs that format the text between the pairs.

- Some formatting codes affect the document forward from the point where they are inserted.

- You can apply appearance attributes to text that has already been keyed by first selecting the text to be formatted.

- Convert Case enables you to change text between uppercase and lowercase.

- Short lines of text can easily be centered between the margins.

- Text can be aligned at the right margin, sometimes using dot leaders between the text at the left and the text at the right.

- The Tab key is used to indent paragraphs and other chunks of text that need to be moved to the right.

- WordPerfect automatically formats envelopes for your letters and adds the mailing address in the proper location.

LESSON 3 REVIEW QUESTIONS

MULTIPLE CHOICE

Circle the best answer to each of the following statements.

1. To turn on Bold, you can press the Bold button on the Property Bar, or you can press
   - **A.** Caps Lock+B.
   - **B.** Shift+B.
   - **C.** Ctrl+B.
   - **D.** Alt+B.

2. If you wish to turn on Italic along with several other appearance attributes, you can do it in the __________ dialog box.
   - **A.** Format
   - **B.** Font
   - **C.** Appearance
   - **D.** Print

3. Formatting codes fall into two categories which are
   - **A.** open codes and closed codes.
   - **B.** closed codes and double codes.
   - **C.** single codes and double codes.
   - **D.** open codes and paired codes.

4. Which of the following ways is NOT a way to change fonts?
   - **A.** Open the Format menu and choose QuickFormat.
   - **B.** Use the QuickFonts list.
   - **C.** Select from the Property Bar drop-down menu.
   - **D.** Press F9 to open the Font dialog box.

5. The QuickFonts feature compiles a list of the most recent ______ you have used.
   - **A.** codes
   - **B.** font faces and sizes
   - **C.** attributes
   - **D.** cases

FILL IN THE BLANKS

Complete each of the following statements by writing your answer in the blank provided.

6. To add attributes to text that has already been keyed, you must first ______________ it before applying the attribute.

7. WordPerfect offers you a feature called ___________________ that enables you to change the case of selected text.

8. By pressing Alt+F7, you will format text with ___________________.

(continued on next page)

9. ALWAYS use the _____________ key to indent lines from the left margin so each paragraph is indented an even amount of space.

10. To create an envelope in WordPerfect, simply choose the Envelope feature from the _____________ menu.

LESSON 3 PROJECT

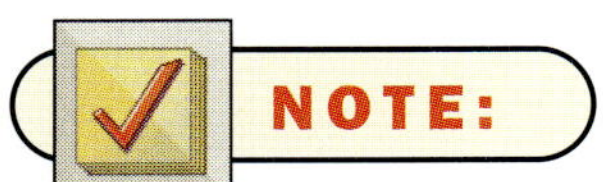

Let's test your understanding of the features learned in Lesson 3. Work quickly and efficiently. How much can you do without referring to the instructions in the lesson?

1. Key the paragraphs illustrated in Figure 3-8. **Center** and **Bold** the title.

2. Use **Tab** to indent the first line of each paragraph. Use **Bold**, **Underline**, and **Italic**, as shown in the figure. (The two hyphens in the first line may change to a dash. That's OK.)

NOTE:

Be careful when you use Bold, Underline, or Italic near the end of a sentence. The period at the end of the sentence should not be formatted with the same formatting applied to the words preceding it.

FIGURE 3-8
Text for Lesson 3 Project

> **The Skeleton**
>
> The SKELETON is composed of two parts: the **axial skeleton** and the **appendicular skeleton**. The **axial skeleton**, consisting of about **80** bones, includes the <u>spine, ribs, sacrum, sternum, and cranium</u>. The **appendicular skeleton**, which contains **126** bones, includes the bones of the <u>arms, legs, pelvis, and shoulders</u>.
>
> Bones are made up of both *organic* and *inorganic* material. The tough outer membrane of the bone is called the periosteum (*per-ee-ahs-tee-um*). If you want to study more about the skeleton, read THE HUMAN FRAME.

3. When you finish keying, save the document as **skeleton proj3 xxx**.

4. Position the insertion point a double space below the second paragraph and insert the Path and Filename code.

5. Select the title and use **Convert Case** to change the title to all uppercase letters.

6. Click in the word *periosteum* in the second line of the second paragraph and change it to **Bold** and **Italic**.

7. Select *THE HUMAN FRAME* in the last line and add **Italic** to the formatting.

8. Press **Ctrl+Home** to move the insertion point to the beginning of the document. Change the font face to **Arial** or some other sans serif font. Change the font size to **14 pt.**

9. Print your document and close it, saving it again with the same name.

CRITICAL THINKING ACTIVITY

The small group assignment for your Environmental Science Class is to research and write a report on the endangered species of Florida's Everglades. Everyone in your group has worked hard searching the Internet for information, as well accumulating material from the library and other sources.

You have offered to key the report using your knowledge of WordPerfect. The report is now 50 pages long, and you want to make it look very professional. What are some of the attributes you could add to enhance the text of your report, and where would you apply them?

WORKING WITH DOCUMENTS

OBJECTIVES

Upon completion of this lesson, you will be able to:

- Discuss the addition of the *.wpd* extension to your document names.
- Change viewing options in the Open File dialog box.
- Delete items from the Favorites list.
- Add items to the Favorites list.
- Insert one document into another.
- Perform a simple Merge operation.
- Discuss the WordPerfect default template.

⏱ Estimated Time: 1 hour

In the previous three lessons you've created text, named documents, and saved them. You've opened documents and resaved them with the same name, as well as saved them with a different name. All of this has taken place while you were learning other things—inserting, deleting, selecting, changing case, aligning with Center and Flush Right, and a variety of other skills.

In this lesson you'll reinforce some things you already know and learn a little more about working with the dialog box that enables you to open and save documents. In addition, you'll learn how to join two documents together, and you'll learn about what's known as the default template—the settings that give you a good-looking document every time.

The Open File Dialog Box

In Appendix B and all of the lessons in this unit, you have been working with the Open File dialog box. You've also worked with the Save File dialog box, and you probably noticed that the two dialog boxes are almost identical. While one is used for saving and the other is used for opening, the two boxes have the same features and work in much the same way.

The illustration in Figure 4-1 shows one version of the Open File dialog box. We will explore this box in the next few pages. Remember that what you learn about the Open File dialog box also applies to the Save File dialog box.

You are about to learn that many of the features showing in the figure are optional; that is, you can choose to display them or not. Let's address the issues one at a time.

Features at the Bottom

The .wpd Extension. As you learned in Lesson 1, documents are automatically saved with the *.wpd* extension unless you specify in the Settings dialog box that *.wpd* should not be used. The *.wpd* extension identifies the files as WordPerfect text files. You need not key *.wpd* as part of the file name. When you list your files, WordPerfect will list all files with all extensions, signified by *.* in the *File name* box.

Last Modified. Near the bottom of the Open File dialog box, note the *Last modified* box. While it normally reports *Any Time*, you can use this option to tell WordPerfect to list only those files modified yesterday, last week, last year, or a variety of other choices. This feature is especially useful when looking for a file for which you can't remember the exact name but you can remember the date on which it was last modified.

File Type. While WordPerfect saves different types of files and attaches different extensions to those types, when *.* is listed in this box, WordPerfect will show all files.

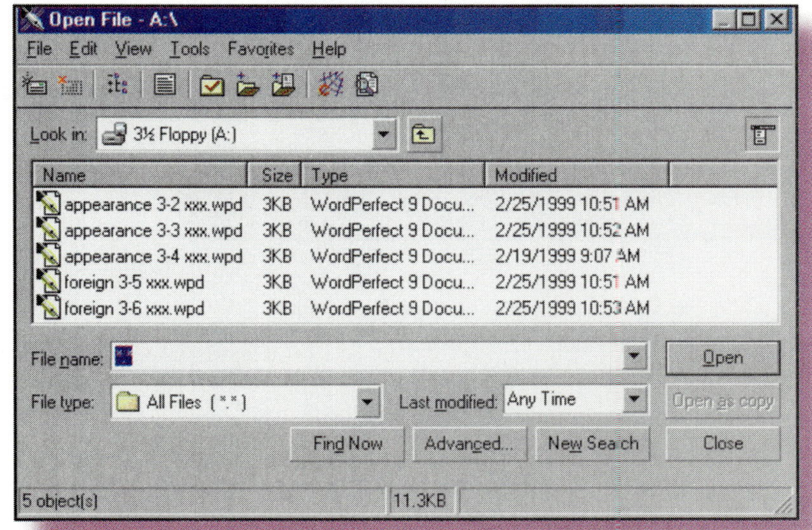

FIGURE 4-1
Open File Dialog Box

View Options

Study the Open File dialog box illustrated in Figure 4-1. You'll see that the following options have been chosen:

- The Menu Bar is displayed. (A button at the right of the *Look in* box controls whether or not the Menu Bar shows.)

- The Toolbar is displayed below the Menu Bar.

- The Status Bar is displayed at the bottom. (This may need to be chosen in the View menu.)

- Preview is deselected. (The button does not appear to be depressed.)

- Details are displayed in the list.

- Files are listed alphabetically by name.

All of these items can be chosen from the View menu. Some can be chosen from the Toolbar. We'll learn about the parts of the View menu and then practice with them.

Toolbar. Note that the Toolbar looks much like the Toolbar in your normal working window. It contains different tools, but you can preview what each button will do by pointing to the button with the mouse pointer and holding it until the QuickTip appears. Your Toolbar may contain more buttons than the Toolbar in Figure 4-1.

Status Bar. The Status Bar tells you how many objects (files) are in the displayed folder and how much space they take (in terms of bytes or kilobytes).

Preview. When selected, Preview displays a miniature version of any document in the list that is highlighted. Preview tends to slow WordPerfect down when you are opening the dialog box, so you probably will not use Preview except in special circumstances.

View. Four choices are provided in the View menu. You can look at your list of files by displaying small icons, large icons, a list, or "details" (as shown). Details lists the name of the file, the size of the file in bytes or kilobytes, the type of file, and the date and time the file was last saved. Sometimes this information is of value to you. Other times, you might not need to see all of that information.

A fifth view option is the Tree view, which can be toggled on and off. The Tree view shows folders and subfolders on your computer.

Arrange Icons by. You can list your files alphabetically by name, by size, by date, or by type of file. The default is to list them by name. Others prefer to see their files in descending order by date—in other words, the most recently opened file will be listed first. For classroom purposes, it would be best to list the files in alphabetic order.

Now that you have all of that information, let's learn how to make changes to this dialog box.

S TEP-BY-STEP ⟹ 4.1

SCANS

1. Click the **Open** button on the Toolbar or open the **File** menu and choose **Open**.

2. If $3^1/_2$ *Floppy (A:)* isn't selected, click the little down arrow beside the *Look in* text box. Compare your Open File dialog box with the one illustrated in Figure 4-1. The list of files should be similar.

3. If your dialog box doesn't display a Menu Bar, click the Menu toggle button at the right.

4. Open the **View** menu in the dialog box and compare it with Figure 4-2.

   a. Notice that at the top of the menu in the figure, **Toolbar** and **Status Bar** are both selected. If your two bars are not selected, choose them. You'll have to do it one at a time.

FIGURE 4-2
Open File Dialog Box View Menu

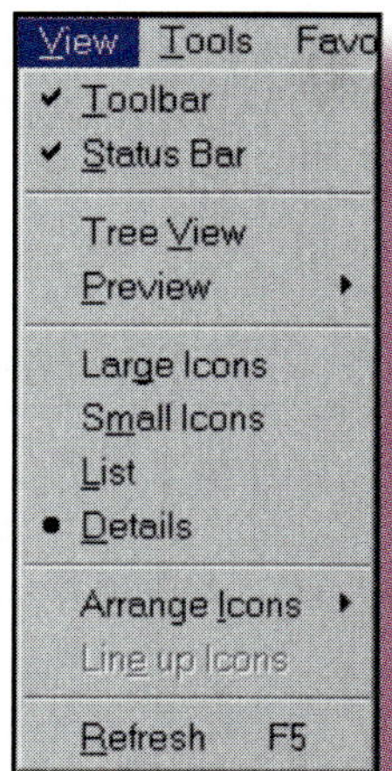

b. Point to any document listed and click once to highlight it. Then click the **Preview** choice. If *No Preview* is preceded by a bullet, click that choice. You'll be returned to the Open File dialog box containing a tiny image of the document. It is too small to read.

c. Open the **View** menu and choose **Preview** again. Click **Use Separate Window**. The document will appear in a separate window. Point to the side of the dialog box. When the pointer becomes a two-headed black arrow, drag to make the dialog box larger. The bigger the box, the larger the document will appear.

d. Close the separate window and open the **View** menu again. Note the choice of large or small icons, the list, or the list with details. In the figure, **Details** is chosen. Make that choice.

e. Return to the **View** menu and click **Arrange Icons**. Look at the choices. Choose **by Date**. Look at your list. Are the most recent files at the top? Return to **Arrange Icons** and choose **by Name** again.

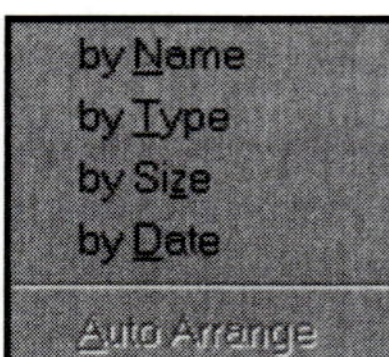

5. Use the **View** menu to change the view of your documents to **Large Icons**. Then try **Small Icons**, **List**, and finally **Details**.

6. Size the Open File dialog box from the side and then from the bottom using the same method you used to size the "Separate Window" in Step 4c. Use the diagonal arrow at the corner to make the dialog box just large enough so you can see all of the information about eight of the files.

7. Keep the Open File dialog box open as you read on.

Favorites

O̶ne way to speed up finding your files when you wish to open one is to add the disk (or folder) you use regularly to the *Favorites* list. This is an easily customizable list that opens with a click of the Favorites button. When it is set up, Favorites can also be used to identify the folder to which your files should be saved.

In Step-by-Step exercise 4.2 it is assumed that you are saving your work on a disk in Drive A of the computer. If you are saving your work in a different folder on the hard drive, please substitute the location for your work whenever reference is made to *3¹/₂ Floppy (A:)*.

S TEP-BY-STEP ⟹ 4.2

1. With the Open File dialog box still displayed, click the button on the Toolbar that shows a file folder with a red check mark. (This is the Favorites button.)

2. Look at the list of favorites. If no one has changed the list, you might see folders for graphics, macros, and personal files in the list.

3. Look for *3¹/₂ Floppy (A:)* in the list. If it is there, continue with this Step-by-Step exercise. If it is not there, skip to Step 5.

4. Position the highlight on *3¹/₂ Floppy (A:)* and open the **File** menu. Choose **Delete**. At the prompt asking if you would like to delete 3¹/₂ Floppy to the Recycle Bin, answer **Yes**. (YOU ARE ONLY DELETING A SHORTCUT!) Was the *3¹/₂ Floppy* item removed? It should have been. Now let's put it back.

5. Click the down arrow beside the *Look in* text box near the top. Use the scroll bar, if necessary, to find the *3¹/₂ Floppy (A:)* item in the list. (It will probably be near the beginning of the list.) Click to select it.

6. With the files on the disk in Drive A showing, click the **Add to Favorites** button. (It is just to the right of the Favorites button.)

7. Click **Yes** at the question about the *.* filter. You want all files listed.

8. Close the Open File dialog box and read on.

With the *3¹/₂ Floppy (A:)* item in your Favorites list, all you have to do when you wish to open a file from that disk or save a file onto that disk is open the Open File dialog box, click the Favorites button, double click the folder containing your documents, and proceed to open or save your file. You won't need to be fishing around in the *Look in* portion of the dialog box for the correct disk or folder.

Learn to always check the *Look in* box just above the names of the files to make certain you are in the correct folder before saving or opening. Finding a misfiled document can be time-consuming.

As you can see from Step-by-Step exercise 4.2, it is easy to add folders to the Favorites list or remove those folders when they are no longer the most important folders for your work. As you progress throughout this course, the folder that contains your lesson Step-by-Step exercises will be used frequently. So you'll want to keep it in the Favorites list. When you are on the job, however, you'll add folders to the list that you are using regularly. That list might change from day to day as the kind of work or the boss for whom you're working changes.

Insert

Occasionally, you wish to join one document to another. This is accomplished by opening one document and positioning the insertion point where you would like the other document to appear. Then you will open the Insert menu, choose File, and choose the file to be inserted.

Let's practice by keying a couple of introductory paragraphs. Then we'll insert a document you created in Lesson 3 at the end of the new document.

S TEP-BY-STEP 4.3

SCANS

1. Key the paragraphs illustrated in Figure 4-3. Indent the first line of each paragraph with **Tab** and press **Enter** twice following each paragraph.

2. When you finish keying, proofread your work carefully. Then save it as **gifts 4-3 xxx**.

3. Position your insertion point a double space below the last paragraph.

4. Open the **Insert** menu and choose **File**. (It's near the bottom.) This will open your Insert File dialog box.

5. Locate the file named **gifts 3-10 xxx**. Double click the file to insert it, or click it once and then click the **Insert** button.

6. Print your file and close it, saving it again as **gifts 4-3 xxx**.

> Customs vary around the world with regard to when to give gifts to business associates, what to give, what is quite improper, when the gift should be presented, and whether or not the gift should be wrapped.
>
> In some countries, it is in very bad taste to arrive giftless. In Japan, you are ALWAYS expected to give a gift. Japan is followed closely in that regard by the countries in the Middle East and the Pacific Rim countries such as Korea, China, Taiwan, Thailand, Malaysia, and Hong Kong. In the Latin American countries, gift giving is quite acceptable but not imperative.

In Step-by-Step exercise 4.3 you inserted the text from the previous lesson at the end of the new file. As mentioned earlier, you can insert text anywhere in a document. When you use Insert, the text is inserted at the location of the insertion point. This is a very useful skill. It saves rekeying!

Mass Mailings Using Merge

Most word processing programs enable you to combine a list of names and addresses with a standard document to prepare identical letters for all of the people on the list. This is sometimes referred to as mass mailing. In WordPerfect it is called Merge. Most of Unit 5 is dedicated to learning about Merge, but Step-by-Step exercise 4.4 will provide you with a brief introduction to the feature.

STEP-BY-STEP 4.4

1. Go to the student **datafile** folder and open **seasons.dat** and study the document. This grid contains mailing information for potential customers. You will send letters to these people.

2. Note the Merge Feature Bar (see Figure 4-4) below your Property Bar (or Ruler, if it is displayed). Click the **Go to Form** button. In the Associate dialog box, click **Create** since you are about to create the standard letter. A new document window will appear, with a different Feature Bar at the top.

3. Press **Enter** until you are about 2" from the top of the page. Key today's date at the left margin. Press **Enter** four more times.

4. Click the **Insert Field** button on the Feature Bar. This will list the titles of the two columns of the grid. Point to *correspondent* and double click. A red FIELD code with parentheses will appear.

FIGURE 4-4
Merge Feature Bar

5. Press **Enter** twice and double click the *greeting* field. Press **Enter** twice. Close the Insert Field box.

6. Open the **Insert** menu and choose **File**. In the student **datafile** folder, find **Jacobson.wpd** and insert it. Save your letter as **seasons.frm**. Keep it open in the window.

7. Click the **Merge** button on the Feature Bar and then click **Merge** again. Your list of

names and addresses will be combined with the letter, and your insertion point will be at the bottom of the fourth letter.

8. Use **Page Up** to go back through the letters, looking at the names and addresses and greetings on each. Save your letters as **seasons 4-4 xxx**. Print the letters and close all files.

That's how simple Merge is. This sample had only four people in the list, but the list could contain hundreds of names. There are many variables with WordPerfect Merge. As mentioned above, you'll learn the terminology and what makes Merge work when you get to Lesson 17.

The Default Template

Every document you create in WordPerfect is formatted by what's known as a *template*. A template is a preformatted document design. If you start a document on a new, blank window, your document will be managed by the default template. That template contains some settings that make it easy for you to begin your document without having to worry about margins, line spacing, tab stop locations, font face and size, and a huge number of other options. Study this list of settings that you'll learn about early in your training.

Margins:	1 inch on all sides—top, bottom, left, and right. The guidelines show you where your margins are.
Tabs:	Set at every half inch.
Line Spacing:	Single
Justification:	Left
Font:	Times New Roman 12 pt.

You should note a couple of things in this list. The one-inch margins support the fact that when your insertion point is at the margin guidelines at the beginning of a document, both the *Ln* and *Pos* indicators report *1"*. Also, when you indented your work with Tab, each time the text was indented a half inch. The font name and point size are the first two items on the default Property Bar. Justification (Left) appears in the middle of the default Property Bar.

As you work with features and formatting in WordPerfect, you will also learn what the default settings are for each feature. It will soon become obvious to you that this program is designed to help you with your work.

Summary

When working with any kind of information processing program, document control is imperative. You need to be able to save your files confidently, knowing exactly where they should go so you can find them when they are needed. In WordPerfect 9 the Open File dialog box is your key to saving and opening files.

In this lesson you learned that:

- WordPerfect automatically identifies your documents as WordPerfect documents with the *.wpd* extension.

- You can customize the Open File dialog box with a Toolbar, Status Bar, Preview Area (not recommended), and a variety of ways to list your files.

- If you include folders that are used frequently in the Favorites list, you will save time locating those folders.

- All WordPerfect documents are formatted by a template. The default template provides margins, font face and size, and a number of other settings to make your documents attractive.

- Mass mailings may be produced with WordPerfect's Merge feature.

LESSON 4 REVIEW QUESTIONS

TRUE/FALSE

Circle the T if the statement is true. Circle the F if it is false.

T F 1. The Open File dialog box and Save File dialog box are almost identical, having the same features and working in much the same way.

T F 2. If the Menu Bar in your Open File dialog box does not display, you need to reinstall your software and specify this choice.

T F 3. One way to speed up finding your files when you wish to open one is to add the file to your Favorites list.

T F 4. When working with Favorites, you must double click the folder to be opened.

T F 5. If you wish to add one document to another, you can do so by opening the File menu and choosing Insert.

T F 6. Mass mailings are easy to prepare using WordPerfect's Merge feature.

(continued on next page)

WRITTEN QUESTIONS

Write your answers to the following questions.

7. The *.wpd* extension identifies files as what type of files?

8. What are four ways you can list your files in the Open File dialog box?

9. Where should your insertion point be when you join one document to another?

10. What feature in WordPerfect formats every document you create with a preformatted document design?

LESSON 4 PROJECT

   In this project we will build on a document with which you have been working. Work carefully and efficiently.

1.   Key the paragraphs in Figure 4-5. Use **Tab** and **Enter**, as shown in the figure.

FIGURE 4-5
Text for Lesson 4 Project

```
     Be cognizant of the culture of the country in which you are
visiting.  In most Arab countries, you would avoid giving alcohol.  In
India, you would not want to give leather objects since cows in India
are sacred.

     Be sensitive of the correct time for the exchange of gifts.  It
shouldn't always be the first thing you do upon meeting an associate
from another country.  Also, don't push for the gift to be opened
immediately.  In some countries, the gift is opened in private later.

     To be safe, carry the gift in a shopping bag or some other way
that's not too obvious.  Then hand the gift to the associate with both
hands (never with the left hand).  It is also a good idea to wrap the
gift in subdued colors, since gifts in bright colors in some cultures
are considered vulgar.

     In some cultures, the best gift is a dinner at a restaurant.  In
Spain and a number of other Mediterranean countries, however, dinner
may not be served until 10:30 or 11 p.m.  Be careful when you eat in
the home of an associate from another country.  In some countries, it
is rude to clean your plate.  In others, it is rude NOT to clean your
plate!
```

2.   When you finish, insert the Path and Filename code a double space below the final paragraph.

3.   Save your file as **gifts proj4a xxx**. Keep it open in the window.

4.   Press **Ctrl+Home** to move your insertion point to the beginning of your document.

5.   Open the **Insert** menu and choose **File**. Insert **gifts 4-3 xxx**.

6.   Delete the Path and Filename code that is in the middle of the document. (Use **Reveal Codes**, if necessary, to find the code.) Adjust the spacing so all paragraphs are separated by a double space.

7.   Save the file again, this time as **gifts proj4b xxx**.

8.   Check your work over once more. Then print the project and close the file.

CRITICAL THINKING ACTIVITY

CANS

You can't remember the exact name of a document, but you can remember when you worked on it. Where would you go in WordPerfect and what would you look at to find this document?

Command Summary

FEATURE	MENU CHOICE	KEYBOARD	LESSON
Bold	Format, Font (Property Bar)	Ctrl+B or F9	3
Caps Lock	—	Caps Lock	3
Center	Format, Line	Shift+F7	3
Close	File	Ctrl+F4	1, Appendix B
Convert Case	Edit	—	3
Delete Line	—	Ctrl+Delete	2
Delete Word	—	Ctrl+Backspace	2
Dot Leaders	—	Alt+F7, Alt+F7	3
Draft View	View, Draft	Ctrl+F5	1
Envelope (Single)	Format, Envelope	—	3
Exit	File	Alt+F4	1, Appendix B
Favorites	File, Open (Toolbar)	F4 or Ctrl+O	4
Flush Right	Format, Line	Alt+F7	3
Font Face	Format, Font (Property Bar)	F9	3
Font Size	Format, Font (Property Bar)	F9	3
Full Page Zoom	View, Zoom (Toolbar)	—	1
Go To	Edit	Ctrl+G	2
Help	Help, Help Topics	F1	Appendix B
Insert	—	Insert	2
Insert File	Insert, File	—	4
Italic	Format, Font (Property Bar)	Ctrl+I or F9	3
Merge	Tools, Merge	Shift+F9	4
Open	File (Toolbar)	F4 or Ctrl+O	1, Appendix B
Page View	View, Page	Alt+F5	1
Path and Filename	Insert, Other	—	2
Print	File (Toolbar)	Ctrl+P	1
QuickMenu	—	—	Appendix B
Redo	Edit (Toolbar)	Ctrl+Shift+Z	2
Reveal Codes	View	Alt+F3	2
Save	File	Ctrl+S	1, Appendix B
Select Text	Edit, Select	F8	2
Soft Page Break	Automatic	—	3

FEATURE	MENU CHOICE	KEYBOARD	LESSON
Tab	—	Tab	3
Two Pages View	View, Two Pages	—	1
Typeover	—	Insert	2
Underline	Format, Font (Property Bar)	Ctrl+U or F9	3
Undo	Edit (Toolbar)	Ctrl+Z	3
View Page	View	Alt+F5	1
Zoom	View (Toolbar)	—	1

DELETING TEXT

KEY	ACTION
Backspace	Erases text to the left of the insertion point one character or space at a time. Hold down this key to delete several characters quickly. The text to the right of the insertion point will shift to the left to close up the space as you press the Backspace key.
Del and Delete	Deletes characters following the insertion point. If you hold the key down, characters will be deleted as they scroll in from the right.
Ctrl+Backspace	Deletes the word in which the insertion point is located. If you hold the Ctrl key and press Backspace several times, you can delete several consecutive words.
Ctrl+Delete	Deletes from the insertion point to the end of the line.

SELECTING TEXT

ACTION	RESULT
double click	selects a word
triple click	selects a sentence
quadruple click	selects a paragraph
click with large white arrow in left margin	selects a sentence
double click with large white arrow in left margin	selects a paragraph

MOVING THE INSERTION POINT

KEY	ACTION	KEY	ACTION
→	one character to the right	↓	one line down
←	one character to the left	Ctrl+↑	up one paragraph
Ctrl+→	one word to the right	Ctrl+↓	down one paragraph
Ctrl+←	one word to the left	Home	to the beginning of the line
End	to the end of the line	Page Down	to the bottom of the window
Page Up	to the top of the window	Alt+Page Up	to the first line on the previous page
Ctrl+Home	to the top of the document	Alt+Page Down	to the first line on the next page
Ctrl+End	to the bottom of the document		
↑	one line up		

UNIT 1 REVIEW QUESTIONS

FILL IN THE BLANKS

Complete the following statements by keying the correct answers on a page to be submitted to your instructor. Center *Unit 1 Review Questions* at the top of the page and triple-space. Number your answers.

1. The _______________ key moves your insertion point to the left margin.

2. The view that shows your document, complete with top and bottom margins, is _________ view.

3. In Reveal Codes [HRt] is the code for a _______________.

4. If you want to add a document on the disk to a document showing in the window, you open the _________ menu and choose ___________.

5. The periods that connect a column at the left with a column at the right are known as _______________.

WRITTEN QUESTIONS

Key your answers to the following questions. Number your answers and double-space between answers. Use complete sentences and good grammar.

6. What is the difference between Save and Save As?

7. When you move around in the text using the scroll bar, what happens to the insertion point?

8. List two different keystrokes that can be used for deleting text and tell what each of them does.

9. Briefly describe the difference between Undo and Redo.

10. Open Help and choose **Help Topics**. Key **template** and open the Help section entitled *about*. What three features from previous versions have been combined into the PerfectExpert feature? What are some of the PerfectExpert projects available?

UNIT 1 APPLICATIONS

Estimated Time: 1 hour

APPLICATION 1

1. Key the memo illustrated in Figure APP-1. Before beginning, press **Enter** until your insertion point is on approximately *Ln 2"*.

2. Center and bold **Memorandum** and triple-space.

3. After keying **TO:**, watch the *Pos* indicator on the Application Bar while you tab to **2"** to key **Hubert Ramon**.

4. Follow the procedure in Step 3 for the other heading lines.

FIGURE APP-1
Text for Application 1

```
                          Memorandum


     TO:       Hubert Ramon
     FROM:     (key your name)
     DATE:     (key the current date)
     RE:       Self-Directed Teams


     We're off to a good start with Total Quality Management in cur
     organization.  Thank you for volunteering to help with the initial
     planning meetings for our staff training.

     As you know, our goal down the pike is to completely convert our
     workforce to self-directed teams.  Your training in this area will be
     of great value to our company.
```

5. When you finish keying the memo, check your work carefully. Then save the Unit 1 Application 1 memo as **quality u1ap1a xxx**, substituting your initials for the *xxx* as always.

6. Insert the Path and Filename code a double space below the last paragraph of the memo.

(continued on next page)

7. Print your document.

8. Position your insertion point following the word *goal* in the first line of the second paragraph. Delete the words *down the pike* and replace them with **for the future**.

9. Following the word *training* in the second paragraph, add the words **and experience**.

10. Select *Memorandum* at the top and use **Convert Case** to change it to all uppercase letters.

11. Following the words *Total Quality Management* in the first line, add (**TQM**), complete with parentheses.

12. Save the document again as **quality u1ap1b xxx**. Print it and close it.

APPLICATION 2

Figure APP-2 illustrates some of the most frequently used proofreaders' marks. Study the marks. Then follow the steps listed to make corrections to a document you've already prepared.

1. Open **gifts proj4b xxx**. Save the file as **gifts u1ap2 xxx**.

FIGURE APP-2
Proofreaders' Marks

Change	Mark	Example	Result
Capitalize	≡	word processing is fun.	Word processing is fun.
Close up	⌒	Word Perfect	WordPerfect
Delete	ℛ	Your work work is good.	Your work is good.
Insert	∧	Word processing *is* fun.	Word processing is fun.
Insert comma	⌃	apples potatoes and peas	apples, potatoes, and peas
Insert space	#	Wordprocessing is fun.	Word processing is fun.
Insert period	⊙	Key the memo	Key the memo.
Lowercase	/lc	Word Processing is fun.	Word processing is fun.
New paragraph	¶	Please call me Tuesday.	Please call me Tuesday.

2. Using Figure APP-3 as a guide, make the corrections indicated to your document.

3. When you finish, check your work carefully. Print the revised document and close it, saving it again as **gifts u1ap2 xxx**.

Customs vary around the world with regard to when to give gifts to business associates, what to give, what is ~~quite~~ improper, when the gift should be presented, and whether or not the gift should be wrapped.

In some countries, it is in very bad taste to arrive giftless. In Japan you are ALWAYS expected to give a gift. Japan is followed closely in that regard by the countries in the Middle East and the Pacific Rim countries such as Korea, China, Taiwan, Thailand, Malaysia, *and* ~~and Hong Kong.~~ In the Latin American countries, gift giving is quite acceptable but not imperative.

Regardless of the country where you are presenting a gift, to ~~a host or business associate,~~ there are some general guidelines regarding international gift giving.

, however, Flowers are acceptable in most cultures, ~~but~~ in many countries, you should avoid red roses because they signify romantic interest. Also, in most European countries, white flowers and chrysanthemums are given only for condolences or sympathy. Avoid giving an even number of flowers, and unwrap the flowers before presenting them to the recipient.

Chocolates or gifts of candy are usually appropriate. Be careful not to give candy manufactured in a rival country.

Gifts with company logos are usually acceptable, providing the logo is small and unobtrusive. In some countries, caps and T-shirts with logos are considered souvenirs, not gifts.

is important. You should be aware that

~~Be cognizant of~~ the culture of the country in which you are

lc visiting. ~~I~~n most Arab countries, you would avoid giving
alcohol. In India, you would not want to give leather objects
since cows in India are sacred.

is also important.

~~Be sensitive of~~ the correct time for the exchange of gifts.
It shouldn't always be the first thing you do upon meeting an
associate from another country. Also, don't push for the gift
to be opened immediately. In some countries, the gift is opened
in private later.

It is in good taste to

~~To be safe,~~ carry the gift in a shopping bag or some other
way that's not too obvious. Then hand the gift to the associate
with both hands (never with the left hand). It is also a good
idea to wrap the gift in subdued colors, since gifts *wrapped* in bright
colors in some cultures are considered vulgar.

in many places

~~In some cultures~~ the best gift is a dinner at a restaurant.
In Spain and a number of other Mediterranean countries, however,
dinner may not be served until 10:30 or 11 p.m. Be careful when
you eat in the home of an associate from another country. In
some countries it is rude to clean your plate. In others, it is
rude NOT to clean your plate!

Follow the example of your host or hostess when dining.

APPLICATION 3

Go to the student **datafile** folder and open the document named **canada**. Use **Save As** to save the document as **canada u1ap3 xxx**. Format by selecting text and adding the following appearance attributes:

- Format all dates using **Italic**.

- Format the names of all explorers using **Bold**.

- Each time the word *Canada* appears, format it with bold and italic.

- Underline the following: *Newfoundland, Atlantic Coast, St. Lawrence River* (twice), and *Hudson Bay.*

When you finish, add the Path and Filename code a double space below the second paragraph. Then save the file again with the same name. Print the file and close it.

You have been hired part time to work for Singing Wheels Tours, a local charter and tour bus company, for a few hours each week. Your boss, Mr. Charlie Becker, knows you are just learning how to use WordPerfect, so he has planned your responsibilities to progress from simple to more difficult. Several Step-by-Step exercises will be included for you at the end of each unit. See how much of the work you can do without special instructions.

JOB 1

Mr. Becker has handed you the paragraphs illustrated in Figure J1. Key the paragraphs and correct all errors. Save the file as **schedule job1 xxx**. (The On-the-Job Step-by-Step exercises will be numbered consecutively throughout the text.) Then insert the Path and Filename code a double space below the second paragraph and print the document. Close the document.

FIGURE J1
Text for Job 1

```
We are sorry for the delay in notifying you of your scheduled trips
for August.  As you know, recent flooding in the Midwest has
necessitated a change in many of our scheduled tours.

The August schedule will be posted later in the week.  Please check
your assignments and make your personal arrangements for the tours on
which you will be serving.
```

JOB 2

Mr. Becker has prepared a tentative list of tours for the first three months of next year. Press **Enter** to space to *Ln 2"* for the heading. Triple-space following the heading. Using your knowledge of Flush Right and dot leaders, prepare the short document illustrated in Figure J2.

When you finish, check your work carefully and save the job as **schedule job2 xxx**. Add the Path and Filename code a double space below the document, print it, and close it.

FIGURE J2
Text for Job 2

```
                        EARLY (year) TRIPS

Southwest Area . . . . . . . . . . . . . . . . . . . . . . . . .  January
Branson . . . . . . . . . . . . . . . . . . . . . . . . . . . .  January
Pacific Northwest . . . . . . . . . . . . . . . . . . . . . . . February
Southern California . . . . . . . . . . . . . . . . . . . . . . February
Phoenix and Flagstaff . . . . . . . . . . . . . . . . . . . . .   March
Key West . . . . . . . . . . . . . . . . . . . . . . . . . . .    March
```

K

WORDPERFECT® BASICS

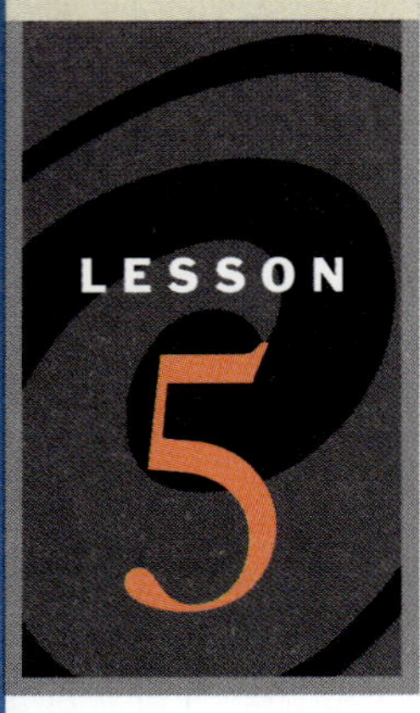

Text Entry Features

Upon completion of this lesson, you will be able to:

- Use various methods of deleting commands.
- Format text with Indent, Hanging Indent, and Double Indent.
- Use QuickIndent to format paragraphs.
- Use the WordPerfect method of creating lists.
- Create lists with the Outline/Bullets & Numbering feature.
- Start a new page using a hard page break.
- Use the WordPerfect Date feature.
- Center text vertically with the Center Page command.
- Format numerals with superscript and subscript.
- Work with various hyphen and space codes.

Estimated Time: 1 hour

Deleting Commands

Sometimes you make a mistake in choosing a menu, dialog box, or feature, and you wish to change your mind. There are different methods of deleting the commands you make in error. For example:

- **Menu**. To close a menu without making a choice, click outside of the menu, press Alt, press Esc, or open a different menu.

- **Dialog box**. To close a dialog box without making any changes, press Esc, click the x in the upper right corner, or, if there is a Cancel button, click Cancel.

Commands like Bold, Italic, and Underline don't open a menu. Nor do they display a dialog box. Instead, they put a code in your document. Some may be removed with the Backspace key. Others can be removed by immediately giving the same command again. Let's try a short practice.

STEP-BY-STEP 5.1

1. Read all three steps in this Step-by-Step exercise. Beginning in a new document window, reveal your codes. Watch your codes as you give each of the commands in Figure 5-1. Then delete the command with one of the following: **Esc**, **Delete**, **Backspace**, or by repeating the command.

2. For each item in the list, jot down which method you used to successfully delete the codes. (The items are numbered for your convenience.)

3. When you finish, check to be sure no codes are remaining in the Codes part of your window except the Initial Style code.

FIGURE 5-1
Practice Instructions for Step-by-Step 5.1

1. Press Ctrl+B (Bold)	6. Press Tab
2. Open the File menu	7. Press F4 (Open)
3. Press F5 (Print)	8. Press Ctrl+U (Underline)
4. Open the File menu and choose Print	9. Press Caps Lock
5. Press Shift+F3 (Save)	10. Open the File menu and choose Open

You can also delete codes that affect your text, such as the Bold, Italic, and Underline formatting codes, by dragging them out of the Reveal Codes window or by using Backspace or Delete. Let's create some text and try these skills.

STEP-BY-STEP 5.2

1. Turn on **Bold** and key your name. Turn Bold off and press **Enter** twice.

2. Turn on **Underline** and key your name. Turn Underline off and press **Enter** twice.

3. Reveal your codes. Point to one of the Bold codes with the mouse pointer and press the left mouse button. Drag that Bold code up and out of the gray Reveal Codes area. Your name should no longer be bolded.

4. Point to one of the Hard Return codes between the two occurrences of your name. Drag that code up and out of the Reveal Codes area.

5. Use **Backspace** or **Delete** to remove one of the Underline codes. Then close your document without saving it.

Indent, Hanging Indent, and Double Indent

You learned in Lesson 3 that Tab is used to indent the first line of a paragraph. The Indent feature may also be used to indent, although the result is quite different. In addition, you can indent with Double Indent and Hanging Indent. Using this variety of tools, you can format your work to make it more easily read or more attractive. While all three of the indent formats can be chosen from the menu that appears when you choose Format and then Paragraph, using keystrokes is easier.

Indent is chosen by pressing F7.
Hanging Indent is chosen with Ctrl+F7.
Double Indent is chosen with Ctrl+Shift+F7.

Let's practice.

STEP-BY-STEP 5.3

1. Beginning in a new document window, open the **Format** menu. Choose **Paragraph**. Look at the indent formats chosen there. Click outside of the menu to close it.

2. Press **F7**. Key the first paragraph in Figure 5-2. Use **Bold** and **Italic** as shown. Double-space between paragraphs.

3. Press **Ctrl+F7** and key the second paragraph in Figure 5-2.

4. Press **Ctrl+Shift+F7** and key the third paragraph in Figure 5-2.

5. When you finish, reveal your codes and look at the codes that format your paragraphs. Add the codes and a description of each to your list in Appendix E.

FIGURE 5-2
Text for Step-by-Step 5.3

```
This paragraph is indented with F7.  This format is simply called
Indent.  It causes all lines to be indented from the left margin
the distance of the first tab stop, which is set by default at one-
half inch.  Indent is canceled when I press the Enter key.

This paragraph is indented with Ctrl+F7.  This is called Hanging
Indent.  All lines except the first will be indented from the left
margin to the first tab stop.  This format, too, is canceled when I
press the Enter key.

This paragraph is indented with Ctrl+Shift+F7.  With Double
Indent, all lines are indented from the left margin to the first
tab stop.  The lines are indented an equal amount from the right
margin.  Pressing Enter ends the format.  The results of this
format don't show very well with left justification.
```

6. Press **Ctrl+Home**. With your codes revealed, press **Delete** to delete the [Hd Left Indent] code that formats the paragraph. Then press **F7** to reformat the paragraph.

7. Look at the second paragraph in Reveal Codes. Use your mouse pointer to drag the two Hanging Indent codes up and out of the gray window. Your paragraph should look like a normal paragraph. Press **Ctrl+F7** to reformat the paragraph with the same format.

8. Check your work carefully and save it as **indent 5-3 xxx**. Insert the Path and Filename code a double space below the Double Indent paragraph.

9. Print the document and close it, saving it as you close it.

QuickIndent

The QuickIndent tool helps you create the indented formats you want for your documents. To use it, press Tab at the beginning of any line of the paragraph except the first.

■ If the first line of the paragraph is already indented with Tab, all lines will be aligned with the beginning of the first line.

■ If the first line of the paragraph is not already indented with Tab, QuickIndent will cause a Hanging Indent format. Let's practice with this timesaving tool.

STEP-BY-STEP 5.4

1. Open **online** from the student **datafile** folder. Use **Save As** to save the file as **online 5-4 xxx**.

2. Position the insertion point at the beginning of the second line of the first paragraph and press **Tab**. Watch as the remaining lines are indented.

3. Delete the [Hd Left Indent] code at the beginning of the first line of the first paragraph. Position the insertion point at the beginning of the second line. Press **Tab**. Watch as your paragraph is given a Hanging Indent format.

4. Insert the Path and Filename code a double space below the final paragraph. Print the file and close it, saving it again as you close.

This was a quick introduction to QuickIndent. It is a tool you are sure to find useful. It's actually quicker and easier to remember than the tools you practiced in the first three Step-by-Step exercises of this lesson. You may practice QuickIndent more at your leisure. Let's move on.

Creating Lists

Indent is useful for formats like the numbered steps in the Step-by-Step exercise you just completed. Imagine how much more difficult it would be to follow the steps if the second and third lines of the steps wrapped to the left margin.

WordPerfect makes it easy for you to create lists like the numbered steps. All you need to do is key a numeral, a period, and press the Tab key and WordPerfect knows you're beginning a list. It inserts a style that automatically inserts the numbers until you delete a number to tell WordPerfect the list is ended. Let's practice.

S TEP-BY-STEP ▷ 5.5

1. Beginning in a new document window, reveal your codes so you can watch what happens. Key **1.** and press **Tab**. Note that WordPerfect adds three codes to your document. (Add them to your list in Appendix E.)

2. Key the first item in Figure 5-3. At the end of the item, press **Enter** twice and key the second item. Note that WordPerfect automatically inserts your second number and indents the text.

3. After Item 2, press **Enter** twice. Since this is the end of the list, press **Backspace** once to delete the numeral. Then key the closing paragraph in the figure.

4. Press **Enter** three times. Save your practice as **numbers 5-5 xxx** and keep the document open as you read on.

FIGURE 5-3
Text for Step-by-Step 5.5

```
1.    This is the beginning of a list that was indented with the
      Tab key.  WordPerfect knew from the format that the text was
      to be indented as if I'd used F7 for indent.

2.    This is the second item in the list.  This text, too, will
      wrap at the tab stop so my list is easy to read.

This sentence indicates that the list is ended.  If I had wanted, I
could have indented this line with Tab and had a normally indented
paragraph.
```

Outline/Bullets & Numbering

The style WordPerfect entered when you began your little list in Step-by-Step exercise 5.5 automatically takes you to the Outline/Bullets & Numbering feature in the Insert menu. When you use this feature, you have a choice of symbols for your list. This includes a number of bullet shapes, as well as a variety of number types.

An interesting facet of this feature is that it "reads" the location of your insertion point when you begin the list and starts the list at that location. For example, if you wanted your numerals to be indented to begin at the first tab stop, you would press Tab to get to that location before beginning the list.

If you lose the format because you accidentally backspace out a number or a bullet, return the insertion point to the end of the previous formatted paragraph and press Enter to restore the numbered or bulleted format. Then you can use Delete to get rid of any extra blank lines and bring your text up to the correct location.

Let's experiment a little more with the bullets. You'll work with the much more powerful outlining tool in Lesson 14.

STEP-BY-STEP ⟩ 5.6

1. With **numbers 5-5 xxx** open, use **Save As** to save the file as **numbers 5-6 xxx**. With the insertion point at the left margin a triple space below the paragraph, open the **Insert** menu and choose **Outline/Bullets & Numbering**.

2. Click the **Bullets** tab and choose a small bullet. In the *Numbering* section at the bottom, click the button that tells WordPerfect to start a new outline or list. Click **OK**.

3. Key a two-line sentence (or two) describing how you got the bullet and indent to begin your list. Then press **Enter** twice and key the Item 2 sentence from Figure 5-3. (It's showing at the top of your window.)

4. Press **Enter** twice and then press **Backspace** once to delete the bullet. Key the final paragraph from Figure 5-3.

5. Press **Enter** three times. Then press **Tab** once to move your insertion point to the first tab stop.

6. Return to the Outline/Bullets & Numbering dialog box and choose a different bullet shape (you get to choose!). Click the **Start**

New… button and then **OK**. Note that the bullet is indented from the left margin at the position of the insertion point when you chose the feature.

7. Key the same text for the first bullet as you keyed in Step 2.

8. Press **Enter** twice and then **Backspace** once. Whoops! You wanted that bullet. Fix it as follows:
   a. Press **Backspace** until your insertion point is at the end of the first item.
   b. Press **Enter** twice to restore the bullet.
   c. Then key the text for the second bullet and the ending paragraph that you keyed in Steps 3 and 4 of this Step-by-Step exercise. (Note that you need to press **Backspace** twice to get the insertion point back to the left margin for the final paragraph because you are working with an indented format.)

9. Save your Step-by-Step exercise again as **numbers 5-6 xxx**. Insert the Path and Filename code a double space below the final paragraph. Print the Step-by-Step exercise. Keep the document open.

New Page

You learned in Lesson 1 that when a page is full, WordPerfect automatically moves the text to a new page. When this happens, a *soft page break* is inserted. Regardless of how full you have a page, you can begin a new page wherever you want by inserting a *hard page break*. You do this by pressing Ctrl+Enter.

Hard page breaks can be removed simply by positioning the insertion point at the beginning of the new page and pressing Backspace, or by revealing your codes and deleting the [HPg] code. Let's work with hard and soft page breaks.

1. With **numbers 5-6 xxx** open in the window, use **Save As** to save the file as **numbers 5-7 xxx**. Press **Ctrl+Home** twice to move your insertion point to the beginning of your document, above all codes.

2. Press **Enter** until the *Ln* indicator in the Application Bar says you are about *5"* from the top of the page.

3. Press **Ctrl+End** to check the bottom of your document. One paragraph and the Path and Filename code should be on page 2.

4. Look at the soft page break and the top and bottom margins separating that final paragraph from the rest of your document.

5. Open the **View** menu and choose **Draft** to see the single line that identifies a soft page break in Draft view. Then change back to **Page** view.

6. Position your insertion point in the line space above the first bulleted item on the first page of your document. Hold **Ctrl** while you press **Enter**. Note that you are now on page 2.

7. Look at the hard page break. It has a black and gray line. Change to **Draft** view to see the double line that indicates a hard page break in Draft view.

8. Page through your document. Note that the final paragraph and the Path and Filename code are still on page 2 because there is enough room for them on that page.

9. Reveal your codes. Find the [HPg] code above the first bulleted item. Remove the code to return the bulleted text to page 1.

10. Close your document without saving it again.

Date

Most computers have an internal clock that keeps track of the date and time. That time is recorded along with the date when you save your documents. You saw the results of that when you looked at *Details* in the Open File dialog box in Lesson 4. Because your computer knows the date, you can insert it into your documents by opening the Insert menu and choosing Date/Time. The dialog box in Figure 5-4 will be displayed. As you can see, this dialog box lists a variety of formats and enables you to customize your format. To insert the date, choose the format and click the Insert button. You may enter the date in a WordPerfect document in one of two ways:

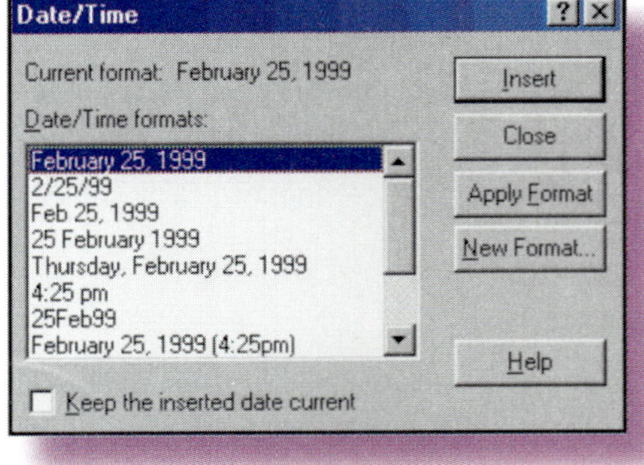

FIGURE 5-4
Date/Time Dialog Box

■ **Date Text** enters today's date at the location of the insertion point as a permanent part of your document. You can also accomplish this by pressing Ctrl+D.

■ **Date Code** enters the date as a code that changes to the current date each time the document is opened. In other words, if you enter the code in a document created today and open the document a week from today, the date on which the document is opened will be the date showing in the document. You can enter the Date Code with Ctrl+Shift+D or by clicking the *keep the inserted date current* check box at the bottom of the dialog box.

STEP-BY-STEP 5.8

1. Beginning in a new document window, press **Ctrl+D** to enter today's date into your window. Is the date correct? If not, have your instructor help you change the date in your computer.

2. Press **Enter** twice and press **Ctrl+Shift+D** to insert the Date Code. Again, the date will appear, but it is entered as a hidden code.

3. Reveal your codes and look at the two dates. Enter the appropriate code(s) in your list in Appendix E.

4. Open **indent 5-3 xxx** into a new document window. With the insertion point at the top of the document, use **Date Text** to enter the current date. Press **Enter** twice.

5. Save the document as **indent 5-8 xxx** and close it. Your previous date practice should be showing. It was hiding behind the **indent** document.

6. Save your "dates" practice as **dates 5-8 xxx**. Keep the file open for the next Step-by-Step exercise.

Center Page

Up to this point, whenever you wanted extra space at the top of a document, you've pressed Enter until the insertion point was the prescribed distance from the top of the page. There's a better way for certain situations. When you have a short document that you'd like centered between the top and bottom margins, you can use the Center Page command. Let's use the Center Page command to move your dates to the center of the page.

STEP-BY-STEP 5.9

1. With **dates 5-8 xxx** open in the window, use **Save As** to save the file as **dates 5-9 xxx**. Move your insertion point to the top of the document.

2. Open the **Format** menu and choose **Page**. Then choose **Center**. The dialog box illustrated in Figure 5-5 will appear.

3. Choose **Current page** and click **OK**.

4. Click the **Zoom** button on the Toolbar and choose **Full Page** to see how your dates look with even top and bottom margins. Use **Zoom** again to return to 100%.

(continued on next page)

5. Position the insertion point at the bottom of the document, a double space below the second date.

6. Insert the Path and Filename code. Print the file. Then close it, saving it when you close it.

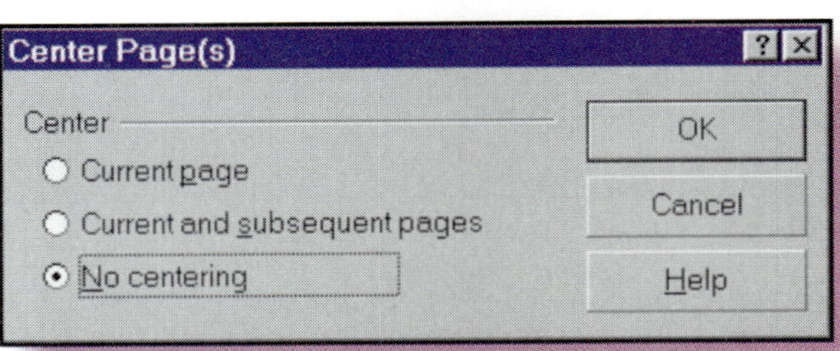

FIGURE 5-5
Center Page(s) Dialog Box

Now that you know how to insert dates and use Center Page, let's put these features to work in a letter. We'll also use Double Indent in this letter.

STEP-BY-STEP ⟹ 5.10

1. Beginning in a new document window, open the **Format** menu and choose **Page**. Choose **Center** and then **Current page**.

2. Press **Tab** to **Pos 4"**. Open the **Insert** menu, choose **Date/Time**, select the format for *month day, year* (i.e., January 1, 2000), and click **Insert**. Press **Enter** four times.

3. Key the inside address and greeting in Figure 5-6 in the usual manner, leaving a blank line above and below the greeting.

4. Use **Tab** to indent the first line of the first, second, and fourth paragraphs. Use **Double Indent** for the third paragraph.

5. Tab to **Pos 4"** for the two closing lines, leaving a quadruple space between them. Press **Enter** twice after the name and key **Enclosures** at the left margin.

6. Press **Enter** twice. Save the document as **sasoot 5-10 xxx**. Insert the Path and Filename code.

7. Prepare an envelope. Then print the letter and the envelope. Close the document, saving it again as you close it.

INTERNET An Internet address is a set of numbers or words that identifies a unique user or computer. Every user and computer on the Internet must have a different address so that the system knows where to send electronic mail and other data.

```
                              (Current Date)

Mr. Paul Weigel
P.O. Box 8760
Beaver Dam, WI 53916-8760

Dear Mr. Weigel:

    It is a pleasure to reply to your inquiry about Sasoot, Graphia.
We are quite proud of our city and of our country and are delighted to
have an opportunity to inform people from other countries about our
people, our products, and our beautiful land.

    The enclosed report will provide you with much of the information
you have requested about Sasoot.  Several brochures are also enclosed
that cover these topics:

    climate, currency used, exchange rate, major cities,
    type of government, housing opportunities, manufacturing. and
    agricultural products

    If we can be of further help, please do not hesitate to write to
me.  If you decide to visit beautiful Sasoot, please look me up for a
personal tour of the city.

                              Sincerely,



                              Reiko Onodera

Enclosures
```

Hyphen and Space Codes

In addition to the formatting tools you've been exploring, WordPerfect has a series of codes that are mostly designed to help at the end of the line. These codes include some special hyphen codes and a special space code. Let's learn about them.

Hyphen. A normal hyphen is used for joining words that always contain a hyphen—words like jack-in-the-box or self-esteem. These hyphens are keyed in the normal way, and they always show as part of a word. If they fall at the end of the line, WordPerfect will automatically divide the parts of the word at the hyphen.

Hyphen Character. A hyphen character is used to join two words that are NOT to be divided at the end of the line. The best example is when a hyphen is used as a minus sign in a formula. Key a hyphen character by holding Ctrl while you key the hyphen (Ctrl+-).

Dash. In typography, a dash is known as an *em dash*. It is longer than a hyphen. Where a hyphen is used to join two closely related words, a dash is used as a pause or break in thought, as illustrated in the Hyphen paragraph about the jack-in-the-box. A dash may occur anywhere on the line. You can create a dash using a WordPerfect shortcut. Key three hyphens (---) and continue keying. The hyphens will become a dash. A dash never has a space before it or following it.

Hard Space. A hard space works like a hyphen character. It keeps two words from being divided at the end of a line. For example, when a date like January 5, 2001, comes at the end of the line, your keyboarding rules tell you that you may (if you must) divide that date after the comma. Keyboarding rules dictate that you should NEVER divide the date between *January* and *5*. Like hyphen characters, a hard space will fool WordPerfect into thinking *January 5* is all one word, and if it falls at the end of the line, the entire "word" will drop to the next line.

Key a hard space using the same procedure as a hyphen character—holding Ctrl while you press the space bar. Hard spaces are used in formulas to keep an entire formula on one line. Look at Figure 5-7. If you key the paragraph in the normal manner, half of the formula will be on one line and half will be on the other. This would make the formula very hard to read. Let's see if we can key it so everything "hangs together." Study all parts of Step 1 before beginning.

All of these codes may be chosen from a dialog box (Format, Line, Other Codes).

STEP-BY-STEP 5.11

1. Beginning in a new document window, key the sentences illustrated in Figure 5-7. Use the following instructions:
   a. For each dash, key three hyphens and then continue keying. Do NOT space before or after the dash.
   b. In the formula, press **Ctrl+space bar** between each of the letters and characters. Key the minus sign with **Ctrl+–**.
   c. For the date, press **Ctrl+space bar** between *January* and *5*.

2. Reveal your codes and check the document against the solution of the document in Figure 5-8. Then add the codes to your list. (The codes for the dashes won't show unless you position your insertion point to the left of them.)

3. Save your paragraph as **codes 5-11 xxx**. At the end of the document, press **Enter** twice and insert the Path and Filename code.

4. Print your document and save it again with the same name. Keep it open.

FIGURE 5-7
Text for Step-by-Step 5.11

The scientists discovered that the best formula—the one that will solve your problem—is a + b - c = x + y. This spectacular formula was developed in Chester, West Virginia, on January 5, 1924.

```
The scientists discovered that the best formula[|: 4, 34]the one that
will solve your problem[|: 4, 34]is
a[HSpace]+[Hspace]b[HSpace]-[HSpace]c[HSpace]=[HSpace]x[HSpace]+
[HSpace]y.  This spectacular formula was developed in Chester, West
Virginia, on January[HSpace]5, 1924.
```

N O T E :

The results of this Step-by-Step exercise may vary according to computer and printer description. If keyed properly, however, the formula and date will remain together on

You no doubt found that inserting all of those dashes, hyphen characters, and hard spaces took some concentration. The result is that you can reformat the text as many different ways as you wish, and the formula and date will both remain intact.

All of the codes you used in this portion of the lesson are available from a dialog box. To display it, open the Format menu, choose Line, and then choose Other Codes. You'll also find quite a number of additional commands in the Other Codes dialog box. You may explore that dialog box at your leisure.

Superscripts and Subscripts

In Lesson 3 you learned about the Font dialog box. The *Position* section of this dialog box enables you to insert superscripted or subscripted numerals in your documents. The formula in Step-by-Step exercise 5.11 provides an excellent opportunity for you to try out this feature.

S TEP-BY-STEP 5.12

1. With **codes 5-11 xxx** showing in the window, position the insertion point immediately following the *a* in the formula. Key a **2** and drag the mouse pointer over the numeral to select it.

2. Open the **Format** menu and choose **Font** (or press F9) to open the Font dialog box. Near the center, find the Position feature.

3. Click the button and choose **Superscript**. Click **OK**. The *2* should now be small and raised.

4. Position the insertion point immediately following the *x* in the formula. Key a **3**, select it, and format it with **Subscript**. It should be small and below the line.

5. Close the document without saving it again.

While a few other applications use superscripts and subscripts, this feature is most frequently used in mathematical calculations and formulas.

Summary

This lesson has provided you with a number of small but important tools for use in creating WordPerfect documents. Some are nice, some are wonderful, and some may not be useful to you at all. You get to choose. In this lesson you learned that:

- There are a variety of ways to delete commands.

- You can indent your text with Indent, Hanging Indent, and Double Indent, as well as with the Tab key.

- The QuickIndent tool is a quick way of formatting indented paragraphs or paragraphs formatted with Hanging Indent.

- The Outline/Bullets & Numbering feature helps you create lists.

- You can begin a new page anywhere you wish in your documents.

- WordPerfect can be told to insert the current date or a code that displays the current date each time a document is opened.

- The Center Page command enables you to vertically center the text of a document.

- Hyphens, hyphen characters, dashes, and hard spaces are useful in protecting your documents from unwanted breaks at your line endings.

- Numerals may be formatted with superscript and subscript using the Font dialog box.

LESSON 5 REVIEW QUESTIONS

FILL IN THE BLANKS

Complete each of the following statements by writing your answer in the blank provided.

1. The _____________________ tool helps you create indented formats.

2. The indented format which has all lines indented from the left margin and the right margin an equal amount is called _____________________.

3. An easy way to create a numbered list is to key a numeral, a period, and press the _________ key.

4. You choose the Outline/Bullets & Numbering feature from the _______________ menu.

5. Regardless of how full you have a page, you can begin a new page by inserting a _____________________.

6. To insert a Date Code into your document, you can open your Insert menu, choose Date/Time, and then choose the format, or you can press the key combination of _____________________.

MATCHING

Write the letter of the term or phrase from Column 2 that best matches the description in Column 1.

Column 1   **Column 2**

____ **7.** The feature used to refer to the position of a character that is printed above the normal line of print.

A. Center Pages

B. Hyphen

____ **8.** This is the feature you would use to keep a date such as October 11, 2001, together on one line.

C. Hyphen Character

D. Dash

____ **9.** Use this feature when you want a short document centered between the top and bottom margins.

E. Hard Space

____ **10.** You can create this feature by keying three hyphens.

F. Superscript

G. Subscript

LESSON 5 PROJECT

This project will have two unrelated parts so you can practice several of the skills learned in this lesson. You'll begin with adding numbers to the most recent version of the **gifts** document.

PROJECT 5A

1. Open **gifts u1ap2 xxx**. Use **Save As** to save the file as **gifts proj5a xxx**. Position the insertion point at the left margin beside the paragraph that begins with the word *Flowers*. It is the fourth paragraph.

2. Press **Delete** once to delete the tab that indents the first line of the paragraph. Then press **Tab** and key **1.** followed by **Tab** again. The entire paragraph should move to align at an inch from the left margin (*Pos 2"*).

3. Position the insertion point after the word *recipient* at the end of the same paragraph. Press **Enter**. Then press **Delete** until the *Chocolates* item lines up with the *Flowers* item.

4. Follow the procedure in Step 2 to add numerals to all of the remaining "gift" paragraphs of the document. (There should be seven in all.)

5. Print the document and close it, saving it again with the same name.

   Now let's format a document that has been created and saved for you.

1. Go to the student **datafile** folder and open **online**. Use **Save As** to save the file as **online proj5b xxx**. With the insertion point at the top of the document, press **Enter** to add some line spaces above the first paragraph.

2. Move your insertion point to the top again. Use **Flush Right** and key your full name at the right margin. Press **Enter** and use **Flush Right** and **Date Text** to position the date below your name.

3. Double-space following the date, and center the title in bold and all caps as shown below. Use **20-pt. Arial** for the title.

COMMUNICATIONS ONLINE

4. Adjust the spacing so one blank line separates the title from the first line of the first paragraph.

5. Return to the top of the document and use the **Center Page** command to center the document vertically.

6. Use **Double Indent** for the second paragraph. Select that paragraph and apply **Bold** to the entire paragraph.

7. In the last sentence, select *free speech*. Change those two words to **Italic**. Do the same with *full exchange of ideas*.

8. Insert the Path and Filename code a double space below the last paragraph. Check your work carefully. Then print it and close it, saving it again with the same name.

CRITICAL THINKING ACTIVITY

SCANS

    As you practice using the Date Text and Date Code features, think about when one would be more appropriate than the other. Make a list of the types of documents in which you would insert Date Text. Make another list of the types of documents in which you would insert a Date Code.

EDITING FEATURES

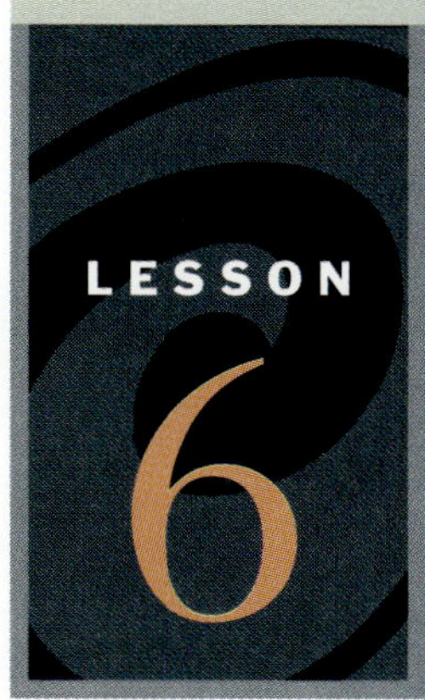

Upon completion of this lesson, you will be able to:

- Use Find to search for unique strings of text.
- Use Replace to replace existing text with different text.
- Use Select for cutting, copying, moving, and pasting text.
- Highlight text to call attention to it with the Highlight tool.
- Use Drag and Drop for editing selected text.

Estimated Time: 1 hour

You have already learned quite a number of ways to edit your text. You learned that to edit, you can:

- Use Backspace to delete text to the left of the insertion point.
- Use Delete to delete text to the right of the insertion point.
- Use Ctrl+Delete to delete from the insertion point to the end of the line.
- Use Ctrl+Backspace to delete the word at the insertion point.
- Delete formatting codes (such as Indent) with the Backspace or Delete keys, depending on where the insertion point is located.
- Delete formatting codes by dragging them out of the Reveal Codes window.
- Select a chunk of text and delete it with the Backspace or Delete keys.
- Select a chunk of text and key new text over the selected text.
- Use Typeover to key new text over existing text.

As you can see, you've learned a lot in five short lessons about how to manipulate the text showing in your window. One of the basic premises of any word processing program is that you should "edit—don't rekey."

In this lesson you will learn about several other powerful features that help support you with this idea of editing. Work carefully in this lesson so you master the concepts covered. They are critical!

Find and Replace

The *Find and Replace* feature enables you to tell the computer to look through the open document to locate specific words, phrases, or codes. It can also be used to replace one piece of text or code with another. Find and Replace can be chosen from the Edit menu, by pressing F2, or by pressing Ctrl+F.

We'll learn about Find and Replace with a couple of simple Step-by-Step exercises, beginning with Find.

STEP-BY-STEP 6.1

1. Open **pc-tv** from the student **datafile** folder. Use **Save As** to save the document as **pc-tv 6-1 xxx**. Keep the insertion point at the top of the file.

2. Open the **Edit** menu and choose **Find and Replace**. The Find and Replace dialog box should open, looking much like Figure 6-1.

3. With the insertion point in the *Find* text box, key **morp** and click **Find Next** or press **Enter**. (The word you are searching for is much longer than what you keyed, but you have enough unique characters so you know WordPerfect will take you directly to the text for which you're searching.)

4. Your insertion point should be moved directly to the word *morphing*.

5. Click outside of the Find and Replace dialog box to make your document window the active window. Press **Ctrl+Home** to return to the beginning of the document.

6. Point to *morp* in the dialog box and click to activate the dialog box. Double click to highlight *morp* in the *Find* text box. Key **tv** in lowercase letters. Then click the **Find Next** button.

7. WordPerfect will stop at the first occurrence of *tv*. Click **Find Next** again. Continue the procedure, counting the number of times *tv* appears in the document. When WordPerfect can find no more occurrences of *tv*, a warning box will tell you that. Click **No** at the Begin again question. Did you find five occurrences?

8. Click outside of the dialog box and return to the top of the document. Keep the document open as you read on.

FIGURE 6-1
Find and Replace Dialog Box

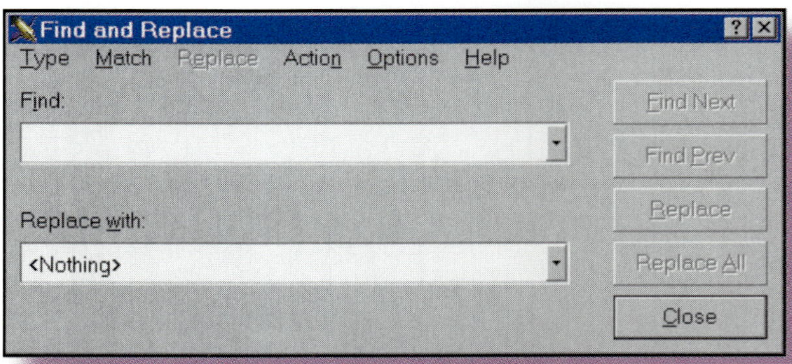

Some of the more important Find and Replace options come from the Match menu. Let's look at the following Match options:

■ **Whole Word**. If you choose Whole Word, WordPerfect will not find the specified text when it is part of another word. For example, if you search for *the* and you don't choose Whole Word, WordPerfect will stop at *weather, them, further, these,* etc.

■ **Case**. In Step-by-Step exercise 6.1 you keyed *tv* in lowercase and Find found it. That's because the default for Find is not case-sensitive. We'll experiment with this shortly.

■ **Font**. This menu choice opens a dialog box where you may choose the font code or appearance attribute for which you're searching.

■ **Codes**. The final choice in the Match menu provides a long list of codes for which you may search.

Now that you have an introduction to these features, let's experiment.

S TEP-BY-STEP ▷ 6.2

1. With your insertion point at the beginning of the document and the Find and Replace dialog box open, open the **Match** menu.

2. Choose **Whole Word**. See how many times WordPerfect will stop at the word *tv* this time. (It should be four times because it won't find the occurrence with the *s*.)

3. Return to the top of the document and choose **Case** from the **Match** menu. Then press **Enter** or click **Find Next**. How many occurrences of *tv* did WordPerfect find? What happened?

4. Return to the top of the document. In the **Match** menu, deselect **Whole Word**. (Case is still selected.)

5. In the *Find* text box, change the text from *tv* to **TV**. Now use **Find Next** to go through the document. Did you find five occurrences of *TV*? Return your insertion point to the top of the document.

6. In the **Match** menu, deselect **Case**. Open the **Match** menu again and choose **Codes**. The resulting dialog box should look much like Figure 6-2.

7. Scroll way down in the list until you find *Hd Left Ind*. Click the code to select it. Then click the **Insert & Close** button. (If *TV* is still in the *Find* box, delete it.)

8. Click **Find Next**. Did Find take you directly to the beginning of the indented paragraph?

9. Close the Find and Replace dialog box, but keep your document open as you read on.

FIGURE 6-2
Find and Replace Codes Dialog Box

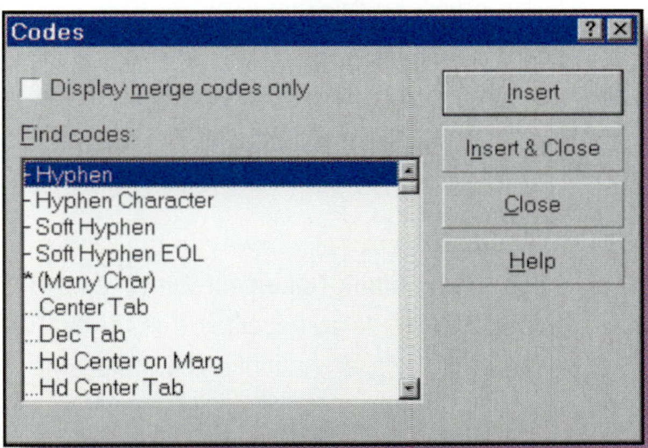

You're doing well. You have already practiced the main parts of Find. Now let's learn about Replace.

Replace uses Find to locate the text that needs to be replaced.

STEP-BY-STEP 6.3

1. With your insertion point at the top of the **pc-tv 6-1 xxx** document, open the Find and Replace dialog box.

2. In the *Find* box, key **tv**. Press **Tab**.

3. In the *Replace with* box, key **bicycle**. (OK. So it's corny. But it's good practice!)

4. Click the **Find Next** button. When WordPerfect stops at the first occurrence of *TV,* click **Replace**. (Note that because *TV* had a capital letter at the beginning, the replacement— *Bicycle*—will also have an initial cap.)

5. WordPerfect will stop at the next occurrence of *TV*, waiting for you to confirm the replacement. This time, click **Replace All**. The remaining four replacements should be made in a jiffy! (Can you count better than WordPerfect can?)

6. Click outside of the Find and Replace dialog box and press **Ctrl+Home** to return to the beginning of your document. Can you use **Replace** to change *Bicycle* back to *TV* on your own?

7. Close the Find and Replace dialog box. Keep your document open in the window as you read on.

While you can easily use Replace All to replace each occurrence of one word with another, it usually isn't safe. Sometimes you need to see the surrounding text to know if other repairs need to be made. For example, assume you had a long document containing the names of Mary Christensen and Harry Christianson. When you keyed the document, you spelled Harry's name like Mary's— Christensen. You can use Replace to fix the error, but you must confirm every replacement so you can look at the surrounding text to see if it is referring to Mary or Harry.

WordPerfect helps you to maintain good grammar with the Word Forms choice in the Type menu. Let's try a little Step-by-Step exercise to see how it works.

STEP-BY-STEP 6.4

1. With **pc-tv 6-1 xxx** still showing in the window, click the **New Blank Document** button on the Toolbar. (On the default Toolbar, it is the first button at the left, and it looks like a piece of paper.)

2. Key the little paragraph in Figure 6-3. Then return the insertion point to the beginning of the document.

3. Open the Find and Replace dialog box. Open the **Type** menu and click **Word Forms**.

4. In the *Find* text box, key **fly**. In the *Replace with* text box, key **swim**.

5. Click the **Replace All** button. Study your sentences. Note that WordPerfect was smart enough to spell *swimming* correctly.

6. Close the Find and Replace dialog box, and close your document without saving it. The **pc-tv 6-1 xxx** document should still be showing in your window. (It was hiding under the other document.) Keep it open and read on.

FIGURE 6-3
Text for Step-by-Step 6.4

```
I have always wanted to learn to fly.  To me there couldn't be
anything more delightful than flying freely with no stop signs.
```

You'll find lots of opportunities to use Find and Replace. You will also find that it is a great time-saver, both for locating specific places in your documents and for replacing text.

Editing with Select

In Lesson 2 you learned that you can select a block of text and delete it all at once. In Lesson 3 you learned that you can select a block of text and format it with appearance attributes such as Bold, Italic, or Underline. It shouldn't come as any surprise to you that you can select blocks of text and move them around in your documents.

You learned that text can be selected using the mouse. You can also turn on Select with F8 or choose it from the Edit menu and use the arrow keys to define the size of a block of text. In this lesson we'll practice both methods, although it is usually faster to select text using the mouse.

We will also use the Windows Clipboard. Whenever you are working in one of the many Windows programs, you can use the Windows Clipboard for cutting, moving, and pasting selected text.

Cut

As you know, once text has been selected, you can cut it from your document with Delete. When you do this, WordPerfect remembers what you've deleted so you can replace the deleted text with Undo. WordPerfect will remember up to 300 changes to your documents.

The text can also be cut to the Windows Clipboard in the following ways:

- By using the Ctrl+X shortcut.

- By clicking the Cut button (scissors icon) on the Toolbar.

- By choosing Cut from the Edit menu.

When you cut text to the Windows Clipboard, it remains there until you cut something else or until you close WordPerfect. Usually when you cut text, your intention is to move the insertion point to a different location where you will choose to paste the text.

Paste

Paste is used to place text that is on the Clipboard back into your document. You can paste from the Clipboard in the following ways:

- By pressing Ctrl+V.

- By clicking the Paste button (clipboard icon) on the Toolbar.

- By choosing Paste from the Edit menu.

Before you paste, you must position the insertion point where you want the text to be pasted. Cutting and pasting is a great way to move text from one location to another. Let's practice. We'll begin by selecting text with yet another method. Position the insertion point at the beginning of the block of text to be selected, hold the Shift key, and click at the end of the block of text to be selected.

STEP-BY-STEP 6.5

1. With **pc-tv 6-1 xxx** still showing in your window, move the insertion point to the beginning of the document.

2. Press **F8**. Press the down arrow key until the first paragraph is selected, along with the line separating the first two paragraphs.

3. Press **Ctrl+X** to cut the paragraph. It will disappear from the document.

4. Press **Ctrl+End** to move the insertion point to the end of the document, a double space below the final paragraph. Press **Ctrl+V** to paste the paragraph at the bottom.

Now we'll move a different paragraph with the mouse and the **Edit** menu.

5. Point to the paragraph in the middle and quadruple click to select the paragraph, together with the blank line following the paragraph.

6. Open the **Edit** menu and choose **Cut**. Press **Ctrl+Home** to move the insertion point to the top of the document. Open the **Edit** menu and choose **Paste** to paste the paragraph at the top.

Let's use the Toolbar to do the same thing.

7. Position the insertion point at the left margin of the first line of the indented paragraph. Hold the **Shift** key while you point with the mouse to the beginning of the first word of the next paragraph. Click once to select the paragraph and the line following it.

8. Point to the Cut tool on the Toolbar—the scissors icon—and click to cut the paragraph. Move the insertion point to the end of the document and click the Paste tool on the Toolbar—the clipboard icon—to paste the paragraph at the end of the document.

9. Keep your document open in the window as you read on to learn the difference between cutting and copying. You'll also read about yet another way to perform these activities.

Copy

Copy is like Cut except that the text you select and place on the Clipboard will also remain in its original position in the document. You might use Copy to copy a phrase, sentence, or paragraph to a different location in a document. Or it is more likely that you would copy a block of text onto the Clipboard so that it could be used in a different document.

Like Cut and Paste, Copy can be selected in the following ways:

- By pressing Ctrl+C.

- By clicking the Copy button (with two "pages") on the Toolbar.

- By opening the Edit menu and choosing Copy.

- From the QuickMenu.

Let's use the same three paragraphs to practice Copy. This time we'll use the QuickMenu.

QuickMenus

As you know, QuickMenus are displayed by clicking the right mouse button. If you have never worked with QuickMenus, you should read about them in Appendix B. The tools available in a QuickMenu depend on where you are pointing and what is happening in your window when you right click.

If text is selected, the QuickMenu includes Cut, Copy, and Paste. It also includes some other tools about which you've been learning. We'll use the QuickMenu in Step-by-Step exercise 6.6.

S TEP-BY-STEP 6.6

1. With **pc-tv 6-1 xxx** still showing in the window, save the file as **pc-tv 6-6 xxx**. Position the insertion point at the beginning of the paragraph in the middle.

2. Select that paragraph (be sure to include the line following the paragraph). Right click to display the QuickMenu. It should look like Figure 6-4. Choose **Copy** to copy the paragraph to the Clipboard.

3. Press **Ctrl+End** to move the insertion point to the end of the document. Point below the final paragraph and right click to display the QuickMenu again. Choose **Paste** to paste the paragraph into place. Now your document should have two paragraphs exactly alike.

FIGURE 6-4
QuickMenu

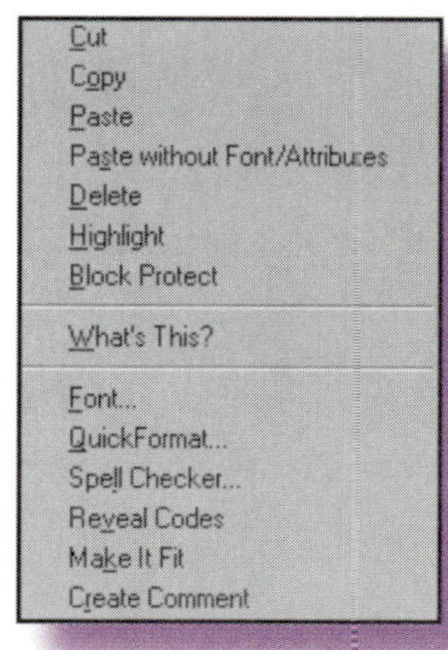

(continued on next page)

4. Study the QuickMenu in Figure 6-4. Notice that it contains some additional features about which you've already learned—Cut, Paste, Font, and Reveal Codes.

5. Double click to select any word in the document. Right click to display the QuickMenu and choose **Highlight**. Reveal your codes and look at the Highlight code. Add it to your list. (We'll discuss this feature shortly.)

6. Practice cutting, copying, and pasting until you are comfortable with the procedure. Then insert the Path and Filename code a double space below the last paragraph.

7. Print your messed-up document and save it again with the same name. Keep it open.

Vertical Spacing

Whenever you use Cut, Copy, and Paste, you should always check the vertical spacing of your document after you've completed the move. It's easy to leave an extra hard return in the old location or end up with two pieces of text too close together in the new location. When that happens, you must add or delete hard returns to make the text correctly spaced. ALWAYS visually check your work when you edit. You'll save yourself much time and frustration.

Methods of Editing

Also, this is a good time to observe that while you normally learn only one way to perform a task, this time you learned FOUR of them! The method you use will depend on where your hands are when you need a feature, and it will also depend on personal preference. Whichever method(s) you choose to use, you will become quite skilled at cutting, copying, and pasting text. It helps you with the "don't rekey" mentality that needs to be developed with word processing. It also helps you save time and errors.

Drag and Drop

One more editing tool deserves mention here. This tool is called *Drag and Drop*. The procedure is to select text to be moved or copied and then use the mouse to drag that selected text to its new position.

If the place where you wish to drag the text is below the text showing in the window, simply drag your mouse pointer into the Application Bar at the bottom. WordPerfect will scroll up in the window until you can see the desired location for the text.

Drag and Drop can be used to move text or to copy text. To move, simply drag it and drop it. To copy, hold the Ctrl key while you drag and drop the text. Let's try it.

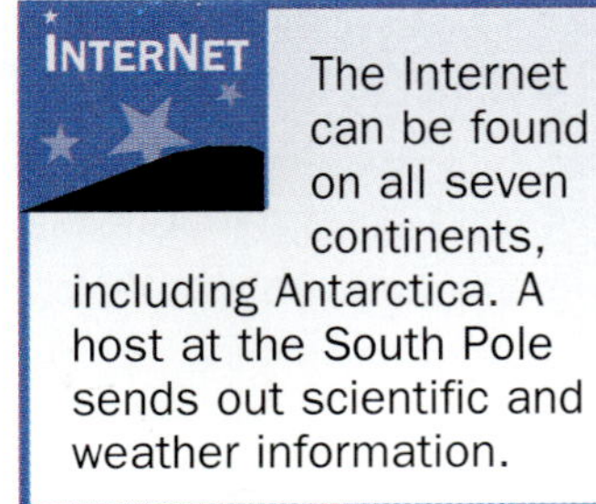

The Internet can be found on all seven continents, including Antarctica. A host at the South Pole sends out scientific and weather information.

S TEP-BY-STEP 6.7

1. With **pc-tv 6-6 xxx** showing in your window, save the file as **pc-tv 6-7 xxx**.

2. Select the indented paragraph—wherever it is in your document. Point to the selected text and depress the left mouse button. Hold it down and move the mouse slightly. The move icon should appear—an arrow with a page attached to the tail.

3. Continue to hold the mouse button and drag the pointer down out of the selected text. You'll see that the mouse pointer is accompanied by a vertical line that's like the shadow pointer.

4. Move the shadow pointer until it is a double space below the final paragraph of the document, just in front of the Path and Filename code. Release the mouse button. The paragraph should be moved to that position. (Repair the spacing around the paragraph and at the top, if necessary.)

5. To copy a paragraph, select the paragraph that is currently second in your document. Hold the **Ctrl** key while you point to the selected text and depress the left mouse button. Hold **Ctrl** and the mouse button as you move the mouse slightly. The copy icon will change from a pointer with two copies of a page to a pointer with a plus sign.

6. Move the mouse and the shadow pointer so the pointer is to the left of the final paragraph and release the mouse button to drop the paragraph there.

7. Practice copying and moving words, sentences, phrases, or paragraphs using the Drag and Drop procedure until you are comfortable with it. Don't worry about messing up the document.

8. When you finish, close the document without saving it.

Highlight

You used Highlight to paint text yellow in Step-by-Step exercise 6.6. Highlight is a way of marking text for shared documents. You can change the color of highlighting and use several colors in the same document. You can also hide the highlighting so it doesn't show in the window or on the printed copy, but the codes remain in the copy so the highlighting can be displayed again.

When you practiced Highlight in Step-by-Step exercise 6.6, you selected the text before selecting Highlight from the QuickMenu. If you prefer, you can turn Highlight on and highlight text by dragging the mouse pointer over text in your document. You probably noticed that highlighted text prints with a shaded background.

Highlight can also be chosen from the Toolbar (the icon near the middle that looks like a yellow marker) or from the Tools menu. In fact, if you wish to change Highlight options, you must choose Tools and then Highlight.

You may explore Highlight at your leisure. Be sure to change it back to the defaults when you finish—with the color as yellow and with Print/Show Highlighting selected.

Summary

In addition to Find and Replace, the major thrust of this lesson had to do with selected text. In this lesson you learned that:

- You can use Find to move the insertion point to a unique string of characters.
- Replace enables you to find text to be replaced and replace it automatically. Text can be replaced one occurrence at a time or globally.
- There are a number of ways to cut or copy text to the Clipboard.
- There are an equal number of ways to paste from the Clipboard.
- If you cut and paste text, it is deleted from the original location.
- If you copy and paste text, you'll have two copies of that chunk of text.
- You can select text and drag or copy it to a new location.
- Text can be marked with Highlight to make it stand out for the attention of others.

LESSON 6 REVIEW QUESTIONS

WRITTEN QUESTIONS

Write your answers to the following questions.

1. Describe the functions of the Find and Replace feature.

2. What three ways can text be cut to the Windows Clipboard?

3. In order to display the QuickMenu that includes features such as Cut, Copy, and Paste, what must be done with your text?

4. The Drag and Drop feature can be used two ways. Name them.

5. What is the name of the feature that can be used as a way of marking text for shared documents and can be chosen from the Toolbar with an icon that looks like a yellow marker?

TRUE/FALSE

Circle the T if the statement is true. Circle the F if it is false.

T   F   6. The default for Find is not case-sensitive.

T   F   7. Once you paste text that is on the Clipboard back into your document, it is removed from the Clipboard.

T F **8.** Copy is like Cut except the text you select and place on the Clipboard will also remain in its original position.

T F **9.** When using Drag and Drop to copy text, hold the Ctrl key while you drag and drop.

T F **10.** You can change the color of highlighting as long as you maintain that same color throughout your document.

LESSON 6 PROJECT

Let's try some of the features you learned in this lesson on a document that has been keyed and saved for you. As always, remember to read through the entire Step-by-Step exercise before beginning. Work efficiently and carefully.

1. Open **gifts proj5a xxx**. Use **Save As** to save the file as **gifts proj6 xxx**. (If you make a mess of the project and need to start again, close this file without saving. Open **gifts proj6 xxx** and begin again.)

2. Use **Find and Replace** to replace the word *vulgar* with the word **offensive**.

3. Using either **Cut and Paste** or **Drag and Drop**, rearrange the first three items in the list into the following order. (Read Step 4 before you begin.)

    1.   *Chocolates . . .*
    2.   *Gifts with company logos . . .*
    3.   *Flowers . . .*

4. Note that the items are automatically renumbered. If you lose a numeral with:
    a. **Drag and Drop:** Click the **Undo** button on the Toolbar and start again. (When positioning the shadow pointer to "drop" the item into place, point in the left margin, opposite the margin guideline. That puts the insertion point in front of the numeral.)
    b. **Cut and Paste:** Position the insertion point at the end of the last line above the missing numeral and press **Enter**. Then delete the spaces to bring the text up to the numeral. (The best way to paste an item before a numbered item so you don't lose a numeral is to first click on the line where the item is to be pasted. Then press **Home** twice to get the insertion point to the left of all codes on the line. Finally, paste the item into place.)

5. Exchange items 4 and 5.

6. Position the insertion point at the beginning of the *Be careful . . .* sentence in the final item. Press **Enter** to give it a number and make it item 8 in the list.

7. Exchange items 7 and 8.

8. Save the file again with the same name. Then print it and close it.

SCANS

One of the members of your small group helping with your Environmental Science Class report just realized she gave you an incorrect spelling of one of the endangered species about which you wrote. The other members have also suggested that the order of the information needs to be changed with some additions and deletions. What are some of the features you learned to use in this lesson that could be put to use with this report?

WRITING TOOLS

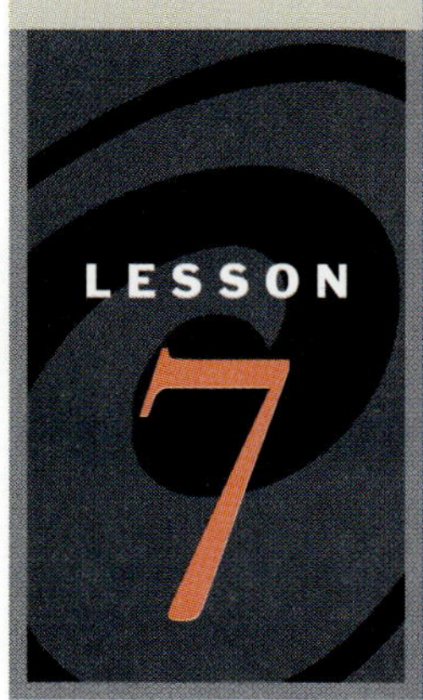

OBJECTIVES

Upon completion of this lesson, you will be able to:

- Discuss the QuickCorrect feature.

- Fix words marked with the WordPerfect Spell-As-You-Go feature.

- Use Spell Checker to find errors in your document.

- Use the WordPerfect Thesaurus to help you find the right word.

- Use Grammatik to check the grammar in your documents.

- Use Prompt-As-You-Go

Estimated Time: 1 hour

WordPerfect has several tools to help you with spelling and keying as you enter your text. Those tools are Spell-As-You-Go, Prompt-As-You-Go, QuickCorrect, WordPerfect Spell Checker, the Word-Perfect Thesaurus, QuickWords, and a grammar checker called Grammatik.

Let's learn about QuickCorrect, Spell-As-You-Go, and Prompt-As-You-Go, and then we'll learn about some of the other tools. QuickWords will be covered in Lesson 11.

QuickCorrect

You learned in an earlier lesson that WordPerfect automatically corrects some of your errors as you key. The program contains dozens of commonly misspelled or miskeyed words, as well as some odd things like ordinals (the *th* in 6th and 1/2). It also makes some changes to capitalization—sometimes they are changes you don't want. When QuickCorrect capitalizes a letter that should remain a lowercase letter, fix it with Backspace or Delete. Sometimes it takes two tries. Let's practice by keying some of the errors QuickCorrect fixes.

The communications structure of the Internet is the global telephone system, which is a network of networks working together. By using the phone system, the Internet has worldwide coverage and significant potential for growth.

1. Watch your window as you key the sentence in Figure 7-1, complete with errors.

2. When you finish, close the practice without saving it.

FIGURE 7-1
Text for Step-by-Step 7.1

THe dog adn cat are in teh barn.

You probably noticed that the correction was made when you pressed the space bar following the word with the error.

QuickCorrect can be customized to fix errors you make frequently. You can also add shortcuts for words and phrases you use often. Then when you key the shortcut, the longer version will appear. Let's try a quick Step-by-Step exercise in customizing QuickCorrect.

1. In a new document window, open the **Tools** menu and choose **QuickCorrect**. The Quick-Correct dialog box should appear, looking much like Figure 7-2.

2. Use the scroll bar to look through the list at the kinds of mistakes QuickCorrect fixes.

3. Browse through the other four tabs and look at the choices available there. Do not make any changes to the options unless your instructor tells you to. Return to the Quick-Correct tab.

4. In the *Replace* text box at the upper left, key **wp**. Tab to the next box. Key **WordPerfect**. Click the **Add Entry** button and then click **OK**.

5. In your document window, key the paragraph illustrated in Figure 7-3. Each time you come to *WordPerfect*, key **wp** and press the space bar. At the end of the paragraph, press **Enter** twice. Did the word expand like you expected it to?

FIGURE 7-2
QuickCorrect Dialog Box

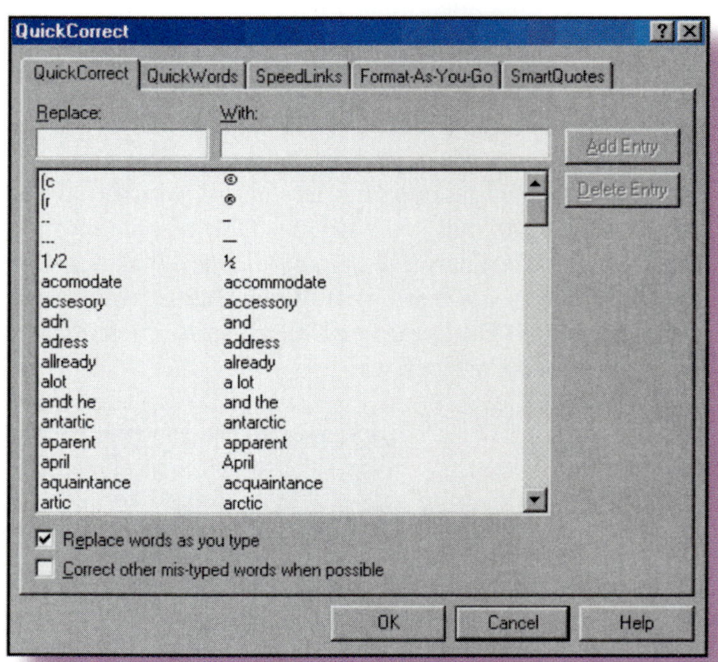

6. Return to the QuickCorrect dialog box. Scroll through the list until you find the *WordPerfect* entry. Highlight it and click the **Delete Entry** button to delete it. Then click **OK** to close the dialog box.

7. Save your paragraph as **fix 7-2 xxx**.

8. Keep the document open in the window as you read on.

FIGURE 7-3
Text for Step-by-Step 7.2

```
    I am in the process of learning about WordPerfect word processing
on a computer.  In the few lessons I have completed, I've learned that
WordPerfect is a great computer application program.  I certainly hope
that when I get a computer at work, I will have a choice of word
processing programs so I can use WordPerfect.
```

Obviously, the shortcut you use must be a unique set of characters. Also, the expanded text is limited to about 125 characters. Do NOT make any changes to QuickCorrect in the classroom unless your instructor gives you permission to add entries. On the job, however, this feature should be of great value to you.

Spell-As-You-Go

Another feature that helps you identify errors in your documents is Spell-As-You-Go. This is the feature that underlines in red words that aren't in the WordPerfect dictionary. Up to this point, you probably have been manually correcting those underlined words. A couple of alternatives are available.

When the insertion point is in a word that is underlined in red, that word is shown in red in the text box at the right of the Property Bar. (Words that are spelled correctly show in black in that box.) The feature is referred to as Prompt-As-You-Go, and it fits together with the Spell-As-You-Go feature. Spell-As-You-Go offers the following two choices:

- When the insertion point is in the incorrect word and the word is red in the Prompt-As-You-Go box, you can click the arrow beside the box and choose the correct spelling of the word.

- When a word is underlined in red, regardless of the position of the insertion point, you can point to it and right click. This displays a short list of possible spellings, as well as some additional options. You can choose the correct spelling from the list.

Let's try a short Step-by-Step exercise so you can see how Spell-As-You-Go and Prompt-As-You-Go work.

STEP-BY-STEP 7.3

1. With **fix 7-2 xxx** showing in the window, use **Save As** to save the file as **fix 7-3 xxx**.

2. Position the insertion point at the end of the document and key the sentence in Figure 7-4.

Do not correct the misspelled words as you key. (Keep an eye on the Prompt-As-You-Go box.)

(continued on next page)

9 3

3. When you finish, click to position the insertion point in *WordPerfct* and click the arrow beside the Prompt-As-You-Go box on the Property Bar. Choose the correct spelling of WordPerfect.

4. Point to *underlning* and right click. Look at the options at the bottom of the menu. Then choose the correct spelling of *underlining* from the list at the top.

5. Use either method to fix *speled*.

6. Read your sentence carefully. Did Spell-As-You-Go find all of the errors? Why do you suppose it missed *sem*? Fix the word.

7. Insert the Path and Filename code a double space below the last paragraph. Click the **Save** button on the Toolbar to save your document again as **fix 7-3 xxx**.

8. Print the two-paragraph document and close it.

FIGURE 7-4
Text for Step-by-Step 7.3

```
WordPerfct helps you by underlning words that don't sem to be speled
correctly.
```

Spell Checker

Spell Checker uses the same WordPerfect dictionary as Spell-As-You-Go for checking the words in your document. With Spell Checker, however, you will probably check the document after you've finished it. Like Spell-As-You-Go, Spell Checker helps you build supplementary dictionaries to fill specific needs.

Spell Checker can be chosen from the Tools menu or the Spell Checker button on the default Toolbar. It pictures a book with a red *s*. Perhaps the best way to get a feel for Spell Checker is to try it on a document containing errors. After practicing, some of the features and cautions regarding Spell Checker will be discussed.

1. Open **errors** from the student **datafile** folder. Use **Save As** to save the file as **errors 7-4 xxx**.

2. Select the parenthetical information in the first line and key your name in its place. Do the same at the bottom of the document. Select the parenthetical information about the school and key the name of your school in that location.

3. Click the **Spell Checker** button on the Toolbar or open the **Tools** menu and choose **Spell Checker**. A dialog box will open that looks like Figure 7-5. Note that the Spell Checker tab is chosen. WordPerfect may stop at your name. If it does, click **Skip All**, because you probably spelled your name correctly.

4. Next, WordPerfect will stop at *lerning*. WordPerfect prompts you to replace the word with *leaning*. Click *learning* in the Replacements box and then click **Replace**. When WordPerfect stops at *WordPerfek*, no suggested spelling is available. In the *Replace with* text box, delete the *k* and replace it with **ct**. Click the **Replace** button.

5. Continue through the document correcting the misspelled words.
   a. If the correct word appears in the *Replace with* text box, click the **Replace** button.
   b. If the correct word is in the list below, click it to select it and then click the **Replace** button.
   c. Some errors may have to be fixed manually. When that occurs, make the correction in the *Replace with* text box and click the **Replace** button. (You can also make the correction right in your text and click the **Resume** button when you are ready to continue spell checking your document.)

6. When WordPerfect tells you that all errors are corrected, confirm that Spell Checker should be closed.

7. Proofread your document carefully. Did Spell Checker find the missing capital letter at the beginning of the last sentence? Did it know that *corse* was not correct? Fix both errors.

8. Add the Path and Filename code a double space below your name and print the document. Save it again with the same name and keep it open.

FIGURE 7-5
Spell Checker Dialog Box

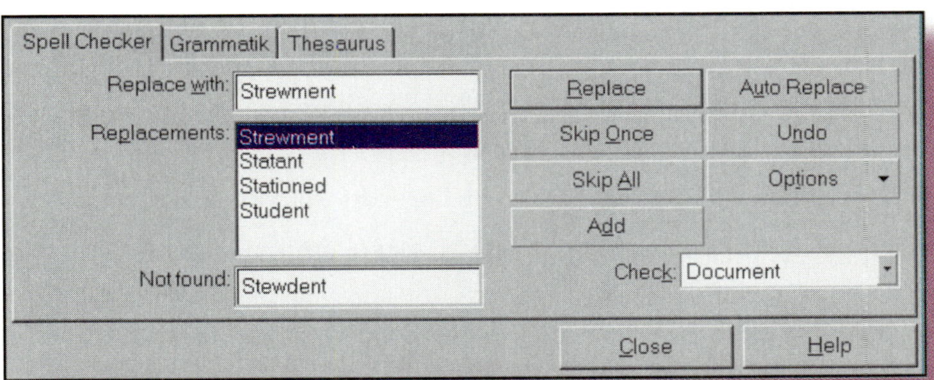

What did Spell Checker do when it came to your name at the bottom of the document? Because you chose Skip All at the top, it should have skipped the one at the bottom without even highlighting it.

This document was filled with foolishly misspelled words that you would have caught and corrected if you had been asked to proofread. Many times, however, even if you've proofread, it's a good idea to run Spell Checker to be certain that all of the words are correctly spelled.

You didn't use all of the choices in the dialog box. Following is a brief explanation of the main buttons in the dialog box:

- **Replace**. Replaces the word or phrase with the text in the Replace with box. You can select one of the suggested replacements or edit the word or phrase in the text box.

- **Resume**. Lets you continue an incomplete spell check if you click in the document while the Spell Checker is displayed.

- **Skip Once**. Skips the current occurrence of the word or phrase.

- **Skip All**. Skips every occurrence of the word or phrase during the current spell check.

- **Add**. Adds the current replacement word or phrase to the user word list showing in the Add to drop-down list. We won't make any changes to the lists in the classroom. If you were on the job, however, you might add your name and your boss's name, and perhaps, the name of your company or city.

- **Auto Replace**. Enables you to define automatic replacements for words as you key them.

- **Undo**. Backs you up to the previous correction.

- **Options**. Gives you some choices regarding how the document is checked. Figure 7-6 shows the Options menu. The User Word Lists choice enables you to go into the word list to delete items. In addition to the multiple user word lists, you can purchase additional main word lists and various language modules. The check marks in the figure show the default settings. If you deselect Auto start, for example, WordPerfect will wait for you to click a Start button before spell checking begins. Don't change any of the options unless your instructor asks you to do so.

FIGURE 7-6
Spell Options Menu

Miscellaneous Spell Checker Notes

Following is a review and some additional information about Spell Checker:

- The document to be checked should be showing in the window.

- Click Close if you wish to discontinue checking.

- Sometimes Spell Checker takes a moment to find the next word. Be patient.

- You can check a block of text by first selecting the text in the usual manner. Then start Spell Checker.

- Spell Checker doesn't recognize an incorrect word if the word is spelled correctly. It can't distinguish, for example, between the correct usage of *house* and *horse*.

YOU MUST PROOFREAD YOUR WORK CAREFULLY, even when you use Spell Checker.

Thesaurus

In addition to Spell Checker, WordPerfect contains a Thesaurus. The Thesaurus helps you find just the right word when you're unsure how to say something. It does this by providing a list of synonyms (words that have the same meaning). You may have noticed the Thesaurus tab when you were using Spell Checker. WordPerfect also offers a list of synonyms for any word that shows in black in the Prompt-As-You-Go box. Let's try the Thesaurus on the corrected document you used for Spell Checker.

9 6

STEP-BY-STEP 7.5

1. With **errors 7-4 xxx** showing in the window, use **Save As** to save the file as **errors 7-5 xxx**.

2. Position the insertion point in the word *beautiful* in the last line of the first paragraph.

3. Click the arrow beside the Prompt-As-You-Go box on the Property Bar and look at the list of possible synonyms for *beautiful*. Press the **Esc** button to close the list.

4. Open the **Tools** menu and choose **Thesaurus**. Look at the dialog box. It looks much like the Spell Checker dialog box. In fact, it is the third tab of the Spell Checker dialog box (see Figure 7-7).

5. The word *beautiful* appears with a definition. Click the **+** at the left of the definition and look through the list of synonyms for *beautiful*.

6. Point to *lovely* in the list and click. A list of definitions for *lovely* will appear.

7. Click the **+** at the left of *Pleasing to the eye….* Click *appealing* and choose **Replace** to replace *beautiful* in your document with *appealing*.

8. Close the Thesaurus and print the document. Save it again as **errors 7-5 xxx**. Keep it open.

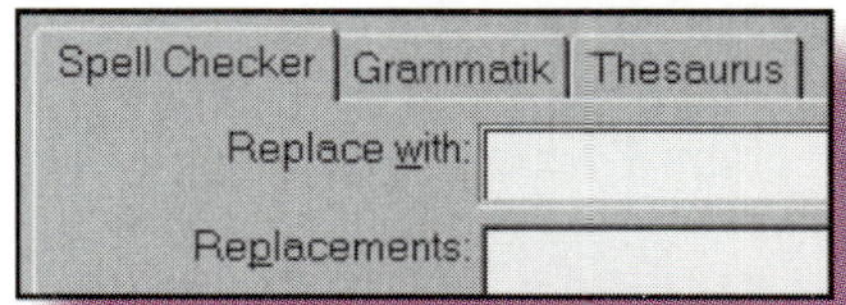

FIGURE 7-7
Tabs in Writing Tools

You can close the Thesaurus dialog box at any time by clicking the Close button. Sometimes you may wish to look up a word in the Thesaurus but not make any replacement in your document. Whether you use the Thesaurus dialog box or the Prompt-As-You-Go drop-down menu, the Thesaurus should be a great help in your writing.

Grammatik

The third tab in the dialog box is a grammar checker called Grammatik. This tool looks for grammar, punctuation, and style flaws in your documents. Even if you have a good command of the English language and write well, Grammatik can help you improve the way you put your words together.

Let's try a short Grammatik exercise so you can see how it works. This Step-by-Step exercise contains your name and the name of your school. Grammatik probably won't find those names in the dictionary. If it doesn't and those names are highlighted, click Skip All.

1. With **errors 7-5 xxx** showing in the window, open the **Tools** menu and choose **Grammatik**. Look at the dialog box. It is the second tab of the dialog box. (If a dialog box appears asking if you'd like the grammar checker closed, click **No**.)

2. Choose **Options** and then **Checking Styles**. If Quick Check isn't selected, choose it.

3. Click **Skip All** for any names that are highlighted. If you are asked if you'd like the grammar checker closed, click **No**.

Grammatik allows you to check your work using a variety of writing styles. Obviously, using Quick Check, the sentences were complete and everything was OK. Let's check the paragraphs using one of the other styles.

1. With **errors 7-5 xxx** still showing in the window, change the Checking Styles from Quick Check to **Student Composition**. Click **Select**.

2. Click **Start**. After it gets past your name and school (click Skip Once if either of these is highlighted), Grammatik will highlight the phrase *in the process of*. Look at the explanation. It says the phrase is wordy, but neither of the suggested solutions fits.

3. Click somewhere in the phrase and delete all of the words that were highlighted. Your sentence will read *I am learning . . . .* Then

click the **Start** button. (If you are asked if you'd like to close Grammatik, choose No.)

4. Grammatik may or may not highlight some of the other sentences or phrases in the paragraphs. If it does, see if you can work your way through the solution without help.

5. Try a couple of other styles to see if Grammatik finds anything else it doesn't like.

6. Change the Checking Styles back to Quick Check. Then read on to see what else Grammatik can do for you.

The Prompt-As-You-Go box shows words in blue when WordPerfect identifies a grammatical error. When that happens, the drop-down list provides some possible "fixes." This document didn't have any screaming errors. Grammatik is good at finding incomplete sentences, subject-verb agreement errors, incorrect punctuation, etc. Whenever you do any original writing of your own, you may wish to use this tool to help make your documents easier to read.

Spell-As-You-Go and Grammar-As-You-Go cannot both be chosen at the same time. To move between them or to turn Prompt-As-You-Go on and off, open the Tools menu and choose Proofread.

One of the other things you can do with Grammatik is check the statistics for your document. When you check for statistics, Grammatik will provide lots of information about the document—the number of words, the number of syllables, and reading grade level. Let's check **errors 7-5 xxx**.

S TEP-BY-STEP ▷ 7.8

1. With **errors 7-5 xxx** still showing in the window and the Grammatik dialog box displayed, click the **Options** button and choose **Analysis**.

2. Then choose **Readability**. Look at the dialog box that is displayed. The **errors 7-5** document will probably be compared with a Hemingway short story. Note that the short story has a grade 4 level, while the **errors** paragraphs have about a grade 9 level. Check the vocabulary complexity.

3. Click the **Basic Counts** button at the bottom of the dialog box. Note the number of words, etc.

4. Finally, click the **Close** button in Basic Counts and the **Close** button for Grammatik. Then close your document without saving it.

This was a very quick introduction to Grammatik. The tool has a number of additional features. For example, you can create a custom writing style for specific documents. You may wish to explore this tool further at your leisure.

Summary

In this lesson you reviewed a couple of WordPerfect tools you learned about earlier, and you were introduced to some additional tools. All of them were designed to help you create documents with few, if any, errors. You learned that:

- QuickCorrect repairs some of your keying errors. Entries can be added to help you with your work.

- Spell-As-You-Go identifies words that may need to be fixed. WordPerfect makes suggestions regarding the correct spelling of those words.

- Spell Checker can be used to check your document after you've finished keying. It finds words that aren't in the WordPerfect dictionaries.

- The Thesaurus may be used to look for the "right" word.

- Grammatik is a grammar checker that can count your words, as well as find errors in your punctuation and sentence structure.

- Prompt-As-You-Go can help you with spelling, grammar, and finding the right word. It is a feature on the Property Bar.

FILL IN THE BLANKS

Complete each of the following statements by writing your answer in the blank provided.

1. The QuickCorrect dialog box is opened from the ______________ menu.

2. The feature, ______________________________, refers to the text box at the right of the Property Bar that shows incorrectly spelled words in red.

3. The feature that underlines in red words that aren't in the WordPerfect dictionary is known as ______________________________.

4. Clicking the icon on the Toolbar that looks like an open book with an *s* will begin the ______________________________.

5. The ______________________ provides a list of synonyms to help you find the right word to use.

6. The tool that looks for grammar, punctuation, and style flaws in your documents is called ______________________________.

7. When WordPerfect identifies a grammatical error, the word in the text box on the right side of the Property Bar is shown in ______________________.

MULTIPLE CHOICE

Circle the best answer to each of the following statements.

8. All of the following are WordPerfect tools that help you with spelling and keying as you enter text EXCEPT
   A. Spell Checker.
   B. Thesaurus.
   C. QuickWords.
   D. CheckWords.

9. QuickCorrect would not correct
   A. hose for house.
   B. adn for and.
   C. sem for seem.
   D. teh for the.

10. When a word is underlined in _____, it means that WordPerfect thinks the word is misspelled.
   A. blue
   B. red
   C. green
   D. yellow

LESSON 7 PROJECT

CANS

Let's practice a couple of the features with which you worked in Lesson 7. We'll begin with Spell-As-You-Go to correct the errors in a document that has been prepared and saved for you.

PROJECT 7A

1. Open **japanese gifts** from the student **datafile** folder. Use **Save As** to save the file as **gifts proj7a xxx**. This document has a number of misspelled words which Spell-As-You-Go has underlined in red.

2. One at a time, point to an underlined word and click the right mouse button. Select the correct spelling of each word.

3. When you finish, check your work over carefully and insert the Path and Filename code a double space below the paragraph.

4. Return the insertion point to the top of the document. Press **Enter** three times. Then press **Ctrl+Home** again to move the insertion point above the hard returns.

5. Use **Flush Right** to move the insertion point to the right of the line. Then use the **Date Code** feature to insert the date.

6. Print the file and close it, saving it again with the same name.

    Now let's use some of the other tools on the same document.

PROJECT 7B

1. Open **japanese gifts** from the student **datafile** folder again. Use **Save As** to save the file as **gifts proj7b xxx**. Insert the Path and Filename code a double space below the paragraph.

2. Start **Spell Checker** and correct all of the words in the paragraph. When asked if you would like to close Spell Checker, choose **No**.

3. Position the insertion point in the word *relish*. Click the **Thesaurus** tab to start the Thesaurus. Find a better word to replace *relish*.

4. Click the **Grammatik** tab and choose **Analysis**. Key the answers to all of the following questions below the Path and Filename code. What is the reading grade level? In which CNE area does the Hemingway comparison show a higher percentage? How many words are in the document?

5. Print your document and close it, saving it again with the same name.

You have started keying one of your documents and notice that your QuickCorrect feature is not correcting some of the common errors you normally make. What is the problem and how do you fix it?

WINDOWS TOOLS AND FILE MANAGEMENT

Quite a number of tools are available in your window at all times to help you with your work. You've already worked with the Menu Bar, the Toolbar, the Property Bar, the scroll bars, QuickMenus, and the Application Bar. You've also practiced using the Next Page and Previous Page buttons to move from page to page.

With the Toolbar and the Property Bar, you've used a few of the buttons as you've learned about a particular feature. But the Toolbar and Property Bar are powerful tools that you will probably customize when you use WordPerfect on the job.

Let's briefly explore those two tools and then we'll look at some other Windows features that will make your work easier.

Finally, you'll learn to manage your files. You've already created quite a number of files, and a full folder is difficult to use. You learned file management basics in Appendix C. You worked with the Open File dialog box in Lesson 4. Now you will create folders into which you can move your files so the basic storage location is more tidy. You'll also learn to delete files that are no longer needed.

Toolbar

You've already used a number of tools on the Toolbar. If you're using the default WordPerfect 9 Toolbar, you've learned the following tools: New Blank Page, Open, Save, Print, Cut, Copy, Paste, Undo, Redo, Highlight, Zoom, and Spell Checker. Can you find each of those buttons?

Other Toolbars. WordPerfect 9 comes with nearly two dozen other Toolbars—each for a specific purpose. You can display the list of Toolbars by pointing anywhere on the Toolbar and right clicking.

Location. The Toolbar can also be located in a number of places in your window. To move it, point to a space on the Toolbar. When the four-headed pointer appears, press the left mouse button and hold it while you drag the Toolbar to the desired location.

Customizing. You can create your own Toolbar that contains buttons for the features you use most often. One way to do this is to name a Toolbar and start from scratch. Another way is to edit one of the existing Toolbars. If you are working in the classroom, you should NOT edit the Toolbar selected for your computer unless you receive permission from your instructor. In the next Step-by-Step exercises, we'll explore Toolbar options. Then we'll create and name a Toolbar. We'll add only a couple of buttons. Then we'll delete the practice Toolbar.

Scroll Bars. The resolution of your video display terminal controls a number of things. One of those is the size of the buttons on the Toolbar and how much space they take. If your Toolbar takes more space than the window allows, a tiny scroll bar will appear at the right of the Toolbar so you can look at the next part of the Toolbar. It is recommended that when you create a Toolbar, you include only as many buttons as will appear in the first window.

Now let's practice all of these Toolbar features.

S TEP-BY-STEP 8.1

1. Point to the Toolbar and right click. Look at the list of available Toolbars. Which one has a black check mark at the left? That's the Toolbar to which you'll return at the end of this Step-by-Step exercise.

2. Choose one of the other Toolbars. Note that the original Toolbar remains displayed with the new one below it. Try a different one. Then, one at a time, deselect all Toolbars except the original one.

3. Point to a blank gray area on the Toolbar. When the four-headed pointer appears, press the left mouse button and drag the Toolbar to each of the following locations and release it:
   a. To the middle of the window.
   b. To the lower right corner of the window.
   c. To the left until a long vertical box appears.
   d. To the top until a long horizontal box appears. Leave it at the top.

4. Point to the Toolbar and right click to display the menu. Choose **Settings**. The Customize Settings dialog box will appear (see Figure 8-1).

FIGURE 8-1
Customize Settings Dialog Box

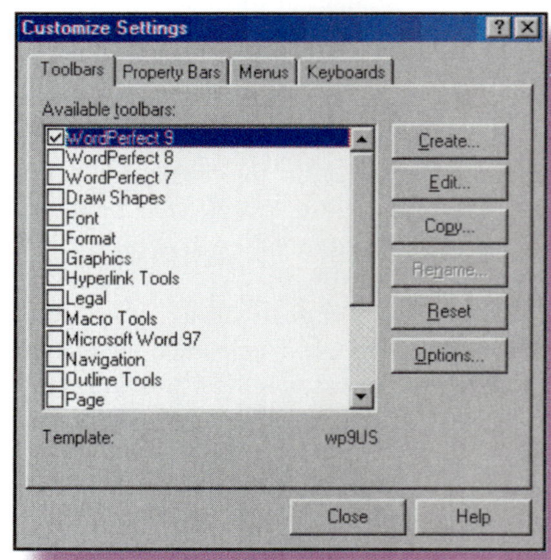

5. Click the **Create** button. Name your Toolbar **practice** and click **OK**. Note that a new, empty bar is displayed between the normal Toolbar and the Property Bar.

6. Look at the Toolbar Editor dialog box. The list of features displayed are from the **File** menu. Click **Close All** and then click the **Add Button** button. See the new button on the Toolbar?

7. In the lower right corner is a separator. Double click it to insert a space between buttons.

8. Click the arrow beside the *Feature categories* text box and choose **Edit**. In that list, choose **Case Toggle**. Either double click the feature to add it to your Toolbar or click it once and click the **Add Button** button. Insert another spacer.

9. Change Feature Categories to **View**. Add a button to the practice Toolbar for Draft.

Now that you have a practice Toolbar, let's learn to rearrange the buttons and delete buttons. Then we'll close the Toolbar Editor dialog box and delete your practice Toolbar.

S TEP-BY-STEP 8.2

1. Point to the Close All button on your practice Toolbar and drag it to the right, so it becomes the third button.

2. Drag the Case Toggle button down and off the Toolbar. You'll see the wastebasket when you "throw it away."

3. Close the Toolbar Editor dialog box. When you return to the Customize Settings dialog box, the **practice** Toolbar will be highlighted. Click the **Delete** button to remove the practice Toolbar from the list.

4. Be sure only the original Toolbar is chosen and close the dialog box.

As mentioned earlier, unless your instructor tells you to do so, you shouldn't make any permanent changes to your Toolbars. Now let's see what can be done with the Property Bar.

Property Bars

WordPerfect 9 comes with more than three dozen Property Bars which are said to be "context-sensitive." This means that the choices available on the Property Bar change according to what you are doing. The main Property Bar is the *Text* Bar, although several bars can be displayed at one time, just as with Toolbars. If you wish to choose a particular Property Bar, go to the same menu you used when creating a Toolbar and choose the Property Bars tab.

No practice is included for Property Bars, because you'll be using many of them as you learn about various WordPerfect features.

Windows

Working with Windows provides you with a number of other features. For example, you can look at more than one document at a time using either *Cascade* or *Tile*. You also can move between open documents—a total of nine documents can be open at any given time. All of these choices come from the Window menu.

In addition, the Application Bar at the bottom enables you to switch from one document to another without even opening a menu. WordPerfect 9 enables you to drag selected text through the Application Bar to move it from one document to another. Let's explore.

STEP-BY-STEP 8.3

1. Beginning in a clear document window, click the **Open** button on the Toolbar.

2. Choose the folder containing your files. Hold the **Ctrl** key while you click each of the following files to highlight them: **music 3-8**, **pc-tv 6-1**, and **skeleton proj3**. Click the **Open** button to open all three files.

3. Open the **Window** menu and choose **Cascade**. Note that each of the documents has its own separate window. Also note that the active file (**music 3-8**) has a blue Title Bar. The others are gray.

4. Point to the Title Bar of **music 3-8** and drag the window down and to the right. Click to make **pc-tv 6-1** the active file.

5. Select the first paragraph in **pc-tv 6-1** and copy that paragraph to the Clipboard. Make **music 3-8** the active file. Position the insertion point a double space below the Path and Filename code in **music 3-8**. Paste the paragraph from **pc-tv 6-1** in that location.

6. Open the **Window** menu and choose **Tile Top to Bottom**. (You probably wouldn't tile more than three files this way.) Now open the **Window** menu and choose **Tile Side by Side**.

7. Click the **Maximize** button (the middle button of the three buttons in the upper right corner) of the **music 3-8** document window.

8. Open the **Window** menu and look at the list of three documents at the bottom of the menu. Change to **pc-tv 6-1**.

9. Find the names of the three documents on the Application Bar at the bottom of the window. Click **skeleton proj3** to make it the active document.

10. Select the second paragraph. When it is selected, point to the paragraph. Press and hold the left mouse button. Drag the mouse pointer to the **music 3-8** button on the Application Bar. Hold the mouse button until **music 3-8** appears. Continuing to hold the

NOTE:

If you don't do Step 10 right, a warning box will tell you that you can't copy to the Application Bar. Click **OK** and try again, remembering to hold the mouse button until you've positioned the insertion point in the **music** document where you'd like the paragraph to be inserted.

mouse button, drag the pointer to the beginning of the Path and Filename code in **music 3-8**. When you release the mouse button, the *bones* paragraph should be in the **music** document.

11. Look at the two sets of Minimize/Maximize/ Restore buttons in the upper right corner of the window. The top set is for WordPerfect.

The lower set is for the document. Close all three documents without saving by clicking the lower *x* for each document.

12. Open your **Window** menu one more time. The documents should no longer be listed. Close the menu and read on.

File Management

Most file management takes place in the File menu of the Open File dialog box. You have already explored much of the Open File dialog box. Now it's time to work with copying, moving, and deleting files. You will also learn to create folders to hold certain groups of files.

Deleting Files

Quite a number of the documents you've saved in the lessons have no future value. Many of them were interim saves of documents that received more formatting later. Others were simply practice. In the next Step-by-Step exercise you will select the files that have no further value and delete them. If you can't find some of these files in your list, don't worry about it. You may have forgotten to save them. Work carefully so you don't delete some files that may be needed later.

S TEP-BY-STEP 8.4

1. Go to the Open File dialog box and open the list of files you have saved.

2. Hold the **Ctrl** key while you click to select the files listed in Figure 8-2.

3. Press the **Delete** key on the keyboard. WordPerfect will ask if you want to send the selected files to the recycle bin. Answer **Yes**.

FIGURE 8-2
Files to be Deleted

appearance 3-1	fix 7-3	gifts proj7a	online 5-4
appearance 3-2	foreign 2-6	gifts proj7b	pc-tv 5-1
appearance 3-3	foreign 2-7	indent 5-3	pc-tv 5-7
appearance 3-4	foreign 3-5	indent 5-8	quality u1ap1a
codes 5-11	foreign 3-6	matter proj1a	seasons 4-4
dates 5-8	gifts 3-10	nasa 2-1	seasons.frm
dates 5-9	gifts 4-3	nasa 2-4	working 2-10
education 1-6	gifts proj4a	numbers 5-5	
errors 7-4	gifts proj4b	numbers 5-6	
fix 7-2	gifts proj5a	numbers 5-7	

Creating Folders and Moving Files

Now that we've gotten rid of all of the extra files, we'll divide the remaining files into three folders. We'll prepare a folder for the regular documents in Units 1 and 2. Then we'll prepare a folder for Applications and another for Mr. Becker's files created in the On-the-Job Simulation. Finally, we'll move the remaining files into the correct folders.

STEP-BY-STEP 8.5

1. With your Open File dialog box showing in the window, open the **File** menu and choose **New**. Then choose **Folder**. A New Folder icon will appear at the bottom of the list with a box around the words *New Folder*. Key **Units 1 and 2** and press **Enter**. Click away from the folder to deselect it.

2. Hold **Ctrl** while you click to select the files listed in Figure 8-3.

3. Open the **File** menu and choose **Move to Folder**. Locate the **Units 1 and 2** folder and double click to select it. Click the **Move** button at the bottom of the dialog box.

4. Back in your regular folder, follow the procedure in Step 1 to create a new folder named **Becker**. Select **schedule job1** and **schedule job2** and move them into the **Becker** folder.

5. In your regular folder, create a folder named **Applications**. Select **canada u1ap3**, **quality u1ap1b**, and **gifts u1ap2** and move them into the **Applications** folder.

6. Look at your regular folder. It should be empty. If it isn't, check the remaining files.
   a. If they are junk that you saved accidentally while you were working on the lessons, delete them.
   b. If they are files that you have created for other classes or personal work, have your instructor help you transfer them to a different location.

7. If you completed the Step-by-Step exercises in Appendix B, your folder will include **move b-9 xxx** and **move2 b-9 xxx**. Delete those files.

8. Finally, close your Open File dialog box and read on.

FIGURE 8-3
Files to Move to the **Units 1 and 2** Folder

education 1-2	online proj5b
errors 7-5	pc-tv 6-6
gifts proj6	sasoot 3-11
matter proj1b	sasoot 5-10
music 3-8	skeleton proj3
nasa proj2	

Miscellaneous

A couple of things need to be noted from Step-by-Step exercise 8.5.

- Do NOT save any personal work or work for other classes with the files for this class. Your disk will be too full for you to complete the course if you do. Instead, if you are saving files for other purposes, save them on a different disk.

- This Step-by-Step exercise utilized the File menu in the Open File dialog box. The menu illustrated in Figure 8-4 shows the File menu when no files are selected. This is the way it looked when you created the file folders. Figure 8-5 shows the File menu when files are selected. As you can see, you can move as well as copy files. You can also rename files. The other useful tool in both menus is the *Print File List* item. This choice actually sends a list of the file names, sizes, and dates to the printer for the folder that is open when the selection is made. You'll have an opportunity to print a file list in Lesson 12.

- "Cleaning out" your folders periodically is very important. This topic is covered in Appendix C. If you have not yet studied Appendix C, take time to do it before you begin Unit 3.

FIGURE 8-4
File Menu in Open File Dialog Box

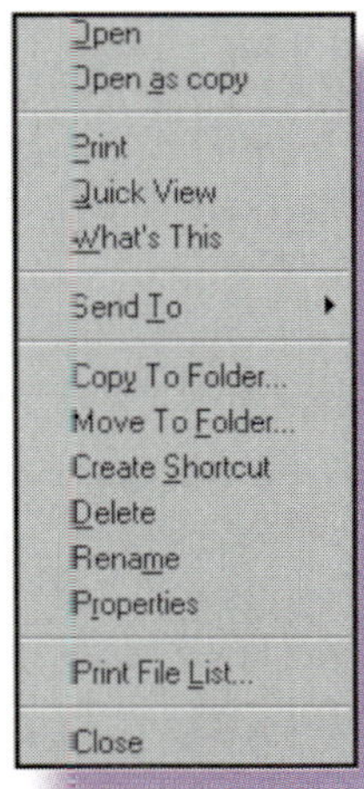

FIGURE 8-5
File Menu in Open File Dialog Box (with Files Selected)

Open as Copy

One of the tools that appears on both of the illustrations of the File menu in Figures 8-4 and 8-5 and is a button at the bottom of the Open File dialog box is the *Open as copy* feature. If you have a document open and try to open it again, a message box will appear telling you the document is either in use or specified as read-only. It goes on to tell you that you can open the document, but you'll have to save it with a different name. In other words, if you choose to continue, you will be opening a copy of the document.

When you choose to open a document as a copy, the part of the document that contains the file name is not included. You can look at the document. You can edit the document, and you can save the document, but it must be saved with a different name.

The *Open as copy* warning message most often serves to remind you that you already have that particular file open in one of your windows.

Recent Files

Another option that is sure to be useful is the list of files at the bottom of the File menu when you are working in your normal document window. WordPerfect remembers the last nine documents with which you have worked. Those documents are listed consecutively in the File menu. If you have recently worked with a file and need to reopen it, the easiest place to go for that file is the File menu.

By selecting the file from the list, you can bypass the Open File dialog box and save yourself a great deal of time.

The World Wide Web is a subnetwork of computers that display multimedia information, including text, graphics, sound, and video clips. Web documents also contain special connections that allow users to switch to other documents that could be on computers anywhere in the world.

Printing

Back in Lesson 1 you learned to print the file showing in the window. In a later lesson, you learned that you can print directly from the file list. In addition to those two methods of printing entire documents, a number of other options are available for special circumstances.

Look at Figure 8-6. It shows the choices for printing. Let's discuss the options.

- **Full document**. This is the choice you've used for all of your printing up to this point. This choice sends the document you are viewing in your window to the printer.

- **Current page**. To print a single page of a document, position the insertion point on the page to be printed and make this choice.

- **Multiple pages**. This choice also enables you to specify pages to be printed. To print pages 1, 3, and 6, choose the Multiple pages tab, and key *1, 3, 6* in the *Page(s)/label(s)* text box before clicking Print. To print from page 5 to the end of a document, choose Multiple pages, and key *5-* before clicking Print. Multiple pages also enables you to print by chapter or volume.

- **Print pages**. With this choice, you can print several consecutive pages of a document. For example, you can tell WordPerfect to print pages 2, 3, and 4 by keying *2* in the *from* box and *4* in the *to* box. In this case, WordPerfect will actually make the Print pages choice for you.

- **Selected text**. To print a chunk of text, select it and choose Print. WordPerfect will automatically make the Selected text choice.

- **Document summary**. You'll learn about document summaries in a later lesson.

- **Document on disk**. If you need a quick printout of a document other than the one on which you're working, you can choose Document on disk and choose the document to be printed.

At the right in the Print dialog box is the place where you can tell WordPerfect how many copies you want of the document to be printed. You can specify whether the documents should be collated or not.

Among the other things you can do with the Print dialog box is check the status of a print job. Click the Status button at the bottom of the dialog box for a list of the last several documents sent to the printer.

With that overview, let's try a few of the features you will probably use when printing your documents.

S TEP-BY-STEP ▷ 8.6

1. Click the **Open** button on the Toolbar. In the folder that should contain the names of your documents, you'll see the three folders you created to hold the documents from Lessons 1 through 7.

2. Point to the **Units 1 and 2** folder and double click to open that folder.

3. Locate **nasa proj2 xxx** and open the file. Position the insertion point somewhere on page 3.

4. Click **Print** on the Toolbar. Choose **Current page**. On the right of the dialog box, change the number of copies to **3**.

5. Then click the **Print** button at the bottom of the dialog box to send the document to the printer.

6. Go to page 2 and select the side heading about flame resistant materials, as well as the paragraphs in that section.

7. Choose **Print** from the Toolbar again. Note that the drop-down menu now suggests **Selected text**. Click **Print** to send the paragraphs to the printer. (If you have text selected and wish to print the entire document anyhow, you can choose Full document and override the Selected text setting.)

Now let's explore a little further.

S TEP-BY-STEP ▷ 8.7

1. Open the Print dialog box again. At the lower left, choose **Document on disk**. Since no document is specified, click the button with the tiny file folder to open the Document on disk dialog box (see Figure 8-7).

2. Locate **canada u1ap3 xxx** in the **Applications** folder and double click to select it.

3. When the document name is showing in the Document name portion of the Print dialog box, click **Print**. Your document will be sent to the printer.

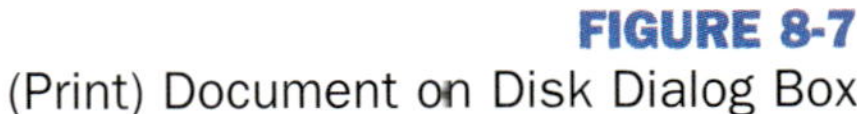

FIGURE 8-7
(Print) Document on Disk Dialog Box

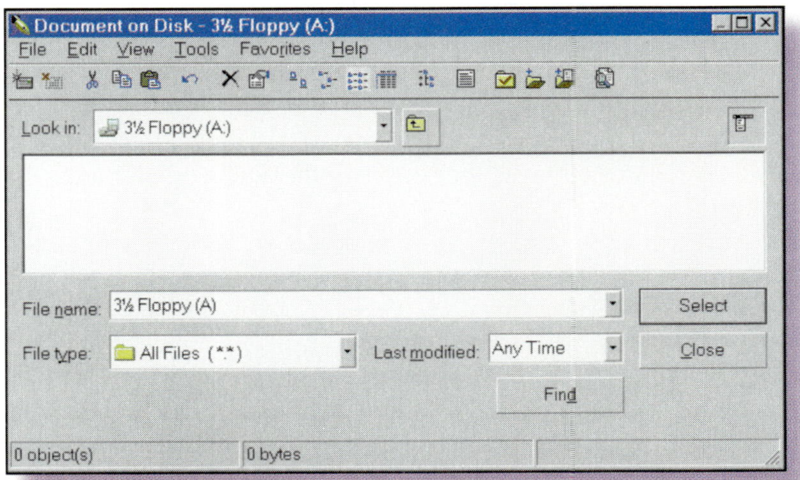

(continued on next page)

1 1 1

4. As soon as you can, return to the Print dialog box and click the **Status** button. Because the **canada** document is so short, you'll see it listed at the top of the Status dialog box as completed.

5. Close the Status dialog box and the Print dialog box. Then close the **nasa** document without saving it.

You should now be more familiar with the Print dialog box and the options available there. You'll be learning more about it later.

Summary

This lesson had less to do with the creating and formatting of documents and more to do with how you work with the Windows environment and how you print your files. In this lesson you learned that:

■ You can customize the Toolbar and choose alternate Toolbars for specific projects.

■ Several Property Bars are available for specific tasks.

■ You can create and name file folders and move files into those folders.

■ It is easy to delete a group of selected files.

■ The Open as copy feature reminds you when you try to open a document that is already open.

■ WordPerfect keeps a list at the bottom of the File menu of the last nine documents with which you've worked.

■ You can print parts of a document instead of the whole document.

■ You can use the Print dialog box to print in a variety of ways.

All of these skills will be useful to you as you progress with your WordPerfect training.

LESSON 8 REVIEW QUESTIONS

MATCHING

Write the letter of the term or phrase from Column 2 that best matches the description in Column 1.

Column 1

_____ **1.** You can use this feature to switch from one document to another without even opening a menu.

_____ **2.** If you have more than one document opened at a time, this arranges your documents so they overlap.

_____ **3.** WordPerfect comes with more than three dozen of these, which are said to be "context-sensitive."

_____ **4.** Tools such as Cut, Copy, Redo, Highlight, and Zoom can be found on the bar.

_____ **5.** Most file management takes place in this dialog box.

_____ **6.** Use this feature if you want your open documents on top of each other but not overlapping.

Column 2

A. Toolbar

B. Property Bar

C. scroll bars

D. Menu Bar

E. Application Bar

F. Cascade

G. Tile Top to Bottom

H. Tile Side by Side

I. Open File dialog box

J. Save As dialog box

FILL IN THE BLANKS

Complete each of the following statements by writing your answer in the blank provided.

7. The print choice that sends the document you are viewing in your window to the printer is _____________________________ printing.

8. To print a chunk of text, select it and choose Print. WordPerfect will automatically make the _____________________________ choice for printing.

9. If you want to print pages 6, 7, and 8, choose _____________________________ in the Print dialog box.

10. Choose _____________________________ if you need a quick printout of a document other than the one on which you are working.

LESSON 8 PROJECT

In this project you will manipulate your files and practice some of the printing options you learned to use in this lesson.

1. Open **errors 7-5 xxx**, **nasa proj2 xxx**, and **schedule job1**. (The first two files listed are in the **Units 1 and 2** folder, and the last one is in the **Becker** folder.)

2. Open the **Window** menu and choose to cascade the documents.

3. Open the **Window** menu and choose **Tile Side by Side**.

4. Open the **Window** menu and choose **Tile Top to Bottom**.

5. Select the first sentence in **errors 7-5 xxx** and copy it to the Clipboard.

6. Paste the sentence at the bottom a double space below the Path and Filename code of each of the other two documents.

7. Use **Save As** to save **nasa proj2 xxx** in the folder where you normally save your files as **proj8a xxx** (no *nasa*). Print only the final page (**Current page**) of the file and close it.

8. Use **Save As** to save **schedule job1 xxx** in the folder where you normally save your files as **proj8b xxx** (no *schedule*). Print the file and close it.

9. Close **errors 7-5 xxx** without saving it.

CRITICAL THINKING ACTIVITY

In Step-by-Step exercises 8.1 and 8.2 you practiced customizing a Toolbar with specific instructions. Now write a list of the tools you would add to your own customized Toolbar and explain why you made those choices.

FEATURE	MENU CHOICE	KEYBOARD	LESSON
Bulleted List	Insert, Outline/Bullets & Numbering	—	5
Cascade Windows	Window, Cascade	—	8
Center Page(s)	Format, Page	—	5
Copy	Edit (Toolbar)	Ctrl+C	6
Create Folder	File, Open	Ctrl+O	8
Cut	Edit (Toolbar)	Ctrl+X	6
Dash (em dash)	—	---	5
Date Code	Insert, Date/Time, Keep…	Ctrl+Shift+D	5
Date Text	Insert, Date/Time	Ctrl+D	5
Double Indent	Format, Paragraph	Ctrl+Shift+F7	5
Drag and Drop	—	—	6
Find	Edit, Find	F2 or Ctrl+F	6
Grammatik	Tools	Alt+Shift+F1	7
Hanging Indent	Format, Paragraph	Ctrl+F7	5
Hard Page Break	Insert, Page Break	Ctrl+Enter	5
Hard Space	Format, Line, Other Codes	Ctrl+space bar	5
Highlight	Tools (Toolbar)	—	6
Hyphen Character	Format, Line, Other Codes	Ctrl+ –	5
Indent	Format, Paragraph	F7	5
New Blank Page	(Toolbar)	Ctrl+N	6
Open as Copy	File, Open	Ctrl+O	8
Outline/Bullets & Numbering	Insert	—	5
Page Break	Insert, New Page	Ctrl+Enter	5
Page Print	File, Print	—	8
Paste	Edit (Toolbar)	Ctrl+V	6
Prompt-As-You-Go	Tools, Proofread (Property Bar)	—	7
Property Bar	View	—	8
QuickCorrect	Tools	Ctrl+Shift+F1	7
QuickMenu	—	—	6
Replace	Edit, Find and Replace	F2	6
Soft Page Break	(Automatic)	—	5
Spell Checker	Tools (Toolbar)	Ctrl+F1	7

FEATURE	MENU CHOICE	KEYBOARD	LESSON
Spell-As-You-Go	Tools, Proofread (Property Bar)	Alt+Ctrl+F1	7
Subscript	Format, Font	F9	5
Superscript	Format, Font	F9	5
Thesaurus	Tools	Alt+F1	7
Tile Windows	Window, Tile	—	8
Toolbar	View, Toolbars	—	8
Windowing	Window	—	7

UNIT 2 REVIEW QUESTIONS

MATCHING

Match the correct term in Column 2 to its description in Column 1 by keying the name of each term on a page to be submitted to your instructor. Center *Unit 2 Review Questions* at the top of the page and triple-space. Number your answers.

Column 1	**Column 2**
	Indent
1. The current date is inserted each time the document is accessed.	
	Hanging Indent
2. All lines are indented from the left to the first tab stop, and they are indented from the right an equal distance.	
	Double Indent
3. All lines of a paragraph are indented from the left to the first tab stop.	Date Code
	Date Text
4. The current date is placed in the document and that date is a permanent part of the document.	
5. All lines, except the first, are indented from the left to the first tab stop.	

WRITTEN QUESTIONS

Continuing on the same page, key your answers to the following questions. Number your answers and double-space between answers. Use complete sentences and good grammar.

6. What is the name of the feature that enables you to tell WordPerfect to look through the open document for a unique string of characters?

7. List the four ways you can copy selected text to the Clipboard.

8. How do you make QuickCorrect fix your errors?

9. After you have selected a list of files to be moved to a different location, how do you tell WordPerfect to move the files?

10. Open Help and key **printing**. In the printing section, find multiple pages. Read about page ranges and keying page numbers. If you want random pages of a document printed and you don't key the numbers to be printed in chronological order, what will happen? Close Help. Open the Print dialog box and click the **Help** button. Click to view print job progress. Then click **Related Topics** and **About Print Status** and **History**. How do you cancel a print job?

UNIT 2 APPLICATIONS 

Estimated Time: 1 hour

APPLICATION 1

1. Key the short memo illustrated in Figure APP-1. Use the **Tab** key to tab as many times as necessary to align the information as shown.

FIGURE APP-1
Text for Application 1

```
TO:        Juan Hernandez
FROM:      (key your name)
DATE:      (use the Date Text feature)
RE:        Quality Training

You have been scheduled for Phase 2 of your quality training. Here are
the particulars about your class:

     Duration:   6 weeks
     Day:        Monday
     Time:       9 to 10:30 a.m.
     Location:   Room A116
     Beginning:  Next Monday

There is no assignment for this first class session.  Please be
prompt.
```

2. When you finish, use **Spell Checker** to check your document and make any necessary corrections. Then save the memo in your regular document folder as **quality u2ap1 xxx**.

3. Check the document with Grammatik set to check at the **Formal Memo or Letter** level. Correct the document as follows:
   a. Use **Skip All** on the comment about *You*.

(continued on next page)

1 1 7

    b. For the *You have been scheduled* problem, click the green *active voice* words at the bottom and read about why Grammatik highlighted the sentence. Click the *x* to close the Active Voice window. Fix the passive voice by choosing the second replacement—*We have scheduled you*—and clicking the **Replace** button.

    c. Fix the *Six* weeks.

    d. Continue through the document until Grammatik is finished. You decide how to fix the errors pointed out by Grammatik. Then close Grammatik.

4. When you finish, insert the Path and Filename code a double space below the last line of the memo.

5. Print and close the document, saving it again as **quality u2ap1 xxx** when you close it.

APPLICATION 2

1. Open **desktop** from the student **datafile** folder. Save the file as **desktop u2ap2a xxx**.

2. Note that the first line in four of the paragraphs are not indented. Select those four paragraphs (all at once) and open the **Insert** menu. Choose **Outline/Bullets & Numbering**. Then choose **Bullets** and the **Diamond** bullet style and click **OK**.

3. At the beginning of each of those bulleted paragraphs is a word or two followed by a period. Beginning with *Graphics*, select the word and format it with bold and italic. Do the same with *Layout*, etc. Be careful not to format the periods.

4. Select the title. Change it to **20-pt. Bold**. Center the title.

5. Press **Ctrl+Home** twice to get above all codes and press **Enter** to add some line spaces. **Flush Right** your name in the upper right corner. Use **Date Text** to put the current date on the line below your name, also using **Flush Right**. Adjust the spaces so two blank lines separate the date from the title of the document.

6. Insert the Path and Filename code a double space below the last paragraph. Save the file again as **desktop u2ap2a xxx** and print it.

7. Use **Cut and Paste** or **Drag and Drop** to move the bulleted items around so the paragraphs are in the following order:

    a. Well-written material

    b. Layout

    c. Graphics

    d. Typography

8. Use **Save As** to save the file again, this time as **desktop u2ap2b xxx**. Print it and close it.

APPLICATION 3

Open **quality u2ap1 xxx**. Use **Save As** to save the file as **quality u2ap3 xxx**. The document is illustrated in Figure APP-2 with corrections. Make the indicated corrections. Then check your work. When you finish, the Path and Filename code should remain a double space below the *Attachment* line. When the file is perfect, print it and close it, saving it again as **quality u2ap3 xxx**.

Corrections for Application 3

```
TO:         Juan Hernandez
FROM:       (key your name)
DATE:       (use the Date Text feature)
RE:         Quality Training

You have been scheduled for Phase 2 of your quality training.  Here
are the particulars about your class:

        Duration:   6 weeks
        Day:        Monday    Tuesday
        Time:       9 to 10:30 a.m.   to noon
        Location:   Room A116    Conference Room A
        Beginning:  Next Monday   Tuesday

There is no assignment for this first class session.  Please be
prompt.
```

Attached is an article that will be discussed at the first class session. Read the article and make a list of questions and comments to bring for discussion. Also be on the lookout for magazine and/or newspaper articles dealing with the aspect of quality discussed in the attached article.

Please be prompt.

Attachment

APPLICATION 4

Key a short paragraph or two, telling how you feel about your training in WordPerfect so far. Which features do you like the best? Which do you like the least? With which features do you have the most problems?

Use any of the formatting features you have learned thus far. When you finish your paragraph, proofread it carefully and save it as **opinion u2ap4 xxx**. Insert the Path and Filename code a double space below the last line of the document. Finally, print a copy of your work for your instructor. Close the document, saving it again as you close it.

APPLICATION 5

The documents that you've created and saved in the Unit 2 Applications need to be moved to the **Applications** folder. Select **quality u2ap1 xxx, desktop u2ap2a xxx, desktop u2ap2b xxx, quality u2ap3 xxx,** and **opinion u2ap4 xxx.** Move them to the **Applications** folder. When your lesson has been approved by your instructor, delete **proj8a** and **proj8b**.

ON-THE-JOB SIMULATION

JOB 3

Mr. Becker has finalized the tour assignments for September. Please key the opening lines illustrated in Figure J3. Tab to **Pos 2"** for *Drivers and Guides* and the related information in the opening lines. Save the file in your normal folder as **schedule job3 xxx**.

With the insertion point a double space below the *SUBJECT:* line, use **Insert** to insert **schedule job1 xxx** into the open document. (The file is in your **Becker** folder.) Make the corrections illustrated in Figure J4.

Add the schedule at the bottom of Figure J4. Proofread and print the document. Then close it, saving it as **schedule job3 xxx**.

FIGURE J3
Beginning Text for Job 3

TO:	Drivers and Guides
FROM:	Charlie Becker
DATE:	(use Date Text)
SUBJECT:	September Schedule

FIGURE J4
Corrections and New Text for Job 3

~~We are sorry for the delay in notifying you of your scheduled trips for August.~~ As you know, recent flooding in the Midwest has necessitated a change in many of our scheduled tours *for September and cancellation of a number of others.*

The ~~August~~ *September* schedule ~~will be posted later in the week.~~ *is listed below.* Please *note the dates you will be working* ~~check your assignments~~ and make your personal arrangements for ~~the tours you will be serving.~~ *your tours.*

```
Sept. 1-4:   Mall of America in Minneapolis; Dennis & Karen
Sept. 6-7:   Fireplace Theater in Madison; Michael & Janie
Sept. 12-28: Vancouver, B.C.: Eric & Shelley
Sept. 14-25: New England; Greg & Karen
Sept. 15-19: Amana Colonies in Iowa; Fred & Janie
Sept. 18-23: Washington, D.C.: Al & Stacey
Sept. 20-27: Branson, Missouri; Tom & Anne
```

JOB 4

Mr. Becker has asked you to write a letter to his good friend, Andrew A. Pitchur, 4561 River Road, Houston, TX 63225. Mr. Becker said, "Tell him I will be in Houston for three days beginning on September 6. I would like to take Andrew to dinner on either the 6th or 7th. Tell Andrew I'll be staying at the Van Gogh Inn on Gallery Drive and that he should call me at my hotel at around 4 p.m. on the 6th to make arrangements."

Spell check your letter and check the writing with Grammatik. Then prepare an envelope, print the letter and the envelope, and close the document, saving it as **houston job4 xxx**.

JOB 5

Mr. Becker tried to find his work on your computer—the work you have saved in the **Becker** folder. He says he never thought to try **Becker**. He was looking for something with the company name. You've decided to change the name of the folder to **Singing Wheels**. While you're at it, you will move the work from Jobs 3 and 4 into that folder.

1. Open the Open File dialog box and locate the **Becker** folder. Click once to highlight it, but don't double click to open it.

2. Using the mouse pointer, point to the highlighted folder and right click to display the QuickMenu.

3. Choose **Rename** from the QuickMenu. The folder name will be enclosed in a box with the words highlighted. Key **Singing Wheels** and press **Enter**.

4. Select **houston job4 xxx** and **schedule job3 xxx**. Move the files to the **Singing Wheels** folder.

5. Check your **Singing Wheels** folder. It should contain the four **job** files.

FORMATTING TOOLS

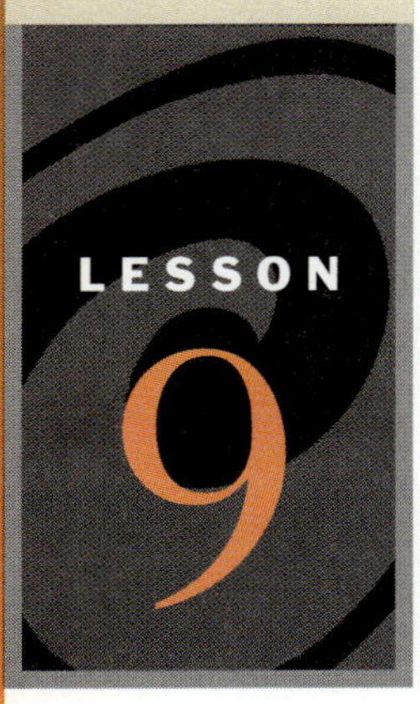

PAGE AND PARAGRAPH FORMATTING

OBJECTIVES

Upon completion of this lesson, you will be able to:

- Discuss the WordPerfect 9 formatting defaults.
- Adjust the line spacing in your documents.
- Work with the five kinds of justification.
- Adjust the margins of your documents.
- Change tab settings to give your documents the right look.
- Use the Ruler for indents, margins, and tabs.

⏱ Estimated Time: 1½ hours

If you've taken a keyboarding or typing class, you've learned to change the appearance of your documents with line spacing, margins, and tab stops. So far in this course, your documents have looked pretty good because the margin, tab stop, line spacing, and justification settings in the default template are designed to give you a good-looking document for most purposes.

In Lesson 9 you will learn to change the most common of those settings. Work carefully and think about what you're doing as you progress through the lessons so that when you finish, you'll be comfortable changing the same defaults on your own.

Formatting Defaults

The formatting with which you'll be working in this lesson is set as follows:

- **Line Spacing**: set to single spacing.
- **Justification**: set to left.
- **Margins**: set so you have equal 1" margins on all sides.
- **Tab Stops**: set with a tab stop at each half inch.

All of these settings can be changed easily so your documents will look exactly as you'd like. Following are some general formatting guidelines:

- Formatting changes that affect an entire document should be inserted at the beginning of a document.

- Formatting changes affect the text forward from the point where the change is made. The text prior to the change is not affected.

- Formatting changes remain in effect until another change to the same format is made. Then only the text following the change is affected.

- WordPerfect automatically positions formatting codes in the proper locations. Paragraph codes are placed at the beginning of the paragraph, and page formatting codes are placed at the beginning of the page.

- The default formats will work for most documents. Use them.

- The default formats are part of the default template. If you find that you are repeatedly changing certain formats, consider creating a customized template that contains the settings you use. WordPerfect Help contains lots of material about templates. In addition, you'll learn more about templates in a later lesson.

- Formatting codes become a permanent part of the document template and are saved with the document. When you close a document, you are returned to the default template.

Line Spacing

So far, everything you've keyed has been single-spaced unless you pressed Enter twice to add a blank line. There will be many times when you want all or part of a document double- or triple-spaced. WordPerfect allows you to space your document using a variety of settings.

It is very important when you want to use spacing other than single for a paragraph that you set line spacing rather than add the extra spaces by pressing Enter twice at the end of the line. When you press Enter, you insert a hard return that makes it impossible for WordPerfect to wrap your text to the next line. This makes quite a mess when you edit the paragraph.

Line spacing is set by choosing Format, Line, and then Spacing to open the dialog box.

STEP-BY-STEP ▷ 9.1

1. Open **record** from the student **datafile** folder. Use **Save As** to save the file as **record 9-1 xxx**, replacing the *xxx* with your initials as usual.

2. With the insertion point at the beginning of the document, open the **Format** menu, choose **Line**, and then choose **Spacing**. The dialog box in Figure 9-1 should appear.

3. Key **2** and press **Enter**.

FIGURE 9-1
Line Spacing Dialog Box

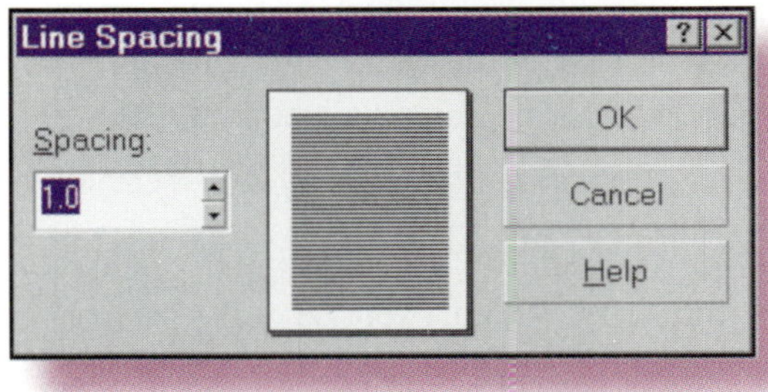

(continued on next page)

1 2 5

4. Look through your paragraphs. Observe the large amount of space between paragraphs. The blank line between the paragraphs was doubled, too, when you chose double spacing.

5. Reveal your codes. Position the insertion point to the left of the Line Spacing code. Note that it tells you what spacing is set. Enter the Double Spacing code on your list in Appendix E. Keep your codes revealed.

6. Move the insertion point to the beginning of the document and use the arrow buttons in

the Line Spacing dialog box to change to **1.5** spacing. Look at the code in Reveal Codes. Use the mouse to drag the Line Spacing code out of the document and return the document to single spacing.

7. Position the insertion point at the beginning of the SECOND paragraph. Set double spacing for that paragraph. Keep the paragraphs showing as you read on.

Single, double, and 1.5 spacing are quite common. WordPerfect also lets you set odd spacing in increments of a tenth of an inch for special documents.

STEP-BY-STEP ⟹ 9.2

1. With **record 9-1 xxx** showing in the window, use **Save As** to save the file as **record 9-2 xxx**.

2. Move the insertion point to the beginning of the first paragraph. Open the Line Spacing dialog box and use the arrow keys to change line spacing to **1.3**. Then click **OK**.

3. Look at the paragraphs. Can you see the difference between the **1.3** spacing and the **2.0** spacing in the second paragraph? What kind of spacing do you suppose formats the line between paragraphs? (If you were on the

first line of the second paragraph when you applied the 2.0 spacing, the space between paragraphs is formatted by the 1.3 spacing.)

4. Go to the end of the document and insert hard returns, if necessary. Press **Enter** twice after the second paragraph and insert the Path and Filename code.

5. Save and print the file. Keep it open for the next Step-by-Step exercise.

In Step-by-Step exercise 9.2 you saw how the Line Spacing code at the beginning of the first paragraph formatted the document up to the Line Spacing code at the beginning of the second paragraph. This illustrates the theory explained at the beginning of the lesson, and is the way formatting works in WordPerfect. Let's learn about another kind of formatting.

"Netiquette" is an Internet phrase that refers to the rules of conduct and behavior on the Net. For example, don't send unwanted advertising, do keep your messages brief and to the point, and don't use ALL CAPS unless you mean to shout.

Justification

WordPerfect offers five kinds of justification, as illustrated in the sample paragraphs in Figure 9-2.

Full:
Researchers have been working on developing a technology that will enable you to not only watch TV on your computer, but also to capture images from the TV to be used in other computer programs.

Center:

Mary had a little lamb.
Its fleece was white as snow,
and everywhere that Mary went,
the lamb was sure to go.

Left:
Researchers have been working on developing a technology that will enable you to not only watch TV on your computer, but also to capture images from the TV to be used in other computer programs.

Right:

Jack and Jill went up the hill
to fetch a pail of water.
Jack fell down and broke his crown
and Jill came tumbling after.

All:

```
W      o      r      d      P      e      r      f      e      c      t
W      o      r      d         P      r      o      c      e      s      s      i      n      g
```

- With *Full justification*, all lines begin and end at the margins, except for a short line at the end of the paragraph. This is commonly used for documents.

- With *Center justification*, all lines are centered between the margins. This style is used for display purposes.

- *Left justification* causes all lines to begin at the left margin and appear ragged at the right. (This is the WordPerfect default setting and is also commonly used for documents.)

- *Right justification* causes all lines to be ragged at the left and to end at the right margin. This is used for special kinds of documents.

- Finally, *All justification* causes each line to spread from margin to margin, no matter how short the line might be. Again, All justification is used for special situations.

Justification can be chosen from the Format menu, from the Property Bar, or with keyboard shortcuts. Let's use the Property Bar to practice justification in Step-by-Step exercise 9.3.

SCANS

1. With **record 9-2 xxx** showing in the window, use **Save As** to save the file as **record 9-3 xxx**.

2. Position the insertion point at the beginning of the first paragraph. Watch the right side of the paragraphs as you use the **Justification** button on the Property Bar to change from Left to **Full**.

3. Position the insertion point at the beginning of the second paragraph. Change from Full to **Right**.

4. Move the insertion point to the end of the second paragraph and press **Enter** twice. Key your name and address on three or four lines the way you normally key your name and address. It should also be aligned at the right margin, just above the Path and Filename code.

5. Click to position the insertion point at the beginning of the second paragraph again. This time open the **Format** menu and choose **Justification**. Choose **Center**. This setting should affect everything in the document except the first paragraph.

6. Position the insertion point at the beginning of the first paragraph and choose **Left** justification.

7. On your own, can you change the second paragraph to **Full** justification, your name and address to **Center** justification, and the Path and Filename code to **Left** justification?

8. Change your name and address to single spacing.

9. When you finish, print your document and save it again as **record 9-3 xxx**.

In addition to choosing justification from the Format menu or the Property Bar, keyboard shortcuts have been assigned to all kinds of justification except All. If you wish, you may use the following:

Ctrl+J = Full   Ctrl+L = Left
Ctrl+R = Right   Ctrl+E = Center

Margins

While WordPerfect provides you with a number of ways to set margins, the easiest is to move the guidelines to the desired locations. No doubt you have seen the tool that moves the guidelines when you've been trying to position the insertion point close to one of the margins. It looks like an intersection with arrows pointing to the left and right (for left and right margins) or up and down (for top and bottom margins).

When you change the margins with the guidelines, the margins will move in increments of about a sixteenth of an inch. You'll know where your margin is at any time because a small box will appear as you're moving the margin, displaying the current position.

For the left and right margins, the margin is set forward from the place on the page where you grab the guideline to adjust the margin. Let's practice.

S TEP-BY-STEP ▷ 9.4

1. With **record 9-3 xxx** showing in the window, use **Save As** to save the file as **record 9-4 xxx**.

2. Point to the left margin just to the left of the beginning of the second paragraph. When the tool with the right/left arrows appears, press the left mouse button and hold it. Watch the box giving you the position of the margin and drag the margin to **2"**.

3. Look at your document. You should see a couple of things.
   a. The first paragraph wasn't affected when you changed the margin.
   b. Everything below the second paragraph was affected—even the centered lines. They are centered between the margins.

4. Reveal your codes. Position your insertion point to the left of the [Lft Margin] code and see where your margin is set. It should report 2".

5. Grab the left margin guideline between your address and the Path and Filename code. Move it back to **1"**.

6. Grab the top margin and drag it to **2"** from the top of the page.

7. Print the document and save it again as **record 9-4 xxx**.

Sometimes you want to set all four margins or, occasionally, you can't get the exact setting you want by dragging the guidelines. In those instances, you should use the Margins portion of the Page Setup dialog box. Let's use it to change your margins.

S TEP-BY-STEP ▷ 9.5

1. With **record 9-4 xxx** showing in your window, use **Save As** to save the file as **record 9-5 xxx**.

2. Press **Ctrl+Home** to move the insertion point to the top of the document.

3. Open the **Format** menu and choose **Margins**. The Margins portion of the Page Setup dialog box will look like Figure 9-3.

4. Are the margins correct? They should report that all of the margins except the top margin are at 1". The top margin should be set at 2".

FIGURE 9-3
Margins Portion of Page Setup Dialog Box

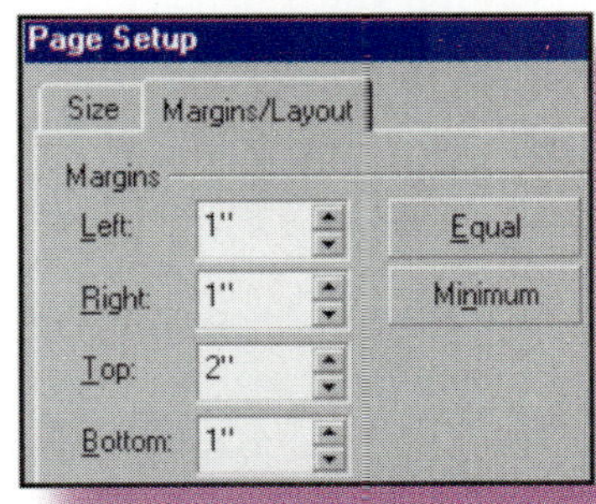

(continued on next page)

5. Key **0** (zero) in the text box for the left margin. Press **Tab** and key **0** again. Continue until you've keyed **0** into each box. (The numbers will change to something else rather than staying at *0*.) Click **OK**.

6. Print your document and save it again as **record 9-5 xxx**. How many Margin Set codes do you have in your document? (Reveal your codes and count.) You should have four of them. Add any new codes to your list. Close the document.

Each printer has what's known as a *no-print zone*. That's an area near the edges of the page where text or graphics can't be printed. When you set the margins at zero and they changed to a different number, that number reported in the Margins portion of the Page Setup dialog box represented the no-print zone on that edge of the paper. These no-print zones range from 0.2" to 0.5" or more, and they might be different on the various sides of your page.

Tabs

As you know, the default tab stops are set at each half inch. You can set one, three, or all tab stops in the Tab Set dialog box. You can also set a variety of tab types. The default type is the Left tab, meaning that when you tab to a location and key text, the text will begin at the tab stop and continue to the right.

Let's first try a Step-by-Step exercise where you change all of the tab stops. Then we'll look at how they can be adjusted and work with the different types of tabs.

S T E P - B Y - S T E P ⇨ 9.6

1. Beginning in a new document window, open the **Format** menu and choose **Line**. Then choose **Tab Set**. The dialog box illustrated in Figure 9-4 should be opened, and a ruler will appear at the top of your window. Look at the half-inch tabs (triangles) on the Ruler.

2. Briefly study the dialog box. Note the following:
a. At the top, the type is set for Left.
b. Below that, the button in the *Tab position* section that is chosen tells WordPerfect to measure the locations for the tabs from the left margin. (This is so when you change the margin, you don't have to reset your tabs.)

c. At the right is a set of buttons.

3. Click the **Clear All** button. Note that all of the tabs are removed.

4. Halfway down at the left, click the **Repeat every** box and key **1.35** in the text box just to the right. Click **Set and Close** to return to your document window.

5. Key the text in Figure 9-5. Begin at the left margin with *corn*. (WordPerfect will capitalize the first letter. Backspace to replace it with a lowercase **c**. It may take two tries.)

6. Tab once and key **eggplant**. Tab once and key **potatoes**. Continue in the same manner, working across and pressing **Enter** at the end of each line.

7. Save your work as **salad 9-6 xxx**. Keep it open as you read on.

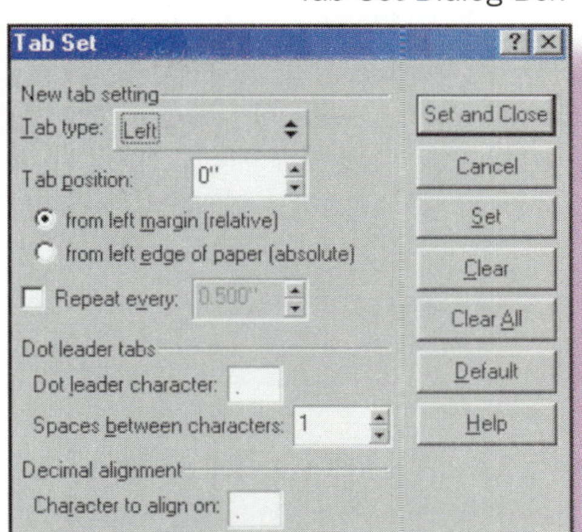

FIGURE 9-4
Tab Set Dialog Box

FIGURE 9-5
Text for Step-by-Step 9.6

corn	eggplant	potatoes	beans	zucchini
okra	cucumbers	lettuce	onions	peppers
peas	broccoli	celery	beets	radishes
yams	tomatoes	sprouts	carrots	cabbage

Look at your work. Because you set evenly spaced tabs and some columns have longer words than the others, the space between columns does not appear to be equal. WordPerfect enables you to reset the tabs to make your columns more attractive. The easiest way to do that is with the Ruler.

The Ruler

The Ruler that appeared when the Tab Set dialog box was opened is another tool you can use for setting and adjusting tabs. It can be used to set margins and indents, too. Look at the left portion of the Ruler, illustrated in Figure 9-6. Observe the following parts:

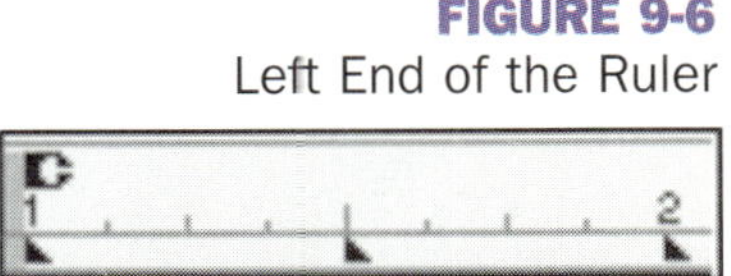

FIGURE 9-6
Left End of the Ruler

- The top part is for setting margins.

- The heavy black marker at 1" is the left margin.

- The two little triangles beside the margin marker are for indents. The top one can be set to automatically indent the first line of a paragraph. The bottom one works like the Indent feature that you learned about in Lesson 5. It indents the entire paragraph.

- The middle part is a scale marked in eighths of an inch.

- The bottom part is for setting tabs.

- The right triangles at each half inch are Left tabs.

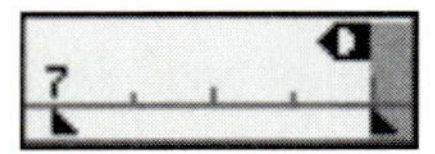

The right portion of the Ruler is illustrated in Figure 9-7. It has a margin marker and only one indent triangle. The triangle is for indenting the right side of a paragraph.

Let's fix our columns of veggies using the Ruler. Then we'll work with the margins and indents.

S TEP-BY-STEP 9.7

1. With **salad 9-6 xxx** showing in the window, use **Save As** to save the file as **salad 9-7 xxx**.

2. If the Ruler is not displayed, open the **View** menu and choose **Ruler**.

3. Press **Ctrl+Home** to move your insertion point to the top of the document. Using your mouse pointer, grab the black triangle tab stop that is near $2^1/2$" on the scale. Drag it to the left and drop it at the **$2^1/8$"** marker. Watch the column of vegetables move.

4. Using the same procedure, adjust the tab stops until your columns appear to have equal space between them.

5. When you finish, insert the Path and Filename code a double space below the columns. Then print the document and close it, saving it again with the same name.

Now let's open a partial document and reset the tabs. Then we'll complete the document using the new tabs.

S TEP-BY-STEP 9.8

1. Open **hostas** from the student **datafile** folder. Use **Save As** to save the file as **hostas 9-8 xxx**.

2. If your Ruler isn't displayed, open the **View** menu and select **Ruler**.

3. Drag the tab stop that's at 1.5" one notch on the scale to the left. Drag the next tab stop two notches to the left. Point to the bar where the tab triangles are located and click a third tab stop three notches from the one you just moved (at $2^1/8$"). The first four tabs should be evenly spaced.

4. Move your insertion point to the bottom of the document. Key the text in Figure 9-8, beginning the first line at the left margin and using **Tab** to indent the lines as shown.

5. When you finish keying and proofreading, return the insertion point to the top of the document and use either the guidelines or the Ruler to change the margins to **2"** on each side (that's **2"** at the left and **$6^1/2$"** at the right). Note that when you move the left margin, the tabs you set move along with the margin.

6. Insert the Path and Filename code a double space below the document. Print the document and close it, saving it again as you close.


```
Large plants (more than 20 inches tall)
   High-priced varieties (more than $10 each)
      Blue Angel
      Fluctuans variegated
   Low-priced varieties (less than $10 each)
      Frances Williams
      Gold Regal
      Gold Standard
```

Now let's use the Ruler to experiment with margins and indents. Then we'll learn about the types of tabs available for your documents.

STEP-BY-STEP 9.9

1. Open **record 9-2 xxx**. Use **Save As** to save the file as **record 9-9 xxx**.

2. Remove the tab that indents the first line of each of the paragraphs. Move the insertion point to the beginning of the first paragraph.

3. Drag the heavy black margin marker to **2"** on the Ruler. Note how your text rearranges itself. Now drag the margin marker back to **1"**.

4. Point to the tiny top triangle beside the left margin marker. Drag it to **1^1/2"** on the scale. Note that both paragraphs are indented as though you pressed Tab at the beginning of the first line.

5. Now point to the tiny bottom triangle. Drag it to **1^1/2"** on the scale. Both paragraphs

should now be indented a half inch from the left margin. The first line indents are still in place, a half inch farther than the other lines.

6. Point to the triangle beside the right margin marker and drag it a half inch to the left. Both sides of the paragraphs should now be indented.

7. Reveal the codes and record all three new codes on your list. Then print the document and save it again as **record 9-9 xxx**.

8. Play with the margins and indents until you are comfortable with what they do. (Remember that the insertion point must be above text you wish to format.) When you are comfortable with the features, close the document without saving it again.

The indents you just set from the Ruler will remain in effect until you change them. Note that for the entire document to be affected, you had to have your insertion point at the top of the document. You can use these tools on individual paragraphs, if you wish, but indenting with F7 and Ctrl+Shift+F7 is probably easier for small parts of a document.

Tab Types

FIGURE 9-9
Tab QuickMenu

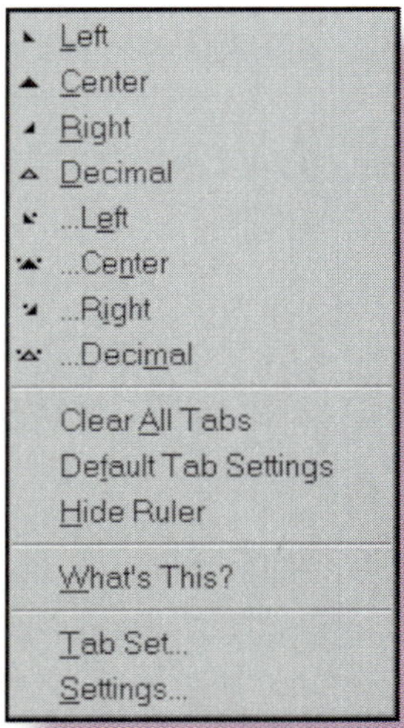

As mentioned earlier, you can set a variety of types of tabs. Those choices can be made from the Tab Set dialog box. They can also be made from the Tab QuickMenu. The Tab QuickMenu is illustrated in Figure 9-9. You can set Left, Center, Right, and Decimal tabs. In addition, you can set the same selection of tabs to be preceded by dot leaders. The QuickMenu can be used to clear all tabs, reset the default tabs, hide the Ruler, or open the Tab Set dialog box.

The various types of tabs provide you with different kinds of formatting, as illustrated in Figure 9-10. Note that each kind of tab has a different shape marker.

- **Left Tab**. This common tab aligns text at the left. The names at the left are aligned with a Left tab set at $1^1/4$" on the scale.

- **Decimal Tab**. This tab type automatically aligns figures at the decimal point. In this case, the series of dots under the tab set marker tell you that dot leaders were included with the tab setting at $2^3/4$".

FIGURE 9-10
Tab Type Samples

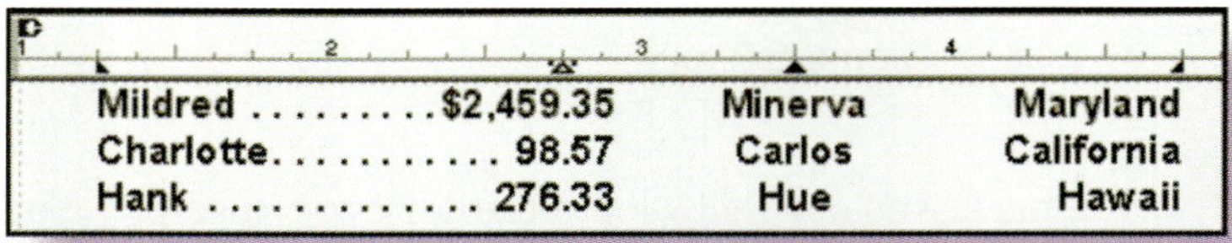

- **Center Tab**. Everything is centered around a Center tab. Minerva, Carlos, and Hue are aligned on the Center tab set at $3^1/2$".

- **Right Tab**. Everything ends at the location of a Right tab. The Right tab in Figure 9-10 is set at $4^3/4$".

Now that you are familiar with the types of tabs, let's go through the steps to create the sample in Figure 9-10.

STEP-BY-STEP 9.10

1. Beginning in a new document window, display your Ruler.

2. Point to the tab portion of the Ruler (the area below the scale) and right click to display the QuickMenu. Choose **Clear All Tabs**. Point to the area just below the $1^1/4$" mark and click to set a Left tab.

3. Display the QuickMenu and choose **...Decimal** (with dot leaders—it's the last choice above the line). Click at $2^3/4$" to set a tab stop there.

4. Use the QuickMenu to change to a Center tab. Click the Ruler to set a Center tab stop at **$3^1/2$"**.

5. Change to a Right tab and set one at **$4^3/4$"**. Save your practice document as **Mildred 9-10 xxx**.

6. Beginning at the left margin, press **Tab** once and key **Mildred**. Tab and key the dollar amount for Mildred. Tab and key **Minerva**. Tab and key **Maryland**.

7. Press **Enter** and do the same for the Charlotte row and then the Hank row.

8. At the bottom of the document, double-space and insert the Path and Filename code. Your document is squished to the left. With the insertion point at the top of the document, adjust the columns as follows:

   a. Move the Right tab to $7^1/4$".

   b. Move the Center tab to $5^1/4$".

   c. Move the Decimal tab with dot leaders to $3^1/2$".

9. Print the document and close it, saving it again with the same name.

Most of your work with changing tab settings in this lesson has been done with the Ruler. You had only a brief introduction to the Tab Set dialog box. While you can set different kinds of tabs in any location using the Tab Set dialog box, doing it that way is awkward and laborious. The Ruler and QuickMenu make the job much easier.

You may have noticed that setting both tab stops and margins using the Ruler is somewhat approximate. If you want precise settings, you must use the Tab Set dialog box for tabs and the Margins portion of the Page Setup dialog box or guidelines for margins.

Summary

This lesson covered a lot of territory with regard to changing default settings for your documents. The theory learned in this lesson will be practiced throughout the rest of your course as you learn to work with different kinds of documents that need different margins, line spacing, justification, and tabs. As a quick review, in this lesson you learned that:

- Settings such as line spacing, justification, margins, and tab stops format forward from the point where they are inserted.

- While the default line spacing is single, you can easily change to different spacing using the Line Spacing dialog box.

- Full and Left are the most common justification choices for business documents.

- Center justification may be used when several lines in a row need to be centered.

- Right and All justification are rarely used in business documents, unless some kind of display is needed.

- Margins may be set by moving the guidelines, keying the desired numbers into the Margins portion of the Page Setup dialog box, or by moving the margin markers on the Ruler.

- Tabs may be set from the Tab Set dialog box or on the Ruler.

- WordPerfect provides you with a variety of tab stops to fit your document creation needs.

- Tab stops can be adjusted after the document has been keyed. (To do this, remember to move your insertion point to the beginning of the text to be adjusted.)

While this lesson wasn't particularly long, you can see from the bulleted list that it contained a wealth of information about margins, tabs, line spacing, and justification. You probably won't remember all of the information in the lesson unless you review it after you finish. It would make good at-home reading!

MATCHING

Match the tab types to the sample below. Put the letter of the tab type from Column 2 in the blank provided in Column 1.

Column 1

_____ 1.

_____ 2.

_____ 3.

_____ 4.

_____ 5.

_____ 6.

Column 2

A. Left tab

B. Decimal tab

C. Center tab

D. Right tab

E. Left tab with Leaders

F. Decimal tab with Leaders

G. Center tab with Leaders

H. Right tab with Leaders

1.	2.	3.
Fax Machine	Office	$299.95 . . . . 20% off
Color Printer	Office & Personal	325.00 . . . . Free with purchase
Answering Machine	Office	39.50 . . . . $5 rebate
Cellular Phone	Car	20.00 . . . . Monthly lease

4.	5.		6.
Betty	van	Town & Country	$31,000.00
Judith	sedan	Avalon	29,900.75
Barbara	convertible	Sebring	23,650.00

MULTIPLE CHOICE

Circle the best answer to each of the following statements.

7. The default formats are a part of
    A. the Tools menu.
    B. the default template.
    C. Reveal Codes.
    D. the Property Bar.

8. All lines begin and end at the margins, except for a short line at the end of a paragraph with __________ justification.

   A. Full
   B. Center
   C. Right
   D. All

9. In addition to setting tabs, the Ruler can be used

   A. to set margins.
   B. to set indents.
   C. to adjust tabs.
   D. for all of the above.

10. Line spacing is set by opening the _______ menu, and choosing Line and then Spacing to open the dialog box.

   A. Insert
   B. Format
   C. Tools
   D. Edit

LESSON 9 PROJECT

Create the short document illustrated in Figure 9-11 as follows:

1. Use **Center Current Page** to center the document vertically on the page. Center the title and key it in all caps and using **16-pt. Bold** and **Italic**. Key all dashes by keying three hyphens.

2. Press **Enter** three times following the title.

3. Double-space both paragraphs and single-space the list. Use **Full** justification.

4. Set the side margins at **$1^1/_2''$**.

5. For the list, set a Left tab at **3''** and a Right tab with dot leaders at **$5^1/_2''$**.

6. Following the list, choose **Default Tab Settings** from the QuickMenu so you can indent the first line of the paragraph in the normal way.

7. When you finish, save the file as **cheese proj9 xxx.** Insert the Path and Filename code a double space below the last paragraph. Print the document and close it, saving it again when you close it.

(continued on next page)

WISCONSIN—NOT JUST FOR CHEESEHEADS

Wisconsin has long been known as the Dairy State. While other states may rank higher in overall production of dairy products, Wisconsin is number one when it comes to making cheese—producing a whopping 32 percent of all cheese made in the U.S. In a recent attempt to rank the states in the nation, the following Wisconsin statistics were assembled:

```
American . . . . . . . . . . . . . . . . . . First
Blue . . . . . . . . . . . . . . . . . . . First
Brick  . . . . . . . . . . . . . . . . . . First
Italian  . . . . . . . . . . . . . . . . . First
Limburger  . . . . . . . . . . . . . . . . First
Muenster . . . . . . . . . . . . . . . . . First
Swiss  . . . . . . . . . . . . . . . . . . Third
```

In addition to those overwhelming numbers, enough processed cheese is manufactured in Wisconsin each year to feed each resident of Wisconsin 15 grilled cheese sandwiches every day. Enough mozzarella cheese is produced in Wisconsin each year to make more than 1 billion pizzas. Are you a cheese lover? If so, Wisconsin is the place to go!

CRITICAL THINKING ACTIVITY

SCANS

You have been using WordPerfect 9 for a while now for both classroom and personal use. Most of the formatting defaults have worked just fine, but you are beginning to realize that you are repeatedly changing certain formats. Consider creating a customized template. What settings would you include?

Document Formatting

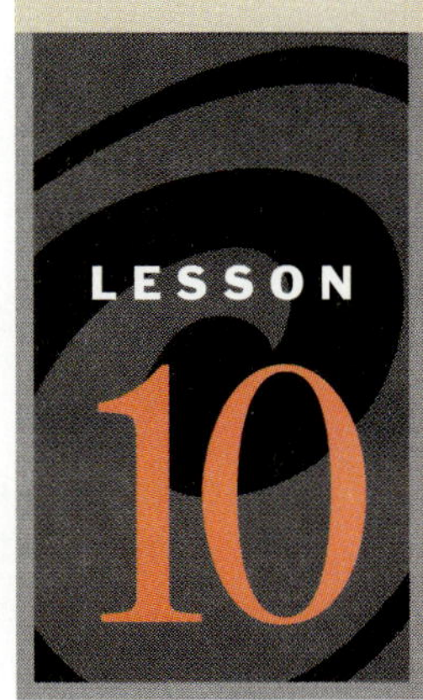

OBJECTIVES

Upon completion of this lesson, you will be able to:

- Format your documents with headers, footers, and watermarks.

- Suppress page numbering and headers on certain pages.

- Use Widow/Orphan protection to give your documents better page breaks.

- Use Center Page(s) in report-type documents.

- Use page numbering in your documents.

- Adjust the page number value.

- Add footnotes to your documents.

- Include endnotes in your document and format the endnote page.

⏱ **Estimated Time: 2 hours**

Look at the book in front of you. Turn to a page that isn't the first page of a lesson and notice the information included at the bottom of the pages. These pieces of information are known as *footers*.

The left-hand page is *always* the even-numbered page. In this book the footer includes a page number positioned all the way to the left. Next to the page number is the number and name of the unit. The right-hand page is *always* the odd-numbered page. In this book only the page number appears in the footer on this page.

Much of the work you do when you create multiple-page documents will be formatted differently from what you see here. This is because most business documents aren't printed with facing pages. Instead, the documents are printed on one side of a page and fastened together at the left. Therefore, you don't need to worry about odd and even footers.

WordPerfect provides many options for how a page will print. All of the options presented in this lesson have default settings that software developers thought would be most practical. In most cases, you can use those settings. The features with which we'll work in this lesson come from either the Insert menu or the Format menu.

This is another lesson that contains many useful skills. Don't try to do it all at once. When you come to a stopping point, you might want to give yourself a mini-break and relax for a moment. When you finish, be sure to review the lesson as at-home reading. It will be difficult to remember everything in this lesson after just one trip through it.

Headers, Footers, and Watermarks

As you learned at the beginning of the lesson, footers are the text that appears at the bottom of pages to tie a document together. The footers may identify the page, document, chapter, etc. Headers are similar text printed at the top of the pages.

Watermarks are a little different. While they are inserted into your document much like headers and footers, watermarks are used to dress up the appearance of a document or to impart some special information. Watermarks might include logos, headlines, art images, or words like *Confidential* printed behind the text on a sheet. While the technical aspect of including watermarks in your documents is much like that for headers and footers, the actual usage is quite different. We'll deal with headers and footers first. Then we'll learn about watermarks.

Headers and Footers

Following are some important facts about including headers and footers in your WordPerfect documents:

- If you are working in Draft view, headers and footers don't show in your window.

- You may have two headers and two footers (a total of four) in one document. With two, you can include different information on facing pages, like the information in the footers in this book. If you don't have facing pages, you probably won't use more than one header or footer in a document.

FIGURE 10-1
Headers/Footers Dialog Box

- Headers and footers are added to your documents by choosing Header/Footer from the Insert menu. When you make that choice, the dialog box illustrated in Figure 10-1 appears.

- In Draft view you are taken to a special header/footer editing window where the rest of your document doesn't show. In Page view your insertion point will be placed in an area enclosed in a dotted line—at the top for a header or at the bottom for a footer. The Header/Footer Property Bar tools (see Figure 10-2) will appear at the top of the window.

FIGURE 10-2
Header/Footer Property Bar Tools

You will enter the text of the header or footer in the special window. When you are finished with the header or footer, choose Close on the Property Bar to return to your document. In Page view you may click anywhere away from the area enclosed in gray to return to your document.

- Many WordPerfect features, such as Margin Set, Center, font changes, and Flush Right may be used in headers and footers.

- A header or footer may exceed one line in length. The first line of a header will begin at the top margin. The last line of a footer ends before the bottom margin.

- WordPerfect automatically adjusts the available space on a page to make room for headers and footers. Both headers and footers are automatically separated from the text by the equivalent of one blank line.

140

- You can use Suppress to prevent a header or footer from appearing on a particular page.

- While in the header/footer edit area, you can define a location for page numbering, and you can tell WordPerfect if you want the header or footer to appear on all pages, odd pages, or even pages.

- You need to enter the header or footer information only once for a document. It will then affect all of the pages of the document from the point where it is inserted.

- Headers and footers are spell checked along with your document.

- Headers and titles are two entirely different things. Here are definitions of each. Do not confuse them.

A *title* is the name of the document. It appears only on the first page of the document, where it is usually keyed two inches from the top of the page. Traditionally, the title is keyed in all capital letters and is separated from the body of the text by a quadruple or triple space. The title is considered to be part of the text.

A *header* may use the same words as the title of the document, but headers rarely appear on the first page of a document. (You'll soon learn how to suppress the header on the first page.) The header appears instead on other pages of the document, and it is frequently keyed in lowercase letters with the first letter of important words capitalized.

Now let's apply what you've learned about headers and footers in a short Step-by-Step exercise. We'll work with both a header and a footer in the Step-by-Step exercise.

STEP-BY-STEP 10.1

1. Open **pcug** from the student **datafile** folder. Use **Save As** to save the file as **pcug 10-1 xxx**, substituting your initials for *xxx* as always.

2. With the insertion point at the beginning of the document, change to double spacing. Remove the extra return between the paragraphs so the document has double spacing throughout. If you are not in Page view, open the **View** menu and choose **Page**.

3. Open the **Insert** menu and choose **Header/Footer**. You should see a dialog box that looks like Figure 10-1.

4. Leave **Header A** as the setting and choose **Create**. The Header/Footer tools will be added to the Property Bar. The insertion point will be in the header area that is outlined by dotted lines.

5. This header consists of two pieces of information, as illustrated in Figure 10-3. Key **PC User Group Meeting** at the left. Give the command for Flush Right (Alt+F7) and press **Ctrl+D** to insert the Date Text. Click the **Close** button on the Header/Footer Property Bar to return your insertion point to the document window.

FIGURE 10-3
Text for Header

```
PC User Group Meeting                              (Current date)
```

(continued on next page)

141

6. Open the **Insert** menu and choose **Header/ Footer** again. This time choose **Footer A**. Click **Create**. With the insertion point in the footer area outlined in gray, center and key the two lines illustrated in Figure 10-4 as the footer for your document. Click the **Close** button to return to your document.

7. Insert the Path and Filename code a double space below the second paragraph. Then Zoom to **Full Page** to view the document, complete with header and footer. Return to **100%**.

8. Reveal your codes and add the Header and Footer codes to your list.

9. Save your document again as **pcug 10-1 xxx** and print it.

FIGURE 10-4
Text for Footers

```
For Discussion Purposes Only
         CONFIDENTIAL
```

As you can see, headers and footers are easy to add to your documents. You'll have more practice with them in later Step-by-Step exercises. Let's try a watermark.

Watermarks

Watermarks are lightly shaded images behind the print on your document. Watermarks don't show in the window in Draft view. We'll learn about watermarks as we add one to the **pcug** document.

STEP-BY-STEP ⟹ 10.2

1. With **pcug 10-1 xxx** showing in the window, use **Save As** to save the file as **pcug 10-2 xxx**.

2. Open the **Insert** menu and choose **Watermark**. Then choose **Create**. The Watermark tools (see Figure 10-5) will be added to the Property Bar.

3. Open the **Insert** menu and choose **Graphics**. Then choose **From File**.

4. Go to your **datafile** folder and find **confidential.wpg**. Double click to insert the image as a watermark.

5. If necessary, center the image by pointing to the *Confidential* image on your page and dragging it so the dotted lines surrounding the image are aligned with the margin guidelines.

6. Click outside of the image (in the margin of the document) to deselect the image. Then click the **Close** button on the Property Bar to return to your document.

7. Save the document again as **pcug 10-2 xxx** and print it. Then close it.

FIGURE 10-5
Watermark Property Bar Tools

Even though you used an image designed to be used as a watermark in this Step-by-Step exercise, any image can be used for a watermark. In addition, watermarks can be edited in a number of ways since they are a graphics application. You'll learn about working with graphics images in Unit 6.

Page Numbering in Headers

WordPerfect is always counting your pages. If you request it, the page number can be printed on the page. You have some choices regarding page numbering. One of those choices is where the page number will be located on the page. Another choice is whether you'll include the page number as part of the header or as a separate feature.

In the next Step-by-Step exercise we'll work with a longer document. This one will have a header that includes page numbering and a watermark.

STEP-BY-STEP 10.3

1. Key the beginning of the document, as illustrated in Figure 10-6.
   a. Press **Enter** until the insertion point is at approximately **2"** from the top of the page for the title.
   b. Center the title in all caps, and press **Enter** three times for a triple space following the title.
   c. Set justification at **Full** and line spacing at **Double**.
   d. Use **Tab** to indent the first line of the first paragraph.
   e. Press **Enter** following the last line of the paragraph.

2. Proofread and correct any errors. Then open the **Insert** menu, choose **File**, and insert **wind** from the student **datafile** folder.

3. Save your document as **wind 10-3 xxx**.

4. Move your insertion point to the top of the document and open the **Insert** menu. Choose **Header/Footer** and **Create** for Header A.

5. Create a header for your document that looks like Figure 10-7. Use **Bold** for the header. Follow these steps:
   a. Key **Wind Power** at the left.
   b. Press **Alt+F7** for Flush Right and key **Page**.

FIGURE 10-6
Text for Step-by-Step 10.3

```
                    THE POWER OF WIND
    In this age of ecology consciousness, we hear more and more about
the best way to provide power to the billions of people inhabiting the
earth.  Power from fossil fuels has long been considered the most eco-
nomical way of producing electricity. Coal, however, is expensive and
dangerous to mine, and the supply is not unlimited.  What's more,
environmentalists are forever attacking the use of fossil fuels
because of the pollution caused by power plant emissions.
```

(continued on next page)

c. Space once and click the **Number** button on the Header/Footer Feature Bar. Choose **Page Number**. A *1* should appear in your document.

d. Click below the header (in the document) to exit the header editing window.

6. Check the appearance of your document using **Two Pages** view. Does the header appear at the top of both pages? Return to **Page** view.

7. Save your document again as **wind 10-3 xxx** and keep it open as you read on.

FIGURE 10-7
Header for **Wind** Document

Wind Power	Page 1

When you used the Header/Footer Property Bar to enter the page number, you actually entered a code telling WordPerfect to number all pages of your document at the location of the insertion point. You don't have to include the word *Page* with your numbers. In fact, pages are usually numbered without any identifying words.

You can put a page number anywhere in a document, even without the Header/Footer feature. Let's take a side trip to learn to do that. Then we'll return to the formatting of the **wind** document.

STEP-BY-STEP 10.4

1. Position your insertion point in the middle of the word *harvesting* in the last sentence of the document.

2. Open the **Format** menu, choose **Page**, and then choose **Insert Page Number**. This will open the Insert Page Number dialog box, as illustrated in Figure 10-8.

3. The settings are fine. Click the **Insert** button and then click **Close**.

4. Look at your document. A number *2* should appear in the word *harvesting*.

5. Reveal your codes. Move the insertion point to the left of the code. Add the code to your list. Then remove the number from the document. You don't really want a page number in the middle of the word.

FIGURE 10-8
Insert Page Number Dialog Box

Insert Page Number			? X
Number:	**Type**	**Value**	
Page	1,2,3,...	2	
Chapter	1,2,3,...	1	
Volume	1,2,3,...	1	
Secondary Page	1,2,3,...	2	
Total Pages	1,2,3,...	2	
Insert	Close	Value/Adjust...	Help

Now let's return to the **wind** document. First, we'll add a watermark. The best place for codes that format the entire document is at the top of the first page.

Text can be used for a watermark. We'll use an image from a previous version of WordPerfect for our watermark.

144

STEP-BY-STEP ▷ 10.5

1. With **wind 10-3 xxx** open in your window, use **Save As** to save the file as **wind 10-5 xxx**.

2. With your insertion point at the top of the first page, open the **Insert** menu and choose **Watermark**. Then choose **Create**.

3. Click the **Image** button on the Watermark Property Bar. When the list of images appears, click your **Favorites** button and change to the drive or folder that contains the **datafile** documents.

4. Find **Windmill.wpg** and double click to select it.

5. Click outside of the image (in a margin) and then click the **Close** button. Look at both pages. Is the windmill watermark there? (It won't show if you are in Draft view.)

6. Save your document again as **wind 10-5 xxx**. Insert the Path and Filename code a double space below the last paragraph. Keep the file open.

Suppress

Sometimes you don't want your headers or your page numbers to appear on certain pages. The **wind** Step-by-Step exercise is a good example. The header looks strange on the top of the first page. You can turn off headers, footers, page numbering, and watermarks by placing the insertion point on the page where you don't want the header, footer, watermark, or page number to appear and by inserting a Suppress code.

Suppress affects only the page on which you place the code. It is accessed by choosing Format, Page, and then Suppress. The Suppress dialog box allows you to select all features to be suppressed on that page. Let's suppress the header on the **wind** document.

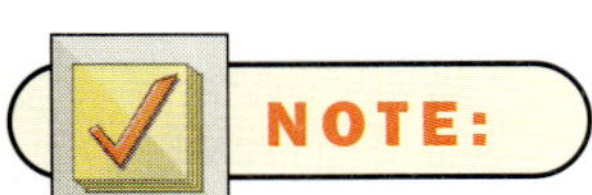

NOTE:

If your page number is included as part of the header, as in the **wind** document, the page number is suppressed when you suppress the header. It can't be suppressed

STEP-BY-STEP ▷ 10.6

1. With **wind 10-5 xxx** open in the window, use **Save As** to save the file as **wind 10-6 xxx**.

2. Move your insertion point to the top of the first page (not in the header area). Open the **Format** menu and choose **Page**. Then choose **Suppress**.

3. Choose **Header A** and click **OK**. You will be returned to your document. Use **Two Pages** view to see if the header still shows on the second page but not the first.

4. When you are satisfied that everything looks as it ought to look, save your document again as **wind 10-6 xxx**. Keep it open.

Widow/Orphan

If you are using the default font—12-pt. Times New Roman—your document still has something wrong with it. Good document formatting rules dictate that a single line of a paragraph should never be by itself at the bottom or the top of a page. Renegade lines of paragraphs are called *widows* and *orphans*.

The Widow/Orphan feature controls those renegade lines. It may be accessed by opening the Format menu, and choosing Keep Text Together. The Widow/Orphan feature is handy because you need to insert it only once, like headers, footers, and watermarks, to take care of an entire multiple-page document.

If your document doesn't have a bad page break, you can use the Widow/Orphan feature anyhow, as a precaution. Let's see how easy it is to add this code to your document.

STEP-BY-STEP 10.7

1. With **wind 10-6 xxx** open, use **Save As** to save the file as **wind 10-7 xxx**.

2. Position your insertion point near the top of the first page. Open the **Format** menu and choose **Keep Text Together**. This opens the Keep Text Together dialog box, as illustrated in Figure 10-9.

3. Click the box below *Widow/Orphan*. Then click **OK** to close the dialog box and return to your document.

4. Use whatever view best displays your document. Check the watermark, the header, and the page end breaks.

5. If everything looks good, print the document. Save it again as **wind 10-7 xxx** and keep it open.

FIGURE 10-9
Keep Text Together Dialog Box

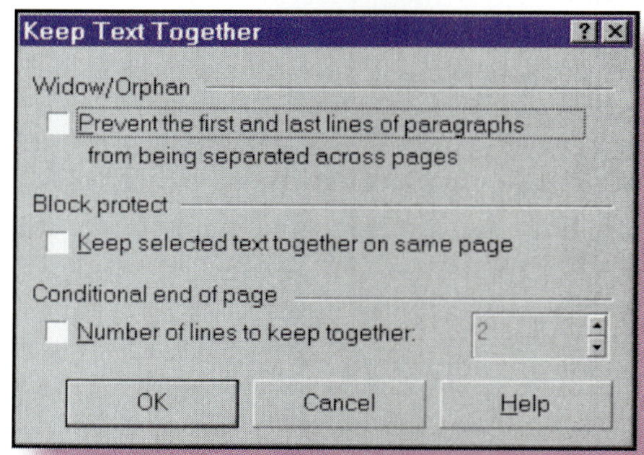

Center Page(s)

Remember the Center Page(s) command? It centers the text from top to bottom on the page. You used it in a couple of earlier documents. We'll use it here to prepare a title page for the **wind** document.

INTERNET

Many Internet connections from schools and homes are dial-in connections. With a dial-in connection, the Internet tools and programs are located on a host computer; your desktop computer can only display what the host processes.

STEP-BY-STEP 10.8

1. Press **Ctrl+Home** twice to position your insertion point at the top of your document, above all codes. Press **Ctrl+Enter** to add a new page at the beginning of the document. Press **Ctrl+Home** again to position the insertion point on the new page.

2. Open the **Format** menu and choose **Page**. Then choose **Center**. Choose the first button—to center the **Current page**. Click **OK**.

3. Back in your document window, click the **Justification** button on the Property Bar and choose **Center** justification.

4. Key the title page information, as shown in Figure 10-10. All lines will be centered, and the text will have even top and bottom margins. Change the title to **24 pt.** and format the name of the course with bold.

5. Zoom to **Full Page** to look at your lovely title page.

FIGURE 10-10
Text for Title Page

```
            THE POWER OF WIND
(press Enter 8 times)
                    by
(press Enter twice)
          (Student Name)
(press Enter 8 times)
       Beginning WordPerfect
(press Enter twice)
          (Current date)
```

6. Check through the document to make sure everything looks OK. If there are any problems, fix them. Save the document as **wind 10-8 xxx**. Print the title page only.

7. Keep the document open as you use another document to learn about page numbering. We'll come back to it in a moment.

Page Numbering

As mentioned earlier in the lesson, page numbering can be a separate feature. For some documents, you'll want page numbering but no header or footer. Let's work with page numbering in a document from a previous unit.

STEP-BY-STEP 10.9

1. Go to your **Units 1 and 2** folder and open **gifts proj6 xxx**. Use **Save As** to save the file as **gifts 10-9 xxx**. Be sure you are in Page view.

2. Press **Enter** a number of times to position the title about **2"** from the top of the page. Center the title **GLOBAL GIFT GIVING**. Follow the title with a triple space.

(continued on next page)

3. Position the insertion point at the beginning of the first paragraph.
   a. Set **1.5** line spacing for the introductory paragraphs.
   b. Change to **Full** justification.

4. Go through the document and remove the extra blank line between paragraphs so the entire document is formatted with 1.5 line spacing.

5. Position the insertion point at the beginning of the numbered items and set line spacing at **1.0**. Look through the document and make sure everything is correctly formatted.

6. Return the insertion point to the top of the document. Open the **Format** menu and choose **Page** and then **Numbering** to display the Select Page Numbering Format dialog box (see Figure 10-11).

7. Click the **Position** button at the top. After looking at the choices, return to **Bottom Center**.

8. Look at the *Page numbering format* section. The highlighted format is fine. Click **OK**.

9. Look at the bottom of both pages. (You'll have to use the scroll bar to see the bottom of page 2.)

10. Save the file again with the same name. Then keep it open as you read on.

FIGURE 10-11
Select Page Numbering Format Dialog Box

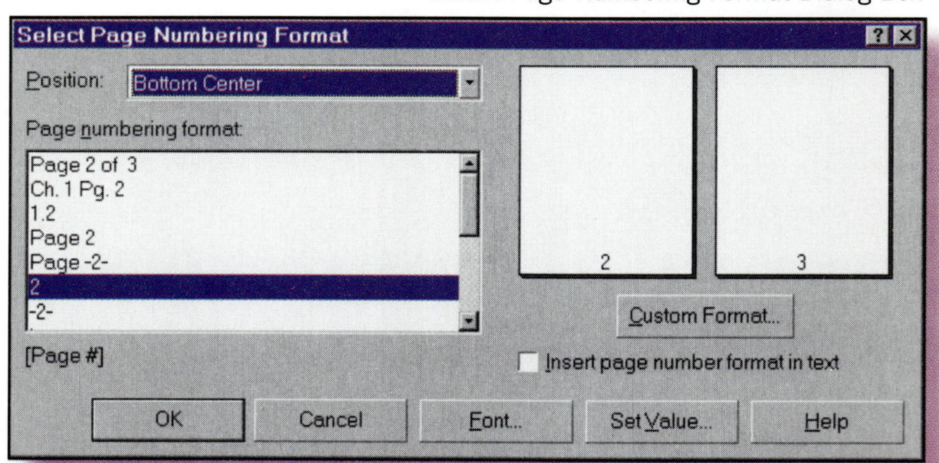

Because the page number is in the document area, you might want to extend the length of your page by changing the bottom margin. It is customary to have a half-inch bottom margin when the page numbers are at the bottom of the page.

Let's drag the guideline for the bottom margin down to a half inch to give your document more room and decrease that unsightly BIG bottom margin.

STEP-BY-STEP 10.10

1. With **gifts 10-9 xxx** showing in your window, use **Save As** to save the file as **gifts 10-10 xxx**.

2. Move the document so you can see the bottom margin on the first page. Using the mouse pointer and the crosshair drag tool, drag the bottom margin guideline down until the little box reports **0.5"**. Release the guideline.

3. Return to the beginning of the first paragraph and display the Ruler. Move the tab marker at $1^1/2''$ to the left so it's between the $1^1/4''$ and the $1^3/8''$ marks. Click to insert an extra tab stop at $1^5/8''$. (Be sure it's a Left tab. You may need to change the type.)

4. Look through your document. In all likelihood, only one or two lines will be on the second page.

5. Return to the beginning of the document and insert a **Widow/Orphan** code (Format, Keep Text Together).

6. Save your document again as **gifts 10-10 xxx**. Print it and close it. (Your **wind** document should be showing now.)

Change Page Number Value

If you looked carefully at your **wind** document after adding the title page, you probably noticed that WordPerfect counted the title page as the first page of the document. Therefore, the second page of text is numbered as page 3. Technically, the title page shouldn't be counted, so the second page of text should be numbered as page 2.

WordPerfect has a feature that enables you to change the value of the page number. WordPerfect will continue numbering from that new page number value. This choice is made in the Select Page Numbering Format dialog box about which you just learned. We'll set the number for the first page of text (after the title page) to 1.

STEP-BY-STEP 10.11

1. With **wind 10-8 xxx** showing in the window, use **Save As** to save the file as **wind 10-11 xxx**.

2. Position the insertion point at the top of the first page of text (following the title page). The insertion point will be at the center because you set Center justification on the title page. Change justification to **Left**.

3. Open the **Format** menu and choose **Page** and then **Numbering**. Click the **Set Value** button.

4. The Values dialog box will open, looking like Figure 10-12. Click in the *Set page number* text box and change from *2* to **1**. Click **OK**.

5. Click **OK** again to return to your document.

(continued on next page)

6. Check the header at the top of the second page of text. It should now report that you are on page *2*.

7. Print only the last page of the document. Then close it, saving it again as **wind 10-11 xxx** as you close it.

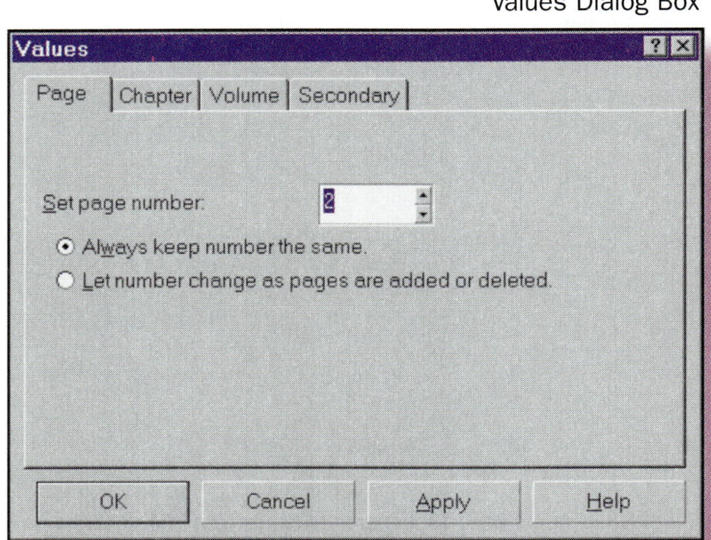

FIGURE 10-12
Values Dialog Box

Footnotes and Endnotes

In technical writing, footnotes and endnotes are used to identify the sources of the information used in a report and provide additional information to the reader. Footnotes are usually numbered consecutively, and each footnote appears at the bottom of the page where the resource is referenced. Footnotes are different from footers, where the same text appears at the bottom of each page.

Endnotes provide the same kind of information as footnotes. The major difference between them is that endnotes are usually at the end of a document—often on a page by themselves. Endnotes, too, are usually numbered consecutively.

WordPerfect helps you create and format footnotes. Numbering is automatic, and footnotes are properly placed and formatted. The same is true of endnotes.

Footnotes

When you are ready to insert a footnote into your document, open the Insert menu and choose Footnote/Endnote. Then choose Create. In Draft view, the reference number will be entered into your document and you will be taken to a special footnote window. In Page view, the reference number will be entered, and you will be moved to the bottom of the page where the footnote is to be keyed next to the footnote number. Both the reference and the footnote numbers are automatically superscripted (small reference numbers raised above the line).

The tools for the Footnote Property Bar appear when you are in the footnote area (see Figure 10-13). The buttons on the bar enable you to restore the note number in case you accidentally lose it, as well as browse through existing notes. The Close button returns you to your document window when you finish keying the note.

FIGURE 10-13
Footnote Property Bar Tools

Following are some miscellaneous considerations for you as you insert footnotes and edit text containing footnotes:

- WordPerfect automatically inserts the footnote numbers. Do not key the number in the text or in the footnote.

- If you want the reference number in the manuscript to appear tight against the preceding text, DON'T SPACE before inserting your footnote.

- WordPerfect indents the first line of each footnote one-half inch.

- WordPerfect inserts the line that divides the footnote from the text on the page.

- Do not press Enter at the end of a footnote. WordPerfect automatically inserts one blank line between footnotes.

- Footnotes do not show in the document in Draft view. When working with footnotes, it is best to work in Page view.

- Footnotes can be inserted as you create the document. You can also go back and insert them after the document is finished.

- If editing affects the footnotes in the document, WordPerfect will automatically renumber and rearrange the footnotes.

- When keying a footnote, you can use most of the features you use with regular text entry, such as Italic, Underline, and Bold.

- Titles of published materials, such as newspapers, magazines, and books, should be italicized.

Let's try a short Step-by-Step exercise to see how footnotes work.

S TEP-BY-STEP ▷ 10.12

1. Key the short paragraph in Figure 10-14. Set line spacing at **Double** at the beginning of the document and indent it as a normal paragraph.

2. When you come to the footnote reference number, don't key the numeral. Instead, create a footnote using these steps:

   a. Open the **Insert** menu and choose **Footnote/Endnote**. Be sure Footnote is selected, and click **Create**.

   b. Key the text of the footnote, as illustrated at the bottom of Figure 10-14. Key the name of the book in italic.

   c. Click the **Close** button on the Property Bar when you finish the footnote. Then complete the paragraph.

(continued on next page)

3. Use **Two Pages** view or Zoom to **Full Page** to see how your footnote looks on the page. (You could also use the scroll bar to see the bottom of the page.)

4. Save your document as **footnote 10-12 xxx**. Insert the Path and Filename code a double space below the paragraph.

5. Print the document and save it again. Keep it open.

FIGURE 10-14
Text for Step-by-Step 10.12

> This is a paragraph that contains a footnote. The footnote number is here.[1] This is the sentence that follows the footnote. It is a thrill to discover how easy creating footnotes can be! Now I can use footnotes in all my school papers.
>
> _______________
>
> [1]Mary Makebelieve. *Practice Footnotes*, (Larsen: Ann Street Press, 1999), p. 85.

Editing Footnotes

Creating the footnote was pretty simple. Editing is just as simple. Let's make a couple of changes to the little document you just created.

S TEP-BY-STEP ⟹ 10.13

1. With **footnote 10-12 xxx** open in your window, use **Save As** to save the file as **footnote 10-13 xxx**.

2. In Page view, use the scroll bar to go to the bottom of the document so you can see the footnote. Click in the word *Mary* to enter the footnote editor.

3. Change *Mary* to **Maria**. Then change the page number from *85* to **25**.

4. Click in the document, above the footnote dividing line, to exit from the footnote editor.

5. Print the document and close it, saving it again as you close it.

Endnotes

As mentioned earlier, endnotes are created and edited much the same as footnotes. The major difference is location. When you put endnotes on a page by themselves at the end of a document, you must add that blank page and format it for the endnotes. Also, endnotes aren't formatted like a paragraph. Instead, they have a kind of hanging indent format, where the number is at the left margin and all other lines are indented. Let's practice.

STEP-BY-STEP 10.14

1. Open **wind 10-11 xxx**. Use **Save As** to save the file as **wind 10-14 xxx**.

2. With your insertion point at the top of the first page of text, reveal your codes and remove the Watermark code. (The watermark isn't necessary for this Step-by-Step exercise, and it slows you down as you move through the document.)

3. Position your insertion point at the end of the paragraph about the *wind turbines in California*.

4. Open the **Insert** menu and choose **Footnote/ Endnote**. Click the **Endnote** button and then **Create**. Your insertion point will be moved to a new line following the Path and Filename code at the end of your document. Endnote number **1.** will be there, with your insertion point next to the number.

5. Press **F7** to indent the text and key the **Melanie Malson . . .** endnote in Figure 10-15. Click the **Close** button on the Property Bar.

6. Position the insertion point at the end of the next paragraph (the one about the *eight-year payback*). Follow the procedure in Steps 4 and 5 to insert the **Donald Swenson . . .** endnote.

7. Experiment with trying to move the insertion point using the arrow keys on the keyboard while it is in an endnote.

8. Click to position the insertion point in the last paragraph of the document. Then click the **Save** button on the Toolbar to save the document with the same name. Keep the document open as you read on.

FIGURE 10-15
Endnotes for Step-by-Step 10.14

```
1. Melanie Malson, "The Winds of Tehachapi," Journal of Power Resources,
   February, 1998, p. 66.

2. Donald Swenson, "That Great, Breezy Midwest," Wisconsota Farm
   Journal, November, 1999, p. 23.
```

As you no doubt discovered, each endnote is an entity. When you try to move the insertion point, you can go left and right, but you can't get to the other endnote, and you can't get to the text of the document. To get out of the endnote "window," use your mouse to click into the document or click the Close button on the Property Bar. Also, when you're in the document, Ctrl+End will take you to the end of the *text* of the document, but it won't take you into the endnote section. You must use the scroll bar to see the endnotes.

Now that the endnotes have been inserted into the document, let's format the documents so the endnotes are on a page by themselves at the end of the document.

1. With **wind 10-14 xxx** showing in the window, use **Save As** to save the file as **wind 10-15 xxx**. Position your insertion point at the end of the Path and Filename code.

2. Press **Ctrl+Enter** for a new page. Press **Enter** several times to move your insertion point to somewhere near **2"** on the *Ln* indicator. (Double spacing is still in effect. Unless you change to single spacing, you won't hit exactly 2". It doesn't matter.)

3. Give the Center command (Shift+F7) and key the word **ENDNOTES** in bold and all caps.

4. Reveal your codes and look through the document at the new codes inserted when you created the endnotes. Add those codes to your list.

5. Print the document. Then close it, saving it again as you close it.

A number of options are available for working with footnotes and endnotes. If these features are important to the work you do, you may wish to spend some time exploring them further. WordPerfect Help contains information about formatting and changing options for both footnotes and endnotes.

Summary

Most of the features you studied in this lesson are primarily useful for documents of more than one page, although all of them can be used in single-page applications. In this lesson you learned that:

- Headers are information put at the top of the page to give a document continuity and to identify the pages.

- Footers provide the same services but are placed at the bottom of the page.

- Watermarks are lightly shaded images in the background on your pages.

- The codes for headers, footers, and watermarks only need to be entered once at the beginning of a document to format the entire document.

- The Widow/Orphan feature prevents a single line of a paragraph from appearing at either the bottom or the top of a page.

- Page numbering can be entered as a separate code, or the header can contain the command to number the pages.

- The value of the page number can easily be adjusted.

- Footnotes are used to identify references. WordPerfect formats footnotes automatically and even provides the reference numbers.

- Endnotes are like footnotes except they appear at the end of the document. If you want your endnotes on a separate page, you can format it after the document has been prepared.

All of the features presented in this lesson have options where you can change from the default settings to achieve an appearance that might be more to your liking. You learned the basics of each of the features. If you wish to explore further, you may do so at your leisure.

LESSON 10 REVIEW QUESTIONS

TRUE/FALSE

Circle the T if the statement is true. Circle the F if it is false.

T   F   1. Headers and footers are similar except that headers appear at the top of a page and footers appear at the bottom.

T   F   2. If you are working in Draft view, headers will show in your window, but footers will not.

T   F   3. If you do not want your header to appear on the first page of your document, you must insert the header at the top of your second page.

T   F   4. Suppress is accessed by choosing Format, Page, and then Suppress.

T   F   5. Single lines of a paragraph at the bottom or top of a page are called leftovers.

T   F   6. In preparing footnotes in Draft view, the reference number will be entered into your document and you will be taken to a special footnote window.

WRITTEN QUESTIONS

Write your answers to the following questions.

7. What is the difference between a footer and a footnote?

8. How do you get out of the endnote "window"?

9. Describe a watermark and list the types of things you might use as a watermark.

10. What command did you use to prepare the title page in Step-by-Step exercise 10.8?

LESSON 10 PROJECT

SCANS

A relatively long document has been created and saved for you to format. It needs a header and some footnotes. You will do more formatting of this document at the end of Lesson 11. Let's get it started here.

1. Beginning in a new document window, open **pc care** from the student **datafile** folder. Use **Save As** to save the file as **pc proj10a xxx**.

(continued on next page)

2. Give the document a header, with **PC Care** in bold at the left and **Page** and the page number in bold at the right.

3. Suppress the header on the first page.

4. Use **Widow/Orphan** to protect the document against awkward page breaks.

5. Go to the bottom of the first page. With the mouse pointer, grab the bottom margin guideline and drag it down to **0.75"**. (That change will affect both pages.)

6. Return to the top of the document. Give the commands to insert a footer that contains the Path and Filename code. Format the footer with **Flush Right** and **8-pt. Arial**.

7. Insert four footnotes into the document. The footnotes are listed in Figure 10-16. Position the footnotes as follows:
    a.   Footnote 1 at the end of the first paragraph in the section about *Equalizing the Power*.
    b.   Footnote 2 following the sentence about *commercial screen savers* in the second paragraph of *Prevent Burn-in*.
    c.   Footnote 3 following the sentence telling about the *15,000 volts*. (You'll need to change the *P* for the page number to lowercase. It may take a couple of tries.)
    d.   Footnote 4 following the second paragraph under *Make Backups*.

8. When you finish, check your work over carefully. If everything is OK, print the document and save it again as **pc proj10a xxx**. If it isn't correct, fix whatever is wrong before printing.

9. You just discovered that you were given an incorrect page number for the second footnote. Change the page number from *61* to **16**. Print only the page containing the correction.

10. Save the file again, this time as **pc proj10b xxx**, and close it.

FIGURE 10-16
Footnotes for Lesson 10 Project

```
1.   Freddy Keelowatt, "Power Up," PC Prognosticators, April 1997,
     p. 42.
2.   "Pixel Protectors," Timely Technology, July 1999, p. 61.
3.   Keelowatt, Op. Cit. p. 37.
4.   Hiam Halpa, "Better Backups," Timely Technology, January
     2000, p. 61.
```

CRITICAL THINKING ACTIVITY

You learned many features in this lesson that you will be using in formatting your documents. You will use some of these features, such as footnotes, page numbering, headers, and footers, frequently, but others have great potential for personal and professional use. Get a multiple-page report from your library, off the Internet, or from a local business. List as many document formatting features as you can find used in that report.

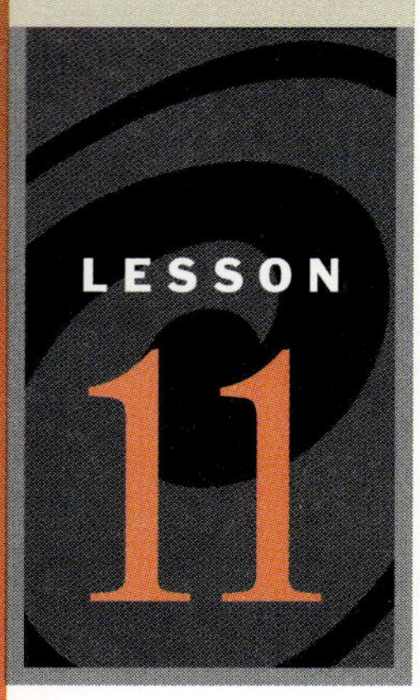

MISCELLANEOUS FORMATTING TOOLS

OBJECTIVES

Upon completion of this lesson, you will be able to:

- Use Advance to set the beginning point in a document.
- Make your document fit the page with Make It Fit.
- Use WordPerfect Symbols for characters not on the keyboard.
- Create and use QuickWords.
- Format portions of your text with QuickFormat.
- Use Block Protect to keep critical pieces of text together on a page.
- Double click parts of the WordPerfect window to open selected dialog boxes.
- Change the default font for documents.
- Use Current Document Style to format the entire document.
- Position text on the page using the Shadow Pointer.

Estimated Time: 1½ hours

WordPerfect has a variety of tools to help you with your work. Some of them are powerful tools that are used with great regularity. Others are tools that perform a small task but are invaluable when needed. In Lessons 9 and 10 you have worked with tools that are important parts of text editing. Tools such as headers, footers, margins, line spacing, and justification are standard tools and belong in the tool case for everyday use. In Lesson 11 you'll learn about a variety of small but useful tools. They don't fit together. In fact, this lesson may seem like a potpourri of features. Some are new; most are old; but all are useful sometimes.

Advance

The Advance tool enables you to position your text anywhere you'd like it on the page. You can use Advance to place text a certain distance from the current location of the insertion point, or you can place text at a specific location on the page measured from the edges of the paper. Usually you will measure from the edges of the paper. Let's try it.

STEP-BY-STEP ▭▶ 11.1

1. Beginning in a new document window, open the **Format** menu. Choose **Typesetting** and then **Advance**. The dialog box illustrated in Figure 11-1 will appear.

2. In the *Horizontal position* section, click **From left edge of page**. Key **4.25"** into the *Horizontal distance* text box.

3. In the *Vertical position* section, click **From top of page**. In the text box, key **5.5"**. Press **Enter** or click **OK**.

4. Key your name. Zoom to **Full Page** to see where your name begins. It should be at the exact center of the page.

5. Print your document and fold it in half in both directions. Does your name begin at the center of the page?

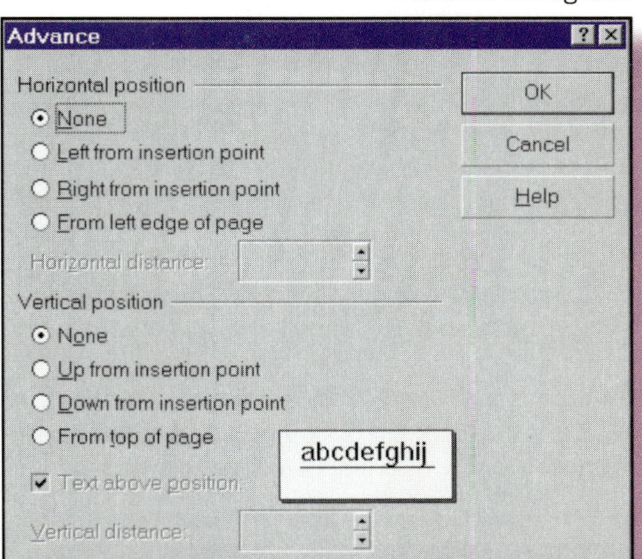

FIGURE 11-1
Advance Dialog Box

6. Close the document without saving it.

Now that you see how it works, let's use Advance to set the top margin of the first page of a document with which you've been working.

STEP-BY-STEP ▭▶ 11.2

1. Open **gifts 10-10 xxx**. Then use **Save As** to save the file as **gifts 11-2 xxx**.

2. Reveal your codes and remove all of the [HRt] codes above the title of the document.

3. Open the **Format** menu and choose **Typesetting**. Then choose **Advance**.

4. In the *Vertical position* section, click **From top of page**. In the text box, key **2.25"**. Click **OK**.

5. Position your insertion point on the title of the document. The Application Bar should report that you are slightly more than 2" from the top of the page.

6. Save the document again as **gifts 11-2 xxx** and keep it open.

Near the bottom of the Advance dialog box is a check box for *Text above position*. If you click to deselect this option, the advanced text will be below rather than above the position measured from the top of the page. That explains why you set Advance at 2.25" and the Application Bar measured only 2.05". In many of the Step-by-Step exercises you will complete in this course, you will be asked to advance from the top of the page 2". It will actually turn out to be about 1.8". Don't be concerned about what seems like a discrepancy in distance.

Make It Fit

If you looked through the document in your window, you probably noticed that very little of the document extended to the second page. If you fiddled with the margins, the line spacing, or the font size, you could get it to fit on one page. WordPerfect has a feature called *Make It Fit* that adjusts your documents so they fit on the number of pages you wish.

Make It Fit can make a number of changes in your document to make it fit in the desired amount of space. The formatting it looks at by default are font size and line spacing. You know how to change both of those items, but it's easier to let WordPerfect adjust your documents for you.

Make It Fit is chosen from the Format menu. Let's learn about Make It Fit as we adjust this **gifts** document so it fits comfortably on one page.

STEP-BY-STEP 11.3

SCANS

1. With **gifts 11-2 xxx** showing in your window, use **Save As** to save the file as **gifts 11-3 xxx**.

2. Open the **Format** menu and choose **Make It Fit**. The dialog box illustrated in Figure 11-2 will appear.

3. Note that WordPerfect is telling you that the document is currently *2* pages long. Be sure *Desired number of pages* is set at **1**.

4. Note also that none of the items in the left column are selected. Only Font size and Line spacing should be checked. If necessary, fix the *Items to adjust* section so it matches Figure 11-2.

5. Click the **Make It Fit** button. WordPerfect will take a minute to complete your task.

6. When WordPerfect finishes squishing your document, it will be on one page. Look at the following things:
   a. Look at the font size reported on the Property Bar. It is now smaller than the default of 12 pt.
   b. Position your insertion point in the first paragraph. Go to the Line Spacing dialog box and check the spacing. It should be less than 1.5.
   c. Look at line spacing with the insertion point in the enumerated items. It should report spacing of less than single (1).

7. Print the document and save it again as **gifts 11-3 xxx**. Close the document.

Make It Fit also works in the opposite direction. If your report is a little short, you can tell WordPerfect to make it fill a little more space. Exercise judgment with this feature. The request must be reasonable. It would have been unreasonable, for example, to have asked WordPerfect to expand the **gifts** document to two pages. If you had, you would have ended up with a gigantic font and very wide line spacing.

In addition, Make It Fit will expand or condense a selected chunk of text to make it fit in a defined space. Simply select the text to expand or condense and tell WordPerfect what to do with it. You may practice more with this feature at your leisure.

Make It Fit is a feature you'll use frequently in this training.

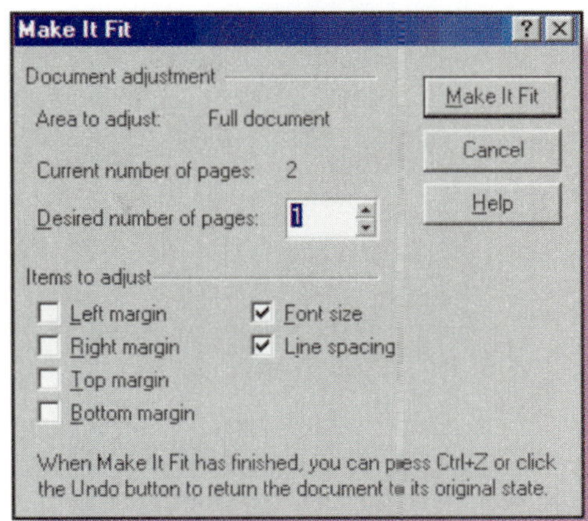

FIGURE 11-2
Make it Fit Dialog Box

WordPerfect Symbols

You learned earlier that you can create an em dash by keying three hyphens. That was one of a few shortcuts available in WordPerfect Symbols. Another way to get different symbols is by using the 15 sets of symbols provided in WordPerfect.

To access special symbols, position the insertion point where you would like the symbols to appear and press Ctrl+W or choose Symbols from the Format menu. In each case a window will open, illustrating a symbol set and waiting for you to choose the desired symbol. The buttons at the bottom of the dialog box offer choices regarding inserting the symbol and closing the dialog box.

Look at Figure 11-3. It shows the WordPerfect Symbols dialog box and Set 4, the set of symbols you'll probably use most frequently.

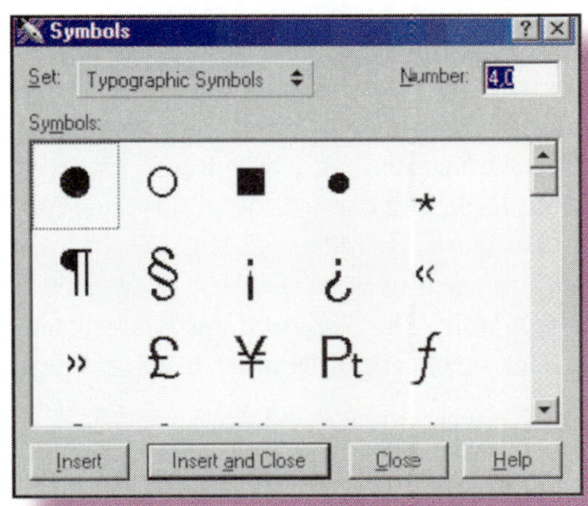

FIGURE 11-3
WordPerfect Symbols Dialog Box

1. Beginning in a new document window, press **Ctrl+W**. Key the numbers **4,67**, with no space following the comma.

2. The number you keyed will appear in the box in the upper right corner. The highlight should move to the $^3/_8$ fraction.

3. Use the scroll bar in the Symbols dialog box and look at some of the symbols. Then return the highlight to $^3/_8$ and click the **Insert and Close** button at the bottom of the dialog box. The $^3/_8$ should appear at the location of your insertion point in your window.

4. Zoom to **200%** so you can see your fraction. Stay at 200% temporarily.

5. Press **Ctrl+W** again. Note that WordPerfect remembered that the last symbol you used was $^3/_8$, so if you wanted $^3/_8$ again, you would only need to press Enter to put the fraction in your document and close the dialog box.

6. Use the scroll bars, if necessary, to find the $^1/_2$ fraction. Double click it to put it into your document. Then click the **Close** button.

7. Press **Enter** twice to prepare for the next Step-by-Step exercise.

Bullets and Check Boxes

Many of the symbols in the 15 sets of symbols are not symbols you will use with regularity. Bullets and check boxes are examples of symbols you might find useful.

You worked with bullets in Lesson 5. If you want a bullet with a different look, you can use WordPerfect symbols to customize the Outline/Bullets & Numbering list, or you can choose a different bullet when starting your own list. Here is a list of the variety of bullets available. The set and number are listed after each bullet.

°	2,27	○	4,45
•	4,0	☻	5,8
○	4,1	○	6,33
•	4,3	°	6,36
●	4,44	►	6,27

Check boxes are little boxes used for choices. Here is how you might use the check box that occurs with 4,38.

☐ Yes or   ☐ No
☐ Male or   ☐ Female

Additional choices for check boxes are ☐ (4,48) and ☐ (5,24). If you think all of these are too small, you can vary the sizes of the check boxes (and all other symbols) by changing the font size. When you do this, extra space might be added between your lines.

While it seems like quite a job to change font size and choose a symbol from the set, you can create the symbol(s) with all the desired changes. Then copy it to the Windows Clipboard and paste it into your document each time you need it.

S TEP-BY-STEP ⟹ 11.5

1. Press **Ctrl+W** and browse through the sets. Practice making some bullets and check boxes. See if you can find a check mark. Vary the sizes of your check boxes and symbols.

2. Zoom to **100%** and press **Enter** twice.

3. Key the sentences in Figure 11-4. Double-space between the sentences. Insert the required symbols using the numbers in parentheses for reference. You do not need to key the numbers in parentheses.

4. When you finish, save your Step-by-Step exercise as **char 11-5 xxx**. Insert the Path and Filename code in a footer. Print the document and close it, saving it again when you close it.

FIGURE 11-4
Sentences for Step-by-Step 11.5

```
It might cost $1.70 or more to buy £ of British money. (4,11)
The cake was baked in a 350° oven. (6,36)
"¿Dónde está su niña?" (4,32) (4,8) (1,59) (1,27) (1,57) (4,31)
I can create check boxes with 4,38 □ and 4,48 □.
```

WordPerfect symbols open a whole new set of doors for document creation. Look for opportunities to use special symbols.

QuickWords

QuickWords may be used for abbreviations that expand into the complete text when you key the QuickWord and then expand it by pressing the space bar, Enter, or Tab. QuickWords work much like QuickCorrect. QuickWords, however, can contain formatting such as Bold, Italic, Underline, and font changes, in addition to a number of formatting features about which you have not yet learned. We'll practice QuickWords here. Then we'll work with it again when you've learned some of those other features.

S TEP-BY-STEP ⟹ 11.6

1. Beginning in a new document window, key your entire name. Select the name and format it with bold, italic, and 24-pt. Arial.

2. Below your name, key your address using **10-pt. Arial** (no Bold or Italic).

3. Select the entire name and address. Then open the **Tools** menu and choose **QuickWords**. The dialog box illustrated in Figure 11-5 will appear.

(continued on next page)

1 6 3

FIGURE 11-5
QuickWords Section of the QuickCorrect Dialog Box

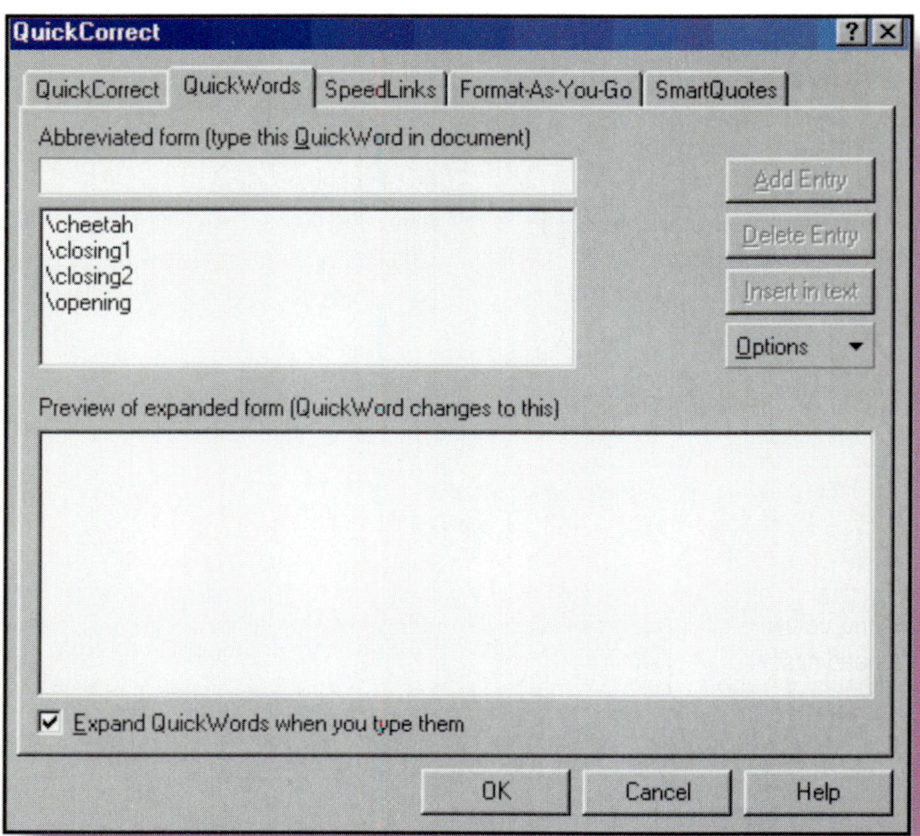

4. In the QuickWords portion of the QuickCorrect dialog box, key the characters that you will use for an abbreviation for your name. If your initials are unique characters, like *dk* for *Donald R. Knowles*, use them.

5. Click **Add Entry**, which closes the dialog box.

6. Back in your document window, move your insertion point to a double space below your formatted name. Key the abbreviation and press the space bar. Watch your name and address appear, complete with formatting.

7. Close your document without saving it.

As you discovered in Step-by-Step 11.6, you aren't limited to one or two words with QuickWords. In fact, you aren't even limited to a single line, as you are with QuickCorrect. You can create as many QuickWords as you wish, and you can use them as often as they are needed. When a QuickWord is no longer needed, you can use Delete to remove it from the list.

Now let's learn about another "Quick" formatting tool.

QuickFormat

QuickFormat is a tool you may use to copy the format from one chunk of text in your document to other chunks of text. You can copy font face, font size, and appearance attributes (such as bold, underline, and italic). For paragraphs, you can also copy spacing, indentation, and borders.

When you choose QuickFormat from the Toolbar or from the Format menu, you have the choice of copying characters or headings. This is an important distinction. We'll review by adding some special formatting to the document. Then we'll practice QuickFormat, trying it both ways.

STEP-BY-STEP ⇒ 11.7

CANS

1. Open **pc proj10b xxx**. Save the file as **pc 11-7 xxx**.

FIGURE 11-6
QuickFormat Dialog Box

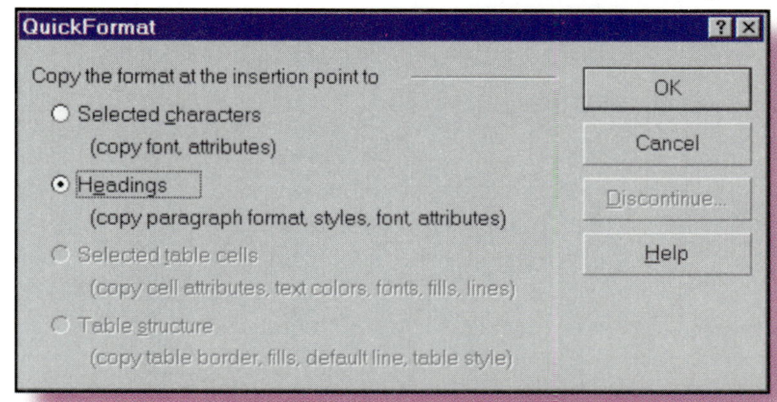

2. Position the insertion point at the beginning of the first paragraph. Change line spacing to **1.5**. Then go through the document and delete the extra blank line above and below each of the side headings.

3. Move the insertion point to the top of the document and use **Advance** to set the first line of the document at **1.5" From top of page**.

4. Select the first side heading (*Equalize the Power*) and format it with Bold, Italic, and Underline.

5. Position the insertion point somewhere in the side heading and click the **QuickFormat** button on the Toolbar. The QuickFormat dialog box, illustrated in Figure 11-6, will appear. Note that WordPerfect knows you're working with a chunk of text surrounded by hard returns, so *Headings* is selected.

6. Click **OK**. Move your mouse and look at the pointer. It should look like a paint roller.

7. Use **Page Down** to move through your document and find the next side heading. Point in the left margin opposite that side heading (your pointer will be a fat white arrow) and click once. The format from the first side heading should be painted onto the second one.

8. Find the other four side headings in the document and paint the format on in the same way. Then click the **QuickFormat** button on the Toolbar to turn QuickFormat off.

9. Check your work over carefully. Then print it and save it again as **pc 11-7 xxx**. Keep it open in the window.

When QuickFormat is used to format paragraphs (headings), it creates a style for those headings. They are all tied together. This is a big advantage, because if you later decide you don't like the style, you only need to change one of the occurrences of the style, and WordPerfect will change all the rest. Let's practice that with the document in the window.

STEP-BY-STEP 11.8

1. With **pc 11-7 xxx** showing in your window, use **Save As** to save the file as **pc 11-8 xxx**.

2. Position the insertion point in any one of the side headings.

3. Press **F9** for the Font dialog box. In the *Appearance* section, deselect **Underline** and choose **Small caps**. Click **OK**.

4. Look through the document. All of the side headings should be formatted with Bold, Italic, and Small caps.

5. Click the **Save** button on the Toolbar and keep the document open in the window as you read on.

With the side headings tied together as a style, you can change the formatting of those lines as often as you like. That "style" is saved with the document when you save it and close the document. It cannot be transferred to another document.

Now that you know what a fine formatting tool QuickFormat is, let's look at the *Selected characters* part of the tool. With the QuickFormat Selected characters choice, the selected formatting is "painted" onto additional text.

STEP-BY-STEP 11.9

1. With **pc 11-8 xxx** open, use **Save As** to save the file as **pc 11-9 xxx**.

2. Click to position the insertion point in the word *computer* in the first paragraph.

3. Click the **Bold** button on the Property Bar. With the insertion point in the bolded word, click the **QuickFormat** button on the Toolbar.

4. Choose **Selected characters** and click **OK**. Your insertion point should look like a paint roller.

5. Look through the document. Each time you find the word *computer* or *computers*, double click to select and format that word. Then move to the next occurrence of the word. The word occurs 15 times!

6. When you finish, turn QuickFormat off by clicking the **QuickFormat** button on the Toolbar again.

7. Position the insertion point in any occurrence of *computer* and change from Bold to **Italic**. (All occurrences should change.)

8. Reveal your codes. Look at the codes by the side headings that are formatted with QuickFormat. Look at the *Auto QuickFormat* codes. Add them to your list. (Auto QuickFormat1 for the side headings and Auto Quickformat2 for the *computer*.)

9. Move your insertion point so it is to the left of one of the side heading Auto QuickFormat codes. Note that it lists all of the appearance attributes you've used to format the side headings.

10. Print your document. Then save it again as **pc 11-9 xxx**. Keep it open.

In this Step-by-Step exercise you could select the text to be formatted by double clicking because it was only one word. If you want to add the format to two or more consecutive words, you must select and format the words by dragging across them with the mouse pointer.

Block Protect

If your document has the specified 1.5 line spacing, Widow/Orphan, and an Advance code positioning the title 1.5" from the top of the page, you probably have a side heading at the bottom of one page and the beginning of the paragraph for that side heading on the next page. Look through your document and find the *Prevent Burn-in* side heading. Widow/Orphan keeps paragraphs together very well, but it doesn't keep TWO paragraphs together (the side heading and the following paragraph).

You can deal with those situations individually as they occur using a tool called *Block Protect*. With Block Protect, you select the text to be kept together on a page, give the proper command, and WordPerfect will keep the text together. Since WordPerfect never violates a margin, it will move the entire block of text to be protected to the next page. Block Protect can be chosen from the Keep Text Together dialog box. An easier source is the Quick Menu. Let's try it on the **pc** document.

S TEP-BY-STEP ⇒ 11.10

1. With **pc 11-9 xxx** showing in the window, use **Save As** to save the document as **pc 11-10 xxx**.

2. Move your document in the window so you can see the *Prevent Burn-in* side heading and at least two lines of the next paragraph. (If you prefer to go to Draft view so the footnote and header don't interfere, it will probably be easier to see what you're doing.)

3. Beginning with the side heading, select the side heading, all of the first line of the next paragraph, and at least a portion of the second line.

4. Point to the selected text. Right click to display the QuickMenu and then choose **Block Protect**. You'll see the side heading move to the top of the second page so it is together with the following paragraph.

5. Save the document again as **pc 11-10 xxx** and print it. Keep it open.

1 6 7

Double Clicking

A couple of other features should be mentioned here that you might find useful when you are formatting your documents. Both of them have to do with double clicking parts of the WordPerfect window.

Property Bar

If you double click the QuickFonts button on the Property Bar, WordPerfect will display the Font dialog box.

Ruler

As you know, if you point to one of the tab set markers on the Ruler and right click, the menu listing the kinds of tabs appears. If you point to one of those markers and double click (with the left mouse button, of course), the Tab Set dialog box will appear.

Pointing anywhere in the margin portion of the Ruler and double clicking will open the Margins portion of the Page Setup dialog box.

Codes

When your codes are revealed, you can point to most of the codes and double click to open the related dialog box. For example, double clicking the Bold, Italic, or Underline code or any of the font codes will open the Fonts dialog box. Double clicking any Tab code will open the Tab Set dialog box. Double clicking the Hard and Soft Return codes will open the Paragraph Format dialog box, where you can set such things as indents and spacing between paragraphs.

Application Bar

If you double click anywhere in the *Pg, Ln, Pos* portion of the Application Bar, the Go To dialog box will open. The Application Bar can be customized. Many users add the current date to the Application Bar. If your Application Bar includes the date, double clicking that date will add the current date to your document at the position of the insertion point.

Let's use the document showing in your window to practice this double clicking. Don't worry about spoiling the document. You'll throw it away when you're finished.

STEP-BY-STEP 11.11

SCANS

1. Point to each of the following items and double click. When the appropriate dialog box appears, look it over and then close it. Some of the dialog boxes may be closed with **OK**. Others may be closed with **Close** or **Cancel**. All of them may be closed by clicking the *x* in the upper right corner.
   a. **QuickFonts** button on the Property Bar.
   b. *Pg, Ln, Pos* portion of the Application Bar.
   c. Margin markers on the Ruler. (You may have to choose the Ruler from the View menu to display it.)
   d. Indent triangles in the margin portion of the Ruler (Paragraph Format dialog box).
   e. Tab set marker on the Ruler.
   f. A font code in Reveal Codes.
   g. Hard Return [HRt] code in Reveal Codes.
   h. **Left tab** code in Reveal Codes.

2. When you've explored this alternate method of displaying dialog boxes and closed those dialog boxes, close the document without saving it.

Selecting Text

While you're learning about miscellaneous formatting tools, one other procedure should be reviewed and expanded. This has to do with selecting odd pieces of text with the mouse. As you know, you can double click to select a word, triple click to select a sentence, or quadruple click to select a paragraph. Or, if you use the fat white arrow in the left margin, you can select sentences and paragraphs with fewer clicks.

It is not uncommon, however, to need to select text that doesn't fall into one of those neat packages (like a word or sentence). Then you are most likely to use the mouse to drag across the text to select it.

If the text to be selected begins at the margin, like the side heading in the Block Protect exercise earlier, it's sometimes difficult to get the first letter of the text without grabbing the margin guideline. In situations like those, it might be easier for you to begin at the opposite end of the text to select it. In the case of the Block Protect exercise, you would have begun in the middle of the second line of the paragraph and dragged the mouse pointer up and to the left until the entire side heading was included in the selected text.

As you work with WordPerfect and edit your documents, practice alternate methods in all you do. You'll soon develop a style that works for you and helps you to be efficient in your work.

Default Font and Current Document Style

In Lesson 10 you learned about formatting whole documents, including extended document parts such as headers, footers, footnotes, and page numbers. In most of those Step-by-Step exercises you worked with the default font face and the default margins. Consequently, you didn't have any problems with odd fonts or margins in your documents.

When you change the font face or the margins, the change only applies to the body of the document. It does NOT extend to the parts of the document in the special editing windows. You must format those document parts separately. A better way is to put the format for the entire document in the Document Default Font or the Current Document Style. Let's look at these two features.

Document Default Font

This tool is for setting a new font for the entire document. The dialog box is opened by choosing File, Document, and then Default Font, or by choosing Default Font in the Font dialog box. When you set the font for a document using the default font, the headers, footers, footnotes, and page numbering will all have the same font. Let's try it.

S TEP-BY-STEP ▷ 11.12

1. Open **pcug 10-1 xxx**. Use **Save As** to save the file as **pcug 11-12 xxx**.

2. With the insertion point at the beginning of the first paragraph, change the font of the text to **Arial**.

3. Check the header and footer. Note that those two parts are still formatted with Times New Roman. Remove the Arial font code you just inserted.

(continued on next page)

4. With the insertion point at the beginning of the first paragraph, open the **File** menu, choose **Document**, and then choose **Default Font**. The dialog box that opens should look like Figure 11-7.

5. Look at the Settings button at the bottom. If you wished to permanently change the font for ALL documents, you would choose *Settings* and make that choice.

6. Choose **Arial** and click **OK**.

7. Check the header and footer. Note that those parts are now formatted with the same font as the text of the document.

8. Save the file again as **pcug 11-12 xxx**. Keep it open as you read on.

FIGURE 11-7
Document Initial Font Dialog Box

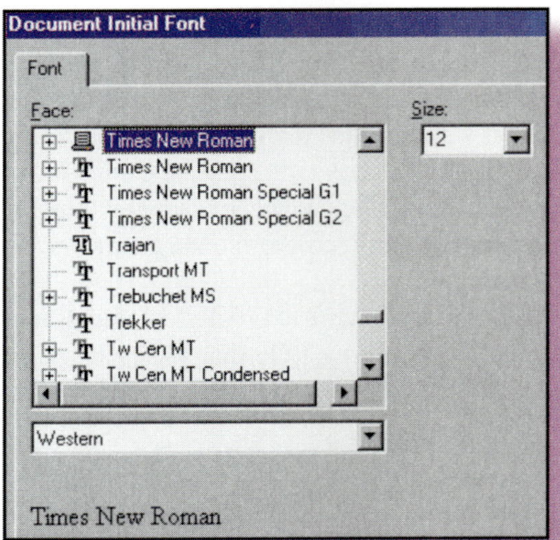

As you can see, if you wanted to change the font of the entire document, it is much easier to do it with Default Font than it would be to have to change the font of the header, the footer, page numbering, or the footnotes individually.

While Default Font is used to change the font face and font size of a document, you can make other changes with the Current Document Style feature.

Current Document Style

Current Document Style may be used for changing fonts, as well as a wide variety of other formats that you want to carry through your entire document. A good example is margins. We'll practice that in Step-by-Step 11.13.

STEP-BY-STEP 11.13

1. With **pcug 11-12 xxx** showing in the window, use **Save As** to save the file as **pcug 11-13 xxx**.

2. Position the insertion point at the beginning of the first paragraph. Use either the Ruler or the Margins portion of the Page Setup dialog box to make **2"** margins on both the left and right.

3. Look at the header in your document. Look at the guidelines surrounding the footer space. As you can see, both of those parts are still governed by the default margin setting.

4. Return the insertion point to the beginning of the first paragraph. Use Reveal Codes so you can see to remove the Left and Right margin settings.

5. Open the **File** menu, choose **Document**, and then choose **Current Document Style**. The Styles Editor dialog box should appear (see Figure 11-8). This is a dialog box you'll see often as you progress through your work.

6. In the Styles Editor dialog box, open the **Format** menu and choose **Margins**. Set the Left and Right margins at **2"**.

7. Click **OK** to close the Margins portion of the Page Setup dialog box and again to close the Styles Editor dialog box.

8. Look at the header and the guidelines surrounding the footer space. As you can see, the margins in those areas now match the margins in the remainder of the document.

9. Save your document again as **pcug 11-13 xxx**. Print it and close it.

FIGURE 11-8
Styles Editor Dialog Box

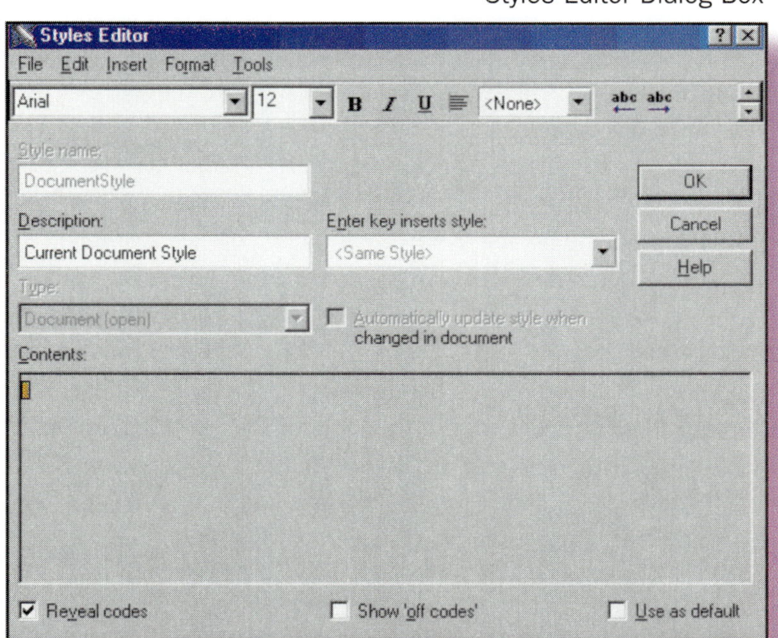

Step-by-Steps exercises 1.12 and 11.13 were short and somewhat exaggerated. But they should have given you a good idea of the value of Document Default Font and Current Document Style. Obviously, both of these tools are valuable when you work with documents that contain extra parts like headers and footers. As mentioned earlier, these features also work for footnotes, endnotes, page numbers, etc.

Shadow Pointer

Earlier in your training, you were told to leave the Shadow Pointer button on the Application Bar in the UP position. That means that your insertion point always looks like an *I*. The Shadow Pointer is actually a very useful tool for certain applications. When it is selected, you can

- point near the middle of the page. If you click when the pointer has an arrow in both directions, the text you key will be centered.

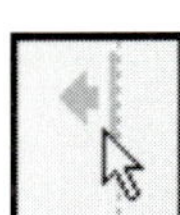

- point near the right of the page. If you click when the point has an arrow pointing to the left, the text you key will be formatted with Flush Right.

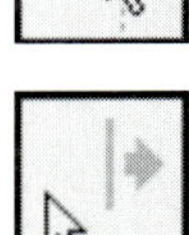

- point anywhere on the page where you would like text to begin. When you click, the insertion point will be positioned at that location, and the space between that location and the previous text will be filled with as many [HRt] and [Left Tab] codes as necessary to position the text.

    Let's practice with the Shadow Pointer (sometimes referred to as the *Shadow Cursor*).

STEP-BY-STEP 11.14

1. Beginning in a new document window, click the **Shadow Pointer** tool on the Application Bar to select it. (When selected, it appears to be depressed.)

2. Anywhere in your window, move the pointer to the horizontal center of the page. When the arrow points right AND left, click. Key your entire name. It should be centered.

3. Point near the right margin (either above or below your name). When the arrow points to the left, click to position the insertion point there and key your name again. It should end at the right margin.

4. Move the pointer to a location on the page where the arrow points to the right. Click there and key your name again.

5. Reveal your codes. Look at all the [HRt] and [Left Tab] codes inserted by WordPerfect.

6. Close your practice without saving it.

Summary

As promised at the beginning of the lesson, lots of interesting tools have been discussed and practiced in this lesson. You've learned that:

- With the Advance tool, you can begin your text anywhere you'd like on the page.

- Make It Fit can be used to compress or expand a document or parts of a document onto a prescribed number of pages.

- WordPerfect Symbols is a tool that enables you to insert a wide variety of symbols and icons into your documents—symbols that don't appear on the keyboard.

- QuickWords can be set up to save you keystrokes. Text entered using QuickWords can contain a wide variety of formats.

- QuickFormat has two settings.

  - If you choose Headings, a style is prepared that you can apply to similar parts of the document.
  - If you choose Selected characters, you can paint the format onto words or phrases in the document.

- Block Protect is a tool that enables you to keep chunks of text together on a page. Block Protect must be applied each time it is needed.

- You can point to a variety of places in your window and double click to open related dialog boxes.

- You can use Document Default Font to insert a font setting that formats all parts of your document.

- Current Document Style is a tool that enables you to make formatting changes that format your entire document.

- The Shadow Pointer enables you to key anywhere on a page.

The federal government links schools, government agencies, colleges, and universities to a network that is much faster than the current Internet. This network is called the National Research and Education Network (NREN).

LESSON 11 REVIEW QUESTIONS

MULTIPLE CHOICE

Circle the best answer to each of the following statements.

1. The tool that enables you to position your text anywhere you'd like it on a page is called
   A. Advance.
   B. Make It Fit.
   C. QuickFormat.
   D. Center Page(s).

2. The Make It Fit feature looks at the following default settings:
   A. margins and font size.
   B. font size and line spacing.
   C. line spacing and line length.
   D. line length and margins.

3. WordPerfect provides ______ sets of symbols.
   A. five
   B. ten
   C. 15
   D. 20

(continued on next page)

4. To change the size of check boxes and all other symbols, you can change
    A. the font size.
    B. to a different symbol.
    C. to a different font face.
    D. by adding Bold.

5. QuickWords may be used for abbreviations that expand into the complete text by pressing any of the following EXCEPT
    A. the space bar.
    B. Enter.
    C. Tab.
    D. Ctrl+Enter.

TRUE/FALSE

Circle the T if the statement is true. Circle the F if it is false.

T   F   **6.** In order to change the font for an entire document, including headers and footers, you can put the format in the Document Default Font or the Current Document Style.

T   F   **7.** QuickFormat is chosen from the Property Bar or the Format menu.

T   F   **8.** If you double click on one of the tab set markers on the Ruler, a Left tab will be set.

T   F   **9.** QuickFormat can copy font face, font size, and appearance attributes.

T   F   **10.** Block Protect is used to keep headings and following paragraphs together.

LESSON 11 PROJECT

SCANS

Follow the steps below to format the **nasa** document you used for practice in Lesson 2.

1. Open **nasa** from the student **datafile** folder. Use **Save As** to save the file as **nasa proj11a xxx**.

2. Use **Advance** to move the title to **2"** from the top of the page.

3. Center the title. Select the title and format it as follows:
    a.   Use **Bold**.
    b.   Select a **20-pt.** font size.
    c.   Go to the Font dialog box and choose **Small caps**.

4. With your insertion point at the beginning of the document, open the **Format** menu and choose **Keep Text Together**. Choose **Widow/Orphan**.

5. Select the first side heading (*Weather Forecasting*). Format it with Bold and Small caps.

6. Use **QuickFormat** to copy the format in Step 5 to the other ten side headings.

7. Look through the document. If any of the side headings are separated from the following paragraphs by a page break, use **Block Protect** to keep the side headings with the following paragraph.

8. Insert a footer that contains the Path and Filename code.

9. On the bottom of the first page, grab the bottom margin guideline (below the footer) and drag it to approximately **0.75"**.

10. Save the document again as **nasa proj11a xxx** and print it.

11. Use **Make It Fit** to make the document fill three pages. Then adjust the document as follows:
    a. After it is expanded, you may need to reset the title at 20 pt.
    b. Look through the document and see if Block Protect is needed anywhere.
    c. If your edits cause the document to stretch to four pages, use **Make It Fit** again.

12. Check your work a final time. Then print it again and save it again as **nasa proj11b xxx**.

CRITICAL THINKING ACTIVITY

The report you are keying is going to be bound at the top, so you have set Advance for a top margin of $2^1/2$". When you begin keying, you notice that the Application Bar is showing Pos 2.3". What do you need to do to make the top margin exactly $2^1/2$"?

ADVANCED FILE MANAGEMENT

OBJECTIVES

Upon completion of this lesson, you will be able to:

- Change the listing order of your files.
- Use QuickFinder to locate files containing specified text.
- Use QuickMarks to help you find your place in a document.
- Use Bookmarks to mark certain parts of the document.
- Work with comments in your documents.
- Save a document in a format different from that of WordPerfect 9.

Estimated Time: 1 hour

In Lesson 8 you learned to create folders, rename folders, delete folders, rename files, and delete files, as well as copy or move files from one folder to another. In Appendix B you learned more about file management. By now you should be quite comfortable with the Open File dialog box and how it may be used for most of your work with files. But there is more to learn.

Working with Files

You learned in Lesson 4 that you can change the order in which the files are listed in the Open File dialog box, and you practiced rearranging the files. You learned that this tool might help you find a misplaced file according to the date on which it was created.

You also learned that the files can be listed in a number of ways. Let's review and try a few more things in the Open File dialog box.

STEP-BY-STEP 12.1

1. Beginning in a new document window, open the Open File dialog box. The View menu provides the choice of listing the files with Large Icons, Small Icons, List, and Details. One at a time, try these options. End with Small Icons. What is the difference between using Small Icons and List?

2. Open the **View** menu and choose **Tree View**. Scroll through the tree view. Note the "depressed" button on the Toolbar. Click it to deselect it.

3. Select the student **datafile** folder that contains your prerecorded documents. Put the insertion point on **ball.wpd**. Click the **Preview** button on the Toolbar. If the viewer is part of the dialog box, the document will be very small.

4. Open the **View** menu, choose **Preview**, and choose **Use Separate Window**. Finally, select **No Preview**.

5. Close the dialog box.

Sometimes WordPerfect remembers how you arranged the files. If they are arranged in order by date or size when you exit from the program, they will be in that same order the next time you start the program. Sometimes another user might leave the setting at something other than Name. If that happens, you might have trouble finding the desired files. You can simply change it back.

QuickFinder

Another way WordPerfect helps you find a file is with QuickFinder. This tool can quickly scan a disk or folder to find files containing a specified word or phrase. It can also look through your folders to find a file by name.

In addition to all of that, QuickFinder Manager is a powerful tool that can also prepare a Fast Search file that indexes all of the words in the documents on your disk or in a folder so that searches can be performed much more quickly.

The Fast Search file can be named. You can prepare different lists of the files in different folders, and choose the particular list you wish to search when you are performing a search. We will not practice with the indexing feature in this text. We will, however, practice finding a file or files that contain specified text. Let's see how it works.

STEP-BY-STEP 12.2

1. Beginning in a new document window, open the Open File dialog box. Choose the folder or disk that contains your practice files for Unit 3.

2. In the **View** menu, make sure the **List** button is chosen. Make sure Preview is not chosen.

3. Be sure the *File type* lists "All Files." Key **hostas** in the *File name* box. Click the **Find Now** button at the bottom of the dialog box. QuickFinder should quickly tell you that **hostas 9-8 xxx** is the only file containing the word *hostas*.

(continued on next page)

4. Click the **Back** button to return to your original list.

5. Click in the *File name* text box again and replace *hostas* with **computer**. Click **Find Now**. WordPerfect will search and list the files that contain that word. It should find more than 20 of them. (Apparently, lots of the documents are about computers!)

6. Close the Open File dialog box and read on.

If you wish to search for a phrase rather than a word, you must put quotation marks around the phrase when you key it in the *Content* text box. For example, if you key **pc care** without quotation marks, WordPerfect will list all files containing *pc* as well as all files containing *care*, but none of the files might contain the words *pc care* consecutively.

QuickFinder can be used to locate files by name and by pattern. For example, you can ask to list all files where the name begins with *pc*. QuickFinder will also locate files with a date range—for example, all files created between January 1 and January 5.

QuickMark and Bookmark

WordPerfect enables you to move quickly from one place in your document to another by using QuickMarks and Bookmarks. Both of these tools are used to mark a specific point in the text. They have similarities—yet they are different.

QuickMark

A document may contain only one QuickMark. The QuickMark doesn't need a name, and if you set a new QuickMark, the old one disappears. You might use a QuickMark while editing a lengthy document to mark your place while you go to a different place to check something or to get additional information. After finding the information, you can use the QuickMark to return quickly to the point of edit.

To set the QuickMark, open the Tools menu, choose Bookmark, and click the Set QuickMark button. An easier way is to press Ctrl+Shift+Q. To return to the place where the QuickMark is set, either press Ctrl+Q or open the Tools menu, choose Bookmark, and click Find QuickMark. Let's try this simple procedure using the keyboard shortcuts.

1. Beginning in a new document window, open **nasa proj11b xxx**.

2. Use **Ctrl+G** for Go To and key **3**. Press **Enter** to go to page 3. Find the side heading *Wheelchairs*. Position the insertion point immediately after that side heading.

3. Press **Ctrl+Shift+Q** to set a QuickMark. Then press **Ctrl+End** to go to the end of the document.

4. Press **Ctrl+Q** to return to the QuickMark. You should be after the word *Wheelchairs* again.

5. Press **Ctrl+Home** to go to the beginning of the document. Press **Ctrl+Q**. Are you back to *Wheelchairs* again?

6. Now set a QuickMark at the end of the first paragraph. Go to the end of the document

with **Ctrl+End**. Press **Ctrl+Q**. Did you return to *Wheelchairs* or the end of the first paragraph?

7. Keep the document open as you read on.

As you can see, when you set a new QuickMark, the old one is removed. You can also see how quickly WordPerfect takes you to the place where the QuickMark is set.

Bookmark

A Bookmark is much like a QuickMark because it marks a specific location so you can return to that location quickly. Bookmarks, however, are named. You may have as many bookmarks in a document as you wish.

You can set a bookmark by selecting the text for the bookmark, choosing Create in the Bookmark dialog box, and clicking OK. If you prefer, you can select the text for the bookmark and give the bookmark a different name in the dialog box. There are times when you might choose either of those methods. In Step-by-Step 12.4 you'll give the bookmarks a different, more meaningful name because you might not remember the text that was selected for the bookmark.

When you tell WordPerfect to search for a bookmark, you can tell WordPerfect to not only find the text marked with the bookmark, but also to automatically select the text when it is located. Then you can copy the selected text to the Clipboard for insertion at a different point in the document.

S TEP-BY-STEP 12.4

1. With **nasa proj11b xxx** showing in the window, use **Save As** to save the file as **nasa 12-4 xxx**.

2. Click in the left margin opposite the first side heading to select that side heading.

3. Open the **Tools** menu and choose **Bookmark**. The Bookmark dialog box will open. Click **Create** to display the Create Bookmark dialog box with the side heading displayed as the Bookmark name (see Figure 12-1).

4. Click **OK** to return to your document. Look at the Bookmark code in Reveal Codes. Move your insertion point to the left of the code. Note that the code identifies the name of the bookmark.

5. Follow the procedure beginning in Step 2 to mark the following side headings as bookmarks: *Water Recycling*, *Dental Braces*, *Wheelchairs*, and *Anti-Corrcsion Paint*.

6. Save the document again as **nasa 12-4 xxx** and keep it open.

FIGURE 12-1
Create Bookmark Dialog Box

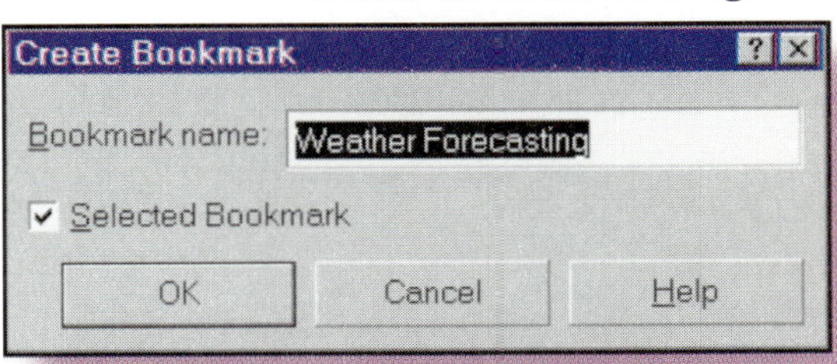

Now that the document has been marked with bookmarks, you can use those bookmarks to jump from one part of the document to another. We'll practice using the bookmarks shortly. This is especially useful in lengthy documents where you need to move between sections frequently.

At the point where you clicked OK to create the bookmark, you had the option of giving the bookmark a name other than the name of the selected text. For example, you could put bookmarks in documents for your coworkers. Then when the coworker opens the document, he or she can use the bookmark(s) to go to the section of the document you've tagged for that person. Let's rename a bookmark, then we'll see how they work.

S TEP-BY-STEP 12.5

1. With **nasa 12-4 xxx** showing in the window, use **Save As** to save the file as **nasa 12-5 xxx**.

2. Open the **Tools** menu and choose **Bookmark**. Your Bookmark dialog box should look like Figure 12-2. Point to the *Weather Forecasting* bookmark and double click to move to that portion of the document.

3. Open the **Tools** menu and choose **Bookmark** again. Point to *Anti-Corrosion Paint* and click once. Then click the **Go To** button.

4. Go to the Bookmark dialog box and click *Weather Forecasting*. Click the **Go To & Select** button to select that side heading.

5. Open the **Tools** menu and again choose **Bookmark**. Point to *Water Recycling* and click once. Then click the **Rename** button in the dialog box. Key the name of a friend and click **OK**. Close the dialog box.

6. Press **Ctrl+Home** to return to the top of the document. Then go to the Bookmark

dialog box. Double click your friend's name to go to the section about *Water Recycling*.

7. Save the document again with the same name. Keep it open.

FIGURE 12-2
Bookmark Dialog Box

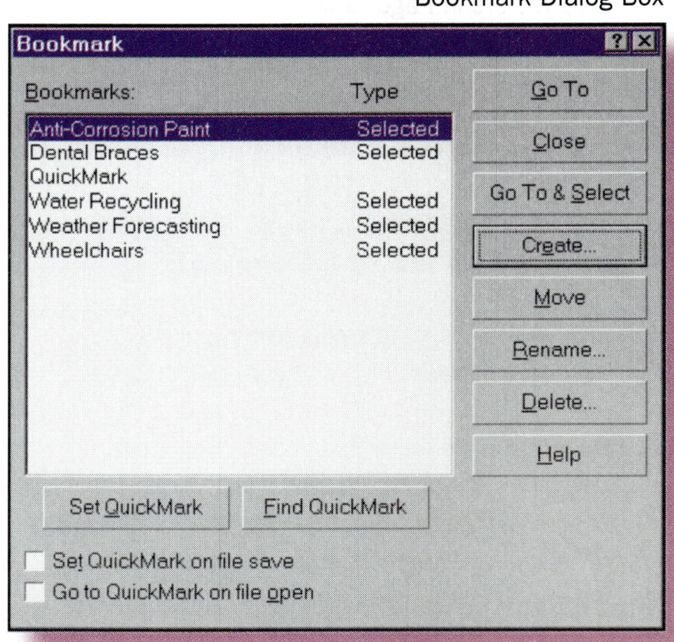

This has been only a sample of how you can use the Bookmark feature in your work. If you are creative, you'll think of lots of ways to use bookmarks to save time and effort in your work.

Comment

A comment is nonprinting text in your document. A comment may give you information about the document, or it may remind you or a coworker to do something with the document. Comments are not printed when you print a document.

Comments don't show in Page view. Instead, a Comment icon appears at the left edge of the left margin. If you click the icon, the text of the comment will appear in a "bubble." In Draft view, a comment shows with a shaded background so you know that the text is a comment.

When you put a comment in a document, a Comment code is inserted. Let's insert a comment telling your friend to read the paragraph about water recycling where you inserted your friend's name as a bookmark.

S TEP-BY-STEP ⟹ 12.6

1. With **nasa 12-5 xxx** showing in the window, use **Save As** to save the file as **nasa 12-6 xxx**. Position your insertion point in the line space below the *Water Recycling* side heading. Be sure you are in **Page** view.

2. Open the **Insert** menu, choose **Comment**, and then choose **Create**. You will be taken to a special Comment editing window. Note the Comment tools on the Property Bar. Key the text in Figure 12-3 as the comment for your friend.

3. Click the **Close** button on the Property Bar to return to your document window. Look for the

icon in the left margin that indicates the presence of a comment. (You may need to use the horizontal scroll bar to see more of the left margin.)

4. Point to the icon with the mouse pointer and click to display the comment. Click the icon again to close the comment.

5. Change to **Draft** view and look at the comment in the document. Return to **Page** view. Save the file and keep it open as you read on.

FIGURE 12-3
Text for Comment

```
Please check the wording in this section about Water Recycling. If you
have suggestions for rewording, please key them into the text using
italic.  Thanks, (your name).
```

Comments can be edited or converted to text. Both of those changes are made from the Insert menu. You can also open the Comment editing window by pointing to the comment or the icon and double clicking. If a comment is no longer needed, it can be removed. To remove a comment, simply delete the Comment code. We'll edit the comment, change it to text, change it back to a comment, and delete it in the next Step-by-Step exercise.

STEP-BY-STEP 12.7

1. With the insertion point near the comment in **nasa 12-6 xxx**, point to the Comment icon and double click. You will be taken to the Comment editing window.

2. Change the word *italic* in the last line to **bold**. Close the editing window.

3. With the insertion point near the comment, open the **Insert** menu, choose **Comment**, and then choose **Convert to Text**. Look at how the comment now becomes part of your document.

4. Select the text that was the comment in your document. Open the **Insert** menu, choose **Comment**, and then choose **Create**. Now the text is a comment again.

5. Reveal your codes and locate the [Comment] code. Double click the Comment code. You should have been taken to the Comment editing window.

6. Close the editing window. Then use your mouse to drag the Comment codes out of the Reveal Codes portion of the window. Your comment has now been deleted.

7. Close your document without saving it again.

File Transfer

With WordPerfect 9, you can open files created in earlier versions of WordPerfect, as well as files created in other kinds of software. WordPerfect checks the file you are opening and converts the file to a WordPerfect file with little interference on your part.

If you have created a file in WordPerfect 9 and wish to use that file in an earlier version of WordPerfect, you must take special steps. Earlier versions of WordPerfect are not able to read some of the WordPerfect 9 codes. For that reason, you must save the file in the format of the version in which you'll be opening it.

In addition, earlier versions of WordPerfect are constrained by DOS file names. The names you've been using for your files are not acceptable to WordPerfect 6.1 for Windows, for example. DOS conventions allow you eight characters for the file name and a three-character extension following a period. If your WordPerfect 9 name is longer than that and you try to find it in a list of files in WordPerfect 6.1, the name will be shortened, and a tilde (~) will appear wherever the WordPerfect 9 name had spaces.

STEP-BY-STEP 12.8

1. Beginning in a new document window, open **footnote 10-12 xxx**.

2. With the document showing in the window, choose **Save As**.

3. In the *File name* text box of the Save As dialog box, change the word *footnote* to **6-1foot**. (Do not change the remainder of the document name.)

4. Click the arrow beside the *File type* text box. Look at all the different formats you can choose to save your WordPerfect 9 documents. (WordPerfect 6/7/8/9 should normally be chosen.)

5. Choose either **WordPerfect 5.0** or **5.1/5.2**. Click **Save** to complete the save and close the document.

6. If your classroom has any copies of WordPerfect 5.0 or 5.1 available, carry your file disk to that machine, start the older version of WordPerfect, and see if you can retrieve the **6-1foot 10-11 xxx** file. (Not all of the name will show in the WordPerfect file list.)

As mentioned earlier, if you want to use a document created in WordPerfect 9 in an earlier version of the program, it is critical that you save it in the format for that version. If you wish to use a document created in WordPerfect 9 in a different word processing program, it would also be a good idea to choose the program from the *File type* list when you save the document. The developers at WordPerfect have tried to provide a good cross section of programs to which you can take your WordPerfect 9 documents.

Summary

This lesson was primarily about working with files. If you are going to be good at WordPerfect or any other word processing program, you have to be able to find your files when you need them. In this lesson you learned that:

- You can look at your files listed by name, date, size, and type.

- You can use QuickFinder to locate files containing specified text or by name.

- QuickMarks help you return to a particular place in the document after you have browsed through it.

- You can have as many bookmarks in a document as you wish.

- Bookmarks may be named by selected portions of text, or they can be given different names.

- Nonprinting comments can be put in your documents as reminders or as additional information about the document.

- If you wish to open a WordPerfect 9 document in a different version of WordPerfect or a different word processing program, you should save the document in that format.

MATCHING

Write the letter of the term in Column 2 that best matches the description in Column 1.

Column 1

_____ 1. The place where you can change the order in which files are listed

_____ 2. A feature used to move quickly from one place to another, which is not named

_____ 3. The tool that is used to quickly scan a disk or folder to find files containing a specified word or phrase

_____ 4. Nonprinting text in your document

_____ 5. A feature used to tell WordPerfect not only to find text, but also to automatically select the text when it is located

_____ 6. In searching for a phrase, you would put quotation marks around the phrase when you key it in this box.

Column 2

A. Bookmark

B. Open File dialog box

C. QuickFinder

D. Bookmark dialog box

E. Comment

F. QuickMark

G. Save As dialog box

H. Content text box

WRITTEN QUESTIONS

Write your answers to the following questions.

7. Why is it important to save your files in the format of the version of WordPerfect in which you will be opening those files?

8. What are the two ways to set a bookmark?

9. What are your four choices on the Toolbar of the Open File dialog box for listing files?

10. If you are working in Page view, how can you tell if a comment has been added to a document?

LESSON 12 PROJECT

Because of the nature of this lesson, the project will consist of a series of small exercises. As you advance in your training, instructions in the Projects and Applications will contain less detail, allowing you to apply your knowledge and skill.

PROJECT 12A

The first exercise reviews the View portion of the Open File dialog box.

1. Open the Open File dialog box and choose the folder that contains your documents. The answers are at the end of the project.
   a. Arrange the files by **Date**. What are the last two files you saved in your folder?
   b. Arrange your files by **Size**. What are the largest two files in your folder?
   c. Arrange the files by **Name**. Which two files are at the top of the list? (Notice that WordPerfect lists files with numerical names before files with alphabetic names.)

2. Close the Open File dialog box.

PROJECT 12B

Now let's work with the Bookmark and QuickMark features.

1. Open **pc proj10b xxx**. Use Save As to save the file as **pc proj12 xxx**.

2. Select the first side heading. With the side heading selected, create a bookmark named **David**. (In the Bookmark dialog box, click Create and key **David** in the *Bookmark name* text box.)

FIGURE 12-4
Bookmarks for Project 12B

SIDE HEADING	BOOKMARK
Keep Your PC Clean	Hue
Prevent Burn-in	Jessica
Defuse Static Electricity	Sandra
Make Backups	Tim

3. Follow the procedure in Step 2 to create a bookmark for each of the side headings, as listed in Figure 12-4.

4. Open the Tools menu and choose Bookmark. Click once to position the insertion point on *David* and click Go To.

5. With the insertion point by the *David* bookmark, create a comment for David that says: **Read this paragraph. Then research surge suppressors and make a recommendation for surge suppressors in our company.**

6. Follow the procedure in Steps 4 and 5 to create comments near the text for the bookmarks in Figure 12-5.

7. Convert each of the comments into text. Print the file and save it as **pc proj12a xxx**.

(continued on next page)

8. Convert each of the comments in the document back to comments.

9. Invite your instructor to watch you use the bookmarks to move through the document and display the comments.

10. Close the document, saving it again as **pc proj12b xxx**.

BOOKMARK	COMMENT
Tim	Prepare a memo to go to all employees, reminding them of the importance of backing up all important company documents on diskettes. The backup diskettes may be stored in the company vault on the first floor.
Jessica	Read this paragraph. Then check the Internet to find a small selection of inexpensive screen savers from which our employees may choose.
Hue	Read this paragraph. Then compose a memo to go to all employees reminding them of the company policy regarding food and drink at company computers.

Answers to Project 12A
Question 1a: **6-1foot 10-11 xxx** and **nasa 12-6 xxx**
Question 1b: **wind 10-8 xxx** and **wind 10-11 xxx**
Question 1c: **6-1foot 10-11 xxx** and **char 11-6 xxx**

CRITICAL THINKING ACTIVITY

SCANS

You have decided that it would be easier to find the files you need if they were listed in the order of the date you worked on them. Describe the steps you would take to arrange your files this way. What might be a reason you would choose this arrangement of files?

Command Summary

FEATURE	MENU CHOICE	KEYBOARD	LESSON
Advance	Format, Typesetting	—	11
All Justification	Format, Justification (Property Bar)	—	9
Block Protect	Format, Keep Text Together	—	12
Bookmark	Tools, Bookmark	—	12
Center Justification	Format, Justification (Property Bar)	Ctrl+E	9
Comment	Insert, Comment	—	12
Current Document Style	File, Document	—	11
Default Font	File, Document	—	11
Endnote	Insert, Footnote/Endnote	—	10
Find QuickMark	Tools, Bookmark	Ctrl+Q	12
Footers	Insert, Header/Footer	—	10
Footnote	Insert, Footnote/Endnote	—	10
Full Justification	Format, Justification (Property Bar)	Ctrl+J	9
Headers	Insert, Header/Footer	—	10
Justification	Format, Justification (Property Bar)	—	9
Left Justification	Format, Justification (Property Bar)	Ctrl+L	9
Line Spacing	Format, Line	—	9
Make It Fit	Format	—	11
Margins	Format, Margins	Ctrl+F8	9
New Page Number	Format, Page, Numbering	—	10
Page Numbering	Format, Page, Numbering	—	10
QuickFinder	File, Open	Ctrl+O	12
QuickFormat	Format, QuickFormat (Toolbar)	—	11
QuickMark	Tools, Bookmark	Ctrl+Shift+Q	12
QuickWords	Tools	—	11
Right Justification	Format, Justification (Property Bar)	Ctrl+R	9
Ruler	View, Ruler	Alt+Shift+F3	9
Shadow Pointer	(Application Bar)	—	11
Spacing	Format, Line	—	9
Suppress	Format, Page	—	10
Symbols	Insert	—	11
Tab Set	Format, Line (Ruler)	—	9

FEATURE	MENU CHOICE	KEYBOARD	LESSON
Watermark	Insert, Watermark	—	10
Widow/Orphan	Format, Keep Text Together	—	10
WordPerfect Symbols	Insert, Symbol	Ctrl+W	11

UNIT 3 REVIEW QUESTIONS

TRUE/FALSE

On a separate page, for each statement below key True if the statement is true or False if it is not. Center *Unit 3 Review Questions* at the top and triple-space.

1. The default setting for margins is 1" on all sides of the page.

2. Using the Ruler, you can set up to four different types of tabs.

3. Page numbering at the top of a page must be set by choosing Page Numbering from the Format menu.

4. Widow/Orphan tells WordPerfect not to leave a single line of a paragraph alone at either the top of the page or the bottom of a page, and it affects the entire document, beginning with the page on which it is inserted.

5. The Headings choice in QuickFormat cannot be applied without selecting the text.

WRITTEN QUESTIONS

Key your answers to the following questions. Number your answers and double-space between them. Use complete sentences and good grammar.

6. How would you describe the difference between a header and a title in a document?

7. What does Make It Fit adjust (default settings) when you are compressing or expanding your documents?

8. What happens when you point to a code in Reveal Codes and double click?

9. What is the difference between a Bookmark and a QuickMark? How many Bookmarks can you have in your document? How many QuickMarks can you have?

10. Open the list of Help topics and find QuickFinder. Double click QuickFinder to look at the list of topics. How many topics are included in that section? Double click to open About QuickFinder (File Open System Help). This section describes Fast Searches. What does QuickFinder do in a Fast Search? What are the three criteria that help you decide whether or not you should use Fast Search?

APPLICATION 1

1. Open **sasoot 3-11 xxx** from the **Units 1 and 2** folder. If you remember, this is the two-page letter with the awkward page break.

2. Use Save As to save the letter as **sasoot u3ap1 xxx**. Look through the letter to remind yourself of how it looks. Then format it as follows:
    a. Insert a Widow/Orphan code at the top of the letter.
    b. Give the letter a header, with the name of the recipient of the letter at the left, the automatic page number code at the center, and the current date (text) flush right, as shown in Figure APP-1.

FIGURE APP-1
Header for Application 1

```
Mr. Antonio Larsen                    1                      (current date)
```

    c. Suppress the header on the first page.
    d. Delete the Path and Filename code at the end of the document.
    e. With the insertion point at the end of the document, insert a footer that contains the Path and Filename code. (Because your insertion point is on the last page of the document, the code will appear only on that page.)

3. Page through the letter, checking the header, the footer, and the page break. (The only way you can see the footer on the last page is to use the vertical scroll bar and scroll all the way to the bottom.)

4. Print the letter and save it again as **sasoot u3ap1 xxx**. Close the file.

APPLICATION 2

1. Open **lighthouses** from the student **datafile** folder. Use Save As to save the file as **lighthouses u3ap2 xxx**. Page through the document to see what's included. Then format it as follows:
    a. Remove the 14 pt. code at the beginning of the document.
    b. Use Advance to advance the title at the top of the first page to 2" from the top of the page.
    c. Center the title and format it with 20-pt. Arial. Quadruple-space following the title.
    d. Select the first side heading. Format it with bold, 16-pt. small caps.
    e. Use QuickFormat to copy that format to the other side headings.
    f. Beginning with the first paragraph, set 1.5 spacing for the entire document.
    g. Remove the extra hard return above and below each of the side headings.
    h. Return to the top and set Widow/Orphan.
    i. If necessary in your copy, use Block Protect to tie the *Illumination* side heading to the paragraph following it.

(continued on next page)

    j. Create a footer that centers the word **Page** followed by the page number at the bottom of each page.

    k. Change the bottom margin of all pages to approximately 0.6".

    l. Create another footer (Footer B) that inserts the Path and Filename code. Position the code flush with the right margin and set it for an 8-pt. Arial font. (Both footers will print on both pages. Actually, all of the information in both footers could be combined in one footer.)

2. Do an interim save of your work. (Develop the habit of saving frequently when you are working with lots of formatting.)

3. With the insertion point above all codes on the first page, press Ctrl+Enter to insert a page at the top of the document. Create a title page as follows:

    a. With the insertion point on the new page at the top, use Center Page(s) to center the text vertically on the current page only.

    b. Set Center justification and key the lines in Figure APP-2. Use Enter to space the lines attractively.

FIGURE APP-2
Information for Application 2 Title Page

```
                        LIGHTHOUSES
                 (A History of Development)
                            by
                     (enter your name)
   (enter the name of the course in which you are learning WordPerfect)
                   (enter your school name)
                       (current date)
```

4. With the insertion point at the beginning of the first page of text, reset the page number value to **1** so the title page isn't included in the page count.

5. Also at the beginning of the first page of text, change from Center justification to Left justification.

6. Position the insertion point at the beginning of the title page and give the document a watermark.

    a. Click the Image button on the Watermark Property Bar and go to the student **datafile** folder.

    b. Find the file named **Lighths** and insert it as the watermark into your document.

    c. Move your insertion point to the beginning of the first page of text and return to the Watermark dialog box. Click the Discontinue button so the watermark appears only on the title page.

7. On the first page of text, insert the same subtitle that's on the title page below the title of the document. Position it a double space below the title, and leave only a triple space between the subtitle and the first line of the first paragraph.

8. Insert the footnotes in Figure APP-3. Position them as follows:

    a. Put the first one following the first sentence in the *History* section.

    b. Put the second one following the third sentence in the *Illumination* section.

c. Put the third one at the end of the first sentence of the third paragraph in the *Illumination* section.

Footnotes for Application 2

[1]Henry McKinnon, *The Seven Wonders of the World*, (London: Plentiful Book Press, 1939), p. 44.

[2]Alfredo Gutierrez, *Lighthouse Lenses*, (New York: Banta, 1989), p. 16.

[3]Mary Madson, "The Fresnel Lens," *Lighthouse Journal*, July 1992, p. 55.

9. Check your work over for accuracy. When it is perfect, print it and save it again as **lighthouses u3ap2 xxx**. Close the file.

APPLICATION 3

FIGURE APP-4
Text for Application 3

1. Beginning in a new document window, key the chart of charges for your bank, as shown in Figure APP-4. Set up the document before keying as follows:

   a. Go to Document Default Font and change to Arial.
   b. Go to Current Document Style and set the side margins at 2".
   c. Use the Center Page(s) feature to give the chart even top and bottom margins.
   d. Display your Ruler and clear all tabs.
   e. For *Price in Dollars*, use Flush Right.
   f. Set a Left tab at 2.25" and a Right tab with dot leaders at 6.25".

2. Center all three titles in bold, all capital letters. Format all three titles using the 14-pt. font size.

**SAFE-DEPOSIT BOX ANNUAL
RENTAL FEES**

	Price in Dollars
3" x 5" box	25.00
4" x 5" box	35.00
5" x 5" box	45.00
5" x 10" box	80.00
10" x 10" box	125.00

**MISCELLANEOUS SAFE-DEPOSIT
BOX FEES**

Lost Key	20.00
Drill Fee	100.00

MISCELLANEOUS FEES

Cashier's Check	3.50
Certified Check	5.00
Lost Passbook or CD	10.00
Money Order	2.00
Overdraft Charge	25.00
Stop Payment	25.00
Return Check Charge	25.00
Wire Transfers	
Domestic	20.00
International	30.00

(continued on next page)

3. Key the description at the left margin. Tab once to key the prices at the right.

4. Save your file as **boxes u3ap3 xxx**.

5. Insert a footer that contains the Path and Filename code formatted in 8-pt. Times New Roman.

6. Print the file and close it, saving it again as you close it.

APPLICATION 4

It's time to make room in the main folder on your disk for your work in Unit 4. Let's move some files and delete some others.

1. Display your Open File dialog box and hold the Ctrl key as you click the files listed in Figure APP-5 for deletion. If you accidentally click one that is not on the list, continue to hold Ctrl as you click that file again to deselect it. Then continue selecting those to be deleted.

FIGURE APP-5
Files to be Deleted

6-1foot 10-11	nasa 12-5	pcug 10-2	record 9-9
char 11-5	nasa proj11b	pcug 11-12	salad 9-6
footnote 10-12	pc 11-7	pcug 11-13	wind 10-14
footnote 10-13	pc 11-8	record 9-1	wind 10-3
gifts 10-9	pc 11-9	record 9-2	wind 10-5
gifts 11-2	pc proj10a	record 9-3	wind 10-6
gifts 11-3	pc proj12a	record 9-4	wind 10-7
nasa 12-4	pcug 10-1	record 9-5	wind 10-8

2. After highlighting the files to be deleted, press the Delete key on the keyboard and confirm that the files are to be deleted.

3. With the Open File dialog box showing in your window and $3^1/2$ *Floppy (A:)* showing in the gray bar above the list of files, open the File menu and choose New. Then choose to create a new folder. Name the new folder **Units 3 and 4**.

4. Select the files listed in Figure APP-6. Open the File menu and choose Move to folder. Choose the **Units 3 and 4** folder and complete the move.

5. Select the following files and move them to the **Applications** folder: **sasoot u3ap1**, **lighthouses u3ap2**, and **boxes u3ap3**.

6. Check any odd files that might be remaining in your main folder. If they are files you need to save for some reason, move them to a different location. If they are junk, delete them, so your main folder is empty as you go to the On-the-Job exercises that follow.

FIGURE APP-6
Files to Move to the **Units 3 and 4** Folder

cheese proj9	pc 11-10
gifts 10-10	pc proj10b
hostas 9-8	pc proj12b
Mildred 9-10	salad 9-7
nasa 12-6	wind 10-11
nasa proj11a	wind 10-15

Mr. Becker has saved a couple of jobs for you to do when you report for work at Singing Wheels Tours today. The first is a schedule of a bus trip to the Mall of America in the Minneapolis area. Part of the document has already been keyed. All you need to do is set up the format and key the first part. Then you will insert the schedule for the last three days of the trip.

JOB 6

1.   Key the text in Figure J5.
   a.   Use Advance to advance the first line 1.75" from the top of the page.
   b.   Center the heading lines, using Bold and Italic as shown.
   c.   Clear all tabs, setting a Left tab at 3.0".
   d.   Bold and italicize the date as shown.
   e.   Use Tab to move from the time column to the activity column.
   f.   Press Enter twice to leave a blank line between each of the items in the itinerary.

FIGURE J5
First Part of Schedule for Job 6

```
                    Mall of America

              Singing Wheels Bus Tours

                    September 1-4
                      Itinerary


September 1, Wednesday

6:30 a.m. sharp      Bus leaves Piggly Wiggly parking lot in Zittau.
7:30-8:30 a.m.       Breakfast at Norma's Nook in Plover.
12:30-1:30 p.m.      Lunch at Harvey's Charcoal Pit in Minneapolis.
2:00-3:30 p.m.       Check in and rest at Happy Haven Hotel in suburban
                     Bloomington.  (Phone 612-555-2293)
3:30-8:15 p.m.       Shopping at Mall of America. Dinner on your own.
8:15 p.m.            Bus pickup at Entrance 32 of the mall. Return to
                     hotel.  Optional cocktails and dancing in the lounge
                     (live band).
```

2.   With your insertion point a double space below the *8:15 p.m.* item, insert **mall** from the student **datafile** folder. Use Save As to save the document in your **Singing Wheels** folder as **mall job6 xxx**.

3.   Use QuickFormat to copy the format from the first date line to the remaining three date lines in the document.

(continued on next page)

4. Position the insertion point at the end of each newly inserted itinerary item and add a hard return to put the blank lines between items.

5. Format the main title by changing to 20 pt.

6. Position the insertion point at the beginning of the first date line and move the tab stop back from 3" to 2.5" to make the columns closer together.

7. Move the insertion point to the top of the document and give it a header with **Mall of America Tour** at the left and **Page** and the page number at the right.

8. Suppress the header on the first page.

9. Position the insertion point at the bottom of the document and insert a footer that contains the Path and Filename code. (It will appear only on the last page because of the insertion point placement.) Format the Path and Filename code with 8-pt. Arial.

10. Position the insertion point at the beginning of the *September 3* date. (Reveal your codes and move the insertion point to the left of the Auto QuickFormat code.) Press Ctrl+Enter to move the whole schedule for September 3 to the second page.

11. Print your schedule. Then close it, saving it again as **mall job6 xxx**.

Now let's format the revised copy of the Policies and Procedures for coach trips. Again, the text has been keyed for you. All you must do is make it look good!

JOB 7

1. Open **coach** from the student **datafile** folder. Save the file in your **Singing Wheels** folder as **coach job7 xxx**.

2. Center the title and format it with 24-pt. Arial. Use Advance to position the title on the first page at 2".

3. Go to Current Document Style and change the side margins to 0.8". Change the bottom margin to 0.5". Return to the document window.

4. With the insertion point at the beginning of the first paragraph, display your Ruler and drag the first-line indent marker to about 1.4" to indent the first line of each paragraph.

5. Change the body of the text to 12-pt. Arial.

6. Insert a header that lists the name of the document at the left.
   a. Format the header with 12-pt. Arial Italic.
   b. Suppress the header on the first page.

7. With your insertion point at the top of the document, insert a footer that contains the Path and Filename code to appear on both pages of the document. Change the font face to Arial and the font size to 8 pt.

8. Use Page Numbering to center the page number at the bottom.

9. In the first line, change *2-1/2* to **2^1/2** using Symbol 4,17 for the $^1/_2$. Do the same for the *3-1/2*.

10. Use Find and Replace to replace all instances of two hyphens (--) with an em dash (4,34).

11. Return to the top of the document and set Widow/Orphan.

12. If necessary, use Make It Fit to make the document fill two pages. (You may need to change the title back to the 24-pt. font after using Make It Fit.)

13. Check your document over. If it looks good, print it. Then close it, saving it again as **coach job7 xxx**.

SPECIAL LAYOUT TOOLS

UNIT 4

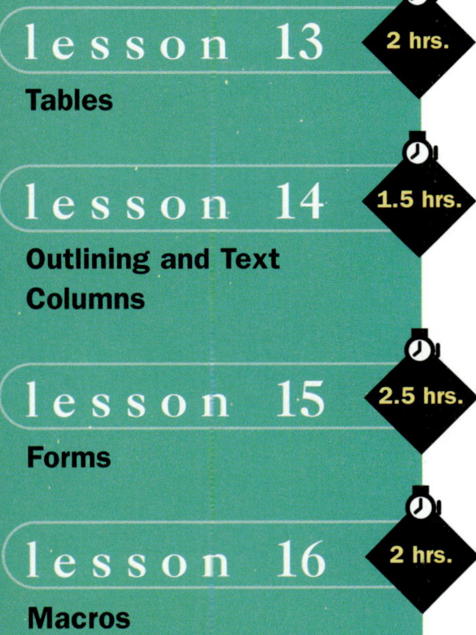

Estimated Time for Unit 4: 9.5 hours

TABLES

OBJECTIVES

Upon completion of this lesson, you will be able to:

- Discuss table terminology.
- Create a table.
- Add rows to a table.
- Join cells in the table.
- Adjust the width of table columns.
- Use a number of methods of formatting your table.
- Do calculations in a table using table formulas.
- Recalculate after a table has been completed.
- Use different means of calculating in a table.
- Use SpeedFormat to format your tables.
- Use floating cells to reference cells in your tables.
- Change tabular text into a table.

Estimated Time: 2 hours

In Lesson 9 you learned to use tabs to arrange your work in columns. You cleared old tab stops, set new tab stops, and rearranged your work when you had finished keying the text if the columns weren't spaced exactly right.

In this lesson you will be introduced to Tables, a more powerful relative of tabs. The WordPerfect Tables feature offers another way to arrange text in columns, but it includes some advantages that the Tab feature doesn't have.

One of the advantages of using the Tables feature to organize your columnar data is that it is faster to set up. It is also easier to add or delete columns than with tabs. Not only that, but you can perform calculations within tables so they can be used for such applications as invoices and time cards. Some documents are composed of several tables that are combined. Many of the documents that use tables won't even look like a table when you finish. You will enjoy working with WordPerfect's Tables feature.

This is a long lesson. You will probably not be able to do it all at once. In addition, there is much to learn. As you read the information and proceed through the Step-by-Step exercises, concentrate and think about what you're doing so when you're faced with some of the same kinds of projects, you won't wonder WHAT to do and HOW to do it.

Table Terminology

A WordPerfect table looks and works much like a spreadsheet. The terminology is also similar. The following terms are peculiar to the use of tables and spreadsheets:

- **Spreadsheet**. A spreadsheet is a grid made up of columns and rows. The columns and rows contain data and/or formulas. Many offices use spreadsheet programs such as Lotus 1-2-3, Excel, or Quattro Pro.

- **Columns**. Vertical collections of information are called *columns*. Columns are labeled with letters (e.g., A, B, C).

- **Rows**. Information is arranged horizontally into *rows*. Rows are labeled with numbers.

- **Cells**. The point at which a row meets a column is called a *cell*. The address of a cell is identified by the column and row. For example, the cell where Column B meets Row 3 is called Cell B3. This location is reported in the Application Bar at the bottom of the window.

Create a Table

You can begin a table by opening the Insert menu and choosing Table, or by clicking and dragging the Tables button on the Toolbar until you have the desired size of the table. Since it is so easy, we'll use the Toolbar method in Step-by-Step 13.1. When you finish, your table will look like Figure 13-3. Pay attention. You'll learn as you go.

STEP-BY-STEP 13.1

1. In a new document window, point to the **Tables** button on the Toolbar. Drag across and down the grid that appears until the table size is 3 x 2, as illustrated in Figure 13-1.

2. When the table is the right size, release the mouse button. When you do that, your table should appear, looking like Figure 13-2. If you don't get it right, click the **Undo** button and try again.

3. Keep your table in your window as you learn how to key text into the table.

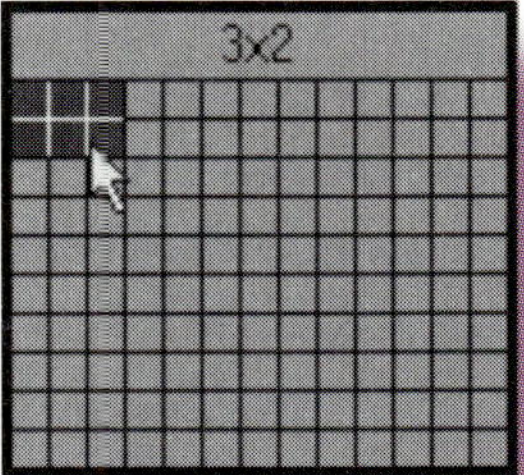
FIGURE 13-1
Table Grid

FIGURE 13-2
3 x 2 Table

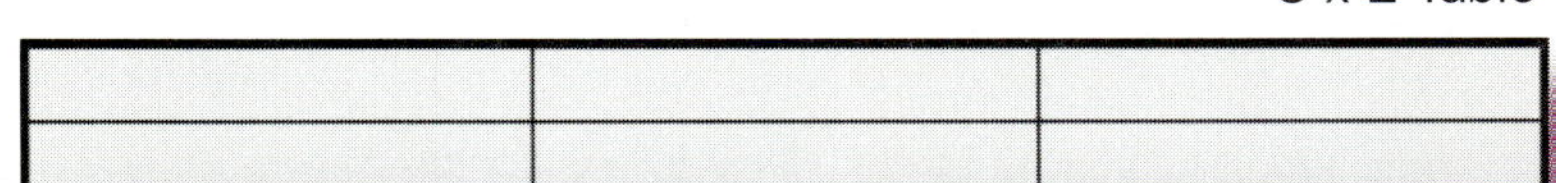

Before keying text, you need to know how to move around in the table. When you key text, move from cell to cell with the Tab key. Do not press Enter, even at the end of a row. When you press Enter, you simply enlarge the cell in which your insertion point is currently located.

After the text has been keyed, you can move the insertion point in the table by clicking with the mouse or by using the following keystrokes:

Tab	Moves the insertion point to the next cell.
Shift+Tab	Moves the insertion point to the previous cell.
Home, Home	Moves the insertion point to the first cell in the row.
End, End	Moves the insertion point to the last cell in the row.

Obviously, your table isn't big enough for all the data in Figure 13-3. When you are working in a table and your insertion point is in the final cell, simply press Tab to add another row to the table. We'll skip the heading rows until later. Also, when you key text into your table, it won't be formatted like Figure 13-3. That will come later, too. Let's enter the data into the table.

FIGURE 13-3
Finished Table of Times

WORLD TIMES

At 12:00 noon Eastern Standard Time, U.S.A.

Bombay	India	10:30 p.m.
Capetown	South Africa	7:00 p.m.
London	England	5:00 p.m.
Manila	Philippines	**1:00 a.m.
Moscow	Russia	7:00 p.m.
Munich	Germany	6:00 p.m.
Paris	France	5:00 p.m.
Rio de Janeiro	Brazil	2:00 p.m.
Tokyo	Japan	**2:00 a.m.
Vancouver	Canada	9:00 a.m.

**Morning the following day.

STEP-BY-STEP 13.2

1. Key **Bombay** and press **Tab**. Key **India** and press **Tab**. Key **10:30 p.m.** and press **Tab**. Do NOT press Enter. If you press Enter by accident, use Backspace to delete it.

2. Continue keying the text in Figure 13-3. Move from cell to cell with the **Tab** key. When you finish, all of the text on the final line will be crowded into the first cell. Also, the information in the third column will be aligned at the left.

3. Reveal your codes and move around in the table. Find the Table Definition code and add it to your list. Notice that instead of [HRt] codes and [SRt] codes, the table has [Cell] and [Row] codes. Add them to your list, too. Which of these two codes comes between rows?

4. Look at the Application Bar, where *Insert* is usually reported. This section of the Application Bar will always report the location of the insertion point in your table. Move the insertion point to Cell B2. Does the prompt at the bottom agree with where you thought you were in the table?

5. Save your table as **Bombay 13-2 xxx**. This is an interim save in case you goof up and need to begin again at this point.

Setting up the table was easy, wasn't it? The best part was that you didn't have to do any figuring. The columns were automatically spaced evenly, but there is much that can be done to make it more attractive. We'll learn how to make adjustments to the table shortly.

Add Rows; Join Cells

Before we change the formatting of the table, let's add a couple of rows for the headings. Then we'll join the cells in the rows so your headings can be centered. We will choose both of those options from the Table QuickMenu, illustrated in Figure 13-4. Follow along carefully.

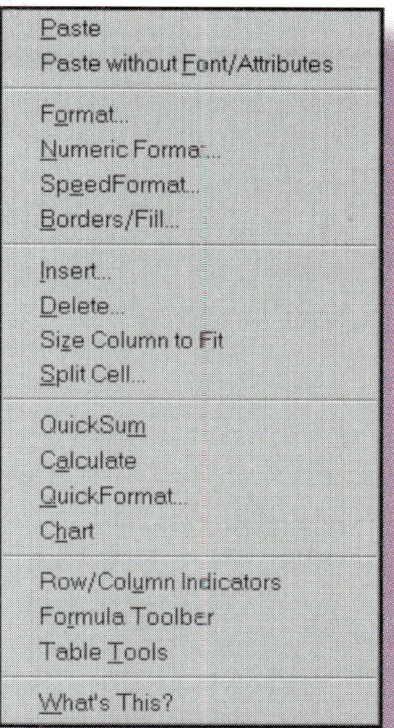

FIGURE 13-4
Table QuickMenu

STEP-BY-STEP 13.3

1. With your insertion point somewhere in the top row of the table, point to the table with your mouse pointer and RIGHT click to display the Table QuickMenu.

2. Choose **Insert** from the QuickMenu to open the dialog box illustrated in Figure 13-5. Note that **Rows** is selected. At the bottom, WordPerfect reports the current size of your table. Note that Placement is set at Before. That means the rows will be added before the location of the insertion point.

3. Change the number in the text box from *1* to **2** and click **OK**. Your table should now have two empty rows at the top.

4. Point to the first row of the table and use the mouse to drag across all three cells to select them. When the cells are selected, they will appear to be black.

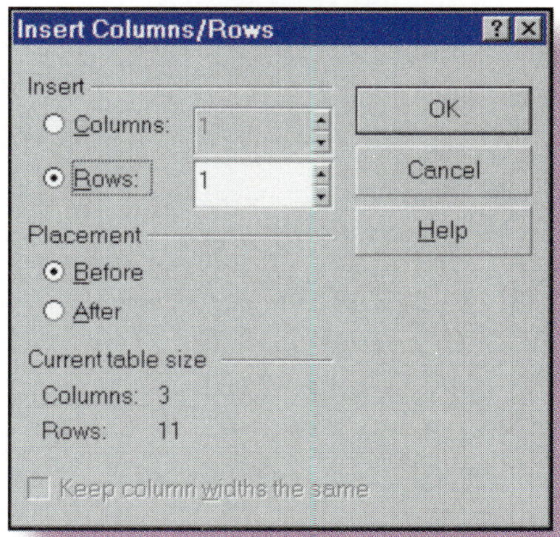

FIGURE 13-5
Insert Columns/Rows Dialog Box

5. Right click to display the Table QuickMenu again. This time, choose **Join Cells**. All of the cells in Row 1 will be joined to form one large cell.

(continued on next page)

2 0 1

6. Point to the **QuickJoin** button on the Table Property Bar and click to select the tool. With the special join cell pointer, drag across the cells in Row 2 to join them. Click the **QuickJoin** button to deselect the tool. (This is a toggle button.)

7. Click to position the insertion point in Row 1. Press **Shift+F7** for Center and key **WORLD TIMES**.

8. In Row 2, center the following:

At 12:00 noon Eastern Standard Time, U.S.A.

9. Use **Save As** to save the file as **Bombay 13-3 xxx**.

You can add rows or columns anywhere in your tables. When you do this, be certain to position the insertion point appropriately and make the correct choices in the Insert Columns/Rows dialog box.

Cells can also be joined as needed. You'll learn more about this later, but you've already learned two ways to make two or three cells into one cell.

When you joined the cells in Rows 1 and 2, you selected the cells to be joined by dragging across them with the pointer. WordPerfect provides another tool to help with selecting text in tables. If you have a steady hand when you point to the top or left side of a cell with the mouse pointer, the pointer will change into a fat white arrow. When the pointer is a fat horizontal arrow, you can select text as follows:

⇦ Click **once** to select the cell.
⇦ Click **twice** to select the row.
⇧ Click **once** to select the cell.
⇧ Click **twice** to select the column.

With either arrow, click **three** times to select the table.

We'll practice with these select tools shortly.

Adjust Column Width

To adjust the width of the columns, simply drag the line separating the two columns. The sizing tool is the same crosshair you used when you adjusted your document margins by moving the guidelines. Let's adjust the width of the columns and practice selecting cells.

1. With **Bombay 13-3 xxx** open in the window, use **Save As** to save the file as **Bombay 13-4 xxx**.

2. Point to the left line in the final row of the table (the row containing the asterisks and the *morning* message). When the fat arrow appears, double click to select the entire row.

3. With the row selected, right click and choose **Join Cells** from the QuickMenu.

4. Use the crosshair pointer to drag the line between the first two columns so it is snug after *Janeiro*. (If you get too close, the word will wrap to the next line. If that happens, grab the table line and drag it a little farther away.)

5. Drag the line between the second and third columns so it is near the end of *South Africa*. Finally, drag the line at the right of the table so it is near the end of the text in the third column.

6. Point to the top of the table. When the fat white arrow appears, triple click to select the entire table. Change the font to **10-pt. Arial**.

7. Drag over Rows 1 and 2 to select both rows. With the rows selected, choose **Bold** from the Property Bar.

8. Point to the line at the left of Row 1. When the fat white arrow appears, click once to select the row. Choose **20 pt.** from the **Font Size** button on the Property Bar.

9. Press **Ctrl+End** to move the insertion point out of the table. Press **Enter** a couple of times to add some space and insert the Path and Filename code. Then save the file as **Bombay 13-4 xxx**. Print it and keep it open as you read on.

As you can see, creating tables and making adjustments to them are easy. You've only begun.

Format a Table

The QuickMenu is only one of the sources of tools when you're working with a table. Let's learn about some of the others. Then we'll do more with this practice table.

Normal Formatting Tools

As you've already learned, many of the formatting tools you use in your normal documents work very well in tables. You've used Center and Bold. You've changed font face and font size. While those choices may also be made from the special tables formatting sources listed below, it's fine to use the tools with which you're familiar whenever they are available.

Table Gridlines

On some computers or when working with very complicated tables, you may notice that you have to wait while your table lines "redraw" in the window. You can speed up this process by using what are called *table gridlines*. Table gridlines are dotted lines surrounding your table cells. With them, you can move around in tables much more rapidly.

The Table Gridlines option is chosen from the View menu. When they are used, the dotted lines simply take the place of the regular lines for viewing purposes. When you print your table, the lines will be printed as usual. We'll work with table gridlines shortly.

Table Property Bar

You may have noticed that when you were working in your table, the Property Bar changed. The buttons to the right of the Justification button are tools for table formatting and editing. You've already used the QuickJoin button. Some of the others that are useful for certain applications include the two to the right of the QuickJoin button–QuickSplit Row and QuickSplit Column. The next is the Insert Row button. You'll use that shortly.

When text is selected, the tools available on the Property Bar change. With your insertion point in your table, periodically check the Quick Tip of the buttons that aren't familiar to you. Some of the tools available on the Property Bar are difficult to find in a menu (such as QuickSplit Row and QuickSplit Column).

Table Menu

One of the buttons on the Property Bar opens the Table menu. That menu contains many of the same tools available in the Table QuickMenu or the Table Property Bar.

With all of these sources of tools available, it might be confusing about where you should go to select your tools. Actually, it doesn't matter. In the next few Step-by-Step exercises you'll be given specific instruc-tions about which source to use so you have an opportunity to try them all. When you create and format your own tables, however, you'll have favorite sources of tools that you'll use for most of your work. And your favorites might be different from everyone else's favorites.

Now let's add some additional formatting to your table. In the process, we'll explore all of the formatting sources listed in this section.

STEP-BY-STEP 13.5

1. With **Bombay 13-4 xxx** open in the window, position the insertion point anywhere in the table.

2. Look at the Property Bar. Beginning with the button to the right of the Justification button, point to each of the tables buttons to see what they do. Many of the tools are new to you. You'll learn about them later in the lesson.

3. Click the **Table** button on the Property Bar. Note that Insert and Join are in that menu as well as the QuickMenu, along with Delete (the opposite of Insert) and Split (the opposite of Join).

4. Open the **View** menu and choose **Table Gridlines**. Look at how the gridlines appear in your table. Return to the **View** menu and deselect **Table Gridlines**.

5. Move your insertion point below the table. Press **Enter** three times to add some space. Then create a 2 x 2 table below your current table.

6. Click the **QuickSplit Column** button. Your insertion point will have two arrows and will be accompanied by a dotted line, as well as a box telling your location.

7. Move the pointer in one of the cells of your practice table until the box reads *1.5" 1.75,"* as shown in the illustration. Click once to add a vertical line at that location. Click the **QuickSplit Column** button again to deselect the feature.

8. Use the **QuickSplit Row** button to split a cell vertically. Note that only one cell is split. Deselect the option.

9. Select your entire practice table and the extra spaces below the Bombay table and delete it. Keep your document open as you read on.

Properties for Table Format

Now that you have a good idea of the sources of tools, let's finish formatting the *World Times* table. The Properties for Table Format dialog box will be used for the following Step-by-Step exercises. This dialog box is like some others that we've used, in that it has several kinds of formatting combined into one dialog box, complete with tabs. The Cell tab, for example, can be used to format a single cell or a group of selected cells. The Table portion has to do with formats that affect the entire table. You'll learn about these choices as you go.

We'll begin by centering the table between the margins.

S TEP-BY-STEP 13.6

1. With **Bombay 13-4 xxx** open, save it as **Bombay 13-6 xxx**.

2. With your insertion point anywhere in the table, click the **Table** button on the Property Bar and choose **Format**. The Properties for Table Format dialog box (from now on to be called Table Format dialog box) will open, looking like Figure 13-6.

3. Look at the tabs across the top of the dialog box. Click the **Table** tab.

4. In the lower left corner is a *Table Position* section. Click the button and choose **Center**.

5. Click **OK** to close the dialog box. Your table should now be centered between the margins.

6. Save the document again as **Bombay 13-6 xxx** and keep it open.

FIGURE 13-6
Properties for Table Format Dialog Box

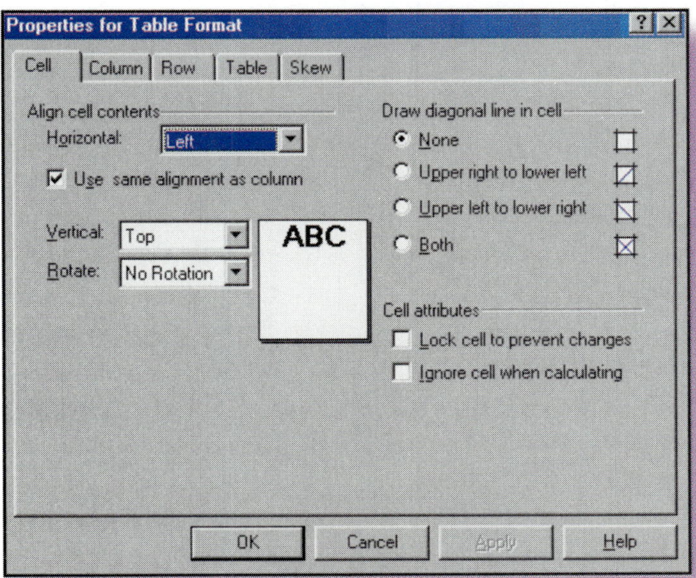

Now we'll add shading (fill) to the subtitle row and align the times in Column 3 at the right.

STEP-BY-STEP 13.7

1. Save **Bombay 13-6 xxx** as **Bombay 13-7 xxx**.

2. Point to the left edge of the row containing the subtitle. When the fat white arrow appears, click to select the row.

3. Click the **Table** button on the Property Bar and choose **Borders/Fill**. A large dialog box will appear, showing choices for lines at the left and fill and a preview area at the right.

4. Click the **X** button beside *Fill*. In the grid of fill patterns that appears, click the second button to the right of the *X*. The grid will look like Figure 13-7. Note that at the bottom, it tells you that you've selected *10% Fill*. This is a common choice because it prints well.

5. At the left of the dialog box, click the button for *Top* and choose the big **X** to tell WordPerfect you don't want a line at the top of the selected cell. The grid should look like Figure 13-8.

6. Click **OK** to close the dialog box. Click away from the selected row to deselect it. Does it look like you expected it to look?

7. Point to the top of the column listing the times (in the cell listing 10:30 p.m. for Bombay). Click the **Select Table Column** button on the Property Bar.

8. Right click to display the QuickMenu and choose **Format**. In the Table Format dialog box, click the **Cell** tab.

9. Locate the *Align cell contents* section. Then click the button to display the pop-up menu and choose **Right**. Click **OK** to close the dialog box. All of the times should now be aligned at the right side of the column.

10. Print your table. Save it again as **Bombay 13-7 xxx** and close it.

FIGURE 13-7
Fill Grid

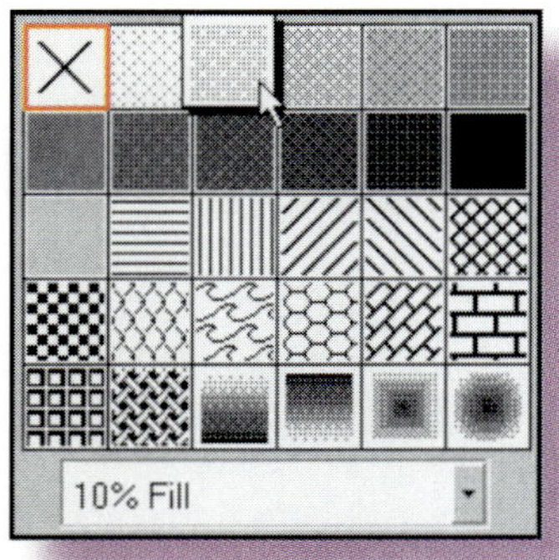

FIGURE 13-8
Lines Grid

You've completed your first table. Does it look wonderful? Perhaps you should take it home and put it on the refrigerator. More importantly, however, is that you have touched on nearly all of the basics with regard to formatting tables in only seven short Step-by-Step exercises.

You can do many more things with tables. For example, as mentioned at the beginning of the lesson, tables can be used like spreadsheets to perform calculations. Let's learn about table formulas. In the process, you will create another table and review many of the things you've learned so far about tables.

Table Formulas

The table you will create in the next series of Step-by-Step exercises shows the first- and second-quarter sales for the top five sales representatives in the company. We'll begin with the raw data. Then we'll learn about tables as we manipulate the table and use the Spreadsheet feature to provide some of the figures for us.

We'll begin this table with only part of the cells needed for the finished product so you can review adding to a table by adding rows and a column. Finally, you'll add quite a lot of formatting. Pay attention to the changes in the appearance of the table as you go. Also, don't ignore the dialog boxes and menus you use to format your table. Soon you'll need to find these features on your own.

S TEP-BY-STEP 13.8

1. Open the **Insert** menu and choose **Table**. Fill in the text boxes to tell WordPerfect to create a table with **3** columns and **1** row. Click **Create**.

2. Using **Tab** to move from cell to cell, fill your table with the text in Figure 13-9. (Remember that when you press Tab at the end of a row, a new row is added.) When you finish, check your work carefully.

3. Whoops! We forgot to allow for the midyear sales figures. We'll add a column at the right. Position your insertion point somewhere in Column C.

4. Choose **Insert** from the QuickMenu. In the Insert Columns/Rows dialog box, change the setting to **Columns**. Change Placement to **After**. Click **OK** to close the dialog box. (Your table now has 4 columns and 5 rows. The spacing of the columns will not be even. Don't worry about it.)

FIGURE 13-9
Text for Step-by-Step 13.8

Johnnie Jacks	499.25	540.00
Phillipe Darling	35.89	648.12
Yang Lin	625.88	569.12
Esther Flores	385.90	485.40
Diane Jones	485.00	1,146.50

5. Follow the Insert procedure to add 2 more rows at the top and 1 more row at the bottom of the table.

6. Select and join the cells in Row 1. Key the following title in Row 1 all on one line at the left. Use all caps but do not use Bold.

QUARTERLY AND MIDYEAR SALES EARNINGS

7. In Row 2 key the column headings, again at the left. Do not use Bold. Key the following four column headings:

Salesperson   **First**   **Second**   **Midyear**

(continued on next page)

8. Key the word **Totals** in Cell A8. Then save the table as **sales 13-8 xxx**. It should look much like Figure 13-10. Keep it open in the window.

Now that you have the basic table created, we'll format the number columns using the Properties for Table Numeric Format dialog box. Figure 13-11 illustrates that box. Quite a variety of number types are available. The columns in this Step-by-Step exercise are money columns, so we'll choose Currency. This choice will add dollar signs to the numbers.

FIGURE 13-10

Example of **sales 13-8 xxx** Document

QUARTERLY AND MIDYEAR SALES EARNINGS			
Salesperson	First	Second	Midyear
Johnnie Jacks	499.25	540.00	
Phillipe Darling	35.89	648.12	
Yang Lin	625.88	569.12	
Esther Flores	385.90	485.40	
Diane Jones	485.00	1,146.50	
Totals			

STEP-BY-STEP ⇨ 13.9

SCANS

1. Point to Cell B3 (499.25). Hold the left mouse button down while you drag to select the cells from Cell B3 to the lower right corner (Cell D8). All three columns (below the column headings) should be selected when you release the mouse button.

2. Display the QuickMenu and choose **Numeric Format**. The Properties for Table Numeric Format dialog box should appear, looking much like Figure 13-11.

FIGURE 13-11

Properties for Table Numeric Format Dialog Box

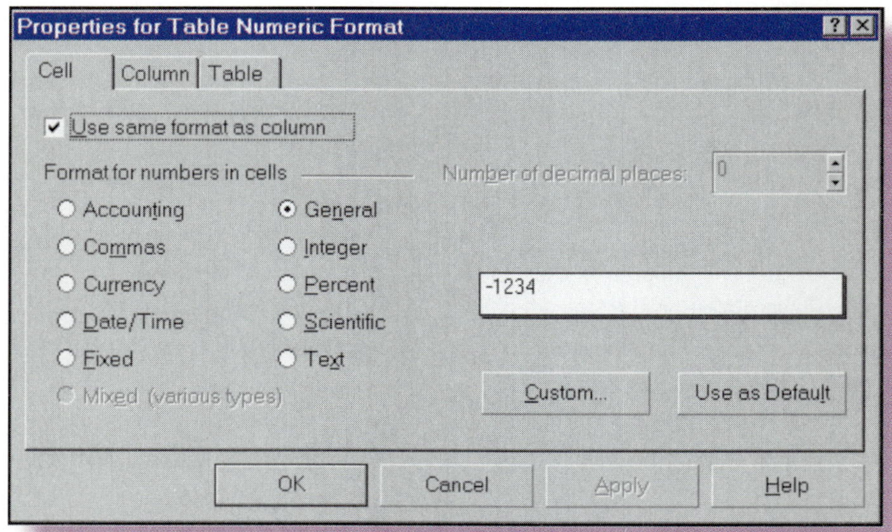

3. In the *Format for numbers in cells* section, choose **Currency**. Click **OK** to close the dialog box.

4. Select the first two rows of the table. Press **F9** to display the Font dialog box and choose **Bold** and **Small caps**. Close the dialog box.

5. With the first two rows still selected, open the Table Numeric Format dialog box and choose **Text**. Close the dialog box.

6. Select Row 3 (any row with all four columns would do) and choose the **Equal Columns** button on the Property Bar. 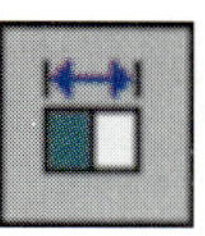

7. Press **Ctrl+End** to move your insertion point out of the table and press **Enter** twice. Insert the Path and Filename code.

8. Save your document as **sales 13-9 xxx**. Save it, and keep it open.

Formatting the first two rows to Text was done as a precaution. It really doesn't affect this Step-by-Step exercise because the title and column heads contain only words. Sometimes, however, you might have numerals in the column heads (such as *1ˢᵗ quarter*). If you don't change those column heads to Text formatting, WordPerfect might include the numerals in the column totals.

Now we'll total the columns with QuickSum and create a formula that will add the first and second quarter amounts for each sales representative, giving the midyear sales.

S TEP-BY-STEP ▷ 13.10

1. With **sales 13-9 xxx** open, save it as **sales 13-10 xxx**.

2. Position your insertion point in Cell B8. Click the **QuickSum** button at the right of the Property Bar. The total of the numbers in Column B should appear. Repeat the same procedure for Column C and Column D.

(WordPerfect will add the totals of Columns B and C for a total in Column D!)

3. Beginning in Cell D7, work UP the column, clicking the **QuickSum** button for each of the horizontal totals.

4. Save your table again as **sales 13-10 xxx** and close it.

In Step-by-Step exercise 13.10 you learned that you can use the QuickSum button to add all of the numbers above a cell. You also used the QuickSum button to add horizontally across the row. It is important to note that WordPerfect adds vertically before it adds horizontally. Had you added the numbers for Johnnie Jacks before the numbers for Phillipe Darling, for example, WordPerfect would have copied Johnnie's midyear total into the cell for Phillipe. That's why you worked UP Column D rather than down the column.

Another way to handle a table such as this would be to select all of the numeric columns. With the columns selected, you can click the QuickSum button for a quick horizontal and vertical total.

SCANS

1. Open **sales 13-9 xxx**. Use **Save As** to save the file as **sales 13-11 xxx**.

2. Position the insertion point in Cell D3. Then choose **Formula Toolbar** from either the **Table** button or the QuickMenu.

3. Click to position the insertion point in the text box just to the right of the blue check mark, and key **b3+c3** to add Johnnie's first- and second-quarter sales. Click the blue check mark to complete the calculation.

4. With the insertion point still in Cell D3, click the **Copy Formula** button on the Formula Bar. Click **Down** and then key **5** into the text box. Your dialog box should look like Figure 13-12.

5. Click **OK**. Look at Column D. Note that in Row 8 there were no numbers to add, so you have only zeros.

6. Use **QuickSum** (the Formula Toolbar also has a QuickSum button) to add Columns B and C. If necessary, click the **Calculate** button on the Formula Toolbar. The Cell D8 total should be filled in automatically.

7. Save your document again as **sales 13-11 xxx**. Keep it open.

FIGURE 13-12
Copy Formula Dialog Box

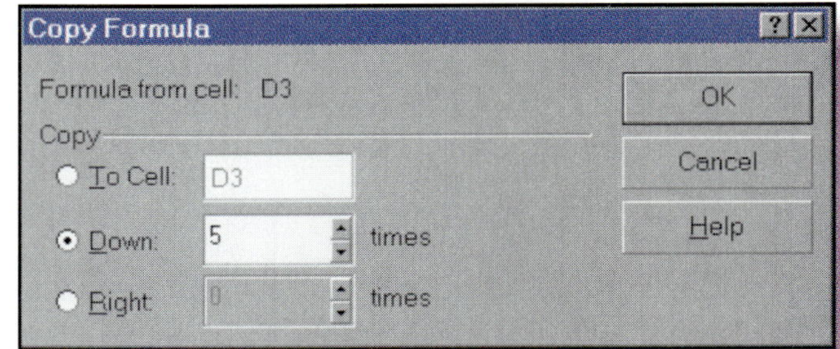

Adjusting Column Size

Most of the time you will let WordPerfect size your columns for you, or you will grab the column margins and size the columns by eye. Sometimes you might want specific sizes for the columns. You can use the Ruler to help you with that task, or you can look at the little boxes that appear beside the column margins when you are making an adjustment. Two buttons on the Tables Property Bar also help you size selected columns. The Equal Columns button makes the selected columns equal in width. The Size Column to Fit button makes a column larger to accommodate a complete word or number.

Let's make the first column in the Step-by-Step exercise wider and the others a little narrower using the size boxes. Then we'll make one of the column headings a two-line heading and align the remaining headings at the bottom.

1. Point to the line between Columns A and B. When the crosshair pointer appears, click and hold it for a minute and look at the two numbers that appear. The first number tells the size of the column to the left of the border and the second number tells the size of the column to the right.

2. Drag the line so Column A is **1.75"**. Column B will become **1.5"**. Adjust Columns C and D so they are both **1.5"** like Column B. Your table won't quite reach from margin to margin.

3. Change *Salesperson* to **Sales Representative**. It will wrap to a second line.

4. Select all of Row 2. Open the **Format** menu and choose **Cell**. In the *Alignment, Vertical* section, click the button and choose **Bottom**. Change Horizontal Alignment to **Center**.

5. Return to your table. The column headings should look like Figure 13-13.

6. With Row 2 still selected, click the **Cell Fill** button on the Property Bar and choose the third choice in the first row. 

7. Position your insertion point in Row 1. Go to the Table Format dialog box and choose the Row tab. Change Row height to **Fixed** and set it at **0.75"**.

8. With the Table Format dialog box still displayed, click the **Cell** tab and change both Vertical and Horizontal Alignment to **Center**. Click **OK** to return to your table. Change the font size of the title of the document to **20 pt.**

9. With the insertion point still in Row 1, go to **Borders/Fill**. Set the line for *Left* to **X**. Do the same with the lines for *Right* and *Top*. Close the dialog box and deselect Row 1 so you can see what the row looks like without lines. (A dotted line will remain to show you the row boundaries.)

10. Select Cells B3 through D8 and set Horizontal Alignment at **Decimal Align**.

11. Save your document as **sales 13-12 xxx**. Then print it and keep it open.

FIGURE 13-13
Column Headings Row in Step-by-Step 13.12

SALES REPRESENTATIVE	FIRST	SECOND	MIDYEAR

Let's take time for a recap on some of the things you did in Step-by-Step 13.12.

- You sized the columns by dragging the column margins.

- You set vertical alignment so the column headings were aligned at the bottom of the cells. The default is for text to be aligned at the top of the cells.

- You specified a measured row height. Normally the row height is determined by the font size, with a 0.083" margin above the text and a 0.04" margin below the text. (You'll work with row margins in a later lesson.)

- You set vertical alignment so the main heading was centered in the space allowed for the heading.

- You added fill to the row containing column headings. Some printers do better with fill than others.

- You were directed to use the Table menu from the Property Bar, the Table QuickMenu, and buttons on the Property Bar as the sources of your formatting choices. In most of the Step-by-Step exercises that follow, you can choose formatting from any of the sources. You get to decide!

- You turned off the lines surrounding the title of the table. The row containing the title remains part of the table, but it appears to stand out by itself above the table.

All of this formatting is easy to perform, and if you spend any time at all with tables, you will find that it becomes second nature to you.

Recalculation

Performing the calculations in the table was easy. In the same way, it is easy to tell WordPerfect to recalculate the table when a change is made. Phillipe wasn't on vacation during the first quarter. Instead, incorrect information was provided. His first-quarter sales should have been $1,035.89, not $35.89. In the next Step-by-Step exercise we'll correct the amount and recalculate so all of the totals are correct. Then we'll remove the lines from the table so you can see what a table looks like without any lines.

STEP-BY-STEP 13.13

1. With **sales 13-12 xxx** open, save it as **sales 13-13 xxx**.

2. Click in Cell B4 between the dollar sign and the *3*. Key **1,0** to change the amount to $1,035.89.

3. Click the **Calculate** button on the Formula Toolbar. Mentally calculate the totals to see if the affected ones increased by $1,000.

4. Use the fat white arrow at the top of any cell and triple click to select the entire table.

5. Choose **Borders/Fill** from one of the several sources. Change *Outside* lines to **None**. Change *Inside* lines to **None**.

6. Save the document again and print it. Keep it open to learn more about formulas.

More Formulas

WordPerfect can do more than add. A wide variety of formulas are available—all of the formulas and functions needed for spreadsheet preparation have been included in this powerful word processing program. Let's look at a couple of others and see how easy they are to use.

STEP-BY-STEP 13.14

1. Select the total in Cell B8 and delete it. Then delete the formula in the text box to the right of the blue check mark in the Formula Toolbar. Position your insertion point in Cell B8.

2. Click the **Functions** button on the Formula Toolbar and double click to choose **AVE(List)**. The *List* portion of the formula tells you that WordPerfect wants to know what cells to average. You could key **B3:B7**. (The colon is

used between cell addresses to designate a *range* of cells.) It's easier to use the mouse.

3. Drag down over the numbers in Cells B3 through B7 to select all of them. (If Word-Perfect asks about deleting a formula, confirm the deletion.) The formula should now read **AVE(B3:B7)**. If it is correct, click the blue check mark to complete the calculation. Did you get $606.38?

4. Delete the contents of Cell B8 again. Then delete the formula in the text box.

5. Position the insertion point in Cell B8 again. Click the **Functions** button again. This time find **PRODUCT(List)**. Double click to choose it.

6. Drag the insertion point over Cells B3 through B4 only to multiply those two numbers. When the text box reads *PRODUCT(B3:B4),* click the blue check mark. Did you get $517,168.08?

7. Close your table document without saving it.

In Step-by-Step 13.14 you worked with formulas provided by WordPerfect to calculate in your document. You learned that you can key the range of cells to be included in the calculation, or that you can drag the mouse pointer across the cells (if they are contiguous) to tell WordPerfect which cells to include in the calculation.

Sometimes it's easier to simply key the desired formula. Four symbols are generally used for calculating on the computer, since the keyboard doesn't provide you with symbols for calculations. Following are the computer symbols for calculating:

*	Multiply
/	Divide
+	Add
–	Subtract

When you multiplied the contents of Cell B3 times Cell B4 in Step-by-Step 13.14, you could have simply keyed B3*B4 in the formula text box and not bothered with the PRODUCT function. If you wished to divide the contents of Cell B3 by the contents of Cell D4, you would key B3/D4 in the formula text box. To subtract the contents of Cell B3 from the contents of Cell D4, key D4-B3. In all cases, be sure to double-check the formula before clicking the blue check mark to complete the calculation.

Now let's practice with WordPerfect functions in a new table.

S TEP-BY-STEP 13.15

1. Prepare the table illustrated in Figure 13-14. Don't bother adjusting the sizes of the cells. Display the Formula Toolbar.

2. Position the insertion point in Cell B4 and click the **QuickSum** button on the Table Formula Toolbar. Repeat the procedure in Cells C4 and D4. Do a quick mental check to see if the sums are correct.

3. Position the insertion point in Cell E1 to enter a formula that adds all three of Patty's numbers. Click the **Functions** button on the Formula Toolbar and key **sum** to move the highlight to the SUM formula. Click the **Insert** button.

(continued on next page)

SCANS

FIGURE 13-14
Text for Step-by-Step 13.15

4. Either key **b1:d1** or drag to select Cells B1 through D1. Click the blue check mark to get the sum (105).

Patty	30	25	50		
Fred	25	45	60		
Sue	15	35	45		
Totals					

5. Position the insertion point in Cell E2 and click in the formula text box. Key **b2+c2+d2**. Click the blue check mark to get the sum (130).

6. Follow any procedure you'd like to get Sue's total (95).

7. Use **QuickSum** to total Column E.

8. In Column F compute the average for Patty. It should be an average of the numbers in Columns B, C, and D. DO NOT include the amount in Column E in the average.

9. Compute the averages for the other three rows. If you wish, you can copy the formula in Row 2 down as you did in Step-by-Step 13.11. Your averages will have many decimal places. We'll work with formatting the numbers shortly.

10. Save your work as **patty 13-15 xxx**. Keep it open for additional formatting.

Now that the calculations are complete in your table, let's add rows for headings and format the table.

1. With **patty 13-15 xxx** open in the window, use **Save As** to save the file as **patty 13-16 xxx**. Add column headings as follows:

  a. Using the **Insert Row** button on the Property Bar, insert two rows at the top of the table. Join the cells in Row 1 and key the title: **QUARTERLY SALES FIGURES**. Format it in any way you wish.

  b. In Cell A2 key **Sales Representative**. Select the cell and find the **Size Column to Fit** button on the Property Bar. Click it. Column A should expand to accommodate the entire column heading.

  c. Key **January** in Cell B2. Select Cells B2, C2, and D2. Find the **QuickFill** button on the Property Bar. Click it. *February* and *March* should automatically appear in Cells C2 and D2.

  d. Key **Quarter** in Cell E2 and **Monthly Average** in Cell F2.

2. Select all of Row 2. Format it as follows:
   a. Align the text at the bottom of the row.
   b. Use **Center** justification for the column headings.

3. Select all of the money columns and format them as follows:
   a. Change the Numeric Format to **Currency**. (That will take care of the extra decimal places in the averages.)
   b. Decimally align the numbers.

4. Insert the Path and Filename code a double space below the table.

5. Save your file again as **patty 13-16a xxx**. Print it and keep it open.

6. Click in the row containing the title of the table. Right click and choose **Delete**. The Delete Structure/Contents dialog box will appear, prompting you to delete one row. Click **OK**.

7. Skew the column at the left and reformat the table as follows:
   a. Point to the table and right click. Choose **Format** to display the Properties for Table Format dialog box. Click the **Skew** tab.
   b. From the Skew settings at the left, choose **Left Down** and click **OK**.
   c. Drag the line between Columns A and B to the left until Column A is **1"** wide.
   d. Select all of Column A. Go to the Cell Format dialog box and set Horizontal Alignment for the cell contents at **Right**.
   e. Select Cells B2:F2. Open the **Table** menu on the Property Bar and choose **Equal Column Widths**.

8. Save your file again, this time as **patty 13-16b xxx**. Print it and close it.

Let's briefly review what you did in Step-by-Step 13.16 and learn a little more about some of the features.

- You learned that the Size Columns to Fit feature will make the column wide enough for the largest entry in the column. This feature doesn't work on the column to the right unless you have room within the margins for it to work. For example, the monthly average can't be spread across the column unless you extend the right margin.

- You used the QuickFill button to fill in a pattern of information. This feature works in a wide variety of applications. For example, it fills in consecutive numbers, numbers in a particular sequence (if you give the sequence), or quarterly dates (if you begin the sequence of dates).

- You learned that QuickFill and Size Columns to Fit are available from the Table menu and from the QuickMenu, as well as from the Table Property Bar.

- You aligned text at the bottom of the cells and reviewed alignment of numbers.

- You deleted a row in a table.

- You skewed the column at the left. In the Skew dialog box you may have noticed that columns at the left and right as well as the row at the top can be skewed. Skewing is a way of fitting more text into a narrower cell.

- You used Equal Column Widths to even the widths of several columns.

Table SpeedFormat

Table SpeedFormat can take a boring-looking table and apply the formatting tools you've already learned for a standard appearance. Some of the formats are especially good for certain kinds of tables, depending on the information in the table and whether it has main headings, column headings, or totals. Let's look at Table SpeedFormat and use it to format your table.

STEP-BY-STEP 13.17

1. Open **patty 13-16a xxx**. Use **Save As** to save the file as **patty 13-17 xxx**.

2. Position the insertion point somewhere in the table.

3. Choose **SpeedFormat** from either the Table QuickMenu or the **Table** menu on the Property Bar. At the left is a list of available formats.

4. Click some of the formats and look at the preview area to see how they work.

5. Go down the list quite a ways and find **Fancy Fills**. Choose that format for your table and click **Apply**.

6. Back in your document window, evaluate the format. Do you like it?

7. Print the file and save it again as **patty 13-17 xxx**. Keep the file open.

As you discovered when you looked through the list of formats, quite a number of them are available. You can try other styles at your leisure. If you like the WordPerfect formats, this feature can save you lots of formatting time.

Floating Cells

WordPerfect has a feature called *floating cell* that allows you to create a tiny table referencing certain cells of a table. The floating cell may not be in the table. Instead, it is usually in the text either above or below the table.

For example, in Figure 13-15, the sentence below the table contains a floating cell that references the total profits. If any of the amounts in the profits column change, total profits change. When total profits change, the total in the text below the table will be updated.

Let's add a floating cell to the Step-by-Step exercise with which you have been working.

FIGURE 13-15
Sample Table with Floating Cell

Location of Office	Fourth-Quarter Profits
New York	$40,500.00
Houston	$32,600.00
San Francisco	$37,800.00
Miami	$28,500.00
Total	$139,400.00

The total fourth-quarter profits from all offices amount to $139,400.00.

1. With **patty 13-17 xxx** showing in the window, save the file as **patty 13-18 xxx**.

2. Make some space between the bottom of the table and the Path and Filename code. Then position the insertion point a double space below the table.

3. Key the sentence in Figure 13-16. When you come to the asterisks (**), don't key them.

FIGURE 13-16
Text for the Floating Cell Sentence

```
The table above illustrates our
sales for the first quarter.
Notice that total sales for the
quarter amount to **.
```

4. Open the **Insert** menu and choose **Table**. The Create Table dialog box will appear. Click to select the **Floating cell** button. The dialog box will look like Figure 13-17. Click **Create**.

5. Reveal your codes and look at the two Floating Cell codes. Your insertion point should be between them.

6. Click to position the insertion point in the formula text box on the Formula Toolbar. Then click in Cell E6 ($330) to tell WordPerfect to reference that cell in the floating cell.

7. Click the blue check mark. After a moment, *330* should appear in the floating cell position. It is not formatted as currency. Key a period at the end of the sentence.

8. Position the insertion point in the floating cell. Change the Numeric Format to **Currency**.

9. Save your document again as **patty 13-18 xxx**. Reveal your codes and add the table codes to your list of codes. Keep the file open.

FIGURE 13-17
Create Table Dialog Box

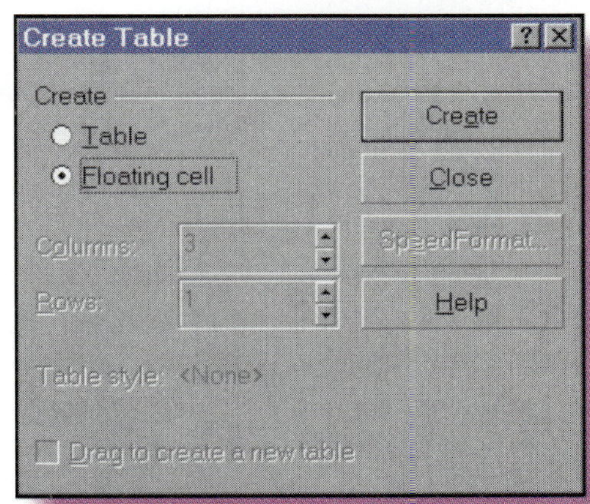

Sue has come up with a plan that should increase her monthly sales by an estimated $20. This would have a positive impact on all of the figures in the table. For the sake of projection, let's increase Sue's sales for January through March and recalculate the table.

STEP-BY-STEP 13.19

1. Save **patty 13-18 xxx** as **patty 13-19 xxx**.

2. Manually increase Sue's sales for January by $20.00. Do the same for her February and March sales.

3. Click the **Calculate** button on the Formula Bar. The floating cell should now show a total of *$390.00*.

4. Print your final table. Then close it, saving it again.

Sources of Tables

Tables can be constructed from a number of sources. Let's look briefly at two of the most common.

Text

Text that has been keyed in columns can be converted to table format. The procedure is simple. Select the text you wish to have in your table. Open the Table menu and choose Create. Let's try it.

STEP-BY-STEP 13.20

1. Open your **Units 3 and 4** folder and open **salad 9-7 xxx**.

2. Select all of the text in the columns. (Do not include the Path and Filename code.)

3. Open the **Insert** menu and choose **Table**. Click **OK** to affirm that you are creating the table from tabular columns.

4. Look at your table. Each vegetable is in a separate cell. This table can be formatted like all of the others with which you've worked in this lesson.

Now let's turn the text back to tabular columns.

5. Reveal your codes. Find the code that defines the table. Delete the code. The dialog box illustrated in Figure 13-18 will appear. Choose to delete the **Table structure**, leaving the text. The text should be returned to the way it was before you turned it into a table.

6. Close the document without saving it.

FIGURE 13-18
Delete Table Dialog Box

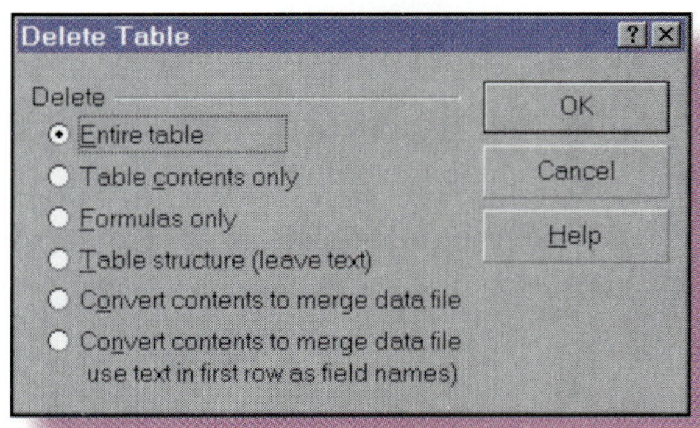

Spreadsheets

WordPerfect has made it possible for you to *import* work sheets prepared in popular spreadsheet programs such as Lotus 1-2-3, Excel, or Quattro Pro. Spreadsheets can also be *linked* to your WordPerfect documents so that as the spreadsheet is updated, it will also update your WordPerfect document. While this sounds difficult, it is really pretty easy. Let's import a simple Quattro Pro work sheet to see how it looks in WordPerfect.

S TEP-BY-STEP 13.21

1. Beginning in a new document window, go to the student **datafile** folder and open the file named **office.wb3**. The Import Data dialog box illustrated in Figure 13-19 will appear.

2. Look at what the dialog box is telling you. You are importing a spreadsheet in table format. The range of cells is listed. Click **OK**.

3. Look at the table that appears. It certainly isn't beautiful, but it can easily be formatted. You could do it on your own with no trouble.

4. Close the document without saving it.

It's that simple to bring a work sheet created in a spreadsheet program into WordPerfect. It's nice to know that you can add work sheets or portions of work sheets to your WordPerfect documents.

Summary

As promised, this was a long lesson. It included all of the basic information about working with tables. In this lesson you learned that:

- Tables can be created from the Toolbar or from the Insert menu.

- You can increase the size of a table by adding columns and rows.

- Many sources of commands are available for table formatting.

- Tables can be used to perform calculations.

- If the numbers in a table calculation change, you can update the entire table with the Calculate button.

- You can reference a table somewhere else in the document using a floating cell.

- Tables can be created from tabular columns or from spreadsheets created in other programs.

FIGURE 13-19
Import Data Dialog Box

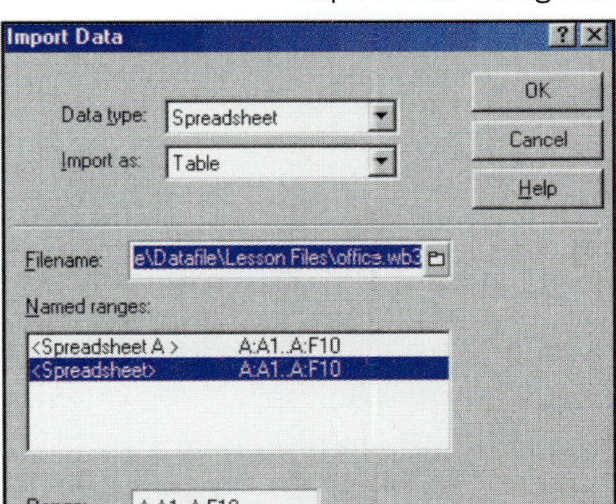

Many more things can be done with tables. They can be part of a larger document, as you'll practice in the Lesson 13 Project. They can be used for forms, as you'll learn in Lesson 15. They can be used to combine standard text with lists of names and addresses or other items. You will use tables in many of the lessons that follow, so you'll get plenty of opportunities to practice your skills with tables.

LESSON 13 REVIEW QUESTIONS

FILL IN THE BLANKS

Complete each of the following statements by writing your answer in the blank provided.

1. A __________ is a collection of information arranged horizontally in a table.

2. You can begin a table by opening the __________________ menu and choosing Table Create.

3. You can also begin a table by dragging the Tables button on the ________________.

4. The location of a cell, such as Cell B3, is reported on the ____________________________.

5. A _____________ is a collection of information arranged vertically in a table.

6. To display the _______________________________, point to the table with your mouse pointer and right click.

MULTIPLE CHOICE

Circle the best answer to each of the following statements.

7. To move the insertion point to the previous cell in a table, press
   A. Tab.
   B. Shift+ Tab.
   C. Home, Home.
   D. End, End.

8. To select the entire table, point to the top or left side of a cell, and when the pointer changes into a fat white arrow, click
   A. once.
   B. twice.
   C. three times.
   D. four times.

9. Which of the following is NOT a button on the Table Property Bar?
   A. QuickJoin
   B. QuickSplit Row
   C. QuickSplit Column
   D. QuickTip

10. The computer symbol for multiplying is
    A. +.
    B. /.
    C. *.
    D. -.

LESSON 13 PROJECT

Prepare the following letter that contains a listing of medical costs and a floating cell. See how much of it you can do without referring back to the Step-by-Step exercises in the lesson.

1. Beginning in a new document window, use Advance to set the beginning line of text 2" from the top of the page. Insert the date text.

2. Key the text in Figure 13-20 as the beginning of a letter to Mrs. Sheri Schneider. Press Enter twice and create a 2-column by 1-row table. Key the table data, as illustrated in Figure 13-21.

FIGURE 13-20
Beginning of Lesson 13 Project

```
Mrs. Sheri Schneider
Box 814
Cranberry Creek, NY 12117

Dear Mrs. Schneider:

Below is a summary of the bill from St. Elizabeth Hospital for your
stay following your automobile accident on July 4, 199x.  As the party
responsible for this accident, you are financially responsible to
remit payment in full to the hospital for these services.
```

3. With the insertion point in Cell B6, do the following:
    a. Display the Formula Toolbar and total the column with QuickSum.
    b. Use Size Columns to Fit.

4. Size Column A to fit.

5. Select all of Column B and format it as follows:
    a. Change Numeric Format to Accounting.
    b. Set Alignment at Decimal Align. (Note that the dollar signs are aligned at the left, whereas, when you used Currency they were directly in front of each number.)

FIGURE 13-21
Table for Lesson 13 Project

Pharmacy	4.90
Medical Surgery Supplies	33.50
X rays	131.00
CT Scan/Head	933.50
CT Scan/Body	1245.00
Total	

6. Go to the Table Format dialog box and set the table Position at Center.

7. Insert a row at the top containing the following column headings: **Item** and **Amount**.

8. Move your insertion point below the table and key the sentence in Figure 13-22 a double space below the table. When you come to the asterisks (**), don't key them. Instead, create a floating cell that references Cell B7. Change the Numeric Format for the floating cell to Accounting.

FIGURE 13-22
Sentence with Floating Cell

```
As you can see, the total
for the bill is **.
```

9. Add the period following the floating cell and key the text in Figure 13-23 to end the letter.

FIGURE 13-23
End of Lesson 13 Project Letter

```
If you have any questions
regarding this bill, please
contact my office.

Sincerely,



(Your Name)
Account Representative
```

10. Check your work carefully. When it is perfect, save the file as **schneider proj13a xxx**.

11. Add a footer that inserts the Path and Filename code at the bottom of the letter. Print the letter and save it.

12. Change the amount of the X rays to **$331.00**. Recalculate the table.

13. Use Table SpeedFormat to apply Double Border Bold.

14. Save the file again, this time as **schneider proj13b xxx**. Print the file again and close it.

CRITICAL THINKING ACTIVITY

SCANS

You have prepared a table to record the number of minutes you spend each week on homework assignments. Across the top of the table, you have named your eight columns Days, Period 1, Period 2, etc., up to Period 7. Down the side you have labeled the rows with the days of the week. At the bottom, you've inserted another row to total the number of minutes per week per class you've spent on homework. Since your first period is Study Hall, you know the total in that column will be zero. However, when you clicked the QuickSum button, a *1* was inserted into the cell. What would cause that to happen and how would you fix it?

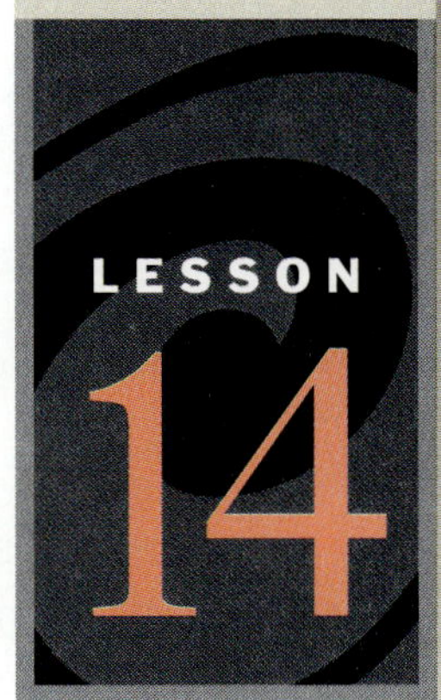

OUTLINING AND TEXT COLUMNS

Upon completion of this lesson, you will be able to:

- Use the WordPerfect Outline tool to create outlines.

- Edit a WordPerfect outline.

- Arrange documents in text columns.

- Use balanced newspaper columns.

- Adjust the widths of the columns.

- Use Hyphenation to fill the lines.

- Discuss the use of one space or two at the ends of sentences.

Estimated Time: 1½ hours

In Lesson 5 you learned that you can create numbered and bulleted lists using the Outline/Bullets & Numbering feature. You also found that WordPerfect automatically continued a list that you began manually with bullets or numbers.

The Outline feature actually is much more sophisticated. We'll find out how powerful it is in this lesson.

Another feature that helps you arrange your text is the Text Columns feature. This is a different kind of column than tabular columns or table columns. You'll also learn about the Text Columns feature in this lesson.

Outlining

One of the biggest areas where Outline is more sophisticated than Bullets & Numbering is with regard to levels. WordPerfect outlines can have as many as eight levels, all numbered differently.

The default outline style is Paragraph. Let's create a short three-level outline in that style.

1. Beginning in a new document window, press **Ctrl+H** to begin a list. The first numeral should appear, and the Outline tools will appear on your Property Bar.

2. Key the text in Figure 14-1.
   a. To change from the first level to the second, press **Tab**. To change to the third level, press **Tab** again.
   b. To return to a higher level from a lower level, press **Shift+Tab**.

3. At the end of the outline, press **Enter** once and backspace once to end the outline and remove the numeral.

4. Check over your work to see that it matches the figure and that everything is correct.

5. Save the file as **outline 14-1 xxx**.

6. Give your file a footer that inserts the Path and Filename code. Save and print the file. Keep it open.

FIGURE 14-1
Text for Step-by-Step 14.1 Outline

```
1.   Level one of the outline.   (This is the first item at this level.
     Note that it is aligned automatically when it wraps.)

2.   Second item at the first level.

3.   Third item at the first level.

     a.   Level 2 item.
     b.   Second item at Level 2, the first indented level.
          i.   First item at Level 3.  (It, too, will wrap automatically
               because the outline style includes Indent after each
               numeral.)
          ii.  Last item at Level 3.  (Now I will press Enter twice and
               then Shift+Tab twice to return to Level 1 to put in the
               final item.)

4.   Final item of the outline.  (Note that this outline has double
     spacing before and after the first level lines and single spacing
     elsewhere.  This is the customary spacing for outlines.)
```

Look at the Outline tools on the Property Bar. They are illustrated in Figure 14-2. This bar contains a number of useful tools.

FIGURE 14-2
Outline Tools on Property Bar

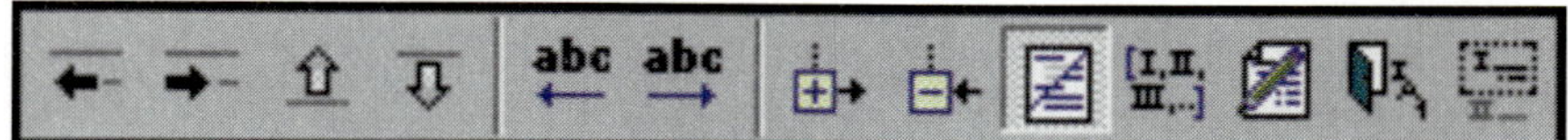

When an item in an outline contains indented items, the entire numbered item in the outline is referred to as a *family*. For example, all of Item 3 in your outline is considered a family. This is important, because you can edit entire outline families, rather than a line at a time.

At the left are four arrows. The first two may be used to change the level of indent for an item. The next two enable you to move a line up or down in the outline. The two buttons with yellow squares allow you to close up an item in the outline, hiding the lower level items in a family and displaying only the first-level items. The final button is similar—it allows you to show as many levels as you wish, rather than all or just one, and it affects the entire outline.

Sometimes an outline contains unnumbered text within the outline. This is called *body text*, and whether it shows or not is controlled with the button that looks like a page. The button with the Roman numerals allows you to change the numbering, and the following button enables you to change the style of the outline.

Finally, the button that looks like a green book is used to display or hide level icons–fat white numbers–in the margin area at the left of the outline. These icons indicate whether an outline item has second- or third-level items and are useful for editing. Let's try some of these buttons.

S TEP-BY-STEP 14.2

1. Save **outline 14-1 xxx** as **outline 14-2 xxx**. Position the insertion point somewhere in the second item of the outline. Click the **Show levels** button and choose **One**. Only the first-level items will show (and the spacing between them may not be equal).

2. Click the **Show levels** button again. Choose **Three**. All of the outline should reappear.

3. Click the **Show/Hide Body** button twice—once to take the blank lines out and again to put them back in. (The blank lines are considered text.)

4. With the insertion point still in the second item, click the black arrow that points to the right. The item should be changed to a second-level item. Now click the arrow that points to the left to return it to a first-level item.

5. If the **Show Icons** button is not depressed, click it and look at the icons.

6. Point at the *1-* at the left of Item 3 and look at the white double-headed arrow. Click once. The entire item should be selected. With the white arrow still in the area of the fat numbers, press the left mouse button and drag the entire section up until the horizontal line across the page is just above Item 2. Release the mouse button.

7. Use the same procedure to return Item 3 to its third-place position.

8. Change some of the other items around and then return them to their original locations. (If you were to leave some of them in their new positions, you would have to do some repair of blank lines.)

9. Keep the outline in the window as you read on.

Ending an Outline

You learned in Step-by-Step exercise 14.1 that you can discontinue an outline by backspacing to remove the final number. This worked with bullets, too. However, if you want a new list later in the same document, the numbering will pick up where you left off in the earlier list. To begin a new outline, you may key the first number and let WordPerfect pick it up from there, or you may specify that you'd like a new outline in the Bullets & Numbering dialog box.

STEP-BY-STEP 14.3

1. Position your insertion point at the end of the final item in the outline. Press **Enter** twice. Then backspace to remove the *5*.

2. Key **This is a line of text in the document that isn't part of the outline**. Press **Enter** twice.

3. Press **Ctrl+H** to begin outlining. The number *5.* should appear. Assume you wanted the new number to be *1*. Backspace to remove the *5*.

4. Open the **Insert** menu and choose **Outline/ Bullets & Numbering**. Click the **Start new outline/list** button at the bottom. Click **OK**. The *1.* for a new outline should appear.

5. Keep the outline open in the window as you read on.

In Step-by-Step exercise 14.3 you began outlining with Ctrl+H. You can do that anytime you wish to start an outline. Although the default is Paragraph numbering, if you have used a different style, WordPerfect will remember that style when you begin an outline with Ctrl+H.

Adding and Deleting Outline Items

You can add text to the outline or delete text from the outline, and WordPerfect will adjust the numbers to accommodate your changes. That is the major reason that outlines are so nice to use for any kind of listing—they are so easy to edit. Let's practice.

STEP-BY-STEP 14.4

1. Position your insertion point at the end of the second item in the outline. Press **Enter** twice. You should get a new *3.* and the items below the new number should be increased by one.

2. Key **This is a new Item 3.**

3. Point to the fat *1-* to the left of the new item. Click once to select the new item. Press the **Delete** key.

4. Your outline should now be back to the original four items. Keep it open as you read on.

Outline Styles

WordPerfect comes with several outline styles. As you know, the Paragraph style is the default. Let's apply some of the others to the outline in your window so you can see how they look.

STEP-BY-STEP ⟩ 14.5

1. Select your entire outline. Open the **Insert** menu. Choose **Outline/Bullets & Numbering**.

2. Choose one of the other styles and note the style name in the gray area near the top of the box. Click **OK**.

3. Select your text again and try some additional styles. Note that some of them don't indent the levels.

4. Close your document without saving it again.

That's enough about outlining for now. Practice will make you better with it. Now let's learn about text columns.

Text Columns

You've already learned a couple of ways to arrange your text in columns. You've learned to do the following:

- Set tabs.

- Create tables.

In both of those cases, the text needed to be arranged horizontally as well as vertically.

A category of WordPerfect columns called *Text Columns* allows you to format your text in columns that snake from one column to the next. Let's explore this feature.

STEP-BY-STEP ⟩ 14.6

1. Beginning in a new document window, open **columns** from your student **datafile** folder. Use **Save As** to save the file with your working files as **columns 14-6 xxx**.

2. Study the contents of this document. It gives you lots of important information about newspaper columns, balanced newspaper columns, and parallel columns.

3. With your insertion point at the beginning of the document, point to the Columns button on the Toolbar and choose **2 Columns**.

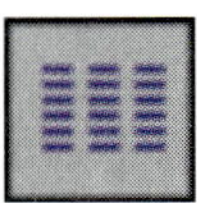

4. Your document should be formatted into columns. Zoom to **Full Page** and compare your document with Figure 14-3. Then return to **100%**.

5. With your insertion point at the top of the file, create a footer that inserts the Path and Filename code. Save your document again as **columns 14-6 xxx**. Keep it open.

(continued on next page)

6. Reveal your codes. Look at the [Col Def] code. Add it to your list of codes. Then delete the code to return the document to its original form.

FIGURE 14-3
Zoom of Columns Document

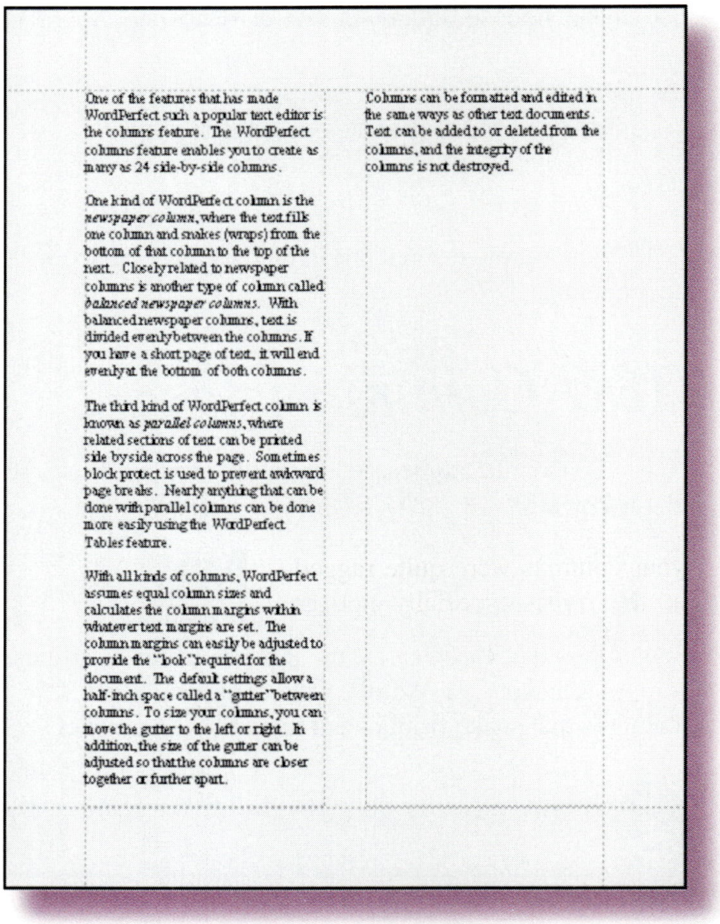

One of the features that has made WordPerfect such a popular text editor is the columns feature. The WordPerfect columns feature enables you to create as many as 24 side-by-side columns.

One kind of WordPerfect column is the *newspaper column*, where the text fills one column and snakes (wraps) from the bottom of that column to the top of the next. Closely related to newspaper columns is another type of column called *balanced newspaper columns*. With balanced newspaper columns, text is divided evenly between the columns. If you have a short page of text, it will end evenly at the bottom of both columns.

The third kind of WordPerfect column is known as *parallel columns*, where related sections of text can be printed side by side across the page. Sometimes block protect is used to prevent awkward page breaks. Nearly anything that can be done with parallel columns can be done more easily using the WordPerfect Tables feature.

With all kinds of columns, WordPerfect assumes equal column sizes and calculates the column margins within whatever text margins are set. The column margins can easily be adjusted to provide the "look" required for the document. The default settings allow a half-inch space called a "gutter" between columns. To size your columns, you can move the gutter to the left or right. In addition, the size of the gutter can be adjusted so that the columns are closer together or further apart.

Columns can be formatted and edited in the same ways as other text documents. Text can be added to or deleted from the columns, and the integrity of the columns is not destroyed.

Balanced Newspaper Columns

With a short document, sometimes it looks better to have the columns end evenly on the page. WordPerfect will end the columns evenly if you choose balanced newspaper columns. Let's convert this document to balanced newspaper columns. We will need to go to the Columns dialog box to do this. The feature can be accessed by opening the Format menu, choosing Columns, and then choosing Define, or by choosing Format from the little menu that appears when you click the Columns button on the Toolbar.

STEP-BY-STEP 14.7

1. With **columns 14-6 xxx** showing in the window, use **Save As** to save the file as **columns 14-7 xxx**. Position the insertion point at the top.

2. Click the **Columns** button on the Toolbar and choose **Format** to open the Columns dialog box (see Figure 14-4).

3. Look at the parts of the dialog box. Then click **Balanced newspaper** in the *Type of columns* section. Click **OK**.

4. How do your balanced columns look? Using the **Justification** button on the Property Bar, change from Left to **Full** justification.

5. Print the document. Then save it again as **columns 14-7 xxx**. Keep it open.

FIGURE 14-4
Columns Dialog Box

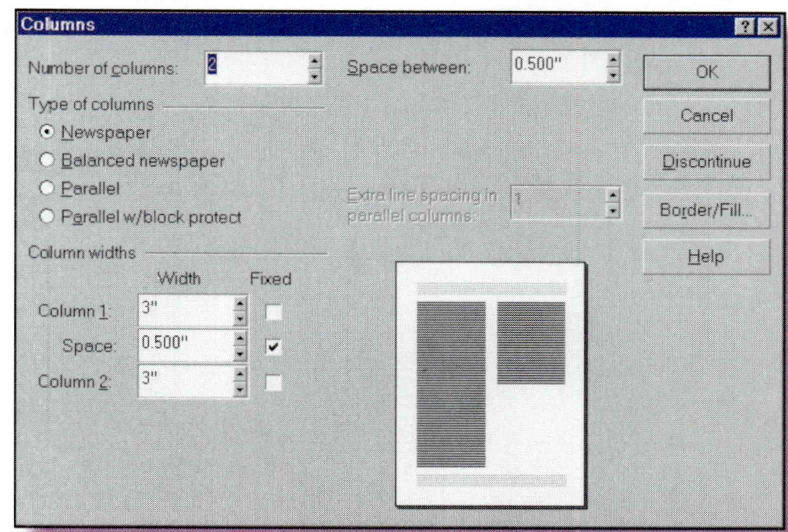

Look at your text. Before you changed to Full justification, your columns were quite ragged at the right—especially notice-able with the short line lengths. All of that excess space at the right was moved into the lines when you changed to Full justifi-cation. Either way, the text isn't particularly attractive.

Hyphenation

One way to even up the line endings and get rid of that "spacey" look is to use Hyphenation. Hyphenation compares the word that falls at the end of the line with the WordPerfect dictionary in which the words have been divided into syllables. WordPerfect then decides whether a word may or may not be divided at the end of the line. If so, the hyphen is inserted and the word is divided.

The hyphen placed in the word is a soft hyphen. When you reformat the text and the word containing the hyphen no longer falls at the end of the line, the hyphen doesn't show. When hyphenation is taking place, WordPerfect may ask you for some help regarding where hyphens should go in and which words may be hyphenated. Figure 14-5 contains a few of the major word division rules, in case you need help in that area.

Let's use Hyphenation in your document.

FIGURE 14-5
Word Division Rules

WORD DIVISION RULES
Divide words only between syllables.
Carry at least three letters to the next line.
Avoid dividing words with fewer than six letters.
Avoid dividing proper nouns.
Avoid dividing more than two lines in a row.
Avoid dividing the last word on a page or in a paragraph.

1. With **columns 14-7 xxx** showing in the window, use **Save As** to save the file as **columns 14-8 xxx**.

2. With the insertion point at the beginning of the first column, open the **Tools** menu, choose **Language**, and then choose **Hyphenation**. The Line Hyphenation dialog box that should appear is illustrated in Figure 14-6.

3. Look at the Hyphenation zone portion of the dialog box. Those settings will be fine for most of your work.

4. Click the **Turn hyphenation on** check box and click **OK**.

5. If WordPerfect has trouble deciding whether a word should be hyphenated, a dialog box similar to the one in Figure 14-7 will appear. Follow the word division rules if you are asked about hyphenation.

6. Look through your document at the hyphenation decisions. Does the document look less ragged?

7. Save the document again as **columns 14-8 xxx** and print a copy.

8. Reveal your codes and use the mouse pointer to drag the [Hyph] code out of your document to turn Hyphenation off. Most of the hyphens will be removed from your text. Keep the document open.

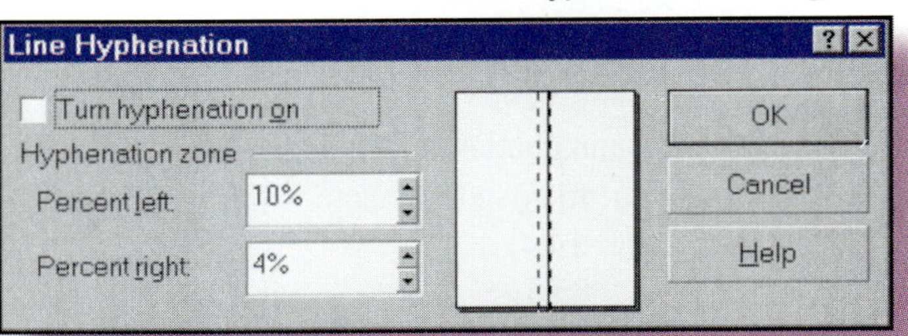

FIGURE 14-6
Line Hyphenation Dialog Box

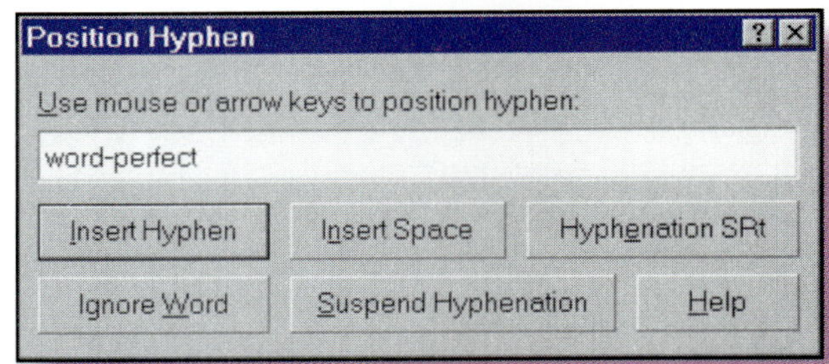

FIGURE 14-7
Position Hyphen Dialog Box

Soft Hyphens

If you wish to even some line endings but don't want to turn on Hyphenation for an entire document, you can manually add hyphens in specific places. This is done by positioning the insertion point and pressing Ctrl+Shift+– using the hyphen key next to the zero in the number row.

WordPerfect relies on you to identify the words that need to be divided with soft hyphens. Soft hyphens are great, because if text is edited so a word no longer falls at the end of the line, the hyphen does not appear.

In Step-by-Step exercise 14.9 you will use the soft hyphen to hyphenate some of the words in the document.

S TEP-BY-STEP 14.9

1. With **columns 14-8 xxx** open in your window, use **Save As** to save the file as **columns 14-9 xxx**.

2. Position your insertion point after the *l* in *columns* at the beginning of the fourth line of the first paragraph. Hold the **Ctrl** and **Shift** keys while you press **–**. The word should be hyphenated at the indicated location.

3. If it will help your document, put soft hyphens in the following words. (If your line endings are different, find other words to which you can add soft hyphens to fill the lines better.)
  a. Paragraph 2, *col-umns* at the beginning of the sixth line.
  b. Paragraph 2, *bal-anced* at the beginning of the eighth line.

4. Save the file again as **columns 14-9 xxx** and print it. Keep the document open.

Editing Column Sizes

While you have the capability of creating as many as 24 columns across the page, you will probably not use more than three or four columns on a standard sheet of paper. WordPerfect automatically spaces the columns evenly across the page. You may have noticed in the Columns dialog box that WordPerfect leaves a half inch between columns. This space is called the *gutter*.

You can edit columns within the Columns dialog box, on the Ruler, or using the column margin guidelines. Let's see how easy it is to change column widths with the guidelines.

S TEP-BY-STEP 14.10

1. With **columns 14-9 xxx** open in the window, use **Save As** to save the file as **columns 14-10 xxx**.

2. Point to the gutter (space between margins). Your pointer will change to a double crosshair pointer.

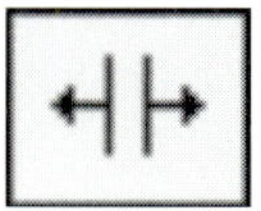

3. Press and hold the left mouse button. The little measurement box will tell you that both columns are 3" wide. Drag the gutter to the left until the left column is **2"** and the right column is **4"**. (If your column spaces out, delete a letter or space in the first line of spread text. Then key it back in after the column has adjusted.)

4. Drag the gutter back to the right to make both columns **3"** wide. Adjust the spaced-out text, if necessary.

5. Drag the right column margin of the first column until the column is **3.25"** wide and the gutter is **0.25"** wide. Adjust the spaced-out text, if necessary.

6. Display your Ruler and use the margin marker to change the right margin of the first column back to **4"**.

(continued on next page)

7. Use the little first-line indent triangle in the margins portion of the Ruler to give the paragraphs a quarter-inch indent. (Drag it to 1.25".)

8. Turn the Ruler off again and Zoom to **Full Page** to check your document. Is it beautiful?

9. Print your document. Then save it again as **columns 14-10 xxx**. Keep it open.

Columns in Part of the Document

Sometimes only a portion of the document should be formatted in columns. You can select the text to be in columns and turn columns on, or you can turn on columns at the beginning of the columnar portion and off at the end. Let's try it both ways in your document.

S TEP-BY-STEP ➡ 14.11

1. With **columns 14-10 xxx** showing, save it as **columns 14-11 xxx**.

2. Reveal your codes and remove the [Col Def] code at the beginning of the document.

3. Position your insertion point at the beginning of the second paragraph. Open the **Format** menu and choose **Columns**. Choose **Balanced newspaper**. Return to your document.

4. Position your insertion point at the beginning of the final paragraph. Click the **Columns** button on the Toolbar and choose **Discontinue**. Look at your document. The first and last paragraph should extend across the page. The center portion of the document should be in columns.

5. Remove the [Col Def] code at the beginning of the second paragraph to return all lines to full length.

6. Drag across the three paragraphs in the middle of the document to select them.

7. Click the **Columns** button on the Toolbar and choose **Format** to open the Columns dialog box. Choose **3** and **Balanced newspaper** columns. Return to your document and deselect the text.

8. With your insertion point at the beginning of the text in columns, choose **Tools**, **Language**, and then **Hyphenation**. Turn Hyphenation on and look at the document. You may need to make some hyphenation decisions.

9. Save the document again as **columns 14-11 xxx**. Print it and close it.

You can adjust your columns in a number of other ways. You'll be able to work it out when you have the need. WordPerfect Help will guide you when you need additional information.

The third kind of text columns—parallel columns—is not covered in this text because tables work so well for the same kind of work. If you want to try parallel columns on your own, check WordPerfect Help for that topic, too.

Spaces Following Periods

In Lesson 1 you learned that you should space twice following the period at the end of a sentence. For business documents, it is the best plan because it makes documents easier to read.

In some arenas, however, only one space following end-of-sentence punctuation is used. In the printing and publishing industry, for example, the rule is to space only once at the end of the sentence because the goal is to get as much text on the line as possible.

The **columns** document, as well as the rest of the prerecorded documents you've been using throughout your training, was prepared using the business standard—two spaces. Those two spaces at the end of each sentence were responsible for some of the unsightly spaces in the columns with which you've been working in this lesson. The extra space is magnified with Full justification and short line lengths.

Normally you should develop the habit of spacing twice at the end of a sentence. When it adversely affects a document as described above, you can use Find and Replace to find instances of a period followed by two spaces and replace them with a period and only one space. It will make your document appear to be more professionally prepared.

Summary

This lesson consisted of two main parts—outlines and columns. You learned about hyphenation along the way. In this lesson you learned that:

- WordPerfect has a number of predefined outline formats.

- Outlines are easy to create and to edit.

- Outlines can be collapsed when you don't want all of the levels to show.

- When using text columns, you can fill one column and allow the text to snake to the next, or you can choose Balanced newspaper columns so the columns end evenly on the page.

- It is easy to adjust the sizes of the columns and the size of the gutter.

- Hyphenation helps fill the lines when they are too spacey.

- Soft hyphens can be inserted when you want control of where the hyphens will be located.

- You should space twice following punctuation at the end of a sentence unless you're working with narrow columns and Full justification, or when you're working in the printing and publishing industry.

MATCHING

Write the letter of the term or phrase from Column 2 that best matches the description in Column 1.

Column 1

_____ 1. First Level 2 item.

_____ 2. Third item at the first level.

_____ 3. First item at Level 1 of the outline.

_____ 4. Second item at Level 3.

_____ 5. Second item at the first level.

Column 2

A. 1. Xxxxxxxxxxxxxxxxxxxxxxxxxxx

B. 2. Xxxxxxxxxxxxxxxxxxxxxxxxxx

C.   a. Xxxxxxxxxxxxxxxxxxxxx

D.   i. Xxxxxxxxxxxxxx

E.   ii. Xxxxxxxxxxxxx

F.   iii. Xxxxxxxxxxxxx

G.   b. Xxxxxxxxxxxxxxxxxxx

H. 3. Xxxxxxxxxxxxxxxxxxxxxxxxxx

TRUE/FALSE

Circle the T if the statement is true. Circle the F if it is not.

T F **6.** WordPerfect outlines can have as many as six levels, all numbered differently.

T F **7.** When an item in an outline contains indented items, the entire numbered item in the outline is referred to as a community.

T F **8.** On the Outline Tools Property Bar, the button that looks like a green book is used to display or hide level icons.

T F **9.** Sometimes only a portion of a document should be formatted in columns.

T F **10.** To discontinue a column, simply backspace to remove the final hard return.

LESSON 14 PROJECT

SCANS

PROJECT 14A

1. Open **wind** from the student **datafile** folder. Save the document as **wind proj14 xxx**.

2. Position the insertion point at the beginning of the second paragraph. Press Enter once to add a blank line between the first two paragraphs.

3. At the beginning of the second paragraph, tell WordPerfect you want two balanced newspaper columns.

4. Turn on Hyphenation and answer the questions about which words should be divided according to good word division rules.

5. Go to the beginning of the document and set a tab stop that changes the indent of the paragraphs from $^1/_2$" to $^1/_4$".

6. Open the Edit menu and choose Find and Replace. In the *Find* text box, key a period and two spaces. In the *Replace with* text box, key a period and one space.

7. Use Advance to move the first line of text 3" from the top of the page.

8. Insert a footer that puts the Path and Filename code at the bottom of the document. Format the footer with 8-pt. Arial.

9. Print your document and save it again as **wind proj14 xxx**. Close the document.

PROJECT 14B

1. Turn on Paragraph numbering and key the outline illustrated in Figure 14-8.

2. When you finish, check your work and end the outline.

3. With the insertion point at the top of the document, clear all tabs. Set tabs to be spaced evenly at 0.4".

4. Save the file as **nasa proj14a xxx**. Insert the Path and Filename code a double space below the last line of the outline.

5. Print the file.

6. Change to Outline style.

7. Move the *Anticorrosion paint* item so it is the second first-level item in the outline.

8. Collapse the outline to only two levels.

9. Save the document again as **nasa proj14b xxx**. Print it and close it.

1. Environmental

    a. Improved methods for weather forecasting
    b. Water recycling

2. Medical

    a. Insulin infusion pump
    b. Vehicle controller for the handicapped
    c. Wheelchairs
        i. New materials to reduce weight
        ii. Mechanism for voice control
    d. Scratch-resistant glasses
    e. Speech autocuer for the hearing impaired
    f. Reading machine for the blind
    g. Laser heart surgery
    h. Flexible metal for dental braces

3. Breathing system for firefighters

4. Flame-resistant materials for mass-transit vehicles

5. Anticorrosion paint

6. Advanced turboprop

CRITICAL THINKING ACTIVITY

SCANS

   You are proofreading a research paper for a friend and notice that several times in the document you come across a word in the middle of a line that has a hyphen inserted, such as *circum-stance*. You ask your friend why, and he doesn't know. What do you think caused this? How can he fix his document?

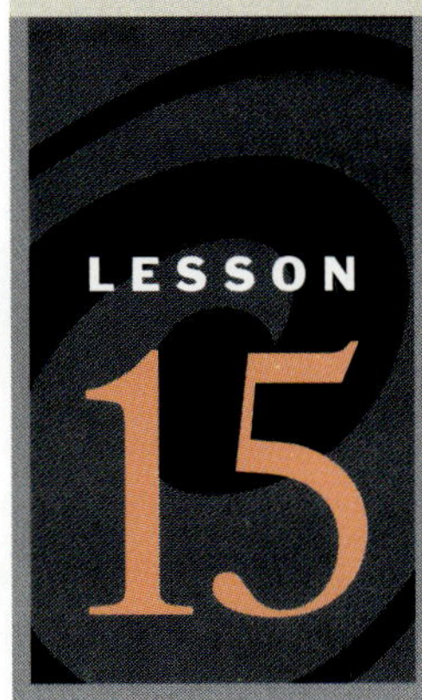

FORMS

LESSON 15

OBJECTIVES

Upon completion of this lesson, you will be able to:

- Use the Underline Tabs feature in creating forms.

- Divide your pages for creating documents smaller than the normal size.

- Construct forms using the Tables feature.

- Change the orientation of the page.

Estimated Time: $2^1/_2$ hours

The preparation of forms is a part of the job that has caused headaches for many office workers. Some forms are prepared and completed all at once. Other forms are prepared for information to be filled in later by hand, by typewriter, or by the computer.

In this lesson you will learn several methods of preparing some sample forms. Fay close attention to the procedure so that when you need to prepare forms of your own, you'll have the necessary skills.

Forms with Tabs

Many forms used in the office consist of words asking for information and blanks where that information can be written in. To create forms using underlined blanks, set tab stops for the text within the form and tell WordPerfect to underline when you tab. The Underline Tabs feature is set in the Font dialog box. We'll begin with a little practice.

STEP-BY-STEP 15.1

1. In a new document window, check to see if your Ruler is displayed. If it isn't, open the **View** menu and choose **Ruler**. Clear all tabs.

2. Set a Left tab at $1^1/4$" and another at $4^1/2$". Press **Enter** twice. (You'll use this space later.)

(continued on next page)

3. Press **F9** or open the **Format** menu and choose **Font** to open the Font dialog box. Click the **Underline** tab and choose **Text & Tabs**. Click **OK**.

4. In your document window, key **Name**. Space once, turn on **Underline**, and press the **Tab** key. Turn **Underline** off and press **Enter** twice.

5. Key **Telephone**, space once, turn on **Underline**, and press the **Tab** key. Turn **Underline** off and press **Enter** twice.

6. Repeat the same procedure for the *Address* line and the *City, State ZIP* line. When you finish, your little form will look like Figure 15-1.

7. Save your practice as **intake 15-1 xxx**. Insert a footer containing the Path and Filename code.

8. Keep the document open.

FIGURE 15-1
Step-by-Step 15.1 Sample Form

Name _______________________________

Telephone ___________________________

Address _____________________________

City, State ZIP ______________________

The Underline Tabs code is positioned in the document at the location of the insertion point when the option is chosen. If you want this feature available for the entire document, your insertion point must be at the top of the document when you choose the feature.

Many forms contain check boxes. You learned to make check boxes when you learned about Symbols. Now you get to use some. Let's finish the form.

STEP-BY-STEP ⟹ 15.2

1. With **intake 15-1 xxx** showing in the window, use **Save As** to save the form as **intake 15-2 xxx**.

2. Go to the top of the form and center **PATIENT INTAKE FORM** in bold, capital letters. Press **Enter** twice.

3. Press **Tab** twice (to the tab stop at $4^1/2"$) and key **COMPLAINTS:** in capital letters.

4. Go to the bottom of the form and complete the form, using the copy in Figure 15-2 for

FIGURE 15-2
Text for Step-by-Step 15.2

Birth Date _________________________
    Male ☐   Female ☐
    Married ☐ Widowed ☐ Divorced ☐
Insurance Company ________________
Policy Number ____________________
Time Admitted ____________________
Admitting Clerk ___________________
Blood Pressure ___________________
Pulse ___________________________
Temperature _____________________

the information. Double-space between all lines. For the indented sections:

a. Tab once, key **Male**, space once, press **Ctrl+W**, and insert check box **4.38**. Space three times and do **Female**.

b. Repeat the procedure for the *Married/ Widowed/Divorced* line. Add *Single* and a check box at the end of the line.

5. Complete the form. Remember that you must turn **Underline** on and off for each line.

6. Check your work over carefully. Then save the form again as **intake 15-2 xxx**. Print it and close it.

Using Tab to insert the lines up to a tab stop when you've chosen to underline the tabs works well. When you wish to underline all the way to the right margin, however, a better method is to use Alt+F7 (Flush Right).

Also make it a habit of spacing once before and after each underline. If you don't put in those spaces, your form will look crowded and unfriendly. Let's create the form in Figure 15-3. This form contains the same information but is arranged in a half-page format.

S TEP-BY-STEP 15.3

1. Beginning in a new document window, clear all tabs and set tabs at **1^1/$_4$"** and **4^1/$_2$"**.

2. Set all four margins at **0.6"**.

3. Create the form in Figure 15-3, as follows:

a. Double-space between all lines.

b. Use **Tab** to insert the underlines that go to the middle of the page.

c. Use **Alt+F7** to insert the underlines that extend to the right margin. (Remember that in each case, you must first turn Underline on and then turn it off after the line has been inserted.)

d. Use WordPerfect symbol **4,38** for the check boxes.

e. For the *Married/Widowed/Divorced/ Single* line, tab after the check box for *Female*. Then space once so all of the lines are aligned.

4. Complete the form. Check your work and save the form as **intake 15-3 xxx**.

5. With the insertion point at the top of the document, give it a footer that positions the

Path and Filename code flush right. Format the footer with **8-pt. Arial**.

6. Zoom to **Full Page** to look at your form. How could you change the document so the footer is aligned with the rest of the text at the right? If you answered *Initial Codes Style*, you are right. Let's fix the footer margins. Zoom to **100%**.

7. Return to the top of the document. Open the **File** menu, choose **Document**, and then choose **Current Document Style**. In the Styles Editor, open the **Format** menu, choose **Margins**, and set all four margins at **0.6"**.

8. Return to your document window. Reveal your codes and move the insertion point all the way to the left at the top of the document. The [Open Style: DocumentStyle] code will show the margins, and the regular margin codes will be removed from the top of the document.

9. Save the file again as **intake 15-3 xxx**. Keep it open.

PATIENT INTAKE FORM

Name ________________________________ Date of Birth ________________________________

Telephone: Home ________________ Work ________________________________

Address ________________________ City, State ZIP ________________________________

    Male ☐   Female ☐ ______________ Married ☐ Widowed ☐ Divorced ☐ Single ☐

Insurance Company ________________ Policy Number ________________________________

Time Admitted ____________________ Blood Pressure ________________________________

Pulse ____________________________ Temperature ________________________________

COMPLAINTS:

With this new arrangement of information, the form is obviously too large for a full sheet of paper. In fact, it would fit very well on a half sheet of paper. You could copy the text to the Windows Clipboard and paste it again on the same page. Then add spaces to push the two halves apart. If you do that, you'll only have the footer on one "page" of forms, and the two halves probably won't be equal. A better way is to use a feature called *Divide Page*.

Divide Page

The WordPerfect Divide Page feature enables you to divide a page into equal sections. You can divide a page by columns or rows. WordPerfect thinks of each section of the page as a *logical page,* while the actual sheet of paper is referred to as a *physical page.*

When you divide a page, you can use nearly any combination of columns and rows. In Step-by-Step exercise 15.4 you'll divide the page into two rows, which gives you the effect of two half pages, one over the other.

Usually when you use Divide Page, you will create your form or document in one of the pages. Then you will copy the form from the first logical page to the second, so that you will have two identical pages. After printing, all you need to do is go to the paper cutter and cut it in half for your two half-page forms.

S TEP-BY-STEP   15.4

1. With **intake 15-3 xxx** showing in the window, use **Save As** to save the file as **intake 15-4 xxx**.

2. With the insertion point still at the top of the document, open the **Format** menu. Choose **Page** and then **Page Setup**. Click the **Margins/Layout** tab.

3. Click the **Off** button beside *Divide page* in the lower right corner of the dialog box and change the choice to **1 x 2** (see Figure 15-4). Click **OK**.

4. Zoom to **Full Page** again to look at your document. Return to **100%**.

5. Open the **Edit** menu and choose **Select** and then **All**. (This is a good way to select the entire document as well as any codes at the beginning.)

6. Copy the selected text to the Clipboard. Press **Ctrl+End** to get to the bottom of the document and **Ctrl+Enter** to go to the next page.

7. Paste the contents of the Clipboard into the next logical page. Look at your document again with **Zoom**. If everything looks wonderful, save the document again as **intake 15-4 xxx**.

8. Print your file and close it.

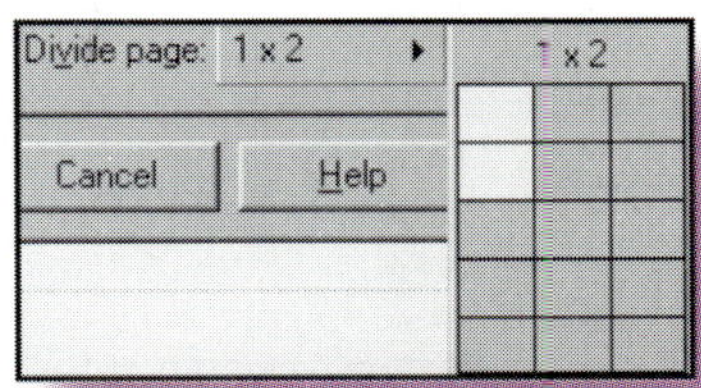

FIGURE 15-4
Divide Page Portion of Page Setup Dialog Box

As you saw when you looked at the physical page after pasting the form from one logical page to the next, both pages were formatted with margins and the footer. Using Divide Page is a clean way of reproducing a document when you want an exact duplicate.

Now let's learn another way to create forms.

Forms with Tables

After your work in Lesson 13 with the Tables feature, it should be no surprise to you that forms can be created with Tables. Study Figure 15-5. This is the shortened version of a form made up of two tables—one directly above the other. In Step-by-Step exercise 15.5 you will create a similar form. Follow along carefully.

STEP-BY-STEP 15.5

1. Create a table consisting of 2 columns and 7 rows.

2. Join the cells in the first row, and center **DAILY TIME SHEET** in bold, uppercase letters.

3. With the insertion point in the first row of the table, go to **Borders/Fill** and set the top, left, and right borders at **None** (X).

4. Move the line dividing the table to the right so Column A is 4.75" wide. Key the remaining headings in the top portion of the form illustrated in Figure 15-5.

(continued on next page)

DAILY TIME SHEET

Employee:			
Department:		Date:	
Company:		Total Hours:	

Job No.	Kind of Work	Began	Finished	Hours

Instructions: Enter the type of work on each job, listing the exact time you started and finished that job. List "Miscellaneous" for time not billable.

5. Beginning at the left and using Figure 15-5 as a guide, use **QuickSplit Column** to create columns with the following widths. (Do not change the side margins of the table.) WordPerfect will provide information about column sizes when you are splitting the columns much like that pictured in Figure 15-6.
   a. *Job No.* = **0.75"**
   b. *Kind of Work* = **3"**
   c. *Began and Finished* = **1"**
   d. *Hours* = **0.75"**

6. Key the column headings. Then center all headings in that row.

7. Split the *Began* and *Finished* columns so each is 0.5" wide.

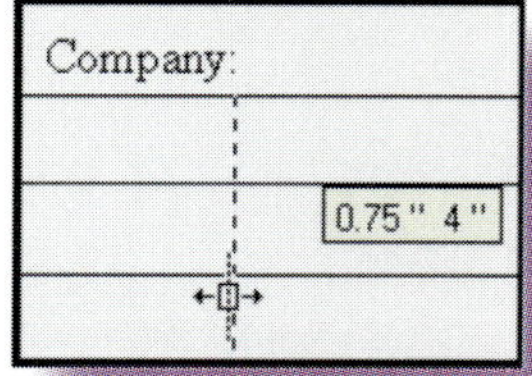

8. Save your evolving table as **time 15-5 xxx**. Insert the Path and Filename code in a footer, formatted with **8-pt. Arial** and positioned at the right. Save the file again and keep it open.

Your form is coming along nicely. Now let's finish it up and make it fill the page.

STEP-BY-STEP 15.6

1. With **time 15-5 xxx** in the window, save it as **time 15-6 xxx**.

2. Select Rows 2-7 of the table. Go to **Borders/ Fill** and set the border for the outside of the table at **Double** (the choice next to *X*).

3. Select Cells B5:B7. Set the border for the left and right at **Double**. Continue selecting portions of the table and setting the border until the form looks like Figure 15-5.

4. Position the insertion point in the final cell of the table and press **Tab** to insert one more row. Join all of the cells in the new row. Then set the left, right, and bottom borders at **None**.

5. Key the text below the table in Figure 15-5 in the row at the bottom of your table.

6. Position the insertion point in either Row 6 or Row 7 of your table. Display the QuickMenu and choose **Insert**. Insert 13 rows into your table. It should now fill the page. If it spills to the next page, delete a blank row so it fits on one page.

7. Check your work carefully. If everything looks good, save it as **time 15-6 xxx**. Print it and close it.

Now that we've created forms for a medical job and a piecework job, let's create an invoice for a law office. We'll use the Tables feature for the invoice.

STEP-BY-STEP 15.7

1. Prepare the document in Figure 15-7 as an invoice for work performed by Manuel Tovar, Attorney at Law.

2. Format the top of the invoice using your choice of fonts and arrangement of information. Figure 15-7 provides the information and a suggested layout.

3. Create a table consisting of 5 columns. Within the standard margins, size all of the columns except the *Description* column at **0.75"**.

4. Format the column headings as follows:
   a. Use **Bold**.
   b. Align the text at the bottom.

   c. Put a double line below the column headings.
   d. Set the rest of the lines around and between the headings at **X**.

5. Key the information into the table as shown. (You don't need to key the dollar signs.)

6. Format the columns as follows:
   a. Select the five cells containing the number of hours and set **Center** alignment.
   b. Select Cells D2:E6. Set Numeric Format at **Currency** and set **Decimal Align**.
   c. Select Cells E7:E9. Set Numeric Format at **Currency** and set **Decimal Align**.

(continued on next page)

7. In Row 7 join Cells A7:D7. Do the same for Row 8. Set Alignment for the joined cells in all three rows at **Right**.

8. Check your work for accuracy. If everything looks OK, save the file as **estate 15-7 xxx**. Keep it open.

FIGURE 15-7
Text for Step-by-Step 15.7

MANUEL TOVAR
Attorney at Law
123 Main Street
Victoria, NJ 08344

INVOICE

(Current Date)

Billing Period: June 1, (year) to July 1, (year)

Mr. & Mrs. Homer Corretja
Box 44
Victoria, NJ 08344

Date	Description	Hours	Per Hour	Total
6/1/year	Introductory meeting with Mr. & Mrs. Corretja	2	$95.00	
6/4/year	Planning meeting with Mr. & Mrs. Corretja	1.5	$95.00	
6/13/year	Library research on tax laws	1.75	$80.00	
6/18/year	Meeting with Mr. & Mrs. Corretja	1.5	$95.00	
6/22/year	Will signing session	.5	$95.00	
			Total Fees	
			State Tax at 5%	
			Total Charges	

Your invoice is complete except for the formulas and the calculations. Let's finish it up.

STEP-BY-STEP 15.8

1. With **estate 15-7 xxx** open in your window, save the file as **estate 15-8 xxx**.

2. Display your Formula Toolbar. In Cell E2 enter a formula that multiplies **C2*D2**. Copy the formula down four times.

3. Complete the calculations as follows:
   a. Use **QuickSum** in Cell E7 to add the numbers above the cell.
   b. In Cell E8 multiply **E7*0.05** to compute the 5% tax.
   c. In Cell E9 add **E7+E8**. The total should be $695.63.

4. Adjust the lines in the table as follows:
   a. Select everything below the double line beneath the column headings. Set all inside lines at **X**. Set left, right, and bottom lines at **X**.
   b. Select Cell E6. Set the bottom line at **Single**.
   c. Select Cell E8. Set the bottom line at **Single**.
   d. Select Cell E9. Set the bottom line at **Double**.

5. Give the document a footer containing the Path and Filename code. Print the document and save it again as **estate 15-8 xxx**. Close the file.

Organizational Charts

One of the toughest pen and pencil jobs in the days prior to good word processing programs was the preparation of organizational charts. The job still takes some time but, using WordPerfect tables, it is much easier and the results are more gratifying.

Whether or not you use organizational charts, the skill used for this application can be transferred to other applications. We'll prepare a sample organizational chart to get the idea of how it works.

Figure 15-8 illustrates where the organizational chart will begin, although your table will be wider than the figure. It is simply a 5 x 4 table. The first thing you'll do is size the columns. In this example you'll be given the figures to use. If you were preparing the job on your own, you'd have to do a little mathematics before beginning. The chart in Figure 15-8 has three boxes across that contain text. Each box will be 2" wide. On a $6^1/2$" line, that leaves $^1/2$" to be divided for the space between the boxes. Follow along carefully.

STEP-BY-STEP 15.9

1. In a new document window create a 5 x 4 table. Size the columns as follows:
   a. Drag the line between Columns A and B to the right so Column A is 2" wide.
   b. Drag the line between Columns B and C so Column B is 0.25" wide.
   c. Make Column C 2" wide.
   d. Make Column D 0.25" wide.
   e. Column E should be 2' wide.

2. Key the text illustrated in Figure 15-8 into your table. If you'd like, you can substitute your name and names of your friends in the table. Are you the boss?

(continued on next page)

3. Display the Tables QuickMenu and choose **Format**. Select the **Table** tab and set Alignment at **Center**.

4. Save the interim table as **boss 15-9 xxx**. Then give the document a footer that contains the Path and Filename code and save the file again.

FIGURE 15-8
Beginning of Organizational Chart

		Top Level Big Boss		
Second Level Boss 1		Second Level Boss 2		Second Level Boss 3

Now that the basic table is created, let's work with the lines. We'll make the lines for the organizational chart double lines and remove all of the remaining lines. When you finish, your chart will look like Figure 15-10.

STEP-BY-STEP 15.10

1. Save **boss 15-9 xxx** as **boss 15-10 xxx**. Position the insertion point in the first cell containing text.

2. Go to the Borders/Fill dialog box and set outside lines at **Double**. Do the same for each of the other cells containing text.

3. Position the insertion point in the cell above *Boss 1*. Use the **QuickSplit Columns** button to split the cell into 2 equal columns.

4. Split the following cells:
   a. Above Boss 2.
   b. Above Boss 3.
   c. Below Big Boss.

5. Select the four-cell square between the Big Boss and Boss 2.

6. Change all inside lines to **Double**.

7. Continue selecting cells and changing lines to **Double** until your chart looks like Figure 15-9.

8. Select blocks of cells and set all remaining lines at **X**. If you make a mistake, click the **Undo** button and redo it so the lines finally look like those in Figure 15-10.

FIGURE 15-9
Carved Out Organizational Chart

		Top Level Big Boss		
Second Level Boss 1		Second Level Boss 2		Second Level Boss 3

9. Select all of Rows 2 and 3. Go to the Format dialog box. Choose the **Row** tab and set Row Height at **Fixed**. Change the amount to **0.15"** so the space between the boxes used isn't so great.

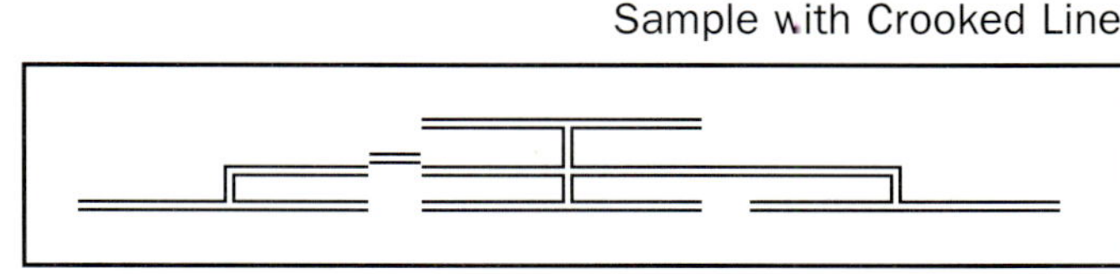

FIGURE 15-10
Final Organizational Chart

10. Save your final organizational chart again as **boss 15-10 xxx**. Print the file and close it.

FIGURE 15-11
Sample with Crooked Line

In an application like the one you just completed, sometimes your lines don't line up. A frustrating jag appears where the lines should be straight. Look at Figure 15-11. It is a sample taken from the table you just completed that illustrates the kind of trouble you can get into when you are formatting table lines.

The raised line that makes the joining line look crooked was applied to the *bottom of the top cell*. The other lines were applied to the *top of the bottom cells*. Obviously, when something like this happens, you know enough about tables and lines that you can go back and fix the problem. Practice with formatting lines will help you in situations such as this.

In WordPerfect tables not all lines are equal. When you have a choice regarding the formatting of the lines between two cells that are above one another, you'll usually be better off formatting the top of the lower cell rather than the bottom of the upper cell. Does that make sense? Practice, practice, practice will make you good at tables!

Orientation

Many times a document doesn't fit on the page in the normal manner—with the $8^1/_2$-inch sides at the top and bottom and the 11-inch sides at the left and right. That normal orientation of the page is called *portrait* orientation.

WordPerfect makes it possible for you to turn the page so the long edges are at the top and bottom and the short edges are at the sides. This arrangement is called *landscape* orientation. WordPerfect can direct most printers to print using landscape orientation. Figures 15-12 and 15-13 illustrate a page in landscape and portrait orientation. Both are divided in two rows and two columns.

FIGURE 15-12
Landscape Orientation Page Divided in Two Columns and Two Rows

FIGURE 15-13
Portrait Orientation Page Divided in Two Columns and Two Rows

247

Landscape orientation can be used for any number of applications. Let's use it to create a large table form.

STEP-BY-STEP 15.11

1. Beginning in a new document window, open the **Format** menu and choose **Page**. Then choose **Page Setup**. Click the **Size** tab. The Size portion of the Page Setup dialog box will look like Figure 15-14.

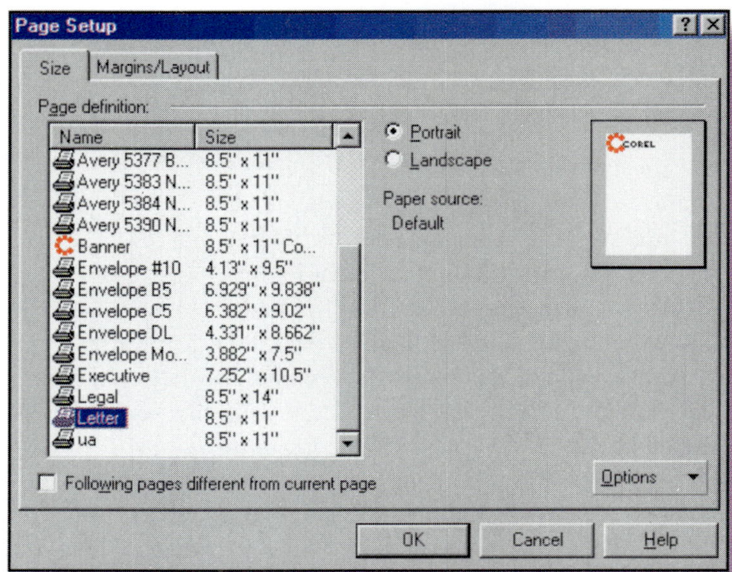

FIGURE 15-14
Size Portion of Page Setup Dialog Box

2. With the **Portrait** button selected, look at the available sizes of paper and the orientations listed.

3. Choose **Landscape** and look at the view of the orientation at the right. Then click **OK**.

4. Back in your document window, Zoom to **Full Page** so you can see the entire page. Zoom to **75%** so you can see most of the page.

5. Create the beginning of an organizational chart—just enough so it looks like Figure 15-8—with six bosses at the second level. Here's a start:
   a. Create a table that's 11 columns by 4 rows.
   b. Join Cells E1, F1, and G1 for the Top Level Boss.
   c. Size the odd columns—those which contain text—at about **1.3"** wide.
   d. Size the columns between the cells containing text at about **0.3"** wide.
   e. Set the entire table for **Center** alignment.

6. Spend no more than 10 minutes on this project. It is just practice.

7. Save the practice table as **landscape 15-11 xxx**. Insert the Path and Filename code a double space below the table.

8. Print the practice table and close it, saving it again as you close it.

When you were in the Size portion of the Page Setup dialog box, you probably noticed that WordPerfect enables you to work with paper in a variety of sizes—nearly all of the sizes commonly available on the market today. Changing the orientation or size of the page doesn't change the other WordPerfect defaults. For example, when you choose Legal or Legal Landscape, the default margins will still be one inch and the tabs will be set at each half inch.

This was just a quick introduction to working with landscape orientation. You'll have another opportunity to use that tool in the project at the end of the lesson.

Summary

You created a number of forms in this lesson. All were sample forms designed to give you the skills needed to create your own forms when the need arises. In this lesson you learned that:

- You can tell WordPerfect to underline the space from one tab stop to another so your lines begin and end at a given location.

- The physical page can be divided into a number of logical pages for forms of different sizes.

- Tables is an ideal tool for the creation of forms.

- You have choices with regard to the size of paper you use for your documents and which way the text is printed on the page.

LESSON 15 REVIEW QUESTIONS

FILL IN THE BLANKS

Complete each of the following statements by writing your answer in the blank provided.

1. The Underline Tabs feature is set in the __________ dialog box.

2. The WordPerfect __________________ feature enables you to divide a page into equal sections.

3. WordPerfect thinks of each section of a divided page as a __________ page.

4. When you arrange a page so that the long edges are at the top and bottom, this arrangement is called __________________ orientation.

5. The best tool to use to create forms is the __________ feature.

WRITTEN QUESTIONS

List at least five features used to create the form shown on page 250 in Figure 15-15, Form for Lesson 15 Project.

Create a quarter-page phone message form.

1. Open the Format menu and choose Page, Page Setup, and Size. Choose Landscape.

2. Open the Format menu again. Choose Page, Page Setup, and Divide Page. Choose 2 columns and 2 rows for the quarter-page look.

3. Zoom to Full Page to look at the layout on the page. Then return to the normal view.

4. Go to Current Document Style and change all four margins to 0.3".

5. Save your form as **message proj15 xxx**.

6. Create a table consisting of 2 columns and 12 rows. The table will not all fit on one page. Select the entire table. Open the Table Format dialog box, choose Row, and set Row Height at Fixed. Change the row height to 0.3" to make the table fit on the quarter page.

7. Look at Figure 15-15. See how quickly you can duplicate this form in your window following these suggestions:
    a. Use a 10-pt. sans serif font for the text.
    b. Join cells where necessary. In the first row the cell containing *Urgent* was created using the QuickSplit Column feature. Notice the different line style around this cell.
    c. Use symbol 4,38 for the check boxes.

8. After *Signed:* in the last row, use Flush Right for the Path and Filename code. Format it with an 8-pt. font size.

9. For an added touch, use reverse video for the *WHILE YOU WERE OUT* cell. Follow these steps:
    a. Select the row and choose Borders/Fill.
    b. Choose the last fill pattern in the second row of patterns. It is black. Close the dialog box.
    c. While the row is still selected (it now looks white and the type doesn't show at all), open the Font dialog box and choose *Color* near the top. In the color palette that appears, choose the white square.

FIGURE 15-15
Form for Lesson 15 Project

For		URGENT ☐
Date	Time	
WHILE YOU WERE OUT		
M	Phone	
Of		
Telephoned ☐	Please Call ☐	
Came To See You ☐	Will Call Again ☐	
Returned Your Call ☐	Wants To See You ☐	
Message		
Signed:	message proj15 xxx	

   d.   In the *Appearance* section at the top, choose Bold.

   e.   Return to the form and deselect the row.

10. When your form is beautiful, open the Edit menu and choose Select All. Press Ctrl+C to copy the form to the Clipboard.

11. Position the insertion point in the next logical page (the next quarter page) and press Ctrl+V to paste the form into that quarter.

12. Repeat Step 11 until the form is in all four quarters of the landscape page. (You may zoom to Full Page to see your page as you complete this step.)

13. Check your work over carefully. When it is perfect, save it again as **message proj15 xxx**, print it, and close it.

CRITICAL THINKING ACTIVITY

SCANS

    A form has been given to you that was created by joining two tables. The first table contains the heading, and the rest of the form has been formatted into the second table. The printed form looks patched with an unusually dark line below the heading. What is causing this problem and how do you fix it?

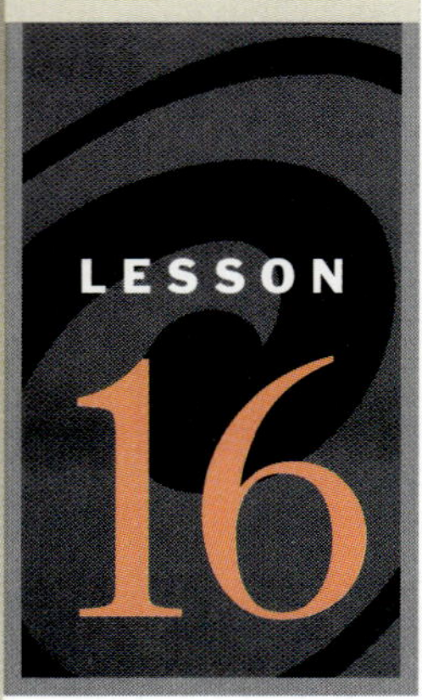

MACROS

OBJECTIVES

Upon completion of this lesson, you will be able to:

- Set preferences.
- Record a macro.
- Play a macro.
- Edit a macro.
- Add a pause to a macro.
- Discuss miscellaneous information about macros.

Estimated Time: 2 hours

In most jobs there are some sets of keystrokes that are repetitive. You key the same thing over and over and wish for some way to streamline the task. WordPerfect provides you with such a feature. You can create what's known as a *macro* to save a series of keystrokes. Then you can play that macro whenever needed to repeat the keystrokes.

WordPerfect macros may be used to save frequently used phrases, paragraphs, or complicated formats. Before you begin this section on macros, you need to set WordPerfect so it can find macros you save on your data disk in Drive A. This setting may have already been made by a previous student. If so, you'll simply check to make sure it has been made. Then we'll learn how to record and play macros.

Settings

In Appendix B you learned that most of the WordPerfect default settings work well, but that they can be changed, if necessary. Working with macros is one of those times, if you are learning in a classroom. The default setting is for macros to be saved in the **Macros** folder.

If you were on the job, had your own computer for your work, and didn't have to share the computer with anyone else, you wouldn't make any changes to the location of your macros. They would automatically be saved along with the WordPerfect system macros in the **Macros** folder.

As a student, however, you want your macros available wherever you are doing your work. If you are saving your work on a diskette in Drive A, your macros should be saved on Drive A. In Step-by-Step 16.1 it will be assumed the macros are to be saved on Drive A. You will be setting that location as the supplemental location for your macros.

S TEP-BY-STEP ▷ 16.1

1. Open the **Tools** menu and choose **Settings**. The dialog box illustrated in Figure 16-1 will appear.

2. Point to **Files** and double click to open the Files Settings dialog box. Click the **Merge/Macro** tab to display the settings for macros and merge (see Figure 16-2).

3. Look at *Supplemental macro folder*. It should say *a:*. If it doesn't, key that information in that text box.

4. When your dialog box is set to look like Figure 16-2, click **OK** to close the dialog box and return to your document window.

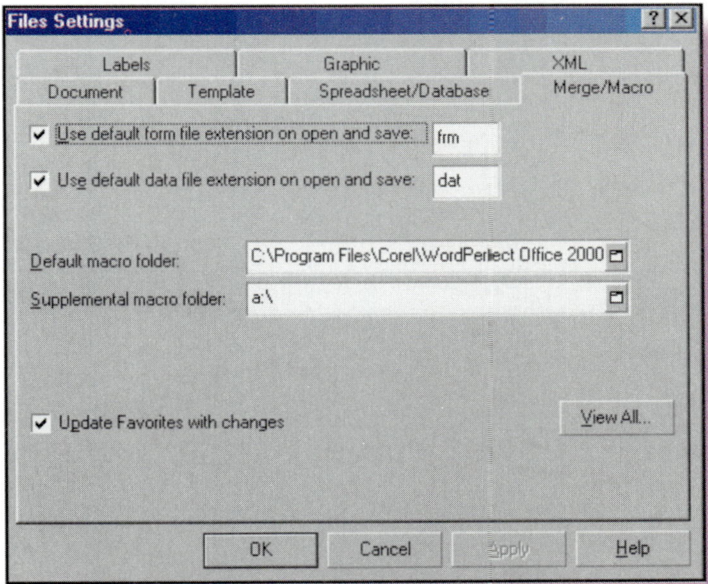

If you have any problem with Step-by-Step exercise 16.1, be sure to have your instructor help you. It is important that these settings be correct. Otherwise, either your macros will be mixed up with those of other students, or WordPerfect won't even be able to find your macros after you record them. When you create your macros, you will send them automatically to the disk in Drive A by including *a:* at the beginning of each macro.

Record a Macro

Assume that you work for a company named Cranberry Creations, and your boss, Francine Berry, likes the company name in the closing lines. You can speed up the preparation of your letters by creating a macro that contains the entire closing of the letters. Let's create the closing macro.

STEP-BY-STEP 16.2

1. Beginning in a new document window, open the **Tools** menu and choose **Macro**.

2. Click **Record**. The Record Macro dialog box should open, looking much like your Open File dialog box.

3. Key **a:\close** as the name of your macro and press **Enter**. Move your mouse. The pointer should look like a circle with a line through it.

4. Look at the Macro Feature Bar that is showing just below the Property Bar or Ruler. It should look like Figure 16-3.

5. Key the information in Figure 16-4. Double-space between the closing and the company name. Press **Enter** five times following the company name.

6. Press **Enter** twice at the end of the macro so the insertion point is in position for the instances where you need to add an Enclosure notation.

7. When you finish, open the **Tools** menu and choose **Macro**. Deselect **Record** to end the recording of the macro.

8. Close the document window without saving the document.

FIGURE 16-4
Text for **close** Macro

```
Sincerely,

CRANBERRY CREATIONS



Francine Berry
```

FIGURE 16-3
Macro Feature Bar

Play a Macro

Congratulations. You've just created your first macro. Let's play the macro. To play it, you can use one of the following methods:

- Open the Tools menu, choose Macro, and then choose Play. Key the name of the macro—in this case, **close**.

- Open the Tools menu, choose Macro, and then choose Play. Locate the macro on disk and double click the name. (This involves clicking the Favorites button and identifying $3^1/_2$ *Floppy (A:)*.)

- Press Alt+F10 and key **close**.

When working with a Windows word processing program, it is normally more natural to use the mouse and the menu system for accessing features. In a case like this, if you know the name of the macro, you will probably choose either the first or third method listed above—and the third one is obviously fastest. We'll play the macro using all three methods. Then you can decide which you prefer.

STEP-BY-STEP ▷ 16.3

1. Beginning in a new document window, open the **Tools** menu, choose **Macro**, and then choose **Play**.

2. In the Play Macro dialog box, locate $3^1/2$ *Floppy (A:)* and then locate the **close** macro. Either click the macro name once and click **Play**, or double click the macro name.

3. Look at the results of the macro in your window. Close the document without saving.

4. Open the **Tools** menu, choose **Macro**, and then choose **Play**. Key **close** and press **Enter**.

5. Look at the results of the macro in your window. Close the document without saving.

6. Press **Alt+F10** and key **close**. Look at the results of the macro in your window. Close the document without saving.

As you can see, playing this little macro is easy. The same is true of all macros, regardless of the length or complexity of the macro. Let's create another macro that you can use frequently as you progress through your learning. Then we'll prepare a document that will use both macros.

STEP-BY-STEP ▷ 16.4

1. Beginning in a new document window, open **pcug** from the student **datafile** folder. (The document is totally unrelated to the Step-by-Step exercise. You just need a document in the window that has a name so you can see your macro as it is prepared.)

2. With the insertion point at the top of the page, open the **Tools** menu, choose **Macro**, and choose **Record**.

3. Key **a:\pf** for the name of the macro and press **Enter** to begin the recording.

4. Give your document a footer that contains the Path and Filename code. Format the footer with **8-pt. Arial**. Close the Footer Property Bar.

5. Open the **Tools** menu, choose **Macro**, and deselect **Record**.

6. Use the scroll bar to go to the bottom of the document. Check to see if the footer is in place and looks like you expect it to look.

7. Close the document without saving it.

Now let's prepare a short letter and use the **close** macro for the closing and the **pf** macro for the Path and Filename code at the bottom.

1. Beginning in a new document window, use the **Center Page(s)** command to vertically center the current page. (Remember? It's Format, Page, Center.)

2. Use **Date Text** to insert the date at the left margin. Press **Enter** four times.

3. Key the mailing address and greeting illustrated in Figure 16-5. When you finish, press **Enter** twice and insert **berry** from the student **datafile** folder. (Remember? It's Insert, File, and then identify the filepath and file.)

4. At the end of the letter, position the insertion point a double space below the last paragraph, and use one of the methods you practiced in Step-by-Step 16.3 to play the **close** macro.

5. With your insertion point at the bottom of the letter, key **Enclosures**.

6. Save your document as **berry 16-5 xxx**. Return the insertion point to the top of the document and play your **pf** macro to put the Path and Filename code in a footer.

7. Prepare an envelope to go with your letter. (Remember? It's Format, Envelope.) Check your work over carefully. Then print both the letter and the envelope.

8. Close the document, saving it again when you close.

FIGURE 16-5
Opening LInes for Step-by-Step 16.5

```
Mr. Joseph Anderson
776 Fourth Street
Blythedale, MD 21903-1918

Dear Mr. Anderson:
```

Edit a Macro

After you got the letter and envelope printed, your boss informed you that she has changed the name of her company to Franberry Creations and that she doesn't need so much room to sign her name. You know that you could recreate the macro incorporating the changes. Macros can be edited, however, so you decide to edit the **close** macro.

1. Click the **Open** button on the Toolbar. Go to your disk and open **close** as a regular document. It will look like Figure 16-6.

2. Look at the format of the macro. Anything that is keyed is identified with the word *Type* and then *Text*. The text is enclosed in parentheses, and the actual words have quotation marks around them. Note that the Hard Return codes also are followed by parentheses.

3. Change *CRANBERRY* to **FRANBERRY**.

4. Delete one of the *HardReturn()* lines between the company name and Ms. Berry's name.

5. Click the **Save & Compile** button on the Macro Feature Bar. (WordPerfect will check to make certain everything in the macro is in order.)

6. Click the **Options** button on the Macro Feature Bar and choose **Close Macro**.

7. In a new WordPerfect window, test your revised macro. If it looks good, close the document and read on. If it has a problem, fix that problem before continuing.

FIGURE 16-6
Close Macro in Editing Window

```
Application (WordPerfect;
"WordPerfect"; Default; "EN")
Type (Text: "Sincerely,")
HardReturn ()
HardReturn ()
Type (Text: "CRANBERRY CREATIONS")
HardReturn ()
HardReturn ()
HardReturn ()
HardReturn ()
HardReturn ()
Type (Text: "Francine Berry")
HardReturn ()
HardReturn ()
```

If you know the macro language, macros are easy to edit. If you don't know the macro language, you can delete items from a macro with ease. Adding them is more difficult. In those cases, you might want to create a small macro that contains the new commands to be added and then copy them to the old macro. In other situations, you may choose to completely redo the macro.

Macro with Pause

You can set up a macro to stop for you to enter information. Then it will continue again. We'll use a fax cover sheet as an example of how you might do this with a macro. Later in your training you'll learn another way to create this same kind of cover sheet.

As you create this macro, note that you don't have full use of the mouse for selecting text and moving the insertion point. You must use the keyboard for these tasks. Work carefully and thoughtfully when you create macros. Remember that the recorder is on, recording all of your actions!

STEP-BY-STEP 16.7

1. Beginning in a new document window, create a macro named **a:\fran fax**. Key the beginning of the macro using the information in Figures 16-7 and 16-8. Stop when you come to *Date:*. Note the following things about the form:
   a. The phone numbers are on the same line as the first two lines of the return address—positioned with **Flush Right**.
   b. Switch to **20 pt.** for the words *FAX TRANSMITTAL*. Switch back to **12 pt.** following the words. Press **Enter** twice.

2. Key **Date:** followed by two spaces with the space bar. Press **Ctrl+Shift+D** to insert the date code. Press **Enter** twice.

3. Key **To:** as illustrated in Figure 16-8. Press the space bar twice and click the **Pause** button on the Macro Feature Bar. Click the **Pause** button again. (To pause and restart the recording of the macro, you must always click the Pause button twice.)

(continued on next page)

FIGURE 16-7
Beginning of Form for **fran fax** Macro

FRANBERRY CREATIONS   Phone: 814-555-4545
123 Sixth Street   Fax: 814-555-4343
Cranberry Ridge, PA 18201

FAX TRANSMITTAL

4. Follow the same procedure to enter the information in Figure 16-8 for the rest of the macro.
   a. Space twice after each colon and add a Pause code.
   b. Press **Enter** twice between each of the lines and at the end.

5. When you finish, look your work over and make any necessary corrections. Open the **Tools** menu, choose **Macro**, and deselect **Record**.

6. Close the document window in which you were working. Do not save the document. (It has already been saved as a macro.)

   Now that the fax form is created, you need to send some information to Joseph Anderson in Blythedale about the craft workshop Francine is attending. Use your fax form to transmit the information.

FIGURE 16-8
Section of **fran fax** Macro with Pause Codes

```
Date:

To:

At Fax Number:

From:

At Fax Number:

Number of pages (including this
page):
```

STEP-BY-STEP 16.8

1. Start the **fran fax** macro. The date should be entered automatically.

2. Key **Joseph Anderson** in the *To:* location. Press **Enter**. Key Mr. Anderson's fax number, **301-555-9811**, and press **Enter**.

3. Can you decide what goes in the next two blanks? The number of pages (including the cover sheet) should be **4**.

FIGURE 16-9
Note for Fax Cover Sheet

```
Here is the setup information
you wanted for my booth at the
craft workshop.  If you have
any questions, please let me
know.

F. Berry
```

4. After the macro is finished, key the brief note a double space below the *Number of pages* line. The text for the note is in Figure 16-9.

5. Check the transmittal sheet over carefully. If everything looks good, save it as **fax 16-8 xxx**. Then play your **pf** macro. Print the document and close it.

Information about Macros

Following are some important things you should know about macros:

- The WordPerfect macro language is a type of programming language. The first time you play a macro, it takes a little longer because WordPerfect has to *compile,* or check, the macro for programming errors. If you have an error, a warning box will appear, telling you which line of the macro to check for an error.

- Programming commands such as CHAIN, LABEL, IF, NEXT, and ENDIF are included in the WordPerfect macro language. These commands enable you to record powerful macros that can take care of just about any circumstance in your work.

- You may *chain* a macro to the end of a different macro to combine them and save more time. The chained macro plays as soon as the original macro finishes.

- WordPerfect automatically applies the *.wcm* extension to your macro names.

- When you are recording a macro, the words *Macro Record* appear on your Application Bar.

- Macros from WordPerfect 6.1, 7, and 8 do not need to be converted to run in WordPerfect 9. A few commands, however, function differently in WordPerfect 9. You can get information about those commands in the macros portion of Help.

- A number of macros come with the WordPerfect program. The **checkbox** macro, for example, inserts a box into which you can add an *X* by simply clicking the box. You may explore the **Macros** folder at your leisure.

- If you make a mistake when creating a macro, you may redo or edit it. If you redo it, WordPerfect will display a warning box telling you that a macro already is saved with that name and asking if you would like to record over the top of the existing macro.

- You can map your keyboards, assigning specific tasks to key combinations. A macro can be assigned to a key combination.

- A macro can be added as a button on the Toolbar or the Property Bar.

Summary

This lesson introduces you to macros. Macros are wonderful, but you must remember to create them and use them. Whenever you find yourself doing something repetitive, that might be a time for you to record a macro and put it to work for you. You can do it because in this lesson you learned that:

- You can set the location where WordPerfect looks to find macros.

- Macros can be named just like you name your regular files.

- Macros automatically get a *.wcm* extension.

- Macros can be played as many times as needed.

- Macros can be edited.

　　You learned how to create some simple macros. If you really get into the macro language, you can create macros that will do wonderful things in helping you with your work.

LESSON 16 REVIEW QUESTIONS

TRUE/FALSE

Circle the T if the statement is true. Circle the F if it is false.

T　F　**1.**　The WordPerfect macro language is a type of programming language.

T　F　**2.**　If you have an error in your macro, the first time you play the macro your screen will remain blank until you correct the error.

T　F　**3.**　Link is the term used to connect a macro to the end of a different macro.

T　F　**4.**　WordPerfect automatically applies the *.wcm* extension to macro names.

T　F　**5.**　When you are recording a macro, the words *Macro Record* appear on your Property Bar.

T　F　**6.**　Macros from WordPerfect 7 and WordPerfect 8 must be converted to run in WordPerfect 9.

T　F　**7.**　There is a Macro button on the default Property Bar.

WRITTEN QUESTIONS

Write your answers to the following questions.

8.　Why would you want to create a macro?

9.　From which menu do you choose Macro?

10.　If you edit your macro, what must you do before you close the macro?

LESSON 16 PROJECT

SCANS

　　In the world of business, many letters consist of more than one page. A second-page heading is necessary to give continuity to the pages and to make sure they are assembled in the correct order. Let's record a macro that can be used to automatically supply the correct information at the top of all of the pages of a letter except the first page. We'll work with the short letter you created in this lesson, since it's easier to create the macro with a letter open.

PROJECT 16A

1. Open **berry 16-5 xxx**. Position the insertion point at the end of the word *Enclosures* and press Ctrl+Enter to add a new page.

2. Return your insertion point to the beginning of Mr. Anderson's name in the mailing address.

3. Create a macro named **a:\header hor** (for *horizontal*). Follow these steps to record your macro:
   a. Press F8 to turn on Select. Press End to move the insertion point to the end of the line. (You have selected the name of the recipient.)
   b. Press Ctrl+C to copy the selected text to the Clipboard.
   c. If the text is still selected, press F8 again to turn Select off.
   d. Create a header.
   e. When the header window appears, press Ctrl+V to paste the name of the recipient at the left margin. Press Shift+F7 for Center.
   f. Key **Page**, space once, and click the Number button on the Header Property Bar. Choose Page Number.
   g. Press Alt+F7 for Flush Right. Press Ctrl+D to insert the date.
   h. Click Close on the Header Property Bar to close the header.
   i. Suppress the header on the first page of the letter.

4. End the macro. Press Alt+Page Down to look at the top of the second page of the document (the fake page you added in Step 1). Is the header there? Is Mr. Anderson's name at the left? Is the page number centered? Is the date at the right? If everything looks good, close the document without saving it.

PROJECT 16B

1. Open **sasoot 3-11 xxx**. It is in your **Units 1 and 2** folder. Use Save As to save the file with your Unit 4 files (not in the **Units 1 and 2** folder) as **sasoot proj16 xxx**.

2. Position the insertion point at the beginning of the name of the recipient of the letter—Mr. Antonio Larsen.

3. Play your **header hor** macro. Check the second page of the letter to see if the horizontal header appears as you expected.

4. Position the insertion point at the top of the letter and choose Widow/Orphan. (Remember? It's Format, Keep Text Together.)

5. Print the letter and close it, saving it again as you close it.

CRITICAL THINKING ACTIVITY

You begin keying a document in class and attempt to play a macro you recorded a couple of days ago, but nothing happens. You open the folder containing your personal macros that you have saved on a disk in Drive A, but cannot find the macro you want. Where is the next place you should look?

Command Summary

FEATURE	MENU CHOICE	KEYBOARD	LESSON
Balanced Newspaper Columns	Format, Columns (Toolbar)	—	14
Columns	Format, Columns (Toolbar)	—	14
Create Macro	Tools, Macro	Ctrl+F10	16
Create Outline	Insert	Ctrl+H	14
Create Table	Insert (Toolbar)	F12	13
Divide Page	Format, Page, Page Setup	—	15
Edit Macro	Tools, Macro	—	16
Edit Table	Table, QuickMenu	Ctrl+F12	13
Hyphenation	Tools, Language, Hyphenation	—	14
Macro, Edit	Tools, Macro	—	16
Macro, Play	Tools, Macro	Alt+F10	16
Macro Record	Tools, Macro	Ctrl+F10	16
Newspaper Columns	Format, Columns (Toolbar)	—	14
Newspaper Columns, Balanced	Format, Columns (Toolbar)	—	14
Outline	Insert	—	14
Page Size	Format, Page, Page Setup	—	15
Pause Macro	Tools, Macro	—	16
Play Macro	Tools, Macro	Alt+F10	16
Record Macro	Tools, Macro	Ctrl+F10	16
Select All	Edit, Select	Ctrl+A	15
Settings	Tools, Settings	—	16
Soft Hyphen	Format, Line, Other Codes	Ctrl+Shift+–	14
Table, Create	Insert, Table (Toolbar)	—	13
Underline Tabs	Format, Font	F9	15

MULTIPLE CHOICE

Select the best response that fits the following statements. Key your answers on a separate page with the heading, *Unit 4 Review Questions*, centered at the top followed by a triple space.

1. When working in tables, you can get formatting commands from the following source:
   - **A.** Tables Property Bar.
   - **B.** QuickFormat.
   - **C.** Create a Table dialog box.
   - **D.** Applications Bar.

2. The correct formula to use to divide the contents of Cell B3 by the contents of Cell D3 is
   - **A.** B3:D3.
   - **B.** D3:B3.
   - **C.** B3/D3.
   - **D.** D3/B3.

3. When keying an outline, you use _________ to go from a higher level of the outline to a lower level.
   - **A.** Ctrl+Tab
   - **B.** Shift+Tab
   - **C.** Alt+Tab
   - **D.** Tab

4. The Underline Tabs feature is chosen from which dialog box?
   - **A.** Tab Set dialog box
   - **B.** Font dialog box
   - **C.** Page Setup dialog box
   - **D.** Typesetting dialog box

5. If your macro isn't exactly right, you can either _______ it or _______ it.
   - **A.** edit, revise
   - **B.** copy, delete
   - **C.** edit, recreate
   - **D.** delete, recreate

WRITTEN QUESTIONS

Key your answers to the following questions. Number your answers and double-space between them. Use complete sentences and good grammar.

6. At the beginning of Lesson 13 you were introduced to the terms related to WordPerfect tables as well as spreadsheets. What is the relationship between columns, rows, and cell addresses?

7. Describe a floating cell and its relationship to the table in the document.

(continued on next page)

8. How would you describe the difference between Newspaper columns and Balanced newspaper columns?

9. Describe the difference between Landscape and Portrait orientation.

10. Go to Help Topics and read about Divide Page. What is the orientation of the sample divided page that is illustrated? Now go to the section about Booklet, Print. WordPerfect will organize and appropriately number the pages of your booklet as it is being printed. What does Help say must be done before you can print a booklet? How many logical pages must you have on a physical page to print a booklet?

UNIT 4 APPLICATIONS

APPLICATION 1

In Project 16 you created a header for continuing pages of multiple-page letters. The letter you used when you created the macro was a block style letter—with all lines beginning at the left margin. The letter to which you applied the header when you played your macro was a modified block style—with the date and closing lines beginning at approximately center and the paragraphs indented.

FIGURE APP-1
Vertical Letter Header

```
Mr. Antonio Larsen
Page (page number code)
(date code)
```

Your header was the correct style for the **sasoot** letter. It would not be correct for a block style letter. Use the **berry** letter, if you'd like, as you create another macro to be used with block style letters. Name this one **header ver** (for *vertical*). When you finish, it should contain the lines in Figure APP-1.

When you finish recording the header, open **sasoot 3-11 xxx**. Save the file with your Unit 4 files as **sasoot u4ap1 xxx**. Play the **header ver** macro. Then play the **pf** macro. Delete the Path and Filename code in the closing lines of the letter. Print the file and close it, saving it again when you close it.

APPLICATION 2

Sometimes Francine Berry uses a fax transmittal sheet on which she writes the information required. Only a half sheet is needed for this form. A suggested sample is illustrated in Figure APP-2.

FIGURE APP-2
Sample Fax Form for Application 2

FRANBERRY CREATIONS
123 Sixth Street
Cranberry Ridge, PA 18201

Phone: 814-555-4545
Fax: 814-555-4343

FAX TRANSMITTAL

Date: ___________________________________

To: _______________________________ At Fax Number: _______________________

From: _____________________________ At Fax Number: _______________________

Number of pages (including this page) _________

1. Prepare for the half-page form as follows:
    a. Divide your page into two rows and one column.
    b. Display the Ruler and clear all tabs. Set a Left tab at 4".
    c. Go to the Current Document Style and change all four margins to 0.8".
    d. Turn on the Underline Tabs option.
    e. Save the file as **fax form u4ap2 xxx**.

2. Create the form illustrated using Underline Tabs, Underline, Tab, and Flush Right.

3. Use your **pf** macro to put the Path and Filename code at the bottom of the form.

4. Check your work carefully. When it is perfect, open the Edit menu, choose Select, and then choose All. Copy the form to the Clipboard.

5. Move your insertion point to the next logical page (go to the end of the form and press Ctrl+Enter) and paste the form onto that page.

6. Save your document again. Print your two half-page forms and close the file.

APPLICATION 3

Figure APP-3 illustrates a portion of a form for the release of medical records. Study it. Then see if you can create a form that is similar. Some suggestions are listed following the sample form. Read through all of the instructions before you begin. It will help you to see the big picture of the formatting.

FIGURE APP-3
Sample Medical Release Form

(continued on next page)

FIRST SECTION

1. Clear all tabs. Set a Left tab at 4.5".

2. Use Underline Tabs to insert the lines for the two pieces of information.

3. Save the form as **release u4ap3 xxx**.

SECOND SECTION

1. Create a 3 x 6 table. Adjust the columns so the first column is 3" wide, the second is 0.5" wide, and the third is 3" wide.

2. Set the lines as follows:
   a. Select Column B and choose X for all lines (inside and outside).
   b. Select Column A and choose X for the left lines.
   c. Select Column C and choose X for the right lines.
   d. Select Cells A5 and A6. Choose None for the inside and bottom lines.

3. Key the text in all of the cells of the table.

4. Select Cell A1. Set the Font Color at White. Set Fill at 100%. Do the same with Cell C1.

5. Select the remainder of the table. Go to the Format menu and apply the following formats:
   a. Click the Column tab. Set the Left Column Margin at 0.02".
   b. Click the Row tab. Set Row Height at Fixed. Make it 0.35" high. Set the Top Row Margin at 0.02".
   c. Set the Font Size at 7 pt.

THIRD SECTION

1. Create a one-cell table. Format it with the same colors as Cells A1 and C1 of the other table.

2. Create the check boxes with Symbol 4,38. Tab to the existing tab stop for the second column of check boxes. Underline Tabs is still on for that final underline.

FINISHING UP

1. Select the entire form. Change the font face to Arial.

2. Proofread your form and check the appearance of the parts. Make any necessary adjustments.

3. Use your **pf** macro to put the Path and Filename code in the footer.

4. Print the form and close it, saving it again as you close.

APPLICATION 4

1. Open **online** from the student **datafile** folder. Save the file with your Unit 4 work as **online u4ap4 xxx**.

2. Remove the blank lines between the paragraphs.

3. Format the document in two Balanced newspaper columns.

4. Drag the left column margin of the second column so Column 2 is 2.5" wide. Drag the right column margin of the first column so the columns are separated by 0.25".

5. Use Find and Replace to replace all instances of a period followed by two spaces with a period followed by one space.

6. Turn on Hyphenation to help fill the lines of the document. Make any hyphenation decisions requested by WordPerfect.

7. Set Full justification.

8. Play your **pf** macro to identify the document. When everything is correct, print the file and close it, saving it again as **online u4ap4 xxx** when you close it.

APPLICATION 5

It's housekeeping time again—time to clear your main folder to make room for your Unit 5 work. Work carefully and confidently. You've done this kind of thing several times before.

1. Display your Open File dialog box and delete the files listed in Figure APP-4.

FIGURE APP-4
Files to be Deleted

berry 16-5	columns 14-7	nasa proj14a	sales 13-11
Bombay 13-2	columns 14-8	online u4ap4	sales 13-12
Bombay 13-3	columns 14-9	outline 14-2	sales 13-8
Bombay 13-6	estate 15-7	patty 13-15	sales 13-9
boss 15-9	fax 16-8	patty 13-16	sasoot u4ap1
columns 14-10	intake 15-1	patty 13-17	time 15-5
columns 14-11	intake 15-3	patty 13-18	time 15-6
columns 14-6	landscape 15-11	sales 13-10	

2. Move the files in Figure APP-5 to the **Units 3 and 4** folder.

3. Move **fax form u4ap2** and **release u4ap3** to your **Applications** folder.

(continued on next page)

4. No files should be remaining in your main folder except your macros. Leave them there so WordPerfect can find them when they are needed. If you have extra files that are unnecessary, delete them. If you have other work in your main folder, move it to a different location where it will be out of your way.

ON-THE-JOB SIMULATION 

SCANS

JOB 8

Mr. Becker is looking for other formats for posting the schedules for the drivers and tour guides. Since you're now an expert at preparing tables, you suggested that perhaps a table format would look good. Now he wants to see how it would look.

Illustrated below is the schedule portion of the memo you prepared in Job 3. It is illustrated as an unformatted table. Begin by preparing the table below. Then format it so it looks MUCH better than the illustration. Use your **pf** macro to insert the Path and Filename code as a footer. Print it and save the document in your **Singing Wheels** folder as **schedule job8 xxx**.

SEPTEMBER TOURS		
Dates	Destination	Driver & Guide
Sept. 1-4	Mall of America in Minneapolis	Dennis & Karen
Sept. 6-7	Fireplace Theater in Madison	Michael & Janie
Sept. 12-28	Vancouver, B.C.	Eric & Shelley
Sept. 14-25	New England	Greg & Karen
Sept. 15-19	Amana Colonies in Iowa	Fred & Janie
Sept. 18-23	Washington, D.C.	Al & Stacey
Sept. 20-27	Branson, Missouri	Tom & Anne

Mr. Becker is still not happy with the appearance of the coach policies list you prepared in Job 7. He has asked you for suggestions regarding other formats.

You've suggested that the items in the list could be numbered, or the list could be prepared in columns. He has asked for samples of both.

1. Open **coach job7 xxx** from your **Singing Wheels** folder. Use Save As to save the file in the **Singing Wheels** folder as **coach job9 xxx**.

2. Change the first-line indent so it is no more than $3/8$". Beginning with the first paragraph, change the font face and size to 12-pt. Times New Roman.

3. Display the Columns dialog box and choose 2 Balanced newspaper columns. In the lower left corner of the box, set the distance between columns at 0.25". Return to your document.

4. Include additional formatting as follows:
   a. Change to Full justification.
   b. Turn on Hyphenation.
   c. Use Block Protect so no item begins in one column and extends to another.
   d. Use Find and Replace to replace all occurrences of a period followed by two spaces to a period followed by one space.
   e. Move the *Memorize your luggage tag* item so it is the last one in the list. Make any necessary adjustments to spacing.

5. Save your document again in the **Singing Wheels** folder as **coach job9 xxx**. Print it. Keep it open.

   Now let's return the file to a single-column format and add numbers to the items.

1. With **coach job9 xxx** showing in the window, use Save As to save the file as **coach job10 xxx**.

2. Position the insertion point at the beginning of the first item. Reveal your codes and remove the [Col Def] code and the [First Ln Ind] code.

3. The insertion point should still be at the beginning of the first item. Open the Insert menu and choose Outline/Bullets & Numbering. Choose Paragraph numbering.

4. One at a time, position your insertion point at the end of the final numbered item. Press Enter twice. Then press Delete twice to move the text up to the line with the numeral.

5. Check your work over carefully. When everything looks good, print the document and close it, saving it again as you close it.

MERGE TOOLS

UNIT 5

Estimated Time for Unit 5: $10\frac{1}{2}$ hours

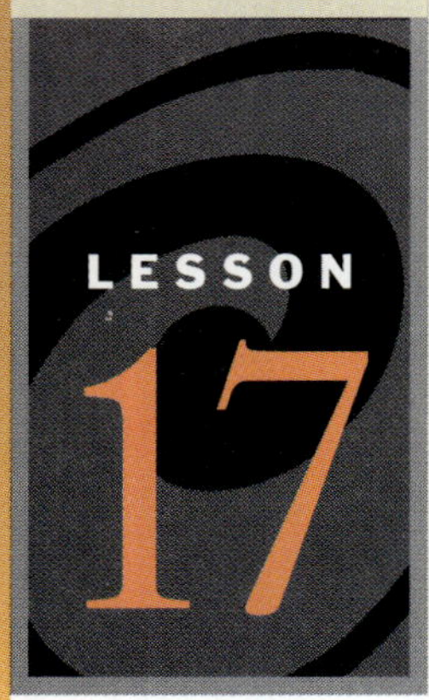

MERGE

No doubt you've received a number of sweepstakes mailings addressed specifically to YOU and telling you that you might be the first person in (your city name) to win $1,000,000. Have you wondered how much work it must be to send a personalized letter to the millions of people who have probably received the same letter? (There must be millions. Why else can't you win??)

In Lesson 4 you learned that the procedure of preparing personalized letters for a number of people is referred to as *merge, mail merge,* or *mass mailing.* In this lesson we will call it *Merge,* and you will discover how easy it is to prepare any number of personalized letters.

Merge Terminology

Every merge requires a *form document.* This is the main form containing text and merge codes. A form document can be merged with information from the keyboard or a *data source* (such as an address list), or a combination of these. In order to work with Merge, you should be comfortable with the terminology.

- **Merge Codes**. Dozens of special codes can be used to help WordPerfect perform merges. The most common are FIELD, ENDFIELD, and ENDRECORD codes.

- **Record**. A record is one complete entry in the list or data file. If you have a list of names, addresses, and phone numbers for a group of people, the complete information for one person is a record. An ENDRECORD code identifies the end of the record. A Hard Page code always follows an ENDRECORD code.

- **Field**. A field is one piece of data in a record. Each of the following could be a field:

      Name
      Street Address
      City, State ZIP
      Telephone

FIGURE 17-1
Sample Record

There is no limit to the number of lines in a field. The first three lines in the above list might be combined into one field and the telephone number might be a second field. Dividing records into more fields with smaller chunks of information makes your data files more versatile. An ENDFIELD code marks the end of a field. It is always accompanied by a hard return. Look at Figure 17-1. Notice how this record has been divided into eight fields.

```
Mr.ENDFIELD
FrankENDFIELD
WeigelENDFIELD
Weigel Wire WorksENDFIELD
453 Rummer RoadENDFIELD
Brunswick, ME 00834ENDFIELD
COM systemsENDFIELD
340-555-1200ENDFIELD
ENDRECORD
```

- **Form Document**. This is the document prepared to be merged with a list. Sometimes it is called a *form file*, or a *main*, or *shell, document*. In earlier versions of WordPerfect it was called a *primary file*. Often it is a letter to be sent to a number of people, although there are no restrictions on the format you might choose to use for a form document.

- **Data Source**. The data source for Merge in WordPerfect may be information from the Address Book, a file from a database program such as Paradox, a data file created in a different word processing program, a data file created in WordPerfect, or a number of other sources. When the data source is created in WordPerfect, these learning materials will refer to that source as a *data file*.

The data source is generally made up of some kind of list containing records. In WordPerfect the number of records in a data file is unlimited. Each record may consist of as many as 255 fields. Figure 17-1 illustrates one record of a WordPerfect data file. As mentioned above, this record contains eight fields, and it is a sample of what you will create in this lesson.

Data Files

The first data file you will create will be a text data file with named fields. It will be a list of potential customers who have inquired about a product. As always, read through the entire Step-by-Step exercise before beginning.

1. In a new document window open the **Tools** menu and choose **Merge**. The Merge dialog box will appear, looking like Figure 17-2.

2. Click the **Create Data** button. The Create Data File dialog box (see Figure 17-3) appears and asks for the names of the fields in your data file.

3. Enter the field names as follows:

  a. Key **title** and press **Enter**. The first field name will be added in the *Fields used in merge* box.

  b. Key **first name** and press **Enter**.

  c. Key each of the remaining names shown in the following list, pressing **Enter** after each:
  last name
  business
  street
  city, state ZIP
  area of interest
  phone

FIGURE 17-2
Merge Dialog Box

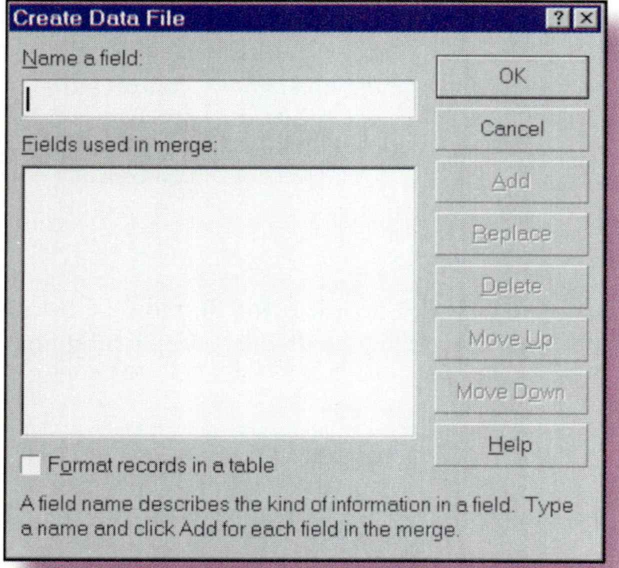

4. When you've keyed *phone* and pressed Enter, click **OK** to tell WordPerfect you are done naming fields. The Quick Data Entry dialog box will appear. Look at the data portion of that dialog box in Figure 17-4.

FIGURE 17-3
Create Data File Dialog Box

FIGURE 17-4
Data Portion of Quick Data Entry Dialog Box

274

5. Key **Mr.** and press **Enter**. Key **Frank** and press **Enter**. Key **Weigel** and press **Enter**.

6. Turn back to Figure 17-1 and key the remaining information for Mr. Weigel. Follow the prompts to the left of the text boxes so you get the correct information in the correct boxes.

7. When you've pressed **Enter** after Mr. Weigel's phone number, WordPerfect should complete the record and put all of the information for Mr. Weigel in the file behind the dialog box.

You have entered the information for the first customer, or *record*, in your first data file. WordPerfect is now prompting you to enter information for the first field of the second record. Let's continue with this process and save your data file.

STEP-BY-STEP ⟹ 17.2

1. The insertion point is in position for you to enter the next record. Enter the data for the potential customers in Figure 17-5.

2. After you have finished with the information for Ms. Oppermann and pressed **Enter** following her phone number, click the **Close** button of the dialog box.

3. WordPerfect will ask if you'd like to save the file. Click **Yes**.

4. Check the folder to be sure you will be saving to your main

folder. Key **micro 17-2 xxx** and press **Enter**. WordPerfect will add *.dat*, which identifies the file to WordPerfect as a data file. Click **Save**.

5. Keep the file open in the window as you read on.

FIGURE 17-5
Customers for Step-by-Step 17.2

```
Mr.                         Ms.
Berndt                      Dorothee
Helmke                      Oppermann
Celle Engineering           Opperthee Sporting Goods
6678 Celle Lane             782 N. Kassel Street
Hamburg, VT 09221           Landeau, ME 00884
micrographics               image printers and plotters
442-555-9866                341-555-7639
```

After saving, the file remains in your window. Study the file, looking for the following:

■ Look at the FIELDNAMES code at the top.

■ Look at the ENDFIELD codes. Does each record have eight of them? This is very important! If you don't have information for a field, the ENDFIELD code must still be included on a line by itself. If you inadvertently miss an ENDFIELD code, weird things will happen when you try to merge the file with a form document.

■ Look at the ENDRECORD codes. Is there one at the end of each of the three records, as well as at the end of the field names?

■ Does a Hard Page code separate the records?

■ Look at the Data File Merge Bar that shows below your Property Bar. It should look like Figure 17-6. If you wish to get back into the Quick Data Entry dialog box, merely click the Quick Entry button on the Merge Bar. If you wish to edit and need to add ENDFIELD or ENDRECORD codes, those buttons are available. We'll explore other parts of the Merge Bar later.

FIGURE 17-6
Data File Merge Bar

Form Documents

Form documents take all shapes. Some are letters, and others are forms similar to those you created in Lesson 15. The one thing that form documents have in common is that they contain merge codes where variable information, such as the information in a data source, will be inserted when the files are merged.

You can start from scratch, creating a form document by choosing Merge from the Tools menu and then clicking the Create Document button. However, if your data file is showing in the window, WordPerfect has made it easy for you to simply click the Go to Form button on the Data File Merge Bar. When you do this, WordPerfect will create a link between the data file showing in the window and the new form document, and also provide the field names.

Let's learn about this process as you create a form document to match your data file. This form document will be a letter, and it will contain much of the same kinds of formatting you have used for your letters in earlier lessons.

STEP-BY-STEP 17.3

1. With **micro 17-2 xxx** showing in the window, click the **Go to Form** button on the Merge Bar. Figure 17-7 illustrates the Associate dialog box that will appear.

2. Click **Create**. A new blank window will open. Look at the buttons on the Form File Merge Bar.

3. Set **Advance** to move the first line of the document **2"** from the top of the page.

4. Click the **Date** button on the Merge Bar to put a red DATE code in your letter.

FIGURE 17-7
Associate Dialog Box

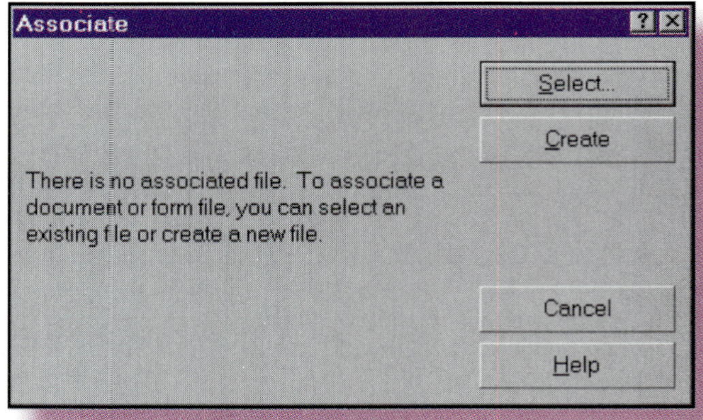

5. Press **Enter** four times and click the **Insert Field** button on the Merge Bar to display the Insert Field Name or Number dialog box (see Figure 17-8). Note that it identifies your data file and lists the names of the fields in your data file.

6. Point to **title** in the dialog box and double click to enter that field name. Press the **space bar** once and double click **first name**. Press the **space bar** once and double click **last name**. Press **Enter**.

7. Double click **business** and press **Enter**. Double click **street** and press **Enter**. Double click **city, state ZIP** and press **Enter** twice.

8. Close the dialog box containing the field names and save your file as **micro 17-3 xxx.frm**.

FIGURE 17-8
Insert Field name or Number Dialog Box

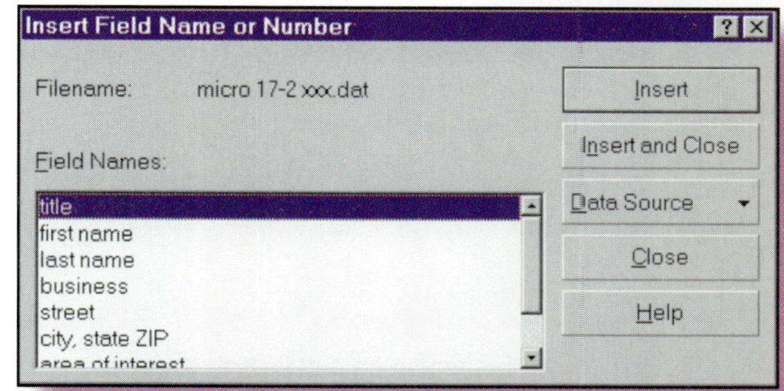

You've just entered the form document codes for the inside address portion of your letter. We'll finish the letter in a moment. In the meantime, let's look at what you have done so far.

The form document contains FIELD codes that match the fields in the data file. When you complete the merge, you will combine the data file with this form document. WordPerfect will know what to put in each "blank" because you've identified the field that contains the desired information.

When entering the FIELD codes for the inside address, be careful with spacing. For example, if you neglected to space between the items on the first line of the mailing address, the names will run together during the merge. This is true whenever you use FIELD codes in documents. Let's finish the form document and put some FIELD codes in one of the paragraphs.

STEP-BY-STEP 17.4

1. With the insertion point a double space below the mailing address of **micro 17-3 xxx**, key **Dear** and space once.

2. Click the **Insert Field** button on the Merge Bar to open the Insert Field Name or Number dialog box again. Double click **title**.

3. Space once and double click **last name**. Key a colon and press **Enter** twice.

4. Open the **Insert** menu and choose **File**. Go to the student **datafile** folder and insert the file named **image**.

5. Add a paragraph between paragraphs 1 and 2 using the information in Figure 17-9. When you come to the location for the first FIELD code, double click **area of interest** in the Insert Field Name or Number dialog box.

(continued on next page)

FIGURE 17-9
Text for New Paragraph 2

```
In your letter, you mentioned
FIELD(area of interest) as the
technology you would like to
research in your effort to
begin using imaging in your
office. In response to that
request, I am enclosing
several brochures on FIELD(area
of interest).
```

6. Continue keying the paragraph and insert the same FIELD code where required. Make sure the spacing is correct above and below the inserted paragraph.

7. Close the Insert Field Name or Number dialog box.

8. Near the bottom of the letter, substitute your name where required. Position your insertion point at the top of the letter and use your **pf** macro to add the Path and Filename code at the bottom of the letter.

9. Check the letter over carefully to make sure everything looks good. Then save the letter again, this time as **micro 17-4 xxx**. (Be sure it has the *.frm* extension.) Keep it open in the window.

Merging the Files

Now that your data file and form document have been prepared, you are ready to combine them into three (in this case) letters customized for the recipients. You'll be pleased to learn how easy it is to merge the two files.

STEP-BY-STEP ⟹ 17.5

1. With **micro 17-4 xxx** showing in the window, click the **Merge** button on the Merge Bar. The dialog box illustrated in Figure 17-10 will appear.

2. Look at the dialog box. Notice the following:
  a. Form document should say *Current Document*.
  b. The Data source is **micro 17-2 xxx**.
  c. Output tells you that the merged file will go to *New Document*.

FIGURE 17-10
Perform Merge Dialog Box

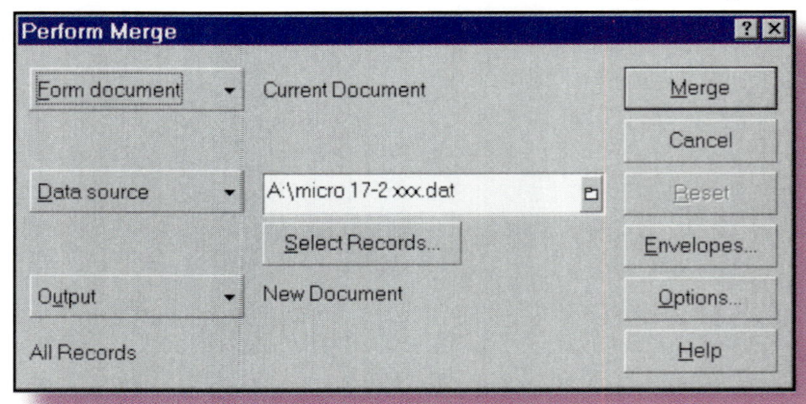

3. Click the **Merge** button to complete the merge. When the merge is finished, your insertion point will be at the end of the final letter.

4. Use **Page Up** to go through the letters. Look at the following:

   a. The Path and Filename code location is empty because the merged file has not yet been saved.

   b. The second paragraph contains the area of interest designated for each potential customer.

   c. The mailing address area is complete with customer name and address. Check the spacing around the parts of the name. (If one letter is spaced correctly, all of the letters probably will be.)

   d. The current date should show on all three letters.

5. Save your letters as **micro 17-5 xxx**. Then print the three letters. Close the document. (The form document should appear. It was hiding behind the merged file.) Close the form document, and the data file will appear. Keep it open.

Editing a Data File

Occasionally you will want to add a record to a data file or remove one. Or perhaps you may want to update a record or make a correction of some type. WordPerfect makes it very easy for you to add, delete, or edit records in an existing data file.

With the data file open, choose Quick Entry from the Data File Merge Bar. Follow these steps to edit your file:

- **Add**. To add a record, move to the end of the file using the Last button and then choose New Record.

- **Delete**. To delete a record, move to the record you wish to delete and choose Delete Record.

- **Edit**. To edit a record, move to the record you wish to edit and make the appropriate changes.

When you close the Quick Data Entry dialog box, you will be prompted to save the changes.

Multiple-Line Fields

Sometimes the information for a field takes more than one line. For example, a street address might consist of the following two lines:

   Suite 982
   921 Plymouth Court

When you are in the Quick Data Entry dialog box, you can't press Enter to add the extra line because Enter takes you to the next field. Instead, whenever you need to add a new line to a field, press Ctrl+Enter. The field text boxes only display one line of a field. Use the up or down arrows to the right of the field box (see Figure 17-4) to view the additional lines.

Let's practice by editing an existing record and adding a new one.

1. Only **micro 17-2 xxx.dat** should still be open in your window. This is your data file. Use **Save As** to save the file as **micro 17-6 xxx**.

2. Position the insertion point somewhere in the second record (Berndt Helmke). Click the **Quick Entry** button on the Merge Bar. The Helmke record will appear in the Quick Data Entry dialog box.

3. Position your insertion point at the beginning of the street address and key **Suite 6B**. Press **Ctrl+Enter** to force the street address to the next line.

4. Use the little arrows at the right of the street address to see the two lines of text in the box. (This is a single field that contains two lines of text.)

5. Click the **Last** button at the bottom of the dialog box. (This moves you to the end of the file.) Now click the **New Record** button and enter the information for the potential customer in Figure 17-11.

6. Press **Enter** after the phone number, and close the Quick Data Entry dialog box. Choose **Yes** to save the file again as **micro 17-6 xxx.dat**.

7. Close the newly revised data file.

FIGURE 17-11
New Record for Data File

```
Mr.
Jacob
Noschang
JN Communications
821 Kingsway Road
Blackwell, ME 04950
micrographics
341-555-7654
```

In addition to being able to merge by clicking the Merge button while the form document is showing, you can merge two files that are saved on the disk or in a folder.

1. Beginning in a new document window, open the **Tools** menu and choose **Merge**. Then click the **Perform Merge** button at the bottom of the dialog box.

2. The Perform Merge dialog box will appear, asking for the names of the files to be merged. Click the folder button beside the *Form document* text box. Note that only form documents are listed, even though your folder contains several other files. Choose **micro 17-4 xxx**.

3. Click the folder button beside the *Data source* text box. Note that only data files are listed. Locate **micro 17-6 xxx** and double click to choose it for your merge.

4. Click the **Merge** button to complete the merge. When the merge is completed, check to see if the changes made to the data file were included.
   a. Check the Application Bar. Are you on page 4?
   b. Use **Page Up** to see if that fourth letter is to Jacob Noschang.
   c. Press **Ctrl+G** and key **2** to go to the second page. Is the suite number listed for Mr. Helmke?

d. If all of your answers aren't *Yes*, go back and repeat Step-by-Step exercise 17.6.

5. Save the merged file as **micro 17-7 xxx** and keep it open.

6. Print only Letters 2 and 4 by opening the Print dialog box, choosing the **Multiple Pages** tab, and keying **2,4** (no space after the comma). Click **OK** and then click **Print**.

7. Close the document without saving it again.

Envelopes

You learned in an early lesson that WordPerfect will automatically position the address of your letter on the envelope when you are working with individual letters. The program will also prepare envelopes to go with your letters when you merge a form document and a data file.

To prepare envelopes, you must insert the FIELD codes in the envelope format. Then as the merge is completed, an envelope will be prepared to match each letter. After the merge, the insertion point will still be at the end of the final letter. The envelopes will be in the same order as the letters, and will follow the letters.

When you print envelopes in the office, you may have a printer designated just for envelopes. In other cases, the envelopes might be loaded in a specified drawer that you will choose when you wish to print an envelope. In the classroom, those conditions are probably not present and you'll need to print your envelopes using the same printer used for your other work. If that is the case, the printer will probably prompt you to insert the envelope to be printed. You have the following choices:

- Your instructor may have a supply of inexpensive envelopes with which you may practice.

- You may be instructed to cut paper to the correct size for envelopes (4.13" x 9.5").

- You can reinsert the letter and print the envelope on the back of the page.

Check with your instructor to see what procedure you should follow for the printing of envelopes. Now let's perform the same merge as in Step-by-Step exercise 17.7 and prepare envelopes for the potential customers.

S T E P - B Y - S T E P ▷ 17.8

1. Choose **Tools**, **Merge**, and then **Perform Merge**. WordPerfect will probably remember the files you were using. If not, choose **micro 17-4 xxx** for the Form document and **micro 17-6 xxx** for the Data source.

2. Click the **Envelopes** button at the right of the dialog box to display the Envelope. The envelope tools will appear on the Property Bar (see Figure 17-12).

3. If a return address shows on the envelope, click the **Return Address** button on the Property Bar and choose **No Return Address**.

4. Click the **Insert Field** button to display a list of the field names. Enter the mailing address as follows:
   a. Double click **title** and space once.
   b. Double click **first name** and space once.
   c. Double click **last name** and press **Enter**.

(continued on next page)

d. Double click **business** and press **Enter**.

e. Double click **street** and press **Enter**.

f. Double click **city, state ZIP**.

5. Click the **Continue Merge** button on the Property Bar.

6. Click the **Merge** button to complete the merge. When the merge is finished, your insertion point will be at the bottom of the final letter. The envelopes will follow the letters. Use **Page Down** to see the envelopes.

7. Zoom to **Full Page** to look at an envelope. Then return to **100%**.

8. Print only one envelope—the one to Jacob Noschang. Save your document as **micro 17-8 xxx** and close all files.

FIGURE 17-12
Envelope Buttons on the Property Bar

If you looked at the results of this merge carefully, you noticed that the first three letters contained the footer with the path and filename. The footer did not appear on the fourth letter. WordPerfect turns the footer off for the envelopes (the Footer End code is at the bottom of the final letter), and for some unknown reason, that command takes effect already on the fourth letter.

Table Data File

When you prepare the data file, you have the choice of formatting it in text format, as you did in Step-by-Step exercises 17.1 and 17.2, or in table format like the data source you used in Lesson 4. When you use table format, the fields are named and the information is entered in the same way, but it appears spread across the page in a table rather than along the left margin with ENDFIELD and ENDRECORD codes.

In the next Step-by-Step exercise you will prepare a short table data file using the same information you used for Step-by-Step exercise 17.2.

STEP-BY-STEP 17.9

1. Beginning in a new document window, open the **Tools** menu, choose **Merge**, and then choose **Create Data**. Key the field names listed in Figure 17-13 into the Field Names dialog box, pressing **Enter** after each name.

2. At the bottom of the dialog box, click the *Format records in a table* check box. Click **OK** to display the Quick Data Entry dialog box.

3. Prepare the data file for the two prospective customers in Figure 17-14. When you finish, close the Quick Data Entry dialog box and save the file as **micro 17-9a xxx**. WordPerfect will add the *.dat* extension.

4. Look at your file. It should look much like Figure 17-15.

5. Click **Merge** on the Merge Bar and merge the file with **micro 17-9a xxx** (the data source in table format).

6. Check your two letters. If they look good, print them and close the file, saving it as **micro 17-9b xxx**. If something isn't right, close the document and go back to the data file to make the necessary repairs. Then merge again and finish the Step-by-Step exercise. Close all files.

FIGURE 17-13
Field Names

```
title
first name
last name
business
street
city, state ZIP
area of interest
phone
```

FIGURE 17-14
Customers for Step-by-Step 17.9

```
Mr.                             Ms.
Frank                           Dorothee
Weigel                          Oppermann
Weigel Wire Works               Opperthee Sporting Goods
453 Rummer Road                 782 N. Kassel Street
Brunswick, ME 00834             Landeau, ME 00884
COM systems                     image printers and plotters
340-555-1200                    341-555-7639
```

FIGURE 17-15
Table Data File

title	first name	last name	business	street	city, state ZIP	area of interest	phone
Mr.	Frank	Weigel	Weigel Wire Works	453 Rummer Road	Brunswick, ME 00834	COM systems	340-555-1200
Ms.	Dorothee	Opperm ann	Opperth ee Sporting Goods	782 N. Kassel Street	Landeau, ME 00884	image printers and plotters	341-555-7639

283

Troubleshooting a Merge

When merging, sometimes your files don't turn out exactly the way you planned. The only way you'll know that is to look through your merged documents to see if the correct information is in the right place. It is costly in terms of time and resources to print your letters or other merged documents before really looking at them. If you find an error, you'll have to print again after fixing that error. Too often, the error occurs on ALL letters, not just one or two.

When something doesn't work, check both the data source and the form document. You can open both of them and choose Tile from the Window menu so you can see both documents at one time. Check to see if the FIELD codes in both documents match. Check to be sure you keyed the correct information in each of the fields. If you find something wrong in either the data source or the form document, make the correction and save the document again before performing the merge again.

Sometimes in a merge, you'll end up with a "blank" form document at the end of your merged letters or other forms. Usually that is the result of an extra hard return or code of some kind following the final Hard Page code in the data file. If that happens, open your data file, reveal your codes, and be sure the [HPg] code is at the end of the file.

You've done well with your merges so far. We'll look at one more kind of merge in this lesson.

Keyboard Merge

Merging form documents and data files is a good way to produce customized documents when you have a number of them to prepare at one time. Another kind of merge is available for situations where you need to prepare only one or two letters or forms at a time. In cases like that, it's not efficient to create a data file for the merge.

A better method is to prepare what's known as a *keyboard merge*. With Keyboard Merge, you prepare only the form document. During the merge you key the variable information. A different merge code is used for a keyboard merge. It is a KEYBOARD code that stops the merge while you key the information. When you've finished keying at that location, you start the merge again with Alt+Enter and WordPerfect will move to the next KEYBOARD code.

You can tell WordPerfect to prompt you with the kind of information to be entered at each stop in the keyboard merge, although the prompts aren't necessary to make the merge work. Let's try a short sample to see how Keyboard Merge works.

S TEP-BY-STEP ➡ 17.10

1. Beginning in a new document window, set line spacing at **2.0** for double spacing.

2. Open the **Tools** menu and choose **Merge**. Click **Create Document** and tell WordPerfect to use the active window. Click **OK**.

3. In the Associate Form and Data dialog box, click **No association** and then **OK**. Look at the buttons on the Form File Merge Bar. Find the **Keyboard** button. You'll use that button in this Step-by-Step exercise.

4. Key the paragraph in Figure 17-16. At the location of the first KEYBOARD code, click the **Keyboard** button on the Merge Bar.

5. In the Insert Merge Code dialog box, key **patient name**. (The prompts are shaded in Figure 17-16.) Press **Enter** to insert the code and prompt into your document. Space once.

6. Continue keying until you come to the next KEYBOARD code. Click the **Keyboard** button and key the prompt. Repeat the process until you have keyed the entire paragraph. The variable information is shown as shaded text in Figure 17-16 to help you pick it out. In your window, the text will appear as normal text with the KEYBOARD codes in red.

7. When you finish, save the document as **referral 17-10 xxx**.

8. Return your insertion point to the top of the document. Play your **pf** macro. Then close the document, saving it again as you close it.

FIGURE 17-16
Text for Step-by-Step 17.10

```
This is a referral of KEYBOARD(patient name) to your care.
KEYBOARD(He/She) lives at KEYBOARD(street address) in KEYBOARD(city,
state and ZIP code).  KEYBOARD(patient name) is a KEYBOARD(male/
female) who is KEYBOARD(age) years old.  KEYBOARD(He/She) has a blood
pressure of KEYBOARD(blood pressure) and is suffering from
KEYBOARD(symptoms).  A complete medical chart is available upon
request.
```

Look at Figure 17-17. It contains the variable information for two patients who are being referred to a specialist. Let's see how easy it is to prepare a document using Keyboard Merge.

S TEP-BY-STEP ⟹ 17.11

1. Open the **Tools** menu and choose **Merge**. Then choose **Perform Merge**. In the location for the Form document, fill in **referral 17-10 xxx**. Look at the *Data source* text box. If it doesn't say *None*, click the **Data source** button and choose **None**. (This merge does not require a data file.)

2. Click the **Merge** button. When your document appears, the insertion point will be in the location for the first piece of variable information. Key **Isabella Legg**.

3. Click the **Continue** button on the Merge Bar or press **Alt+Enter** to move the insertion point to the next variable. Following the prompt, fill in the correct information from Figure 17-17.

4. Work carefully. After the final KEYBOARD code, click **Continue** or press **Alt+Enter** one more time to end the merge.

5. Check your work. Then save it as **referral 17-11 xxx**. Position the insertion point at the end of the paragraph and press **Ctrl+Enter** to go to a new page.

(continued on next page)

6. Open the **Tools** menu, choose **Merge**, and then choose **Perform Merge**. In the Perform Merge dialog box click the **Output** button and change it to **Current Document**.

7. Continue the merge procedure in Steps 1-4 to complete the referral for Mr. Hartmann.

8. Print your two referrals and save them again with the same name. Close the file.

FIGURE 17-17
Data for Keyboard Merge

```
Patient 1:                      Patient 2:
Isabella Legg                   Harley Hartmann
333 Erie Street                 77 Yoman Court
Epsonville, IA 49876            Yaleston, IA 49879
Female                          Male
Age: 33                         Age: 77
Blood Pressure: 98/58           Blood Pressure: 180/95
Symptoms: dizziness             Symptoms: chest pains
                                          and shortness
                                          of breath
```

This was a brief introduction to Keyboard Merge. You'll have a number of additional opportunities to work with this feature in future lessons.

Viewing File Extensions

Up to this point, you have learned that most of your documents have a *.wpd* extension. Macros have a *.wcm* extension, form documents have a *.frm* extension, and data files have a *.dat* extension. These extensions identify the particular file types to WordPerfect. They also help you to identify your files when you see them in the Open and Save As dialog boxes.

Your computer might be set up so that the extensions don't show. This is a choice that's made in the Windows desktop. It is not a WordPerfect setting. If you have been able to see all of the extensions on your document names as you've progressed through your training, that's good. If you haven't been able to see the extensions, check with your instructor to find out whether or not you should do Step-by-Step exercise 17.12. In this Step-by-Step exercise we will go to the Windows desktop and change the settings so your extensions show.

The Step-by-Step exercise is written for Windows 95. In the cases where the step is different in Windows 98, the Windows 98 instruction is shown in parentheses. Please note that if your classroom is networked, this Step-by-Step exercise may not work because the critical settings are locked.

STEP-BY-STEP 17.12 (optional)

1. Check with your instructor to see if you should proceed with this Step-by-Step exercise!

2. Click the dash button in the upper right corner of your WordPerfect window to minimize WordPerfect to a button on the Windows Task Bar.

3. Find the **My Computer** button on the desktop. Double click to open the My Computer dialog box, if it isn't already open.

4. Open the **View** menu and choose **Options** (in Windows 98, it's **Folder Options**). Then click the **View** tab.

5. At the bottom of the dialog box, be sure the final choice is deselected (Hide MS-DOS file extensions for file types that are registered). (In Windows 98, click to deselect **Hide file extensions for known file types**.)

6. In Windows 95, check to make sure that none of the other options are chosen.

7. Click **OK** to close the dialog box. Close the My Computer dialog box. Then click the **WordPerfect** button on the Task Bar to maximize your WordPerfect window again.

8. Display the Open dialog box and see if the extensions now show on your documents. If not, check with your instructor to see if something else needs to be done to display the extensions.

Summary

This has been an introduction to Merge and the kinds of tasks that can be completed using this feature. In this lesson you got the basics. You learned that:

- Merge is sometimes referred to as "mail merge."

- A data file contains the variable information for a merge.

- Every merge must have a form document.

- WordPerfect helps you insert the fields for your form document by making the data source field names readily available.

- To join a data source with a form document, all you need to do is tell WordPerfect to merge and then name the files to be merged.

- Data files can be in text format or table format.

- Data files can be edited after they have been created.

- You can prepare an envelope for each letter as part of a merge.

- Keyboard Merge is used for situations where a small number of letters or forms are prepared at one time.

In the next three lessons you will continue to work with Merge and explore some of the ways you can put it to work for you.

MATCHING

Write the letter of the term or phrase from Column 2 that best matches the description in Column 1.

<table>
<tr><td>**Column 1**</td><td>**Column 2**</td></tr>
</table>

_____ **1.** One complete entry in a list.

_____ **2.** The document prepared to be merged with a list.

_____ **3.** Dozens of special codes used to help WordPerfect perform merges.

_____ **4.** One piece of data in a record.

_____ **5.** Press Alt+Enter to start this merge again.

_____ **6.** A file generally made up of some kind of list.

A. Mail merge

B. Merge codes

C. Record

D. Field

E. Form document

F. Data source

G. Table Data File

H. Keyboard merge

I. Keyboard codes

MULTIPLE CHOICE

Circle the best answer to each of the following statements.

7. A data source may consist of as many as _____ fields.
- **A.** 25
- **B.** 255
- **C.** 55
- **D.** 555

8. A form document contains _____ codes.
- **A.** ENDFIELD
- **B.** ENDRECORD
- **C.** FIELD
- **D.** FILE

9. The default is to merge all documents
- **A.** onto one page.
- **B.** onto as few pages as possible.
- **C.** onto two pages per record if possible.
- **D.** onto one page per record.

10. When a merge is completed between a form letter and mailing list, the insertion point will be
- **A.** at the beginning of the first letter.
- **B.** at the end of the first letter.
- **C.** at the beginning of the last letter.
- **D.** at the end of the last letter.

LESSON 17 PROJECT

This project will consist of several small tasks. Work carefully but efficiently. How much can you do without referring back to the lesson?

PROJECT 17A

Create a memo form with KEYBOARD codes. It should look like Figure 17-18 when you finish. The instructions will help you set up your form.

1. Create a form document. There is no associated data source. Center the heading in bold, all capital letters with a 20-pt. type size. Use a font face of your choice.

FIGURE 17-18
Memo Form

MEMORANDUM

TO: KEYBOARD(memo recipient)
FROM: KEYBOARD(memo author)
DATE: DATE
SUBJECT: KEYBOARD(subject of memo)

KEYBOARD(body of memo)

2. Display the Ruler and remove the tab stop at 1.5". Set a Right tab at 1.75". Tab once and key **TO:**. Tab again and insert the KEYBOARD code as shown. Press Enter twice to separate the parts of the opening lines with a double space. Follow the same procedure for the four opening lines. Use the DATE button on the Merge Bar for the date.

3. After inserting the KEYBOARD code for the body of the memo, save the file as **memo** (with the *.frm* extension). Return the insertion point to the top of the memo and play the **pf** macro. Then close the file, saving it again as **memo.frm**.

FIGURE 17-19
Records for Project 17B

```
Mr. Miguel Zedillo              Mr. Kim Lee
Bits and Chips                  Lee Electronics
441 Main Street                 42 Leeward Way
Springvale, ME 04083ENDFIELD    Leeds, ME 04263
Mr. ZedilloENDFIELD             Mr. Lee
multimediaENDFIELD              COM
Andreas WernerENDFIELD          Pedro Costilla
2 p.m.ENDFIELD                  8:30 a.m.
Thursday, March 23ENDFIELD      Monday, March 20

Mrs. Rosemary Waldman
Wally's Wallpaper Shop
554 Walnut Street
Waldo, ME 04915
Mrs. Waldman
image printing and plotting
Marcus Schmidt
1 p.m.
Friday, March 24
```

PROJECT 17B

Create a data file using the data in Figure 17-19. Use the following field names: *customer, greeting, area of interest, representative, time, date*. In this data file the entire customer name and address will be

(continued on next page)

keyed into one field. That means you must press Ctrl+Enter following the customer name, the name of the business, and each line of the mailing address. After the ZIP code, press Enter to move the insertion point to the text box for the greeting. Follow the usual procedure to enter the data for the three records. Note that the ENDFIELD codes are shown for the first record only. When you finish, check your work. Each record should have six ENDFIELD codes, with the first one following the ZIP code number. Make any necessary corrections, and save the file as **im spec proj17b xxx**.

PROJECT 17C

Click the Go to Form button on the Merge Bar and choose Create. Create the form document illustrated in Figure 17-20. Begin by giving the Center Page(s) command to center the current and subsequent pages. Press Enter four times following the date. Click the Insert Field button on the Merge Bar to help you in entering the FIELD codes.

When you finish, save the file as **im spec proj17c xxx**. Then play the **pf** macro to add the Path and Filename code in the footer. Save the file again.

FIGURE 17-20
Form Document for Project 17C

```
DATE

FIELD(customer)

Dear FIELD(greeting):

Thank you for choosing Image Specialists to install imaging equipment
in your company.  As we agreed in our phone conversation yesterday,
part of our service to your company is to provide training for those
employees who will be using the imaging equipment.

Our consultant for FIELD(area of interest) equipment,
FIELD(representative), will meet you at your company at FIELD(time) on
FIELD(date) to discuss your company's needs and how the installation
of the FIELD(area of interest) equipment will be handled.  At that
time, arrangements for the training of your employees will be made.

Again, the staff of Image Specialists would like to thank you for your
confidence in our organization.  We are looking forward to providing
you with the best in FIELD(area of interest) equipment and service.

Sincerely,


(your name)
Imaging Manager
```

PROJECT 17D

Click the Merge button on the Form File Merge Bar to merge your form document and data file. Click the Envelopes button in the Perform Merge dialog box. You'll only need to enter one FIELD code—*customer*—for the mailing address on the envelopes.

Complete the merge. Check the letters and envelopes carefully. If everything looks good, print all three letters and envelopes. If the spacing around the variable information is incorrect or if something is wrong with the format of your letter, make the appropriate corrections to the form document or data file, save the files again, and then merge again, printing the letters and envelopes. Save the merged file as **im spec proj17d xxx** and close all files.

CRITICAL THINKING ACTIVITY

You have just completed a merge between a letter (form document) and the mailing list of all club members (data source). As you proofread the merged documents, you notice that the names in the inside address run together. What is the first thing you should check and how would you fix this problem?

PUTTING MERGE TO WORK

In Lesson 17 you learned the terminology associated with Merge and the basics of creating form documents and data files. You learned to combine those form documents and data files into finished documents. Best of all, you learned that a great deal of time can be saved by using Merge to streamline your work.

In Lesson 18 you will learn that there are a number of things you can do to expand the power of Merge in your work. None of the applications here are difficult, providing you take the time to think about what you are doing and how you are being asked to do it. What's more, these applications might give you some ideas about how you can use Merge in your work.

Planning Data Files

While you can break up your data files into as many parts as you wish, you learned in Lesson 17 that the smaller the pieces of information in each field, the more flexible your data file will be.

Usually you know ahead of time how the information in a data file will be used. You can configure the fields in the records so that they will best fit your needs. In designing a data file, it is important to remember that all records in the entire file must be prepared in the same way. Figure 18-1 illustrates four possible schemes that might be used for a data file. All four schemes include the same information.

Look at Scheme 4. Notice that the entire name and address section is one field. This arrangement doesn't allow you to work individually with the parts of a person's name. The same is true of Scheme 2. Note that the title is separate, but the entire name is in one field.

You could debate the advantages of each of the schemes. Each of the illustrated schemes is best for a certain situation. Most important is that you understand the options so you can make an educated choice when asked to create a data file.

		Scheme 1	Scheme 2	Scheme 3	Scheme 4
Field	1	title	title	title	mailing address
Field	2	first name	name	first name	telephone
Field	3	middle initial	company	last name	
Field	4	last name	street address	company	
Field	5	company	city	street address	
Field	6	street address	state	city, state ZIP	
Field	7	city	ZIP	telephone	
Field	8	state	telephone		
Field	9	ZIP			
Field	10	telephone			

Missing Data

Notice that in Scheme 1 a separate field is used for the middle initial. If you don't know the initial, an ENDFIELD code must still be included for that field. You must have the same number of ENDFIELD codes in each record of a file.

It is not unusual to not know all of the information called for in a data file. The way you deal with the missing data differs, however, depending on what information is missing and where it should be positioned when the merge is completed.

- **Data on a line by itself**. If the missing data is a company name, for example, it will usually fall on a line by itself. WordPerfect is set to delete a line if it doesn't include any information. You can change this setting in the *Options* portion of the Perform Merge dialog box.

- **Data between other variables**. If the missing data is a middle initial as discussed above, additional merge codes need to be inserted to deal with it. If you don't, WordPerfect will leave two spaces between the adjacent words. In this case, it would be the space before AND AFTER the missing initial.

Let's create a data file where each record has 13 fields. Then we'll experiment with the way the data can be used in several kinds of merges.

S TEP-BY-STEP ➡ 18.1

1. Beginning in a new document window, create a new data file. Use the following field names: *account number, title, first name, middle initial, last name, company, street, city, state, ZIP, phone, amount due, months overdue.*

2. Enter the three records for this data file using the data in Figure 18-2. Save the file as **flowers 18-1 xxx.dat**.

(continued on next page)

293

3. Use **Go to Form** to create a form document that looks like Figure 18-3. Save the form document as **flowers 18-1 xxx.frm**.

4. Click the **Merge** button on the Form File Merge Bar to display the Perform Merge dialog box. It should show that you are merging the current document with **flowers 18-1 xxx.dat**. Complete the merge.

5. When your merge is finished, all three addresses will be on separate pages. Open the **View** menu and choose **Draft** so you can see all three at once.

6. Look at the three sets of information. Note the following:
   a. No blank line was left for Mr. Bloom's missing company name.
   b. Look at the extra space between first and last names for the other two customers. This space is so large because you spaced before and after the FIELD code for the middle initial, which isn't included for either of those customers.

7. Close the file without saving. You will be returned to your form document. Keep the form document and the data file open.

FIGURE 18-2
Records for Step-by-Step 18.1

account number	3349	2399	5488
title	Mr.	Mrs.	Ms.
first name	Bill	Daisy	Pearl
middle initial	B.		
last name	Bloom	Ditson	Poppy
company		Dixie's Dilemma	Puppies and Pets
street	543 Bixby Street	7632 Ann Street	6732 Polk Street
city	Bloomington	Dixonville	Pittsburgh
state	OK	DE	WI
ZIP	74562	19811	54461
phone	405-555-9975	302-555-1490	715-555-4453
amount due	789.56	45.39	125.90
months overdue	1	4	2

FIGURE 18-3
Form Document for Step-by-Step 18.1

```
FIELD(title) FIELD(first name) FIELD(middle initial) FIELD(last name)
FIELD(company)
FIELD(street)
FIELD(city), FIELD(state) FIELD(ZIP)

FIELD(amount due)
```

Let's address the problem of the missing middle initial, first. Then we'll learn about some other options. The WordPerfect Merge language contains a large number of powerful commands, each designed for a particular job. Two of those commands can solve the problem of the missing middle initials.

Figure 18-4 illustrates the same portion of a form document illustrated in Figure 18-3. The IFNOTBLANK and ENDIF commands tell WordPerfect that if the initial is there, it should be included. If it is not included, the FIELD code for the middle initial should be ignored. The black dots indicate where the spaces should go. (Note that because the merge commands take so much room, the first line of the form document is wrapped to the next line. It will be OK when you merge.)

FIGURE 18-4
Form Document with IFNOTBLANK and ENDIF Codes

```
FIELD(title)•FIELD(first name)•IFNOTBLANK(middle initial)FIELD(middle
initial)•ENDIF FIELD(last name)
FIELD(company)
FIELD(street)
FIELD(city),•FIELD(state)•FIELD(ZIP)

FIELD(amount due)
```

Let's amend the **flowers 18-1 xxx.frm** file to include the IFNOTBLANK and ENDIF codes.

S TEP-BY-STEP ⇒ 18.2

1. With **flowers 18-1 xxx.frm** showing in the window, use **Save As** to save the file as **flowers 18-2 xxx.frm**.

2. Leave the space following the *first name* field, and delete to the end of the line with **Ctrl+Del**.

3. Click the **Merge Codes** button on the Form File Merge Bar to open the Insert Merge Codes dialog box. It should look like Figure 18-5. If necessary, point to the dialog box name and drag the box down so you can see your work.

4. Key **ifn** to move the highlight to **IFNOTBLANK**. Click the **Insert** button.

5. WordPerfect will ask you for the field in question. Key **middle initial** and press **Enter**.

6. Click the **Insert Field** button to open the Insert Field Name or Number dialog box. Drag this box down beside the other one. Then double click **middle initial** to enter a FIELD code for the middle initial.

FIGURE 18-5
Insert Merge Codes Dialog Box

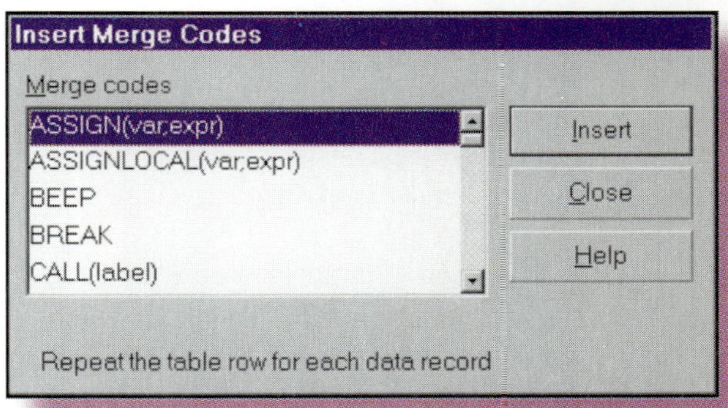

7. Space once with the space bar. Click in the Insert Merge Codes dialog box to activate it. Scroll back through the codes to find the **ENDIF** code. Click **Insert** to insert it. Then click **Close** to close the dialog box.

(continued on next page)

2 9 5

8. Double click **last name** in the Insert Field Name or Number dialog box to insert the FIELD code for the last name. Close the dialog box.

9. Compare your form document with Figure 18-4. Do you have a space only in the places marked with a dot in the figure? When everything is correct, save your file again as **flowers 18-2 xxx.frm**. Keep it open.

Now let's merge the two files and see if the extra space in the name has been taken care of.

STEP-BY-STEP 18.3

1. Click the **Merge** button on the Merge Bar to merge the current file with **flowers 18-1 xxx.dat**. (You may need to go to your files to select the data file.) Complete the merge.

2. Change to **Draft** view so you can compare the three merged pages. Reveal your codes, if

necessary, to be sure that the first and last names for Mrs. Ditson and Ms. Poppy have only one space separating them. Return to **Page** view.

3. Close the file without saving it. Keep the form document and the data file open.

Now that you've learned how to remove that extra space when information is missing on the same line with other FIELD codes, let's look at some of the options available during a merge.

Merge Options

Usually when you merge, you want each record to end up on a page by itself. Letters would look pretty funny, for example, if one began where the other left off, all on the same page. Sometimes, however, you want the records to merge onto one page. It would have been easier to compare the records in the merge you just completed if all three sets of information had been on one page.

The Merge Options dialog box offers you the place to change that setting. It also allows you to make multiple copies of a merge, and it allows you to tell WordPerfect not to remove the blank line that results from a missing field if you should want it to appear.

Let's try our merge one more time and work with all of these options.

STEP-BY-STEP 18.4

1. Check the bottom of your form document. The FIELD code for Amount Due should be followed by two hard returns. If the hard returns aren't there, please add them.

2. Click the **Merge** button on the Merge Bar to display the Perform Merge dialog box. Then click the **Options** button to open the Perform Merge Options dialog box (see Figure 18-6).

296

3. Click the **Separate . . .** item at the top to deselect it.

4. Change Number of copies . . . to **2**.

5. Change the *Remove Blank Line* button to **Leave Blank Line**. Click **OK**.

6. Back in the Perform Merge dialog box, click **Merge**.

7. Save your merged file as **flowers 18-4 xxx**. Print it and keep it open as you read on.

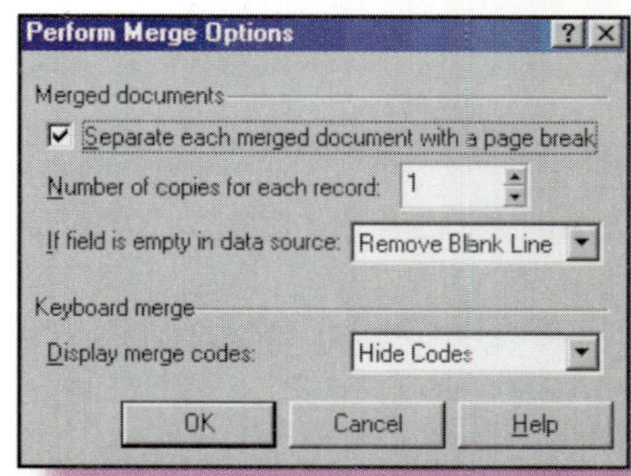

FIGURE 18-6
Perform Merge Options Dialog Box

Look at your merged file. Notice the following things about the file:

■ Each person appears twice. You asked for two of each in the Perform Merge Options dialog box.

■ All six records appear on the same page. You requested that, too.

■ Note that Mr. Bloom has a blank line in both occurrences of his address. What's supposed to be in that blank line? If you answered that the company name is missing, you are correct. In your earlier merges that blank line was suppressed. You told WordPerfect to leave the blank line in this merge.

After you've changed some of the options in a merge, it is important that you remember to click the Reset button if you wish to return to the default settings. Since your next merge will be quite different from this one, let's finish up the previous Step-by-Step exercise and take care of Reset.

S TEP-BY-STEP ▷ 18.5

1. Close **flowers 18-4 xxx**. You don't need to save it again.

2. Back in the form document, click the **Merge** button on the Merge Bar. Click the **Reset** button and then the **Close** button.

3. Keep the form document and the data file open for the next Step-by-Step exercise.

POSTNET Bar Codes

POSTNET bar codes can be added to any of your envelopes. If you are working with a single letter and are creating an envelope, you only need to go to Options and tell WordPerfect where you'd like the bar code—above or below the address.

When you merge, you must have the ZIP code in a field by itself to add bar codes to your envelopes. In the next Step-by-Step exercise we'll convert your **flowers** form document into a brief letter. Then we'll merge. We'll include envelopes, and we'll add POSTNET bar codes to the envelopes.

STEP-BY-STEP 18.6

1. With **flowers 18-2 xxx.frm** showing in the window, use **Save As** to save the file as **flowers 18-6 xxx.frm**.

2. Delete the *Amount Due* section from the form. Replace it with a greeting that begins with **Dear** and includes the title and last name. Put a colon at the end of the greeting.

3. Return to the top of the document and tell WordPerfect to center the current and subsequent pages. Insert the DATE merge code and press **Enter** four times.

4. Position the insertion point a double space below the greeting and prepare the rest of the letter, using the information in Figure 18-7.

5. When you finish, check your work over carefully. Play the **pf** macro, and save your document again as **flowers 18-6 xxx.frm**.

FIGURE 18-7
Text for Step-by-Step 18.6

```
SUBJECT: Account #FIELD(account number)

It has been a great pleasure doing business with you for a number of
years.  In all likelihood, the business relationship between our
companies has benefitted both our company and yours.

We are concerned, however, about your overdue account in the amount of
$FIELD(amount due).  Your account is now FIELD(months overdue) months
overdue, and we will have to put you on our cash-only account list if
we don't hear from you within 10 days.

Please maintain your good credit and send us a check for $FIELD(amount
due) today.

Sincerely,

GAILLARDIA GARDEN SUPPLY



Gabby Gaillardia, Account Manager
```

Now let's prepare the merge and tell WordPerfect to put the POSTNET bar code on each envelope. We'll set the option and then identify the field that contains the ZIP code number.

S TEP-BY-STEP ⟩ 18.7

1. With **flowers 18-6 xxx.frm** showing in your window, click the **Merge** button on the Merge Bar to open the Perform Merge dialog box.

2. Choose **Envelopes** and enter the FIELD codes to address the envelope. Use IFNOTBLANK and ENDIF to insert the middle initials.

3. Press **Enter** following the ZIP code and find **POSTNET (string)** in the Merge Codes. Insert that code.

4. With the insertion point between the parentheses, insert ZIP from the Insert Field Name dialog box. Close both *insert* boxes. The address on your envelope will look like Figure 18-8.

5. Click the **Merge** button and complete the merge.

FIGURE 18-8
Envelope Field Codes

```
FIELD(first name) IFNOTBLANK(middle initial)FIELD(middle
initial) ENDIF FIELD(last name)
FIELD(company)
FIELD(street)
FIELD(city), FIELD(state) FIELD(ZIP)
POSTNET(FIELD(ZIP))
```

6. Look at your letters and envelopes. Is the spacing correct around the variables in the letters? Do the envelopes contain the POSTNET bar codes below the addresses? If not, close the merged file without saving. Can you go back and think your way through the problem?

7. Read through the letter to Bill Bloom. Can you find an error that needs to be corrected?

8. When your letters and envelopes are correct, save the merged file as **flowers 18-7 xxx**. Print all three letters and envelopes and close all three files without saving again.

Merge into Tables

A different set of commands is used if you wish to merge into a table format. When you do this, you begin with a table that's too small to contain all of the records. WordPerfect will make the table the correct size for the merge.

Look at Figure 18-9. The following three new codes are chosen from the Merge Codes list on the Merge Bar:

- **LABEL(top)** tells WordPerfect where to loop back to in merging the records. It should be placed in the first cell of merged text. Put the first FIELD code directly after the LABEL code.

- **NEXTRECORD** must be in the cell with the final FIELD code. It tells WordPerfect to go to the next record (Obviously!).

- **GO(top)** tells WordPerfect to loop back to the *top* label with the information for the next record.

Name	Amount Due	Months Overdue
LABEL(top)FIELD(title) FIELD(first name) IFNOTBLANK(middle initial)FIELD(middle initial) ENDIF FIELD(last name)	FIELD(amount due)	FIELD(months overdue)NEXTRECORD
GO(top)		

Let's perform a merge using this form document so you can see how the LABEL and NEXTRECORD codes work.

S TEP-BY-STEP ▷ 18.8

1. Beginning in a new document window, create a 3-column by 3-row table. Key the column headings, as shown in Figure 18-9, and position the insertion point in Cell A2.

2. Open the **Tools** menu, choose **Merge**, and then choose **Create Document**. Tell WordPerfect to convert the file in the active window to a form document. Use **flowers 18-1 xxx.dat** as the associated data source.

3. Click the **Merge Codes** button to open the list of merge codes from which you may choose the LABEL, NEXTRECORD, and GO codes. For both the LABEL and GO codes, key **top** in the label box. Click the **Insert Field** button to get the fields for the names, the amount overdue, and the number of months overdue. Insert the spaces between the name codes as before.

4. When you finish creating the form document so it looks somewhat like Figure 18-9, save the file as **flowers 18-8 xxx.frm**.

5. Merge the form document with **flowers 18-1 xxx.dat**. Check your final table. Is the spacing between the parts correct?

6. Format the table to make it attractive. Give it the title **OVERDUE ACCOUNTS**.

7. Save the finished document as **accounts 18-8 xxx**. Use your **pf** macro to insert the Path and Filename code. Print the file and save it again.

8. Close all open files.

Step-by-Step exercise 18.8 provided a small example of how you can use tables as form documents for merges. Regardless of the size of the table or the number of records, the three special merge codes that made Step-by-Step exercise 18.8 work will be the same.

Document Assembly

Another way you can use Merge to speed up the preparation of documents is to put information that is used repeatedly into the fields of a data file, and retrieve those pieces of text to make up a customized document. This prerecorded text is sometimes called *standard text,* or *boilerplate.*

A data file to be used for document assembly doesn't have named fields. In fact, you never really HAVE TO name your fields as you have done for your previous data files. You can let WordPerfect number the fields and just work with field numbers.

Let's begin to learn about document assembly by creating a data file. Then we'll learn how to use the information in that data file.

S TEP-BY-STEP 18.9

1. Beginning in a new document window, open the **Tools** menu and choose **Merge**. Then choose **Create Data**.

2. In the Create Data File dialog box click **OK**. In the Number of Fields dialog box click **Cancel**. Click on the blank page to position your insertion point there. The Data File Merge Bar will be at the top.

3. Key the first sentence in Figure 18-10. Space two times following the period. Then either click the **End Field** button on the Merge Bar or press **Alt+Enter**. WordPerfect will insert an ENDFIELD code and a hard return.

4. Key the second sentence in Figure 18-10. Follow the same procedure until all three sentences have been keyed and are followed by ENDFIELD codes.

5. Check your work and make any necessary corrections. With your insertion point on the line below the third field, open the **Insert**

menu and choose **File**. Insert **ziepke.dat** from the student **datafile** folder to give you the other 20 fields in the data file.

6. Check the spacing. Each field should begin on a new line and be followed by an ENDFIELD code.

7. Use **Save As** to save the file as **ziepke 18-9 xxx.dat** and close it.

FIGURE 18-10
Three Fields for the Ziepke Data File

```
Thank you for your phone call
regarding our line of automated
office equipment. ENDFIELD
Thank you for your letter
inquiring about our automated
office equipment. ENDFIELD
Thank you for stopping at our
booth at the recent PC trade
show in your area. ENDFIELD
```

Now let's see how we can use all of this standard text to create letters responding to inquiries by potential customers. In Step-by-Step exercise 18.10 you will prepare a form document that contains four skeleton letters. Each letter will look somewhat like the first letter, which is illustrated in Figure 18-11. The four letters will be separated by hard page breaks. When you merge, all four letters can be merged with the data file at one time. Follow these steps to create your form document.

1. Beginning in a new document window, create a form document using **ziepke 18-9 xxx.dat** as the associated data file.

2. Use the **Center current and subsequent page(s)** command.

3. Click the **Date** button on the Merge Bar to insert a DATE code. Press **Enter** four times.

4. Key the name and address of the potential customer, as shown in Figure 18-11. Key the greeting as shown and press **Enter** twice.

5. Click the **Insert Field** button on the Merge Bar and insert Fields 1 and 4 for the first paragraph. Do not space between the two FIELD codes. The spaces between sentences were taken care of when the sentences were keyed.

FIGURE 18-11
First Letter in Document Assembly Form Document

```
DATE


Mr. Samuel Sampson
14 Singletary Circle
South Bend, SD 77401

Dear Mr. Sampson:

FIELD(1)FIELD(4)

FIELD(6)FIELD(7)FIELD(11)

FIELD(13)FIELD(19)FIELD(21)

FIELD(23)
```

FIGURE 18-12
Data for Step-by-Step 18.10

```
Miss Sing Ho Lee, 992 Lighthouse Lane, Los Altos, AR 77227
Paragraph 1: Fields 2 and 5
Paragraph 2: Fields 10, 12, and 14
Paragraph 3: Fields 15 and 17
Paragraph 4: Field 23

Mrs. Stella Severson, 17 Sensenbrenner Lane, Sarasota, NC 32413
Paragraph 1: Fields 3 and 5
Paragraph 2: Field 9
Paragraph 3: Fields 18, 20, and 22
Paragraph 4: Field 17
Paragraph 5: Field 23

Mr. James Jillian, 731 Jackman Way, Jonesboro, WI 54911
Paragraph 1: Fields 1 and 10
Paragraph 2: Fields 12, 22, and 11
Paragraph 3: Field 16
Paragraph 4: Field 23
```

6. Press **Enter** twice and insert the FIELD codes for Fields 6, 7, and 11.

7. Repeat the procedure until you have entered the FIELD codes, as shown in Figure 18-11.

8. Press **Ctrl+Enter** to move the insertion point to a new page. Create a letter for Miss Sing Ho Lee using the information in Figure 18-12.

When you finish the letter for Miss Lee, create one for Mrs. Severson and another for Mr. Jillian.

9. When you finish all four form letters, check your work carefully. Then save the file as **ziepke 18-10 xxx.frm**. Play the **pf** macro and close the file, saving it again.

With the form letters prepared, you are ready to merge them with the data file. This will be easy for you. You've merged so many times already.

S TEP-BY-STEP ▷ 18.11

1. Beginning in a new document window, begin a merge. Identify the form document as **ziepke 18-10 xxx.frm** and the data source as **ziepke 18-9 xxx.dat**. In the Perform Merge dialog box, click the **Reset** button unless it is already grayed.

2. When you finish, look at your four letters. Do they look good? Do any adjustments need to be made? If spacing adjustments need to be made in the form document, close your completed merge without saving. Open the form document and make the corrections. Save the form document and close it. Then perform the merge again.

3. Save the merged document as **ziepke 18-11 xxx**. Print your four letters. Then close the document, saving it again when you close it.

Reference Document

The Step-by-Step exercise you just completed was easy to prepare because you were told which field numbers to include to suit the request for information from each of the four potential customers. If you were preparing letters on the job, however, you'd need to have the data file in front of you to know which sentences to include. And then you wouldn't know what the sentence numbers were.

For this reason, part of preparing standard text for a document assembly application is to prepare what's known as a *reference document*. That document includes the standard text and the field numbers. With a reference document, anyone can decide which sentences should be used in the form documents. The reference document might be used by the boss or by the administrative assistant. Imagine the scenario of a boss receiving a letter asking for information about a product. He or she could use the reference document to identify the sentences to be used in a "form letter" to be sent back to that prospective customer and jot those numbers on the letter for the assistant. Let's prepare a reference document for the data file in Step-by-Step exercise 18-9.

1. Beginning in a new document window, center **ZIEPKE ELECTRONICS**. Center **Standard Sentences** in bold a double space below the title. Press **Enter** twice.

2. Identify the document as a form document with **ziepke 18-9 xxx.dat** as the data source.

3. Key a **1.** at the left margin and press **Tab** for QuickIndent.

4. Click the **Insert Field** button on the Form File Merge Bar and double click **Field 1** to insert the FIELD code after the *1*. Press **Enter** twice. Unless your automatic bullets and numbers are turned off, the next numeral will appear automatically. Insert Field 2. The first part of your form document will look like Figure 18-13.

5. Continue keying numbers, using **Indent**, and entering FIELD codes until you run out of fields. (There are 23 of them.)

6. When you finish, check your work. Then save the file as **ziepke 18-12 xxx.frm**. Play your **pf** macro to insert the Path and Filename code at the bottom of all pages.

7. Save the file again and close it.

8. Use **Merge** to combine **ziepke 18-12 xxx.frm** with **ziepke 18-9 xxx.dat**.

9. When your merge is finished, look over the reference document. Then print it and close it, saving it as **reference 18-12 xxx**.

FIGURE 18-13
Beginning of Step-by-Step 18.12 Form Document

```
          ZIEPKE ELECTRONICS

          Standard Sentences

  1.    FIELD(1)

  2.    FIELD(2)
```

If the form document is kept, the reference document can be redone each time the standard text in the data file is revised.

Address Book

A feature apart from the data files used in merge applications is the CorelCENTRAL Address Book feature. This feature may be used to keep frequently used addresses, phone numbers, e-mail addresses, etc., together in one place. The information stored in the Address Book can be used on envelopes, letters, labels, mass mailings like those prepared with Merge, and e-mail (if you have a modem or network connection). You can also use the Address Book to dial phone and fax numbers.

The Address Book feature makes it possible for you to have multiple address books. Available books are listed at the left in the CorelCENTRAL section of the main Address Book window.

Create an Address Book

For practice, let's create an Address Book using the names and addresses you used for the Ziepke letters in Step-by-Step exercises 18.9 through 18.12. Then we'll see how those names and addresses can be used in a merge.

STEP-BY-STEP ⟹ 18.13

1. Beginning in a new document window, open the **Tools** menu and choose **Address Book**.

2. Look at the left side of the CorelCENTRAL Address Book dialog box. It should look somewhat like Figure 18-14. Is *Ziepke* in the CorelCENTRAL list? If *Ziepke* is there:

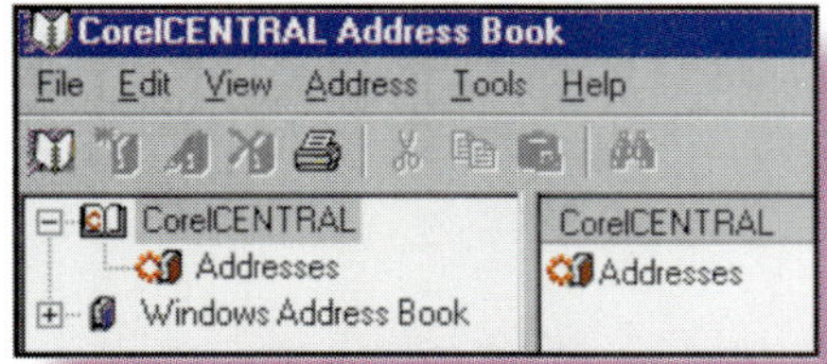

FIGURE 18-14
CorelCENTRAL Address
Book Dialog Box

   a. Click that book name and look at the names included in the book.

   b. Point to *Sing Ho Lee* and double click.

   c. Look at the tabs and the kinds of information that may be entered for Sing Ho. For this book, you will need the prefix, first name, last name, home address, home city, home state, and home ZIP code. Are all of those parts present? If not, turn to Figure 18-12 and complete the address.

   d. Check the other three addresses for completeness and make any necessary repairs.

3. If no *Ziepke* book appears, choose **File** and **Open**. Look for *Ziepke* in the list of closed books. If you find it, choose it. If no *Ziepke* book appears in that list, you will need to create one. Close the Open dialog box and follow these steps:

   a. Click the **File** menu and choose **New**. Affirm *CorelCENTRAL* by clicking **OK**. Key **Ziepke** as the name of the new book and click **OK**. *Ziepke* should now show in the CorelCENTRAL list at the left.

   b. Click **Ziepke** to choose that book. Open the **Address** menu and choose **New**. Choose **Person** and click **OK**.

   c. With the *General* tab chosen (see Figure 18-15), key Samuel Sampson's name and address (from Figure 18-11) into the appropriate text boxes.

   d. Click the **Personal** tab and choose the personal title from the **Prefix** drop-down list. Key the greeting. Click **OK**.

   e. Click the second button on the Toolbar (Create a new address entry) and follow the procedure in Steps 3c and 3d to enter the information about the other three customers in Figure 18-12. Be sure to supply appropriate greetings.

4. Close the Address Book.

FIGURE 18-15
Person Properties Dialog Box

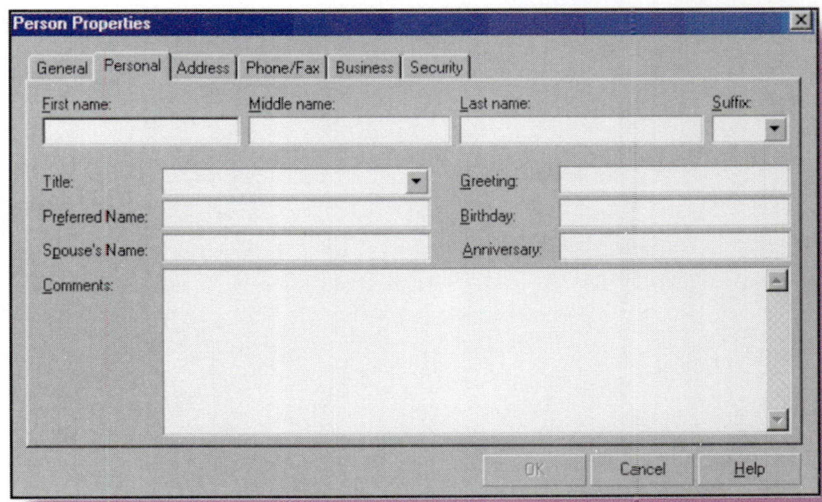

Merge with an Address Book

Now that you have an Address Book with which to work, let's use Merge to send a sample letter to the four addresses.

STEP-BY-STEP 18.14

1. Create a form document. In the Associate Form and Data dialog box, click **Associate an address book**.

2. In the drop-down menu beside that choice, change to **Ziepke** (see Figure 18-16). Then click **OK**.

3. In your document window, set up a form document, including the following features:
   a. Center pages vertically.
   b. Insert the DATE code using the Merge Bar.
   c. Insert FIELD codes using the **Insert Field** button. (Note that the available codes match the fields in the Address Book and that the *Greeting* field is near the bottom of the list.)

4. Key the short letter in Figure 18-17.

5. When your letter is finished, save it as **ziepke 18-14 xxx.frm**. Play your **pf** macro and save the file again.

6. Click the **Merge** button on the Merge Bar. Note that Form document is *Current Document* and Data source is *Ziepke*. Complete the merge.

7. Print the four short letters and close the file, saving it as **interest 18-14 xxx**.

FIGURE 18-16
Associate Form and Data Dialog Box

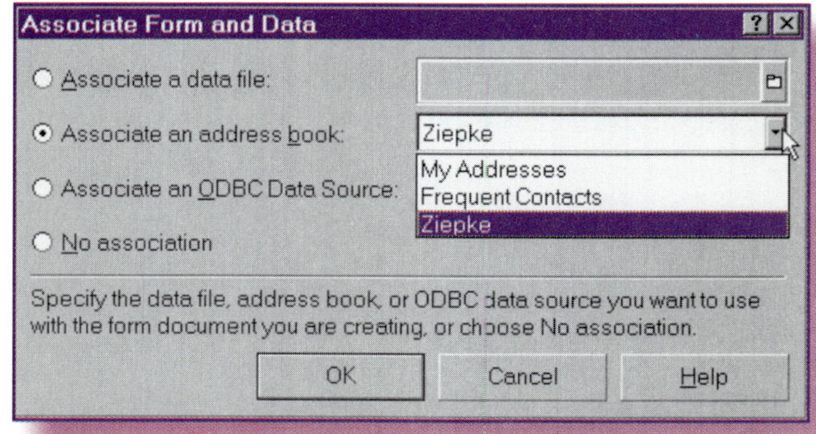

```
FIELD(Prefix) FIELD(First Name) FIELD(Last Name)
FIELD(Street)
FIELD(City), FIELD(State/Province) FIELD(Zip/Postal Code)

FIELD(Greeting):

Thank you for your interest in our company.  We look forward to doing
business with you.  Please keep in touch.

Sincerely,

ZIEPKE ELECTRONICS



Felix Rodriguez, Manager
```

Summary

This lesson took Merge several steps farther than the basics you learned in Lesson 17. In the process of discovering that WordPerfect Merge is a powerful tool, you learned the following:

- Data files can be arranged in a variety of ways.

- The smaller the chunks of data in a data file, the more flexibility you will have in your merge.

- WordPerfect takes care of data missing from a field if the field falls on a line by itself.

- WordPerfect merge codes may be used to deal with missing data if it falls between two other fields on the same line.

- If the ZIP code is in a field by itself, you can include a POSTNET bar code on your envelopes.

- Several special merge codes must be used to merge a data file into a table format.

- Merge can be used for boilerplate, or standard text, letters.

- WordPerfect's Address Book feature can be used for a variety of applications, including merging.

Before leaving Merge, it is important to note that in all of the Merge Step-by-Step exercises you've completed in Lessons 17 and 18, you have been instructed to save the data file, the form document, and the completed merge. In actual practice you probably won't ever save the documents that result from the completed merge. Having the form document and the data source makes it simple to remerge the documents, if necessary, and saving the same letter to a number of people uses disk space unnecessarily.

FILL IN THE BLANKS

Complete each of the following statements by writing your answer in the blank provided.

1. The smaller the pieces of information in each field, the more flexible your _____________________ will be.

2. The IFNOTBLANK and ____________ commands tell WordPerfect that if information is there, it should be included.

3. After you change options in the Perform Merge Options dialog box, it is important to click the ____________ button if you wish to return to the default settings.

4. If you wish to add the POSTNET bar codes to your envelopes in a merge, you must have the ________________ in a field by itself when you are setting up your data source.

5. When merging into tables, _____________________ tells WordPerfect where to loop back to in merging records.

6. When merging into tables, _____________________ must be in the cell with the final FIELD code.

7. WordPerfect's _______________________________ may be used to keep frequently used addresses, phone numbers, e-mail addresses, etc., together in one place.

TRUE/FALSE

Circle the T if the statement is true. Circle the F if it is false.

T   F   8. WordPerfect takes care of missing data from a field if the field falls on a line by itself.

T   F   9. In document assembly, a reference document is used as the form document.

T   F   10. Prerecorded text is sometimes called standard text, or boilerplate.

LESSON 18 PROJECT

Keyboard Merge can be combined with document assembly. It involves putting KEYBOARD codes in the fields of the data file prior to the merge. In this project we will revise two of the fields of the Ziepke data file and then merge that data file again with the form document you created for the Ziepke inquiries. Follow along carefully.

1. Open **ziepke 18-9 xxx.dat**. Save the file as **ziepke proj18 xxx.dat**.

2. Move the insertion point to Field 15 (you can see the field numbers at the right on the Application Bar).

3. Position the insertion point following the word *area* and key a comma and a space.

4. Click the Merge Codes button on the Merge Bar and key **keyb** to move the insertion point to the KEYBOARD code. Click Insert and key the prompt, as illustrated in Figure 18-18 Press Enter to enter the code. Key a comma.

FIGURE 18-18
Modified Fields for Lesson 18 Project

```
Our salesperson for your area, KEYBOARD(district salesperson), will
call you within the next few days.

The business card for our salesperson in your area, KEYBOARD(district
salesperson), is enclosed with this letter. Please call
KEYBOARD(him/her) at KEYBOARD(salesperson's telephone number) to
arrange for a demonstration of any of our products.
```

5. Follow the same procedure to put KEYBOARD codes in Field 16. Note that this field gets three KEYBOARD codes.

6. Save the file again with the same name and close it.

7. Merge **ziepke proj18 xxx.dat** with **ziepke 18-10 xxx.frm**. During the merge, you will be asked to key the information requested in the KEYBOARD codes. Your document will look like a mess when the prompt appears at the bottom of the window. When a prompt appears, key the required information and press Alt+Enter to move to the next prompt. Following is the information you'll need in the order you should enter it:

District Salesperson:	Joan Jackson
District Salesperson:	Amy Evans at 414-555-6755

(continued on next page)

8.   Save the four letters as **ziepke proj18 letters xxx**. Print only the letters that contain the information about district salespersons and close all files.

With this kind of merge, it is difficult to prepare envelopes. The regular Envelope feature (in the Format menu) can be used for the first letter in the merge. After printing the letters, you could prepare the first envelope and print it, then delete the first letter and prepare an envelope for the next letter, and so on. It doesn't seem to be very efficient, but it is one possible solution.

CRITICAL THINKING ACTIVITY

SCANS

You have recently gone on-line and have access to the Internet. One of the services you are using frequently is e-mail. What WordPerfect feature could be used to enhance your use of e-mail?

Sort, Extract, and Select

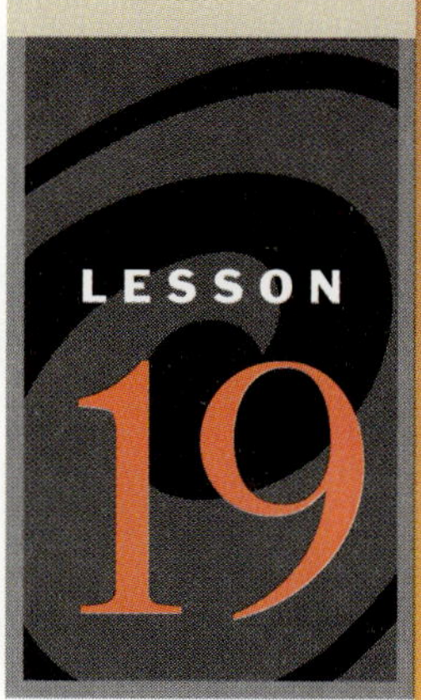

OBJECTIVES

Upon completion of this lesson, you will be able to:

- Use Line Sort.
- Use Paragraph Sort.
- Use Merge Sort.
- Use Table Sort.
- Extract and select records.

⏱ Estimated Time: 2 hours

In the last two lessons you've been working with Merge. While a variety of documents might be created using Merge, combining a standard, or shell, document (the form document) with a list of names and addresses is probably one of the most frequently used applications.

If the list of names and addresses to be merged is relatively small, hand sorting the documents for distribution after printing isn't a big problem. When the list is large, however, and post office requirements for ZIP code order are taken into account, hand sorting can be a big job.

With WordPerfect, hand sorting is unnecessary because WordPerfect has a tool called Sort that enables you to sort the records in a data file before it is ever merged with a form document. What's more, you get to direct the sort. The list can be sorted in any number of ways. For instance, a data file can be sorted in alphabetic order by name, in ZIP code order, by ZIP code and alphabetized within each ZIP code grouping, by company name, by amount owed, or by months overdue for payment.

Depending on your needs and the content of the data source, the list can be sorted by just about any other criteria. In addition, WordPerfect can be directed to select certain records from your lists.

Types of Sort

WordPerfect can be used to sort records in the following five formats:

Line	Any groupings of text separated from each other by a hard return or soft return.
Paragraph	Groupings of text separated by two hard returns.
Merge Data File	Rows in data files separated from each other with ENDRECORD codes.
Table Row	Horizontal rows of cells in WordPerfect tables.
Column	Parallel columns separated by hard page breaks.

Let's learn about Sort as you practice some examples in each of the types except Column Sort. We didn't prepare any parallel columns because tables do the work so much more easily.

Line Sort

We'll begin with Line Sort. Follow the steps in Step-by-Step exercise 19.1.

STEP-BY-STEP 19.1

1. Key the following list of names in a single column at the left margin. Add your name as indicated.

Alberta	**Dale R.**
Carol	**Judy Anne**
Elizabeth	**Pedro**
Walter	**Betty**
Earl	**Carol**
(your name)	

2. With the list showing, open the **Tools** menu and choose **Sort** to display the Sort dialog box, as displayed in Figure 19-1.

3. If it is not already highlighted, select **First word in a line**. Click the **Edit** button and check the parameters in the middle of the Edit Sort dialog box: Alpha, Ascending, 1, and 1. Click **OK**.

4. Click **Sort**. Voila! Your list should instantly be alphabetized.

5. Save the list as **sort 19-1 xxx**. Play your **pf** macro to identify the file. Keep it open.

FIGURE 19-1
Sort Dialog Box

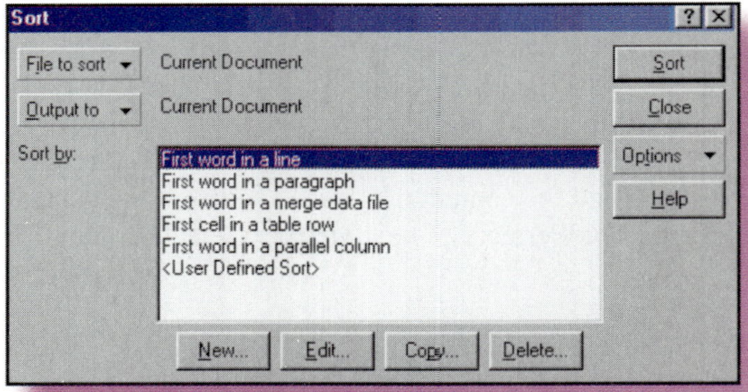

That was pretty easy, wasn't it? That's about as basic as Line Sort can be. The people in our list, however, probably wouldn't normally be sorted by first name. Let's give them last names and learn more about Line Sort.

In Step-by-Step exercise 19.2 we'll create a User Defined Sort category that will be edited for each sort in this lesson.

STEP-BY-STEP 19.2

1. With **sort 19-1 xxx** open in the window, use **Save As** to save the list as **sort 19-2 xxx**. Amend your list by adding a surname for each of the people in the list as follows:

   Alberta Weigel
   Betty Boneske
   Carol Anderson
   Carol Morgan
   Dale R. Nelson
   Earl Wiesemann
   Elizabeth Reichert
   Judy Anne Boneske
   Pedro DePino
   Walter Anderson

2. Add **Pam Anderson** to the list. Include your own last name.

3. Open the **Tools** menu and choose **Sort** to return to the Sort dialog box. Look at the Sort choices. Note that there is a choice for each type of sort listed at the beginning of this section.

4. Do you see *<User Defined Sort>* in the list? If so, choose it and click **Edit**. If not, click **New**. The Edit Sort or New Sort dialog box, illustrated in Figure 19-2, should appear.

5. Look at the dialog box. The **Line** button should be chosen in the *Sort by* section at the top. In the *Keys (sorting rules)* section, only one "Key" should appear. If your dialog box shows more than one, get rid of all but the first by clicking in the *Field* box for any additional Keys and then clicking the **Delete Key** button.

6. In the Key 1 section set Field at **1** and Word at **-1**, and click **OK** and then **Sort**. This will bring you back to your document, and the list should now be alphabetized by last name. (Don't worry about it if the Andersons are out of order for now.)

7. Save the list again as **sort 19-2 xxx**. Then open the **Tools** menu and choose **Sort** again so you can look at these dialog boxes as you learn about them.

FIGURE 19-2
Edit Sort Dialog Box

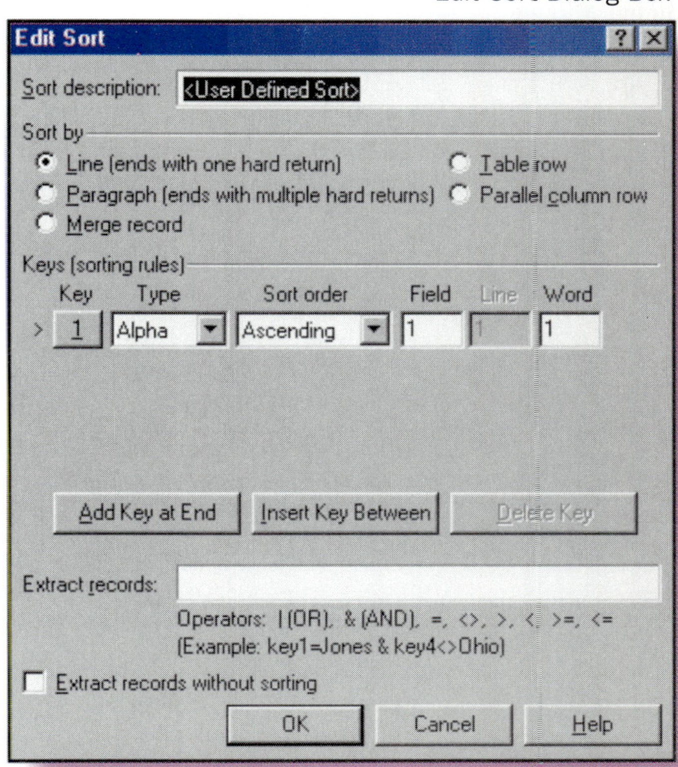

The *<User Defined Sort>* choice should be highlighted. We'll highlight that choice and choose Edit for all sorting in this course. On the job, you might wish to set the criteria for a specialized kind of sort you use often. Then you can name it so it is easy to choose from the list each time you need it. If you don't use a sort that's listed, it can be deleted to make room for those you DO use.

At the top of the Sort dialog box are a couple of naming options. You don't have to have a document showing in the window to sort it. You can direct WordPerfect to sort a file that is on disk and save it with a different name. Usually you will sort a document that's showing in the window. In that case, you won't work with File to sort and Output.

Now click Edit to open the Edit Sort dialog box. This dialog box is pretty simple, once you get a handle on it. In the *Keys (sorting rules)* section you can make your choices about how you want the document sorted. A "Key" is a term used to tell WordPerfect the priorities regarding how you want the list sorted. The default setting has only one Key, but you may set more Keys.

Because WordPerfect remembers your last sort, the current settings in the *Keys (sorting rules)* section for Key 1 are:

Alpha   Ascending   Field 1   Word -1

- **Type**. You can set your sort to be alphabetic (Alpha) or Numeric.

  - **Alpha** may contain words, a combination of letters and numerals, or numbers of equal length, like Social Security or telephone numbers.

  - **Numeric** includes numbers of unequal length or numbers containing periods or commas, like 3,451 or $5.30.

- **Sort Order**. You may change the order from Ascending (A to Z) to Descending (Z to A).

- **Field**. This is the same kind of field with which you worked in Merge. In Line Sort, fields are separated by tabs or indents. We'll work with fields shortly.

- **Line**. This choice is currently grayed because it is used only with Merge or Paragraph Sort.

- **Word**. *Alberta* is Word 1 and *Weigel* is Word 2, but *Anne* is word 2, also. To be consistent in identifying the last name, count from the right by adding a hyphen. In your list, the last name is always Word -1 of Field 1.

We'll work with some of the other choices in the dialog box shortly. Now we'll learn how to deal with first and last names and more information. Then we'll set some tab stops for Step-by-Step exercises coming up.

The names in your list are considered Field 1 of the information to be sorted. The addresses you'll add in Step-by-Step exercise 19.3 will be considered Field 2 information because they will be separated from Field 1 by a tab. Then we'll sort the list—first by ZIP code and then by city. As always, read through the entire Step-by-Step exercise before beginning.

STEP-BY-STEP 19.3

1. With **sort 19-2 xxx** open, save the file as **sort 19-3 xxx**.

2. Choose **Tools**, **Sort**, and then **<User Defined Sort>**. Click **Edit**. In the Edit Sort dialog box click the **Add Key at End** button. The criteria is Field 1, Word 1 (the first name).

3. Perform the sort. Are Carol, Pam, and Walter Anderson in order, now? Let's adjust the file and include addresses.

4. Display the Ruler. Clear all tabs. Set a Left tab at **3.5"** and a Decimal tab at **6.75"**.

5. Each city, state, and ZIP code in Column 2 represents Field 2 of the list. Key the addresses as follows:

   a. Press **End** to move your insertion point to the end of Carol Anderson's name and press **Tab**.

   b. Key Carol's city, state, and ZIP code, as shown in Figure 19-3.

   c. Press the down arrow key and **Tab** to position the insertion point for Pam's information.

   d. Use hard spaces (**Ctrl+space bar**) between the parts of *Butte des Morts*, *Stevens Point*, and *Wisconsin Dells* to make WordPerfect think each of them is all one word.

   e. Include your own address opposite your name.

6. Let's sort by ZIP code. Open the Edit Sort dialog box. Set Key 1 as follows:

Alpha Ascending   Field 2   Word -1

FIGURE 19-3
Addresses for Step-by-Step 19.3 Sort

```
Carol Anderson        Stevens Point, WI 54481
Pam Anderson          Neenah, WI 54955
Walter Anderson       Phoenix, AZ 88471
Betty Boneske         Oshkosh, WI 54901
Judy Anne Boneske     Neenah, WI 54955
Pedro DePino          Butternut, WI 54914
Carol Morgan          Wisconsin Dells, WI 53965
(your name)           (your address)
Dale R. Nelson        Butte des Morts, WI 54927
Elizabeth Reichert    Milwaukee, WI 53211
Alberta Weigel        Hendersonville, NC 18739
Earl Wiesemann        Ladysmith, WI 54848
```

7. Leave Key 2 in place, but change it so the sort is by last name. To do that, change Word to **-1**. (Note that only two people have the same city. If you didn't set Key 2 at **-1**, Boneske might end up before Anderson after the sort.)

8. Click **OK** and then **Sort** to perform the sort. Check your list over to see if it did what you expected. Print it and save it again as **sort 19-3 xxx**. Keep it open.

STEP-BY-STEP 19.4

Can you sort this list by the name of the city? You're on your own. (HINT: The city is the first item in Field 2.) When you finish, keep the document open for Step-by-Step exercise 19.5.

Let's take this Step-by-Step exercise one step further and use it to learn about a Numeric Sort.

1. With your sort from Step-by-Step exercise 19.4 showing in the window, use **Save As** to save the file as **sort 19-5 xxx**.

2. Use a method similar to Step-by-Step exercise 19.3 to add the following dollar amounts at the Decimal tab you set. It doesn't matter who gets which number.

455.00	24.00	110.00
786.00	998.00	2390.00
15.00	567.00	1334.00
1199.00	3.00	1.50

3. Go to the Edit Sort dialog box. Set Key 1 at **Numeric Ascending 3 1**. (This is a Numeric Sort on Word 1 of Field 3. Do you understand that setting? By now, you should. If you don't understand, ask your instructor to help you. It's important!)

4. Click somewhere in the Key 2 line. Click the **Delete Key** button to delete Key 2.

5. Click **OK** and then **Sort** to perform the sort. Did the list rearrange so the person with the smallest debt is at the top?

6. Return to the Edit Sort dialog box. Change Key 1 from *Ascending* to **Descending**. Sort again. Were the results what you expected?

7. Play your **pf** macro to identify the document. Then print it and close it, saving it again as **sort 19-5 xxx** as you close it.

Congratulations! You are now an expert with Line Sort. All of the principles you learned here will be applied in the other kinds of Sort. Be sure you are comfortable with Line Sort before moving on.

Paragraph Sort

Anything separated by two hard returns can be sorted in Paragraph Sort. It can be one line or several, and the lines in the paragraph may end either with a soft return or a hard return. Paragraph Sort may be used to arrange bibliography entries in alphabetic order. You could also use Paragraph Sort for names and addresses. Let's increase the size of the **flowers** data file and merge it with a simple format. Then we'll be able to sort the list using Paragraph Sort.

1. Beginning in a new document window, open **flowers 18-1 xxx.dat**. Use **Save As** to save the file as **flowers xxx.dat**.

2. Position the insertion point at the end of the file. Go to the student **datafile** folder and insert **flowers**. You should now have 16 records in your file. Save the large file.

3. Click the **Go to Form** button and create a form document that looks like Figure 19-4. Press **Enter** twice following the *amount due* line.

4. Save the form document as **list 19-6 xxx.frm**. Prepare to merge it with **flowers xxx.dat**. In the Perform Merge dialog box click **Options** and tell WordPerfect not to put the merged records on separate pages.

5. Save the merged file as **flower list 19-6 xxx**. Play your **pf** macro to identify the file.

6. If your file extends to a third page, use **Make It Fit** to squeeze it onto two pages.

FIGURE 19-4
Form Document for Step-by-Step 19.6

```
FIELD(first name)  FIELD(last name)
FIELD(company)
FIELD(street)
FIELD(city),  FIELD(state)
FIELD(ZIP)
FIELD(amount due)
```

Look at the names, addresses, and amounts in the file. Each of those customers is considered a paragraph with regard to sorting. You can sort by just about any criteria.

S TEP-BY-STEP ➡ 19.7

1. With **flower list 19-6 xxx** showing in the window, go to the Edit Sort dialog box and click the **Paragraph** button at the top. (WordPerfect may have already done that for you.)

2. Set Key 1 to sort by last name. That's Line 1, Field 1, Word -1. Complete the sort and check your work.

3. Sort the list in the following ways:
   a. By amount due with the greatest number at the top (Numeric, Descending, Line -1, Field 1, and Word 1). Note that you can't count the line number from the top because some customers have a company name and others don't.
   b. By ZIP code (Alpha, Ascending, Line -2, Field 1, and Word -1).
   c. By state. (Can you figure it out?)
   d. By city name.

4. Resort the list so the last names of the customers are in alphabetic order.

5. Print the file and close it, saving it again as **flower list 19-6 xxx** as you close it. Close all open files.

That was a simple Step-by-Step exercise in Paragraph Sort. Obviously, it can be used for other kinds of paragraphs, as well as for the names and addresses of our blooming customers.

Merge Sort

In the previous Step-by-Step exercise using Paragraph Sort you got rid of the merge codes in the original list. In Merge Sort you work with the data files, complete with their merge codes. The ENDFIELD codes separate one field from another.

1. Open **flowers xxx.dat**. With the data file showing in the window, open the Edit Sort dialog box. If necessary, change to **Merge record**.

2. Sort alphabetically by the last name of the customer. (That's Field 5.) Check your work. Are Adelbert Aster and Bill Bloom at the top of the list?

3. Insert the correct field number and sort numerically by account number in Ascending order. Are Zola Zinnia and Charles Cosmos at the top of the list?

4. Change to Descending order. Are Mari Gold and Dandi Lyons at the top?

5. Change the field number and sort by the amount owed in Descending order. Are Gary Gardenia and Petunia Peters at the top?

6. Sort by ZIP code number in Ascending order. Are Rose Ramirez and Mari Gold at the top?

7. Close the file without saving it again.

Those sorts were easy because each field only contained one piece of information. Let's try something a little more challenging.

1. Open **im spec proj17b xxx.dat**. Save the file as **im spec 19-9 xxx.dat**. Study the fields. Note that the entire inside address is one field.

2. Note, too, that each customer has a company name. Delete the *Bits and Chips* line from Miguel Zedillo's record and close up the space.

3. Sort the list by last name. You should set Field 1, Line 1, and Word -1. You should get Lee, Waldman, and Zedillo.

4. Sort the list by ZIP code. (Because Field 1 has an unequal number of lines, you'll have to use Line -1. Did you remember that the best way to identify the ZIP code number on a line that includes city and state is by using Word -1? You should get Zedillo, Lee, and Waldman.

5. Close the file without saving and open **micro 17-6 xxx.dat**. Look at the way the fields are arranged.

6. Sort the list by last name. You should get Helmke, Noschang, Oppermann, and Weigel.

7. Sort the list by ZIP code. You should get Weigel, Oppermann, Noschang, and Helmke. Close the file without saving it.

As you can see, Merge Sort isn't difficult when you have an understanding of how the merge data files are organized. You should be able to sort any data file now. Let's look at a different kind of sort.

Table Sort

Table Sort is used for sorting the rows in a table. For sort purposes, table rows are divided into columns. Let's create a table to sort. Then we'll practice.

STEP-BY-STEP 19.10

1. Beginning in a new document window, merge **flowers 18-8 xxx.frm** with **flowers xxx.dat**. Look at the resulting table. It is unformatted, but that doesn't matter for our sort. Save it as **table 19-10 xxx**.

2. Select the entire table except the first row that contains the column headings. (When you select, the cells should stay all black, not just black in the center. If you drag your insertion point below the bottom of the table when selecting, you'll need to drag it back up into the table so the cells stay black.)

3. Open the Edit Sort dialog box. If necessary, choose the **Table row** button at the top. Then tell WordPerfect to sort the list by the last names of the customers.

4. Select all rows of the table except the first row again. Can you figure out how to sort the customers by amount owed—in Descending order? Do it. Then play your **pf** macro to identify the file. Print it and close it, saving it again.

In Step-by-Step exercise 19.10 you selected the rows to be sorted, so the row containing the column headings wasn't affected. This is an especially useful technique when you want to sort only part of a table. A better way, when you are sorting all of the data in a table, would be to use your table formatting knowledge to set the row containing the column headings as a Header Row. Then WordPerfect knows that the row must always stay at the top. To do this, you would position your insertion point in the row and choose Format, Row, and Header Row.

Now that you're so good with Sort, let's learn how we can work with only part of a list.

Extract

WordPerfect enables you to separate certain records from a list. There are several ways to do this. One of those ways is in the Edit Sort dialog box. Normally you will extract (or select) the records to be used from the data file before completing a merge. Let's work with the **flowers** file and learn to extract based on several criteria.

When you extract files, the original list is lost unless you have it saved. In this Step-by-Step exercise you will work with the **flowers** list of customers. BE CAREFUL not to save after you use Extract. If you do save, give your file a new name. Otherwise, your partial list will take the place of the complete list of customers on your disk.

1. Beginning in a new document window, open **flowers xxx.dat**. Go to the Edit Sort dialog box and set Key 1 at **Field 10** to point to the ZIP code numbers. Set an Alphabetic sort in Ascending order.

2. In the *Extract records* text box at the bottom, key **Key 1>55000**. (The *greater than* symbol is the shift of the period key.)

3. Perform the sort. You should end up with 8 customers, and the first two are Betty Blum and Lily Larsen. (If you press Ctrl+End and look at the *Pg* indicator, you'll see *10*. One of the records is the blank one in which your insertion point is positioned. The other is the Field Names record at the top.)

4. Close the file without saving and open **flowers xxx.dat** again.

5. This time we'll sort the customers alpha-betically, and we'll extract only those cus-tomers who owe more than $500.00. Set the sort and extract as follows:
   a. Set Key 1 for last names.
   b. Set Key 2 to identify the field containing amounts due. Remember that it is numeric.
   c. In the *Extract records* text box, key **Key 2>500.00.**
   d. Perform the sort and extract.

6. Check the records. You should have six records, beginning with Adelbert Aster and Bill Bloom. Close the file without saving.

Always check two things in the Edit Sort dialog box before beginning a sort:

- Make sure the setting at the top matches the kind of sort you are performing.

- Check the *Extract records* text box at the bottom. WordPerfect doesn't automatically clear the *Extract records* text box. If your next sort doesn't involve Extract, the formula must be deleted!

7. Open **flowers xxx.dat** again. Select the accounts where the balance is equal to or greater than 4 months overdue. (HINT: Identify the field to be sorted and put it in any Key. In the *Extract records* text box identify that Key and specify that it should be **=>4**.) Arrange the accounts in Ascending order according to the amount owed. THINK!

8. Check your work. You should end up with Petunia, Zola, Gina, Daisy, and Peter. If you didn't do it right, close the file without saving and try again. If you did it right, congratulate yourself and close the file without saving it.

Select Records

One more method of separating out records for a mailing is Select Records, which may take place during a merge. When you select records during the merge, your data file remains complete, but only the selected records will be used during the merge.

Select Records offers two options. You can specify conditions, like we did when we specified that the amount due should be in excess of $500.00, or you can manually select the records you wish to include. We'll try it both ways.

STEP-BY-STEP 19.12

1. Beginning in a new document window, fill in the Perform Merge dialog box to merge **list 19-6 xxx.frm** with **flowers xxx.dat**. Before clicking the **Merge** button, choose **Options** and deselect **Separate each merged document with a page break**. Click **OK**.

2. Back in the Perform Merge dialog box, click the **Select Records** button. Look at the Select Records dialog box. It should look like Figure 19-5.

3. Notice the two round buttons near the top. Click the **Mark records** button. In the *First field to display* box click the down arrow and choose **amount due** from near the bottom of the list. Then click **Update Record List**.

4. Look at the Record List. It should show the amounts due, with the number of months overdue in brackets. Go through the list and click to put a ✓ at the left of each account balance that is less than $100.00.

5. Complete the merge. It should include Daisy, Mari, Rose, Peter, Gina, and Dandi. (They might be in a different order. There is no way to arrange the records when you use Select Records.)

6. Save your merged file as **small 19-12 xxx** because it includes customers with small balances. Play the **pf** macro to identify the file, print it, save it again, and close it.

7. Return to the Perform Merge dialog box and choose **Select Records** again. This time, click the **Specify conditions** button. Click the arrow beside the text box under the word *Field* over the first column. Change to **amount due**.

(continued on next page)

8. In the *Cond 1* text box key **<100.00** to choose all accounts of less than $100.00. Complete the merge and look at the results. You should have the same six customers.

9. Close all files without saving.

FIGURE 19-5
Select Records Dialog Box

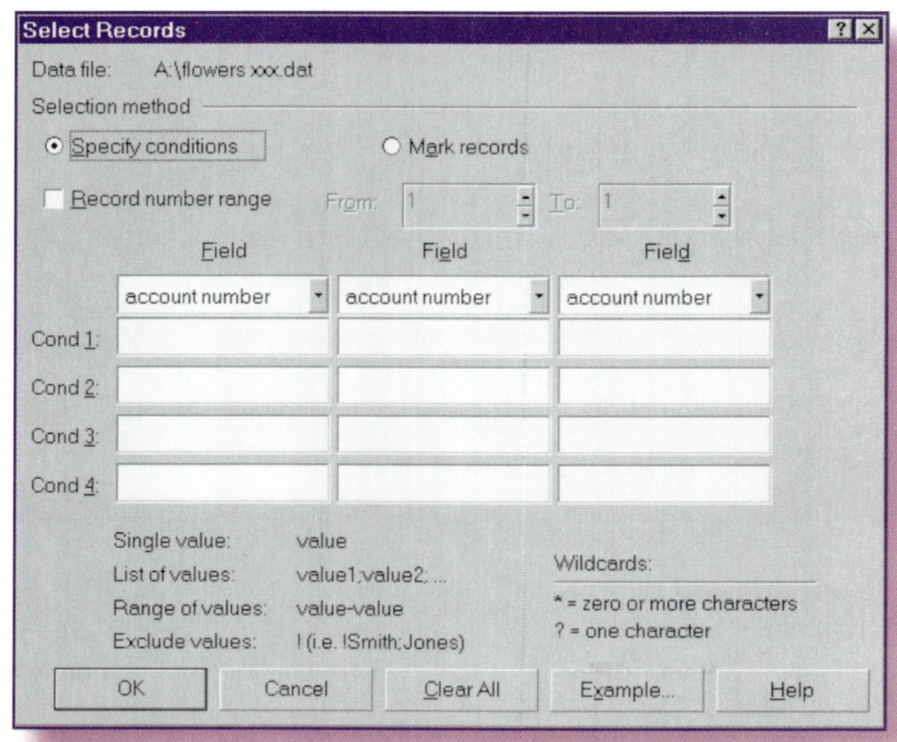

Obviously, this was a brief introduction to Select Records. If you are confused about the different ways to select records, study Figure 19-6. It explains the differences between the two features.

FIGURE 19-6
Feature Comparison

Extract Using Sort	**Select Records During Merge**
Extract using Sort is done BEFORE the merge.	Select Records takes place when you are setting up the merge.
When the desired records are extracted, all other records are deleted. (Be sure not to save the extracted list over your complete list!)	The complete list of records remains intact, although only the selected records are merged.
During the Extract process, your records can be sorted in a specified order.	Records must be sorted before the merge if you want them in a specified order after the merge.

Summary

This lesson was mostly about Sort—arranging things in order. You had a lot of practice so you would grasp what Sort is all about. You also learned about selecting records. You learned that:

- Lines of text can be sorted in a number of ways.

- A variety of types of information can be sorted with Paragraph Sort.

- Merge Sort enables you to rearrange data records before the merge, saving hand sorting after the merge.

- Records bearing certain characteristics can be separated out from a complete data file using Extract.

- Select Records enables you to select certain records to be used in a merge during the merge.

You should be an expert at Sort, Extract, and Select by now, but you'll get a little more practice in Project 19.

LESSON 19 REVIEW QUESTIONS

MULTIPLE CHOICE

Use the columns of information about the customers of XYZ Corporation below and circle the best answer to each of the following statements.

Name	Home Office	Amount Owed	Phone Number
Barbara Ann Valette	Tampa, Florida	15.00	813-555-0222
Joni Loock	Madison, Wisconsin	99.00	608-555-2348
Tica Hayes	Knoxville, Tennessee	35.00	423-555-9838
Cherryl Gene Pritts	San Antonio, Texas	44.00	512-555-5560
Jennifer Jarosik	Madison, Wisconsin	76.00	608-555-3348

1. To sort by customer last name, you would set Key 1 at
   A. Field 2, Word 2.
   B. Field 1, Word 2.
   C. Field 1, Word -1.
   D. Field 1, Word 1.

2. To sort by amount owed, you would set Key 1 at
   A. Field 1, Word 1.
   B. Field 2, Word 1.
   C. Field 2, Word -1.
   D. Field 3, Word 1.

3. To sort by name of city, you would set Key 1 at
   A. Field 2, Word 1.
   B. Field 2, Word -1.
   C. Field 1, Word -2.
   D. Field 3, Word 1.

(continued on next page)

323

4. To sort by state, you would set Key 1 at
    A. Field 2, Word 2.
    B. Field 2, Word -1.
    C. Field 1, Word 2.
    D. Field 1, Word -1.

5. To arrange the third column so that the largest number is on top, you would set
    A. Alpha, Descending.
    B. Alpha, Ascending.
    C. Numeric, Descending.
    D. Numeric, Ascending.

6. To extract only the customers owing more than $25.00, you would set Key 1 to identify the field containing the amounts due and then key ______________ in the *Extract records* text box.
    A. Key 1 = 25.00
    B. Key 1>25.00
    C. Key 1<25.00
    D. Key 1=<25.00

TRUE/FALSE

Circle the T if the statement is true. Circle the F if it is false.

T   F   **7.** Extract using Sort is done before the merge.

T   F   **8.** When the desired records are extracted, all other records are deleted.

T   F   **9.** During the Extract process, your records can be sorted in a specified order.

T   F   **10.** Select Records during a merge enables you to keep your complete list of records intact while only the selected records are merged.

LESSON 19 PROJECT

In this project you will prepare letters for a selected portion of a customer list. All of the data files have been prepared. You must prepare the form document and extract the customers to whom the letters will be sent. Read through the entire project before beginning.

1. Open **im spec proj 17b xxx.dat**. Save the file as **im spec proj19a xxx.dat**.

2. Position the insertion point at the bottom of the file and insert **micro** from the student **datafile** folder.

3. Sort the file by last name of customer. Be sure to remove any extra Keys in the Sort dialog box and remove any Extract commands. After sorting, save the file again with the same name.

4. Using the open file as the associated data file, create a form document for a letter to be sent to selected customers. You get to insert the date, mailing address, and greeting. The body and closing of the letter are illustrated in Figure 19-7. Insert your name in the closing lines.

FIGURE 19-7
Body of Letter for Lesson 19 Project

```
Thank you for choosing Image Specialists to bid on the installation of
imaging equipment in your company offices.  As we agreed in our phone
conversation yesterday, included in the bid will be training for your
employees who will be using the imaging equipment we install if we
should win the contract.

Our consultant for FIELD(area of interest) equipment,
FIELD(representative), will personally bring our bid to you at
FIELD(time) on FIELD(date).  At that time, please ask any questions
you might have about our company and procedures.

Again, the staff of Image Specialists would like to thank you for your
confidence in our organization.  We are looking forward to working
with you should we be selected to install FIELD(area of interest)
equipment at your office.

Sincerely,

IMAGE SPECIALISTS



(your name)
Imaging Manager
```

5. Save the form document as **im spec proj19b xxx.frm**. Play your **pf** macro and save the form document again.

6. Merge the form document with the data source. Use either Extract (in the Sort dialog box) or Select Records (in the Perform Merge dialog box) to prepare letters ONLY for those customers interested in *multimedia* systems. (When you merge, use Reset to return the Perform Merge dialog box to the defaults. If you use Select Records, do that AFTER you click the Reset button.)

7. Print the letters and save them as **im spec proj19c xxx**. Close all files.

CRITICAL THINKING ACTIVITY

In a list of names you want sorted alphabetically by last name, the name Cindy Van Horne keeps showing up after Robin A. Hood instead of before Reggie Voiers. You have checked the New Sort dialog box and confirmed that Key 1 is set at Field 1, Word -1. What could be causing the problem?

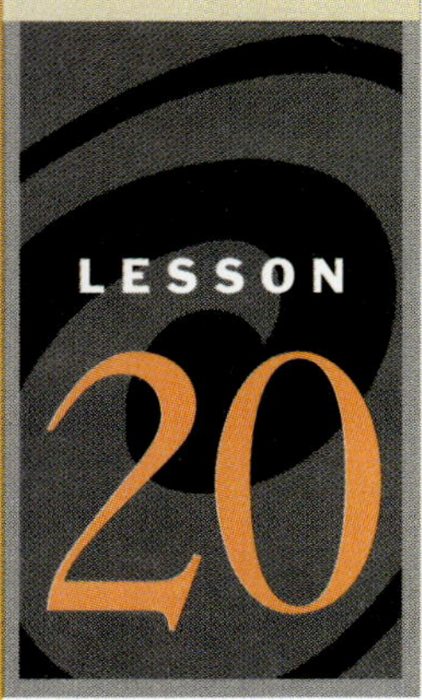

LABELS

OBJECTIVES

Upon completion of this lesson, you will be able to:

- Key and print labels.

- Prepare merged labels.

- Add the POSTNET bar code to your labels.

- Create name badges.

- Create numbered tickets.

Estimated Time: 2 hours

In Lessons 17 through 19 you've worked with mailing lists. You created lists and sorted them. You created form letters or documents, and you combined those forms with mailing lists. With those tools, you discovered how easy it is to prepare documents to be sent to a number of addresses, whether it is several or several thousands.

All of those letters or documents, however, don't do you or your company much good stacked on your desk. You must come up with a way of distributing them. You have a number of alternatives for distribution:

- facsimile (fax)

- electronic mail

- special courier services (using labels and special packaging)

- the postal service (using envelopes, labels, or window envelopes)

You've already learned how to prepare envelopes—both for individual letters and for bulk mailings. To use window envelopes, you simply need to position the mailing address in a specific location on the letter. Advance works well for locating the address, whether you create individual letters or form letters. As you know, you can even include POSTNET bar codes on your envelopes.

The third alternative in preparing mailings is using labels. There are lots of reasons why a company might choose to use labels for their mailings. By the same token, there are a lot of things you can do with the WordPerfect Labels feature besides creating labels for mailings. For example, you can use the feature to prepare name badges for a meeting. You can also prepare diskette labels, file folder labels, and numbered tickets. We'll try a variety of these uses in this lesson.

Labels for Mailing

WordPerfect comes with definitions for more than 250 labels, tabs, business cards, note cards, and name badges. The predefined labels are listed and described when you open the Format menu and choose Labels. Some of the labels are appropriate for laser printers because they can be printed on a standard size sheet of paper. Others are appropriate for dot matrix printers because they come on a roll or are fanfolded in a box so they can be fed continuously.

On the job you'll choose the definition that fits the labels you can use with your printer. When you've selected the correct label description, you can key the text directly onto the labels or you can define a form document, complete with FIELD codes so you can merge the data source with the label form.

When working with labels, WordPerfect considers each individual label as a logical page. The entire sheet of labels is considered a physical page. If you wish to print only one label, you must print the Current Page. Normally, of course, you will print all of the labels on a page.

One of the most widely used styles of labels has the following characteristics:

- 30 labels per page (3 columns of 10 rows)

- each label measures 1 inch x 2.63 inches

- standard $8\frac{1}{2}$- x 11-inch paper

- specifically manufactured to be printed on a laser printer

- narrow strip at the edges of the page to make allowance for the printer's no-print zone

We'll use a label definition with those characteristics in Step-by-Step exercise 20.1.

STEP-BY-STEP 20.1

1. In a new document window, open the **Format** menu and choose **Labels** to display the Labels dialog box.

2. Study the dialog box. Notice that below the Labels window are the details of the label that is highlighted. Move the highlight to *Avery 5160*. Your dialog box should look like Figure 20-1.

3. Look at the description and information about the label. Then click **Select** to choose the label and return to your working window. If you are in Draft view, change to Page view to see how the label looks.

4. Key your name and address. Then press **Ctrl+Enter** to move to a new page, and key the name and address of a friend. Repeat the procedure two more times so you have a total of four labels.

5. Press **Ctrl+Home** to move your insertion point to the beginning of YOUR address. Open the **Format** menu and choose **Page**. Center the current and subsequent pages. Return to your page of labels. Your labels should look like Figure 20-2.

6. Zoom to **Full Page**, if you'd like, to look at the page. Then return to **100%**.

(continued on next page)

FIGURE 20-1
Labels Dialog Box

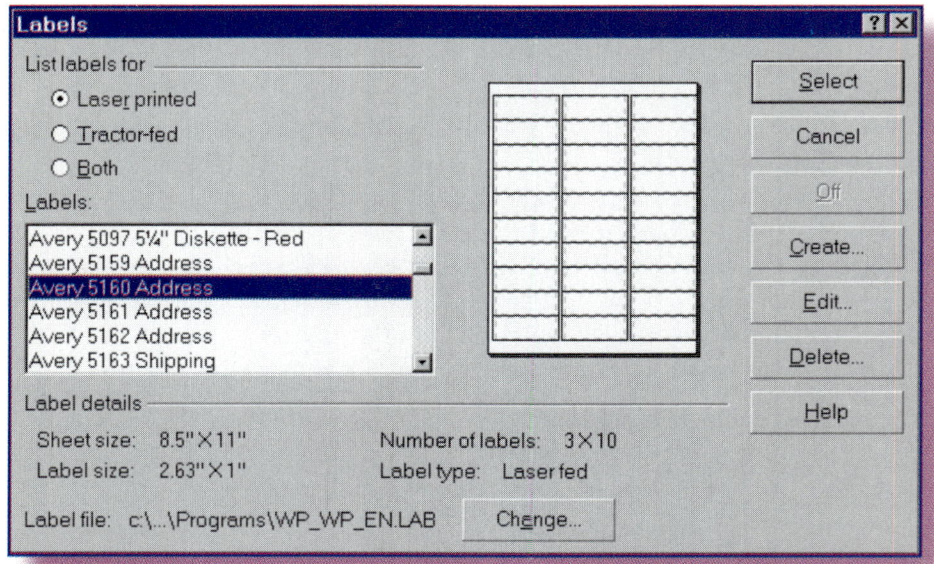

FIGURE 20-2
Sample Labels

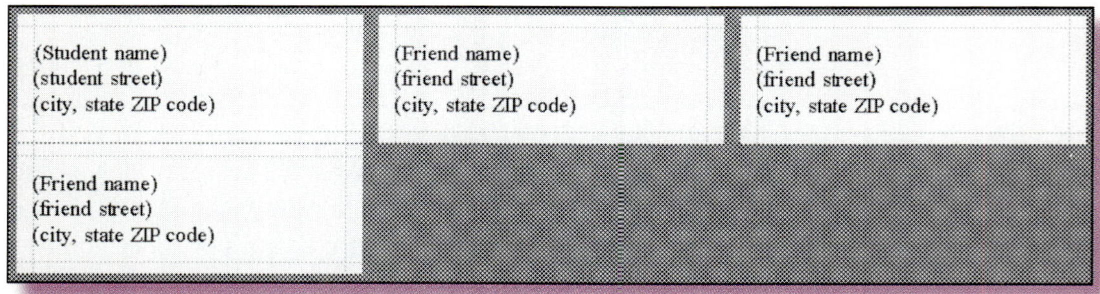

7. Save your labels as **labels 20-1 xxx**. Press **Ctrl+End**. Then press **Ctrl+Enter** to go to Label 5. Insert the Path and Filename code to identify the job.

8. Print the page of labels, save, and close the file.

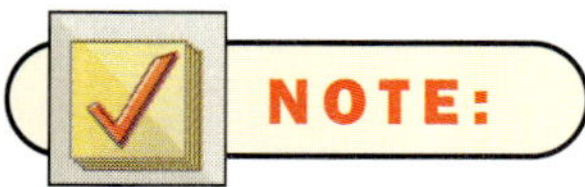

NOTE:

If you are using a laser printer, the display window in the printer will probably prompt you to manually feed a sheet of labels. Laser printers aren't normally stocked with labels in the feed trays. With most printers, you can feed any sheet of paper through the sheet feed portion of the printer.

Now let's use the same label description for merged labels. Read all of the instructions for the Step-by-Step exercise before beginning.

S TEP-BY-STEP ⟹ 20.2

1. Open the **Format** menu and choose **Labels**. As in the last Step-by-Step exercise, choose the **Avery 5160** label description.

2. Insert the command to center the current and subsequent pages.

3. Turn the current document into a form document, using **flowers xxx.dat** as the associated data file.

4. Enter the FIELD codes for the names and addresses on the labels. You don't need the middle initial. Because the FIELD codes are so long, your form document will look like Figure 20-3 when you finish.

5. Save the label form document as **labels 30.frm** because it is for a form document with 30 labels per page.

6. Merge **labels 30.frm** with **flowers xxx.dat**. Look at the labels that result. Zoom to **Full Page** to check them. Then return to **100%**.

7. Save the page of labels as **labels 20-2 xxx**. Position the insertion point in the final label. Press **Ctrl+Enter** to add one more label. Insert the Path and Filename code on that label.

8. Print the page and close it, saving it again.

FIGURE 20-3
Sample Form Document for Step-by-Step 20.2

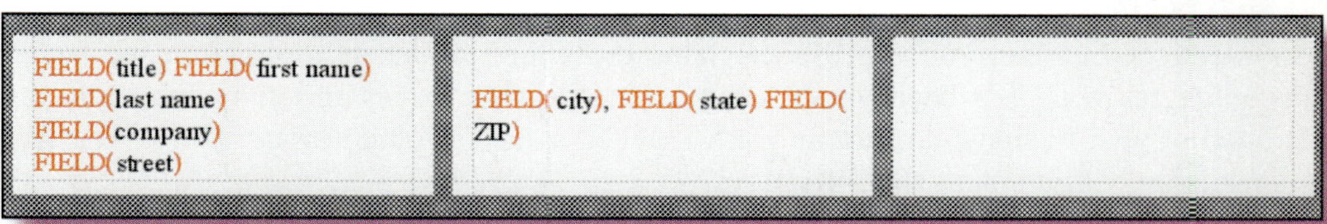

That was pretty easy, wasn't it? Your sample data file was small, so your sheet of labels was partly empty. You can print hundreds of labels this way. By way of review, following is the basic procedure for preparing labels:

1. Choose the label description.

2. Create a form document and name the associated data source. Insert the merge codes.

3. Combine the form document with the data source and print the labels.

Before we go to something different, let's amend the label form you prepared in Step-by-Step exercise 20.2 and add a POSTNET bar code to the address. You'll need a label description that provides a larger label than the Avery 5160 label. We'll use the Avery 5162 label description.

1. The **labels 30.frm** file should be showing. Go to the Current Document Style dialog box. Move your insertion point to the left of the codes.

2. Open the **Format** menu, choose **Labels**, and select **Avery 5162**. Close the Styles Editor and move your insertion point to the line below the FIELD codes for city, state, and ZIP code. (You may need to press Enter.)

3. Click the **Insert Field** button on the Merge Bar to open the Insert Field dialog box. Move it to the lower left corner of your window.

4. Click the **Merge Codes** button on the Merge Bar and key **po** to move to POSTNET(string). Insert it and double click **ZIP** in the Insert Field dialog box to put *ZIP* between the parentheses. Close both dialog boxes.

5. Look at the code for the POSTNET bar code in your label form. Note that *ZIP* has two sets of parentheses. That's OK. Use **Save As** to save the labels form as **labels 14.frm**.

6. Merge your files. Because Avery 5162 provides 14 labels per page, the labels will extend to a second page. That's fine.

7. Save your labels as **labels 20-3 xxx**. Add a label at the end and insert the Path and Filename code, as you did in Step-by-Step exercise 20.2.

8. Print your labels. Then save the file again and close all open files.

Name Badges

As mentioned earlier, you can use the same procedure for labels to create name badges for programs and meetings. Let's begin by creating a data file with names and companies for an office demonstration of your equipment. Assume you've invited some customers along with your employees to a demonstration of equipment and software.

1. Create a data file using the names and company names in Figure 20-4. Use the following field names: *first name, last name, company*.

2. Sort the list alphabetically by last name and save it as **names 20-4 xxx.dat**.

3. Create a form document to be associated with the data file. In the Current Document Styles Editor, put a code for **Avery 5390** name badges. Include a **Center Page(s)** command and a **Center** justification command. Return to your working window.

```
Miguel Zedillo        Milton Mason         Marcus Schmidt
Bits and Chips        Milty's Millions     Image Specialists


Rosemary Waldman      Wally Williams       Pearl Binder
Wally's Wallpaper Shop Williams Electronics East Wisconsin Wire


Kim Lee               Bertha Bertals       Dick Dawson
Lee Electronics                            Dawson, Hughs, & Park
                      Nchoua Thor
Joshua Jacobs         Image Specialists    Mary Winter
                                           Winter & Sons Electric

Sandee Simpson        Diego Marchetti
Simply Computing      Image Specialists    Ruth Anne Remmel
                                           Roffler Mfg. Co.

Natasha Nichols       Andreas Werner
Nickelodeon Nightmare Image Specialists    Ira Ibsen
                                           Ibsen Ink Products

Peggy Perkins         Pedro Costilla
Perticular PCs        Image Specialists
```

4. Enter the FIELD codes for the name badges, as shown in Figure 20-5.
   a. Put each field on a line by itself.
   b. Separate the *last name* field from the *company* field with a double space.
   c. Use a **36-pt.** font size for the first name (it may not fit on one line) and a **14-pt.** font size for the other two lines.

5. Save the form document as **badge xxx.frm**.

6. Merge the form document and the data file. Look at the badges. Save the finished badges as **badge 20-4 xxx**.

7. Go to the end of the file and press **Ctrl+Enter** to create another badge. Insert the Path and Filename code on that badge.

8. Print your badges (all three pages) and close the file, saving it again as **badge 20-4 xxx**. Close all files.

FIGURE 20-5
Form Document for Step-by-Step 20.4

FIELD(first name)
   FIELD(last name)

   FIELD(company)

Are your name badges beautiful? The different styles of name badges or name tags that can be chosen from the label definition list can be found on the shelves of your favorite office supplies store. It is a good idea to shop for the badges first. Then come back and choose the label definition that matches the badges you've purchased.

3 3 1

Numbered Tickets

You can also number your labels. This procedure requires the use of a couple of merge codes you have not yet used. If you follow along carefully, you shouldn't have any trouble with this procedure.

In this instance you don't need to put your Paper Size code in the Current Document Style because there is no data file. Otherwise, most of the codes for the format will be the same codes you used for the previous Step-by-Step exercises.

S TEP-BY-STEP ⟹ 20.5

FIGURE 20-6
Insert Merge Code Dialog Box

1. Beginning in a new document window, create a form document that has no associated data file.

2. Define a label using **Avery 5390 Name Tag**. Back in your document, choose **Center Page(s)** and **Center** justification.

3. Click the **Merge Codes** button to open the Insert Merge Codes dialog box. Key **fo** and choose **FORNEXT**. The dialog box illustrated in Figure 20-6 will appear.

4. Fill in the following information, pressing **Tab** to move from text box to text box. When you finish, click **OK**. (The Insert Merge Codes dialog box will remain open.)

    Variable = **x**
    Start = **1**
    Stop = **23**
    Step = **1**

(In this set of codes, *x* tells WordPerfect that another *x* will appear somewhere in the document to identify the position for the number. The first *1* tells WordPerfect to start numbering at *1*, while *23* tells WordPerfect to stop numbering at *23*. The final *1* tells WordPerfect to count in increments of *1*. You have the option of setting it to number only even numbers, such as 2, 4, and 6, or only odd numbers, such as 1, 3, and 5.)

FIGURE 20-7
Text for Step-by-Step 20.5

```
FORNEXT(x;1;23;1) IMAGE SPECIALISTS

            Spring Show
          Monday, April 1
         8 a.m. to 4 p.m.
        (by invitation only)

       Ticket #VARIABLE(x)
```

5. Back in your document window, you'll see the results of the code you entered. Continue on the same line, keying the first line of the text for the ticket, as illustrated in Figure 20-7. Continue keying the text until you have keyed the number sign (#) after the word *Ticket*.

6. Click in the Insert Merge Codes dialog box to activate it and key **v** to move to the *Variable* section. Choose **VARIABLE**. At the prompt for the variable, key **x** and click **OK**. Your form should now look like Figure 20-7.

7. Press **Ctrl+Enter** for a hard page break. Your insertion point will move to the next ticket. Then activate the Insert Merge Codes dialog box and choose the **ENDFOR** code. (This code ends the loop that tells WordPerfect to go back and repeat the text and add the next numeral.)

8. Save your ticket form as **ticket xxx.frm**. Merge the form.

9. When the merge is completed, look at your 23 tickets. (One space is left on the final page for your Path and Filename code.)

10. Save the merged tickets as **show 20-5 xxx**. Go to the blank ticket at the end and insert the Path and Filename code. Print the three pages of tickets and close the file, saving it again. Close all files.

The tickets you just created are the same size as the name tags you prepared in Step-by-Step exercise 20.4. You could use any of the label definitions if you wished to prepare tickets of a different size. This application was set up for just three pages of tickets. You could print hundreds this way, all numbered, if that was what you needed.

Summary

In this lesson you learned many of the things you can do with the Labels feature. You learned that:

- You can key directly onto the labels after you've defined them.
- You can use labels as a form document to merge with a data source for names and addresses.
- You can add the POSTNET bar code to your labels.
- If one size label doesn't fit, you can try a different size.
- You can use the Labels feature to create name badges.
- Labels can be used to create tickets—even with consecutive numbering.

Quite a number of other tasks can be completed with the Labels feature. As you experiment with it, you will surely have other ideas for its use.

LESSON 20 REVIEW QUESTIONS

FILL IN THE BLANKS

Complete each of the following statements by writing your answer in the blank provided.

1. WordPerfect comes with definitions for more than _________ labels, tabs, business cards, note cards, and name badges.

2. The predefined labels are listed when you open the _____________ menu and choose Labels.

(continued on next page)

3. When working with labels, WordPerfect considers each individual label as a ______________ page.

4. WordPerfect considers the entire sheet of labels a ______________ page.

5. If you wish to print only one label, you must select ______________ in the Print dialog box.

6. In order to number your labels, tickets, or badges, you first click the Merge Codes button to open the Insert Merge Codes dialog box. Then key fo and choose ______________ to insert the variable, start, stop, and step codes.

7. In preparing tickets, press ______________ to move to the next ticket.

WRITTEN QUESTIONS

Write your answers to the following questions.

8. If one size label doesn't fit, what should you do?

9. How would you use labels in a merge if you wanted to use a list of names and addresses you already have?

10. Name three things the WordPerfect Labels feature can be used for.

LESSON 20 PROJECT

Your instructor is running behind today. He has asked you to make some diskette labels for him to distribute to a class of 16 students that begins this evening. He expected you to write on each label by hand, but you found a box of Avery 5096 Red Diskette Labels that he has given you permission to use if you can prepare them on your own.

Figure 20-8 shows what he would like on the labels. Create the form document and choose the label description. Center the first three lines. For the *Name* line, key **Name** at the left. Then use Underline Tabs and Alt+F7 to create the line for the students to fill in their names. Save the form document as **diskette xxx.frm**.

To merge the 16 labels, begin the merge. In the Perform Merge dialog box choose Options and set the number of copies at 16. Complete the merge.

When you finish, look at your diskette labels. Create one more label at the end for your Path and Filename code.

Save your diskette labels as **disk proj20 xxx**. Print the labels and close the file.

FIGURE 20-8
Text for Diskette Labels

```
        ADVANCED  WORDPERFECT
        November 23, (year)


        Shareware Clipart Files

Name_________________________________
```

CRITICAL THINKING ACTIVITY

If you wanted to number all advanced-sale tickets up to 1,000 beginning with 100 using only even numbers printed on the tickets, what information would you key in the following text boxes of the Insert Merge Codes dialog box?

Variable = _________

Start = _________

Stop = _________

Step = _________

FEATURE	MENU CHOICE	KEYBOARD	LESSON
Address Book	Tools, Address Book	—	18
Document Assembly	Tools, Merge, Merge	Shift+F9	18
ENDFIELD Code	Tools, Merge, Data Source	Alt+Enter	17
ENDRECORD Code	Tools, Merge, Data Source	Ctrl+Shift+Enter	17
Envelope (Merge)	Tools, Merge, Merge	—	17
ENDFOR Code	Tools, Merge, Form	—	20
ENDIF Code	Tools, Merge, Form	—	19
Extract	Tools, Sort	Alt+F9	19
Field Names	Tools, Merge, Data Source	—	17
FORNEXT Code	Tools, Merge, Form	—	20
GO(label) Code	Tools, Merge, Form	—	20
IFNOTBLANK Code	Tools, Merge, Form	—	18
KEYBOARD Code	Tools, Merge, Form	—	17
Labels, Create	Format, Labels	—	20
LABEL(label)	Tools, Merge, Form	—	20
Line Sort	Tools, Sort	Alt+F9	19
Merge	Tools, Merge, Merge	Shift+F9	17
Merge Sort	Tools, Sort	Alt+F9	19
Name Badges	Format, Labels	—	20
NEXTRECORD Code	Tools, Merge, Form	—	20
Paragraph Sort	Tools, Sort	Alt+F9	19
POSTNET Bar Code	Tools, Merge, Merge	Shift+F9	18
Select Records	Tools, Merge, Merge	Shift+F9	19
Sort	Tools, Sort	Alt+F9	19
Table Sort	Tools, Sort	Alt+F9	19

TRUE/FALSE

On a separate page, key True if the statement below is true or False if it is not. Center *Unit 5 Review Questions* at the top and triple-space.

T   F   **1.**   A keyboard merge enables you to enter variable information as the merge takes place.

T   F   **2.**   If you prepare the form document before you prepare the data source, you can use the field names in the form document.

T   F   **3.**   If you are missing information in a data source, the ENDRECORD code must still mark that spot.

T   F   **4.**   To extract the records where the ZIP code is larger than 65000 and the ZIP code location is identified as Key 2, Extract Records should be set at Key2>65000.

T   F   **5.**   A *physical page* is the term used when referring to an entire sheet of labels.

WRITTEN QUESTIONS

Key your answers to the following questions. Number your answers and double-space between them. Use complete sentences and good grammar.

6.   Describe the differences between a data source and a form document.

7.   Name four kinds of Sort you learned about in Lesson 19. Which of those is used for merge data files?

8.   When performing a sort on a field containing amounts of money, should you set the sort to be Alpha or Numeric?

9.   Why must you be careful in saving your data source after you have used Extract?

10.   Sometimes when you are working with data files and you are proofreading, the ENDFIELD codes get in the way. Go to WordPerfect Help and find out how you can hide the merge codes so they don't show in your documents. How do you make the codes show again? Go to the data file section and read About Data Files. What are some of the other programs from which you may convert data files?

UNIT 5 APPLICATIONS

APPLICATION 1

In Lesson 17 you created a keyboard merge form named **memo.frm**. Use that form for a keyboard merge, and prepare a memo for your instructor with the subject *Merge Topics*. Briefly describe how you feel about the merge tools you learned in Unit 5. Which tools do you like the best? Which do you like the least? Which do you think you could put to use immediately? Save the memo as **memo u5ap1 xxx**. Print the memo. Then close it, saving it again.

APPLICATION 2

Open **seniors** from the student **datafile** folder. Use Save As to save the file on your disk as **seniors u5ap2a xxx**. Play your **pf** macro to identify the file.

You will sort this list in a number of ways. For some of the sorts, you will need to set more than one Key. When you don't need a Key, click in the row of the extra Key and delete it. Always check all parts of the Sort dialog box before you complete a sort.

1. Sort alphabetically by last name. Add Key 2 to sort by first name so the people with the same last name are in alphabetic order. Check your work and print the file. Save it again with the same name.

2. Sort alphabetically by school. Set the sort so if two people are attending the same school, they will be arranged alphabetically by last name and then by first name. (HINT: If you choose the *Insert Key Between* button, the new key will be added above the existing key. Then you just need to set the new Key 1 to point to the schools.) Print the sorted list and save it as **seniors u5ap2b xxx**.

3. Extract the females. (HINT: Identify the school in any Key. In the *Extract records* text box, key **Key?=Female**, substituting the Key number where you have Field 3 for the question mark.) At the same time you extract, sort the list alphabetically by last name. Check your work. Print the list and close it, saving it as **seniors u5ap2c xxx**.

4. Open **seniors u5ap2a xxx** and extract the males. Sort the list alphabetically by school. Print and close, saving this sort as **seniors u5ap2d xxx**.

APPLICATION 3

Assume that you are Manuel Tovar's secretary, and you are tired of preparing an invoice form each time you bill a customer. We'll convert an invoice file to one that can be prepared with Keyboard Merge. Then we'll try it out with a couple of invoices.

Go to your **Units 3 and 4** folder and open **estate 15-8 xxx**. Convert it to a form document, with no associated data source. Save the file as **invoice xxx.frm** and adjust it as follows:

1. Delete the current date and replace it with the DATE code.

2. Delete the billing period information and replace it with a KEYBOARD code prompting the user to key the billing period.

3. Delete the name and address of the customer and replace it with a KEYBOARD code prompting the user to key the name and address of the customer.

4. In the table, delete the first date and replace it with a KEYBOARD code prompting the user to enter the first date of service to be billed. (The entire KEYBOARD code may not show because it's too large for the cell. That's OK.)

5. Delete all of the remaining information in the Date, Description, Hours, and Per Hour columns. DO NOT delete anything in the Total column. Leave the words to the left of the totals near the bottom. Recalculate the invoice.

Save the form again as **invoice xxx.frm** and close it.

APPLICATION 4

Mr. Tovar has given you information for invoices for two clients for the period of September 1, (year), to October 1, (year). The information is illustrated in Figure APP-1.

1. Use Keyboard Merge to prepare the first invoice.

2. When you have entered the first date of service, press Alt+Enter to conclude the merge.

3. Then fill in the table in the usual table manner. Calculate the invoice.

4. In the row that contains only zeros (00.00), highlight those zeros and delete them.

When you finish the first invoice, press Ctrl+Enter to go to a new page and merge again. This time, in the Perform Merge dialog box, choose Current Document for Output. Both invoices will be in one document.

Save the finished invoices as **invoice u5ap4 xxx**. Print the invoices and close all files.

FIGURE APP-1
Information for Invoices in Application 4

```
Mr. & Mrs. Junior Washington
1776 Cherry Tree Lane
Victoria, NJ 08344

9-6-00      Office Visit        1 hr. @ 80.00
9-10-00     Title Search        3 hrs. @ 75.00
9-14-00     Office Visit        0.5 hrs. @ 80.00
9-28-00     Office Visit        1 hr. @ 80.00

Ms. Munira Dughish
5723 N. Dexter Street
Victoria, NJ 08344

9-3-00      Office Visit        1 hr. @ 90.00
9-11-00     Office Visit        2 hrs. @ 90.00
9-26-00     Court Appearance    1 hr. @ 90.00
```

1. It's housekeeping time again—time to delete some files and move others. Begin by creating a **Units 5 and 6** folder with the **Units 1 and 2** folder and the **Units 3 and 4** folder. Move the files in Figure APP-2 from your normal folder into the **Units 5 and 6** folder.

2. Move the files **seniors u5ap2a**, **memo u5ap1**, and **invoice u5ap4** to the **Applications** folder.

FIGURE APP-2
Files to Move to **Units 5 and 6** Folder

badge xxx.frm	labels 30.frm
diskette xxx.frm	memo.frm
flower list 19-6 xxx	micro 17-4 xxx.frm
flowers 18-8 xxx.frm	micro 17-6 xxx.dat
flowers xxx.dat	micro 17-9a xxx.dat
im spec proj19a xxx.dat	sort 19-5 xxx
invoice xxx.frm	ticket xxx.frm
labels 14.frm	ziepke 18-9 xxx.dat

3. Figure APP-3 lists files that should be deleted. Work carefully. When you finish, your main folder should contain only your macros.

FIGURE APP-3
Files to Delete

accounts 18-8 xxx	interest 18-14 xxx	seniors u5ap2b xxx
badge 20-4 xxx	labels 20-1 xxx	seniors u5ap2c xxx
disk proj20 xxx	labels 20-2 xxx	seniors u5ap2d xxx
flowers 18-1 xxx.dat	labels 20-3 xxx	show 20-5 xxx
flowers 18-1 xxx.frm	list 19-6 xxx.frm	small 19-12 xxx
flowers 18-2 xxx.frm	micro 17-2 xxx.dat	sort 19-1 xxx
flowers 18-4 xxx	micro 17-3 xxx.frm	sort 19-2 xxx
flowers 18-6 xxx.frm	micro 17-5 xxx	sort 19-3 xxx
flowers 18-7 xxx	micro 17-7 xxx	table 19-10 xxx
im spec proj17d xxx	micro 17-8 xxx	ziepke 18-10 xxx.frm
im spec proj17b xxx.dat	micro 17-9b xxx	ziepke 18-11 xxx
im spec proj17c xxx.frm	names 20-4 xxx	ziepke 18-12 xxx.frm
im spec 19-9 xxx.dat	reference 18-12 xxx	ziepke 18-14 xxx.frm
im spec proj19b xxx.frm	referral 17-10 xxx.frm	ziepke proj18 letters
im spec proj19c xxx	referral 17-11 xxx	ziepke proj18 xxx.dat

JOB 11

Mr. Becker has just handed you the list of customers in Figure J6 who had signed up for the October tour to Disney World. Registrations have been light, and the tour had to be canceled.

He would like you to prepare letters to send to the customers. Create a data file and a form document (see Figure J7) and merge them to complete the letters. Include an envelope with each letter. Save the data file in the **Singing Wheels** folder as **dis job11a xxx.dat** and the form document as **dis job11b xxx.frm**. Save the completed merge as **disney job11 xxx**.

FIGURE J6
Addresses for Job 11

```
Mr. & Mrs. Neverat Holme
773 3rd Street
Manawa, WI 54949

Mrs. Lottie Baggs
22 Sunny Court
Shawano, WI 54166

Miss Norma Nomad
3411 Jonquil Lane
Junction City, WI 54443
```

FIGURE J7
Letter for Job 11

```
(current date)

(Customer)

Dear (greeting):

I am sorry to inform you that the tour you had planned to take with us
to Disney World in Florida beginning on October 22 has been canceled
due to lack of registrations.  A check in the amount of your down
payment is enclosed.

It is extremely rare that we are forced to cancel a tour.  From what
we can tell, registrations were low because so many of our customers
chose instead to go on the November tour to Disney World.  We still
have some openings for that tour and would like to encourage you to
check your calendars.  Perhaps you could go with us on November 15
instead of in October.

Please call within the next week if you are able to arrange to join us
in November.  We would very much like to have you with us at that
time.  Either way, thank you for your business.  It is customers like
you that keep our wheels singing!

Sincerely,

SINGING WHEELS TOURS



Charlie Becker

Enclosure
```

JOB 12

Mr. Becker just received three more reservations for the November Disney World trip. The names and addresses of the customers are listed in Figure J8. Use Merge to prepare and print a letter and envelopes for these customers. A letter named **disney** is in the student **datafile** folder for this job. (Only the body of the letter and the closing have been prerecorded for you. Insert the merge codes for the date, mailing address, and greeting. Then use Insert to insert the **disney** file.)

Note that the data file includes a field for the middle initial. Not all of the customers have middle initials, so you'll have to set up your merge accordingly for the letters. Include POSTNET bar codes on the envelopes. Do not include middle initials on the envelopes. Save the data file in the **Singing Wheels** folder as **dis job12a xxx.dat** and the form document as **dis job12b xxx.frm**.

After merging, print all three letters and envelopes. Save the merged file as **disney job12 xxx**. Close all files.

FIGURE J8
Customers for Job 12

```
Mr. & Mrs.              Mr.                     Mrs.
Mickey                  Sylvester               Minnie
M.                      A.
Arodent                 Katt                    Marvin
9811 Arkdale Lane       51 Kettleson Creek      3557 Mead Street
Marinette               Kaukauna                Marion
WI                      WI                      WI
54143                   54130                   54950
414-555-7728            414-555-0023            414-555-8893
```

JOB 13

The body and closing of the letter used for Job 12 is generic enough so it could be used each time a registration and deposit arrives for most of the Singing Wheels trips. Open the **disney** document from the student **datafile** folder. Save it in the **Singing Wheels** folder as **deposit.frm**.

Convert the document to a keyboard merge form document, including the DATE code and KEYBOARD codes for the mailing address, the greeting, and the four places where question marks (??) have been inserted in Figure J9. Remove the question marks, of course. Use your **pf** macro to insert the Path and Filename code. Then print the form document and save the file again.

FIGURE J9
Body of **deposit** Keyboard Merge Letter

```
Thank you for your reservation for our trip to ?? leaving on ??.  We
are excited about this trip and hope that it will be everything you
are expecting.  It should be a good time of the year to visit ??.

Your ?? deposit has been recorded, and our usual questionnaire about
your preferences and any possible physical restrictions is enclosed.
Please return the completed questionnaire to us along with your final
payment no less than 30 days before the tour begins.

Again, welcome to what promises to be a fun adventure.  We are looking
forward to having you along for the ride.
```

JOB 14

You finished converting that file to a keyboard merge document just in time. Mr. Becker just received another registration for the trip to Disney World leaving on November 15. Please prepare a letter like the others for the Disney World tour for Mrs. Lila Lingstrom, 647 3rd Avenue, Larsen, WI 54947. Mrs. Lingstrom sent a $50 deposit. Save the completed file in the **Singing Wheels** folder as **disney job14 xxx**. Include the Path and Filename code in a footer. Prepare an envelope, including the POSTNET bar code. Print the letter and envelope.

JOB 15

Mr. Becker has given you the list of names and addresses of the first ten people who will be on the November bus tour to Disney World. Three of the folks who had signed up for the canceled October tour (Job 11) will be able to go along in November. They are Neverat and Hazel Holme and Mrs. Baggs.

Please use the the name badge form you created in Lesson 20 to make name tags for these three people, as well as for seven other people (see Figure J10). You may send friends and relatives—in fact, you get to provide the seven names and addresses. (Position the city and state where the company name was positioned on the name tags in Step-by-Step exercise 20-4. Save the modified form document in the **Singing Wheels** folder as **badge job15 xxx.frm**.)

Prepare the data file for the ten people. Be sure to include the Holmes couple and Mrs. Baggs. Save the data file in the **Singing Wheels** folder as **names job15 xxx.dat**. When you have both files ready, complete the merge. Save the finished document in the **Singing Wheels** folder as **badges job15 xxx**. Add an extra name tag at the end to identify the document. Print the document and save it again. Close all files.

FIGURE J10
Form Document
for Job 15

```
First Name
Last Name

City, State
```

GRAPHICS TOOLS

Estimated Time for Unit 6: 7$\frac{1}{2}$ hours

GRAPHICS BOXES

OBJECTIVES

Upon completion of this lesson, you will be able to:

- Insert a graphics box containing an image.
- Select, move, size, and add captions to your graphics boxes.
- Discuss graphics box styles.
- Change the border and fill of your graphics boxes.
- Customize the captions on your boxes.
- Work with wrap options.
- Create and adjust text boxes.
- Use the Drag to Create feature.
- Insert an image From File.

Estimated Time: 1½ hours

Quite often when we think about word processing and graphics, we are thinking about working with page layouts—that is, designing attractive pages for multiple production. The documents might be newsletters, brochures, business reports, resumes, or magazine articles.

Regardless of the final product, the design elements are the same. Page layout is simply the arrangement of type, white space, and graphics. If it is attractive and easy to follow, people will read it. If it is neither attractive nor easy to follow, no matter how interesting, people probably won't read it.

WordPerfect provides you with a number of design elements that enable you to produce attractive documents. These design elements include columns (which you already know how to create), graphics images, graphics lines, borders, and fonts of every imaginable size!

WordPerfect graphics enables you to insert drawings, photos, Clipart images, and a variety of other types of graphics into your documents. In this lesson you'll learn to insert images as well as make changes to the appearance of your images. In the other lessons of this unit you'll work with some of the other graphics elements.

Insert an Image

The first step in working with graphics is to insert an image into your document. More than 100 Corel images are copied to your computer when a standard installation is performed. The remainder are on the CD on which the program is shipped. The images are in a compressed format, but if they were saved individually, each would have a *.wpg* extension, which makes them easy to distinguish from other types of files.

In Step-by-Step exercise 21.1 we'll preview some of the images that come with the program.

STEP-BY-STEP 21.1

1. In a new document window, open the **Insert** menu, choose **Graphics**, and choose **Clipart**. WordPerfect will display the Scrapbook.

2. Use the scroll bar to preview the thumbnails of the images. Note that they are arranged alphabetically.

3. Choose an image that appeas to you. Double click to insert it into your document. The image will be inserted at the top and left margin guidelines.

4. Close the Scrapbook and keep the image displayed as you read on.

With the image in the window, let's learn about working with images.

Selecting, Moving, and Sizing Boxes, and Adding Captions

When you insert an image into your document, it is placed in a frame called a graphics box. Unless you place a border around the image or select a certain type of image, that frame doesn't show. You'll learn to work with graphics box frames shortly.

To work with an image, it must be selected. When the image is selected, it is surrounded by black squares called "sizing handles," and they can be dragged to make your image the size or shape you would like it to be. Also when an image is selected, the graphics tools will appear on the Property Bar. This bar is one source of tools for working with images. The other source of tools is the QuickMenu. Most of the same choices are available from these two sources. We'll choose tools from both of these sources in the next few Step-by-Step exercises.

Let's begin by exploring the tools available when an image is selected.

STEP-BY-STEP 21.2

1. Click away from the image. Then point to it again and click to select it. Note the sizing handles.

2. With your mouse pointer, grab the handle at the middle right and drag it to the right about an inch. Look at your image. Is it distorted? Unless the default settings have been changed, it looks strange.

(continued on next page)

3. Click away from the image to deselect it and use **Undo** on the Toolbar to return the image to its original proportions.

4. Select the image again and point to it with your mouse pointer while you right click. The QuickMenu, illustrated in Figure 21-1, should appear. Look at the eight items at the bottom of the QuickMenu. We'll be concentrating on those items in this lesson.

5. Click away from the QuickMenu to close it. Is your image still selected? If not, click it to select it. Click the **Graphics** button at the left of the Property Bar. The menu should look like Figure 21-2.

6. If you have a good memory, you'll see that most of the tools at the bottom of the QuickMenu are in the menu in Figure 21-2.

7. Choose **Content**. Look at the dialog box that appears. This box provides a number of options regarding how the image appears in the area that surrounds it. At the bottom is a check box for preserving the image width/height ratio. If a check mark doesn't appear in that box, click the box so it DOES have a check mark. Then click **OK** to close the Content dialog box.

8. Grab the handle at the middle right and drag about an inch to the right. Did the image remain the same size and shape? It should have, although it probably moved to the horizontal center of the box area.

9. Click outside of the Image box to deselect it and click the **Undo** button on the Toolbar to return the Image box to its original size and shape.

FIGURE 21-1
Graphics QuickMenu

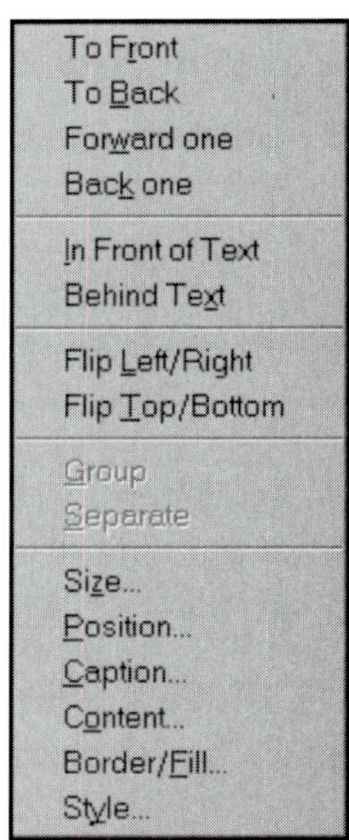
FIGURE 21-2
Graphics Menu

Image Width/Height Ratio

The default setting in WordPerfect is that the check box for preserving the ratio of width and height is not selected. Even though you've preserved the ratio of the current image, WordPerfect may not remember when you size your next image. That means that each time you work with an image, you could possibly distort the image. Later in your training you will learn how to permanently change graphics styles.

Since you are probably in a classroom and your preferences might not match those of other students, we won't mess with defaults at this time. Instead, we'll try to remember to go to the Content dialog box and choose that setting for each image with which we work. Remember that if you choose it immediately, you can use Undo to return the image to its original size and shape if you accidentally distort it.

Sizing Graphics Boxes

One way to size graphics boxes is to drag the handles as you did in Step-by-Step exercise 21.2. If you want to set exact measurements for your box, you can choose Size from either the QuickMenu or the Graphics menu. The Box Size dialog box looks like Figure 21-3. When you bring a graphics box into a document, it will always be 1.50" wide. WordPerfect will not distort a box if you leave one of the settings at *Maintain proportions*. Let's practice.

S TEP-BY-STEP ⟹ 21.3

1. With the image showing in your window and the box selected, point to the image and right click to display the QuickMenu. Choose **Size**.

2. In the Box Size dialog box, change the width of the box to **3.0"** and click **OK**. Back in your document window, look at the large image.

3. With the box selected, click the **Graphics** button on the Property Bar to display the Graphics menu and choose **Size**. Change Width to **Maintain proportions**. Change Height to **Full**. Click **OK**.

4. Zoom to **Full Page** to look. Then return to **100%**.

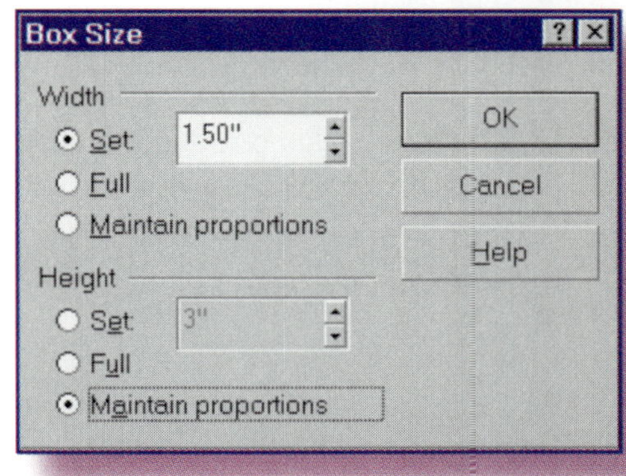

FIGURE 21-3
Box Size Dialog Box

5. Now return to the Box Size dialog box and change Height to **Set** and **3.0"**. Click **OK**.

Captions

Now that you've sized the graphics box, let's give it a caption.

S TEP-BY-STEP ⟹ 21.4

1. With the image showing in your window and the box selected, use either the QuickMenu or the Graphics menu to choose **Caption**.

2. In the Box Caption dialog box (we'll come back to this box later) click the **Edit** button at the right. *Figure 1* will appear at the bottom left of the box containing the image.

3. Backspace once to delete the automatic caption and key a two- to three-word caption that identifies the image. Click outside of the box to deselect it.

Moving

When a graphics box is selected, you can drag it to move it to the desired location. The moving tool is a four-headed arrow. You can also set a measured position by choosing Position from either the QuickMenu or Edit menu. We'll move the image by dragging it.

STEP-BY-STEP 21.5

1. With the image showing in your window and the box selected, point to the image and use the four-headed arrow to drag the image to the right. Then align it at the margin guidelines in the upper left corner of the window again.

2. Zoom to **Full Page** so you can see the entire page. Drag the image to the lower right corner, aligned with the edges of the paper. Note that when you release the mouse button, the image will move about a quarter of an inch away from the edges of the paper. That's the no-print zone, and it will vary according to your printer description.

3. Finally, move it to the upper right corner of the page and return to normal view (100%).

4. Deselect the image and read on.

Graphics Box Styles

Sometimes when you use graphics boxes in your documents, you'd like a different appearance. WordPerfect has saved you formatting time by providing a variety of graphics boxes from which you may choose. Characteristics of the box styles vary, such as location of the caption, whether or not WordPerfect counts the caption for a listing of figures, and whether or not the box is surrounded with a line. The following 14 styles are available:

- *Image.* This is a box with no borders that is best used for images, drawings, and charts.

- *Text.* The Text box usually contains text for information to be set apart from the rest of the text in a document.

- *Equation.* An Equation box is used for formulas and equations.

- *Figure.* A Figure box is like the Image box, but contains the image in a single-line border.

- *Table.* A Table box normally contains a table. In the box, the table can be numbered or rotated. Using boxes, two tables can be placed side by side.

- *User.* The User box is much like a Figure box, but it doesn't have a border.

- *Button.* Button boxes are most often used to put buttons in your document, representing a link to another part of the document. WordPerfect has what's known as Hypertext capabilities. Hypertext links two or more parts of a document so the user can quickly move from one place to another.

- *Watermark.* You've already used Watermark to put an image behind the text of your document.

- *Inline Equation.* This type of box enables you to put an equation right in the line of text that you are keying. It becomes part of the sentence.

- *OLE 2.0 Box.* This type of box is linked to another application. When the object is altered in the other application, it is automatically updated in the linked document. Since we aren't working with other applications, we won't use this type of box.

- *Inline Text.* The Inline Text box allows you to apply special formatting to normal text.

- *Draw Object.* This kind of box is positioned behind the text.

- *Draw Object Text.* This is a box like the Draw Object box, but one that contains text. It is used for grouping text with an image.

- *Sticky Note Text.* This kind of box has a yellow background, and it covers everything behind it.

The kind of work you do will determine which styles of graphics boxes you use most often. Let's look at how the different styles affect the graphics box in your document and then try some other options.

STEP-BY-STEP 21.6

1. Click to select the box. Then right click to display the QuickMenu.

2. Choose **Style** and try some of the other styles as follows:
   a. Change from an Image box to a **Figure** box. Deselect the box and look at the lines and the caption.

   b. Change to a **User** box.
   c. Change to a **Table** box.
   d. Finally, return to an **Image** box.

3. Close the document without saving and read on.

Image from File

One of the choices available to you when you open the Insert menu and choose Graphics is to insert an image *From File*. This choice allows you to get images from other sources. (You'll learn about a number of other sources in Lesson 22.) The *From File* choice can also be used to insert WordPerfect graphics images that are stored in places other than the Clipart Scrapbook.

Several WordPerfect images from previous versions of the program have been saved for your use in the **datafile** folder. We'll use some of those images as you continue to learn about WordPerfect graphics.

Border/Fill

Another way to change the appearance of the lines surrounding the image is by adjusting those lines with the Box Border/Fill option. Let's use *From File* to get a different image as we review what you've learned so far and work with border and fill.

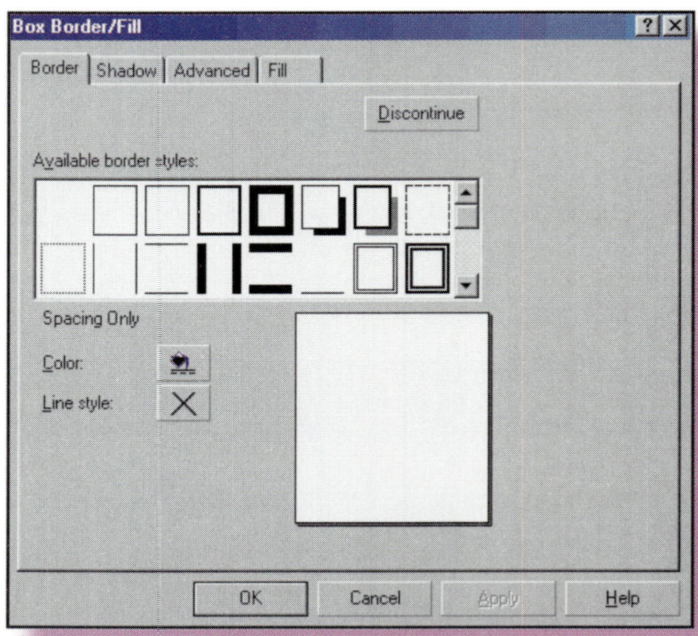

FIGURE 21-4
Box Border/Fill Dialog Box

1. Beginning in a new document window, open the **Insert** menu, choose **Graphics**, and then choose **From File**.

2. In the Insert Image dialog box, go to the **datafile** folder, find **rose.wpg**, and double click to insert it. Save the file as **rose 21-7 xxx**.

3. Set the height of the rose at **3"** and move it to the upper right corner. Give the rose a caption: **A Rose by Any Other Name . . . .**

4. Display the QuickMenu and choose **Border/Fill**. The dialog box in Figure 21-4 will appear.

5. Scroll to the top of the border choices using the little scroll bar. Choose a heavy black border and look at the preview.

6. Click the **Fill** tab and choose the third button from the left (10%). Try a couple of other border and fill patterns. Then return to the heavy border and 10% fill.

7. Click the **Shadow** tab and look at the variety of shadows you can give your image box.

8. Click the **Advanced** tab. At the top left, you can set the size of the inside space surrounding your image in the box, as well as the outside space separating your box from the surrounding text.

9. In the *Corner radius* section, change the radius from *0* to **0.2"**. Notice the round corners in the preview. Click **OK**.

10. Save the document again and play your **pf** macro. Print the document and keep it open.

Customizing a Caption

Your graphics box already has a caption, so you don't need to learn to add one. However, you can do many things to customize your captions. Let's adjust the caption for the rose.

S TEP-BY-STEP ⟹ 21.8

1. With your rose showing in the window, select the image and go to the Box Border/Fill dialog box. Click **Discontinue** in the upper right corner. This removes the border and the fill.

2. Point to the selected image and display the QuickMenu. Choose **Caption** to display the Box Caption dialog box. It should look much like Figure 21-5.

3. In the upper left corner, change *Side of box* to **Left** and change *Position* to **Bottom**.

4. Rotate the caption **90 degrees**. Click **OK** and look at the way the caption runs along the side of the image.

5. Move the graphics box to a different location. Then return it to the left, aligning it with the top and left guidelines.

6. Display the QuickMenu and choose **Edit Caption**. Delete all of the caption except *A Rose . . . .* Click the **Close** folder on the Property Bar.

7. Return to the document and use **Save As** to save your file as **rose 21-8 xxx**. Keep it open.

FIGURE 21-5
Box Caption Dialog Box

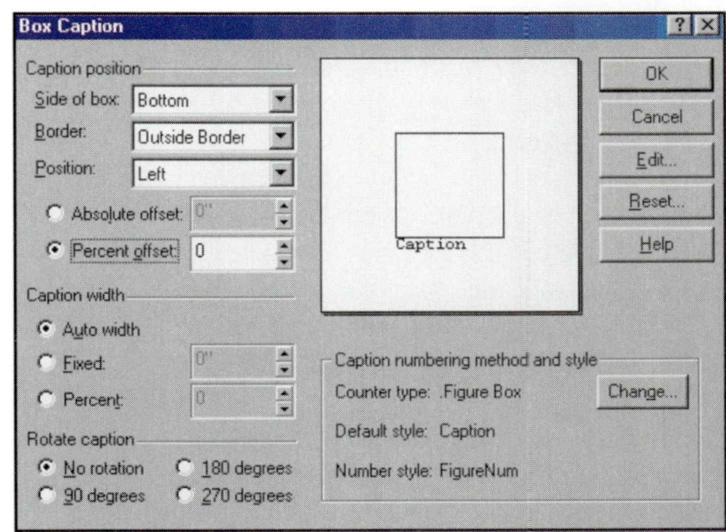

As you can see, the caption is easy to manipulate. Now let's add some text to see how the graphics box works within the document.

Wrap

When text surrounds a graphics box, you have a number of choices regarding how the text wraps around that box. The default is for the text to respect the entire box that contains the image. However, if you prefer, you can tell WordPerfect to forget about the box and wrap the text around the image. What's more, you can designate the sides of the box that the text wraps around. Let's try it.

A browser is a software program that gives access to most Internet services. A browser is required to connect to the multimecia documents on the World Wide Web.

STEP-BY-STEP 21.9

1. With your rose in the upper left corner of the window and the caption running up the left side of the box, open your **Insert** menu and choose **File**. Go to the student **datafile** folder and choose **columns**.

2. Display the QuickMenu and choose **Wrap**. Look at the Wrap Text dialog box (see Figure 21-6).

3. Choose **Contour** and **Largest side**. Click **OK**. Look at how the text wraps around your image. Move the image to the upper right corner and deselect it.

4. Return your insertion point to the top of the document and change from Left justification to **Full justification**. Note that the words crowd the image a little more with Full justification. Return to **Left justification**.

5. With the insertion point still at the beginning of the text, change to **2 Balanced newspaper columns**.

6. Drag the image to the middle of the page, centered on the gutter.

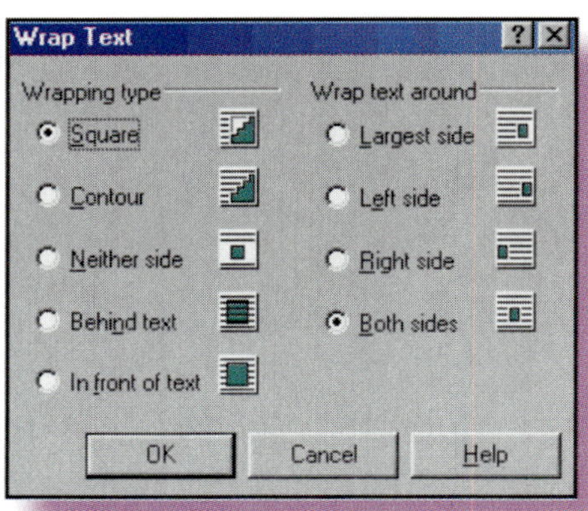

FIGURE 21-6
Wrap Text Dialog Box

7. Experiment with some of the other Wrap choices. Then return to **Contour** and **Both sides** (although Contour/Largest side would work with columns).

8. Save your document as **rose 21-9 xxx** and print it. Keep it open.

As you can see, you can customize how the image is surrounded by text in a number of ways. Now let's look at how the image is positioned on the page.

Position

A graphics box may be attached, or anchored, in the document in one of three ways. This is called the *Position* of the box. Position affects how the box will react when text is added to or deleted from the page on which the box is located.

- **Paragraph.** When a graphics box is attached to a paragraph, it becomes part of the paragraph. Text added or deleted above the paragraph will cause the paragraph to move on the page. The box will move with the paragraph.

- **Page**. A graphics box that is attached to the page remains in the same position, regardless of changes to the text surrounding the box. Page anchor is the default setting.

- **Character**. A graphics box that is anchored to a character is treated as a single character in the line of text. The box moves with the line as changes are made in the text.

The default setting for Position is Page.

STEP-BY-STEP 21.10

1. Go to the beginning of **rose 21-9 xxx** and remove the [Col Def] code to return to a single line length.

2. Open the Box Size dialog box and set the Height at **Maintain proportions**. Set the Width at **1"**. Set Wrap at **Contour** and **Largest side**.

3. Move the box to the left margin. Align the top of the box with the beginning of the third paragraph.

4. Select the entire second paragraph (double click in the left margin). Copy the paragraph to the Windows Clipboard.

5. Deselect the paragraph. Position the insertion point at the beginning of the second paragraph and paste the paragraph on the Clipboard into the document at that location. (The second paragraph is now repeated.)

6. Look at what happened with the image. It stayed in the same place on the page. Delete the second paragraph.

7. Select the rose image. Display the QuickMenu and choose **Position**. Change *Attach box* from Page to **Paragraph** (see Figure 21-7). If necessary, realign the image with the beginning of the third paragraph.

8. Position the insertion point at the beginning of the second paragraph. Paste the paragraph into the document again. Your image should have moved down, along with the original third paragraph because it is attached to that paragraph.

9. Delete both occurrences of the second paragraph. Now the rose should move up with the paragraph to which it is attached.

10. Select the rose and drag it down. Align the top of the box with the top of the new third paragraph. Keep the document open as you read on.

FIGURE 21-7
Attaching the Image

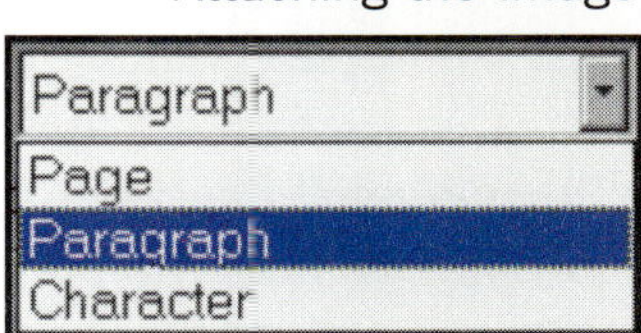

You may not have noticed it, but when the box is attached to the paragraph when you move it, a pushpin at the left identifies the beginning of the paragraph to which it is attached. When you moved from the second to third paragraph, the pushpin moved, too. When the pushpin moves, the [Box] code in Reveal Codes also moves. If you would delete the paragraph to which the box is attached, the [Box] code would also be deleted.

Now let's learn about attaching the box to a character.

1. Select the graphics box in your document. Copy the selected image to the Windows Clipboard.

2. Move the insertion point to the end of the document. Paste the copied rose to that position. Make the following changes to the settings of the new box:

   a. Size. Change the Width to **0.3"** and leave the Height set at **Maintain proportions**.

   b. Caption. Go to the Caption dialog box and click the **Reset** button. WordPerfect will ask if you'd like to delete the caption. Confirm the deletion.

   c. Position. Change the setting so the box is anchored to **Character**.

3. Select the image and use **Cut** to remove it from your document.

4. Position your insertion point at the beginning of the last sentence of the first paragraph. Paste the tiny rose box at that location.

5. Save your practice Step-by-Step exercise as **rose 21-11 xxx** and print it. Close the file.

When you attach a graphics box to a character as you did in this Step-by-Step exercise, you can expect some strange spacing in your paragraph unless your image is really tiny. In this case, the little rose image pushed the third line of the paragraph down an extra line. If you have occasion to attach graphics boxes to characters, you'll have to work on achieving exactly the right look for your documents.

Text Box

All of the Step-by-Step exercises in this lesson have involved an Image box. At one point, you set it to be a User box, but it still contained an image. While any of the box styles can contain images or text, a Text box is created in the keying mode. After keying, click outside of the box to exit the keying mode and deselect the box.

If you wish to edit the contents (text) of the box, click in the box to return to the keying mode. Little diagonal lines will surround the box. If you wish to edit the box itself, you must select the box. Selecting the box by pointing to it with the mouse and clicking is tricky. Sometimes you'll enter the edit mode and sometimes the box will be selected. Normally, when you want the Text box selected, it is because you will format it with a choice from the QuickMenu. Simply point to the box and right click. The box will be selected and the QuickMenu will be displayed. A couple of tricks for selecting the box without the QuickMenu include: 1) After right clicking, choose Select Box. 2) After right clicking, press the Esc key to close the menu.

Text boxes may be used as sticky notes in documents. When formatted as a sticky note, the box will cover the text behind it. The sticky note can be placed anywhere on the page, and is often used to give comments to the reader of an electronic (not paper) document.

STEP-BY-STEP 21.12

1. Beginning in a new document window, open the **Insert** menu and choose **Text Box**.

2. Key the sentences in Figure 21-8. Click outside of the box to exit the keying mode. Then point to the box and right click to display the QuickMenu.

3. Choose **Style** and change the style to a **User** box. Then change it to a **Figure** box. As you can see, the box contents are unaffected by the box style.

4. Change the Width to **2"** and leave the Height setting at **Maintain proportions**. With the box selected, point to the box border. When the four-headed arrow appears, align the box with the left and top margin guidelines.

5. Click in the Text box to edit the contents. Format the words *TEXT BOX* with **Bold** and **Italic**.

6. Deselect the box and save the file as **box 21-12 xxx**. Play your **pf** macro to identify the document. Keep it open in your window.

7. Go to your student **datafile** folder and open **columns**. With the document open in the window, create a Text box that says:

   This is a sample sticky note.

8. Click outside of the box to exit the edit mode. Then display the QuickMenu and choose **Style**. At the bottom of the list, choose **Sticky Note Text**.

9. Position the sticky note in different places on the text. Then close the practice without saving. The **box 21-12 xxx** file will remain open.

FIGURE 21-8
Text for Step-by-Step 21.12

```
This is a TEXT BOX. It is one
of the graphics box styles, and
it is enclosed in a single-line
border.
```

While Text boxes may have different contents than graphics boxes containing images, the theory is the same. All of the things you can do when working with graphics boxes containing images can be done with Text boxes. In fact, you now should be an expert at working with graphics boxes.

Let's learn about another way to create a graphics box.

Drag to Create

Another way to insert a graphics image into your document is by using Drag to Create. When the Shadow Pointer is selected, your pointer turns into a tool that enables you to draw a box in the document window. Then WordPerfect takes you to a QuickMenu from which you may choose a graphics option.

Let's try Drag to Create in our practice document.

1. With **box 21-12 xxx** open, click the **Shadow Pointer** button on the Application Bar at the bottom of the window to choose that option.

2. Beginning to the right of the Text box, press the left mouse button and hold it. Move the mouse slightly. Your mouse pointer will look like a hand holding a piece of paper.

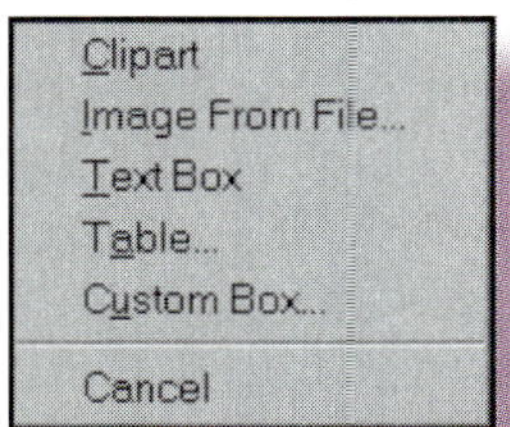

3. Hold the mouse pointer as you draw a box that is about two inches wide and a half inch high.

4. Release the mouse pointer. A QuickMenu will appear, giving you a choice of graphics options (see Figure 21-9). Choose **Text Box** and key your entire name.

5. Click outside of the box to exit the edit mode. Select the box. Use the sizing handles so the border fits snugly around your name.

6. Drag to create another box. (Any size will do.) From the QuickMenu, choose **Image From File**.

7. Go to the **datafile** folder and insert **dog.wpg**. Center it in the middle of the page, below the Text boxes, and deselect the graphics box.

8. Select the dog box, display the QuickMenu, and choose **Wrap**. At the left of the dialog box, choose **Behind text**. Click **OK**.

9. Back in your document window, deselect the image. With the shadow pointer still chosen, point at the left of the dog's paper. When the gray arrow points right, click to position the insertion point. Using the **space bar**, move the insertion point into the box and key **I'm Fido**. (If the words aren't exactly centered, move the Image box until they are and your image looks like Figure 21-10.)

10. Save the file as **box 21-13 xxx**. Print it and close it.

FIGURE 21-9
Drag to Create Options

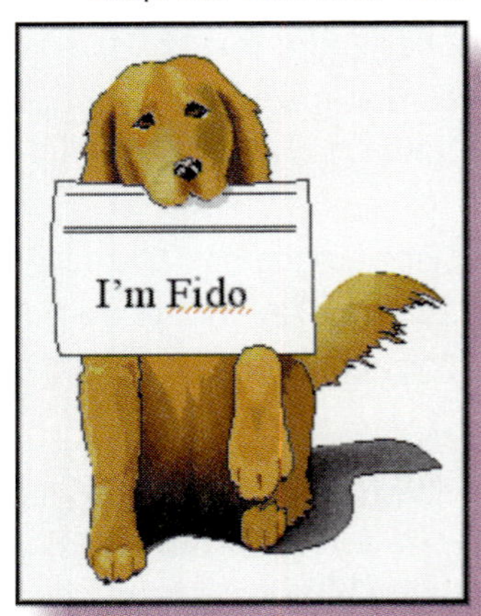

FIGURE 21-10
Graphics Box with Text

Look at your Fido document. The dog image from the Clipart collection is one of only a few images designed so the text will fit within a frame. When you use those images with text placed on the page with hard returns and tabs, the text is firmly positioned on the page. If you wish to move the image, you must also adjust the placement of the text. What's more, in order for this to work, you must tell WordPerfect to put the image behind the text with the Wrap setting. We'll learn another way to combine text with an image in Lesson 22.

Let's review with a final Step-by-Step exercise.

STEP-BY-STEP 21.14

1. Beginning in a new document window, open the **Insert** menu and choose **Graphics**. Then choose **From File**.

2. In the Insert Image dialog box, locate your student **datafile** folder and double click to insert the **Friends2.wpg** image.

3. Save the file as **friends 21-14 xxx**. Play your **pf** macro to identify the document.

4. Center the word **Friends** as a caption for the image. Format the caption with a **10-pt.** sans serif font using **Italic**.

5. Display the QuickMenu and choose **Position**. Set the Horizontal Position at **Center of Margins**.

6. Display the QuickMenu again and choose **Content**. In the Box Content dialog box, click the button displaying the file folder beside the *Filename* text box. You will be returned to your **datafile** files. Double click to choose **Friends.wpg** and confirm that you would like this image to replace the current contents of the box.

7. Print the file and close it, saving it again with the same name.

Summary

This lesson has provided you with the basics of working with graphics boxes. You learned that the boxes can contain images or text. Specifically, you learned that:

- You can use graphics boxes to dress up documents.

- Graphics boxes can contain text or images.

- WordPerfect comes with several dozen images.

- You can move graphics boxes by dragging them.

- You can size graphics boxes by dragging a sizing handle or by using the Box Size dialog box.

- If you want to preserve the width/height ratio of your graphics images, you must make that choice in the Content dialog box.

- You can manipulate your graphics boxes using the QuickMenu or the Graphics button on the Graphics Property Bar.

- You can enclose your graphics boxes in different border styles and apply different fill options, if you wish.

- Your text can be wrapped around the box in a number of ways.

- A variety of box types are available from which you may choose for the look you want.

- Captions can be manipulated so they appear where you wish and say what you'd like them to say.

- If you prefer to draw a box in your document and fill it with an image or text, you can use the Shadow Pointer for the Drag to Create feature.

- You can insert an image that has been saved as a file.

LESSON 21 REVIEW QUESTIONS

MULTIPLE CHOICE

Circle the best answer to each of the following statements.

1. WordPerfect graphics images have a _______ extension.
   - **A.** *.cgm*
   - **B.** *.wpg*
   - **C.** *.wcm*
   - **D.** *.sty*

2. To insert a graphics image into your document, you must choose _______ from the ______ menu.
   - **A.** Image, Tools
   - **B.** Image, Insert
   - **C.** Graphics, Format
   - **D.** Graphics, Insert

3. When an image is selected, it is surrounded by
   - **A.** a heavy black line.
   - **B.** moving handles.
   - **C.** sizing handles.
   - **D.** a fine black line.

4. When an image is selected, the graphics tools will appear on the _________
   - **A.** Property Bar.
   - **B.** Toolbar.
   - **C.** Application Bar.
   - **D.** Ruler.

5. The other source of tools is the _________
   - **A.** QuickGraphics.
   - **B.** QuickMenu.
   - **C.** QuickFormat.
   - **D.** QuickImages.

6. When you bring a graphics box into a document, it will always be _______ wide.
   - **A.** 1"
   - **B.** 1.25"
   - **C.** 1.50"
   - **D.** 2"

7. You can move a graphics box with the moving tool, which is _________
   - **A.** a black square on each corner.
   - **B.** a fat white arrow.
   - **C.** a four-headed arrow.
   - **D.** a dotted square.

MATCHING

Write the letter of the term or phrase from Column 2 that best matches the description in Column 1.

Column 1

____ **8.** Contains text for information to be set apart from the rest of the text in the document.

____ **9.** Used for images but contains the image in a single-line border.

____ **10.** Most often used to put buttons in your document, representing a link to another part of the document.

Column 2

A. Image box

B. Text box

C. Equation box

D. Figure box

E. User box

F. Button box

G. OLE 2.0 box

LESSON 21 PROJECT

Let's apply what you've learned about working with graphics boxes in three short projects. Your instructions are more general than specific. Make your documents lovely!

PROJECT 21A

Open the **wind** document from the student **datafile** folder. Save it with your documents as **wind proj21a xxx**. Give the document a title (you get to create it). Position the title $1^1/2$" from the top of the page. Format the document with double spacing.

Insert the **Windmill.wpg** graphics image from the student **datafile** folder. Position the image in the lower left corner, and set Wrap to Contour and Right. Make the image 4" wide with Height set to Maintain proportions.

Play your **pf** macro to identify the document. Make sure the image doesn't cover the footer. If necessary, use Make It Fit to get the entire document and image on one page. Print the document and close it, saving it again with the same name.

Figure 21-11 illustrates an old WordPerfect graphics image with text keyed over the image with Wrap set at Behind Text. It is in your **datafile** folder and is called **blob**. It is illustrated with the paper in landscape orientation and the Width set at Full and Height set at Maintain proportions. The text is keyed using 30-pt. Times New Roman, although you can use any font you like.

To get the text in the correct location, deselect the image and press Enter until the insertion point is on the correct line. Then center the text. Because the space for the text in the image is off center, you may wish to use the space bar to push the text a little farther to the right.

When you finish, save the file as **party proj21b xxx**. Play the **pf** macro and print the file. Close it.

FIGURE 21-11
Solution for Project 21B

PROJECT 21C

Open **wind proj21a xxx**. Use Save As to save the document as **wind proj21c xxx**. Change the document so it is formatted with Balanced newspaper columns. Drag the inner column guidelines toward the gutter so each column is 3.13" wide and the gutter is 0.25".

Adjust the size of the graphics box containing the windmill so it is only 3" wide. Maintain the proportions in the Height section. Zoom to Full Page so you can see what you are doing as you move the graphics box to the exact center of the page. Keep the text contoured (largest side) around the box. The document should still be contained on one page. If it isn't, use Make It Fit to adjust it to fit on one page.

When your page looks good, save it again as **wind proj21c xxx**, print it, and close it.

CRITICAL THINKING ACTIVITY

You have just finished keying the first draft of your small group's report on democratic countries of the world. The report highlights the six largest countries, and with WordPerfect's Clipart capabilities, you have added graphics images of each country's flag plus one or two more images that were appropriate to each country. After adding and deleting text from the suggested revisions, you print the report, but notice that the images are no longer where you inserted them. What could have happened and how would you fix this problem?

WORKING WITH IMAGES

OBJECTIVES

Upon completion of this lesson, you will be able to:

- Discuss the sources of graphics images to be used in WordPerfect.
- Use the Image Tools palette to edit images.
- Discuss changing defaults for box styles.
- Group graphics boxes and change their order.

Estimated Time: 1 hour

While you might have thought you learned all there was to know about working with graphics boxes in Lesson 21, you'll be pleased to know that a whole set of tools have yet to be explored. These tools are the Image Tools, which can be chosen from either the graphics box QuickMenu or the Graphics button on the Graphics Property Bar.

The tools you used in Lesson 21 were primarily concerned with how and where the graphics box appears in your document. The Image Tools palette concentrates on the image itself and how you can use it to make your documents more attractive.

Before we begin working with the Image Tools, let's briefly discuss images and where you might get the images you need for your work.

Sources of Images

The images you used in your graphics boxes in Lesson 21 were all WordPerfect images. Some of them were from WordPerfect Office 2000. Others were from earlier versions of WordPerfect.

Graphics can be acquired from hundreds of sources. Following is a list of some of the sources of graphics images that can be used in your WordPerfect documents:

- You can purchase packages of clipart at any computer supply store or from mail-order catalogs.
- Graphics images can be downloaded from a computer bulletin board or the Internet. (When you download, be sure to check the files for computer viruses.)
- Pictures and images can be scanned from hard copy.
- Digital cameras can be used to take pictures that are recorded on disks. Some digital cameras can be plugged into your computer for transfer of the pictures to your computer.

- You or a talented friend can create images in a draw program.

- Programs are available that allow you to capture images in your window. These programs convert the captured image to a file that can be used in WordPerfect.

When you download images from a bulletin board or the Internet, be careful not to violate copyrights. Most "cute" images like Disney characters shouldn't be used because companies such as Disney own copyrights for those characters.

WordPerfect will recognize images saved in a variety of formats. Some of these include *.wfm, .tif,* and *.pcx.* As you already know, all WordPerfect images have a *.wpg* extension.

Corel Images

An obvious source of graphics images is right in your WordPerfect program. When you inserted your first image, you saw many more images in the **ClipArt** folder. If you choose From File and go to the **WordPerfect Graphics** folder, you'll find another set of folders that includes **backgrounds**, **borders**, **ClipArt**, **photos**, **Pictures**, and **textures** (see Figure 22-1). Each of these folders contains another set of folders, categorizing the images so it is easier for you to find what you want.

FIGURE 22-1
Graphics Folders

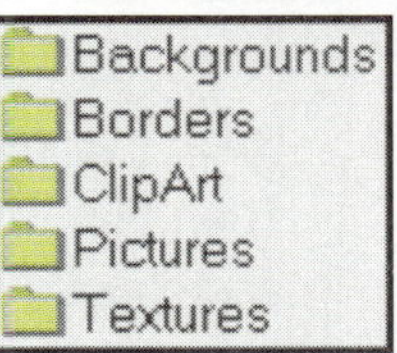

Backgrounds provide continuity to slide shows prepared using the presentations portion of WordPerfect Office 2000. *Borders* are useful for page borders. (You'll learn about borders in Lesson 23.) The *Textures* folder contains wood grains, bricks, and a variety of other backgrounds to be used for specific purposes such as Web pages.

Pictures are bitmapped pictures. For some documents, you'll find them to be rather grainy. Let's preview the pictures. (Your instructor may need to help you locate the **Corel Graphics** folder.)

Have your instructor direct you to the Corel folder. Choose WordPerfect Office 2000 and then Graphics.

S T E P - B Y - S T E P ⇨ 22.1

1. Beginning in a new document window, open the **Insert** menu and choose **Graphics**. Then choose **From File**.

2. If you have a standard WordPerfect Office 2000 installation, begin at the root. Choose **Program Files**, **Corel**, **WordPerfect Office 2000**, **Graphics**, and then **Pictures**.

3. Click the **Preview** button on the dialog box Toolbar. Browse through the folders and look at the pictures using the following guidelines:
   a. Time yourself. Don't spend more than 5 minutes looking at the images in the folders. (Some images can't be previewed.)
   b. To select a folder, double click.
   c. To return to the "parent folder," click the folder icon just to the right of the *Look in* text box.
   d. When you finish, click the **Preview** button again to deselect that option and close the dialog box.

4. Close your empty document window without saving.

Bitmapped images can be edited a single dot at a time. That's a topic for a graphics course, not a word processing course. If you are interested, WordPerfect Help contains information about editing bitmaps.

Image Tools Palette

The Image Tools palette provides you with a whole set of features to help customize your images. Let's explore the palette using an image from an earlier version of WordPerfect.

Rotate and Move

Let's begin with the tools at the top of the palette.

1. Open the **Insert** menu. Choose **Graphics** and **From File**. Go to your student **datafile** folder and choose **Mallard.wpg**.

2. Display the QuickMenu and choose **Content**. Be sure the image width/height ratio is preserved.

3. With the image selected, choose **Image Tools** from the QuickMenu. The Image Tools palette will look like Figure 22-2.

4. Beginning in the upper left corner, click the **Rotate** button. The selected image will have another set of black squares around it. The new squares with little lines beside them are *rotate* handles.

5. Grab one of the rotate handles and tip the duck forward to the right, as shown in Figure 22-3. When you release the mouse button, part of his head will be hiding behind the edge of the box.

6. Drag the Image Tools palette to the right. Then grab the sizing handle at the center right of the graphics box and drag it so the box containing the duck fills half of the page between the margin guidelines. (The duck will move to the middle of the box.)

7. Click the **Move** button in the Image Tools palette and use the **Move** tool to drag the duck to the right, so its bill is just inside of the graphics box area. If you move too far, move it back.

8. Close the Image Tools palette and deselect the duck. Save the file as **duck 22-2 xxx**. Play your **pf** macro and save the file again.

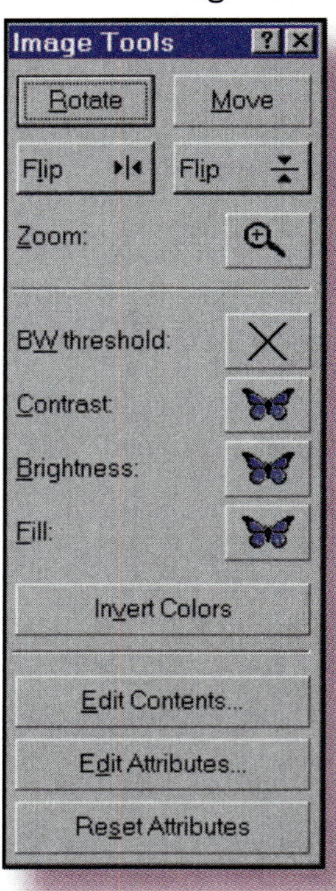

FIGURE 22-2
Image Tools

FIGURE 22-3
Rotating the Duck

When you enlarged the graphics box, the duck moved to the middle. It didn't get fatter because you told WordPerfect to preserve the width/height ratio. In the last couple of steps you moved the duck to one end of the graphics box. The entire area between the sizing handles is the graphics box. Sometimes you want a box that is larger than the image, and you want part of the box to remain empty. The Move tool enables you to position the image anywhere you want it in the graphics box.

Flip

The two Flip buttons enable you to turn your images around. Good page layout dictates that an image usually faces toward the center of the page, not toward the edge of the page. Rarely will you have an image that you can turn upside down!

S TEP-BY-STEP ⇨ 22.3

1. With the **duck 22-2 xxx** document in the window, drag the graphics box from the left margin to the right margin. Align it with the top and right margin guidelines.

2. Display the Image Tools palette and use the **Rotate** tool to make your duck stand upright again (not tipped).

3. Turn your duck upside down with the **Flip** button on the right. Then tip him upright again.

4. Use the **Flip** button on the left to make the duck face the left. With the duck facing the left, use the **Move** tool to move him a little closer to the right edge of the graphics box. Don't lose any tail feathers.

5. Keep him in that position and read on.

Zoom

The Zoom button is three-tiered. Let's try each of the tiers and learn as we work with them.

S TEP-BY-STEP ⇨ 22.4

1. With your duck showing and the Image Tools palette displayed, click the **Zoom** button in the Image Tools palette. Compare your pop-out menu with Figure 22-4.

FIGURE 22-4
Zoom Portion of Image Tools

2. Choose the first tool—the one that looks like a magnifying glass with a plus sign in the middle. This turns your mouse pointer into a floating crosshair to be used for drawing an "elastic" box around a part of the image.

3. Draw a box that includes only the duck's head. When you release the mouse pointer, your image will  include only the part of the duck around which you made the elastic box.

(continued on next page)

4. Deselect the graphics box. Then save your file as **duck 22-4 xxx** and print it.

5. Display the Image Tools palette again and choose the middle **Zoom** tool. This displays a scroll bar which you can use to increase or decrease the view of the duck. Experiment with it. Then return to the head shot.

6. Choose the third **Zoom** tool. This restores the duck. Finally, click the **Reset Attributes** button at the bottom of the Image Tools palette. This returns the duck to its original proportions, and it will be facing to the right again.

7. Keep the duck in the window as you read on.

When you displayed the head of the duck only, you didn't really crop that portion from the duck. The rest of the image was still there. It was just hiding, waiting for you to restore the entire image.

Color

The next four buttons—BW threshold, Contrast, Brightness, and Fill—have to do with the colors of the image and how bright they are. Because the duck is in color, the BW (black/white) threshold is set at None. Contrast and Brightness can move in either direction. The default is the center choice. With a color image, Fill won't be adjusted. The big button at the bottom of that section allows you to invert colors—to look at the colors that are complementary to the regular colors.

STEP-BY-STEP 22.5

1. Spend no more than 5 minutes playing with the five color choices on the Image Tools palette. You may choose any settings you wish for your duck.

2. Do NOT click the Edit Contents button. That button takes you to the draw program. It takes a long time to load on most computers, and you need to keep moving.

3. When you have a good idea of what happens with the color choices, click the second button from the bottom—**Edit Attributes**. This displays a dialog box containing all of the tools with which you've been working.

4. Spend a few minutes exploring the choices in that box. Then click **Reset All** to see how easy it is to restore the duck. Close your duck file without saving it again.

As you can see, your options are unlimited regarding what you can do to make the Clipart images fit attractively in your documents.

Box Styles

As discussed earlier, some of the default settings may not be satisfactory as you use WordPerfect on the job and use images in your documents. One of the settings you may decide to change will be the one in the Content dialog box where you told WordPerfect to maintain the width/height ratio. Another is the setting that attaches images to the page rather than to the paragraph.

368

Whether you need to edit those defaults to make you more efficient on the job will depend on the kind of work you do. In the classroom, however, you don't want to change ANY defaults. Otherwise, it will be confusing to other students.

So that you can learn how easily those defaults can be changed, however, we'll try a Step-by-Step exercise in which you DO change the defaults. Then we'll cancel the changes as we return to the working window. Follow along carefully.

S TEP-BY-STEP 22.6

1. Beginning in a new document window, open the **Insert** menu. Choose **Graphics** and **Custom Box**. Click the **Styles** button.

2. Be sure **Image** is selected. (When you make changes to box styles, you must change each type individually.)

3. Click **Edit** to display the Edit Box Style dialog box, as illustrated in Figure 22-5.

4. Note that at the top, it reinforces that you are editing the Image style. Look at the buttons at the left. Do they look familiar?

5. Click **Content** and choose the **Preserve...** choice at the bottom. Click **OK**.

6. Click **Position** and change to **Paragraph**. Click **OK**.

7. Now, because you don't want to save those changes, click **Cancel** and then **Close** and **Cancel** to return to your document window.

FIGURE 22-5
Edit Box Style Dialog Box

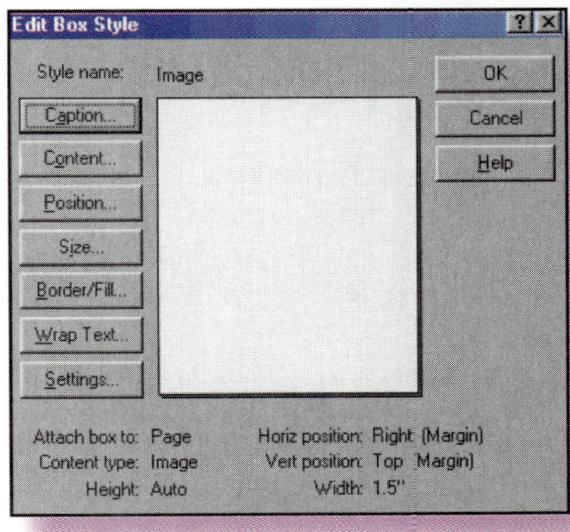

INTERNET In certain browsers and other Internet programs, a bookmark or hotlist is a special file used to save addresses and locations. By saving and recalling addresses, it is easy for you to visit your favorite sites over and over.

Had you accepted the changes you made in those dialog boxes, WordPerfect would have remembered the settings, and you would not have needed to make either of them in your work with future images.

Grouping and Arranging Graphics Boxes

When you have more than one graphics box occupying the same space, WordPerfect enables you to decide which box is on top. You can rearrange the order of the boxes as often as you wish. You can also group two or more boxes so that they can be sized or moved together.

Remember Fido? We'll use that same image for practice.

1. Beginning in a new document window, insert the **dog** from the **datafile** folder. Size the image to 2" wide. Maintain the proportions for height.

2. Save the file as **fido 22-7 xxx**. Play your **pf** macro to identify the document.

3. Position the image Centered between Margins and 1" from the top margin.

4. Return to the **datafile** folder and insert the **litebulb.wpg** image. Size it so it's 0.75" wide.

5. Move the lightbulb so the base of it is over the dog's head. With the lightbulb selected, display the QuickMenu and choose **Order**. Choose **To Back**. (The base of the lightbulb should now be behind Fido's head.)

6. Create a Text box that contains the words **I have an idea!**. Press **Enter** after the word *have* so the text is on two lines.

7. Click outside of the box to exit the edit mode. Display the QuickMenu, choose **Border/Fill**, and set the border at **None** (the first choice in the first row of borders). Size the box so the handles are close to the text on all sides.

8. With the Text box still selected, use the moving tool (the four-headed arrow) to move the Text box to the paper in Fido's mouth. For practice, with the box still selected, choose **Order** from the QuickMenu and move the text to the back. Click away from the box to deselect it.

9. Point to the place where the Text box is hiding. Select the Text box again. Use the QuickMenu and choose **Order** again to move it to the front.

10. Your file should look like Figure 22-6. Save it again with the same name. Keep it open.

FIGURE 22-6
Layered Graphics Boxes

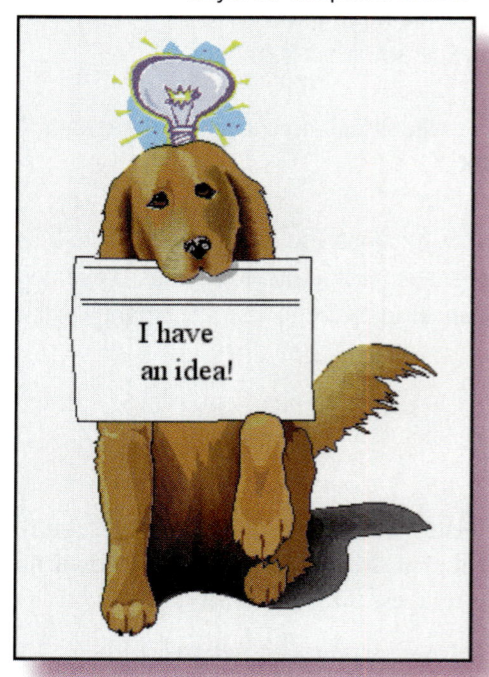

Your picture now has three graphics boxes. You aligned them so they look good together. But they are still separate items. If you move one of them, the others will stay in the same place. Let's learn to group the boxes so you can move them as one.

STEP-BY-STEP 22.8

1. With **fido 22-7 xxx** showing in the window, save it as **fido 22-8 xxx**. For practice, move the lightbulb away from the dog. Then move it back. It is a separate item.

2. Click the lightbulb to select that image. Hold the **Shift** key while you select the Text box. (One set of sizing handles will surround those two boxes.)

3. Still holding the **Shift** key, click Fido's tail to select the dog. The sizing handles should now contain all three graphics boxes. (If you get dashed lines around the images, cl ck away from them and start again.)

4. Display the QuickMenu and choose **Group**. Point to any part of the grouping and drag it to a different position on the page. All three parts of the grouping should move.

5. Use a corner sizing handle to make the image larger or smaller. The parts should be adjusted together. (If you use the Size dialog box to size a set of grouped boxes, they will fall apart.)

6. Select the grouped images and display the QuickMenu again. Choose **Separate** to change them back into individual boxes.

7. Select the lightbulb and make it 0.5" wide. Reposition it behind Fido's head.

8. Print your practice and save it again with the same name. Close the document.

Summary

This short lesson provided you with additional information about working with graphics images. In this lesson you learned that:

- You can buy Clipart images.

- You can download images from bulletin boards and the Internet.

- WordPerfect Office 2000 comes with a large number of images.

- Images can be rotated and moved within the graphics box area.

- You can flip an image vertically or horizontally.

- Color brightness and intensity can be adjusted.

- After making adjustments to an image, it is easy to return the image to its original size, shape, and color.

- If you find yourself constantly making the same change(s) to graphics boxes, you can change the default settings.

■ You can adjust the position of two or several boxes to the front or back.

■ Multiple graphics boxes can be grouped to behave as one box.

LESSON 22 REVIEW QUESTIONS

FILL IN THE BLANKS

Complete each of the following statements by writing your answer in the blank provided.

1. The Image Tools can be chosen from either the graphics box QuickMenu or the _______________ on the Graphics Property Bar.

2. When you choose From File and go to the WordPerfect Graphics folder, you'll find another set of folders that includes Backgrounds, Borders, ClipArt, _______________, and Textures.

3. Click the _______________ button on the dialog box Toolbar to browse through the folders and look at the pictures.

4. With the image selected, choose Image Tools and the Image Tools ___________ will be displayed.

5. The __________ tool enables you to position the image anywhere you want it in the graphics box.

6. The two ___________ buttons enable you to turn your images around.

7. The ___________ button is three-tiered; the first one looks like a magnifying glass with a plus sign in the middle.

TRUE/FALSE

Circle the T if the statement is true. Circle the F if it is false.

T   F   8. The Textures folder contains images of wood grains, bricks, and a variety of other backgrounds.

T   F   9. You can download images from the Internet and use them free of charge because you have already paid for on-line services.

T   F   10. You can rearrange the order of the boxes once, from front to back.

LESSON 22 PROJECT

In this project you get to apply your skills with regard to inserting and editing graphics images. You will work on your own, with few directions. Following is the general idea of what you are to do:

1. Open **Brazil** from the student **datafile** folder and save it as **Brazil proj22 xxx**.

2. Use the **pf** macro to identify the file.

3. Increase the size of the top margin on the first page. Format the title and side headings using different font sizes and bold, if you wish. After formatting one side heading, use QuickFormat to apply the formatting to the others, making it easy to reformat if you should change your mind.

4. Use Widow/Orphan control or Block Protect, if necessary, to achieve an attractive page break.

5. Use at least two of the three graphics images listed. Get them from your student **datafile** folder. Position, size, and edit the images so they complement the document, not detract from it. (You may use other graphics images, if you wish. Do not use more than three graphics boxes in a document of this length.)
   a. **Brazil flag.wpg**
   b. **Brazil map.wpg**
   c. **Tropics.wpg**

6. Select the first sentence in the second paragraph about Economics. Copy it to the Clipboard. Then create a Text box. Paste the sentence into that box. Adjust the size of the box so it is 2" wide. Align it at the right margin. Change the text in the box to 14-pt. italic. Go to Border/Fill and choose the fifth border in the second row (Thick Top/Bottom). This type of box that highlights certain information in a document is called a "pull quote." You have no doubt seen pull quotes in magazines and newspapers.

7. When you finish, save the file again, print it, and close it.

CRITICAL THINKING ACTIVITY

You have been working with the red lobster image that you have inserted into your document. With the Image Tools palette displayed, you notice that the BW threshold button has an X in it. Why is that selection unavailable?

GRAPHICS LINES, BORDERS, AND FILL

Like graphics boxes, graphics lines, borders, and fill are used to enhance the appearance of documents. Much of what you learned in Lesson 21 can be applied to working with lines, borders, and fill. The features are closely related. A graphics border is actually made up of graphics lines. The basic difference is that a border goes all the way around a page, paragraph, or column, while a line simply goes straight from one point to another.

Let's begin by taking a look at graphics lines.

Graphics Lines

WordPerfect will automatically insert horizontal or vertical lines for you if you tell the program what you want. Graphics lines can be chosen from the Insert menu. If you prefer, you can use Ctrl+F11 for a horizontal line and Ctrl+Shift+F11 for a vertical line.

STEP-BY-STEP ➡ 23.1

1. Beginning in a new document window, press **Ctrl+F11** to insert a horizontal line. Press **Enter** twice.

2. Open the **Insert** menu, choose **Line**, and choose **Horizontal Line**. Look at your two lines. They are identical, except the second is two returns below the first.

3. Press **Ctrl+Shift+F11** to insert a vertical line. Press **Tab** twice.

4. Open the **Insert** menu, choose **Line**, and choose **Vertical Line**. Look at your two lines.

5. Zoom to **Full Page** to get a bird's-eye view of your lines. Keep the lines showing in the window as you read on.

The lines you created in Step-by-Step exercise 23.1 are the default lines. Each of them extends from margin to margin and is 0.013" thick. If you wish to create a line with any other characteristics, you must create a custom line. Let's practice with custom lines by creating four of them. We'll do all of the formatting and placement of the lines in the Create Graphics Line dialog box.

STEP-BY-STEP ➡ 23.2

1. Reveal your codes. Look at the line codes. Move your insertion point to the left of one of the codes and look at the description of the line in the code. Record the codes in your list of codes. Close the document without saving it.

2. Open the **Insert** menu, choose **Line**, and choose **Custom Line**. The Create Graphics Line dialog box should appear, looking like Figure 23-1.

3. We will be creating four lines. The first line is easy. In the buttons at the left is one for *Line thickness*. Click it and look at the selection of lines. At the bottom is a number reporting the current thickness. Change that number to **0.10"**. (That's ten hundredths of an inch or a tenth of an inch.) Click **OK** to return to your document and look at the line. It's thick!

4. Return to the dialog box and make the following changes for the second line:
  a. Near the bottom, click the button beside *Horizontal* and change from Full to **Centered**.
  b. Just below Horizontal is *Vertical*. Change from Baseline to **Set**. In the box to the right, key **1.5"** so the second line will be a half inch below the first line.
  c. In the Length box, just above the *Position* section, key **5"**. (The first line was 6.5" long. It went from margin to margin. This line is 1.5" shorter.)
  d. Change thickness to **0.08'**. Click **OK** to return to your document.

5. Create a third line as follows. Then return to your document and look at it.
  a. Set Horizontal at **Centered**.
  b. Set Vertical at **2"** from the top of the page.

(continued on next page)

c. Set Length at **3.5"**.

d. Set thickness at **0.06"**.

6. Finally, create a fourth line. You probably can guess the settings, but here they are:

a. Set Horizontal at **Centered**.

b. Set Vertical at **2.5"**.

c. Set Length at **2"**.

d. Set thickness at **0.04"**.

7. Back in your document window, look at your lines. They should look like Figure 23-2. Save the file as **lines 23-2 xxx**.

8. Play your **pf** macro to identify the document. Print it and keep it open.

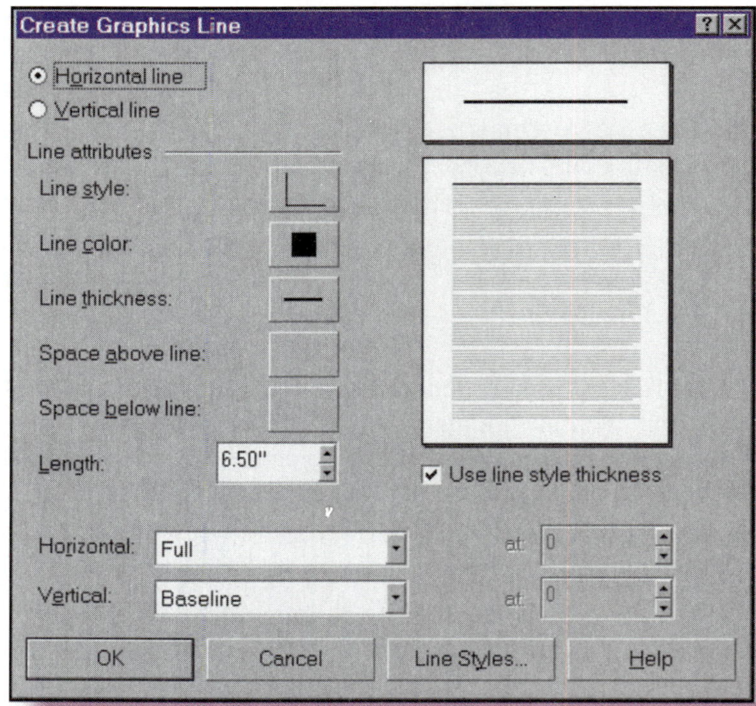

FIGURE 23-1
Create Graphics Line Dialog Box

FIGURE 23-2
The Lines for Step-by-Step 23.2

Once you have created a line, you can edit it or move it to a different location. Let's practice editing lines using the lines in your window.

S TEP-BY-STEP ▷ 23.3

1. Zoom to **Full Page** and save your document as **lines 23-3 xxx**.

2. Point to the first line carefully. When your white mouse pointer arrow points to the right, drag the line to the bottom of the document. (The line will have sizing handles.) Align it at the top of the footer area. Align the ends of the line with the guidelines at the sides of the page.

3. Point to the middle line at the top and drag it so it's about halfway between the 2-inch line and the 6.5-inch line at the bottom. Then point to the sizing handle at the bottom center of the line and drag it down until the line is about a half inch thick. (Make it BIG and BLACK.)

4. Point to the line that's on top and click to give it handles. Then grab a handle on the left end with a two-headed arrow and drag the end of the line as close to the edge of the page as you can get it. (The line should get longer.)

5. Point to the 2-inch line (the only one you haven't edited) and double click to open the Edit Graphics Line dialog box. Change the color of the line to red.

6. Still in the Edit Graphics Line dialog box, click the **Line Styles** button and look at the line styles available. Choose the second line style in the first row. Click **OK** to return to your document.

7. Save your document again as **lines 23-3 xxx**. Print it and close it.

By now you have a pretty good idea of what you can do with horizontal lines. Vertical lines are no different. Simply click the Vertical line radio button in the Create Graphics Line dialog box before setting up the line. Let's create some vertical lines that might be used to dress up a letterhead.

S TEP-BY-STEP ▷ 23.4

1. Beginning in a new document window, create a vertical line that violates the margins of your document. That's OK because the margins will still hold the text. In the Create Graphics Line dialog box, click the button at the top for a **Vertical** line. Set the line up as follows:

  a. Choose **Set** in the Horizontal Position box and key **0.5"** from the left edge of the page.

  b. Choose **Set** in the Vertical Position box and key **0.5"** from the top of the page.

  c. Set the Length at **10"**.

  d. Set thickness at **0.05"**. Click **OK**.

2. Create another vertical line that is the same length, **0.75"** from the left, **0.5"** from the top, and **0.05"** thick. Set the color to a shade of gray. (If you have a color printer, you might want to choose a color that matches your company or school logo.)

3. Return to your document and check your lines. The difference in shading might not be obvious until you print your document.

4. Save the document as **lines 23-4 xxx**. Play your **pf** macro. Then print the document and close it, saving it again.

You can create a different effect by piling your lines up. Look at Figure 23-3. We'll go to the Footer dialog box to position these lines. Then we'll put the Page Number code between them so you can use the whole thing as a fancy footer in your documents.

FIGURE 23-3
Footer Lines

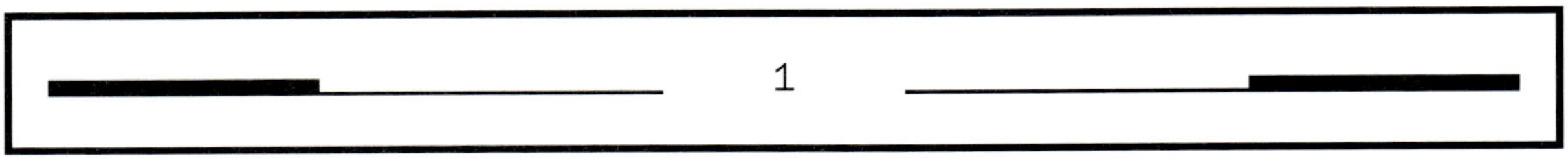

STEP-BY-STEP 23.5

1. Beginning in a new document window, open the **Insert** menu and choose **Header/Footer**. Then choose **Footer A** and **Create**.

2. In the Footer A space, create four horizontal lines, one at a time. Following are the criteria for those lines:
   a. Line 1 — Horizontal Position **Left**, Length **2.5"**
   b. Line 2 — Horizontal Position **Left**, Length **1"**, Thickness **0.05"**
   c. Line 3 — Horizontal Position **Right**, Length **2.5"**
   d. Line 4 — Horizontal Position **Right**, Length **1"**, Thickness **0.05"**

3. Give the **Center** command and click the **Number** button on the Footer Property Bar. Choose **Page Number**. Your page number should appear between your lines.

4. Click the **Close** button on the Property Bar. Use the scroll bar so you can see your footer at the bottom of the page.

5. Save the file as **footer 23-5 xxx**. With your insertion point at the top of the page, open the **Insert** menu, choose **Other**, and then choose **Path and Filename** to identify this non-document. Print it and close it.

These were just a few short Step-by-Step exercises with lines. It should be pretty clear to you at this point that the possibilities for the use of lines in your documents are endless.

Shapes

WordPerfect offers you a wide variety of shapes, such as polygons, polylines, rectangles, circles, and arrows. Each shape is a graphics box that can be edited much as you've edited other graphics boxes. Let's practice with a few of the shapes.

STEP-BY-STEP 23.6

1. Open **columns** again so you have some text in your window. Then open the **Insert** menu and choose **Shapes**. Choose **Basic**. Look at the choices, and choose the first shape—a rectangle. Click **OK**.

2. Beginning somewhere near the left of the first paragraph, draw a rectangle. When you release the mouse button, the rectangle will be filled with the color that was used last, and the Property Bar will change to include some new tools. (You'll learn about working with those tools in Lesson 29.)

3. With the image selected, display the QuickMenu and choose **Wrap**. Choose **Behind text**.

4. Deselect the shape. Open the **Insert** menu, choose **Shapes**, **Lines**, and then the first line. Click **OK**.

5. Beginning in the upper right corner of the document, draw a diagonal line that extends down and to the left, right over the text of the document. End the line by double clicking.

6. With the line selected, display the QuickMenu and choose **Wrap**. Choose **Contour** and **Both sides**. Note how the line bisects your text. Deselect the object.

7. Open the **Insert** menu and choose **Shapes** again. Choose **Basic** and the **Rounded Rectangle**. Draw a rounded rectangle that fits closely around the word *Columns* at the beginning of the last paragraph. Choose **Wrap** and position the shape behind the text.

8. Select the rounded rectangle and drag it so it surrounds the last word of the paragraph instead of the first. Size the box so the entire word is enclosed in the rectangle.

9. Save your practice as **shapes 23-6 xxx**. Play your **pf** macro and print the document before closing it.

Borders

Using the Borders feature isn't much different from the Graphics Line feature. Several line styles have been prepared to save you work in defining what the borders should look like and where they should be placed. Unless you have some unusual application, the predefined styles should meet most of your needs. We'll begin with Paragraph borders.

Paragraph Borders

Paragraph borders enclose one or more paragraphs. You have a choice of Paragraph border styles. Let's try a few of them.

Gopher is a program that uses a series of menus to lead users to files of information. Gopher is named for the Golden Gophers of the University of Minnesota, where the program was developed.

1. Beginning in a new document window, go to the student **datafile** folder and choose **columns**. (This document is beginning to look familiar, isn't it?) Use **Save As** to save the document as **borders 23-7 xxx**.

2. With the insertion point at the beginning of the first paragraph, open the **Format** menu, choose **Paragraph**, and then choose **Border/Fill**. The Paragraph Border/Fill dialog box will open, looking like Figure 23-4.

3. Choose the first border. (It's actually the second button in the first row of borders.) Look at the box at the bottom of the dialog box. The *Apply border to current paragraph only* option should be checked. Click **OK**.

4. Position the insertion point at the beginning of the second paragraph.

5. Choose **Format**, **Paragraph**, and then **Border/Fill**, to return to the Paragraph Border/Fill dialog box.

6. Choose the sixth button in the first row (the one with the black dropped shadow). Click **OK**.

7. Position the insertion point at the beginning of the third paragraph and put a border around that paragraph. This time you'll use the scroll bars so you can choose the second border in the third row. Click **OK**.

FIGURE 23-4
Paragraph Border/Fill Dialog Box

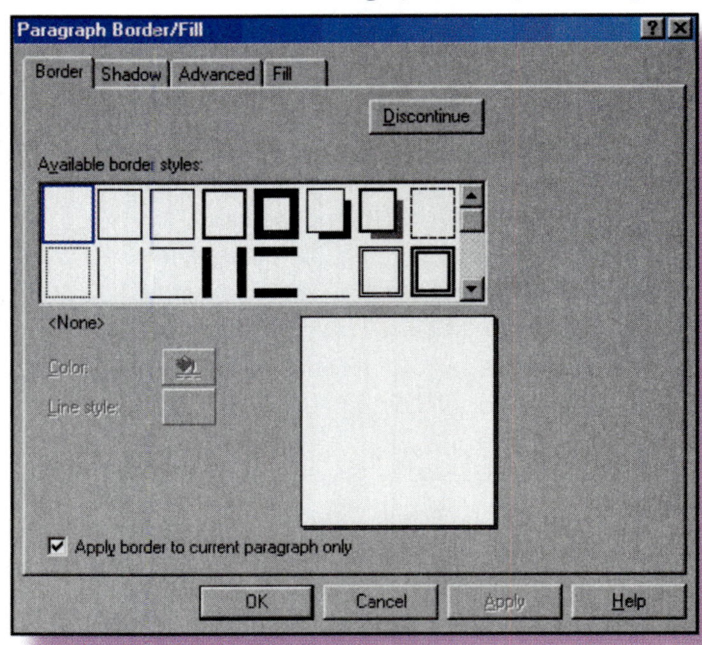

8. Your document has two more paragraphs. Select those paragraphs. Then go to the Paragraph Border/Fill dialog box and choose one last border for these two paragraphs. Note that because they were selected, one border contains both paragraphs.

9. Return to your document window. Save the document again as **borders 23-7 xxx**. Play your **pf** macro and print the document. Save it again, and keep it open.

Sometimes you want more space between the text in the paragraph and the border surrounding the paragraph. WordPerfect will put as much space as you'd like. In the process, the border extends into the margin of the document. The text doesn't change. Let's try it.

STEP-BY-STEP 23.8

1. With **borders 23-7 xxx** showing in the window, position the insertion point at the beginning of the first paragraph.

2. Reveal your codes and find the [Para Border] code for the first paragraph. Point to that code and double click. (You could open the dialog box in the normal way, too, to edit the border.)

3. Look at the top of the dialog box. Find the **Advanced** tab and click it. In the *Spacing* section in the upper left corner, click the button beside **Inside**.

4. Point to the first bar in the right-hand column and click to choose it. Watch your paragraph as the dialog box closes and the change is made. You should see the border expand and move away from the paragraph.

5. Close your document without saving it again.

As you can see, it was easy to adjust the inside space of the border. Most of the time, however, you will probably be satisfied with the default inside space.

Page Borders

Page borders work a lot like Paragraph borders. A major difference is that for Page borders, you get to choose between *Line* borders (like the Paragraph borders) and *Fancy* borders. When you use Line borders, you may choose an option that tells WordPerfect to put the border only on the current page. When you use Fancy borders, the border will appear on all pages of the document following the page where it was inserted. Let's modify our **columns** document and add a Page border that continues to the second page.

STEP-BY-STEP 23.9

1. Beginning in a new document window, open the **File** menu, find **columns** in the list at the bottom, and open that file again. Use **Save As** to save the file as **borders 23-9 xxx**.

2. With the insertion point at the beginning of the document, change to double spacing (2.0). Then open the **Format** menu, choose **Page**, and then choose **Border/Fill**.

3. Look at the *Border type* section at the top. If *Fancy* isn't selected, click the button and choose it.

4. Click below the scroll box six times. Choose the second border in that row. It looks kind of fluffy when it is in miniature. Click once to select it and then click **OK**, or double click to select the border.

5. Back in your document window, look at the shapes that surround your page. Press **Ctrl+End** to look at the second page of the document. Zoom to **Full Page** to see the page in full. Then return to **100%**.

6. Save your document again as **borders 23-9 xxx**. Play your **pf** macro to identify the document. Print the document and keep it open.

If you want the border to appear only on the first page, you can tell WordPerfect to discontinue the border beginning on a particular page. That will turn the border off for the remainder of the document. Let's tell WordPerfect to discontinue the border on the second page.

1. Position the insertion point somewhere near the beginning of the second page of **borders 23-9 xxx**.

2. Return to the Page Border dialog box. Click the **Discontinue** button near the upper right corner.

3. Look at both pages of the document. The first should have a border. The second shouldn't. Close your document without saving it.

You probably noticed as you looked through the borders that some of them would work better for announcements than for pages of text. Let's try one of the really fancy ones.

1. Beginning in a new document window, go to the Page Border/Fill dialog box and choose the fancy border near the bottom that looks like people in front of a stage.

2. Use **Center** justification and prepare the poster illustrated in Figure 23-5. Use whatever font size looks good. You can customize the words, if you don't happen to know an "Amazing Anne."

3. When you finish, save your flyer as **borders 23-11 xxx**. Press **Ctrl+Home** to move the insertion point to the top of the document. Go to the **Insert** menu and insert the Path and Filename code. It should show through the curtain at the top. Print the flyer, save it, and close it.

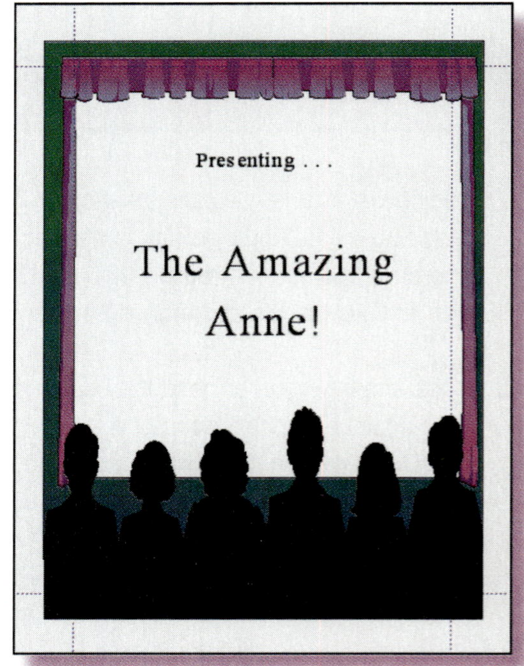

FIGURE 23-5
Flyer for Step-by-Step 23.11

Now let's go back to the Page Border/Fill dialog box and look at the Line borders.

S T E P - B Y - S T E P ▷ 23.12

1. Open **columns** again from the list at the bottom of the **File** menu. Save the file in your normal folder as **borders 23-12 xxx**.

2. With the insertion point at the beginning of the document, set double spacing.

3. Go to the Page Border/Fill dialog box and change *Border type* to **Line**.

4. Look at the variety of Line borders. Choose the last border on the right of the second row of borders.

5. Look at the bottom of the box. Does a check mark tell WordPerfect to put the border on the current page only? If it doesn't, click that option to select it and click **OK** to return to your document window.

6. Look at the first page. Look at the second page. The border should appear only on the first page.

7. Play your **pf** macro. Print the document and close it, saving it again.

Column Borders

The third kind of border is the Column border. Column borders can only be chosen if your text is in columns. Two styles of Column borders are available—with only a line between the columns, or with the columns completely enclosed within the border.

Let's open our **columns** document yet again and try the two border styles available for columns.

S T E P - B Y - S T E P ▷ 23.13

1. Beginning in a new document window, go to the **File** menu and open **columns**. Use **Save As** to save the file as **borders 23-13 xxx**.

2. With the insertion point at the beginning of the document, go to the Columns dialog box and change to **2 Balanced newspaper** columns. Keep the dialog box open.

3. With the Columns dialog box still displayed, click the **Border/Fill** button.

4. Choose the seventh border style in the last full row of borders and look at it in the Preview window. It is simply a line between the columns.

5. Choose the fifth border in the same row.

6. Click the **Shadow** tab. Choose the fourth shadow in the second row. Change the color of the shadow to blue.

7. Click the **Advanced** tab. Note that you can change inside and outside border space for Column borders, just as you did for Paragraph borders.

8. Click **OK** twice to return to your document. Play your **pf** macro. Then print the file and close it, saving it again as **borders 23-13 xxx**.

Actually, you can apply any page border style to your columns, but the two with which you experimented in this Step-by-Step exercise are the only two that will put a line between the columns.

Fill

Finally, let's take a look at fill. As you know, *fill* is the term that refers to shading the background of something. You used fill in the background of your rose in Lesson 21. The theory is the same. Choose the fill style and/or darkness. Let's work with fill for paragraphs.

STEP-BY-STEP 23.14

1. Open the **columns** document from the student **datafile** folder one more time. Use **Save As** to save the file as **borders 23-14 xxx**.

2. Position the insertion point at the beginning of the second paragraph. Choose **Format**, **Paragraph**, and **Border/Fill**. Click the **Fill** tab and look at the variety of Fill styles available.

3. Choose the Fill style third to the right of *None*. Close the Paragraph Border/Fill dialog box.

4. Play your **pf** macro, print the document, save it, and close it.

As you can see, WordPerfect offers you a wide variety of fill styles. In addition, a number of options are available that you can explore at your leisure.

Summary

This lesson was all about dressing up your documents. You learned quite a number of things you can do for that "certain" look. In this lesson you learned that:

- Horizontal, diagonal, and vertical lines, as well as drawn shapes, can be inserted to dress up your documents.

- WordPerfect provides you with a wide variety of borders for paragraphs, pages, and columns.

- You can use fill with or without borders to cause portions of text to stand out from the rest.

LESSON 23 REVIEW QUESTIONS

MULTIPLE CHOICE

Circle the best answer to each of the following statements.

1. If you wish to create a custom line, open the Insert menu, choose _______, and choose Custom Line.
   - **A.** Line
   - **B.** Graphics
   - **C.** Shape
   - **D.** Image

2. The default length of a horizontal graphics line is
   - **A.** $6^{1}/_{2}$ inches.
   - **B.** $8^{1}/_{2}$ inches.
   - **C.** 9 inches.
   - **D.** 11 inches.

3. If you create a vertical line with Ctrl+Shift+F11, your line
   - **A.** can be set at two inches.
   - **B.** will extend from the left margin to the right margin.
   - **C.** will extend from the top margin to the bottom margin.
   - **D.** will extend from the left edge of the page to the right edge.

4. To enclose a paragraph with a border, open the _______ menu, choose Paragraph, and then choose Border/Fill.
   - **A.** Format
   - **B.** Insert
   - **C.** Graphics
   - **D.** Tools

5. When enclosing the text on a page with a Page border,
   - **A.** the text must first be selected.
   - **B.** the insertion point can be anywhere on the page.
   - **C.** the border must be applied before text is keyed.
   - **D.** the border is formatted in a new document and the text is inserted from another file.

6. The third kind of border you learned about in this lesson was the _______ border.
   - **A.** Table
   - **B.** Image
   - **C.** Graphics
   - **D.** Column

Write your answers to the following questions.

7. Define the term *fill.*

8. What is the easiest way to move a line?

9. When you choose Page borders, your choices are between what type of borders?

10. What are the two styles of Column borders?

LESSON 23 PROJECT

SCANS

The project for Lesson 23 consists of several short exercises reviewing what you learned in the lesson. Work quickly and efficiently. See how much you can do without having to look back into the lesson for help.

PROJECT 23A

Open **lighthouses u3ap2 xxx**. Save the document as **lighthouses proj23a xxx**. Give the title page of the document a border. You may choose a Line border or a Fancy border. Be sure that the border is on the title page only. If you use a Fancy border, you'll have to discontinue it on the first page of text.

When you finish, save the document again and print the title page only. Close the document.

PROJECT 23B

Use one of the Fancy borders to create a one-page poster, flyer, or handbill. Consider a poster advertising a school dance or party. Perhaps you want to create a flyer urging your classmates to vote for a particular candidate.

When you are satisfied with your work, save the document as **proj23b xxx**. Identify it with the Path and Filename code, either in the footer with the **pf** macro or somewhere else on the page where it will be visible. Print and close the file, saving it again when you close it.

PROJECT 23C

Create a simple letterhead for your home or business using the sample in Figure 23-6 as a guide. Use at least two graphics lines, and vary their width or length to make your letterhead attractive. Vary the font sizes to stress the important parts of your letterhead.

When you finish, save the sample letterhead as **proj23c xxx**. Use your **pf** macro to identify the page. Then print it and close it, saving it again when you close it.

MYCORP MANUFACTURING
1492 Highland Drive
Hometown, OH 44135

Phone 216-555-2525   Fax 216-555-2526

CRITICAL THINKING ACTIVITY

You have just printed out a document in which you have used Paragraph borders to highlight some of the information. You are not pleased with the appearance of the document because it looks too crowded. You think that if you had more space between the border and the text of the paragraph it would improve the layout. What can you do and how do you do it?

FEATURE BONANZA

OBJECTIVES

Upon completion of this lesson, you will be able to:

- Use TextArt to create lovely display documents.
- Add drop caps to the beginning of your paragraphs.
- Work with the Equation Editor.
- Rotate the text in a Text box.
- Mark text with Redline and Strikeout.
- Remove the Redline and Strikeout markings.
- Use Compare to compare similar documents.
- Number your lines with Line Numbering.
- Print a document using Booklet Printing.

 **Estimated Time: 1½ hours**

In Lessons 21, 22, and 23 you've learned about a variety of graphics tools to help you dress up your documents. You've worked with graphics boxes, images, lines, borders, and fill. You're probably pretty good with all of those tools.

In this lesson you will be introduced to a set of additional tools. Not much time will be spent on any one of them. Pay attention so you learn as much about each of them as possible.

INTERNET The most efficient form of Internet connection is a direct connection. With communications hardware physically connecting you to the Net, data is transferred between hosts and your computer at the highest possible speeds and with the highest reliability.

TextArt

TextArt enables you to turn text into art for display-type documents. To learn about this feature, we'll prepare a one-page flyer that will look much like Figure 24-1 when you are finished. You may prepare the flyer using the information provided in the Step-by-Step exercise, or you may prepare an equivalent project using information of interest to you. It's really easy, so enjoy yourself!

FIGURE 24-1
Flyer with TextArt

S TEP-BY-STEP ⟹ 24.1

1. Beginning in a new document window, open the **Insert** menu, choose **Graphics**, and then choose **TextArt**. The TextArt dialog box will appear, looking like Figure 24-2.

2. The largest part of the dialog box reflects what your image will look like with the choices you make. Near the bottom at the left is the place to key. Key **WINNECONNE**.

3. Look at the three black shapes in the *Shapes* section. The shape selected is whichever one was used last.

4. Click the **More** button and look at all the shapes that are available. Click to choose the shape that's third from the right in the first row. The one you are selecting is the shape of *Winneconne* in Figure 24-1.

5. Click **Close** to close the TextArt dialog box. Look at your TextArt image. It has handles like a graphics box—because it IS a graphics box. Drag it so the top of the box is about an inch from the top margin guideline. Click outside of the graphics box to deselect it.

6. Open the **Insert** menu, choose **Graphics**, and choose **TextArt** again. This time, key **Sovereign State Days**. Choose the shape that's sixth from the right in the first row, and click **Close** to close the TextArt dialog box.

7. Drag the second TextArt box so the text snuggles below the first TextArt box. The boxes will actually be overlapping, but that's OK because no lines surround the TextArt boxes. The text shouldn't touch.

8. Save your emerging flyer as **days 24-1 xxx**. Keep it open as you read on.

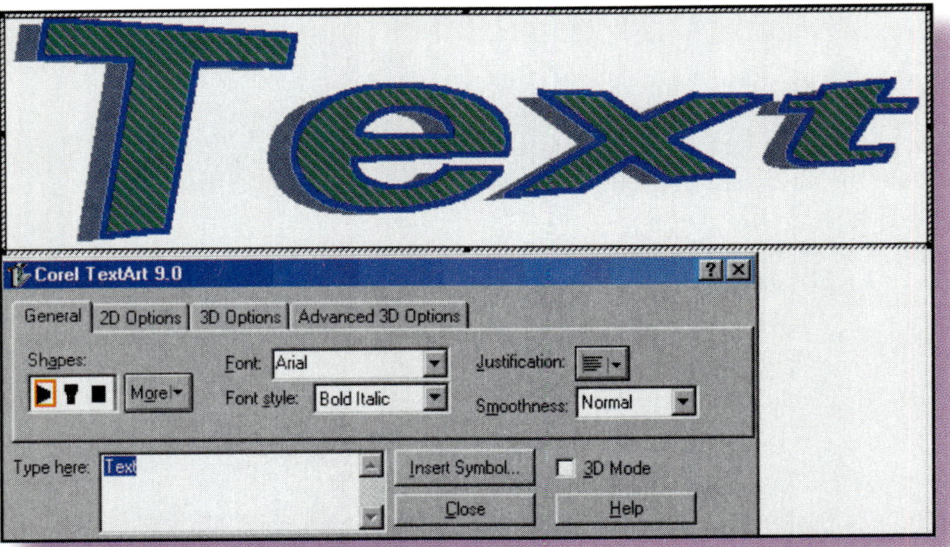

Now let's change the colors and finish the flyer. When working with color, you can adjust four parts of the TextArt letters. Each letter has a body color, an outline, a pattern, and a shadow. We'll look at all four, and you can make some choices. After you've finished, you can explore the options at your leisure.

STEP-BY-STEP 24.2

1. Return your insertion point to the top of the flyer. Press **Enter** until your insertion point is a little ways below the second TextArt box.

2. Change to **Center** justification and key the text illustrated in Figure 24-3. You can vary the font faces and font sizes as you wish. When you finish, check your work and save it with the same name.

3. Point to the *WINNECONNE* TextArt box and double click to select it. Look at the choices available in the TextArt dialog box.

4. Notice *Justification* and *Smoothness* at the right.

FIGURE 24-3
Text for Step-by-Step 24.2

Thursday through Sunday
July 20-24

SCHEDULED EVENTS INCLUDE:
Venetian Parade
Pancake Breakfast
Ecumenical Church Service
Softball Tournament
Pie & Ice Cream Social
Parade
Carnival & Street Dance
Toll Bridge

Call 920-555-5822 for Information
Winneconne, Wisconsin 54986

5. Click the **2D Options** tab and look at the choices. Click the **Pattern** button and change the pattern to **None** (first choice in the second row). Click the **Shadow** button and set a shadow size and location of your choice. Also, in the Shadow box, set the color of the text and the color of the shadow. (You get to choose the colors.)

6. Click the **Outline** button. Set the width of the outline (the first choice below *None* is the default) and the color of the outline. Note that

TextArt shows you the letter color here to help you pick a complementing color.

7. Click **Close** to return to your document. Double click the second TextArt box and make the same changes to color and outline that you made in the first box.

8. With your insertion point at the top of the document, play your **pf** macro. Then print the flyer, save it again as **days 24-1 xxx**, and close it.

TextArt boxes are like any other graphics box with regard to sizing and location. In the Step-by-Step exercise you just completed you allowed the boxes to fill the space between the margins, but the boxes can be any size you choose. You also may choose the font face and justification, as well as use WordPerfect in your TextArt boxes.

You probably noticed the 3D and Advanced 3D tabs in the Corel TextArt dialog box. Those options are not installed in a normal installation, so they are not covered here. If they are available, you may explore them on your own.

Drop Cap

One of the attention-getting devices used in magazine articles is known as a *drop cap*. The first letter of this paragraph has a modified drop cap. A drop cap is simply a large first letter at the beginning of the paragraph or article. Normally, drop caps extend below the line. The one at the beginning of this paragraph extends above the line.

WordPerfect has a flexible Drop Cap feature that creates the drop cap for you and allows you to customize the look of the letter. Let's practice.

STEP-BY-STEP 24.3

1. Beginning in a new document window, go to the student **datafile** folder and open **wind**. Save the file as **wind 24-3 xxx**. Play your **pf** macro.

2. Position the insertion point just to the left of the *N* of *Nuclear* in the first paragraph. Open the **Format** menu, choose **Paragraph**, and then choose **Drop Cap**. The beginning of your document should look like Figure 24-4.

3. Normally a paragraph beginning with a drop cap isn't indented. Delete the tab that indents the paragraph.

FIGURE 24-4
Sample with Drop Cap

(continued on next page)

4. Look at the Drop Cap Property Bar. Click the first button to display the Drop Cap palette. Experiment with the different styles and sizes of drop caps.

5. Choose a style and size of drop cap that looks good to you. Click away from the drop cap to close the Property Bar, but keep the document open.

Equation Editor

The Equation Editor in WordPerfect enables you to build complex equations for use in your documents. It doesn't solve equations, but it does enable you to create graphical representations of equations. The Editor is based on a series of more than 100 templates into which you insert the data to create the equation.

When your equation is finished, it is entered into your document as a graphics box. The default setting for the box is an Inline Equation. If you wish to have the equation on a line by itself, simply change the box style to Equation.

Equation Editor is an install-as-you-go feature. It is not available after a standard installation. If you try to create an equation and a message box tells you that you need the WordPerfect Install disk, ask your instructor to follow the prompts to install the feature for you. Let's learn to use the equation editor by creating simple equations. We'll begin with a simple formula that doesn't involve the use of any of the templates.

1. Move your insertion point a double space below the final paragraph in the document. Save the document again as **wind 24-4 xxx**.

2. Open the **Insert** menu and choose **Equation**. The Equation Editor will open, looking much like Figure 24-5. Look at the rows of buttons at the right. Each of those buttons contains a number of templates. Browse through a few of them and look at the descriptions of the symbols. Whenever you see a gray box, information can be entered at that location.

FIGURE 24-5
Equation Editor

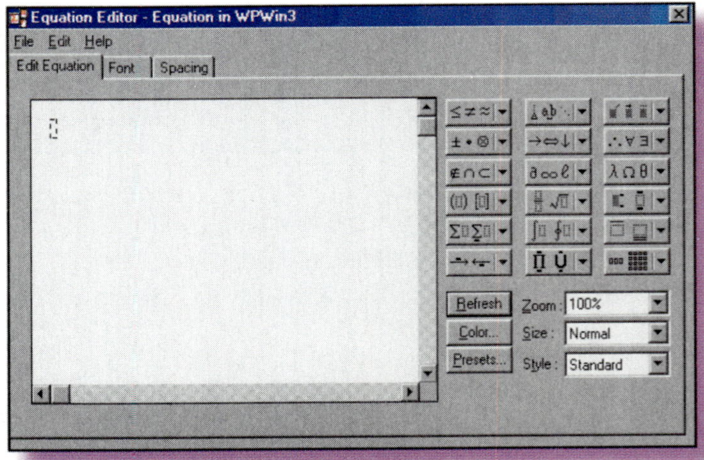

3. Without choosing a template, click the **Refresh** button to activate the editor. Key **a+b=c**. The equation will appear in the white area. Open the **File** menu and choose **Exit and Return to . . . .** Your equation should appear at the left margin, enclosed in sizing handles. Click away from the equation to deselect the graphics box and press **Enter** twice.

4. Open the **Insert** menu again and choose **Equation** to return to the Equation Editor to create a new equation. Key **a+**. Choose the second button in the fourth row of template buttons and choose the first template on that button.

5. Position your insertion point in the top box and key **b**. Click to position your insertion point in the bottom box and key **d**. Click to the right of the box and key **=c**. Return to your document window.

6. Point to the equation you just completed and double click to return to the Equation Editor. Click to position the insertion point just to the right of the *b*. Choose the third button in the fourth row and choose the **Superscript** template. Key **2** in the box.

7. Position the insertion point to the right of the *d* and choose **Superscript** again. This time, key **3** in the box. Return to your document. Your equation should look somewhat like Figure 24-6.

FIGURE 24-6
Second
Equation

$$a + \frac{b^2}{d^3} = c$$

8. Figure 24-7 illustrates a third equation. Can you create it on your own? Here is a little help:

   a. The entire first part of the equation is prepared using the fraction template you used for the *b over d* section of the second equation.

   b. The brackets come from the first set of templates on the fourth row. The square bracket is the second button in the set.

FIGURE 24-7
Third Equation

$$\frac{a + \left[x^2 y\right] + b}{d} = c^2$$

   c. If the equation looks messy, open the **File** menu and choose **Update**. The equation will be updated in your document.

9. When you finish this equation, return to your document. With the equation selected, display the Graphics QuickMenu and choose **Style**. Change to **Equation**.

10. Save the document again as **wind 24-4 xxx**. Keep it open in the window.

This was only a brief introduction to equations. If you use them in your work, you probably already have ideas about how easy it will be to prepare equations using the WordPerfect Equation Editor.

The Equation Editor for WordPerfect versions 5.1 though 7 is also installed with WordPerfect 9. If you are familiar with the earlier version of the Equation Editor and wish to use it, open the Tools menu, choose Settings, and then choose Environment. Click the Graphics tab and select the WordPerfect 5.1 to 7 Equation Editor. A check box can be checked to make a choice of equation editors available each time you wish to create an equation.

Rotate Text

Graphics Text boxes provide you with the unique ability to rotate text. The Rotate choice is in the Content dialog box.

STEP-BY-STEP ⟹ 24.5

1. Position the insertion point below the equations in **wind 24-4 xxx**, and create a Text Box. In the box, key your entire name and address the way you would key it on an envelope or label.

2. Choose **Content** from the QuickMenu and choose to rotate the text **90 degrees**. Then size your box so it looks much like Figure 24-8.

3. Drag the box so it's about a half inch below the paragraphs and aligned with the right margin guideline.

4. Save the document as **wind 24-5 xxx**. Print it and close it.

FIGURE 24-8
Graphics Box with Rotated Text

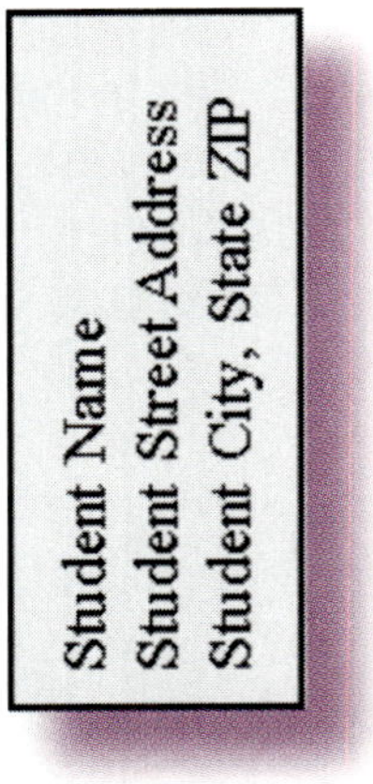

The ability to rotate text in graphics boxes can save you a good deal of time in cutting and pasting. It is easy to do, and you know enough about graphics boxes to create the "look" you want for your documents.

Line Numbering

If you request it, WordPerfect will count the lines on your page and put a number in the left margin opposite each line. This feature is useful in situations where a document must be discussed. The lines can be referred to by number. Give the command to number the lines at the beginning of the document. A code will be placed at that point. To turn Line Numbering off, either deselect the feature or remove the code. We'll practice with Line Numbering in your next Step-by-Step exercise.

Redline and Strikeout

Redline and Strikeout are used to prepare suggested corrections to documents so others may have input regarding how the final document will look. Redline is used to mark text to be added. Strikeout is used to mark text to be deleted. After the decisions are made about the changes to the document, one step will remove all text marked with Strikeout and remove the Redline markings from text marked with Redline.

Redline and Strikeout are in the Font dialog box. They are also part of the Legal Toolbar. Accessing them from the Toolbar is easier than continually going to the Font dialog box. In the next Step-by-Step exercise we'll display the Legal Toolbar as well as mark a document from an earlier lesson for discussion by company officials.

STEP-BY-STEP 24.6

1. Look at Figure 24-9. Note that some of the text has a line through it. That text is marked with Strikeout. Note that some of the text (in addition to the FIELD codes) is in red. That text is marked with Redline.

2. Look at the spaces between words. It is important that when the Redline text is added and the Strikeout text is deleted, the spacing between words is correct.

FIGURE 24-9
Text Marked with Redline and Strikeout

```
Our consultant for FIELD(area of interest) equipment,
FIELD(representative), imaging equipment will personally bring our bid
to you at FIELD(time) on FIELD(date) next week.  Please call 1-800-
555-2345 for an appointment.  At that time, please ask any questions
you might have about our company and procedures.

Again, the staff of Image Specialists would like to thank you for your
confidence in our organization.  We are looking forward to working
with you should we be selected to install FIELD(area of interest)
imaging equipment at your office.
```

(continued on next page)

3. Point to your Toolbar and right click. Choose **Legal** to display the Legal Toolbar below your normal Toolbar. Use Quicktips to find the Redline and Strikeout buttons.

4. Open the **Insert** menu, choose **File**, and insert **im spec.frm** from the student **datafile** folder. Save the file as **redline 24-6 xxx**.

5. With the insertion point at the top of the document, open the **Format** menu and choose **Line**. Then choose **Numbering**. At the top of the large Line Numbering dialog box (which you may study at your leisure), click the **Turn line numbering on** option. Click **OK**. Look at the numbers in the left margin of your document.

6. Working with one chunk of text at a time, click the **Redline** button on the Legal Toolbar and add the text that is shown in red in Figure 24-9.

7. Then, again working with one chunk of text at a time, select the text with a line through it. When exactly the right amount of text is selected, click the **Strikeout** button on the Legal Toolbar.

8. Double-check the spaces around your Redline and Strikeout markings. When everything looks good, save the document again as **redline 24-6 xxx** and print it. Keep it open.

The document has been discussed, and all of the suggested changes have been approved except the one in Line 9. It is the wish of the people who approved the document to leave *and procedures* in the document. Let's remove the markings from that phrase. Then we'll finish what we started with the Redline and Strikeout markings, turn Line Numbering off, and take away the designation of *form document* for the document since it no longer contains any merge codes.

STEP-BY-STEP ➡ 24.7

1. With **redline 24-6 xxx** showing in your window, click the **Options** button on the Form File Feature Bar and choose **Remove Merge Bar**. A prompt will ask if it's OK to delete the data file association. Confirm your actions. Use **Save As** to save the file as **redline 24-7 xxx**.

2. Reveal your codes and remove the Strikeout markings from Line 9. Open the **File** menu and choose **Document**. Then choose **Remove Markings**. The dialog box illustrated in Figure 24-10 will appear.

3. Make sure the first choice is selected. Then click **OK**. Your document will miraculously be updated. Check spacing and general accuracy. If everything is correct, display your codes and remove the [Ln Num] code.

FIGURE 24-10
Remove Markings Dialog Box

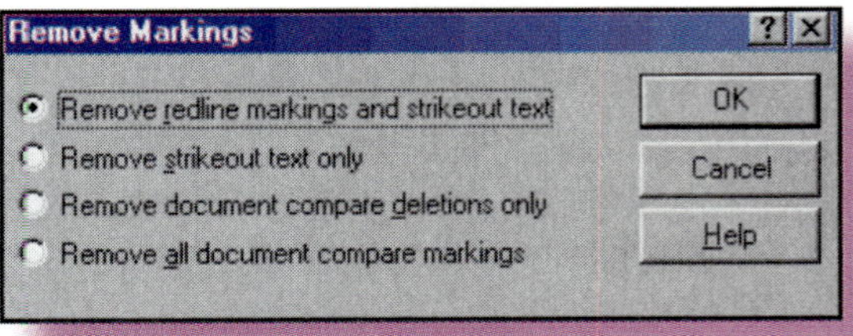

4. Print the document. Then close it, saving it again as **redline 24-7 xxx**.

5. Point to the Legal Toolbar and right click. Click **Legal** to deselect the bar.

Compare

You may compare two documents using two methods. Both methods end up with the differences between the documents marked with redline and strikeout in whichever document you choose—the new document (the one on disk) or the old document (the one you have open in the window)—and show the marked-up document in a new window.

Compare/Review asks you to enter your name and initials, with the assumption that after you've reviewed the document, it will be passed on to someone else for review. *Compare* marks the changes and gives you a summary of the changes made to the document. In either case, you can remove the markings for changes you don't want made and use the WordPerfect *Remove Markings* tool to make the rest of the corrections. Let's try it.

STEP-BY-STEP ▷ 24.8

1. Open **redline 24-7 xxx**. Then open the **File** menu and choose **Document**. Choose **Compare**. Study the options in the dialog box.

2. Click the arrow beside the *With* box and choose **redline 24-6 xxx**. Your dialog box should look like Figure 24-11. Click **Compare/Review**.

   a. Fill in the boxes for your name and initials. Click **OK**.

   b. Look at the document. View the Quick Tips on the Compare bar.

   c. Choose **File**, **Document**, and **Remove Markings**. Click **OK** to accept the first choice. WordPerfect will remove the strikeout text and add the redlined text.

   d. Close the revised document without saving it.

3. With **redline 24-7 xxx** open in your window, return to the Compare dialog box. **Redline 24-6 xxx** should still be identified. Choose **Compare Only**.

FIGURE 24-11
Compare Documents Dialog Box

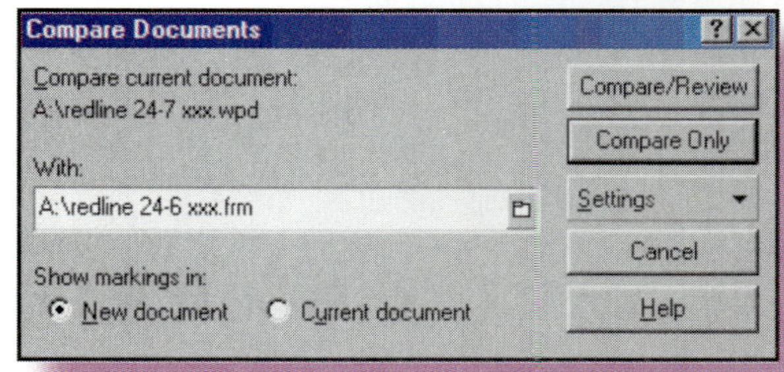

   a. Look at the Document Compare Summary.

   b. Scroll down and look at the document.

   c. Open the **File** menu, choose **Document** and then **Remove Markings**. In the Remove Markings dialog box, click **OK**. The result should be the same as before.

   d. Close all files without saving them.

Redline, strikeout, and compare are very useful in certain environments. They may be of little use in your work. If you should need them, you now know how easy these features are to use.

Booklet Printing

A very useful feature for some applications is one called *Booklet Printing*. This feature works only when you have your page subdivided into two columns and one row. The purpose of the feature is to arrange the pages in proper booklet order, saving you the trouble of cutting and pasting all the pages of your booklet either before or after printing (to make it ready for mass production). Programs, church bulletins, and a variety of other applications can be easily prepared using Booklet Printing. Let's see how easy it is to use Booklet Printing.

STEP-BY-STEP 24.9

1. Beginning in a new document window, open **nasa proj11a xxx**. It is in your **Units 3 and 4** folder. Use **Save As** to save the file as **nasa 24-9 xxx**.

2. With the insertion point at the top of the document, open the **Format** menu, choose **Page**, and choose **Page Setup**. Change to **Landscape** orientation.

3. Click the **Margins/Layout** tab. Choose **Divide Page**. Tell WordPerfect you want **2** columns and **1** row (2x1). Click **OK**.

4. Back in your document window, open the **File** menu, choose **Document**, and then choose **Current Document Style**. Using the **Format** menu in the dialog box to choose **Margins**, set all four margins at **0.5"**. Return to your document window.

5. Give the document a header that includes the word *Page* followed by a space at the flush right position. Use the **Number** button on the Header Property Bar to insert the page number.

6. Move the insertion point out of the header area and use **Suppress** to suppress the header on the first page of the document.

7. Look through your document. If it extends to a fifth page, use **Make It Fit** to make the document fit on four pages. (This doesn't have anything to do with Booklet Printing. It just makes this particular job a little neater.)

8. Open the Print dialog box and choose the **Two-Sided Printing** tab at the top. In the middle at the right is a **Print as booklet** check box. Select that option. Then print your document.

As the document prints, you will be asked to "Reinsert page 1." Wait until the printer stops. Put the piece of paper in the bypass tray when it comes out of the printer and click **OK**. If you have trouble with this, ask your instructor to help you.

9. When you have your lovely four-page booklet document, close the document, saving it again as **nasa 24-9 xxx**.

This was a quick introduction to Booklet Printing. If you wanted, you could make a pretty fancy document with this feature. The length of the document doesn't matter. WordPerfect will arrange the pages perfectly for you, whether you have 4 pages or 40.

Summary

You learned about a group of miscellaneous tools in this lesson. Most of them were related in one way or another to graphics images. All of them will probably be useful to you at one time or another. All were easy to use. In this lesson you learned the following:

- The TextArt feature provides many options for putting text into your documents in a decorative manner.

- A drop cap can be added to the beginning of any paragraph to add eye appeal and capture the reader's attention.

- The Equation Editor is a flexible tool for anyone who wishes to use equations in their writing.

- Text that is in a Text box can be rotated 90 degrees, 180 degrees, or 270 degrees.

- Redline and Strikeout can be used to indicate text to be added to or deleted from a document.

- Line Numbering puts numbers in the left margin, opposite the lines of the document, to make it easier to discuss a document.

- The WordPerfect Compare feature enables you to compare two similar documents. It puts Strikeout and Redline text in the document to be compared, showing the areas of difference.

- If requested, WordPerfect will print your divided pages in booklet format, arranging the pages in perfect order.

Again, the project consists of several small jobs, enabling you to review some of the features learned in Lesson 24.

LESSON 24 REVIEW QUESTIONS

MULTIPLE CHOICE

Circle the best answer to each of the following statements.

1. To open the TextArt dialog box, first open the _______ menu.
    - **A.** View
    - **B.** Insert
    - **C.** Format
    - **D.** Tools

2. In order to add a drop cap to your work, you must first open the _______ menu.
    - **A.** View
    - **B.** Insert
    - **C.** Format
    - **D.** Tools

3. All of the following statements are true concerning the Equation Editor EXCEPT:
    A. It does enable you to create graphical representations of equations.
    B. It solves the equation you've created.
    C. It enters the equation into your document as a graphics box.
    D. It is based on a series of more than 100 templates.

4. Redline and Strikeout are used primarily for
    A. changing the appearance of your documents.
    B. adding variety to your writing style.
    C. making final changes to a manuscript in preparation for printing.
    D. making suggested changes to a document that other people have to approve.

5. Redline is used in documents to indicate text that is to be
    A. deleted.
    B. bolded.
    C. added.
    D. formatted with italics.

6. When WordPerfect compares two documents, it
    A. adds Redline and Strikeout markings to show additions and deletions.
    B. adds Redline markings to show additions first time through.
    C. adds Strikeout markings to show deletions first time through.
    D. converts your window to Two Pages view, placing the documents side by side.

7. In order to use the Booklet Printing feature, you must choose ________ in the Print dialog box.
    A. the Details tab
    B. the Multiple Pages tab
    C. the Two-Sided Printing tab
    D. the Print/Booklet tab

TRUE/FALSE

Circle the T if the statement is true. Circle the F if it is false.

T F   8. Booklet Printing works only when you have your page divided into two columns and one row.

T F   9. Normally, a drop cap extends above the line.

T F   10. The Equation Editor inserts an equation into a document as an Inline Equation as the default setting.

LESSON 24 PROJECT

PROJECT 24A

Look at the formula in Figure 24-12. Your boss has given you a document with this formula in it and requested that you prepare a copy. For now, just prepare the formula.

Key the formula in a new document window. When it is perfect, save it as **formula proj24a xxx**. Insert the Path and Filename code a double space below the formula and print the document. Close the file, saving it again.

$$\frac{d}{dx}\,[7y^4]\,\frac{d}{dx}\,x^3y\;+\;\frac{d}{dx}\,[x]\;=\;0$$

PROJECT 24B

Go to your **Units 3 and 4** folder and open **cheese proj9 xxx**. Save the file as **cheese proj24b xxx**. Position the insertion point at the beginning of the first paragraph and delete the tab that indents the line. Create a drop cap. Format the drop cap as follows:

- Choose the second style in the last row of the Drop Cap palette.

- Click the Size button and tell WordPerfect to make the drop cap 2 Lines High. The beginning of your paragraph should look like Figure 24-13.

When the document is lovely, print it and close it, saving it again as you close it.

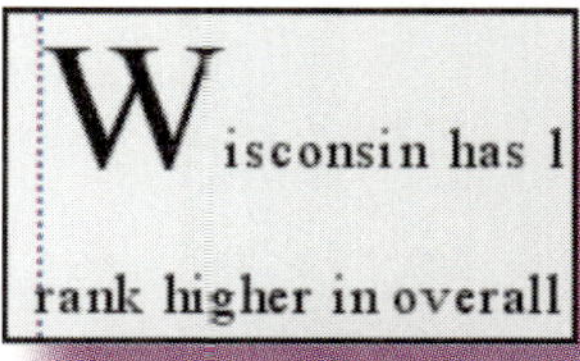

PROJECT 24C

Open **nasa proj11a xxx** again. It is in your **Units 3 and 4** folder. Select the first paragraph and copy it to the Clipboard. Close the file. Paste the paragraph from the Clipboard into a new document window.

Use Redline and Strikeout to mark the changes illustrated in Figure 24-14. Turn on Line Numbering.

The scientists at the National Aeronautics and Space Administration are continually working to develop technology to help them with issues raised as they progress aid in the space program. Many of their developments have been applied to make life easier or better for the general population populace. A small number of the technologies that have been developed for the space program that have been put to use in other ways developments are discussed in the following sections.

Save the file as **nasa proj24c1 xxx**. Insert the Path and Filename code a double space below the paragraph. Print the file.

After discussion among the staff in your office, you decide to NOT change *populace* to *population* in Line 4. Remove the word *population* and the markings around *populace*. Go to the File menu and choose Document. Remove the Compare Markings in such a way that the Redlined text is added and the text marked with Strikeout is removed. Check your work for accuracy. Then save it again, this time as **nasa proj24c2 xxx**, print it, and close it.

CRITICAL THINKING ACTIVITY

SCANS

You are excited about learning to use the Booklet Printing feature of WordPerfect because you have volunteered to prepare the program for this year's Charity Auction. You thought you had all the settings and format correct, but when you printed the first program, the information on the inside was upside down. What could have happened?

Command Summary

FEATURE	MENU CHOICE	KEYBOARD	LESSON
Booklet Printing	File, Print, Two-Sided Printing	Ctrl+P	24
Column Border	Format, Columns, Border/Fill	—	23
Compare	File, Document	—	24
Draw Shapes	Insert, Shapes	—	23
Drop Cap	Format, Paragraph	Ctrl+Shift+C	24
Equation	Insert	—	24
Fill	Format, Paragraph or Page, Border/Fill	—	23
Graphics Box	Insert, Image	F11	21
Graphics Line, Custom	Insert, Line, Custom Line	—	23
Graphics Line, Horizontal	Insert, Line, Horizontal Line	Ctrl+F11	23
Graphics Line, Vertical	Insert, Line, Vertical Line	Ctrl+Shift+F11	23
Group Graphics Boxes	QuickMenu, Property Bar	—	22
Horizontal Line	Insert, Line, Horizontal Line	Ctrl+F11	23
Image Tools	(QuickMenu)	—	22
Inline Equations	Insert, Equation	—	24
Line Numbering	Format, Line	—	24
Page Border	Format, Page, Border/Fill	—	23
Paragraph Border	Format, Paragraph, Border/Fill	—	23
Redline	Format, Font	F9	24
Shapes	Insert	—	23
Strikeout	Format, Font	F9	24
TextArt	Insert, Graphics, TextArt	—	24
Vertical Line	Insert, Line, Vertical Line	Ctrl+Shift+F11	23

UNIT 6 REVIEW QUESTIONS 

FILL IN THE BLANKS

Complete each of the following statements by keying your answer on a separate page. Center the title, *Unit 6 Review Questions*, followed by a triple space.

1. If you want text to fit around parts of an image, choose _____________ in the Wrap Text dialog box.

2. If you want the width/height ratio of a box preserved, choose that option in the _____________ dialog box.

3. The _____________ tool in the Image Tools palette enables you to tilt and turn an image.

4. The _____________ button at the bottom of the Image Tools palette returns the image to all of the default settings.

5. In addition to varying the length, location, color, and style of a line, you can also vary the _____________ of a graphics line.

6. _____________ is the feature to use to bend text in all kinds of different shapes.

WRITTEN QUESTIONS

Key your answers to the following questions. Number your answers and double-space between them. Use complete sentences and good grammar.

7. What are the two ways you can size a graphics box?

8. When you are working with a Text box, how do you get back into edit mode so you can make changes to the text in the box?

9. What is the name of the tool that puts numbers in the left margin opposite the lines of your documents? When might you use this feature?

10. Open the Help menu and go to the section on Graphics Boxes. Find Changing Contents. How do you replace the image in a graphics box with a different image? Go to the section about Booklet Printing. In that Help box, click Related topics. How can WordPerfect help you if you want to bind the document?

UNIT 6 APPLICATIONS

APPLICATION 1

Let's combine some of your previously gained skills and create an invitation to a party. Because this application has so many parts, the steps are quite specific. Learn as you go!

1. Change all margins to 0" (or as small as your printer will allow). Then divide the page into 2 columns and 2 rows. (HINT: Choose Format, Page, Page Setup, and then Divide Page.)

2. In the first logical page, create a Text box.
   a. Set Center justification and key the text showing in Figure APP-1.
   b. Use a 16-pt. font.
   c. Change to a User box with both Height and Width set at Full.
   d. Choose Content from the QuickMenu and rotate the contents of the box 180 degrees.

3. Save your evolving document as **beach u6ap1 xxx**. Go to the third logical page (press Ctrl+Enter to get there). Create another Text box. In this box, key the following partial phrase:

   When you care enough . . . .

   Press Enter and insert the Path and Filename code. Both lines should be centered.

4. Format the Text box as follows:
   a. Make it a User box and set the Width at Full.
   b. Go to the Box Position dialog box and check to make sure the box is attached to Page.
   c. Set Vertical (at the bottom of the dialog box) at Bottom Margin.
   d. Format the text with a 6- or 8-pt. font size.

5. Press Ctrl+Enter to go to the final logical page and give it a Page border. Select the border that has a crane in the rushes (see Figure APP-2).

6. Using Left justification, key **BEACH PARTY**, as shown in Figure APP-2. You may use the font face and font size of your choice.

7. When you are finished, check your work and print your document. Fold it in quarters like a greeting card. Make any necessary adjustments. Save and close the file.

FIGURE APP-1
Text for Application 1

```
Last Fling of Summer

Sunday, September 2
      2-8 p.m.

Harry's Place on the
        BEACH!

Bring a dish to pass
   and your own
  meat to grill.
```

FIGURE APP-2
Sample Invitation

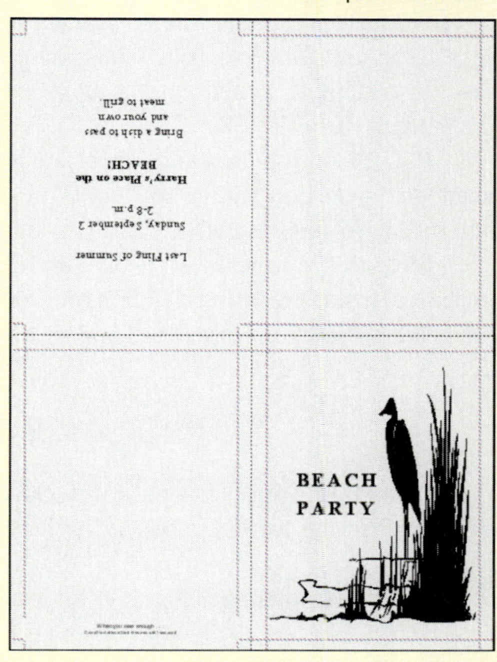

APPLICATION 2

Now that you have the idea of the greeting card in your head, create one on your own. Include at least three of the following:

- graphics images

- graphics lines

- graphics borders

- graphics fill

- TextArt

- Drop Cap

Your greeting card may be prepared in quarters like the one in Application 1. Another acceptable alternative is to prepare it using Booklet Printing with Divide Page.

Plan a birthday party, a wedding or baby shower, a corn-husking bee, a quilting party, or make a regular greeting card for one of your friends who is ill or an invitation to a surprise party for someone who is celebrating a birthday. Try your hand at creating a beautiful card!

When you finish, save the card as **greeting u6ap2 xxx**. Put the Path and Filename code in an obscure location. Print the card and close it.

APPLICATION 3

Look at Figure APP-3. It is a suggested letterhead for the attorney for whom you created an invoice form in an earlier lesson. Create a letterhead that looks much like the one in the figure. You may choose a font that appeals to you. The graphics image in the illustration is **Scale.wpg**. It is in the student **datafile** folder.

Put all of the opening lines and the graphics image in a header so you don't have to deal with them when you use the letterhead. Work efficiently. The text is illustrated in Figure APP-4.

Save the letterhead as **tovar u6ap3 xxx**. For identification purposes, insert the Path and Filename code on the first line below the header. Print your letterhead and save it again before closing it.

FIGURE APP-3
Suggested Header for Letterhead in Application 3

FIGURE APP-4
Text for Letterhead

Attorney at Law
123 Main Street
Victoria, NJ 08344
Phone 413-555-2345

APPLICATION 4

Open **lighthouses proj23a xxx**. Save the file as **lighthouses u6ap4 xxx**. Prepare the document for Booklet Printing using the following features:

1. Set Landscape orientation.

2. Divide the page in 2 columns and 1 row.

3. Insert a hard page break between the title page and the first page of text so the back of the cover will be blank. (Depending on where your insertion point is when you enter the Hard Page command, you may need to move the footer code to the first page of text and discontinue the watermark.)

4. Set the page number value for the first page of text at 1 (one).

5. Set margins of 0.7" on all four sides in Current Document Style.

6. Remove Footer B (which contains the Path and Filename code) and put the Path and Filename a double space below the last line of the document.

7. Change the indent for paragraphs to a quarter inch.

8. On the first page, open the Insert menu, choose Watermark, and then choose Edit. In the Watermark edit window, display the Image Tools palette. Choose the Move tool and move the image down in the window so it's just inside of the bottom margin guidelines. Return to your document window.

When you have the document formatted to your satisfaction, print it using Booklet Printing. Save and close the document.

APPLICATION 5

It's time to clear your disk of unneeded files and store away those that might be helpful to you at some point in the future. The procedure is the same as in other lessons.

Select the following four files: **Brazil proj22**, **days 24-1**, **lighthouses proj23a**, and **nasa 24-9**. Move them to your **Units 5 and 6** folder. Work carefully.

Select these four files to be moved to your **Applications** folder: **beach u6ap1**, **greeting u6ap2**, **lighthouses u6ap4**, and **tovar u6ap3**.

Figure APP-5 lists the files to be deleted. When you finish, check to see if any random files remain in your main folder. If so, delete those that are of no use to you and file the others in a safe place. Remember to keep the macros (with *.wcm* extensions) in your main folder.

FIGURE APP-5
Files to Delete

borders 23-11	duck 22-2	lines 23-4	rose 21-7
borders 23-12	duck 22-4	nasa proj24c1	rose 21-8
borders 23-13	fido 22-7	nasa proj24c2	rose 21-9
borders 23-14	fido 22-8	party proj21b	shapes 23-6
borders 23-7	footer 23-5	proj23b	wind 24-3
borders 23-9	formula proj24a	proj23c	wind 24-4
box 21-12	friends 21-14	redline 24-6	wind 24-5
box 21-13	lines 23-2	redline 24-7	wind proj21a
cheese proj24b	lines 23-3	rose 21-11	wind proj21c

Now that you know how to use all of the graphics tools you learned about in this unit, you can really begin to produce attractive documents for Singing Wheels Tours. We'll create a new type of document in the first job. Then you'll have an opportunity to go back and "pretty up" some of your previous documents.

JOB 16

Go to the student **datafile** folder and open **new england**. Save the file in your **Singing Wheels** folder as **new england job16 xxx**. Add the title section illustrated in Figure J11.

Splendor of New England

September 14-25, (year)—11 days   (Tour #1745)

Format your document in 2 Balanced newspaper columns. Use your **pf** macro to identify the file.

Since you didn't have an opportunity to key the document, read the article about the New England tour to get an idea of what the tourists will do on the tour. With your insertion point at the bottom of the document, insert an image to enhance the document. Look through the Corel images. If you can't find an appropriate Corel image, **Lights**, **Shore**, **Bridge**, and **Sailing** are in the **datafile** folder. Use one of them.

Grab the bottom margin guideline and drag it down to approximately 0.5". Set the Width of the image at Full, and line the image up at the bottom margin guidelines. Since you want the entire document on one page, either use Make It Fit or set Wrap at No Wrap (Through). Some of the suggested images will fit better with the document than others. If you can't read the writing where the text goes across the image, display your Image Tools palette and decrease the brightness of the image a little.

When you finish, print your lovely document and close all files.

JOB 17

Open **coach job9 xxx** from your **Singing Wheels** folder. Save it as **coach job17 xxx**. Replace the title of the document with some TextArt that says the same thing. You can create two TextArt images and move them close together like you did in the **Winneconne** document, or you can put the entire heading in one or two lines of a single TextArt image.

Add a couple of horizontal or vertical lines in the heading section. Since the document is already two pages long, you don't need to worry about conserving space. Spend a little time playing with this so it is attractive when you finish. Figure J12 shows one possible solution. Can you make it even more beautiful?

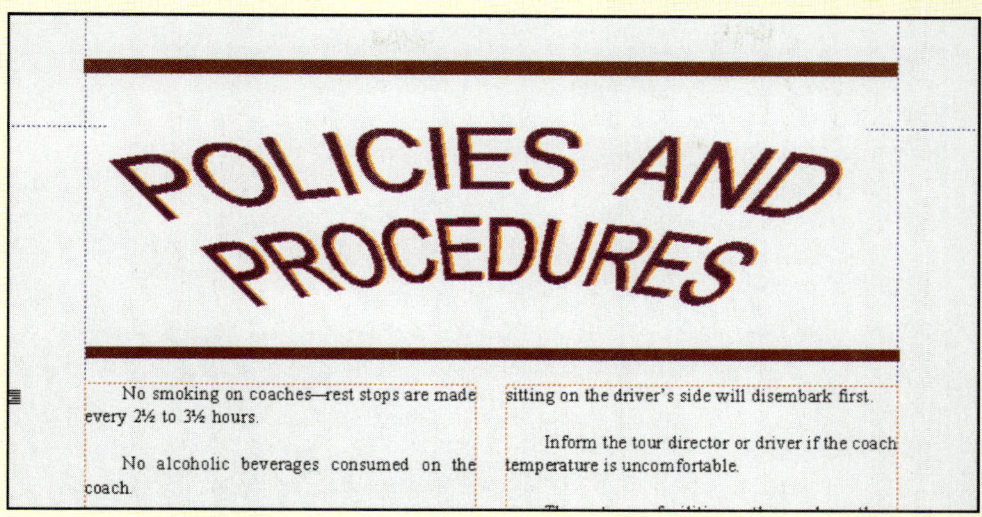

JOB 18

Choose any other document that you created for Singing Wheels. Reformat the document using at least three of the following:

Borders and/or Fill	Drop Caps
Graphics Lines	Booklet Printing
Graphics Boxes and Images	Rotate Text
TextArt	Special Font Faces

When you submit the document to your instructor, include a list of the features you used, including font faces and sizes, kinds of graphics boxes, etc. Make your work look as if it was professionally done. (It was—by you!)

K

MORE POWER TOOLS

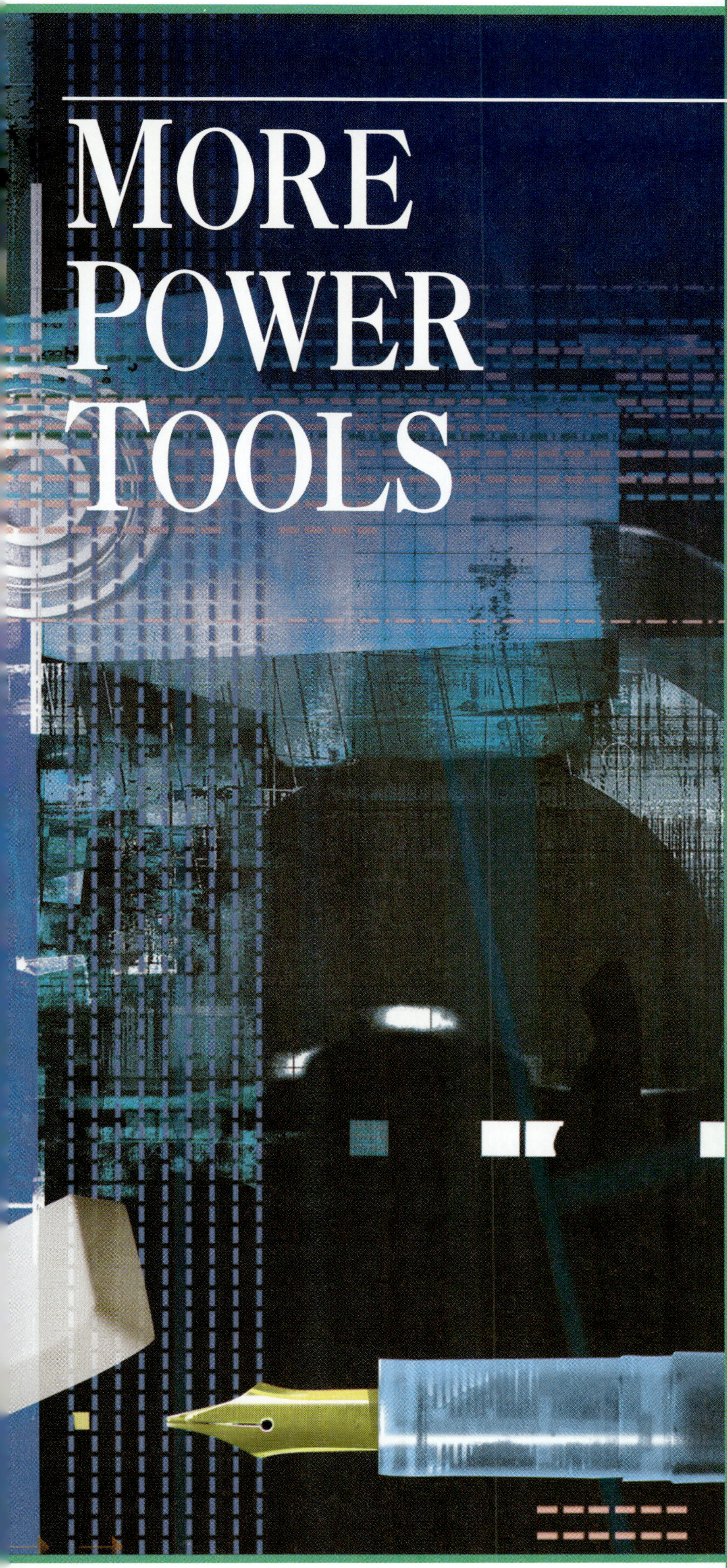

UNIT 7

lesson 25 — 2 hrs.
Address Book

lesson 26 — 1 hr.
Templates, Styles, and PerfectExpert

lesson 27 — 1.5 hrs.
Table of Contents and Index

lesson 28 — 1 hr.
Table of Authorities, Hypertext, and Master Document

Estimated Time for Unit 7: 7$^1/_2$ hours

ADDRESS BOOK

You learned in an earlier lesson that the Address Book can be used as an information center for all your address needs. You used the Address Book to create a short list of customers for Ziepke's Imaging. Then you merged the names and addresses in the Address Book with a letter.

That was a simple, yet powerful, application of the Address Book. Basically, it enables you to keep lists of people that can be manipulated and used for envelopes, letters, labels, etc. Let's learn more about the Address Book.

Importing and Exporting Books

Each Address Book is saved as a file in WordPerfect. That file can be exported so you can put the Address Book on another computer or network location. When you have exported it from one computer, you may import it on a different computer.

The list of "flower" customers with which you worked in Lesson 18 has been saved in your student **datafile** folder as a book for the Address Book to save you keying time. In the first Step-by-Step exercise you'll import the book. Then you'll export it to save it with the solutions of your Step-by-Step exercises so you can remove it from the computer when you finish working with it. Export is much like Save As. The book will be saved in a different location, but it still appears in the window so you can continue to work with it.

STEP-BY-STEP 25.1

1. Open the **Tools** menu and choose **Address Book**. When the main Address Book window appears, the upper left corner of the Address Book dialog box will look much like Figure 25-1.

FIGURE 25-1
Portion of CorelCENTRAL
Address Book

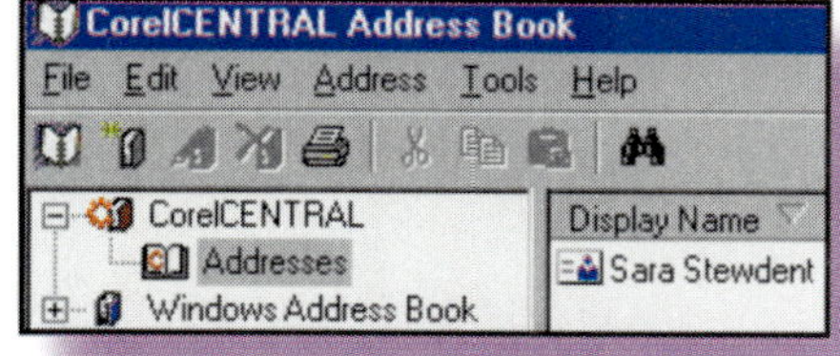

2. Open the **File** menu and choose **New**.

3. Click **OK** to create a CorelCENTRAL Address Book and key **Flower Customers** as the name for the book. Press **Enter**.

4. Select the **Flower Customers** book and open the **File** menu again. Choose **Import**. In the Import dialog box, *.txt* will appear in the *File name* text box.

5. Identify the location of your student **datafile** folder and choose **Flower Customers.txt**. Click **Open**. Click **OK** in the ASCII Delimiter dialog box. Field Mapping will show that all columns are mapped. Click **OK**. WordPerfect will report a successful import.

6. With the *Flower Customers* book selected, open the **File** menu and choose **Export**. Identify the folder where you are saving your work, call the book **Flower Customers**, and click **OK** in the ASCII dialog box. In the Columns dialog box, deselect E-mail.

7. Add check marks to select the following columns: *First Name, Last Name, Street, City, State/Province, Zip/Postal Code, Business Phone, Job Title, Organization*, and *Prefix*.

8. Complete the export. WordPerfect will report a successful export. Close the Address Book dialog box.

Commas and *Crlf* codes are common delimiters. Commas separate fields within a record; Crlf codes separate records within a file. Other delimiters may be used when you are importing files into the Address Book from other software applications. In this course you will work with the default delimiters.

Opening and Closing Address Books

You can have any number of Address Books. When an Address Book is open, the name of the book will appear in the CorelCENTRAL section of the left panel (see Figure 25-1). If you don't use a particular book often, the book can be closed—so an entry doesn't appear in the CorelCENTRAL list.

STEP-BY-STEP 25.2

1. Open the **Tools** menu and choose **Address Book**. Look at the books listed under CorelCENTRAL. You should see *Flower Customers* and *Addresses*. Is the *Ziepke* book there from Lesson 18?

2. One at a time, look at the other books. In the classroom you might find a variety of entries. Return to *Flower Customers*.

3. Open the **File** menu and choose **Close**. *Flower Customers* will disappear from the list.

4. Open the **File** menu again and choose **Open**. The list of closed books will appear. Choose **Flower Customers** to reopen that book. Keep it open as you read on.

Viewing and Sorting Columns

The default in Address Book is to display only the Display Name and E-mail Address columns. You can display as many columns as you have room for in the window. In Step-by-Step exercise 25.3 we'll size the dialog box, if necessary, and display all columns of the *Flower Customers* Address Book. When you export an Address Book, WordPerfect will automatically choose the displayed columns for export. If only a few columns are displayed, you will need to manually select all columns to be exported as you did in Step-by-Step exercise 25.1. If a column isn't exported and the Address Book is deleted from your Address Book dialog box, the columns won't be available for import when you import the Address Book and the information contained in those columns will be lost.

While it doesn't matter in what order the columns are displayed in the Address Book, arranging the displayed columns in a particular order might be helpful to you in your work. You can easily change the arrangement of the columns.

The default order for entries in the Address Book is alphabetically by the first name in the Display Name column. WordPerfect will quickly sort the entries by whichever column you want, in either ascending or descending order.

STEP-BY-STEP 25.3

1. Does your Address Book fill the window from side to side? If not, grab the left side of the dialog box and drag it to the left side of the window. Do the same at the right so the dialog box fills the window from left to right. Make it "tall" enough that you can see all entries.

2. With the *Flower Customers* Address Book chosen, open the **View** menu and choose **Columns**. The dialog box you used for exporting the Address Book to your solutions file will appear.

3. Click to deselect *E-mail address*. Then select the following columns: *First Name*, *Last Name*, *Street*, *City*, *State/Province*, *Zip/Postal Code*, *Business Phone*, *Job Title*, *Organization*, and *Prefix*. Click **OK**.

4. Size the columns by grabbing the line between the buttons above the columns and move them to the right or left. When you finish, you should see most of the information about all customers.

5. Grab the **Prefix** button and drag it to *First Name*. Drop the column there. Then rearrange the other columns so they are in the order illustrated in the portion of the Address Book in Figure 25-2.

6. Click the **First Name** heading to sort the list alphabetically. Click the button again to sort the list in descending order.

7. Click the **ZIP code** heading to sort the list by ZIP code. Sort by State. Finally, sort the list alphabetically by last name. Keep the *Flower Customers* Address Book open.

FIGURE 25-2
Part of the *Flower Customers* Address Book

Display Name	Prefix	First N...	Last Name	Job T...	Organization	Street	City	Stat...	Zip/P...	Business Phon
Adelbert Aster	Mr.	Adelbert	Aster	Mana...	Angler Alley	67 An...	Anchorage	FL	33412	305-555-8642
Betty Blum	Miss	Betty	Blum		Buttons and ...	657 Jo...	Jackson	MN	56143	218-555-8225
Bill Bloom	Mr.	Bill	Bloom			543 Bi...	Bloomington	OK	74562	405-555-9975
Charles Cosmos	Mr.	Charles	Cosmos		Visions of C...	90-C C...	Canton	CA	93518	619-555-5664
Daisy Ditson	Mrs.	Daisy	Ditson		Dixie's Dilem...	7632 ...	Dixonville	DE	19811	302-555-1490

Adding Entries to an Address Book

You learned in Lesson 18 how easy it was to create an Address Book. In the same way, you can add entries to an existing book. We'll add five more flower customers to the list.

A set of tabs helps you sort personal and business information (see Figure 25-3). For entries like those in the *Flower Customers* Address Book, you'll need the Personal tab for the Prefix (Mr., Mrs., Miss, etc.) and the Business tab for customers with Job Titles. The remaining information can go in the General tab. (If you key the entire name of the customer in the *Display Name* text box, WordPerfect will separate the first and last names appropriately.) Be sure to put the phone number in the Business phone text box.

FIGURE 25-3
Person Properties Dialog Box

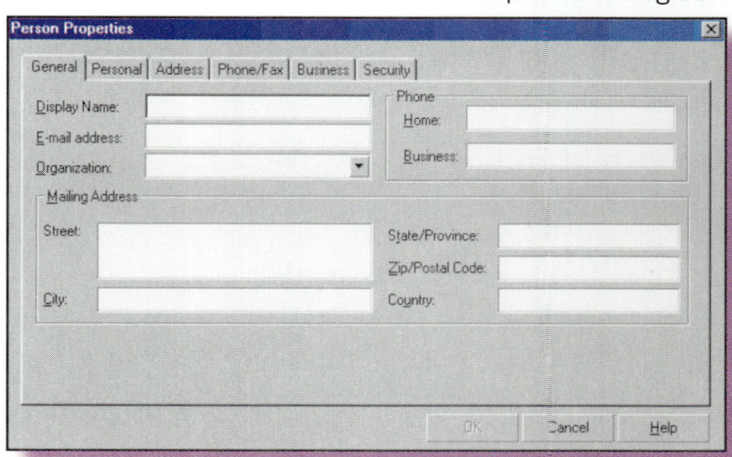

FIGURE 25-4
New Entries for Step-by-Step 25.4

1. With the *Flower Customers* Address Book selected, click the second button on the toolbar to add a new entry. Click **OK** when *Person* is prompted.

2. Key the name, phone number, and address for Victor Verbena (see Figure 25-4) into the appropriate text boxes in the General tab.

3. Change to the Personal tab and choose **Mr.** from the Prefix drop-down list.

4. Change to the Business tab and enter Victor's job title. Click **OK**.

5. Repeat the procedure to enter the remaining customers in Figure 25-4.

6. When you finish entering the customers, sort the list alphabetically by last name. Keep the book open in the window.

```
Mr. Victor Verbena
Title: President
Vic's Variety Store
1776 Varsity Avenue
Victory Hills, PA 15063
Phone: 456-555-7621

Miss Susan Blackeye
17 Bilge Court
Blackhawk, IN 46805
Phone: 872-555-9800

Ms. Chris Santhemum
CS Specialties
4C Baker Square
Churchtown, NJ 08070
Phone: 997-555-2355

Miss Violet Voiers
Vi's Variety
14 Vertigo Valley
Verdi, VA 22435
Phone: 804-555-7136

Mrs. Agnes Astilbe
Title: Manager
Astounding Accessories
3421 Asheby Avenue
Astoria, OR 97103
Phone: 973-555-2385
```

Copying Entries Between Books

People who are in one book can easily be copied or moved to a different book. To move, simply drag the person from the panel on the right to the destination book listed in the panel at the left. To copy, hold the Ctrl key when you drag the entry from one book to the other. Let's practice.

1. Open the **File** menu and choose **New**. Create a new CorelCENTRAL book named **Practice**.

2. Open the *Flower Customers* book and click **Chris Santhemum**. Press the mouse button and drag Chris to the *Practice* book. That book will open and Chris will be the only entry.

3. Open the *Flower Customers* book and check. Is Chris missing from the book? She should be!

4. Move Chris back to the *Flower Customers* book. Now the *Practice* book is empty.

5. Copy Chris to the *Practice* book. The procedure is the same, except you must hold the **Ctrl** key. (When you begin to move the mouse, the pointer will show a small plus sign to indicate that you are copying the entry.) Check to see if Chris is in both books.

6. Keep your Address Book open while you read on.

Deleting an Address Book

When an Address Book is no longer needed, it can be deleted, just like you delete a file. You can also delete an Address Book after you have exported it, knowing that you can import the book again when it is needed. In the classroom where other students may be using your computer, it is a good idea to export and delete your Address Books whenever you leave the computer. Otherwise, other students might make changes to your book. Also, when your book has been deleted, the next student can practice using all the features you've been learning in this lesson.

It is important to note that the notion of removing a useful Address Book from your computer is strictly a classroom procedure. If you were in the office, you would probably want to export your active Address Books regularly to a backup location for safekeeping, just like you save your important files and documents in more than one place. But if you were the only person using the computer, there would be no need for you to ever delete an active Address Book.

We are finished with the *Practice* Address Book, even though it contains an entry. Let's get rid of it. Then, since you've added entries to the *Flower Customers* Address Book, we'll review exporting and importing. (Remember that to import an Address Book after you've deleted it, you must first create a book. Then import the book into the newly created book.)

S·TEP-BY-ST·EP ⟹ 25.6

1. Click the *Practice* book to select it.

2. Open the **File** menu and choose **Delete**. Confirm that you would like to delete the *Practice* Address Book.

3. Export your *Flower Customers* Address Book to your solutions file. Be sure to export ALL COLUMNS that contain information. (Otherwise, that information will be lost.) You may save the book over the one already there with the same name.

4. Delete the *Flower Customers* Address Book from your computer and close the Address Book.

5. In an empty WordPerfect window, move the insertion point to **2"** from the top of the page. Insert the current date. Follow the date with four hard returns. (This is the start of a letter. We'll return to it soon.)

6. Open the Address Book and open the **File** menu. Choose **New** and create a new CorelCENTRAL book named **Flower Customers**. Import the *Flower Customers* book from your solutions file.

7. Keep the *Flower Customers* Address Book open as you read on.

Inserting an Address; Customizing the Format

Each time you use the Address Book to insert an address, WordPerfect will ask you what format you'd like. The CorelCENTRAL Address Book comes with four standard formats, but you can create as many custom formats as you wish. If each of your Address Books contains information in the same fields, you can use the same format for all of your addresses. If the information in the fields varies between Address Books, you may need to create a custom format for each Address Book. For example, your *Flower Customers* Address Book contains a Prefix (Mr., Miss, etc.). If you would like to use that prefix in your mailing addresses, you'll choose that field in the custom format. If you would prefer to skip the prefix for some documents, you'll need to create a custom format WITHOUT the prefix.

If you get a message about MAPI books not being available, click OK. (It may happen twice.)

The letter you began in Step-by-Step exercise 25.6 is to go to Chris Santhemum. Let's create a letter using the address from the *Flower Customer* Address Book. At the same time, we'll create a customized format that includes the prefix along with Chris's name and address. Then we'll use the Address Book to create an envelope for a mailing to Lily Larsen.

S TEP-BY-STEP ➡ 25.7

1. With the *Flower Customers* Address Book open, click **Chris Santhemum** and then click the **Insert** button at the bottom of the dialog box.

2. In the Format Address dialog box, look for a format called *Flowers Org*. If it is not there, click **Custom**.

3. Position the insertion point to the left of [Display Name] in the *Format* box. Scroll down the *Fields* list to **Prefix**. Double click to insert that field.

4. Add and delete fields in the *Format* section of the Custom Address Format dialog box until your dialog box looks like Figure 25-5. (Note that Chris doesn't have a job title, but some of the entries in the Address Book do.)

5. When everything looks right, click the **OK** button and name your custom format **Flowers Org**.

FIGURE 25-5
Custom Address Format Dialog Box

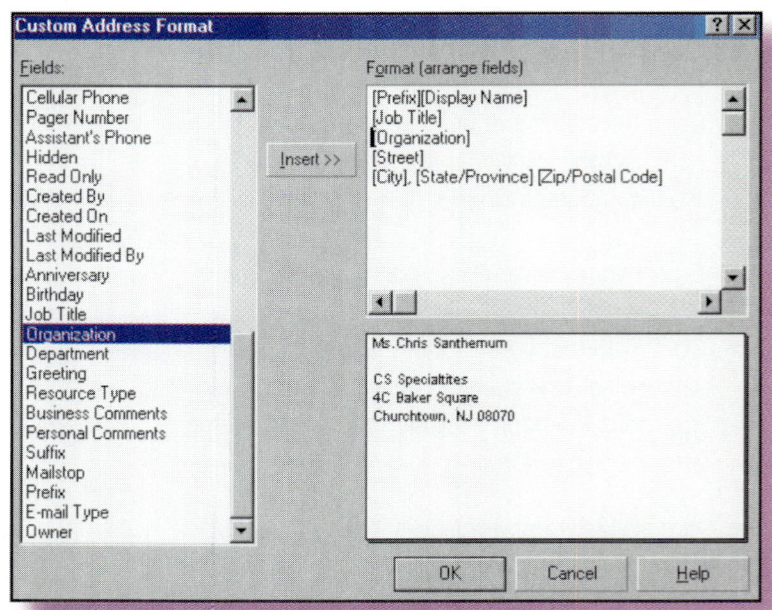

6. Click **OK** to complete the insertion. Chris's name and address should drop into the correct place in your document. Double-space and key an appropriate greeting followed by another double space.

7. Insert **gaillardia** from your **datafile** folder. Check your letter for appearance and save it as **gaillardia 25-7a xxx**. Play your **pf** macro. Print the letter, save it again, and close it.

8. Beginning in a new document window, open the **Format** menu and choose **Envelope**. Then use the Address Book to create an envelope for Lily Larsen. After inserting the address, include the POSTNET Bar Code below the address. Can you do it on your own? Print the envelope and close it, saving it as **envelope 25-7b xxx**.

Working with Parts of Address Books

Some Address Books may contain hundreds of names. In those cases, it is unlikely that you will work with all of the names on a regular basis. Instead, you might wish to work with smaller groups of names within the Address Book. You can do this in a number of ways:

Address Groups

Within an Address Book, you can select certain entries, place the entries in a group, and give that group a name. You might create groups of customers who you deal with frequently because they buy certain products or live in a particular marketing area. When the group is created, you can merge using only the entries in the named group.

Filtering

The View menu of the Address Book has a filtering tool that enables you to separate out entries meeting certain criteria. An easy-to-understand example would be to filter out all entries with ZIP codes greater than 66000. After filtering, the Address Book will hide the entries that do NOT match the filtering criteria until you return to the View menu and remove the filter. As with the address groups, you can perform a merge using only the entries that are selected using the filter process.

Select Records

You learned in Unit 5 that you can select certain records from a data file to be used during a merge. The same is true when you are merging with entries in an Address Book. With address groups and filtering, the groups are determined before the form document is prepared. You can select entries from an Address Book to be used in a merge at the time the merge is taking place.

In the next Step-by-Step exercises you will create a form document that you will merge with a list of entries chosen in each of the methods discussed above. Pay attention as you go along so you gain a good understanding of how the Address Book can be used to prepare mailings.

S TEP-BY-STEP ⟹ 25.8

1. Beginning in a new document window, create a merge form document using the *Flower Customers* Address Book as the associated data file.

2. Insert a DATE merge code about **2"** from the top of the page. Space down an appropriate amount of space to the position of the mailing address.

(continued on next page)

419

3. Click the **Insert Field** button and insert the field (column) codes from the *Flower Customers* Address Book for the mailing address so the completed address matches the format of the address in Figure 25-5. You'll need to scroll around in the Insert Field Name dialog box to find all of the address parts.

4. A double space below the mailing address, create a greeting that begins with *Dear* and

includes the Prefix and the Last Name codes. Follow the name with a colon.

5. A double space below the greeting, insert **gaillardia** from the **datafile** folder. Check your letter over for appearance and spacing and make any necessary adjustments.

6. Save the letter as **gaillardia 25-8 xxx**. Play your **pf** macro and save the letter again. Keep the letter open for the next Step-by-Step exercises.

Now we'll merge from the Address Book using only selected entries for the merge. First we'll manually select the entries. Then we'll try it again using the Address Book filter, choosing only those customers with ZIP codes larger than 85000.

STEP-BY-STEP ⟹ 25.9

1. With the **gaillardia 28-5 xxx** form document showing in the window, click the **Merge** button on the Merge Bar.

2. With *Flower Customers* showing in the *Data source* text box in the Perform Merge dialog box, click the **Select Records** button below the text box.

3. Hold the **Ctrl** key while you choose **Agnes Astilbe**, **Susan Blackeye**, **Chris Santhemum**, and **Victor Verbena**. Click **OK** in the Address Book and **OK** in the Format Address dialog box. (It will probably remember that you want the *Flowers Org* format.) Complete the merge.

4. Look over your letters. If you find any problems with spacing or accuracy, close the merged document, return to the form document, make any needed changes, and perform the merge again.

5. When you have four lovely letters, save the file as **gaillardia 25-9 xxx**. Print the letters and close the file.

6. With the **gaillardia 28-5 xxx** form document showing, click **Merge** and **Select Records** to return to the Address Book. Select the *Flower Customers* book, open the **View** menu and choose **Filter**.

7. In the Filter dialog box, click the arrow beside the first text box at the bottom and choose **Zip/Postal Code**. Click the second button and choose **Greater Than or Equal**. In the text box at the right, key **85000**. When you finish, your dialog box will look much like Figure 25-6.

FIGURE 25-6
Filter Dialog Box

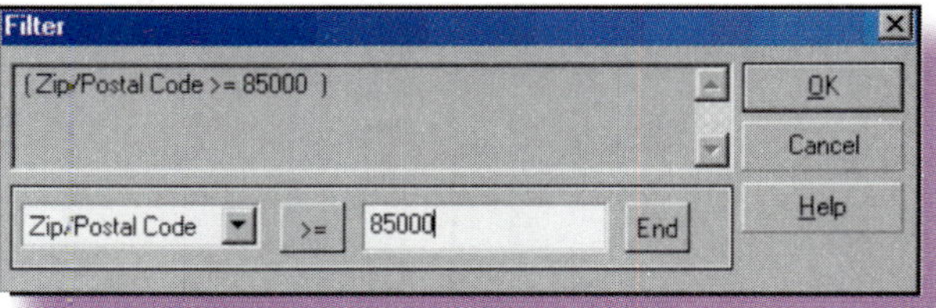

8. Click **OK**. Back in the Address Book, press **Ctrl+A** to select all three entries. Click **Insert**. Verify the *Flowers Org* format and complete the merge.

9. Look at your three letters. Close the file without saving it.

The filter remains in the Address Book until you remove it. We'll do that in the next Step-by-Step exercise, where we will also create an Address Group to merge with your very flexible form document. This time we'll create a group that includes the same four entries you used when you selected entries during the merge.

S TEP-BY-STEP ⟹ 25.10

1. Return to your *Flower Customers* Address Book. Open the **View** menu and choose **Remove Filter**.

2. Open the **Address** menu and choose **New**. Choose **Group** and click **OK**. Name the new group **Best Customers**.

3. Click the **Add/Remove Members** button to display a little list of the entries in the *Flower Customers* Address Book. Point to each of the following entries and double click to add them to the group: **Agnes Astilbe**, **Susan Blackeye**, **Chris Santhemum**, and **Victor Verbena**.

4. Click **OK**. Your Group Properties dialog box should look much like Figure 25-7.

5. Click **OK**. Look at the *Best Customers* group. It should be in the tree structure at the left and at the top of the entries in the Address Book. Practice switching between the *Flower Customers* list and the *Best Customers* group in the larger list.

6. Close the Address Book dialog box. Your **gaillardia 25-8** form document should still be displayed.

7. Click **Merge** and choose **Select Records**. Go to the *Best Customers* group and press **Ctrl+A** to select all four of the customers.

8. Complete the merge as before. When you finish, confirm that your letters go to the correct four individuals.

9. Close all open documents without saving them. Then return to the Address Book and export the *Flower Customers* book to your solutions file one more time. Delete the *Flower Customers* Address Book from your computer so it isn't in the way for other students.

FIGURE 25-7
Group Properties Dialog Box

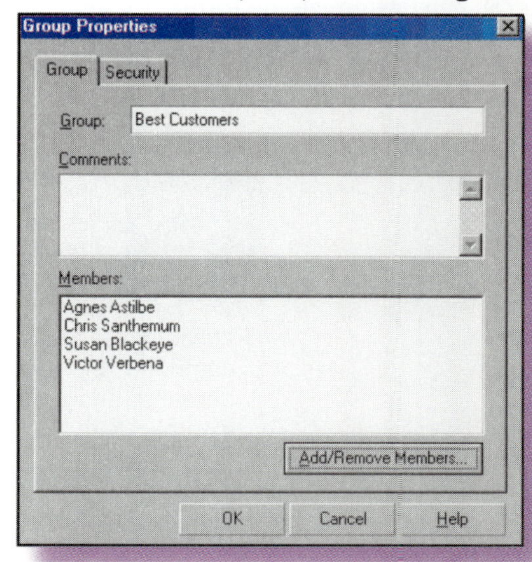

Custom Fields

The default columns (fields) in the CorelCENTRAL Address Book fill most of your needs for information storage. If you wish to include information that doesn't fit in any of the default fields, you can create custom fields. To do so, simply choose Custom Fields from the Edit menu and name the fields. A *Custom* tab will appear in the Person Properties dialog box for use when you are filling in the information.

On the job, custom fields can be created and used with ease. However, custom fields cannot be imported with an Address Book, so no practice is included for classroom use where you are asked to delete your Address Book when you leave your computer.

Summary

You now have an additional tool at your disposal to help you with your work. By now you should be quite comfortable with the manipulation of the information in the Address Book and what you can do with it. In this lesson you have learned the following about the Address Book:

- You can save an Address Book on a floppy disk or send it to another user over a network with the Export feature. You can reverse the procedure to import an Address Book.

- Entries in an Address Book can be sorted and filtered in a variety of ways.

- It is easy to add entries to an Address Book.

- If an Address Book is no longer needed, it can be removed from the computer.

- Address Book can be used for a merge.

- You can divide the entries in an Address Book into groups and save those groups for future use.

- You can customize the format for an address to be inserted into a document.

Combining your telephone, computer, and television, future super-networks will expand the power of the Internet and its successors. You will be able to talk to your computer and television, order movies on demand, and play computer and video games with partners across the world.

LESSON 25 REVIEW QUESTIONS

FILL IN THE BLANKS

Complete each of the following statements by writing your answer in the blank provided.

1. Each Address Book is saved as a ______________ in WordPerfect.

2. The Address Book can be ______________ from one computer and ______________ to a different computer.

3. When an Address Book is open, it shows as a branch of the file structure at the _________ of the main Address Book dialog box.

4. When entries are put into the Address Book, WordPerfect automatically alphabetizes the entries by the first word of the ________________.

5. To delete an Address Book, simply open the File menu and choose ____________.

6. You can select entries that match a certain criteria by opening the ____________ menu and choosing ____________.

TRUE/FALSE

Circle the T if the statement is true. Circle the F if it is false.

T   F   7. When merging a form document with a few entries in an Address Book, you must first copy the desired entries to a data document, save it as a file, and then complete the merge.

T   F   8. Exporting an Address Book is like using Save As, because it is saved in a different location but still appears in the window.

T   F   9. The default for columns to be displayed in the Address Book includes name, address, phone number, birthday, and other important dates.

T   F   10. If you want the list of names in your Address Book sorted by State, simply select the address column and choose Sort from the Tools menu.

This project will consist of two parts. You will create a small (just a sample) Address Book and export it to your disk so you can use it on other computers. Then you will create a letter to be sent to the people in the Address Book. Finally, you will remove the Address Book from your computer. Work efficiently. How much can you do without looking back at the instructions in the lesson?

PROJECT 25A

Study Figure 25-8. It contains the names and addresses of five people from other countries that attended a recent management seminar conducted by your company. Create an Address Book called *Foreign* and enter these names and addresses.

Before you start entering data, study the addresses. Notice that the addresses aren't parallel. Some contain ZIP codes, and some contain states. All contain personal titles (Prefix). Note that the country name is always keyed in all capital letters, and it always goes on a line by itself at the bottom of the address.

Foreign Characters. The first address contains an *a* with an accent that you'll have to get from the Multinational symbols. Since you can't access the symbols in the Address Book, close the Address Book and key **Paraná** in your regular document window. Then select the word, copy it to the Clipboard, reopen the Address Book, edit Joanna's entry, and use Ctrl+V to paste *Paraná* into the location for the state.

Follow the same procedure for the final address. These special letter characters (the Ç and the ü) are also in the Multinational symbols. You'll have to copy and paste three times, for *Hüseyin, Çimrin,* and *Çamlik.*

When you finish, check your work carefully. Then export the book to your normal work folder.

FIGURE 25-8
Names for *Foreign* Address Book

```
Ms. Joanna Brown
address: Caixa Postal 12125
city:    82401-970 Santa Felicidade
state:   Paraná
country: BRAZIL

Mr. Peter Szymski
address: 201 St. Clair Avenue
city:    Georgetown
state:   ON
ZIP:     Y6B 4T8
country: CANADA

Mr. Berndt Scholz
address: Schonbornstr 25
city:    Zeusleben
ZIP:     8727
country: GERMANY

Mrs. Suzan Seitz
address: 4 Pelikano Street
city:    Nikosia
ZIP:     2338C
country: CYPRUS

Mr. Hüseyin Çimrin
address: Yeni Çamlik Caddesi Sokak
         No: 4-17, 4 Levent
city:    Istanbul
ZIP:     80660
country: TURKIYE
```

PROJECT 25B

Figure 25-9 contains the body of a letter to be sent to the people in the *Foreign* Address Book. Prepare a form document associated with the *Foreign* Address Book. Save the form document as **proj25 xxx.frm**. Use your **pf** macro to identify the file. Then merge the form document with all five names in the *Foreign* Address Book. Normally you would prepare envelopes to go with this kind of letter. Today you can skip the envelopes because the letter will be enclosed in a package of materials being sent to these people.

After merging, save your letters as **foreign proj25 xxx** and print them. Close all files. Delete the *Foreign* book from the Address Book main window.

FIGURE 25-9
Body of Letter for Project 25

```
It was a pleasure to have you attend our management seminar in Chicago
last week.  Our seminar presenters enjoyed working with you, getting
to know you, and learning more about management styles in your
country.

Enclosed is the material you requested at the end of the seminar. It
is my hope that the materials, as well as the information presented at
the seminar, will be of use to you and that your company will continue
to grow and flourish as a result of what you learned in Chicago.

A number of our seminar leaders have expressed an interest in
presenting seminars in other countries.  If you wish to work with us
to plan a seminar in your city, please let me know.

Sincerely,

MM MANAGEMENT SEMINARS, INC.



Mona Magnusson, Manager

Enclosures
```

CRITICAL THINKING ACTIVITY

You have created a group of six entries within a large Address Book that you wish to merge with a form document. When you perform the merge, you choose Select Records and specify the address group containing the six names. You can't complete the merge, however, because the OK button at the bottom of the Address Book is grayed. What must you do to complete the merge?

TEMPLATES, STYLES, AND PERFECTEXPERT

OBJECTIVES

Upon completion of this lesson, you will be able to:

- Use templates for the preparation of documents.
- Enter personal information to speed up the preparation of documents.
- Edit a template.
- Discuss creating personalized templates.
- Discuss the WordPerfect Internet tools.
- Discuss two ways of creating styles.
- Create styles to format your documents.
- Apply the styles to your document parts.
- Discuss the differences and similarities among styles, templates, and macros.
- Discuss the PerfectExpert tool.

⏱ **Estimated Time: 1 hour**

Every document you create in WordPerfect is based on a template. A template is a document form. You have been using a template called the *default template* for each document you've created in WordPerfect. Although it seems like an empty document, the default template includes the margins, justification, tab settings, font face and size, line spacing, Toolbar, and a host of other defaults about which you've been learning as you progress through your lessons.

The program also enables you to create *Styles* for formats you use frequently. WordPerfect 9 has a feature called *PerfectExpert* that helps you in the creation and formatting of documents and lets you create and save frequently used projects. We'll begin by learning about templates.

Templates

WordPerfect comes with a number of preformatted templates to help you with certain kinds of tasks, such as faxes, memos, newsletters, and calendars. To see what templates are available, choose New from Project from the File menu. Not all of the templates that come with WordPerfect are installed during a standard installation. A special installation to "Add New Components" must be performed to ensure availability of all templates. We'll begin our exploration of templates with a monthly calendar. If the calendar isn't available in your list of templates, ask your instructor to add the WordPerfect 9 components.

S TEP-BY-STEP ⇒ 26.1

1. Beginning in a new document window, open the **File** menu and choose **New from Project**. (You can also use Ctrl+T or Ctrl+Shift+N.) The PerfectExpert dialog box will appear, as illustrated in Figure 26-1.

2. Check the text box at the top. If it doesn't say [WordPerfect 9], click the arrow beside the box and make that choice.

3. Look through the list of templates available in this box. Then choose **Calendar**, **Monthly** and **Create**. Wait while the feature loads. When it finishes, the calendar for the current month will be showing, along with the Calendar Information dialog box (see Figure 26-2).

4. Change the month and year to be the month following the current month. Click **Finished**. Look at the calendar. Notice the PerfectExpert panel at the left. This panel provides you with quick access to a variety of formatting options.

5. Click the **Change Abbreviations** button. Look at the available options and choose **Abbreviate Weekday Names**. Note the effect of the change on the calendar. Access the same button and choose **Expand Weekday Names** to return the names to their original format.

6. Click **Change Table Look** and choose **Striped Horizontal**.

7. Click the small blue **X** in the upper right corner of the PerfectExpert panel to close the panel. We'll return to it shortly.

8. Save the calendar as **calendar 26-1 xxx**. Keep it open.

FIGURE 26-1
Corel PerfectExpert Dialog Box

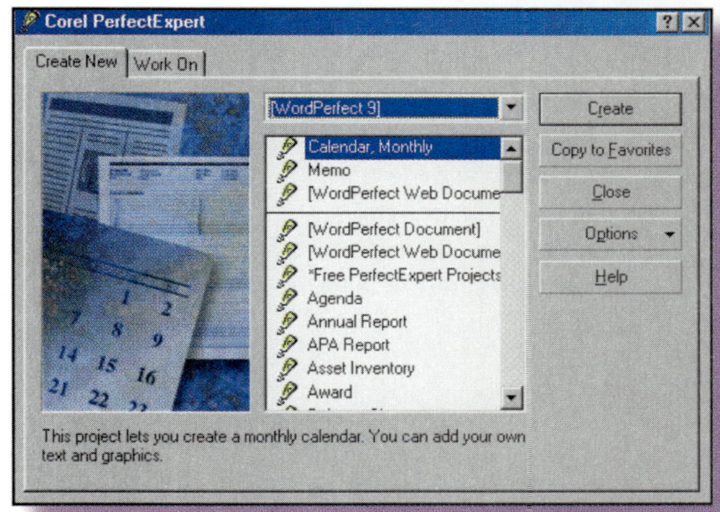

FIGURE 26-2
Calendar Information Dialog Box

4 2 7

Many of the WordPerfect templates use a table format. The Calendar template is no exception. In the original format, most of the lines remained. With the Striped Horizontal format, some of the lines have been removed. If you want to see the layout of the table, open the View menu and choose Table Gridlines. Then return to the striped view. Each of the numbers was inserted with Drop Cap. (You can see those codes if you reveal your codes.)

Now let's key the appointments already on your boss's calendar for next month.

S TEP-BY-STEP 26.2

1. Choose a percentage of Zoom with which you are comfortable and key the appointments listed in Figure 26-3. Double-space between items scheduled for the same day so additional items can be penciled in. (Figure 26-4 illustrates a sample day from the calendar.)

2. Insert the Path and Filename code in the final blank cell of the table. Format the cell so the code is in the lower right corner. Change the font of the code to **6-pt. Arial**.

3. Save the file again. Then print it and close it.

FIGURE 26-3
Appointments for Calendar

Every Monday	9–10	Staff Meeting
Every Wednesday	11:45	Lunch with Fred
1st Monday	10:30	Barbara Voiers
	11	M&M Rudy Anderson
1st Tuesday	9:15	Jon Jacobs
1st Thursday	10	Nan Cartwright
	1:15	Elmer Futte
1st Friday	9:15	Frank Jeloca
2nd Monday	11	Barbara Voiers
2nd Tuesday	10:15	Frances Fargo

FIGURE 26-4
Sample Day

10 9-10 Staff Meeting

11 Barbara Voiers

As you can see, using a template is easy. When you finish, you have an ordinary WordPerfect document that you can edit to your heart's content.

Personal Information

WordPerfect considers a specified entry in the Address Book as *personal information*. That information is automatically included on the templates that require information about the person or business doing the work.

You can change the current personal information default in the PerfectExpert dialog box. If you haven't specified personal information, WordPerfect will prompt you to enter the information.

Let's create a new book for the Address Book. You'll include information about yourself (bogus information if you wish to protect your privacy from other students) and then specify the information about you to be the default personal information.

S TEP-BY-STEP 26.3

1. Open the Address Book and create a new book named **Gaillardia** for Gaillardia Garden Supply.

2. Choose **Address**, **New**, and **Person**. Create an entry for yourself as follows:

   a. Put the Gaillardia address (from Figure 26-5) in the normal address boxes and your home address in the *Other address* locations.

   b. Enter your home phone number, the Gaillardia phone number in *Business Phone 1*, and the Gaillardia fax number appropriately identified in *Business Phone 2*.

   c. Use the **Business** tab to enter the organization name, your job title, and your department.

3. Add entries for Mabel and Perry (see Figure 26-5) exactly like yours, except you'll skip their home addresses and phone numbers.

4. Add an **Organization** entry for Gaillardia, putting the address in the normal address (not *Other*) location. (You should now have three personal entries and one organization entry.) Export the *Gaillardia* book to your disk. Be sure to choose all fields that contain information.

5. Close the Address Book dialog box. Open the **File** menu and choose **New from Project**. Click the **Options** button and choose **Personal Information**. Click **OK** at the information box, and the Address Book will open.

6. Open the **Gaillardia** book. Double click your name for personal information. Click **OK** to close the Properties dialog box. Click **Insert** to tell WordPerfect your information should be saved as Personal Information.

7. Close the PerfectExpert dialog box.

FIGURE 26-5

Information for *Gaillardia* Address Book

```
GAILLARDIA GARDEN SUPPLY
47 Garland Drive
Garden City, NY 11530
Phone: 723-555-8787
Fax: 723-555-8788

Mabel Maples and Perry Pine
Sales Representative
Department: Sales
```

Now that you have told WordPerfect what you would like to use for personal information, let's combine the Address Book with a template.

1. Beginning in a new document window, press **Ctrl+T** or choose **New from Project** from the **File** menu.

2. Choose **WordPerfect 9** in the top box. Below the line, find **Letter, Business**. Click **Create**. The PerfectExpert panel will appear at the left of a letter skeleton (see Figure 26-6) that contains your personal information in the letterhead area.

3. Complete the letter as follows:
   a. Click the **Fill in Heading Info** button. After a moment, the Heading Information dialog box will appear.
   b. Click the **Address Book** button beside the *To* slot. Open the **Ziepke** book and click **Stella Severson**. Click **Insert**, choose **US Standard**, and click **OK**.
   c. Still in the Heading Information dialog box, click in the *Greeting* slot and key **Dear Stella:**. Click **OK**.
   d. Back in the letter, click the **Choose the Look** button on the PerfectExpert panel. Choose **Contemporary**.
   e. Click the **Change the Body** button on the PerfectExpert panel. The letter body choices illustrated in Figure 26-7 will appear. Scroll down and choose the fourth **Accept Credit Application** body and click **Apply**.
   f. Still in the PerfectExpert panel, click **Fill In Entry Fields**. WordPerfect will move to the first entry field in the first line. Key **Gaillardia Garden Supply**.
   g. Click the **Fill In Entry Fields** button again and insert the company name in the last paragraph.
   h. Click the arrow at the left of the house at the top of the PerfectExpert panel to return to the main choices.
   i. Click **Fill in Closing Info** on the PerfectExpert panel and be sure only *Complimentary Closing* has a check mark. Click the arrow beside *Sincerely* for the drop-down list and choose **Respectfully**. Click **OK**.
   j. Make any necessary adjustments to spacing in the closing lines. Check the information in the letterhead and carefully make any necessary edits.

4. Save your letter as **stella 26-4 xxx**. Play your **pf** macro to identify the letter. Print the letter but keep it open.

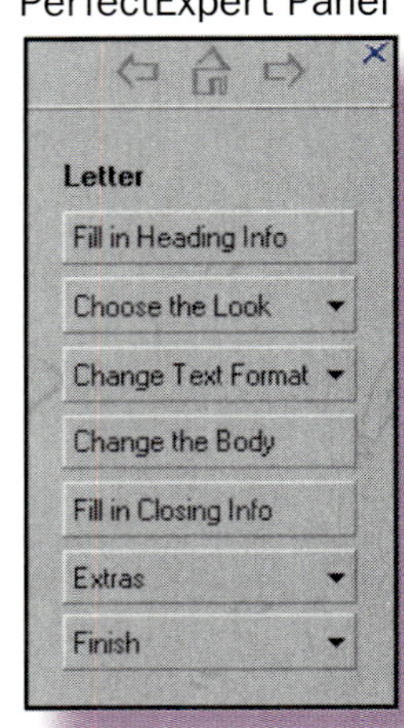

FIGURE 26-6
Personal Letter PerfectExpert Panel

5. Browse through the choices on the PerfectExpert panel. Look at some of the other available letters. If you wish to see the body of a letter, click **Apply** or double click to put the body into your letter. (You don't need to worry about spoiling your letter because you won't save it again.)

6. Experiment with changing the look of the letter and the text format.

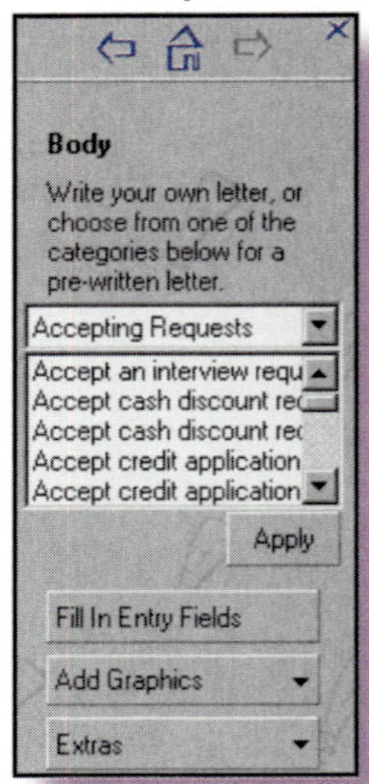

FIGURE 26-7
Letter Body Choices

7. Finally, click the blue **X** on the PerfectExpert panel to close it. Then close your letter without saving it again.

Creating Templates

If you are willing to begin from scratch, you can create your own templates in much the same way you create WordPerfect documents. The major difference is that templates may contain prompts, like those you used to make choices when you used the letter template.

Gaillardia Garden Supply has an expense report form used by the sales representatives that was created in table format. In the next Step-by-Step exercise you will turn that form into a template, complete with prompts. Then you'll use the template to complete the expense report to be submitted to

STEP-BY-STEP 26.5

1. Press **Ctrl+T** to go to the PerfectExpert Document dialog box. Choose **Options** and then choose **Create WP Template**. You will be taken to a new document window, with the Template Property Bar showing at the top (see Figure 26-8).

2. Open the **Insert** menu and choose **File**. Insert **exp.wpd** from your student **datafile** folder. Click **Yes** at the Overwrite Current Styles prompt. (The document will look awful. Zoom to **Full Page** to rewrite the form. Look at the layout of the document. Then return to **100%.**)

3. Click the **Build Prompts** button and click **Add**. Key **Employee Name** for the first prompt. In the *Link . . .* box below, click the arrow for the drop-down menu and choose **Display Name**. Click **OK**.

4. Follow the same procedure for **Employee Title**, choosing **Title** from the drop-down menu. Continue to build prompts in the same way using the following information:

Department	Department
Telephone	Business Phone
Supervisor	<None>
Purpose of Trip	<None>

5. Paste the prompts into the proper locations on the expense report. Work carefully as follows:

   a. With the highlight in the dialog box on *Employee Name*, click to the right of *Employee Name* on the form behind the Prompt Builder dialog box. (You'll have to click twice to exit the dialog box and position the insertion point.)

   b. Click the **Paste** button in the dialog box. The prompt will appear in the form.

   c. Move the highlight in the dialog box to *Employee Title*. Paste that prompt in the appropriate location on the form.

   d. Continue until all prompts have been pasted. Click **OK** to close the Prompt Builder dialog box.

6. Open the **File** menu and choose **Save As**.

   a. In the Save Template dialog box, key **Gaillardia Expense** in the *Description* text box.

   b. For *Template Name*, key **a:\Gaillardia Expenses xxx** (replacing **xxx** with your initials). (Insert the correct filepath if you are saving your files in a different location.)

(continued on next page)

c. For *Template Category*, choose **Business Forms**. Click **OK**.

7. Click the **Close** button on the Template Property Bar to close the template.

FIGURE 26-8
Template Property Bar

| Build Prompts... | Copy/Remove Object... | Associate... | Description... |

the supervisor.

If you were on the job, you would have simply keyed the name of the template, not inserted a filepath when you saved the template. For this course, however, you want your templates where other students can't mess them up. The program will remember that you created the template and saved it on the disk in Drive A, so you'll be able to use the template whenever your disk is in Drive A. Other students will NOT be able to access your template unless they have a template with the same name on their disk in Drive A.

As a precaution, it would be a good idea to tell WordPerfect where you are saving your templates. In the next Step-by-Step exercise you'll set Drive A to be a secondary location for templates. If you are saving your work somewhere other than on the disk in Drive A, customize the Step-by-Step exercise accordingly. Then we'll use the new template.

STEP-BY-STEP ➩ 26.6

1. Beginning in a new document window, open the **Tools** menu and choose **Settings**. Double click the **Files** icon and choose the **Template** tab.

2. In the text box for *Additional template folder*, key **a:**. Then click **OK** and **Close** to return to your working window.

3. Press **Ctrl+T** to begin a new template. You will probably be in the Business Forms section. If not, click the arrow beside the top box and choose **Business Forms**. Choose **Gaillardia Expenses xxx**. (WordPerfect sometimes remembers which templates you've used recently.) If it isn't at the top, find it in the alphabetic list and click **Create**.

4. The Template Information dialog box will appear, asking for information. You are the person submitting the expense report. Click the **Address Book** button to open the Address Book and choose **Gaillardia**. Highlight your name and click **Insert**. Choose **US Standard** format.

5. A dialog box will appear, asking for information about your sales trip. Fill in any missing information, including **Gabby Gaillardia** as the supervisor and **Sales Contacts** as the purpose of the trip.

6. Click **OK** and look at the expense report. Save the beginning of the expense report as **expense 26-6 xxx**. Keep it open in the window.

You're ready to begin entering expenses in the expense report. The work of the template is finished, and you're now working with a normal WordPerfect table. The table already has formulas in place so that when you finish, the totals can be calculated. In Step-by-Step exercise 26.7 you'll complete the report.

STEP-BY-STEP ⟹ 26.7

1. Position your insertion point in Cell A14 to enter the date. Key **10-27** and press **Tab**. (Note that the year is automatically added to the date, and the date is formatted.)

2. Using **Tab** to work across and to skip the cells for which there is no information, enter the data in Figure 26-9.

3. When you finish, display the Table QuickMenu and choose **Calculate**. Zoom to **Full Page** to look at the entire form. You should have $406 coming in reimbursement.

4. Save your expense report as **expense 26-7 xxx**. Play your **pf** macro to identify the file. Then print it and close it, saving it again when you close it.

FIGURE 26-9
Data for Step-by-Step 26.7

```
Date:            10-27
Description:     Travel to East Windsor, NH
Travel:          8
Lodging:         103
Breakfast:       6
Lunch:           7
Dinner:          25
Date:            10-28
Description:     Travel to Hartford, CT
Travel:          17
Lodging:         98
Breakfast:       5.5
Lunch:           8
Dinner:          20
Entertainment:   54
Date:            10-29
Description:     Return to Garden City
Travel:          18
Lodging:         (None. Tab past this cell.)
Breakfast:       4.5
Lunch:           10
Dinner:          22
```

Editing Templates

When using templates on the job, you may find that you are constantly performing the same edits on the documents created with the templates. In the same way that WordPerfect enables you to create new templates, you can also edit templates you've created or those that come with the program.

Your supervisor has decided that rather than entering a dollar amount for travel, she would like to know the number of miles you've traveled so you can be reimbursed at a set amount per mile. This is the way the Internal Revenue Service deals with transportation expenses. Let's edit the expense report template to include miles.

1. Open the **File** menu and choose **New from Project**.

2. With **Gaillardia Expenses xxx** highlighted, click **Options** and then click **Edit WP Template**. Your expense report template will appear in the edit mode.

3. Open the **File** menu and choose **Save As**. In the *Description* text box, key **Expense with Mileage**. For the template name, key **a:\Mileage Expense xxx**. Choose the **Business Forms** group and click **OK**.

4. Make the following changes to the left side of the table. When you finish, the first five columns will look like the miniature in Figure 26-10.
   a. Drag the table line between Columns A and B to the left until column A is **0.625"** wide.
   b. Use the **QuickSplit Columns** button on the Tables Property Bar to draw a line down the middle of Column B, beginning in the word *Description* and ending above *TOTALS*, splitting the column into two columns.
   c. Delete the *Description* column heading. Title the new Column B **Purpose** and the new Column C **From-To**.
   d. Replace *Travel* with **Miles** and make the column approximately **0.5"** wide.

5. Check your work against Figure 26-10. If it looks good, click **Save** for an interim save and continue reading.

FIGURE 26-10
New Expense Report Columns

Date	Purpose	From-To	Miles	Lodging

We'll delete some of the rows in the expense part of the table and add rows at the bottom to make room for the mileage information at the bottom of the expense report, and adjust the formulas to accommodate the new column. In order to adjust the formulas, you'll need to unlock some cells that were locked in the original document to make sure the contents of the cells would not be changed. Then we'll lock them again. Follow along carefully.

1. Adjust the table and format the cells.
   a. Position your insertion point in Row 20 and display the QuickMenu. Choose **Delete** and change from *1* row to **3** rows. Complete the 3-row deletion.
   b. Position your insertion point in Row 32 and insert 2 rows.
   c. Select the two cells above the final zeros. Format them with bold. Set Numeric Format at **Currency** and Alignment at **Right**.
   d. In the cell to the left of the first of those cells, Flush Right the label **Subtotal**. In the next cell down, Flush Right the label **Mileage**.

2. Fix Row 33 so it looks like Figure 26-11.

   a. Beginning three cells down from *TOTALS*, Flush Right and Bold the words **Total Miles**.

   b. Format the next cell with a single line all the way around.

   c. Join the next two cells. Key **at $0.30 per mile**. Select the next four cells and format them with **40%** fill.

3. Position your insertion point in the cell next to the word *TOTALS* in the *Miles* column (see Figure 26-11). Drag your insertion point across the formula in the Formula Toolbar and delete the formula by pressing **Delete** and clicking the blue check mark.

4. Format the cell with **40%** fill. (The total miles figure is several rows down.)

FIGURE 26-11
Bottom of Expense Report

TOTALS		0.00	0.00	0.00	0.00		0.00		0.00
						Less Advances and charges to company			
							Subtotal		$0.00
Total Miles	.00	at $0.30 per mile					Mileage		$0.00
									$0.00
									TOTAL

Now that all of the formatting is completed, let's work with the formulas.

STEP-BY-STEP 26.10

1. Let's begin by fixing the formula for the totals at the right of the table.

   a. Select the cells in the final column (TOTALS) down to the cell above *TOTAL*.

   b. Right click and choose **Format**. In the Cell format dialog box, click to deselect *Lock cell to prevent changes* in the lower right corner. Click **OK**.

   c. Position the insertion point in the first cell of the *Totals* column. (That might be Column M or N, depending on how WordPerfect named the columns when you edited the form.)

   d. Look at the formula in the Formula Toolbar. Carefully adjust the formula so it captures all expenses, beginning with *Lodging* and ending with *Other*. Click the blue check mark to enter the formula.

   e. Copy the formula down 15 times.

   f. Position the insertion point in the cell beside *Subtotal*. Enter a simple formula that subtracts the amount of the advance from the total expenses (i.e., M30-M31).

   g. Position the insertion point in the cell beside *Mileage*. Enter a formula that multiplies the number of miles in the Total Miles box at the left times the 30¢ reimbursement per mile (i.e., D33*0.3).

   h. Position the insertion point in the final total cell and enter a formula that adds the Subtotal to the Mileage reimbursement amount (i.e., M32+M33).

   i. Select the entire final column and reverse Step 1b, locking the cells again.

(continued on next page)

4 3 5

2. Format the *Miles* column as follows:
   a. Select all of the cells in the *Miles* column, above the shaded box. Set Numeric Format at **Fixed**. Change the number of decimal places to **0**. Click **OK**.
   b. Position your insertion point in the cell that will hold the total miles. Click the **Functions** button on the Formula Toolbar and key **sum** to move to that function in the list.
   c. Insert the SUM function and choose the range of cells to be totaled by selecting the cells in the *Miles* column. Click the blue check mark to insert the formula.
   d. Align the contents of the cell at the right.

3. Play your **pf** macro and save the expense report again. Close the form.

Now that you have created your personalized template, complete with a mileage column, you may use it any time you wish to prepare an expense report. You'll have an opportunity to use your customized form in Project 26.

WordPerfect Projects

WordPerfect remembers the work you do when using templates. Any job that you do that begins by going to the PerfectExpert dialog box is considered a *project*. Those projects are included in the list in the PerfectExpert dialog box, and some of the data in the project are remembered from one use to the next.

In this course you have saved your templates with your other work (usually on the disk in Drive A), so although the projects may appear in a list in the PerfectExpert dialog box, the projects aren't readily available unless your disk is in the drive. On the job you will save the projects to the hard drive, so they will always be available. You'll no doubt find the idea of projects very useful, since most jobs call for repetition of the same tasks over and over.

Internet Template

A very special template is the template that enables you to create a Web document for the Internet. This template may be accessed by opening the File menu and choosing Internet Publisher. This choice opens the Internet Publisher dialog box, pictured in Figure 26-12.

Look at the four choices available in this dialog box.

■ The first choice takes you to a window where you can design a Web document from scratch, using the tools you've been learning about.

■ The second choice in the menu allows you to take a document that has already been prepared and convert it to a format acceptable on the Web.

■ The third choice saves your document in HTML format.

■ The final choice in the menu can be used to connect your computer to the Internet so you can access the information available there. Of course, in order to do this, your computer must be connected to a modem, and you must have Internet access already established.

In Lesson 30 you'll have an opportunity to design a Web page. Unless your classroom has Internet connections, you won't be able to publish the page, but you'll get the design experience. Ask your instructor if your classroom has Internet access so you can learn to use this popular tool.

Create Styles

Styles provide another easy way to format similar types of text, such as headings and lists. Use a style repeatedly to save time and to give your documents a consistent format. If you change your mind about the format, you can edit the style to update all text where the style has been applied.

Styles often are a combination of formatting codes (and sometimes text) that can be called upon when needed. Styles are given a name and can be grouped together for certain kinds of documents. They are saved with the documents they format. Styles can be associated with a template. You can make the styles available wherever you are working in WordPerfect by copying a style document to your disk.

Styles can be created in two ways. In the next few Step-by-Step exercises we will use both of the following methods:

- Identify the style and key the codes in the Styles dialog box.

- Position the insertion point in text that already has the desired format, and name the style using the QuickStyle feature.

QuickStyle

We'll try the second method first. We'll create styles using QuickStyle.

STEP-BY-STEP 26.11

1. Beginning in a new document window, go to the student **datafile** folder and open **backup**. Save the file with your work as **backup 26-11 xxx**.

2. Select the first side heading and format it with Bold, Italic, and a 16-pt font size.

3. Deselect the side heading and click to position the insertion point somewhere in the side heading. Open the **Format** menu and choose **Styles** (at the bottom). Click the **QuickStyle** button. The QuickStyle dialog box, as illustrated in Figure 26-13, will appear, asking for a style name for the style and a description.

(continued on next page)

4. In the *Style name* box, key **side heading**. Tab to *Description* and key **bold, italic, 16-pt. formatting**. Click **OK**. Then click **Close** to close the Style List dialog box.

5. Move in the document to the second side heading. Position the insertion point somewhere in the heading.

6. Click the **Styles** button on the Property Bar to open the Style List. Click **side heading** to apply that style to the side heading.

7. Use the procedure in Steps 5 and 6 to format the third side heading.

8. Return to the top of your document. Select the title and format it with a 20-pt. font size and Bold. Choose **Format** and **Styles**, and click the **QuickStyle** button again.

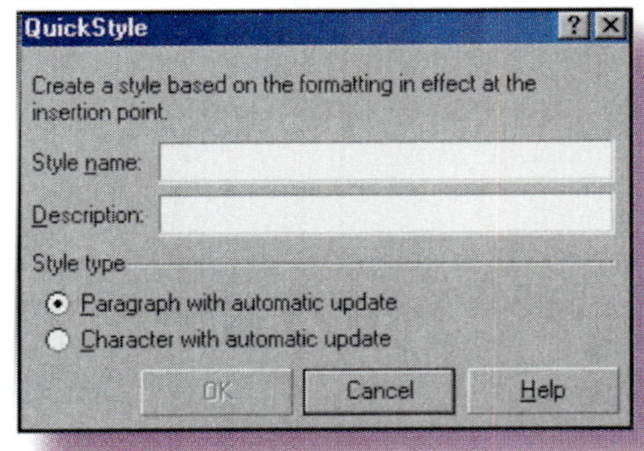

FIGURE 26-13
QuickStyle Dialog Box

9. Give this style **title** as the style name and **20-pt. bold** as the description. Click **OK** and then **Close**.

10. Play your **pf** macro and save the document again as **backup 26-11 xxx**. Keep it open.

NOTE:

You can open the Style List with Alt+F8.

The side heading style that you created in your document worked much like working with QuickFormat. When you learned QuickFormat, you learned to determine the format and then copy it to other parts of the document. In both cases, if you make a change to the style, the document is automatically updated to reflect that change.

The major difference between using styles and QuickFormat is that QuickFormat may only be used to format the document in the window. With styles, you can save the style so it can be used on other documents. We'll learn about that in a minute. First, let's look at the other way of creating a style.

Create a Style with Codes

You can open the Styles Editor and add the codes needed for the style. This procedure is much like when you inserted margin and font codes in the Current Document Codes Style. In fact, the dialog box is identical. We'll create one style using that method.

STEP-BY-STEP ⇒ 26.12

1. With **backup 26-11 xxx** showing in the window, open the **Format** menu and choose **Styles** to display the Style List dialog box. Click **Create** to display the Styles Editor (see Figure 26-14).

2. In the *Style name* box at the top, key **just paragraph** for justified paragraph. For *Description*, key **report paragraph format**.

3. Click to position your insertion point in the *Contents* box. Open the **Format** menu and choose **Justification** and **Full**. Return to the **Format** menu and choose **Line** and then **Tab Set**.

4. In the *Tab position* box, key **0.25**. Click the **Set** button. Then key **0.75** and click the **Set and Close** button.

5. Look at the codes in the Styles Editor. You should see a justification and a tab set code.

6. In the *Type* section of the dialog box, click the button to display the drop-down menu. Choose **Document (open)**. Then click **OK**. Click the **Close** button in the Style List dialog box to return to your document.

7. With the insertion point positioned at the beginning of the first paragraph, apply the **just paragraph** style to the entire document.

8. Use **Save As** to save the file as **backup 26-12 xxx**. Print the document.

FIGURE 26-14
Styles Editor

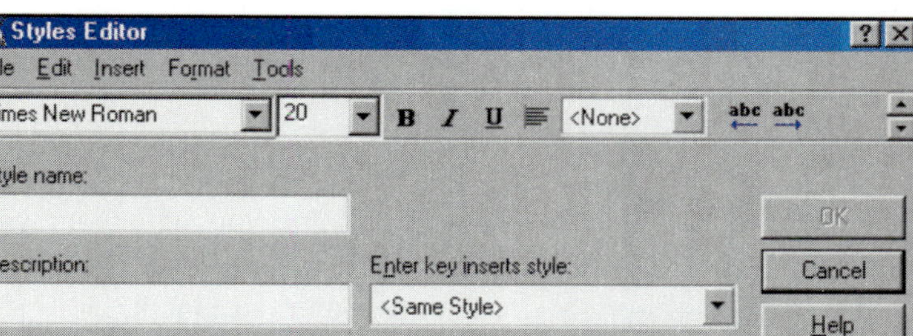

Now that all three styles have been created—two of them using QuickStyle and one of them the traditional way—let's save the set of styles so you can apply them to another document.

1. With **backup 26-12 xxx** showing in your window, choose **Format**, **Styles**, and **Options**. Then choose **Save As**.

2. Click the folder beside the *Filename* text box and locate the folder containing your files. When it is specified, key **report style** in the *Filename* box and click **Select**.

3. In the Save Styles To dialog box, click the button at the bottom for **User styles**. Then click **OK**. Close the Style List. Close your document without saving it again.

4. Go to the student **datafile** folder and open **pc-care**. Use **Save As** to save the file as **pc 26-13 xxx**.

5. With the insertion point at the top of the document, open the **Format** menu, choose **Styles**, and click the **Options** button. Choose **Retrieve**.

6. Click the folder beside the *Filename* text box and locate your **report style** document in your folder. Retrieve that file.

7. When you are returned to the Style List, apply the **just paragraph** style at the beginning of the first paragraph. Then click in the document title and apply the **title** style.

8. Go through the document and apply the **side heading** style to each of the six side headings.

9. Play your **pf** macro to identify the file. Then print it and close it, saving it again as **pc 26-13 xxx**.

PerfectExpert

PerfectExpert is another way that WordPerfect helps you with your work. The PerfectExpert panel was displayed at the left of the window when you were working with the first two templates in this lesson. It gave you a choice of options for the particular document.

You can also use PerfectExpert separate from templates. This tool can be used to help you create documents, format the documents, make the documents pretty, edit the documents, and finish them. The PerfectExpert provides the steps for you to progress through these tasks. Let's browse through the PerfectExpert tools.

1. Beginning in a new document window, open the **Help** menu and choose **PerfectExpert**. The PerfectExpert panel will be displayed at the left of your window, looking like Figure 26-15. (The yellow button near the right on the default Toolbar also displays the PerfectExpert panel.)

2. Look at the top of the panel. The *X* may be used to close the panel. You may click the little house in the middle at the top to return to the main panel—the one that is displayed in the figure.

3. Click **Write a Draft**. Look at the outline option. Then click the **Home** icon to return to the main panel.

4. Try each of the buttons, looking at the options available, before returning to the main panel. Note that the PerfectExpert contains very few tools about which you haven't already learned.

5. When you have finished looking at the options, click the blue **X** to close the panel.

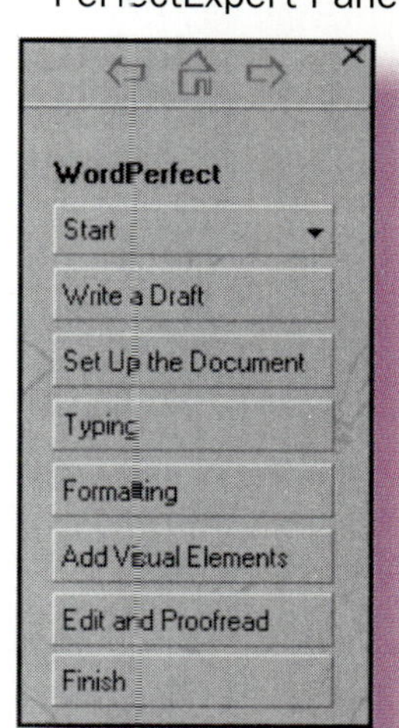

FIGURE 26-15
PerfectExpert Panel

The PerfectExpert might be useful to you for certain documents. You'll learn in Lesson 30 to use the PerfectExpert when you create a Web document to be published on the Internet. That PerfectExpert is different from the one you used in this lesson, since the PerfectExpert tool is context-sensitive—it changes according to the feature you're using when you access it.

As you discovered when you looked at the tools available in PerfectExpert, you've already learned to do almost all of the formatting provided in PerfectExpert on your own. You don't need to go through the extra steps required to access the PerfectExpert features. Congratulations!

Summary

This lesson contained not much more than an introduction to templates and styles. You worked with each of the features to format your documents. In this lesson you learned that:

- WordPerfect has provided you with a wide variety of preformatted templates to help you prepare certain kinds of documents.

- The Address Book is closely connected to templates, making your work easier.

- With your name and address in the Address Book, that information can easily be added to documents prepared with templates.

- You can create WordPerfect templates complete with prompts to help you do your work.

- WordPerfect templates can be edited just like other WordPerfect documents.

- WordPerfect comes with an Internet Publisher that helps you prepare documents to be formatted by HTML for the Web.

- Styles can be used to add consistent formatting to your documents.

- You can format a portion of a document and then create the style with the QuickStyle button, or you can enter the codes for the style in the Styles Editor.

- You can save sets of styles to be retrieved into other documents to provide consistent formatting of the documents.

- Styles, templates, and macros have many similarities as well as many differences.

- The PerfectExpert can be used to create and format your documents.

■ Many of the tasks you can perform with styles and templates can be performed with macros or even Keyboard Merge. Figure 26-16 provides you with a comparison among three features—macros, templates, and styles.

Macros	Styles	Templates
Purpose: Macros are used to record keystrokes so they can be played back.	**Purpose:** Styles are used to reduce formatting work and to ensure formatting consistency between documents or in templates.	**Purpose:** Templates are files that are used to set up documents.
Explanation: Macros are played back by choosing Tools and Macro, and then selecting the desired macro. Macros are files that end with a *.wcm* extension. Therefore, macros can be opened, copied, deleted, edited, or renamed. A number of macros come with WordPerfect.	**Explanation:** Styles consist of various formatting codes. Text can also be included in your styles. Various styles are included with WordPerfect, but you can also create styles to suit your specific needs. A group of styles can be saved and retrieved to be applied to other documents.	**Explanation:** All templates end with the *.wpt* extension. Every document in WordPerfect is based on a template. WordPerfect comes with groups of templates. You can edit existing templates, or you can create your own. Templates are like containers that can "hold" objects such as Tool-bars, macros, styles, Menu Bars, Property Bars, abbreviations, and keyboards.
Length: No limit exists on the number of keystrokes in a macro. Macros may be short or complex. Macros can contain text and keystroke commands. Macros may contain a description to remind you what the macro does.	**Length:** Styles can contain an unlimited number of formatting commands as well as text. You may add a description to help you remember what the style does.	**Length:** Templates are files. There is no limit to the number of keystrokes that can be stored in a template. You can add a description to remind you what the template does.
Location: Macros are stored in a template; typically, the *default* template. However, macros can be attached to any template.	**Location:** Styles are saved in the document or template with which you are working. To use a style, retrieve a group of styles. You can also open the document or create a document using the template where the styles are stored. Then choose the desired style from the Styles button on the Property Bar.	**Location:** Templates are files that are saved in a group category. To use a template, open the File menu and choose New. Then locate the desired template and choose it.
Example: You could prepare a macro that creates a memo heading for page 2 of a memo. The macro could also be used to suppress the header from the first page of the memo. Another macro could be used to save and print the memo.	**Example:** You could create styles that format various sections of a memo, such as the side headings, enumerated items, and body text.	**Example:** You could create a memo template that contains the macros and styles that are necessary to create the memo. The template would be for the margins of the memo, the font face and size, and to prompt you for the fill-in lines of the heading.

LESSON 26 REVIEW QUESTIONS

WRITTEN QUESTIONS

Key your answers to the following questions. Number your answers and double-space between them. Use complete sentences and good grammar.

1. The formatting for every document you create in WordPerfect is based on something. What is that something?

2. Name three of the formats controlled by your answer to Question 1.

3. What is the name of the panel that appears at the left of the screen to help you format your documents?

4. What choice must you make from the File menu to see the available templates?

5. When you create a job based on a template, WordPerfect saves it as a special kind of document that can be used and reused. What is that kind of document known as?

6. What choice must you make in the File menu to create a Web document for the Internet?

7. If you wish to create a style from already formatted text, what choice must you make in the Styles dialog box?

MATCHING

Write the letter of the term or phrase from Column 2 that best matches the description in Column 1.

Column 1	Column 2
_____ **8.** Used to reduce formatting work and to ensure formatting consistency between documents.	**A.** Forms
_____ **9.** Files that are used to set up documents.	**B.** Macros
_____ **10.** Used to record keystrokes so they can be played back.	**C.** Styles
	D. Templates

SCANS

PROJECT 26A

Let's assume you are temporarily working for Gaillardia Garden Supply. Two of the sales representatives have submitted expense reports for sales trips they made to contact prospective customers. The information for the trips is illustrated in Figure 26-17.

FIGURE 26-17

Information for Two Expense Reports

Employee Name: Mabel Maples   Perry Pine
Employee Title: Sales Representative   same
Department: Sales   same
Telephone: 723-555-8787   same
Supervisor: Gabby Gaillardia   same
Purpose of Trip: Sales Contacts   same

Mabel:

Date	Purpose	From-To	Miles	Lodging	Breakfast	Lunch	Dinner	Entertainment
10-22	Sales Contact	GC to Boston	222	56.00	4.75	8.75	25.00	
10-23	Same	Boston to Bangor	249	48.00	5.55	10.85	38.00	54.00
10-24	Same	Bangor to GC	471		8.00	12.85	15.35	

Perry:

Date	Purpose	From-To	Miles	Lodging	Breakfast	Lunch	Dinner	Entertainment
10-22	Sales Contact	GC to Buffalo	430	88.00	6.55	8.75	28.95	
10-23	Same	Buffalo to Pittsburgh	224	73.00	7.95	6.00	23.75	40.00
10-24	Same	Pitts. to Wash. D.C.	259	93.00	10.55	15.00	42.00	
10-25	Same	Wash. D.C. to GC	203		9.95	14.50		

Use your Expense Report with Mileage template to prepare their reports. In the *Personal Information* section of the Template Information dialog box, go to the Address Book and choose Gaillardia Garden Supply. Don't bother keying any of the zeros after the decimal points. WordPerfect will add them automatically.

When you finish the first report, save it as **mabel proj26a xxx**. Play your **pf** macro to identify the file. Print it and close it, saving it again. Do the same with the second, naming it **perry proj26a xxx**.

How quickly can you fill in the required information and calculate the totals for these two expense reports?

PROJECT 26B

Most of the WordPerfect templates contain named regions. Let's take a moment to explore a couple of templates, checking on how the templates work. Follow these steps:

1. Press Ctrl+T to open the PerfectExpert dialog box. In the WordPerfect 9 group, choose Agenda. Note that the insertion point is in the *Meeting Title* section.

2. Reveal your codes. Look at the paragraph style. Click the Change the Heading button on the PerfectExpert panel and choose Meeting Title. The document is set up to go directly to the QuickMark and select the prompt so you can key the replacement text.

3. Press Tab. Note that the same thing happens for the next field to insert the information. Move the insertion point to the left of one of the opening *Named Region* codes. Note that the code expands to show the name of the "region."

4. Click in the *Persons Attending* section and press Tab. Note that the cells that contain numerals are locked so you can enter information into the blanks without worrying about numbered cells. Close the agenda without saving it. Start a couple of other templates and look at the codes that make the templates and prompts work.

5. Finally, choose Memo. Look at the codes. Open the Format menu and choose Styles. Look at the styles included with the memo. Close the style list and browse through the buttons on the PerfectExpert panel. Note that the style list is the same as the choices in the PerfectExpert.

6. Click the first button on the PerfectExpert panel to position the insertion point to fill in the heading information. Enter your instructor's name in the *To* location and **Templates** in the *Subject* location.

7. Key a short paragraph telling why you think WordPerfect used tables, named regions, and styles to help format the templates. Save the file as **proj26b xxx**. Submit the paragraph to your instructor, along with the rest of the lesson.

Instead of sending and reading written documents as e-mail, in the future you will use the Internet for video and voice mail. If the person you want to reach is not available, you will be able to leave a message for video playback later.

Now that you know how to create your own template, you've decided to create a template for your health class assignment. Your teacher wants you to keep track of your caloric intake on a daily basis, including the amount of fat (saturated, unsaturated, polyunsaturated) and the percent of calories from fat. Since this is an eight-week project, creating a template seems like a good idea. How would you set up this template and what functions would you have WordPerfect perform for you?

TABLE OF CONTENTS AND INDEX

OBJECTIVES

Upon completion of this lesson, you will be able to:

- Mark text for a table of contents.

- Define a table of contents.

- Generate a table of contents.

- Use Delay Codes to appropriately number the pages of your documents.

- Create a concordance file for an index.

- Define an index.

- Generate an index.

- Discuss other kinds of lists that can be created in WordPerfect.

Estimated Time: $1^1/_2$ hours

In a number of previous lessons you've worked with lists of one kind or another. You've learned that WordPerfect provides you with helpful tools to number paragraphs, outlines, and bulleted lists.

WordPerfect can help you prepare other kinds of lists. Two of them are covered in this lesson—a table of contents and an index. Both of these features are quite useless for short documents. However, when you are preparing a longer document, the features can be wonderfully helpful. This lesson contains a multiple-page document that you will mark for a table of contents. You'll also use it to prepare an index. You'll learn as you go!

Table of Contents

You will use the Table of Contents Feature Bar to mark the text to be included in the table of contents. In addition, a decision must be made regarding how the table of contents is to be displayed. When the document is completely marked, you will tell WordPerfect where you want the table of contents. Then another click of the mouse button tells WordPerfect to look at all of the marked text and the page numbers on which the text is located. A table of contents is then generated, complete with page numbers and dot leaders.

Look at Figure 27-1. This is a portion of the table of contents you will be preparing in this lesson. You will be referred to this figure later.

Preparing the Text

When working with a document in which you'd like an automatically generated table of contents, you may mark the text as you are keying. An alternative is to key the text and then go back to mark it for the table of contents. In the Step-by-Step exercises that follow, the document has already been keyed and saved for you, so all you have to do is select the text to be included in the table of contents and mark it.

TABLE OF CONTENTS

STEP-BY-STEP 27.1

1. Beginning in a new document window, go to the student **datafile** folder and open **ergo**. Use **Save As** to save the document as **ergo 27-1 xxx**.

2. Open the **Tools** menu and choose **Reference**. Then choose **Table of Contents**. The Table of Contents Feature Bar should appear, looking like Figure 27-2.

3. Select the first side heading (*Introduction*) and click the **Mark 1** button on the Feature Bar. You have just marked that side heading as a Level 1 entry for your table of contents.

4. Select the next side heading (*Computer Terminals*) and mark it in the same way.

5. Look at Figure 27-3. It shows the first two paragraphs in the *Computer Terminals* section, with the items to be included in the table of contents circled and the level for the table of contents indicated beside the circle. Mark all five items at the appropriate level.

6. Play your **pf** macro to identify the file. Then save your document again as **ergo 27-1 xxx**. Keep it open.

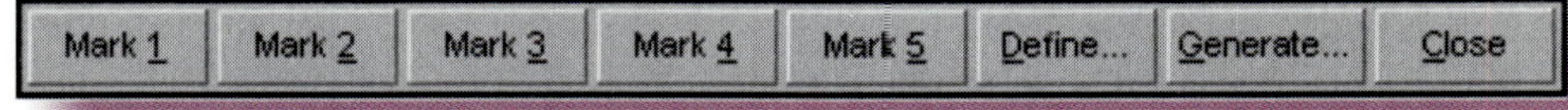

Computer Terminals

    Computer terminals have been blamed for many ailments and maladies among workers. Research has steadfastly refused to prove that there is any substance to the complaints that computer terminals are to blame for those ailments. A common-sense approach to terminals in the workplace, however, can prevent even the complaints.
    Monitors. Many factors need to be considered in the installation of computer monitors (VDTs or display screens). One factor is the clarity of the character in the window. What about character size? Can the illumination be adjusted? How bright is the color of the picture? What about flicker? Much of this can be assessed by spending a little time using the monitor before the decision to purchase is made.

The remainder of this document has been marked for you. Obviously, it isn't too difficult. Now you'll define the location of the table of contents. Usually the table of contents goes before the first page of text and is preceded by a title page.

Defining the Table of Contents

To tell WordPerfect where the table of contents should go, you must insert a *Define* code. Let's add a page and define the table of contents for your document.

S TEP-BY-STEP ▷ 27.2

1. With **ergo 27-1 xxx** showing in the window, press **Ctrl+Home** twice to position the insertion point before all codes on the page. Press **Ctrl+Enter** to add a new page at the beginning.

2. Move your insertion point to the new page (above the page break) and tell WordPerfect to vertically center the current page. Center **TABLE OF CONTENTS** in bold, using all caps. Press **Enter** twice.

3. Click the **Define** button on the Table of Contents Feature Bar. Change the number of levels to **3**. Your dialog box should look like Figure 27-4.

4. Click **OK** to return to your document. A code will appear showing you where your table of contents will be generated. Look at the code in Reveal Codes and add it to your list.

5. Click the **Generate** button on the Feature Bar. In the little dialog box that appears, the first option should be checked. The second option should NOT be checked. Click **OK**.

(continued on next page)

449

6. After a moment, your table of contents should appear in the window. Look it over. Look at the format. Notice that the first page of text is *page 2*.

7. Save your file as **ergo 27-2 xxx** and keep it open.

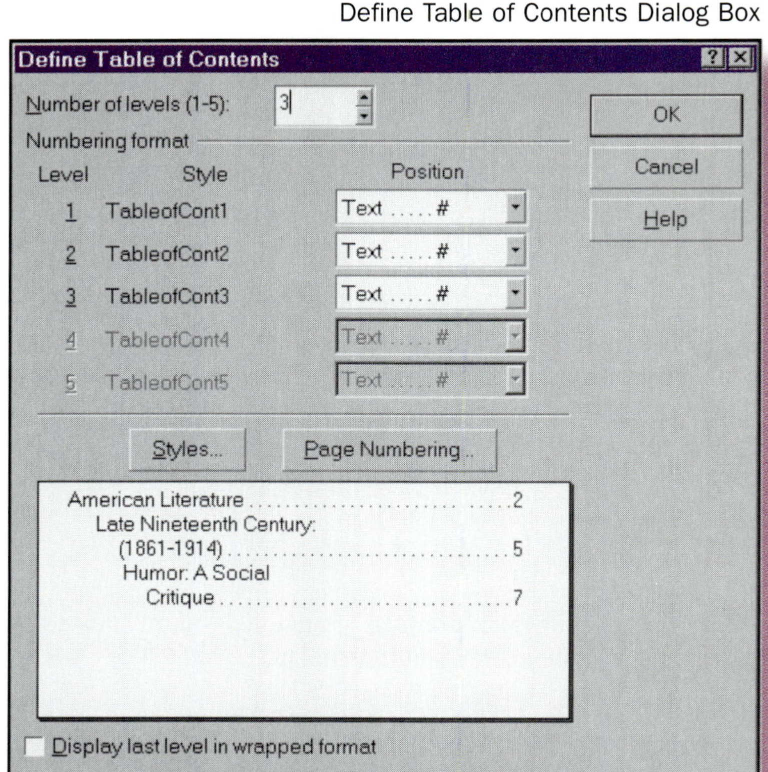

FIGURE 27-4
Define Table of Contents Dialog Box

Delay Codes

WordPerfect has a feature called *Delay Codes* that enables you to number your pages but not have the page numbers start immediately. That feature is perfect for a document with front matter such as a table of contents because you want the first page of text to be considered *page 1*. We'll add a title page. Then we'll put a Delay Codes code on that title page telling WordPerfect to begin numbering on the first page of text, and add another code that tells WordPerfect the first page of text will be *page 1*.

STEP-BY-STEP ⟹ 27.3

1. With **ergo 27-2 xxx** showing in your window, use **Save As** to save the file as **ergo 27-3 xxx**.

2. Press **Ctrl+Home** twice to move your insertion point above all codes, and press **Ctrl+Enter** to add another new page at the top of the document. Format the title page as follows:

a. Center only the current page vertically.

b. Center the following title: **OFFICE ERGONOMICS**. Select and format it with **20-pt. Times New Roman** in bold all caps. Below the title, press **Enter** four times. Key the remaining text, as shown in Figure 27-5, to complete the title page.

c. Put a Page border on the page. Go to **Line** borders and choose the fourth border in the last full row.

FIGURE 27-5
Text for Title Page

OFFICE ERGONOMICS

by

(Student name)
(Course name)

(Current date)

3. Press **Ctrl+Home** twice to move your insertion point to the top of the page. Open the **Format** menu and choose **Page**. Then choose **Delay Codes**. Set the number of pages to delay at **2**. (One of the two pages is the title page and the other is the table of contents page.) Click **OK**.

4. This will take you to a special window where you can enter all of the codes you'd like delayed. Enter the following codes:

a. Open the **Format** menu and choose **Page** and **Numbering**.

b. Choose **Bottom Center** as the location for the page number. Choose a simple **1** format for the page number.

c. Choose **Set Value**. Make sure *1* is showing in the *Set page number* box. Click **OK** twice to return to the Delay Codes window.

d. Click **Close** on the Delay Codes Feature Bar to return to your document.

5. Page through the document and look at the page numbers. They should begin at the bottom of the first page of text, and that page should be page 1. If you have something different, remove your Delay Codes codes at the beginning of the document and repeat Steps 3 and 4.

6. Your Table of Contents Feature Bar should still be showing at the top of the window. Click the **Generate** button and **OK**. Your table of contents should be regenerated, and the page numbers should now be correct.

7. Compare your table of contents with the portion illustrated in Figure 27-1. Do they contain the same information? If so, you are ready to move on. If not, go back and see if you can identify the problem.

8. When your table of contents is beautiful (the text of the document isn't beautiful, yet!), save the document again as **ergo 27-3 xxx**. Keep it open.

Formatting Review

Now that the table of contents and title page are in place and the page numbering is set up, let's make the document a little more attractive. We'll use the **report style** style you created in Lesson 26 to format the document parts, and we'll revise one of the styles slightly.

1. Position your insertion point at the beginning of the first page of text, just to the left of the title of the document.

2. Change Line Spacing to **2.0**.

3. Open the **Format** menu and choose **Styles**. Click the **Options** button and choose **Retrieve**.

4. Locate the **report style** file in your file folder and retrieve it to your style list. Position the insertion point on *title* and click the **Edit** button. Edit the style as follows:

  a. Press **Enter** twice to put two hard returns above the title.

  b. Give the **Center** command (Shift+F7) to center the title.

  c. Click **OK**.

  d. Back in the Style List dialog box, click the **Options** button and choose **Save As**. Save the style again as **report style** in its original location so the revised *title* style is saved for future use.

  e. Then click **Insert** to format the title with the edited *title* style.

5. Format the five side headings with the *side heading* style. The side headings are listed in Figure 27-6.

6. Look through your document. In all likelihood, you will see a problem that should be fixed with Widow/Orphan. Return to the top of the first page of text. Insert the **Widow/Orphan** code.

7. Save your lovely document again, this time as **ergo 27-4 xxx**. Keep it open.

FIGURE 27-6
Side Headings to Format

```
Introduction
Computer Terminals
Lighting and Decor
Furniture
Summary
```

If you've been thinking at all about what you've been doing, you know that your table of contents is now out of date. All of the page numbers are wrong because the document is five pages long, not just two. That's OK. We'll come back and deal with that later. Now let's learn about a new feature.

Index

An index could be described as an alphabetical listing of topics or terms and where they can be found in a document. The index is usually the very last item in a document. Turn to the index at the back of this book and study it. Note that not only are the topics listed alphabetically as individual terms, but also, in some instances, they are listed in indented format under main sections.

In the next Step-by-Step exercises you'll learn to create an index to accompany your ergonomics document. Your index will look much like the portion of an index illustrated in Figure 27-7.

As with the Table of Contents feature, you must mark the text to be included in the index. Marking text for an index is

FIGURE 27-7
Sample Portion of an Index

ambient lighting, 3
breaks, 2
chair, 4
character size, 1
color, 1, 3
computer terminals, 1, 2
decor, 1, 2
desk, 3, 4

usually a little more complex than marking the text for a table of contents. In an index, reference is made to EACH OCCURRENCE of the word or phrase. In the table of contents, topics are listed as they are introduced.

You may mark the text for an index manually—that is, go through the document and select each word or phrase to be included in the index and mark that word or phrase, much like you did for the table of contents. There is a better way . . . .

The Concordance File

It is usually much more efficient to prepare what is known as a *concordance file*. The concordance file is a separate document containing a list of all the terms to be included in the index. With the list prepared, WordPerfect will search the text for each occurrence of each word and will insert the page numbers for each entry into the index.

When using a concordance file, the first step is to choose the words to be included in the index and key them as a list. The words or phrases can be keyed in any order and sorted alphabetically before generating the index. WordPerfect Sort will sort your list quickly.

The words and terms illustrated in Figure 27-8 might be included in an index for the document about office ergonomics. You should still have it open in your window. Let's learn about creating an index with a concordance file.

S TEP-BY-STEP ⟩ 27.5

1. Click the **New Blank Document** button on the Toolbar or press **Ctrl+N**. Key the terms in Figure 27-8 in a single column at the left margin.

2. Go to **Sort** and choose **First word in a line** to alphabetize the list. If the first letter of *computer terminals* is uppercase, change it to lowercase.

3. Save the alphabetized list with your other documents as **concord** and close it.

FIGURE 27-8
Words for the Concordance File

computer terminals	furniture
display screen	character size
illumination	color
flicker	VDT
keyboard	glare
decor	breaks
direct lighting	ambient lighting
desk	task lighting
disk drives	chair
monitor	lighting
mouse	morale

Defining and Generating the Index

As with the table of contents, you must tell WordPerfect where you'd like the index to be generated. While you can position the index anywhere in a document, the usual place is at the end of the document.

As with the table of contents, you must tell WordPerfect how you'd like the index to look. When you define the index, WordPerfect puts a code at the position of the insertion point. The index will be generated at the location of that code. WordPerfect offers you several index styles.

STEP-BY-STEP ⟹ 27.6

1. With **ergo 27-4 xxx** still open, use **Save As** to save the file as **ergo 27-6 xxx**. Press **Ctrl+End** to move the insertion point to the end of the document.

2. Press **Ctrl+Enter** for a hard page break and change from double spacing to single spacing. Center **INDEX** about 2" from the top of the page, followed by a triple space.

3. Open the **Tools** menu and choose **Reference**. Then choose **Index**. Look at the Index Feature Bar (see Figure 27-9).

4. Click the **Define** button and look at the Define Index dialog box. Click the **Position** button and choose **Text, #** (the last choice in the pop-up list). This tells WordPerfect to list the word, a comma, and then the page number of each item.

5. Click to position your insertion point in the *Concordance file* text box at the bottom of the dialog box. Key the filepath and **concord**, or click the arrow beside the text box and select **concord** from your files.

6. Click **OK** to close the dialog box. You should see the message telling you where the index will be generated.

7. If everything looks OK, click the **Generate** button on the Feature Bar. Click **OK** in the Generate dialog box. (All lists, including the table of contents, are regenerated when you give the Generate command.)

8. Check the index. Does it look good? Look at your table of contents. Does it have the right page numbers for your expanded document?

9. Save your document again as **ergo 27-6 xxx** and print it. Close the document.

FIGURE 27-9
Index Feature Bar

This was a simple index with all items aligned at the left margin. The Heading and Subheading tools on the Feature Bar could be used to create an indented format for some of the items so they would look like the index in this text. We won't practice that feature here, but it is a fairly simple process to work with the concordance file to identify which items are to appear at the left margin and which will be indented as subheadings. You may work with that feature at your leisure.

Lists

Using WordPerfect, you can create a variety of other kinds of lists for your documents. For example, you can create a list of tables (you'd mark the Table boxes in the document) or a list of figures (you'd mark the Figure boxes). Lists of figures are sometimes included at the beginning of research papers or other literary works. The Reference choice from the Tools menu is the source for all of those features. Figure 27-10 shows the menu item from which you chose Index and Table of Contents. As you can see, Lists and Cross-Reference are other choices in this menu. You can work with these features as you need them.

The only other feature about which you will learn is Table of Authorities. You'll learn to create a table of authorities in Lesson 28.

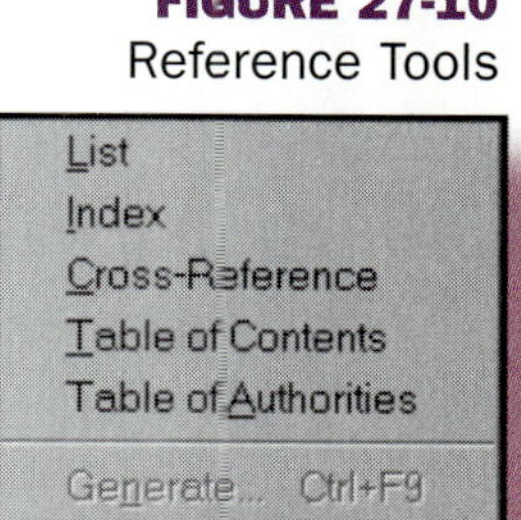

FIGURE 27-10
Reference Tools

Summary

This lesson provided a brief introduction to the listing features included in WordPerfect. These are very powerful tools. Once your text is marked for a table of contents, for example, you can edit the document to your heart's content. Whenever you generate the document, WordPerfect will find the marked items and report the page number where that item is located. The same is true of the index. While you didn't edit the document in this lesson, you did learn about these features. You learned that:

- The Table of Contents Feature Bar makes it easy to mark text for a table of contents.

- You format a table of contents page in the same way you format other document pages—you just have to add a Define code to tell where the table of contents should appear.

- Generating a table of contents is easy. WordPerfect does all the work!

- Delay Codes can be used to tell WordPerfect to wait a bit before beginning certain prescribed features. In this case, you delayed the numbering of the pages and set a new page number.

- Marking a document for an index can be tiresome and time-consuming. An easier way is to use a concordance file.

- The concordance file is a list of words to be included in the index.

- An index can be generated at the same time the table of contents is generated.

- WordPerfect can generate a variety of lists for your documents.

INTERNET Hypertext is an information retrieval system in which certain keywords or pictures are linked to information in the same or a different document. Clicking on a hypertext word or picture instructs your Browser to find and load the information selected.

MULTIPLE CHOICE

Circle the best answer to each of the following statements.

1. The procedure for identifying the text to be included in the table of contents is called
   A. identifying.
   B. marking.
   C. coding.
   D. formatting.

2. Open the _______ menu, choose Reference, and then choose Table of Contents.
   A. Edit
   B. Insert
   C. Format
   D. Tools

3. The Table of Contents Feature Bar contains buttons to mark up to _______ levels.
   A. five
   B. four
   C. three
   D. two

4. To tell WordPerfect where the table of contents should go, you must insert a _____
   A. Position code.
   B. Format Page code.
   C. Define code.
   D. Table Def code.

5. In an index, reference of the word or phrase is made _________
   A. only once.
   B. for each occurrence.
   C. at least twice.
   D. no more than three times.

6. The ________ file is a separate document containing a list of all the terms to be included in the index.
   A. tickler
   B. index data
   C. accordance
   D. concordance

7. Items in an index
   A. are at one level only.
   B. may have a heading level under the subheading level.
   C. may have a subheading level under the heading level.
   D. may have as many as four levels.

WRITTEN QUESTIONS

Write your answers to the following questions.

8. What are the choices available from the Reference Tools menu?

9. Where is an index normally found in a document?

10. What is the WordPerfect feature that enables you to number your pages, but not have the page numbers start immediately?

LESSON 27 PROJECT

Create a document complete with title page, table of contents, page numbering, and index. Use **lighthouses** from the student **datafile** folder. Following is a list of things to do with the document. Very few specific steps are given. If you can't remember how to do something, look back in the lesson for the specific steps. See how much you can do on your own.

FIGURE 27-11
Words for **lighthouse concord** File

1. After opening **lighthouses**, save the file as **light proj27 xxx**.

2. Add two pages at the beginning, one for a title page and one for the table of contents. Create the title page, using any kind of border. (The border should be only on the title page.) Make the title page pretty.

3. Since the title page and the table of contents will take up two pages, insert a Delay Codes code that tells WordPerfect to begin page numbering two pages later. Set the value of the page number at 1.

4. Change the document to double spacing. Delete all of the extra line spaces above and below the side headings.

5. Retrieve your **report style** styles, and format the title and side headings.

6. Display the Table of Contents Feature Bar. Mark all four side headings as Level 1 entries for the table of contents.

7. Set up your table of contents page and enter the Define code. You will have only one level of entries for this table of contents.

8. Add a page at the end of the document and play your **pf** macro so the document name appears only on the last page of the document.

9. Format the page for an index. Go to a new document page and create a concordance file using the words and phrases in Figure 27-11. Save the concordance file as **lighthouse concord**.

```
Phoenician
structure
Egyptian
beacon
Roman
stone
wood
masonry
England
Smeaton
illumination
Swiss
coal
oil
gas
petroleum
kerosene
mirror
Fresnel lens
optical
prisms
incandescent
solar
electricity
sound
radio
radar
```

(continued on next page)

10. Define the index.

11. Look through your document to see if everything is in order. Especially look for the need for Widow/Orphan or Block Protect.

12. Generate both the table of contents and the index at once. (It doesn't matter which Feature Bar is displayed when you choose Generate, since both lists are generated at once.)

13. Look at the finished document. If everything is perfect, print it. If not, go back and make repairs. Then print it and save it when it is perfect. Save it again as **light proj27 xxx**.

CRITICAL THINKING ACTIVITY

You have just finished marking your text for the table of contents, added a new page with a title, and defined your table of contents. You click OK and return to your document. A code appears in your document, but your table of contents does not appear. What is wrong?

TABLE OF AUTHORITIES, HYPERTEXT, AND MASTER DOCUMENT

In Lesson 27 you learned about creating several kinds of lists. In this lesson you'll learn about one more kind of list—the table of authorities. We'll also explore a feature called Master Document. This feature enables you to break up very long documents into parts. Then the parts can easily be assembled for generating a table of contents or index, or both.

Table of Authorities

A table of authorities is part of a legal document that lists all references cited in a legal document and identifies the position of each reference in the document by page number. The references might be cases, statutes, laws, or other sources, and those references are usually divided by groups in the table of authorities.

The finished table of authorities closely resembles a table of contents. In fact, the procedure for preparing a table of authorities and a table of contents is the same—mark the text to be included, define, and then generate the table. Figure 28-1 shows a sample table of authorities listing cases and statutes. The table of authorities is placed at the beginning of a document, between the table of contents and the first page of the text.

CASES

Becton Dickinson & Co. v. C.R. Bard, Inc., 922 F.2d 792, 795-96 (Fed.Cir.1990) 2

Johnston v. IVAC Corp., 885 F.2d 1574, 1577, 12 USPQ2d 1382, 1384
(Fed.Cir.1989) 2, 3

Wilson Sporting Goods Co. v. David Geoffrey & Assoc., 904 F.2d 677, 683,
14 USPQ2d 1942, 1947-48 (Fed.Cir.1990) 3

STATUTES

15 U.S.C. § 1125(a) (1982) 1

Lanham Act § 43(a) 1

Minnesota Deceptive Trade Practices Act ("MDTPA"), Minn. Stat. § 325D.44 1

Defining the Table

We'll begin by defining the table of authorities for a sample document.

STEP-BY-STEP 28.1

1. Beginning in a new document window, open **patent** from the student **datafile** folder and save as **patent 28-1 xxx**.

2. With the insertion point at the top of the document, insert a hard page break and format the new page for a table of authorities as follows:

   a. Use **Delay Codes** to delay one page. In Delay Codes, set page numbering at bottom center, use a simple **1** for the page number, and set the numbering value at **1**.

   b. Center **TABLE OF AUTHORITIES** about 2" from the top of the page.

   c. Press **Enter** three times and key **CASES** in bold caps at the left margin. Press **Enter** twice.

3. Open the **Tools** menu, choose **Reference**, and choose **Table of Authorities**. The Table of Authorities Feature Bar will appear, looking like Figure 28-2.

4. Click the **Define** button. A dialog box that looks like Figure 28-3 will appear.

5. Click the **Create** button to open the Create Table of Authorities dialog box.

6. Key **cases** (lowercase is fine) in the *Name* text box at the top. Keep the dialog box open as you read on.

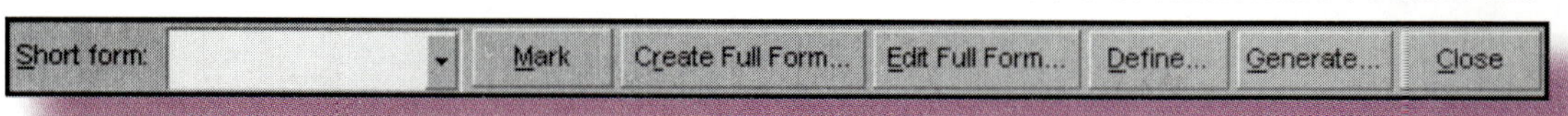

FIGURE 28-2
Table of Authorities Feature Bar

FIGURE 28-3
Define Table of Authorities Dialog Box

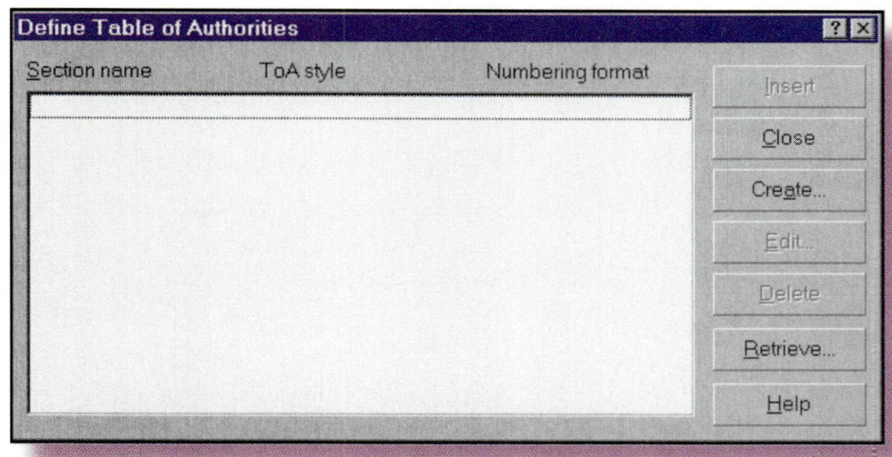

The default format for the table of authorities allows long items to extend all the way to the right margin where your page numbers are to be printed. We'll change the layout and set some indents for the longer items.

STEP-BY-STEP ⟹ 28.2

1. With the Create Table of Authorities dialog box, open (see Figure 28-4), click the **Change** button. In the Table of Authorities Style dialog box, be sure *TableofAuth* is highlighted. Click **Edit**.

2. Welcome to the Styles Editor. Does it look familiar? Press **Ctrl+Shift+F7** to indent the text from both sides.

3. Press **Ctrl+Shift+Tab** to move the first line back to the left margin.

4. Click **OK** to return to the Table of Authorities Style dialog box. Click **Select** to choose **TableofAuth**. Click **OK** to return to the Define

Table of Authorities dialog box, and click **Insert** to put the definition into your document.

5. Press **Enter** twice and key **STATUTES** in bold caps. Press **Enter** twice.

6. Click the **Define** button on the Feature Bar again and click **Create**. Key **statutes** and click **OK**. Then click **Insert** to insert the definition into your document. Beneath the title, your table of authorities page should look like Figure 28-5.

7. Save your document as **patent 28-2 xxx** and keep it open.

Full and Short Form

A case or statute might be referred to several times in a document. You don't want a complete entry in the table of authorities for each time a case or statute is mentioned.

You can mark a reference as a *full form* entry or a *short form* entry. The first time a reference is marked, the entire reference is marked. At the time you mark the entire reference, the case or statute is given a "nickname," which is referred to as the short form entry. This short form is used to mark subsequent references to the same case or statute. Short form nicknames are suggested in the Step-by-Step exercises in this lesson.

When you generate the table of authorities, WordPerfect will create an entry for each full form reference and the page on which it appears. Then it will list the page numbers of the subsequent references that are marked as short form references.

Marking the References

In the next Step-by-Step exercise you will select the reference, tell WordPerfect whether it is a case or a statute, and give it a nickname. Sometime during the marking process, reveal your codes and look at the [ToA] code. Position your insertion point to the left of the code and see how it identifies the section and the short form name.

Create Table of Authorities Dialog Box

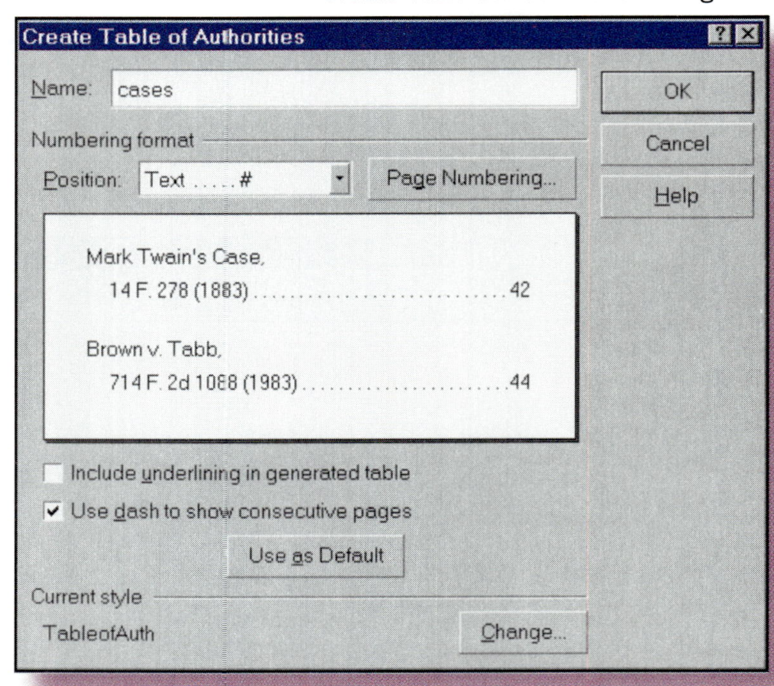

Table of Authorities Definitions

CASES

<< Tables of Authorities will generate here >>

STATUTES

<< Tables of Authorities will generate here >>

1. Use **Save As** to save **patent 28-2 xxx** as **patent 28-3 xxx**.

2. Scroll down in the document to *Lanham Act § 43(a)*. Select that text and click the **Create Full Form** button. The Create Full Form dialog box, illustrated in Figure 28-6, will appear.

3. Click the arrow beside the *Section name* text box and choose **statutes**.

4. Position your insertion point just to the right of the *m* in *Lanham* and press **Ctrl+Delete** to delete everything to the right of *Lanham*. (This will be the short form.)

5. Click **OK**. This takes you to an editing window where you can review the section name, the long form, and the short form. If it looks OK, click **Close** to complete the marking of the reference.

6. Follow the procedure in Steps 2-5 for *15 U.S.C. § 1125(a) (1982)*. This time, make the short form simply **15**.

7. Mark *Minnesota Deceptive Trade Practices Act ("MDTPA"), Minn. Stat. § 325D.44*. Make the short form **Minnesota**.

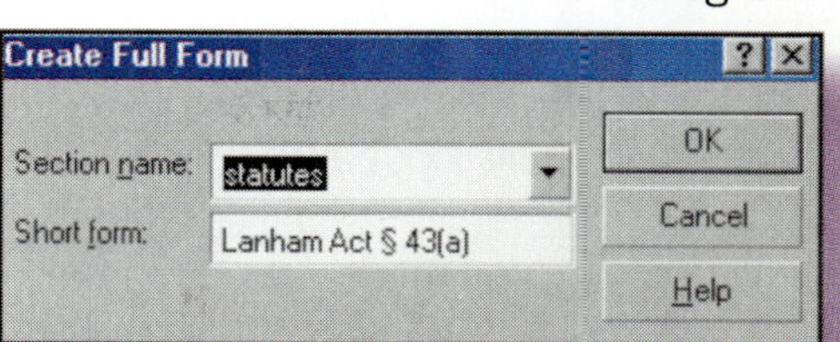

FIGURE 28-6
Create Full Form Dialog Box

8. Save your document again as **patent 28-3 xxx**. Keep it open.

Now that the statutes are marked, let's mark the cases in this sample document. One of them is referred to a second time, so you'll have an opportunity to mark a short form reference.

STEP-BY-STEP 28.4

1. With **patent 28-3 xxx** open, use **Save As** to save it as **patent 28-4 xxx**.

2. Go to the next page and select the Johnston reference, beginning with the *J* of *Johnston* and ending with the close parenthesis after *(Fed.Cir.1989)*. Click the **Create Full Form** button, change to **cases**, and make the short form **Johnston**. Finish marking that entry.

3. Mark the Becton Dickinson case, again ending with the parenthesis following the year. Make the short form **Becton**.

4. On the third page, position the insertion point to the left of the *J* of the Johnston reference. Click the arrow for the **Short form** drop-down menu on the left of the Table of Authorities Feature Bar (see Figure 28-2), and choose **Johnston**.

5. Click the **Mark** button on the Feature Bar to mark this reference as a short form reference tied to the long form Johnston reference.

6. Finally, mark the Wilson Sporting Goods reference, making the short form **Wilson**.

7. Save your file again as **patent 28-4 xxx**. Keep it open.

Generating the Table of Authorities

Now that the references are all marked, you can generate the table of authorities in the same way you generated the table of contents in Lesson 27.

4 6 3

1. With **patent 28-4 xxx** open, save it as **patent 28-5 xxx**. Then click the **Generate** button on the Table of Authorities Feature Bar.

2. Look at the table of authorities that was generated. Does it look like Figure 28-1? It should. If not, go back and figure out what you did wrong.

3. Finally, save the file again and print the table of authorities. Keep it open.

Hypertext

As you learned earlier, WordPerfect has the ability to add hypertext links to a document like a table of contents or table of authorities. Hypertext is a feature that links parts of a document together so you can jump quickly from one location to another.

In a table of contents the page numbers can be hypertext numbers, so if you point to one with the mouse pointer and click, your insertion point will be taken directly to the reference in the text.

Building hypertext links is part of the generate process. Since you already know you can regenerate, let's regenerate this practice table and build hypertext links.

1. Position your insertion point on the table of authorities page so you can see your table of authorities as you work.

2. Click the **Generate** button again. In the Generate Options dialog box, click to select **Build hyperlinks**. Then click **OK**.

3. When WordPerfect is finished, look at the page numbers in your table of authorities. They should be blue and underlined (although it's hard to see the underlines).

4. Use the hand pointer to point to the *3* for the Wilson Sporting Goods reference and click once. Your insertion point should be moved to the beginning of the Wilson reference.

5. Return to the table of authorities page and click the number of a different reference.

6. Click the **Generate** button again. Deselect the hypertext option and complete the generation.

7. Close your document without saving it again.

After you have chosen to build hypertext links, that option will remain chosen for all generate functions (including a table of contents or an index) until you deselect it. The hypertext link in the table of authorities is a one-way link. You can use the link to jump to the reference, but there is no reverse link that jumps you back to the table of authorities. Using WordPerfect, you CAN build hypertext links that work in both directions. If you are interested in learning more about hypertext, check the WordPerfect Help feature.

Master Document

The Master Document feature enables you to break very large documents into smaller parts, called *subdocuments*, for easier handling. Then, when you are ready to apply consecutive page numbering, a table of contents, or an index, you will create a *master document* that links to the subdocuments.

When you wish to print or display the entire master document, the subdocuments must first be *expanded*. You have the choice of expanding all or only some of the subdocuments. When the subdocuments are expanded, you can look at the text in the window. If you wish, you can edit the text of the subdocuments.

To close or save the master document, you must first *condense* the subdocuments. (During the condense step, you should save any subdocuments that were edited.) Once the subdocuments are condensed, they will be represented by a subdocument icon that shows the subdocument names.

Prepare the Subdocuments

Normally, you will create documents that will be combined with the Master Document feature and save them individually. In this case, however, we will save some work by taking the **ergonomics** document that is already marked for a table of contents and breaking it into segments to be used as the subdocuments.

STEP-BY-STEP ⟹ 28.7

1. Beginning in a new document window, open **ergo 27-1 xxx**. Select the title and the first section of text (up to *Computer Terminals*).

2. With the text selected, open the **File** menu and choose **Save As**. The Save dialog box will appear (see Figure 28-7), asking if you'd like to save the entire file or the selected text. Choose **Selected text** and name the file **nom1** (for ergoNOMics).

3. When you are returned to your document window, the text will still be selected. Delete it.

4. Select the next section of the document (*Computer Terminals* up to *Lighting and Decor*). Save this selected text as **nom2** and delete it from the original document.

FIGURE 28-7
Save Dialog Box

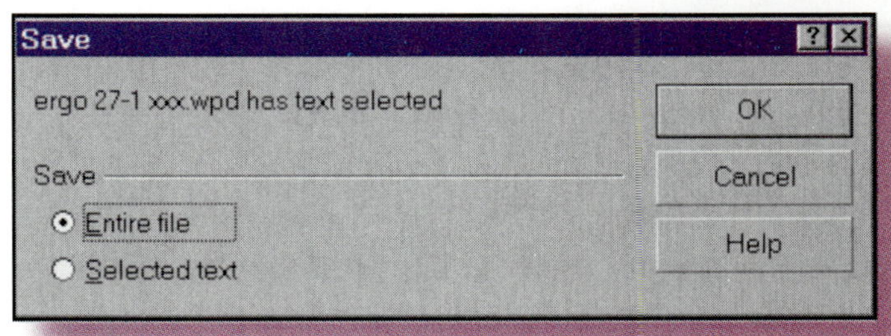

5. Continue saving and naming the chunks of text as follows. Delete each chunk of text after it has been saved.

   nom3 *Lighting and Decor* (up to *Furniture*)
   nom4 *Furniture* (up to *Summary*)
   nom5 *Summary*

6. Close the empty document without saving it.

Prepare the Master Document

Now let's use the five **nom** documents for the preparation of a master document. If the subdocuments were chapters in a book or thesis, for example, each would begin on a new page. So we'll put page breaks between the sections of our practice document.

1. Beginning in a new document window, open the **File** menu and choose **Document**. Then choose **Subdocument**. The Include Sub-document dialog box will appear, looking suspiciously like your Open File dialog box.

2. Find **nom1** and double click to select it. Back in your document window, look for some indication that you just added a subdocument.
   a. If you are in Page view, a small icon will appear at the far left side of the left margin. You may need to use your horizontal scroll bar to see the icon.
   b. If you are in Draft view, a gray bar will appear, listing the name of the subdocument.

3. Go to **Draft** view and stay there for now. Press **Ctrl+Enter** to add a hard page break.

4. Open the **File** menu, choose **Document**, and then choose **Subdocument**. Get the **nom2** subdocument and add another hard page break.

5. Repeat the process until you have brought all five **nom** documents into your master document as subdocuments. If you are saving your work on a disk in Drive A, your window will look like Figure 28-8.

6. Save your master document as **master 28-8 xxx**. Keep it open.

7. Return to the first page. Change to **Page** view. Click the icon at the left and look at it. Click away from the "bubble" to close it.

8. Open the **File** menu, choose **Document**, and then choose **Expand Master**. The Expand Master Document dialog box (see Figure 28-9) will appear, asking which documents to expand. Since you want them all, click **OK**.

9. Keep the expanded master document open in the window as you read on.

FIGURE 28-8
Master Document in Draft View

Subdoc: A:\nom1.wpd
Subdoc: A:\nom2.wpd
Subdoc: A:\nom3.wpd
Subdoc: A:\nom4.wpd
Subdoc: A:\nom5.wpd

Now all five parts of your document are showing in your window. The gray bars show the beginning and end of each subdocument. In Page view, subdocument icons indicate the beginning and ending of each subdocument. Let's check the icons. Then we'll apply your **report style** styles to the document to format it.

FIGURE 28-9
Expand Master Document Dialog Box

STEP-BY-STEP 28.9

1. Return to the top of the document and click one of the icons to see the bubble that identifies the subdocument. With your insertion point at the top of your document, change to double spacing.

2. Open the **Format** menu, choose **Styles**, and retrieve your **report style** styles from your folder.

3. Apply the *title* style to the title of your document. Apply the *side heading* style to each of the side headings. (These will appear in the table of contents.)

4. Add a page at the beginning of the document for a table of contents. With your insertion point on the top of the new page, play your **pf** macro to identify all pages of the document.

5. Format the new page for a table of contents, and define the table of contents using one level of entries and any style you wish.

6. Insert a **Delay Codes** code at the beginning of the first page that delays numbering one (1) page.
   a. Within Delay Codes, set page numbering to appear at the bottoms of the pages.
   b. Set the value for the first page at **1**.

7. Check your footer and page numbers. Generate the table of contents.

8. Print the table of contents page only. Do not save this master document yet. Keep the document open in the window as you read on.

Condense the Master Document

You should not save a master document when it is expanded. If you do, the subdocuments will be saved with the master document and take double the space on your disk. Instead, it's better to condense the master document, leaving only the subdocument icons.

Let's condense the master document, saving all subdocuments (because they have been formatted), and then save the master document in a separate file.

INTERNET

HyperText Markup Language, or HTML, is a set of computer commands. HTML is used to create World Wide Web documents that can be viewed by a browser program.

1. Open the **File** menu and choose **Document**. Choose **Condense Master**. The Condense/Save Subdocuments dialog box will appear (see Figure 28-10).

2. Note than a ✓ appears before each subdocument for saving and for condensing. Click **OK**.

3. Look at what remains of your master document. Check it in **Draft** view.

4. Save the master document with your other files as **master 28-10 xxx**. Close the file.

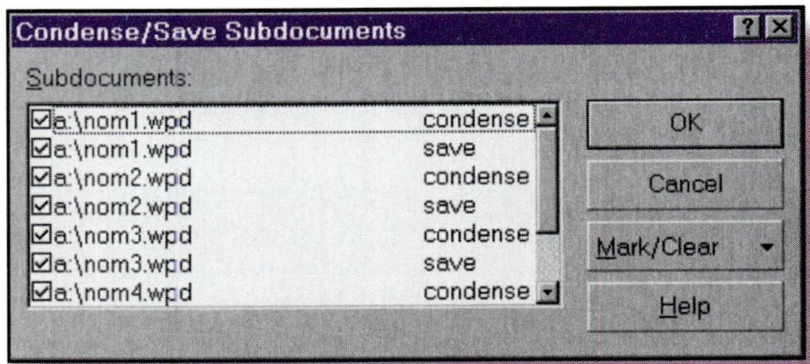

FIGURE 28-10
Condense/Save Subdocuments Dialog Box

A table of contents can be generated without first expanding the master document. It takes longer, because WordPerfect has to go to the disk to find the marked text in the subdocuments.

The Master Document feature is quite flexible. You can edit the subdocuments as individual files and resave them. Then when you expand the master document, the edited versions of the subdocuments will be included. If you prefer, you can open the master document and expand only the file to be edited and make the necessary changes. When you condense the master document, the edited subdocument will be saved in its edited form on your disk.

Remember that the master document is a shell with links to the subdocuments on disk. If the subdocument references are to a disk in Drive A and you have a different disk in Drive A, the master document can't be expanded. In the same way, if the subdocument references are in a directory on the hard drive of a particular computer and you carry the disk containing your master document to a different computer, your master document won't be able to find the subdocuments.

Summary

As mentioned at the beginning of the lesson, the features learned in this lesson are primarily features that would be used for lengthy documents. You learned that:

- A table of authorities lists the cases, statutes, and laws referenced in a legal brief.

- Preparing a table of authorities is much like preparing a table of contents.

- When preparing a table of authorities, the first time a case or statute is referenced, it is given a full form reference. When it is referenced again, it is marked as a short form reference.

- When you generate a table of authorities or a table of contents, you can tell WordPerfect to create hypertext links.

- A hypertext link enables you to jump from the reference directly to the portion of text where the reference is marked.

■ A master document is used to temporarily join parts of a long document for the creation of an index or a table of contents or to number the pages.

■ A master document may be expanded so the whole document shows in the window.

■ A master document should be condensed before it is saved.

In addition to all of the good things you learned about in this lesson, you also reviewed a number of the features learned in Lesson 27. You should be good at generating lists and using Delay Codes by now.

LESSON 28 REVIEW QUESTIONS

FILL IN THE BLANKS

Complete each of the following statements by writing your answer in the blank provided.

1. A _________________________________ is part of a legal document that lists all references cited and identifies the position of each reference.

2. The first time a reference is marked, the entire reference is marked as a _______________.

3. The "nickname" you give a reference is referred to as the ___________________.

4. _____________________ is a feature that links parts of a document together so you can jump quickly from one location to another.

5. In a table of contents the _______________________ can be hypertext numbers.

6. When you select Build hyperlinks while in a table of authorities, the page numbers become _______________________.

7. The _______________________ feature enables you to break very large documents into smaller parts.

TRUE/FALSE

Circle the T if the statement is true. Circle the F if it is false.

T F **8.** A document must be expanded before a table of contents can be generated.

T F **9.** A master document is a shell with links to the subdocuments on disk.

T F **10.** A master document should be condensed before it is saved.

SCANS

Open **brake3** from the student **datafile** folder. Save the file as **brake proj28 xxx**. This is a portion of a larger document you'll work with in the Unit 7 Applications. For practice, create a table of authorities for this document as follows:

1. Add a page at the beginning of the document and format it for a table of authorities.

2. Key **STATUTES** at the left margin and press Enter twice. Go to the Table of Authorities Feature Bar and create a section named **statutes**.

3. Change the TableofAuth formatting by using Ctrl+Shift+F7 and Ctrl+Shift+Tab to indent the entries. Insert the section.

4. Key **CASES** at the left margin and press Enter twice. Create a section named **cases**. Insert the section.

5. Locate the following cases and create them as full form references in the *cases* section. You may decide on the short form for each.

    Adam B. Wanty Co. v. Western Sys., Inc., 742 F.2d 1388, 1892, 222 USPQ 943, 948
      (Fed.Cir.1984)
    Grandy v. Jack Buck Co. 383 U.S. 1, 17-18, 86 S.Ct. 684, 693-94, 15 L.Ed.2d 545,
      152 USPQ 459, 467 (1966)
    Royal, 837 F.2d at 1050, 5 USPQ2d at 1438

6. Locate the second *Grandy* reference and mark it as a short form.

7. Locate the following statutes and create them as full form references:

    54 U.S.C. § 103
    U.S. Patent 3,480,115
    Fed.R.Civ.P. 52(a) (1995)

8. Play your **pf** macro to identify all pages.

9. Generate the table of authorities.

10. Check your work over carefully. If everything is in order, save the file again as **brake proj28 xxx**. Print the table of authorities only.

11. Delete the page at the beginning containing the table of authorities. (Check your codes to be certain all codes before the Bold code for the side heading are deleted.) Save the marked file as **brake3 xxx**.

CRITICAL THINKING ACTIVITY

SCANS

You are working with a legal document and have prepared a table of authorities with hypertext links. As you proofread the document, you think there is a mistake in one of the references so you use the link to jump to the reference. You try to "jump back" but nothing happens. What's wrong?

470

Command Summary

FEATURE	MENU CHOICE	KEYBOARD	LESSON
Address Book	Tools	—	18, 25
Condense Master	File, Document	—	28
Create Template	File, New from Project	—	26
Define Index	Tools, Reference, Index	—	27
Define T. of Auth.	Tools, Reference, T. of Auth.	—	28
Define T. of Cont.	Tools, Reference, T. of Cont.	—	27
Delay Codes	Format, Page	—	27
Edit Template	File, New from Project	Ctrl+T	26
Expand Master	File, Document	—	28
Generate	Tools	Ctrl+F9	27, 28
Hypertext	Tools, Reference	—	28
Internet Publisher	File, Internet Publisher	—	26
Lists	Tools, Reference, List	—	27
Master Document	File, Document	—	28
PerfectExpert	Help (Toolbar)	—	26
Styles, Create	Format, Styles	Alt+F8	26
Styles, Edit	Format, Styles	Alt+F8	26
Table of Authorities	Tools, Reference, T. of Auth.	—	28
Table of Contents	Tools, Reference, T. of Cont.	—	27
Templates	File, New from Project	Ctrl+T	26

UNIT 7 REVIEW QUESTIONS

TRUE/FALSE

On a separate page, key True if the statement below is true or False if it is not. Center *Unit 7 Review Questions* at the top and triple-space.

T F 1. When you close an Address Book, you are not saving it.

T F 2. When working with any of the template experts, you are given some choices regarding format.

(continued on next page)

T F   **3.** It is a bigger job to mark entries for a table of contents than it is for an index.

T F   **4.** Hypertext links are typically shown on the window in a different color.

WRITTEN QUESTIONS

Key your answers to the following questions. Number your answers and double-space between them. Use complete sentences and good grammar.

5. If you want to merge a selected group of entries from an Address Book with a form document, how do you tell WordPerfect which names are to be used?

6. How does the Address Book help you when preparing a template document?

7. What four Internet tasks have been integrated into the WordPerfect program?

8. What is the difference between a style and a template?

9. What is the purpose of the Master Document feature?

10. Open your Address Book and choose the Help menu. Choose Address Book Help. Click Related Concepts at the bottom and choose About Dialing from the Address Book. What utility is opened when you dial from the Address Book? How many numbers may you list for each associate?

Close the Address Book and open the Help menu. Double click Internet and choose About Creating Internet Documents. What would be the advantage of creating a Web document in WordPerfect? What does WordPerfect do with your document when you want to put it on the Web?

UNIT 7 APPLICATIONS

⏱ **Estimated Time: 2 hours**

APPLICATION 1

In this application you will be preparing a master document that will contain five subdocuments, a title page, a table of contents, a table of authorities, and an index. The text is already marked for the table of authorities. You must prepare the files to be included, mark the text for the table of contents, and prepare the concordance file. This application has many parts. Read through all of the information about it before beginning. Then attack the application in a methodical manner.

Begin by going to the student **datafile** folder. Open **brake1**, **brake2**, **brake3**, **brake4**, and **brake5**. Save each of the files in your working folder with your initials (e.g., **brake1 xxx**).

FIGURE APP-1
Title Page for Application 1

```
        B.G. Woolworth
     Plaintiff-Appellants

             v

Breaker Braking Systems Corporation
             and
   Anderson-Smith, Incorporated
   Defendants/Cross-Appellants
```

Arrange the parts of the master document in the following order:

- *Title Page*. Use a Page Line border to dress it up. Figure APP-1 provides the information for the title page.

- *Table of Contents*. Use the five bolded side headings in the subdocuments as the items to be marked for the table of contents.

- *Table of Authorities*. (The text is already marked. Make a section for **cases** and another for **statutes**.)

- *Subdocuments*. **brake1**, **brake2**, **brake3**, **brake4**, and **brake5**. Do NOT put hard page breaks between the subdocuments. They should be joined into one continuous document.

- *Index*. Use the words and terms in Figure APP-2. Name your concordance file **brake concord**.

- *Page Numbering*. Use Delay Codes to begin the first page number at the bottom center of the first page of text, and set the value there at 1. (Think! How many pages must you delay?)

FIGURE APP-2
Terms for **brake concord** File

```
obviousness
patent de novo
rotors
inventor
Patent and Trademark Office
United States District Court
Court of Appeals
inequitable conduct
aircraft brakes
expert witness
patentee
end plates
inventor
stators
carbon disks
Dunsirn
carbon utilization
'017 patent
'895 patent
brake assembly
thick-thin assembly
```

Before expanding the master document, save it as **master u7ap1 xxx** and play your **pf** macro to identify all pages.

After defining the table of contents, the table of authorities, and the index, generate the document. Then condense the master document, saving all files. Save the master document, again as **master u7ap1 xxx**.

Print the master document. (It will consist of only the title page, the table of contents, the table of authorities, a blank page that holds the subdocument codes, and the index.) Close all documents.

APPLICATION 2A

You and some of your friends have decided to form a football fan club. You've decided that the best way to keep track of the members of the club is to use the Address Book feature to create a book containing their names. Most of the names have been saved for you, but you need to enter a few of them. Create a book named **Football Club** and enter the names, addresses, and home phone numbers listed in Figure APP-3.

FIGURE APP-3
Football Club Members

```
Roberta Butler              Bernardo Clavelle
8730 Rodden Road            P.O. Box 982
Sycamore, IL 60178          St. Charles, IL 60175
708-555-1511                708-555-4240

Erica Rivera                Dinny Diaz
23 Shoal Creek Ave.         301 Del Rey Lane
Elmhurst, IL 60126          Bloomington, IL 61701
708-555-5377                708-555-1252

(Add your own name)

(Add a friend's name)
```

(continued on next page)

4 7 3

When you finish with all six names and addresses and have checked your work, open the File menu in the Address Book and import **football.txt** from the student **datafile** folder. Use Export to save the book in your folder as **football xxx.txt**. Close the Address Book.

APPLICATION 2B

The membership of the club has decided that everyone should have a copy of the membership roster. You've been asked to prepare a list of all members using the WordPerfect Tables feature. Create a form document associated with the Address Book. Identify **Football Club** as the associated Address Book.

Use Page Setup to turn your page to landscape. Then create a three-column table listing the complete member name in the first column, the complete address on one line in the second column (separate the parts of the address with commas), and the phone number in the third column.

You learned in Lesson 18 that you need three special merge codes to merge into a table format: LABEL(label), NEXTRECORD, and GO(label). Can you get them in the right places without checking Lesson 18? When your table form is attractive, save it as **football u7ap2 xxx.frm**. Then merge it with the *Football Club* Address Book.

Format your two-page roster so it is attractive, including a title, the current date, and column headings. Select all of the information in the table except the heading rows at the top, and sort the club members by last name. Save the merged file as **football u7ap2b xxx**. Play your **pf** macro and save the file again. Then print it and close it.

APPLICATION 2C

Several of the club members have indicated an interest in helping you get mailings out to the membership regarding special meetings or parties. The president has planned a meeting/party to be held during the Monday night football game on the first Monday in November. You have a couple of weeks to get some help with the mailing.

- Go to your Address Book and create and save a list named **helpers**. Include Gary Dotson, Erica Rivera, and Noel Koonce.

- Create a form letter asking these three people to meet at your house next Saturday (include the date) at 7:30 p.m. to help assemble a mailing. Ask them to please come with ideas for producing an attractive brochure for the meeting/party. You might entice them with the offer of refreshments. Save the form letter as **form u7ap2c xxx.frm**.

- Merge the form letter with the **helpers** list in your *Football Club* Address Book. When you merge, click the Select Records button in the Perform Merge dialog box. In the Address Book, double click the **helpers** entry and click OK. The form document should merge with the three names in the **helpers** list.

- Save the three letters as **football u7ap2c xxx**. Identify the three letters with the **pf** macro. Then print the three letters and close all files.

APPLICATION 3

It's time to delete files and move files to make room in your folder for the final unit. Begin by moving **master u7ap1 xxx** and **football u7ap2 xxx.frm** to your **Applications** folder.

Create a **Units 7 and 8** folder and move **flower customers.txt**, **football.txt**, **Foreign.txt**, **Gaillardia.txt**, and **Mileage Expense.wpt** to the **Units 7 and 8** folder.

Finally, delete the files listed in Figure APP-4. If any files remain when you are done, check to see if they are worth keeping. If so, transfer them to another location. Otherwise, delete them. Remember that your macro files and **report style** file should remain in your main folder.

backup 26-11	ergo 27-1	gaillardia 25-7a	nom5
backup 26-12	ergo 27-2	gaillardia 25-8 (frm)	patent 28-1
brake concord	ergo 27-3	gaillardia 25-9	patent 28-2
brake proj28	ergo 27-4	light proj27	patent 28-3
brake1	ergo 27-6	lighthouse concord	patent 28-4
brake2	expense 26-6	mabel proj26a	patent 28-5
brake3	expense 26-7	master 28-10	pc 26-13
brake4	football u7ap2b	master 28-8	perry proj26a
brake5	football u7ap2c	nom1	proj25 (frm)
calendar 26-1	foreign proj25	nom2	proj26b
concord	form u7ap2c (frm)	nom3	stella 26-4
envelope 25-7b		nom4	

ON-THE-JOB SIMULATION

JOB 19

Mr. Becker and the Singing Wheels staff are preparing the tour catalog for next year. The tour to the Mall of America was so successful that they are making it one of their regularly offered tours.

The write-up in the catalog for next year will follow a standard format for all tours. Luckily, the format will use some of the same styles you prepared for your **report style** styles in Lesson 26. You will need to create one more style for the subtitles.

Key the tour information illustrated in Figure J13.

After you've keyed the document, proofread it. Then retrieve your **report style** styles file and apply the *title* style to the heading. Apply the *side heading* style to the "Day" side headings.

Create a new style for the subtitles. Call it **subtitle** and key the description **Subtitles at Top of Document**. Format the new style as follows:

- Paragraph (paired) Type

- Center

- Small Caps, Bold, and 14 pt.

Apply the new style to the two subtitles individually. Then open your Style List and use Save As to save the style again as **report style**.

(continued on next page)

MALL OF AMERICA SHOPPING

September 1-4, (year) (Tour #2113)
4 Days

Day 1, Tuesday

    We spend the day traveling to Minneapolis. Lunch is in Plover at
Norma's Nook. Accommodations in the Minneapolis area are at the Happy
Haven Hotel in Bloomington. Get in some late afternoon and evening
shopping after checking into the motel and resting.

Day 2, Wednesday

    You have a full day of shopping today at the mall. Lunch is on
your own. In the evening, we have reserved seats for dinner and the
theater at the Bloomington Playhouse. The play is the off-Broadway
musical Power Shopping Patsy, where guests get a glimpse of what
really goes on behind the scenes in our country's largest shopping
malls.

Day 3, Thursday

    Today is another full day of shopping at the mall. In the
evening, you may continue to shop or take an optional tour of the
Minneapolis night spots (at a cost of $35 per person). Dinner at the
Riverfront is included in the cost of the optional tour.

Day 4, Friday

    Today we're covering the miles for the trip home.

Finally, return to your document and position the insertion point at the beginning of the *Day 1* side heading. Open the Columns dialog box and tell WordPerfect you would like the document formatted with 2 Balanced newspaper columns. Make it lovely! Save the document in the **Singing Wheels** folder as **mall job19 xxx**. Play your **pf** macro to identify it. Then print it and close it, saving it again.

JOB 20

Now that you've learned more about Address Book, you're excited about the possibilities at Singing Wheels. You think of all the work you did earlier keying a data file for name badges and some of the letters you sent to customers. Now it looks like all of the Singing Wheels "tourists" could be put in an Address Book and separated out for special kinds of mailings. In fact, you have a couple of those mailings to do today. But you have time to enter quite a few names and addresses.

For this job, create an Address Book for Singing Wheels called **Singing Wheels** and enter the names, addresses, and phone numbers in Figure J14. When you finish, check your work. Export the Address Book to your **Singing Wheels** folder. Name it **tourists xxx.txt** .

With the *Singing Wheels* book open, import **new tourists.txt** from the student **datafile** folder. Export the complete book to your **Singing Wheels** folder again as **tourist xxx.txt**.

FIGURE J14
Names for Singing Whee's Address Book

Neverat Holme 45 Creekside Drive Manawa, WI 54949 neverath@example.com 920-555-7853	Lottie Baggs 45 Main Street Shawano, WI 54166 lottieb@example.com 920-555-7866	Kim Kittleson 234 Kiel Street Kimberly, WI 54136 920-555-7896
Hazel Holme 45 Creekside Drive Manawa, WI 54949 920-555-7853	Fred Feldman 8722 Farmhill Road Little Chute, WI 54140 fredf@example.com 920-555-7869	Darcy Dobberstein 5693 Township Drive Darboy, WI 54911 920-555-7879

JOB 21

A number of Singing Wheels customers have called or written inquiring about next year's tour catalog. The new catalog won't be available until the first week in January.

Using the *Singing Wheels* Address Book as the associated data file, create a form letter thanking the customers for their interest and telling them when the new catalog of tours will be available. Tell them that you will be adding their names to the list of customers who are eager to get copies of the catalog. Their copy will be shipped as soon as the catalogs arrive. Save the form document as **catalog xxx.frm** and play your **pf** macro to identify the letter.

The customers who inquired about catalogs are Kim Kittleson, Joanie Tokheim, Pam Wall, and Jeff Hauser. Your company has agreed that it is OK to address the customers by their first names in the greeting.

Start the merge and choose the *Singing Wheels* Address Book. Then click Select Records and select the four people to receive the letter. Complete the merge.

After merging the letters, print them and close all files, saving the letters as **catalog job21 xxx**.

ADVANCED GRAPHICS TOOLS

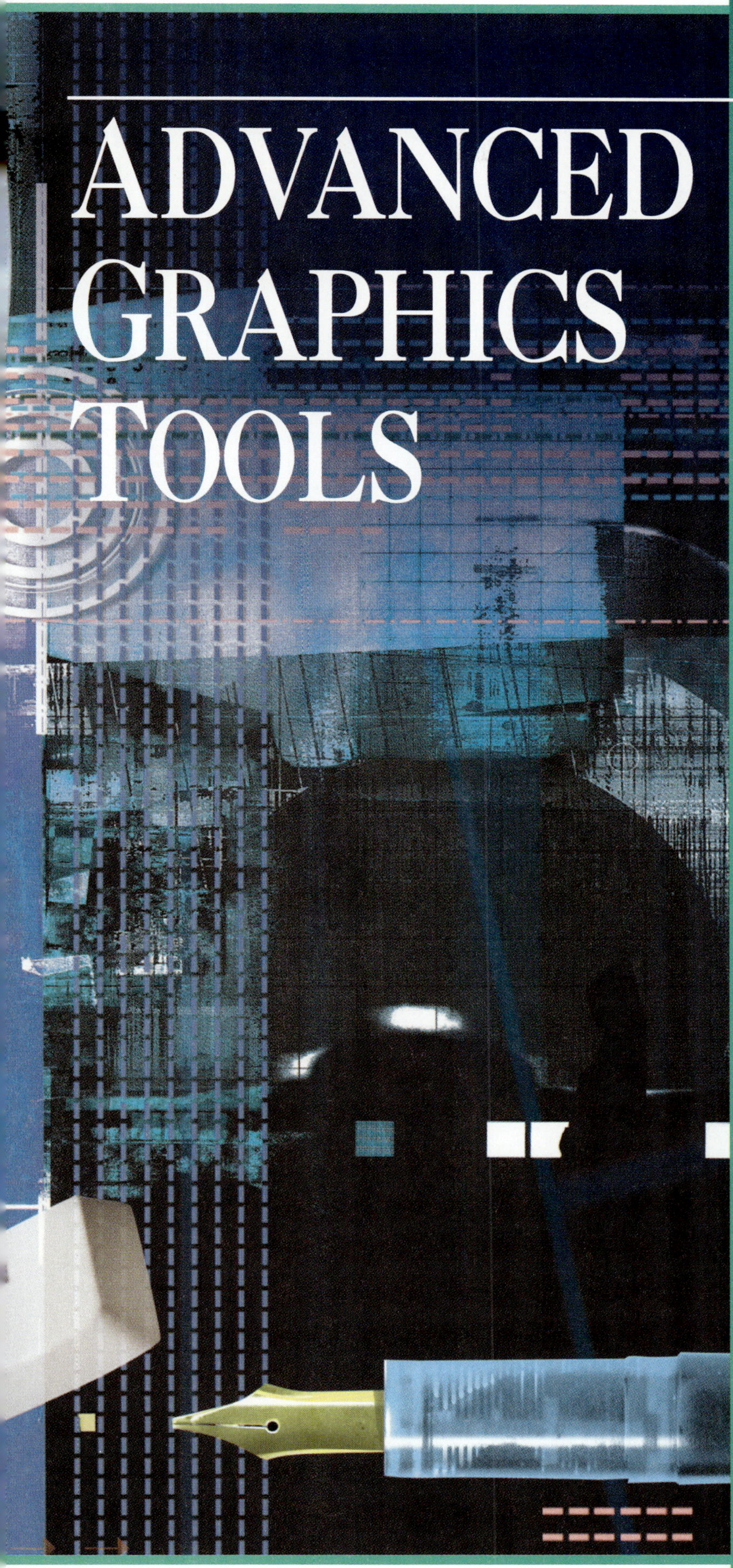

lesson 29 — 2 hrs.
Drawing and Charting

lesson 30 — 2 hrs.
Keyboard Mapping; Designing a Web Page

lesson 31 — 2.5 hrs.
Designing Marketing Tools

lesson 32 — 2.5 hrs.
Designing a Newsletter

Estimated Time for Unit 8: 11 hours

DRAWING AND CHARTING

Wordperfect comes complete with a Draw feature and a Chart feature. Both of these tools help you create graphics that add interest and information to your document. In this lesson you'll edit some WordPerfect images, create some drawings of your own, and learn to use the Chart feature.

Editing Images

The Draw feature can be used to edit the images that come with the WordPerfect program. We'll begin with a crane image.

As you work with the Draw program, you will be using a variety of buttons on the Graphics Toolbar and the Draw Property Bar. Occasionally these buttons will be described. More often, you'll be expected to use the Quick Tip to choose the appropriate button. Pay attention as you do this so you don't waste a lot of time looking for new buttons.

1. Beginning in a new document window, open the **Insert** menu, and choose **Graphics** and **From File**. Go to the student **datafile** folder and choose the **Crane.wpg** image.

2. Set the size of the image so it is 4 inches wide. Maintain height proportions. Drag the image so it is lined up with the margin guidelines in the upper left corner of the page.

3. Point to the image and double click to enter the Draw program. When it is loaded, the upper left portion of your window will look like Figure 29-1. (It may take a while for the program to load. Be patient!)

4. Look at the new tools on the Toolbar and the Tool Palette at the left. In addition, the choices in the menus are different.

5. Grab the lower right handle of the Draw box and enlarge the box by about an inch at the right and at the bottom. The size of the crane won't change.

6. Point inside the Draw window (away from the image) and right click. Choose **Select All** from the QuickMenu. (All parts of the image will be selected and have sizing handles.)

7. Point anywhere in the selected image and drag it so it's about in the middle of the Draw box. Deselect the image by clicking away from the image but still in the Draw box.

NOTE:

Clicking outside of the image closes the Draw program. If you click outside by accident, you can reenter the program by double clicking the image again.

FIGURE 29-1
Draw Window with Image

Before we go on, let's summarize what you did. You opened an image from the student **datafile** folder, made the image larger, double clicked to enter the Draw program, and enlarged the Draw box. Note that when you enlarged the Image box before entering Draw, the image grew with the box size. When you enlarged the Draw box after entering the Draw program, the image stayed the same size and only the box got larger.

In the next Step-by-Step exercise we will size two parts of the crane. When you size his beak, watch the head. The whole black area of the head will be elongated. Each color or part of the image is separate from the others, so you must be careful when you work with individual parts not to lose the continuity of the image.

1. With your image still showing in the Draw program, locate the **Zoom** button on the Toolbar. Choose **Zoom To Area**.

2. Use the magnifying glass pointer to draw a small "elastic box" that begins at the left of the crane's head and includes the head. Your window will look much like Figure 29-2. When you let go of the mouse button, only the head will fill your Draw window. Note the scroll bars at the bottom and right of the window.

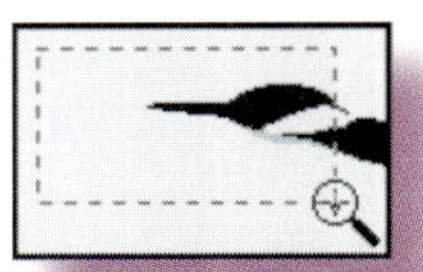

FIGURE 29-2
Zoom of Head

3. Point to the beak and click to give it sizing handles. Grab the handle at the left and drag it to the left, making the crane's beak longer. As you do this, the entire portion of the head stretches out. When you are satisfied with the adjustment, return to the **Zoom** button and choose **Previous View** or **Margin Size**.

4. Use the same procedure to make the crane's tail feather longer. Then click outside of the Draw window to exit the Draw program and deselect your image.

5. Save your edited crane as **crane 29-2 xxx**. Keep it open.

By selecting parts of a drawing, you can edit each one individually. For example, you could have edited each of the crane's features. You can make other changes at your leisure. Let's work with text in the drawing.

1. Point to the image and double click to return to the Draw program. Click the **A** tool on the Tool Palette for text mode. Use the "hand" tool to draw a box about 2 inches wide near the bottom of the Draw box.

2. Check Font Size on the Property Bar. If it isn't set at *36 pt.*, make that choice. Turn on **Bold** and key **HARVEST MIGRATION** in all caps.

3. Use the sizing tools to adjust the box so both words are on one line and the box is snug around the text.

4. Click outside of the Text box, but still inside of the Draw box, to exit the text edit mode. Center the box below the image.

5. Click outside of the Draw box to close it and deselect the image. Save the document as **crane 29-3 xxx**. Play your **pf** macro, print the document, and close it.

HyperText Transfer Protocol, or HTTP, are computer instructions for displaying and sending hypertext documents from computer to computer. Most World Wide Web addresses begin with the letters "http."

Now that you have learned how easy it is to edit images, let's see what you can do with Draw.

Drawing

The various tools on the Draw Tool palette can be used for creating your own images. We'll try just a few of them so you get a feel for the Draw program. Look at Figure 29-3. We'll begin by drawing these four shapes.

STEP-BY-STEP 29.4

1. Open the **Insert** menu, choose **Graphics**, and then choose **Draw Picture**. This opens the Draw window with no image in it.

2. On the Draw Tool palette, find the **Basic Shapes** button. (It looks like a rectangular box.) Click the little arrow beside the button and select the third tool in the top row (the ellipse).

3. Begin on one end and draw an ellipse that looks like the first object in Figure 29-3.

4. Pretend you don't like your ellipse. Press **Delete** to remove it. (That was for practice, in case you want to get rid of an object.)

5. Choose the tool again and draw another ellipse.

6. Choose the same tool and hold the Shift key to draw a perfect circle below the ellipse. Then choose the **Rectangle** tool (the first basic shape). Draw a rectangle beside the ellipse.

7. Hold the **Shift** key as you use the same tool to draw another object next to the circle. (The Shift key enables you to make a perfect square.) Stay in the Draw program.

FIGURE 29-3
Step-by-Step
29.4 Shapes

Now let's see what else can be done with the objects.

STEP-BY-STEP 29.5

1. Click to select the first object. With the pointer on the object, right click and choose **Rotate** from the QuickMenu. Look at the handles around your object.
   a. The handles at the corner are rotate handles.
   b. The handles in the middle of the sides are skewing handles.

2. Point to the rotate handle on the upper left corner. When your pointer turns into a two-headed arrow, drag it up and to the right so your ellipse is higher on the left than on the right.

(continued on next page)

3. Select the square object and choose **Rotate** from the QuickMenu again. Grab the skewing handle at the middle of the top of the square. Drag it to the right so your square leans to the right.

4. Rotate the rectangle so the right end is higher than the left.

5. Select the circle. Use a corner handle and move it toward the center of the circle to make your circle smaller. When you finish, your four objects should look somewhat like Figure 29-4.

6. Click outside of the Draw box and save your file as **objects 29-5 xxx**. Play your **pf** macro. Select the Draw box and press **Ctrl+C** to copy it to the Clipboard.

FIGURE 29-4
Edited Objects

7. Click outside of the box to deselect it. Then press **Ctrl+V** to paste another copy of the box into your window. Drag the new box so it is directly below the first box. Double click in the new box to return to the Draw window.

As you have already discovered, you can size and manipulate your graphics objects separately. You can also treat them as a single object. To do that, you must select them all at one time. Let's try it.

STEP-BY-STEP ⟹ 29.6

1. The **Select** tool is the pointer on the Draw Tool palette. Be sure that tool is chosen. Begin in the upper left corner (being sure to be above and to the left of all objects). Draw an elastic box that completely contains all four objects in the new box.

2. Grab the sizing handle at the lower right and drag it up and to the left so the elastic box is about a quarter of the size of the Draw box.

3. Keep the four objects selected. Then click the **Fill Pattern** button on the Draw Tool palette. Click **More** and choose a style pattern.

4. Click outside of the box of objects to ungroup them. Then click the circle object. Change the Foreground Fill Color, and drag it so part of it

covers the square and the rectangle. It will be behind those objects.

5. With the circle still selected, right click and choose **To Front** to move the circle in front of the other two objects. Then push it to the back again.

6. Choose a straight line from the Line Shapes Tools and draw a line across the bottom of the Draw area. Using the **Zigzag** tool, draw a triangle as follows: Click to begin the first line. Click each time you want a joint. Finally, double click to end the line.

7. Select the triangle. Grab a center handle and distort the proportions of the triangle.

8. Click the **Curve** tool (the last tool in the first row of Line Shapes) and make a wave across the box. Click each time you wish to change direction. Double click to end the curve.

9. Click the **Text** tool. Drag to draw a box. Change to **12 pt.** and key your name in the Text box.

10. Spend no more than 5 minutes working with the other tools, clicking to begin and bend, and double clicking to end. Press **Delete** to delete any selected object.

11. When you are finished, click outside of the Draw window to close Draw. Print your masterpiece and close it, saving it as **objects 29-6 xxx**.

Now let's go back to the crane and use our drawing skills to enhance that picture.

S TEP-BY-STEP 29.7

1. Open **crane 29-3 xxx**. Double click on the image to enter the Draw program.

2. Make the Draw box wider by dragging the right line to the right margin guideline. Point under the crane's legs and right click. Choose **Select All**. Drag the image as far to the right as you can without cutting off his legs.

3. Draw a circle about the size of a quarter to the left of the crane. Drag the circle so it is on top of the crane's head. With the circle selected, right click and choose **To Back**.

4. Change the color of the circle so it looks like a harvest moon. You may also need to change the Line Color. Center the text attractively in

the picture. Then click outs de of the Draw window to exit the Draw program. Your picture should look like the miniature in Figure 29-5.

5. Save your new crane drawing as **crane 29-7 xxx**. Print it and close it.

FIGURE 29-5
Crane Picture

Charting

The WordPerfect Chart feature provides you with a variety of chart styles and options for formatting your charts. You can customize your own charts, or you can choose one of the many charts in the gallery. The Chart window is like the Draw window, in that if you click outside of it, the editor is closed. Then you need to double click to reopen the editor.

STEP-BY-STEP ⟹ 29.8

1. Open the **Insert** menu, and choose **Chart**. Look at the Chart Toolbar and Property Bar (see Figure 29-6). Look at the Quick Tips for the specialized buttons. Note that the Tool Palette is grayed at the left.

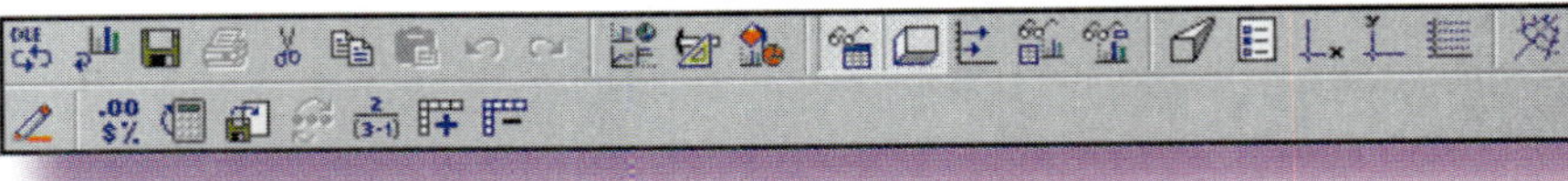

2. Click the button to the right of Redo and explore the Data Chart Gallery. Be sure the View Datasheet button and the 3-D Chart button are depressed.

3. To clear the sample data, open the **Edit** menu and choose **Clear All**. Affirm that you would like all data cleared.

4. In the Datasheet, click to positon the insertion point in the Legend column, opposite Label 1. Key **Patty**. Tab once and key **30**. Continue positioning the insertion point, keying data, and tabbing until you have entered all of the information in Figure 29-7.

5. Look at your chart. One salesperson was forgotten. George's numbers are 40, 20, and 55. Position the insertion point in Row 2 of the Label column. Open the **Edit** menu and choose **Insert**. Insert a row between Patty and Fred, and key the information for George.

6. Try some of the chart styles for your chart. Then choose the style that looks like Figure 29-8.

Patty	30	25	50
Fred	25	45	60
Sue15	35	45	

Now that the chart is created, let's add a title and some labels.

STEP-BY-STEP ⟹ 29.9

1. Point to *Title of Chart* and click to select it. Then double click to open the Title Properties dialog box. At the top, name the chart **DAHLIN'S DAIRY** and click **OK**.

2. Open the **Chart** menu, choose **Axis**, and then choose **Primary Y**. Select **Display labels**. In the same dialog box, choose the **Title Options** tab and key **$ in Thousands**. Click **OK**.

3. In the Datasheet, opposite labels, key **January** under *A*, **February** under *B*, and **March** under *C* to add those labels to your chart.

4. Open the **Chart** menu, choose **Axis**, and choose **X**. Choose the **Title Options** tab and insert **Monthly Totals** for the label.

5. If no subtitle area appears in the chart, open the **Chart** menu, choose **Subtitle**, choose to display the subtitle, and key **Quarterly Sales**. Click **OK**.

6. Click the white space outside of the chart to return to your document window. Your chart should appear in your document, looking somewhat like Figure 29-8.

7. Use your Graphics Box Quick Menu to size the box to **4"** wide. Maintain height proportions.

8. Save the chart as **chart 29-9 xxx**. Play your **pf** macro. Print the document, save it, and close it.

This is just a brief introduction to the Chart feature. You'll have another opportunity to create a chart in Project 29. Beyond that, you can explore this feature as you have a need for it.

Summary

All of the graphics features introduced in this lesson are accessed from the Graphics menu. They widen your horizons regarding what you can do with graphics in WordPerfect. Specifically, in this lesson you learned the following:

FIGURE 29-8
Finished Bar Chart

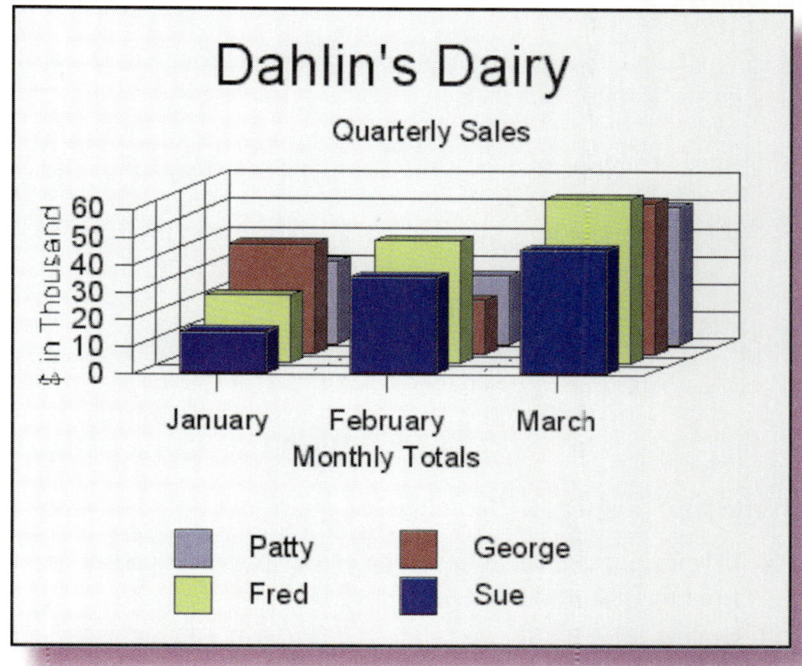

- The Draw feature can be used for editing graphics images.

- The Draw feature can be used to create objects and drawings of your own. If you have artistic talent, this tool will probably be very useful to you.

- The Chart feature enables you to create a wide variety of charts. Those charts can be customized using the tools in the Chart program.

- Charts and graphics boxes containing objects created or edited in the Draw program can be sized and formatted in the same way that you size and format the normal WordPerfect graphics boxes.

FILL IN THE BLANKS

Complete each of the following statements by writing your answer in the blank provided.

1. The ___________________ feature can be used to edit images that come with the WordPerfect program.

2. If you don't know what a button is on the Draw Tool palette, use the ___________________ to choose the appropriate button.

3. Clicking outside a selected image ___________________ the Draw program.

4. When you enlarge the Image box before entering the Draw program, the ___________________ grows with the box size.

5. By selecting parts of a drawing, you can ___________________ each one individually.

6. If you want to draw your own images, open the Insert menu, choose Graphics, and then choose ___________________ .

7. To reopen the Chart editor window, ___________________ to reopen the editor.

WRITTEN QUESTIONS

Write your answers to the following questions.

8. If you want to change the shape or size of only a part of an image, how do you separate that part from the rest of the image?

9. When you click the arrow beside the Basic Objects Tools button, how many objects are there for you to choose from?

10. What type(s) of chart(s) do you think you would use most frequently in your school assignments?

LESSON 29 PROJECT

In the final part of the lesson you were introduced to the Chart feature, where you created a bar chart. In this project you will create a pie chart. Pie charts must be made up of figures that add up to 100 percent. In the example used for the bar chart, we looked at a number of variables. In order to chart the sales of Patty, Fred, George, and Sue, we need to look at their totals only, so those totals can add up to 100 percent.

Study Figure 29-9. You will prepare this pie chart, and you will do it mostly on your own, using your knowledge of the Chart feature and your willingness to explore the dialog boxes to find the feature you wish to use. If you want to make your chart fancier than the one illustrated, that's OK, too. Here are just a few helpful hints:

- Add the January, February, and March sales figures from Step-by-Step exercise 29.8 for each salesperson to get the totals to be used in the chart.

- Key the names of the salespersons in the Legend column.

- Key the quarterly totals in the Pie 1 column.

- Add a title, subtitle, and percentage data labels.

    When you are finished, check your work carefully. Then save the chart document as **pie proj29 xxx**. Identify it with your **pf** macro and print it. Close the file.

FIGURE 29-9
Suggested Pie Chart

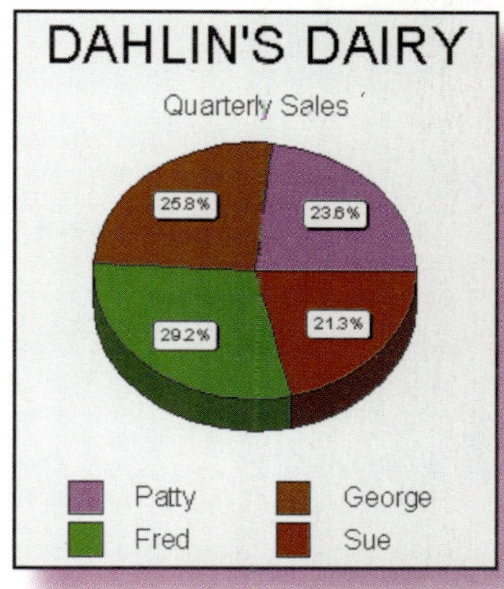

CRITICAL THINKING ACTIVITY

You are working with an image in a document and want to make the image larger. However, when you try to use the sizing handles to widen the selected image, only the box around the image gets larger. What's the problem?

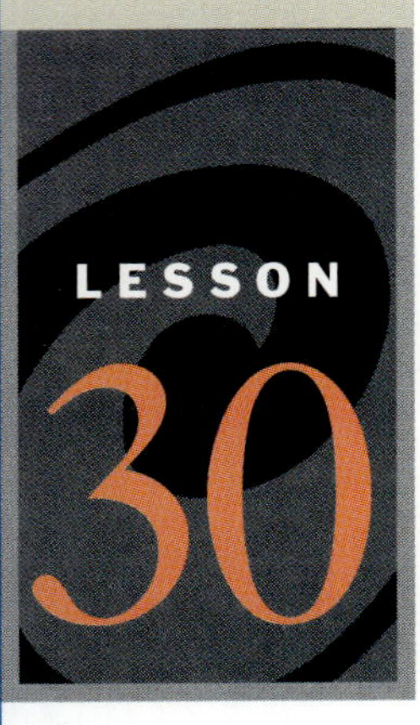

KEYBOARD MAPPING; DESIGNING A WEB PAGE

OBJECTIVES

Upon completion of this lesson, you will be able to:

- Map a keyboard containing special characters.

- Choose a mapped keyboard.

- Use the mapped keyboard for creating a document.

- Discuss the different methods of using the Internet Publisher to create a Web page.

- Create a sample Web page, complete with hypertext links.

⏱ **Estimated Time: 2 hours**

Keyboard Mapping

Ever since you learned about WordPerfect Symbols in Lesson 5, you've needed characters periodically. In some offices you use specific characters so often, it would be useful to have those characters on your keyboard. WordPerfect enables you to map the keyboard so it contains those frequently used keys. When you have a mapped keyboard and you press a mapped key, the mapped character appears instead of the regular character.

The best way to access special characters is to create a customized keyboard and switch to the customized keyboard when you need the special characters it contains. You can have several customized keyboards—one for Spanish, another for French, and a third for Portuguese, if you prefer.

In the next few Step-by-Step exercises we'll create a German keyboard (because it only involves customizing a few keys) and learn to choose that keyboard when it is needed. Then we'll key a letter using the German keyboard. Finally, we'll delete the German keyboard so the next student can create one for practice.

Hypermedia means using hypertext links to connect different types of media. Examples of different media are animation, graphics, pictures, sound, text, and video.

UNIT 8: ADVANCED GRAPHICS TOOLS

STEP-BY-STEP 30.1

1. In a new document window, open the **Tools** menu and choose **Settings**. Double click the **Customize** icon and click the **Keyboards** tab. The *WPWin 9 Keyboard* should be highlighted.

2. Look at the listed keyboards. The keyboards that come with WordPerfect CANNOT be edited. Click the **Create** button.

3. Name your new keyboard **German** and click **OK**. Look at the Keyboard Shortcuts – German dialog box, as illustrated in Figure 30-1.

FIGURE 30-1
Keyboard Shortcuts – German Dialog Box

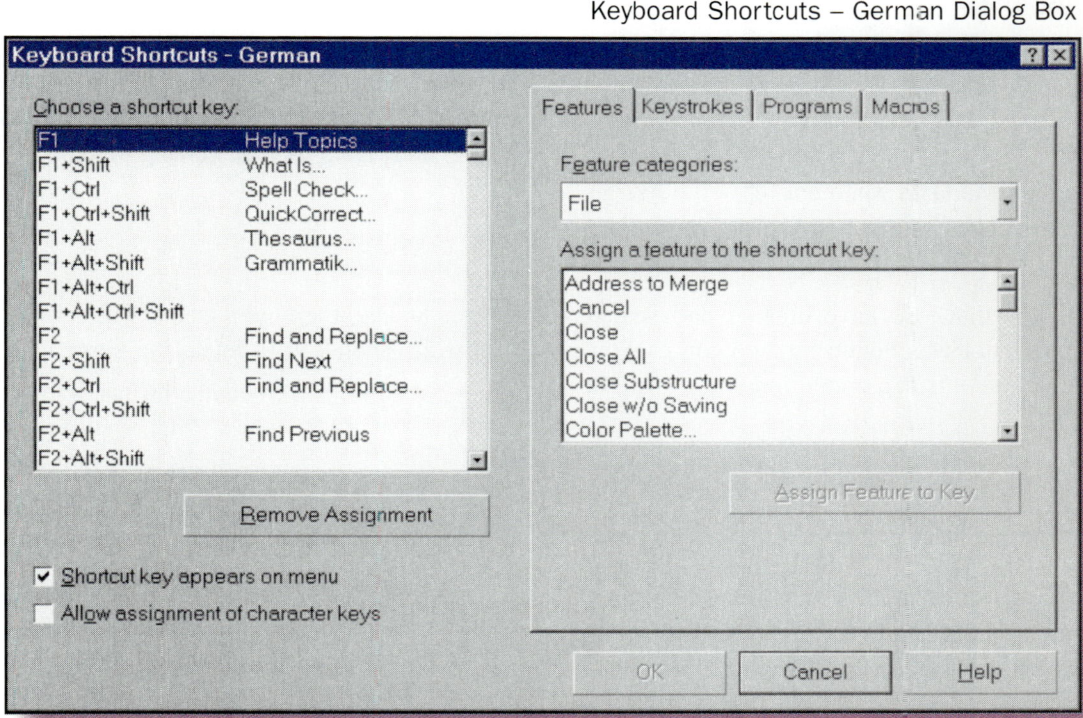

The list on the left of the Keyboard Shortcuts – German dialog box includes all possible key combinations using Shift, Ctrl, and Alt together with the alphabetic, numeric, and function keys. As you can see, many of the key combinations have already been assigned. You know, for example, that Ctrl+B turns on Bold and Ctrl+C chooses Copy. Because there are so many possibilities, however, lots of the combinations haven't been assigned. We'll use some of those unassigned combinations for our German characters.

SCANS

1. With the Keyboard Shortcuts – German dialog box open, scroll through the list of keyboard assignments until you come to the *A* section of the alphabet. Click to position the highlight on the **A+Alt** combination.

2. Click the **Keystrokes** tab. Your insertion point will be in a large white box. Press **Ctrl+W** to display the Symbols dialog box. Key **a"**. (If you prefer, you can change to the Multinational Symbol Set and find the *ä* character.) Insert the character and close the dialog box.

3. Below the large white box, click the **Assign Keystrokes to Key** button. The assignment

should appear in the *shortcut key* box at the left. Delete the *ä* in the large white box.

4. Move the highlight to the **A+Alt+Shift** combination. Click in the large white box at the right. Follow the procedure above to assign the **Ä** character.

5. Follow the same procedure to assign the small **ö** and capital **Ö** to the *O* keystrokes and the **ü** and **Ü** to the *U* keystrokes.

6. Click **Select**, select the **German** keyboard, and return to your working window.

Now that you have created and selected the German keyboard, you can try the keyboard. A German letter was begun by a coworker. You get to finish it. Then you'll delete the German keyboard so other students can create one.

SCANS

1. In a new document window, go to the student **datafile** folder and open **will**. Save the file as **will 30-3 xxx**.

2. Open the **Tools** menu, choose **Settings** and **Customize,** and then click the **Keyboards** tab. Choose the **German** keyboard. (It may already be selected.)

3. Add the final paragraph and closing lines to the letter. The text is illustrated in Figure 30-2. When you need a lowercase German character, hold the **Alt** key while you key the letter. If you need an upper-case German character, hold both **Alt** and **Shift** while you key the letter.

FIGURE 30-2
Text for Step-by-Step 30.3

Bitte überprüfen Sie alle Akten und sollten keine Änderungen notwendig sein dann machen Sie einen Termin mit meinem Büro, wo wir die Testamente unterschreiben können.

Ich verbleibe lhr,

(Student name)
Rechtsanwalt

Einlage

4. Finish the letter and check your work.

5. Play your **pf** macro to identify the document. Print the letter. Save it again as **will 30-3 xxx** and close it.

6. Open the **Tools** menu and choose **Settings** and **Customize**. Click the **Keyboards** tab.

7. Move the highlight to the *German* keyboard and click the **Delete** button. Affirm the deletion of the keyboard.

8. Click **Close** twice to return to your WordPerfect window.

That's a brief introduction to keyboard mapping. As you can see, it is a relatively simple process to map a keyboard. If you need lots of special characters on the job, the easiest way to get them is to map a special keyboard and choose it when you will be doing work that requires the special characters.

Web Page

Most documents published on the World Wide Web are written in HTML (Hypertext Markup Language). WordPerfect's Internet Publisher will publish WordPerfect formatting into HTML language, so you don't need to buy a special program or learn the HTML language if you wish to create documents for the World Wide Web.

You may create Web pages in one of three ways:

- Format the document in WordPerfect and then convert it to HTML format.

- Use the WordPerfect Web PerfectExpert template to provide the tools for creating a Web page.

- Use a blank page template for preparing a Web page in HTML format.

Regardless of the method you use, your finished document must be in HTML format before it can be published on the Internet. Since you are probably learning WordPerfect in a classroom, you won't be asked to publish your home page. You can learn about working with HTML by creating a sample home page using the WordPerfect Internet Publisher.

Web pages are used for a variety of reasons. Individuals might have Web pages to offer information about themselves, and they communicate with the people who contact them. Companies have Web pages to offer information, request information, provide help, or advertise goods and services. WordPerfect has a Web page to provide information about new products, and one branch of that page may be used to get technical assistance from the WordPerfect help team.

Like the WordPerfect page, many Web pages consist of several parts, and the person accessing the page can move from one part to another using hyperlinks (hypertext links). In the next few Step-by-Step exercises you will create a five-page Web document that is in HTML format. The first page will be an introductory page that contains a list of contents of the entire document. The contents items will be hyperlinked to the other pages. This is a simple example, but it illustrates one way to create a document and link the pages.

STEP-BY-STEP 30.4

1. Open the **File** menu and choose **New from Project**. Be sure **WordPerfect 9** is selected in the box at the top of the list of templates. Then choose **[WordPerfect Web Document]** from near the top. Click **Create**.

2. A gray window will appear, with the PerfectExpert panel at the left. Look at the Web Toolbar and Property Bar (see Figure 30-3). You may explore the buttons on both bars at your leisure. For these Step-by-Step exercises we'll use the PerfectExpert panel.

3. Click the **Font/Size** button on the Property Bar and choose **Heading 1**.

4. Key **Gaillardia Garden Supply** and press **Enter**.

5. Click the PerfectExpert **Extras** button and choose **Add a Horizontal Line**. Press **Enter**.

6. Click the **Font/Size** button and choose **Indented Quotation**. Then key the text in Figure 30-4, press **Enter**, and insert another horizontal line.

7. Click the **Justification** button on the Property Bar and change to **Center** justification.

8. Click the **Font/Size** button again and choose **Heading 3**. Key **Contents** and press **Enter**.

9. Key the four page references illustrated in Figure 30-5. Press **Enter**.

10. Keep your document open as you read on.

FIGURE 30-3
Web Toolbar and Property Bar

FIGURE 30-4
Text for Step-by-Step 30.4

```
Let us satisfy all of your
gardening needs. Visit this
page regularly to learn about
specials and to learn new ways
to make your garden the best in
town.
```

FIGURE 30-5
Page References for Step-by-Step 30.4

```
Gabby's Gobbledygook
Garden Supplies
The Bird Connection
Nursery Stock
```

You can view your template in HTML format or in WordPerfect format. Most of the time, you'll prefer to work in HTML format because the formatting is applied. Sometimes you'll prefer to work in WordPerfect format. A button on the Toolbar enables you to jump back and forth between the two formats. When you return to HTML format, a warning will tell you that only Web-compatible formatting will be included.

Graphics images can be used to make your Web pages more attractive. In the next Step-by-Step exercise you'll insert our favorite rose image and format it. Then you'll save your page as a Web page.

STEP-BY-STEP ⟹ 30.5

1. Click the PerfectExpert **Extras** button and choose **Add a Graphic from File**.

2. Go to the **datafile** folder and locate the **rose.wpg** image. Insert it.

3. With the rose selected on your page, display the QuickMenu and choose **Position**. Note that you can't set the position at *Page*. Click **Cancel** to close the dialog box.

4. Deselect the image and click the **Change View** button to go to the WordPerfect view of the page. 

5. Select the rose and change the position to **Page**. Then align the rose just below the second horizontal line and at the left. Deselect the image.

6. Click the **Change View** button to return to HTML format and click **OK** at the warning box. Position the rose attractively on the page.

7. Using the PerfectExpert buttons, click **Change Colors** and choose **Yellow**. Click the **Change Background** button and choose **Hatch**.

8. Use **Save As** to save your Web template as **a:\web1**. Close the file.

STEP-BY-STEP ⟹ 30.6

1. For page 2 of your Web document, repeat Step 1 above to create a new Web template. Change to **Center** justification and choose **Heading 2**. Key **Gabby's Gobbledygook** and press **Enter**.

2. Add a horizontal line and key: **Keep up with the latest in gardening tips and deals!**

3. Press **Enter** and add another horizontal line. Change to **Left** justification and key the tips in Figure 30-6.

4. Press **Enter** twice, choose **Center** justification, and key **Contents Page**.

5. Select the *Contents Page* text and click the **Add a Hyperlink** button on the PerfectExpert panel. The dialog box illustrated in Figure 30-7 will appear.

FIGURE 30-6
Text for Step-by-Step 30.6

```
Tip 1:
Plant a butterfly bush. It flowers in the
autumn and is loved by all varieties of
butterflies.

Tip 2:
Don't kill those milkweed plants that seem to
be such a nuisance. Instead, plant a milkweed
patch especially for the butterflies in your
life.
```

(continued on next page)

6. Click the folder button beside the *Document* text box and locate your **web1** document. Choose it and click **Select**. When you return to your **web2** document, the *Contents Page* words will be a different color, indicating that they now are part of a hyperlink.

7. Use **Save As** to save the page as **a:\web2**.

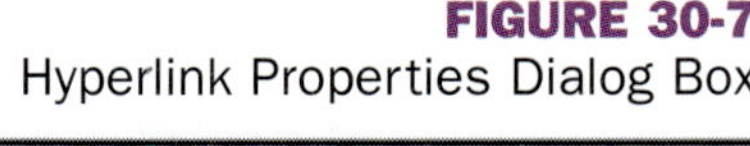

FIGURE 30-7
Hyperlink Properties Dialog Box

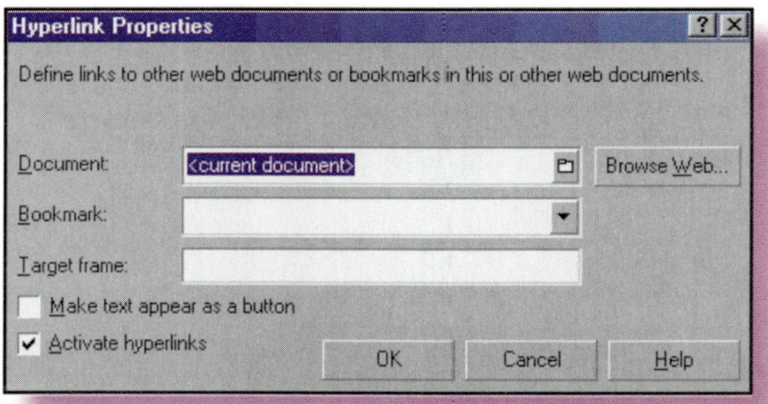

STEP-BY-STEP 30.7

SCANS

1. For page 3 of your Web document, create another page for *Garden Supplies*, similar to the one in Step-by-Step exercise 30.6. Center the title and use **Heading 2**. Following the heading, press **Enter** and insert a horizontal line. You may add any information you'd like to the page, or you may leave the page blank.

2. Add the **Contents Page** line at the center, a few lines below the horizontal line. Select **Contents Page**, and create a hyperlink to the **web1** contents page as in Step-by-Step exercise 30.6.

3. Save the document as **a:\web3** and close it.

STEP-BY-STEP 30.8

1. Create **web4** and entitle it, **The Bird Connection**. Add Clipart from the Scrapbook or other sources to your pages, if you wish. Press **Enter** and insert a horizontal line.

2. Key **Send us your bird stories. We'll publish them right here!** Press **Enter** and insert another horizontal line. Change to **Left** justification.

3. Insert a Heading 4 line at the left that reads, **Clean Crows**. Open the **Insert** menu, choose **File**, and insert **crow** from the student **datafile** folder.

4. Center the *Contents* line at the bottom, and create a Hyperlink as in earlier Step-by-Step exercises. Save the page as **a:\web4** and close it.

5. Create **web5** entitled **Nursery Stock**. Key the text in Figure 30-8. Choose **Bulleted List** from the **Font/Size** drop-down menu for the services.

6. Add the *Contents* line and create a hyperlink as in earlier Step-by-Step exercises. Save the page as **a:\web5** and close it.

FIGURE 30-8
Text for Step-by-Step 30.8

```
Watch this space for specials. Come in and check the prices.

August Specials: Pyramidal Arborvitae, 4-ft. Maple Trees
September Specials: Globe Arborvitae, Apple and Pear Trees
October Specials: Potentilla and Weigela Shrubs

Services:
• Landscape Design Service
• Expert Advice for the Do-It-Yourselfer
```

After the pages have been created and saved, they can be edited at any time. Let's add two more services to the list on the **web5** page. Then we'll add a graphics image.

STEP-BY-STEP 30.9

1. Open **web5**. Click the **Perfect Expert** button on the Toolbar.

2. Between the two services listed, add **Planting and Removal** and **Fitting the Pieces of Your Yard Together**.

3. Insert **puzzle.wpg** from the **datafile** folder. Position it at the right, opposite the list of services. (You'll probably need to change Position to Paragraph to get it to stay where you want it.)

4. Save the page again. Then test the hyperlink one more time to go to **web1**.

Let's add hyperlinks to the Contents page so people can go to the various pages of your document from the Contents page. Then we'll add background formatting to the remaining pages so they look like the **web1** page.

1. With **web1** showing in the window, select **Gabby's Gobbledygook**. Create a hyperlink that links the document to **web2**. Add links to the other pages as follows:

   Garden Supplies to **web3**
   The Bird Connection to **web4**
   Nursery Stock to **web5**

2. Save **web1** again.

3. Use the hyperlink to go to each of the other pages—one at a time—and change the color to **Yellow** and the background to **Hatch**. Save each modified page before using the hyperlink to jump back to the Contents page.

4. Close all files and click the **X** on the PerfectExpert panel to close it.

Summary

In this lesson you worked with a mapped keyboard and received a brief introduction to the use of the WordPerfect Web PerfectExpert. While you didn't actually publish the Gaillardia Garden Supply Web page to the Internet, you learned enough about creating a page so you could do it on your own.

In this lesson you learned that:

- It is easy to create a keyboard with special characters for when you need to key documents with characters that are not on the normal computer keyboard.

- You can use WordPerfect to create Web pages.

- In order for Web pages to be used on the Internet, they must be published to HTML (Hypertext Markup Language).

- Hyperlinks can be used to jump from Web page to Web page.

If you are interested in exploring the Internet Publisher in depth, you can use the normal Help menus or you can access the *WordPerfect Reference* on CD-ROM. Just key **Web** as the lookup term. WordPerfect will take you to additional topics that will give you more information about working with Web documents.

In addition to the Internet Publisher that you used to create the Web pages in these Step-by-Step exercises, WordPerfect Office 2000 contains a more sophisticated Web page tool called Trellix. Trellix is included in the extra components your instructor installed so you could use the WordPerfect templates in Lesson 26. If you are interested in Web page design and would like to learn more about Trellix, the following two sources are available:

1. The Reference Center on the WordPerfect Office 2000 CD-ROM contains an extensive manual on the use of Trellix.

2. An interactive multimedia tutorial is included with the Trellix program. Simply open any document and choose Publish to Trellix from the File menu. Click OK at the first two opportunities to go to the Trellix dialog box. Choose Help and then QuickTour. You may take this tour whenever you have some spare time.

LESSON 30 REVIEW QUESTIONS

MATCHING

Write the letter of the term or phrase from Column 2 that best matches the description in Column 1.

Column 1

____ **1.** The language you must use in order for Web pages to be used on the Internet.

____ **2.** One of the choices you can select when defining links in a Web document.

____ **3.** A customized keyboard is created using this feature.

____ **4.** These are used to jump from Web page to Web page.

____ **5.** Key combinations using Shift, Ctrl, and Alt together with alphabetic, numeric, and function keys.

____ **6.** WordPerfect uses one on the Internet to provide information about new products.

Column 2

A. Web page

B. Hyperlinks

C. HTML

D. Keyboard mapping

E. COBOL

F. Bookmark

G. Keyboard Shortcuts

H. Keystrokes

MULTIPLE CHOICE

Circle the best answer to each of the following statements as it relates to information found in your Keyboard Shortcuts - German dialog box.

7. The shortcut key for Spell Checker is
   A. F1+Alt+Ctrl.
   B. F1+Alt+Shift.
   C. F1+Ctrl+Shift.
   D. F1+Ctrl.

8. The four tab choices are the following EXCEPT
   A. Features.
   B. Functions.
   C. Keystrokes.
   D. Macros.

9. You would select the _________ tab to key text to be inserted into your document when the shortcut key is pressed.
   A. Features
   B. Keystrokes
   C. Programs
   D. Macros

(continued on next page)

10. All of the following key combinations can be used for assigning functions on a customized keyboard EXCEPT

    A. Alt+Ctrl.

    B. Alt+Ctrl+Shift.

    C. Ctrl+Shift.

    D. Ctrl+Alt+Del.

LESSON 30 PROJECT

Most of your projects have given you specific instructions for the document to be prepared and how to prepare it. In this case, you have some choices. Think carefully about your choices and pick one that is most meaningful to you and your interests. Choose from the following:

FIGURE 30-9
Sample Art

■ Create a Web page of your own—one that includes topics of interest to you. You will need to use a different set of names—anything will do. Include at least one graphics image and at least two topic pages in the table of contents. When you finish, print the pages of your Web page and submit them to your instructor. Save your Web pages when you close the document.

■ Continue with the Gaillardia Web page. Fill in the remaining topics and make any desired changes to the ones prepared in Step-by-Step exercises 30.4 through 30.10. Add more graphics images. If you can't find any that fit in the Clipart Scrapbook, go to the Draw program and create your own, like the lovely tree in Figure 30-9. When you finish, print the pages you changed and submit them to your instructor. Save the Web pages when you close the document.

■ Map a keyboard for a language that you know and/or use. Then write a short paragraph or two using the language and the appropriate characters. If you don't have something else you'd like to write about, tell what you think about the Internet. When you finish, save your document as **proj30 xxx**, identify it with the **pf** macro, print it, and submit it to your instructor.

CRITICAL THINKING ACTIVITY

As you are keying information using your customized keyboard, you try your shortcut for Sort, but nothing happens. You open the Tools menu to look for the keyboard shortcut, but it isn't there. Why not?

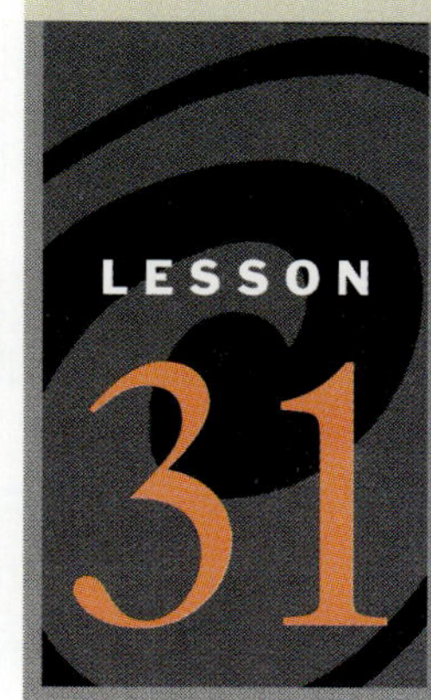

DESIGNING MARKETING TOOLS

OBJECTIVES

Upon completion of this lesson, you will be able to:

- Discuss using WordPerfect templates for the creation of brochures and business cards.

- Create a brochure.

- Create business cards using the Labels feature.

⏱ Estimated Time: 2$\frac{1}{2}$ hours

Many jobs involve marketing of some kind. Sometimes the commodity being sold is merchandise. Sometimes the commodity being sold is services. In some cases, the commodity being sold is a person—for example, when you apply for a job.

WordPerfect helps you with quite a number of marketing documents by providing templates that are preformatted and that contain suggested arrangements of the information. As you already know, templates can be very helpful. However, during the standard installation of WordPerfect, most of the templates aren't loaded. If you are at a computer with the WordPerfect CD-ROM disk in the drive, the templates are probably available. Also, if you are on a network or if your instructor performed the special installation, the templates might also be available.

As you know from your previous practice with templates, templates can be used to help you through the process of setting up the text for a particular layout. The templates use the same tools you've been learning about in your lessons. In fact, you know how to do nearly everything included in most of the templates.

Since you may not have the templates available to create the business forms needed in this lesson, we'll create them using the WordPerfect tools. If you have the brochure and business card templates available, you can explore those tools on your own.

Brochure

We'll begin by checking to see if your computer can access the templates for the brochures and business cards. Then we'll proceed to create those marketing documents using the skills you already possess.

S TEP-BY-STEP ▷ 31.1

1. Open the **File** menu and choose **New from Project**. Choose the **WordPerfect 9** group of templates and look through the list for **Brochure**.

2. Double click to choose the Brochure template. Read some of the information in the sample brochure about the creation of brochures.

3. Close the document without saving it.

4. Follow the same procedure with the **Business Card** template. Reveal your codes and look at each of the codes. Note that the template picked up your personal information.

5. Close your document without saving it, just in case any codes were entered on the page. If the PerfectExpert panel is still displayed, close it by clicking the **X** in the corner.

Now let's create a brochure advertising a certificate program for the local business college. In the following Step-by-Step exercises you will create a document that has three panels on each side of the paper. Each panel is illustrated. The Step-by-Step exercises provide all the information you need to prepare the panels. Work quickly and efficiently. How rapidly can you produce an accurate, attractive brochure?

S TEP-BY-STEP ▷ 31.2

Panel 1: Figure 31-1 (next page)

1. Go to the **Format** menu, and choose **Page** and **Page Setup**. Choose **Landscape**.

2. Click the **Margins/Layout** tab. Divide the page into three columns (3x1). Set all four margins at **0.4"**. Click **OK**.

3. Set an extra tab stop midway between the left margin and the first tab that affects your document.

4. The entire panel is in Times New Roman. The title is centered in bold with a 20-pt. font size.

5. The graphics image is in the student **datafile** folder. It's an old WordPerfect graphics image called **Ladderup.wpg**.

6. When you complete the panel, save the evolving brochure as **brochure 31-2 xxx**. (Save often!)

About This Certificate

This six-course certificate program provides essential computer skills used in today's modern offices. Designed for those seeking a fast track toward employment, only core computer classes are required for completion. To gain the necessary skills for employment in this short time span, a minimum keying speed of 45 words per minute is a requirement for entry.

Benefits to You:
- Only specific computer skills—no costly extras
- Fast track to a career
- Courses available day or evening

What Is a Certificate?

A certificate is the recognition given by Butte des Morts Business College for academic achievement in a particular field of study. The Office Computing certificate includes courses from the Administrative Assistant associate degree program. Credits from this certificate can be transferred into more than 60 technical diploma or associate degree programs available at Butte des Morts Business College.

This certificate is earned by students who successfully complete the following Butte des Morts Business College courses:

Course No.	Course Title	Credits
1348	Beginning WordPerfect	1
1350	Advanced WordPerfect	1
1388	Beginning Quattro Pro	1
1408	Integrated Software: WordPerfect Office 2000	1
1415	Desktop Publishing: Microsoft Publisher	1
1422	Word Processing Simulation	1
Total Credits		6

Path and Filename Code

Make everything illustrated in the panel here fit your first panel. Zoom to Full Page regularly, so you can see the results of your work.

Panel 2: Figure 31-2

1. Position the title the same distance from the top of the page as you did in Panel 1.

2. Create a three-column table for the listing of courses. Turn off all lines except the line

TIP

In order to make the information fit comfortably in the table, use 10-pt. Arial for the entire table.

separating the credit for the Word Processing Simulation from the total number of credits.

Can you make your table look as good as this one—or even better? Remember that everything illustrated in Figure 31-2 must fit in Panel 2, including the Path and Filename Code at the bottom.

S TEP-BY-STEP 31.4

Panel 3: Figure 31-3

This panel should be easy for you to prepare. Note that Center justification is used for the italicized paragraph in the lower half.

The Butte des Morts Business College logo is saved in the student **datafile** folder as **bbc.wpg**. Size it and position it attractively in the panel.

S TEP-BY-STEP 31.5

Panel 4: Figure 31-4

This panel will be the most difficult with regard to space. Use whatever font size will fill the page. The text MUST fit on this panel.

The sections listing the course names are a single-cell table filled with **10%** fill. The lines on the right and left have been removed. To decrease the amount of space above each course name, position the insertion point in the table and choose **Format** from the QuickMenu. Click the **Row** tab. In the *Row margins* section, set the top margin at **0.04"**.

TIP

Format one "table." Reveal your codes so you can select all of the table codes and copy that table to the Windows Clipboard. Then paste it into place for each of the other courses, changing the wording as needed.

How to Get Started

For registration information, contact:

Butte des Morts Business College
Business and Marketing Division
1483 Lakeside Way
Kansas City, MO 64101
(816) 555-9162

or

Butte des Morts Business College
(Regional Center)
87 Riverside Road
Fox Haven, MO 64083
(816) 555-3411

http://www.buttedesmorts.net

Butte des Morts Business College endeavors to meet the needs of area workers who either want to learn new skills or upgrade existing ones. Our goal is to provide timely business-related training through specific courses for those who wish to earn a certificate. Courses will be offered both days and evenings.

Course Descriptions

Beginning WordPerfect

Students will be given basic instruction in word processing using WordPerfect 9. Students learn editing, formatting, text enhancement, tables, columns, and outlining.

Advanced WordPerfect

Students learn additional features, including merge, macros, labels, graphics, and forms.

Beginning Quattro Pro

This course introduces the students to the basic operations of the PC using spreadsheets and Quattro Pro. Students will develop and construct accounting-related work sheets and reports using the spreadsheet software.

Integrated Software: WordPerfect Office 2000

In this course, students explore the world of software integration while learning to use word processing, spreadsheet, database, and presentation tools. They also will learn how to make these tools work together to create and electronically communicate documents that meet their needs.

Desktop Publishing: Microsoft Publisher

In this course, students develop additional skills for working with multiple-page documents—brochures, newsletters, and reports. Students will learn about page layout, graphics, styles, and fonts, as well as how to create letterheads, borders, and logos.

Word Processing Simulation

This one-credit, 36-hour course requires students to complete a simulation utilizing various word processing features. Time management, communication skills, and proofreading skills are stressed.
Prerequisite: Advanced WordPerfect

INTERNET FTP stands for File Transfer Protocol. FTP software transfers files of data from one computer to another.

Panel 5: Figure 31-5

Study Panel 5. Both pieces of information are included in Text boxes—the first is changed to a User box so no lines surround it. The second remains as a Text box so it is enclosed in a single line.

1. Create the return address Text box and key the information. Change the box style and go to **Content** to rotate the box **90 degrees**.

2. Position the return address box in the return address corner. Zoom to **Full Page** so you can see the entire panel at one time. Be careful of the no-print zone of your printer. (WordPerfect may refuse to put the box too close to the edge of the paper.)

3. Create the second Text box and key the information. Rotate the box, and position it approximately where the address label would be applied if the brochure was going to be mailed. (This box provides additional advertising if the brochures are distributed without address labels.)

Panel 6: Figure 31-6

1. Create four vertical graphics lines of decreasing width for the design at the left. Make them full height.

2. Choose a color that matches one of the colors in the college logo for the vertical lines.

3. Simply tab to the starting location for the text on the page. Vary the fonts and formatting to make the text inviting and readable.

4. At the bottom, use the **bbc.wpg** graphics image again. Size it so it looks good.

5. When you finish, save your work again, this time as **brochure 31-7 xxx**.

6. Go back and check each panel for accuracy. Zoom to **Full Page** to look at the two pages from a distance to make sure everything fits and looks good.

7. Print your finished brochure on two separate pages and close the file. Congratulations on a job well done!

FIGURE 31-5
Information for Panel 5

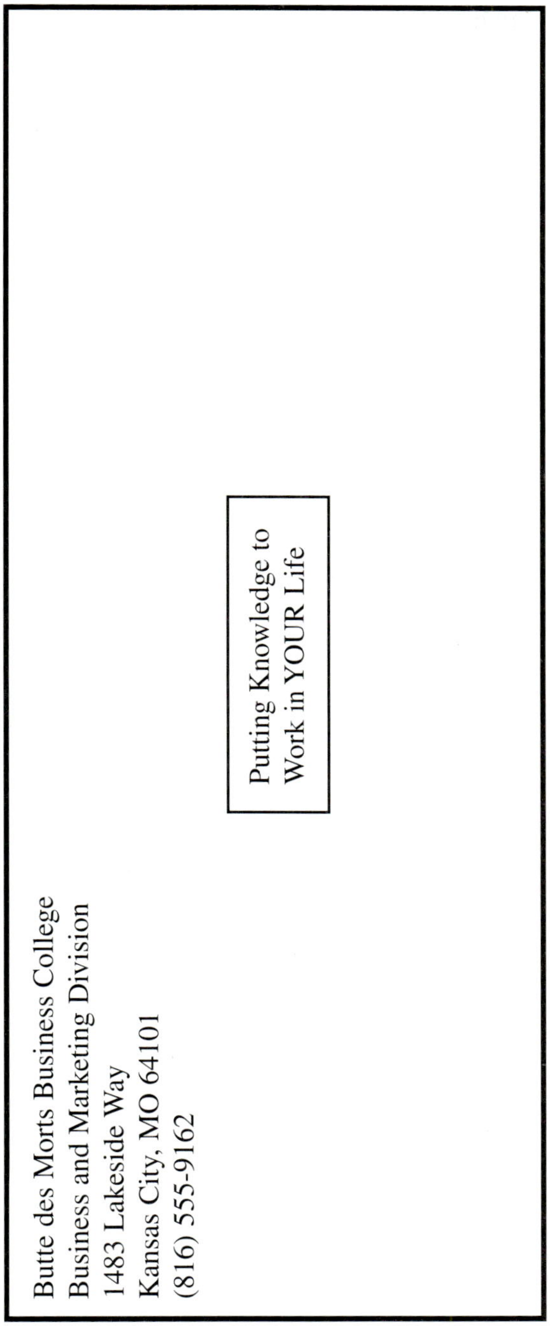

FIGURE 31-6
Information for Panel 6

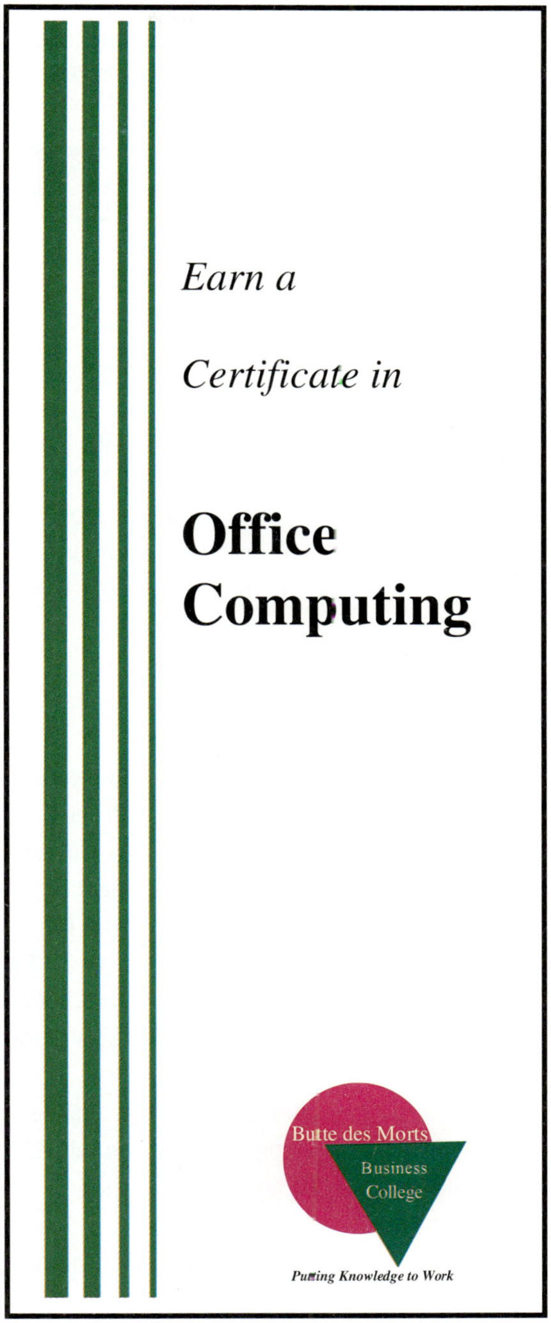

Putting Knowledge to
Work in YOUR Life

Butte des Morts Business College
Business and Marketing Division
1483 Lakeside Way
Kansas City, MO 64101
(816) 555-9162

Earn a

Certificate in

**Office
Computing**

Butte des Morts
Business
College

Putting Knowledge to Work

NOTE:

When you create a brochure such as this one, the finished product will be printed on both sides of a sheet of paper. If you are having multiple copies produced, the original pages should NOT be printed back-to-back for the print shop because the type on one side might show through in the duplication process. Instead, print on separate sheets of paper.

507

Business Card

Now let's create your own business card for Gaillardia Garden Supply. This will give you practice so you can create one for yourself in the project at the end of the lesson.

STEP-BY-STEP 31.8

1. Look at Figure 31-7. It is a simple business card for Gaillardia Garden Supply. Note that it has three parts.

2. Open the **Format** menu and choose **Labels**. Click **Laser** and scroll through the list until you find **Avery 5371**. Along the way, you might notice that a number of other business card labels have been included.

3. Add the following parts of the business card and format them as follows:

   a. The **rose.wpg** graphics image that you used for this company on the Web page. Size the image so it is small and position it in the upper right corner (not too close to the edge—you have plenty of room). Attach the image to **Page** so it stays in place when you reproduce the business card. Use **Flip** so the rose is facing the center of the card.

   b. Your name and business title for the company. Simply tab from the left edge for these two lines. Format them attractively.

   c. The company name, address, and phone numbers. Those lines are centered in Figure 31-7, with the two phone numbers separated by several spaces using the space bar. Perhaps you can come up with an arrangement you like better.

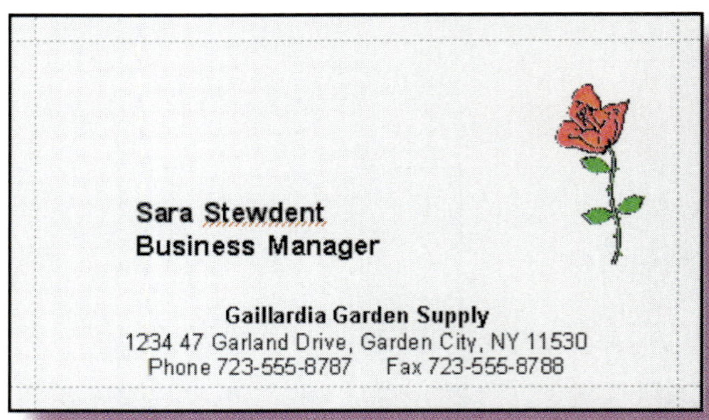

FIGURE 31-7
Gaillardia Business Card

4. Check your work carefully, and save the card as **card form xxx**.

5. Open the **Tools** menu, choose **Merge**, and then choose **Perform Merge**. Set Data source to **None**. Click the **Options** button and tell WordPerfect to make **9** copies of the card.

6. Complete the merge. Save the file as **card 31-8 xxx**. Press **Enter** to position the insertion point on the last card on the page. Add some space and insert the Path and Filename code.

7. Print your lovely business cards and close the file, saving your work again as you close. Close the form document.

Summary

You produced some attractive documents in this lesson, and you discovered that it wasn't especially difficult! You learned a few things, too. In this lesson you learned that:

- WordPerfect has templates for the creation of brochures and business cards.

- A brochure can be created using Landscape orientation and Divide Page.

- When entering the information for the brochure, you key the text and enter graphics images and lines in the normal manner.

- Business cards can easily be created using one of the Avery label formats.

- Text and images can be added to the business card form, and you can make multiple copies with the Merge process.

LESSON 31 REVIEW QUESTIONS

FILL IN THE BLANKS

Complete each of the following statements by writing your answer in the blank provided. All of these statements will relate to the Step-by-Step exercises you completed in this lesson.

1. In Panel 1 you opened the Format menu, chose Page and Page Setup, and then clicked the ______________________ tab before choosing Landscape.

2. Still in Panel 1, you clicked the ______________________ tab, chose Divide Page, and chose 3 columns with 1 row.

3. You were advised to use ______________________ regularly to see the results of your work.

4. In Panel 4 the sections listing the course names are a single-cell table filled with ______________________ fill.

5. The return address in Panel 5 does not have lines surrounding it because it is a ______________________ box.

6. You had to rotate the box styles ______________________ in Panel 5.

7. Business cards can easily be created using one of the Avery ______________________ formats.

(continued on next page)

TRUE/FALSE

Circle the T if the statement is true. Circle the F if it is false.

T   F   **8.** You can make multiple copies of a business card form with the Merge process.

T   F   **9.** WordPerfect has templates for the creation of brochures and business cards.

T   F   **10.** During the standard installation of WordPerfect, most of the templates are loaded.

LESSON 31 PROJECT

PROJECT 31A

Create a business card for Pierce Jameson, Dean of Business at Butte des Morts Business College. Use the Avery 5371 label for your business card.

Get the address of the college from the return address on the brochure. Use the **bbc.wpg** logo somewhere on the card. (Remember to attach it to the Page.) You may also choose to use one or two vertical lines to add interest to the card. Be creative!

When you finish, save your card form as **proj31 card form xxx**. Use Merge to fill up the page with business cards except the last one. Save your card as **bbc proj31 xxx** and put the Path and Filename code on the last card. Print the page of cards and close all files, saving again as you close. (In real life, of course, you would merge all ten cards and print multiple copies on your printer.)

PROJECT 31B

Complete one of the following two personalized projects:

1.   Create a business card for yourself or someone you know who could use one. If you can't find Clipart to use on the card, use vertical or horizontal lines to give it interest, or create some image using the Draw program (like the Butte des Morts Business College logo you used in this program).

2.   Create a six-panel brochure for some school or community event. Browse the Graphics and Clipart images to find one that fits your needs. Use TextArt, if you'd like, to design decorative text for your brochure.

When you finish, save your completed project as **proj31b xxx**. Identify it with the Path and Filename code, print the project, and close it. Submit your work to your instructor.

CRITICAL THINKING ACTIVITY

You have just completed a six-panel brochure and printed it back-to-back. When you tried making multiple copies on the office copier, the text from the back side showed through to the front. How can you correct this?

Looking Ahead . . .

Congratulations! You've almost finished your last unit. You have only one lesson to go. You've been doing a great job of learning all of the WordPerfect features that have been introduced. Some have been lots of fun. Others have been a little more difficult. In all likelihood, you've learned about a few features that you can't see any use for.

Depending on where you work and what you do with WordPerfect when you finish your training, you probably will NOT use all of the features you've learned. That's fine. At least you know about the features so you can come back and review if you ever find a need for them.

That brings up another point. Will you remember everything you've learned? Probably not. Nobody can remember all of the WordPerfect features, especially when you get to some of the more complicated applications. At that point, you need a good reference. The Quick Reference at the end of this text might be the reference you need. Perhaps the entire textbook will be the reference you will take with you when you go on the job.

It is important that you continue to learn and to be flexible. In all likelihood, when you get your first office job, you'll be asked to use a different version of WordPerfect or even a different word processing program. That's fine, too. Because you have such a good basic understanding of text processing using WordPerfect, you can carry your knowledge of what the program CAN do over to the new program or different version. Then it's up to you to find the way to do it. That's flexibility, and it is one of the prerequisites for success on the job.

Now you're ready for Lesson 32. In this lesson you will be applying many of the skills you have acquired up to this point. By the time you finish Unit 8, you will be able to call yourself a WordPerfect expert! Good luck!

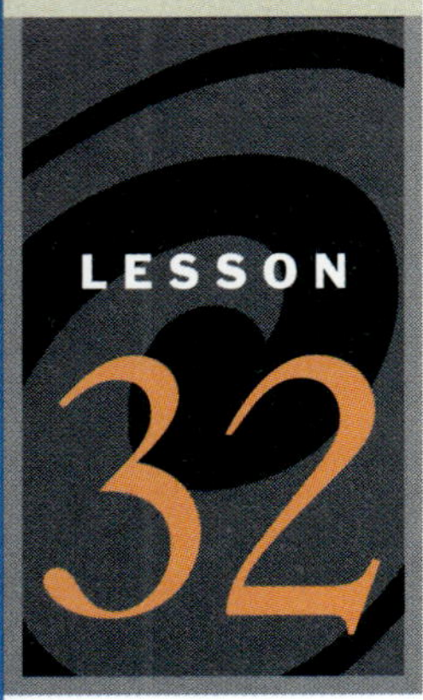

DESIGNING A NEWSLETTER

Upon completion of this lesson, you will be able to:

- Create a newsletter template.
- Prepare the styles for the template.
- Use the template to assemble the newsletter.

Estimated Time: 2½ hours

When you design a newsletter, you should pay special attention to the top portion of the first page of the newsletter. As with a newspaper, that top portion is called a *masthead*. The masthead should be the same from one issue of the publication to the next. The masthead gives the newsletter a "look" of consistency so your readers will be comfortable with it.

Other parts of the "look" include headers, footers, columns, etc. For consistency, you will create a template named **newsty** containing styles for the formatting of the newsletter.

WordPerfect has a template that sets up a newsletter. As in the case of the brochures and business cards, we'll bypass the WordPerfect template (you can explore it as needed) and create one of our own.

Creating the Template

We'll begin by telling WordPerfect we're going to create a template. Then we'll create the styles for the template. Remember that when you are working in the Styles Editor dialog box, most of your choices must be made from the menus in this dialog box. Choices may not be made from the Toolbar or Property Bar. Also, when you are in the Styles Editor dialog box, you may work by looking at a preview of the "document" or by looking at the codes. The Reveal Codes check box at the bottom of the Styles Editor dialog box allows you to move back and forth between those two views as you work.

A Home Page contains text, graphics, and links to other Internet resources. The information on a Home Page is related to a particular topic, such as finance or medical care.

STEP-BY-STEP ⟹ 32.1

1. In a new document window, choose **File** and then **New From Project**. Choose the **WordPerfect Document** group.

2. Click the **Options** button and choose **Create WP Template**. Note the prompts on the Template Toolbar that is now displayed.

3. Open the **File** menu. Choose **Document**, and then choose **Current Document Style**. Set all four margins at **0.60"** and close the Styles Editor dialog box.

4. Use **Save As** to save the template as **a:newsty xxx**. For the description, key **Newsletter Format** and choose the **Publish** category from the list at the bottom.

Now that you have established the newsletter template, you can start adding parts. We'll create a style for the masthead, a style for a header to appear on all pages except the first, and a style for a footer.

STEP-BY-STEP ⟹ 32.2

1. With your **newsty** template showing in the window, open the **Format** menu and choose **Styles** to display the Style List dialog box.

2. Click **Create**. For the name, key **masthead**. For *Description*, key **Masthead for Newsletter**. Set Type at **Document (open)**.

3. Click the *Contents* box. Working from the **Format** menu in the Styles Editor dialog box, choose **Widow/Orphan**.

4. Select or deselect the check box for Reveal Codes at the bottom of the window, depending on whether you want to see formatted text or codes. In the *Contents* box, add a code to create a footer as follows:

   a. Tell WordPerfect that you would like to create Footer A.

   b. In the Footer window, choose the **Arial 10-pt.** font.

   c. The footer will be two lines long. Set Justification at **Center**.

   d. Key the text illustrated in Figure 32-1. For the bullets, use bullet **4,0**.

   e. Notice the scroll buttons at the right on the Property Bar in the Styles Editor. (It's too long to fit in the dialog box.) Click the down arrow to see the rest of the tools and click the **Close** button.

FIGURE 32-1
Text for the Footer

```
                    Kapaa Publisher
        44 Hilo Road • Kapaa, HI 96746 • 808-555-8733
```

FIGURE 32-2
Text for the Header

```
    HOOK,  LINE,  &  SINKER ━━━━━━━━━━━━━━━━━━        2
```

(continued on next page)

5. Continuing in the Styles Editor dialog box, create a header that will appear on the second and following pages (when the newsletter is more than two pages long). The header will be a wider version of Figure 32-2, although you probably won't be able to see all of it. Part of the time, you will be working "blind." Follow these criteria for the header:

  a. Click the *Contents* box and choose **Arial 12-pt. Italic**.

  b. Key **HOOK, LINE, & SINKER**. Space once and create a custom line. For Horizontal Position, choose **Set**. Set the length at **5.2"**. Set the thickness using the first style in the second column. Click **OK**.

  c. Press **Alt+F7** for Flush Right.

  d. On the Property Bar, click the **Number** button and choose **Page Number**.

  e. Turn off Italic.

  f. Click **Close** on the Property Bar to return to the Styles Editor dialog box.

6. Tell WordPerfect to **Suppress** the header on the current page.

7. Look at the codes in your **masthead** style. You should see the following codes: [Wid/Orph] [Footer A][Header A][Suppress].

Now that you have completed the header and footer and you have the margins set, let's add the information that will show at the top of the first page. When you finish, the top of your page will look much like Figure 32-3. You'll be using the Property Bar and a variety of dialog boxes for formatting the parts of your newsletter. Unless told otherwise, return to the Styles Editor dialog box after making the settings as directed in each of the dialog boxes.

STEP-BY-STEP 32.3

1. Create a custom line. For Line style, choose the fourth style to the right of *None*. Return to the Styles Editor dialog box and press **Enter** twice.

2. Still in the Styles Editor dialog box with your insertion point following all codes, change to **35-pt. Arial**.

3. Center **HOOK, LINE, & SINKER**. Before pressing **Enter**, change the font size to **12 pt**. Then press **Enter** twice.

4. Create a single-cell table. In the table, change to **10-pt. Arial**. Use **Italic** to key

Published in Kapaa, HI at the left. Flush right the Date code, also in italic. Then turn Italic off.

5. Still in the table, be sure Reveal Codes is deselected at the bottom of the window so you can see part of your table. Set Fill at **10%**. Set the Top, Left, and Right lines at **None**. Set the line at the bottom of the cell at **Heavy** (the first button in the third row).

FIGURE 32-3
Masthead Format

HOOK, LINE, & SINKER

Published in Kapaa, HI   *(Current date)*

6. Press **Ctrl+End** to get out of the table. Then press **Enter** following the table and go to the Columns Define dialog box (Format, Columns). Tell WordPerfect you would like **2 Balanced newspaper** columns. Click **OK**.

7. Go to the Font dialog box and choose any other font. Then choose **Times New Roman**. Choose **11 pt.** (See note below.)

8. Click **OK** to close the Styles Editor dialog box and return to the Style List dialog box.

NOTE:

Sometimes you must make a change in a setting for WordPerfect to enter the setting in the dialog box. Since Times New Roman was already chosen before you got to Step 7, you had to change the setting and then come back to 11 pt. Times New Roman for the setting to be entered.

You're doing well. Your masthead is completed. Now let's create the other styles for the newsletter.

STEP-BY-STEP 32.4

1. In the Style List dialog box, click **Create**. Name the new style **text**. For the description, key **Article Body Text**. The Type for this style should be **Document (open)**.

2. In the *Contents* box, add codes for the style as follows:
   a. Set Justification at **Full**.
   b. Open the **Format** menu, choose **Line**, and choose **Tab Set**. Click the **Repeat Every** check box and change to **0.250"**.
   c. Set **11-pt. Times New Roman**.
   d. Return to the Style List dialog box.

3. In the Style List dialog box, click **Create**. Name the new style **title**. For the description, key **Title of Articles**. The Type for this style should be **Paragraph**.

4. In the *Contents* box, use the following codes to format the article titles:
   a. Set Justification at **Center**.
   b. Set **Bold** and **16-pt. Times New Roman**.
   c. Return to the Style List dialog box.

5. In the Style List dialog box, click **Create**. Name the style **drop cap**. For the description, key **Drop Cap for Beginning of Article**.
   a. Set Type as **Paragraph**.
   b. In the *Contents* box, choose **Drop Cap** from the **Format Paragraph** menu.
   c. For Style (the first button on the Drop Cap Property Bar), choose the third style in the third row.
   d. Return to the Style List dialog box and close it.

6. Click the **Close** button on the Template Property Bar and save the changes. Close the document window.

Assembling the Newsletter

Now that you have the styles in place in your newsletter template, you can use them again and again, whenever the newsletter needs to be produced. Of course, the newsletter template can be fine-tuned if changes need to be made, but you have done the bulk of the work for this project.

The articles you will use in this newsletter have been saved in the student **datafile** folder. Step-by-Step exercise 32.5 lists the steps for assembling the newsletter. Also, some of the articles may have extra space at the top or at the bottom. Make any necessary adjustments so the articles are separated by one blank line.

STEP-BY-STEP 32.5

1. Open the **File** menu. Choose **New from Project**, change to the **Publish** group (top box), and choose **newsty xxx**.

2. Choose **Create**. Choose **Format**, **Styles**, **Masthead**, and **Insert**. Your lovely masthead should appear.

3. Your insertion point will be in the outline for the columns. Open the **Insert** menu and choose **File**. Go to your student **datafile** folder and locate **cat**. Double click to put that article into your newsletter.

4. Press **Ctrl+End** to get to the end of the article. Press **Enter** twice to put some space between the articles. Insert the document named **romance**.

5. Continue adding space between articles and inserting articles until the following four articles have been added to your newsletter: **health**, **mustang**, **ball**, and **golf**. You will end up about a third of the way down the second page, with text in both columns.

6. Return to the first paragraph of the first article. Position the insertion point in the blank line space between the article title and the first line of the article. Choose **text** from your style list. The font size and indents will be adjusted for the entire newsletter.

7. Position the insertion point in the title of the first article. Choose **title** from the style list.

8. Format the other five titles in the same way.

9. Save the newsletter as **hook 32-5 xxx**. Keep it open as you read on.

Your newsletter is beginning to take shape. The articles are in place, and the titles are formatted. If you look carefully, however, you probably noticed that each sentence is followed by two spaces. That's great for business articles—it's not so great for tight columns. We'll fix that. We'll also format the beginning of each article with drop caps and add some graphics images.

STEP-BY-STEP 32.6

1. Position the insertion point at the beginning of the first article. Open the Find and Replace dialog box and key a period and two spaces in the Find box. In the Replace with box, key a period and one space. Click the **Replace All** button.

2. Return the insertion point to the beginning of the first paragraph and delete the tab that indents the paragraph. Open the style list and choose **drop cap**.

3. Go to the beginning of each of the other five articles, delete the tab, and format the first word of the paragraph with the **drop cap** style.

4. Position the insertion point at the beginning of the second paragraph of the first article.
   a. Insert the **limb.wpg** image from the student **datafile** folder.
   b. Display the Image Tools palette and flip the image so the cat's back is toward the left margin.
   c. Move the image so the cat's ear just touches the margin guideline.
   d. Contour the text around the largest side of the image.

5. Position the insertion point at the end of the fourth paragraph of the article about Dwight's car (following the word *garage*).
   a. Insert **mustang.wpg** from the student **datafile** folder.

   b. Size the auto so it is **2"** wide (maintain height proportions).
   c. Contour the text around the auto on the largest side.
   d. Park the car just inside the margin guidelines in the lower right corner of the page (above the footer guideline).

6. Position the insertion point at the end of the newsletter.
   a. Insert **bee.wpg** from the student **datafile** folder.
   b. Flip the image so the bee is facing toward the center of the page.
   c. Size the bee so it's large enough to see but not large enough to be scary.
   d. Contour the text around the image on the largest side.
   e. Position the bee in the lower right corner of the article.
   f. If the text is spacey around the bee, change the Position of the image from *Page* to **Paragraph**.

7. Position the insertion point at the end of the newsletter. Click the **Columns** button on the Toolbar and choose **Discontinue** to turn the columns off. Insert the Path and Filename code, formatted at **9 pt**.

8. Save your newsletter again, this time as **hook 32-6 xxx**. Print it and close it.

Summary

This entire lesson has been about creating a template, complete with styles, to format a newsletter. In this lesson you learned that:

- When you create a template, you begin with a new blank document.

- Styles are used to format parts of a document that are repeated or that need continuity from one publication to the next.

- A template can contain any number of styles.

- When you use the template to begin the document, the styles can be applied to the document parts in the same way that you use styles for a normal document.

- For templates and styles to work, everything must be set up exactly right!

LESSON 32 REVIEW QUESTIONS

WRITTEN QUESTIONS

Write your answers to the following questions as they relate to this lesson, *Designing a Newsletter*.

1. What is the top portion of the newsletter called?

2. Name three other parts of the newsletter that are included to give the newsletter a "look" of consistency.

3. When working in the Styles Editor as you create a template, from where will most of your choices be made?

4. While you are in the Styles Editor dialog box, you may work by looking at what two features, and what allows you to move back and forth between those two views?

5. Where will the headers appear in your newsletter?

6. What WordPerfect feature did you use at the beginning of the first paragraph of each article?

7. What feature did you use to change the two spaces following your sentences to one space?

MATCHING

Write the letter of the term or phrase from Column 2 that best matches the description in Column 1.

Column 1	**Column 2**
_____ **8.** The option chosen from the Publish group used to design your own newsletter template.	**A.** Contour
_____ **9.** The justification you used for the footers.	**B.** Center
_____ **10.** The feature you used to keep the header from showing on the first page.	**C.** Create WP Template
	D. Suppress
	E. Left
	F. New Template-Create

LESSON 32 PROJECT

PROJECT 32A

One thing you might do to add interest to the articles in your newsletter is put some kind of decoration between the articles. The decoration might be one of the "enders" from the **Graphics** Clipart folder. In some newspapers or newsletters, the articles are separated with a simple line. In the next Step-by-Step exercise we'll add one more style to the **newsty.wpt** style. That style may be used to put a wide gray line between the articles.

Since we've already created our document using the template, there is no way to edit the template and have it fix our document automatically. We'll add this style to the newsletter document. Follow along carefully.

1. Open **hook 32-6 xxx**. Save the document as **hook proj32 xxx**.

2. Open the Format menu and choose Styles to open the Style List dialog box. Create a new style named **line**. For the description, key **Dividing Line between Articles**. For Type, choose Document (open).

3. In the *Contents* box, create a custom horizontal line as follows:
   a. For Horizontal Position, choose Left and set the line length at 3.40".
   b. Set the thickness of the line by choosing the last style in the first column of thickness styles (0.060").
   c. Set the color of the line to gray. Choose the first of the two gray colors in the middle of the first row of colors.
   d. Return to the Style List dialog box.

4. Close the Style List dialog box. Position the insertion point at the end of the last paragraph of the first article. Press Enter twice and apply the **line** style from the list of styles.

(continued on next page)

5. Use the same procedure to add space and put the line at the end of each of the articles. (Your car may move to the next page. We'll fix it in the next step.)

6. Zoom to Full Page and move the document in the window so you can see the car.

7. Select the car and drag it to its original location—in the bottom right corner of the first page.

8. Check your document over for appearance and accuracy. When everything looks good, save it again as **hook proj32 xxx**. Print it and keep it open.

PROJECT 32B

Now let's copy the codes to the Windows Clipboard and paste them into the template in edit mode.

1. Open the Style List dialog box. Click to position the highlight on the **line** style. Click the Edit button.

2. Position the insertion point to the left of the code in the *Contents* box. Press F8 to turn on Select. Press the right arrow key to move past the Line code. Press Ctrl+C to copy the code to the Windows Clipboard. Click Cancel and Close to return to your document.

3. Open the File menu, choose New from Project, and highlight the **newsty xxx** template. Choose Edit WP Template from the Options button to take you to the template. Go to the Style List dialog box.

4. Create a new style named **line**. For the description, key **Dividing Line between Articles**. For Type, choose Document (open).

5. Position the insertion point in the *Contents* box. Press Ctrl+V to paste the codes into the box.

6. Click OK or Close to return to your document window. Click the Close Template button and save the changes as you exit. Now your template is ready for use, complete with the dividing line.

CRITICAL THINKING ACTIVITY

Get a copy of a local newsletter from your school, a local service organization, a local utility company, etc. Study the newsletter and write down the "parts" of the newsletter you know how to create using your knowledge of WordPerfect.

FEATURE	MENU CHOICE	KEYBOARD	LESSON
Bar Chart, Create	Insert, Graphics, Chart	—	29
Chart	Insert, Graphics, Chart	—	29
Draw	Insert, Graphics, Draw Picture	—	29
Images, Draw	Insert, Graphics, Draw Picture	—	29
Images, Edit	Insert, Graphics, Draw Picture	—	29
Internet Publisher	File, Internet Publisher	—	30
Keyboard Map	Tools, Settings, Customize, Keyboard	—	30
Pie Chart, Create	Insert, Graphics, Chart	—	29
Web Page	File/New from Project or File, Internet Publisher	—	30

UNIT 8 REVIEW QUESTIONS

FILL IN THE BLANKS

Complete each of the following statements by keying your answer on a separate page. Center the heading, *Unit 8 Review Questions*, followed by a triple space.

1. To select all of the parts of the image at once, open the _____________________ menu and choose Select All.

2. When you choose Rotate in the WordPerfect Draw window, you can identify the _____________________ tools because they are in the middle of the sides.

3. For a _____________________ chart, all of the data must add up to 100 percent.

4. The _____________________ is at the bottom of a chart; the _____________________ is at the side.

5. On a Web page you can tell which items have hypertext links because _____________________ .

(continued on next page)

Key your answers to the following questions. Number your answers and double-space between them. Use complete sentences and good grammar.

6. When you wish to edit a WordPerfect graphics image, how do you get to the editing program without using the menu?

7. When using the WordPerfect Draw program, how do you tell WordPerfect that you want to work with all objects at one time?

8. When you are working in Draw and you put one object on top of another, how do you tell WordPerfect which object should be on top?

9. The abbreviation, HTML, stands for what?

10. WordPerfect offers on-line help for WordPerfect users. That means that if you have a modem and you are connected to a telephone line via a communications network, you can ask questions about the use of software. Open the Help menu and choose Help Online. What service or services are listed in your dialog box? Close the dialog box and return to Help Topics. Read the Help Online section. What are the three links available in the Documentation home page?

UNIT 8 APPLICATIONS

SCANS

Estimated Time: 2 hours

APPLICATION 1

You have been asked to prepare a one-page document about the virtues of adult cereals for distribution to the local consumer-advocate group. A set of statistics was given to you, along with the text for the document. You need to format the document and add two charts to illustrate the data. Following are the particulars:

- The document is in the student **datafile** folder. It is named **cereal**. After opening the document, retrieve your **report style** styles to format the title and the side headings.

- Chart 1: Create a bar chart using the information in Figure APP-1. The figure also contains the title and subtitle for the chart.

- Give Chart 1 a caption. WordPerfect will automatically name it Figure 1. Space once, key a hyphen and a space, and key **Comparison of 1995 and 1996 Prices**.

- Chart 2: Create another bar chart using the information in Figure APP-2.

- Give Chart 2 a caption. Following the Figure 2 caption, put a space, a hyphen, a space, and **Calories in a Cup of Raisin Bran**.

FIGURE APP-1
Data for Chart 1

Leading Cereal Brands		
Cost Per Box		
	1995	1996
KFF	$3.86	$3.34
PGN	$3.42	$2.53
QCC	$3.21	$2.39
RCC	$2.94	$3.18
GMC	$2.49	$2.58

- For Chart 2, include labels at the tops of the bars. Do this by opening the Chart menu, choosing Data Labels, and choosing Outside.

- Size both charts so they are 3" wide. Maintain height proportions. Position them near the references.

- When you finish, save your document as **cereal u8ap1 xxx**. Play your **pf** macro to identify the document, and use Make It Fit, if necessary, to make the document fit on one page.

- Print the document and close it, saving it again with the same name.

APPLICATION 2

Illustrated in Figure APP-3 is a suggested format that you can use to prepare a resume to take as you seek employment. It contains some horizontal and vertical lines to dress up the appearance of the resume. Prepare a resume for yourself that looks somewhat like the one in Figure APP-3.

Vary the locations, shading, and thickness of the lines and the spacing between sections of text, as necessary, to prepare an attractive resume. You may use a table to format this resume, or you may clear all tabs and set a tab stop for the material at the right. Adjust the length of the vertical line so it doesn't bump any of the other lines.

When you finish, save your resume as **resume u8ap2 xxx** and identify it with your **pf** macro.

FIGURE APP-2
Data for Chart 2

Raisin Bran Calories	
PU	253
SA	200
PO	190
KE	170
SF	160

FIGURE APP-3
Sample Resume

SARA STEWDENT
2726 North Bluemound
Menasha, WI 54952
414-555-7890

EMPLOYMENT OBJECTIVE	To be employed as an administrative assistant in a company that uses WordPerfect.
EXPERIENCE	Hug-a-Leg Hosiery Co., Fox Haven, MO Internship position, Administrative Assistant (1995 to present)
	Clara's Computers, Kansas City, MO Part-time Administrative Assistant (1994-1995)
	Schimmelpfennig Schimmelpfennig Krizenesky Hall & Vanderlinden SC, Kansas City, MO High School Co-op Position, Secretarial (1993-1994)
	Singing Pines Girl Scout Camp, Fox Haven, MO Scout Leader and Counselor (1991-1993)
	Leo's Custard Stand, Kansas City, MO Carhop (1991-1993)
EDUCATION	Butte des Morts Business College, Kansas City, MO Administrative Assistant—Information Processing Associate Degree, May 1996
	Fox Haven High School, Fox Haven, MO Graduated in 1994
HOBBIES AND INTERESTS	Scouting, church youth group, sewing, knitting, bicycling, hiking, reading, and gardening
REFERENCES	Available upon request.

Path and Filename code

APPLICATION 3

Look at Figure APP-4. Begin by choosing Landscape orientation. The certificate uses the last Page border in the first row of Fancy borders. Create a certificate for yourself using Figure APP-4 as a guide. You may make adjustments, as necessary, to fit your situation. Size the font face so it looks good. (Choose Landscape orientation and Zoom to Full Page to complete the exercise.)

When you finish, save the certificate as **certificate u8ap3 xxx**. Put the Path and Filename code at the right on the last line of the page. Print your certificate and close it, saving it again with the same name.

FIGURE APP-4
Sample Certificate

APPLICATION 4

Using the **newsty.wpt** template that you created in this lesson and information you gather on your own, create a newsletter, complete with graphics. A one-page newsletter is fine, if you have a limited amount of information or time. Make your newsletter lovely.

When you finish, save the newsletter as **newsletter u8ap4 xxx**. Identify it with the Path and Filename code. Print it, and close it, saving it again with the same name.

It's time once more to delete files and move others. In this case, you will be mostly deleting. Only one of the documents that you created in this unit should be saved for future use. That is the **newsty.wpt** document. Move it to the **Units 7 and 8** folder. Move **cereal u8ap1**, **resume u8ap2**, **certificate u8ap3**, and **newsletter u8ap4** to your **Applications** folder.

Figure APP-5 lists the remaining files you created and saved in this unit. Please delete them.

bbc proj31	crane 29-2	objects 29-5	web1
brochure 31-2	crane 29-3	objects 29-6	web2
brochure 31-7	crane 29-7	pie proj29	web3
card 31-8	hook 32-5	proj31 card form	web4
card form	hook 32-6	proj31b	web5
chart 29-9	hook proj32	proj30	will 30-3

ON-THE-JOB SIMULATION

JOB 22

Occasionally Singing Wheels Tours goes beyond where a bus can go. One of those tours is a yearly trip to Hawaii where guests have an opportunity to visit four of the islands and enjoy many of the activities that have made Hawaii a paradise in the Pacific.

Set the Page Size and Divide Page for a six-panel brochure. Set the margins at 0.4" on all sides. Insert **Hawaii** from the student **datafile** folder. Save the file in the **Singing Wheels** folder as **Hawaii job22 xxx**. The prestored text should fit in the first five panels. Use **bird-of-paradise.wpg** (from the student **datafile** folder) in a couple of places on the first three panels, if you'd like, to break up the continuous text. Remember that you can use Image Tools to flip it over so it looks toward the page if you position it at the right. A few other images that you might decide you'd like to use in your brochure are **Hula.wpg**, **beach.wpg**, and **Island.wpg**. They are also in the student **datafile** folder.

On the fifth panel, put the company name and return address in the return address location and rotate it 90 degrees. In the address label position, put another Text box containing **ALOHA** in a 30-pt. font, with the Path and Filename code under it in a very small font.

Panel 6 should contain the information that is provided in Figure J15. Size the fonts and arrange the text attractively. Include some art to dress up the panel.

```
       FOUR-ISLAND
     HAWAIIAN HOLIDAY
         14 Days
   January 13-26, (year)


 Visit Maui, Kauai, Oahu,
and the Big Island of Hawaii
```

(continued on next page)

Figures J16 and J17 show you in miniature what your finished brochure might look like. In the illustration, the **Island.wpg** graphics image was taken to the Draw program, and the sun was deleted. Then the cropping tool in the Image Tools palette was used to get rid of most of the soil at the base of the tree. Try your hand at customizing some of the images.

When you finish, check your work for accuracy. Then check it for appearance. Is it attractive? When it looks good, print it and save it again in the **Singing Wheels** folder as **Hawaii job22 xxx**.

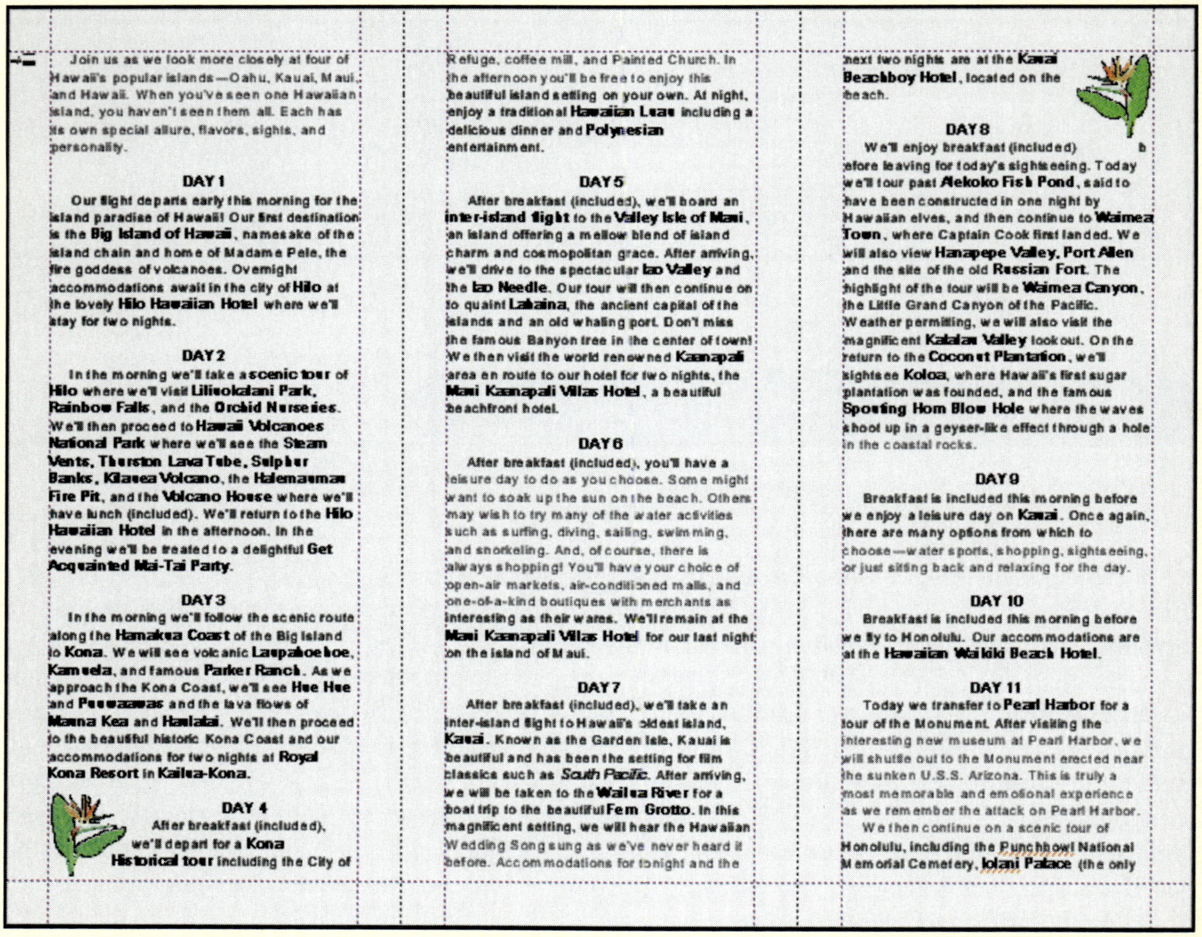

Join us as we look more closely at four of Hawaii's popular islands—Oahu, Kauai, Maui, and Hawaii. When you've seen one Hawaiian island, you haven't seen them all. Each has its own special allure, flavors, sights, and personality.

DAY 1

Our flight departs early this morning for the island paradise of Hawaii! Our first destination is the **Big Island of Hawaii**, namesake of the island chain and home of Madame Pele, the fire goddess of volcanoes. Overnight accommodations await in the city of **Hilo** at the lovely **Hilo Hawaiian Hotel** where we'll stay for two nights.

DAY 2

In the morning we'll take a scenic tour of **Hilo** where we'll visit **Liliuokalani Park, Rainbow Falls**, and the **Orchid Nurseries**. We'll then proceed to **Hawaii Volcanoes National Park** where we'll see the **Steam Vents, Thurston Lava Tube, Sulphur Banks, Kilauea Volcano**, the **Halemaumau Fire Pit**, and the **Volcano House** where we'll have lunch (included). We'll return to the **Hilo Hawaiian Hotel** in the afternoon. In the evening we'll be treated to a delightful **Get Acquainted Mai-Tai Party**.

DAY 3

In the morning we'll follow the scenic route along the **Hamakua Coast** of the Big Island to **Kona**. We will see volcanic **Laupahoehoe, Kamuela**, and famous **Parker Ranch**. As we approach the Kona Coast, we'll see **Hue Hue** and **Puuwaawaa** and the lava flows of **Mauna Kea** and **Haulalai**. We'll then proceed to the beautiful historic Kona Coast and our accommodations for two nights at **Royal Kona Resort** in **Kailua-Kona**.

DAY 4

After breakfast (included), we'll depart for a **Kona Historical tour** including the City of Refuge, coffee mill, and Painted Church. In the afternoon you'll be free to enjoy this beautiful island setting on your own. At night, enjoy a traditional **Hawaiian Luau** including a delicious dinner and **Polynesian** entertainment.

DAY 5

After breakfast (included), we'll board an **inter-island flight** to the **Valley Isle of Maui**, an island offering a mellow blend of island charm and cosmopolitan grace. After arriving, we'll drive to the spectacular **Iao Valley** and the **Iao Needle**. Our tour will then continue on to quaint **Lahaina**, the ancient capital of the islands and an old whaling port. Don't miss the famous Banyon tree in the center of town! We then visit the world renowned **Kaanapali** area en route to our hotel for two nights, the **Maui Kaanapali Villas Hotel**, a beautiful beachfront hotel.

DAY 6

After breakfast (included), you'll have a leisure day to do as you choose. Some might want to soak up the sun on the beach. Others may wish to try many of the water activities such as surfing, diving, sailing, swimming, and snorkeling. And, of course, there is always shopping! You'll have your choice of open-air markets, air-conditioned malls, and one-of-a-kind boutiques with merchants as interesting as their wares. We'll remain at the **Maui Kaanapali Villas Hotel** for our last night on the island of Maui.

DAY 7

After breakfast (included), we'll take an inter-island flight to Hawaii's oldest island, **Kauai**. Known as the Garden Isle, Kauai is beautiful and has been the setting for film classics such as *South Pacific*. After arriving, we will be taken to the **Wailua River** for a boat trip to the beautiful **Fern Grotto**. In this magnificent setting, we will hear the Hawaiian Wedding Song sung as we've never heard it before. Accommodations for tonight and the next two nights are at the **Kauai Beachboy Hotel**, located on the beach.

DAY 8

We'll enjoy breakfast (included) before leaving for today's sightseeing. Today we'll tour past **Alekoko Fish Pond**, said to have been constructed in one night by Hawaiian elves, and then continue to **Waimea Town**, where Captain Cook first landed. We will also view **Hanapepe Valley, Port Allen** and the site of the old **Russian Fort**. The highlight of the tour will be **Waimea Canyon**, the Little Grand Canyon of the Pacific. Weather permitting, we will also visit the magnificent **Kalalau Valley** lookout. On the return to the **Coconut Plantation**, we'll sightsee **Koloa**, where Hawaii's first sugar plantation was founded, and the famous **Spouting Horn Blow Hole** where the waves shoot up in a geyser-like effect through a hole in the coastal rocks.

DAY 9

Breakfast is included this morning before we enjoy a leisure day on **Kauai**. Once again, there are many options from which to choose—water sports, shopping, sightseeing, or just sitting back and relaxing for the day.

DAY 10

Breakfast is included this morning before we fly to Honolulu. Our accommodations are at the **Hawaiian Waikiki Beach Hotel**.

DAY 11

Today we transfer to **Pearl Harbor** for a tour of the Monument. After visiting the interesting new museum at Pearl Harbor, we will shuttle out to the Monument erected near the sunken U.S.S. Arizona. This is truly a most memorable and emotional experience as we remember the attack on Pearl Harbor. We then continue on a scenic tour of Honolulu, including the **Punchbowl** National Memorial Cemetery, **Iolani Palace** (the only

Royal Palace on American soil), the **Hawaii State Capitol, China Town**, the historic **Kawaiaho Church**, and much, much more. Later we'll return to our hotel where the rest of the afternoon and evening are yours to enjoy at your leisure.

DAY 12

Our final day in Hawaii will be spent at your own pace. This is an excellent chance to rest, shop, or enjoy area sightseeing. Oahu is the site of Hawaii's state capital and business center, and is the most populated island in the chain. You can shop in Waikiki or browse through Chinatown's fascinating shops. You might want to walk along the beautiful Honolulu beaches.

DAYS 13-14

Our flight home begins later in the day as we fly through the night, arriving on the mainland early the next morning.

TOUR COST PER PERSON:

Double Occupancy	$2095.00
Single Occupancy	$2645.00

- Tour cost subject to change due to fluctuating airfare.
- $200 deposit per person due within ten days of making reservation.
- Balance due approximately 60 days prior to departure. The exact date will be indicated on the deposit receipt.

ALOHA
A Singing Wheels Hawaii tour '22 xxx

Singing Wheels Tours
77 Travel Way
Neenah, WI 54956
414-555-7777

FOUR-ISLAND HAWAIIAN HOLIDAY

14 Days
January 13-26, 199x

Visit Maui, Kauai, Oahu, and the Big Island of Hawaii

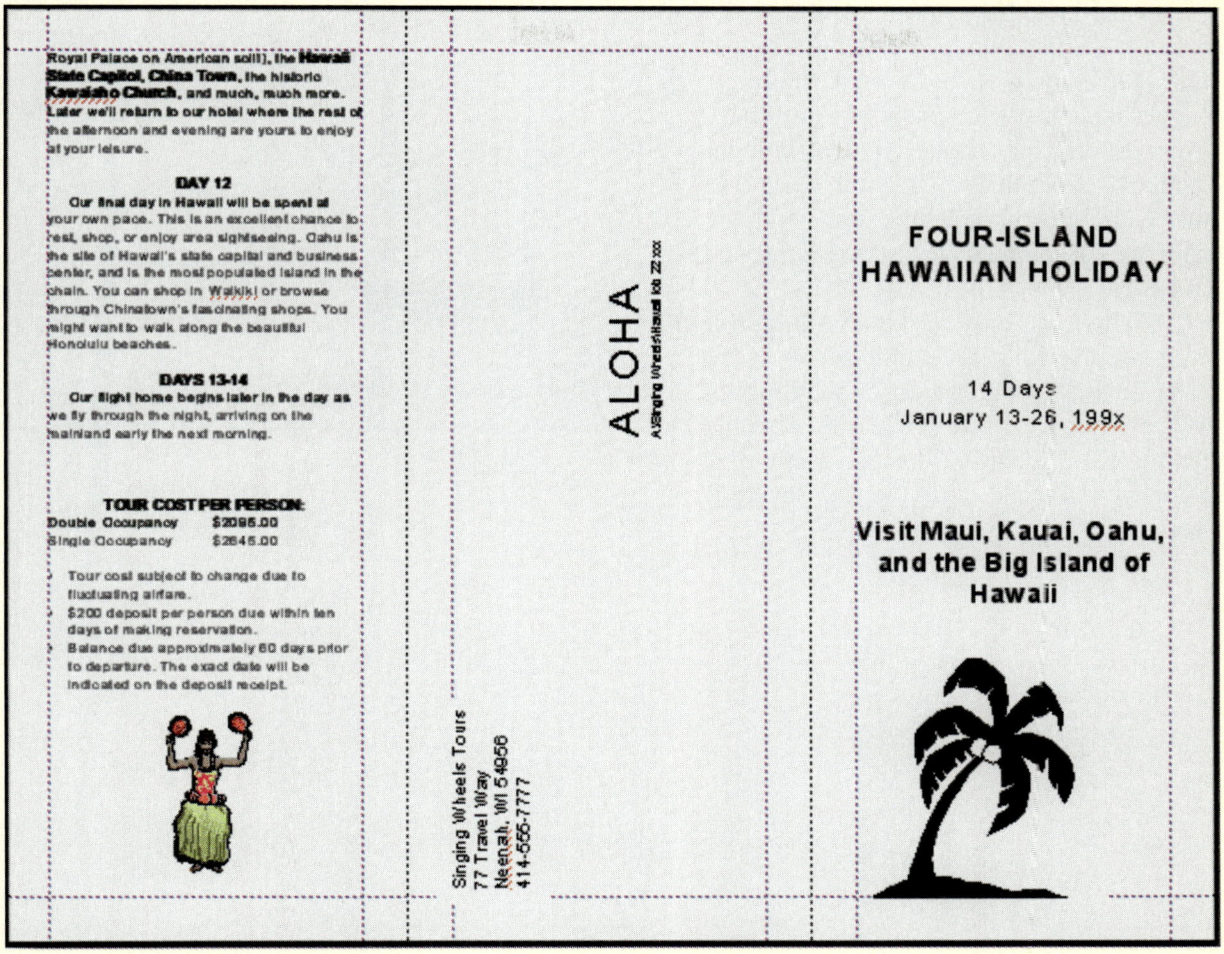

Also included in the student **datafile** folder is an image called **bus.wpg**. Use that image on a business card for Mr. Becker. A suggested card is illustrated in Figure J18. You can probably create one that is more attractive. Note that the bus was taken into the WordPerfect Draw program, and the name of the company was added to the side of the bus.

When you have designed a beautiful card, use Merge to make nine copies of the card. Save the merged cards in the **Singing Wheels** folder as **bus job23 xxx**. Use the tenth card to identify your file. Print your business cards and close the file, saving it again.

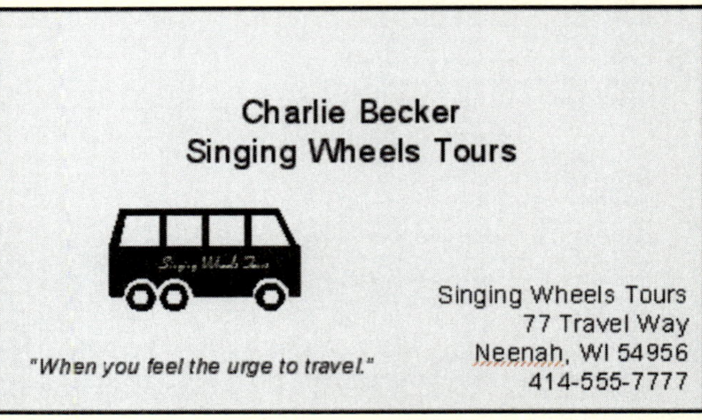

CAPSTONE SIMULATION

Introduction

At a recent meeting of the Eden Chapter of the International Association of Administrative Professionals™ (IAAP™), your group decided to put together an educational seminar for the membership and other local administrative support staff. You eagerly (?) volunteered to use your considerable WordPerfect skills to help with this project.

In this simulation you will be preparing the necessary paperwork for the seminar planning committee. Your work will usually be as a result of the planning meetings held by the seminar committee. The committee meets the first Tuesday of each month, beginning in September of the current year. Nearer the seminar date, additional meetings may be held. The seminar is scheduled for the following April 1.

It will be your responsibility to prepare the advertising materials, assemble the list of those to be invited to the seminar, distribute those materials to the people on the list, follow up on the contacts with prospective speakers, make arrangements for seminar attendees to receive continuing education credits (CEUs) for the seminar, handle the registrations as they are received, prepare an agenda for each meeting, and prepare the seminar program, among other things.

The committee has already made arrangements to hold the seminar at the Adams Hotel at 276 Wisconsin Avenue in downtown Eden, Wisconsin, ZIP code 53019. While most of the people who attend the seminar will be from the Eden area, Eve Warren, manager of the Adams, has agreed to set aside a block of rooms for seminar attendees who wish to spend a night or two. The hotel ballrooms have been reserved for the day of the seminar, along with a series of smaller meeting rooms to be used for the concurrent sessions.

This simulation begins with a training manual that includes the names of the committee members with whom you will be working and their responsibilities on the committee. Also included in the training manual is a copy of a sample letter on Eden IAAP Chapter letterhead and a copy of an agenda prepared using Eden IAAP Chapter letterhead. The training manual provides general instructions about preparation of the documents in the simulation and the saving of those documents on your disk.

Training Manual

Your work will be coming to you from the members of the seminar committee. Here are their names, responsibilities, and phone numbers.

Georgia Gates, CPS ....Chairperson 555-3778
Becky Brown ....Speakers 555-7812
Joanne Dahleen...................Food and Flowers 555-6234
Rhonda Evers, CPS..............Registration 555-3791
Francis Fiera, CPS ....Facilities...555-0665
Tica Hayes ....Corporate Sponsors.........................555-2468
Jacob Jensen, CPS ....Publicity 555-2871
Erv Thorson, CPS ....Seminar Treasurer..........................555-2276
Whitney Woo, CPS ....Exhibitors and Door Prizes..............555-1357
(your name).........................Word Processing Specialist...............555-____

The Letterhead

The Eden IAAP Chapter letterhead is available for your use as a document that you can retrieve each time you need the letterhead. It is called **letterhead** and is in the **datafile** folder. Each time you wish to use it, open it and press Ctrl+End to move the insertion point below the letterhead.

If you are feeling really entrepreneurial, you might try your hand at creating a letterhead template for your work with the Eden IAAP Chapter. Maybe you could get extra credit for doing that.

The Student Datafile Folder

Included in the **datafile** folder are a number of the formats needed for the simulation. The document formats could be created "from scratch," but most of them are forms. Re-creating them would be time-consuming.

Also included in the **datafile** folder are two IAAP logos. The IAAP graphics used in this simulation are **IAAPColr.jpg** and **iaap-oneline.wpg**. These logos will be used in various jobs.[1]

Letters

All letters should be prepared in block style on the Eden IAAP Chapter letterhead. If possible, use a 12-pt. proportional font with serifs. The date should be a double space below the letterhead, and it should be followed with at least a quadruple space. In the case of very short letters, adjust the position of the letter on the page by leaving more space between the date and the inside address. The one-inch default margins are fine. Study Figure Sim-1 to see how your letters should look.

---

[1] The IAAP logos used in this simulation are the registered trademarks of International Association of Administrative Professionals™. They are to be used exclusively for the purposes of this simulation. Any other use of the logos requires written permission from International Association of Administrative Professionals, 10502 N.W. Ambassador Drive, P.O. Box 20404, Kansas City, MO 64195-0404.

International Association of
Administrative Professionals™

Eden Chapter
P.O. Box 552
Eden, WI 53019

(Current date)

Ms. Susan Fenner, Ph.D.
Education and Professional Development Manager
International Association of Administrative Professionals
10502 NW Ambassador Drive
P.O. Box 20404
Kansas City, MO 64195-0404

Dear Dr. Fenner:

Enclosed is the application for Continuing Education Units for the participants of our spring seminar on April 1, (year). As you can see, we are expecting about 100 secretaries and administrative assistants to attend.

I am enclosing $15 for 100 blank certificates along with the required $20 processing fee. Also enclosed are brief biographical sketches on the keynote speaker as well as the six speakers for the concurrent sessions and a copy of the seminar brochure.

Plans are going well for our seminar. We are proud to be offering it with IAAP endorsement since any affiliation with IAAP adds credibility and substance to a seminar.

Sincerely,

Rhonda Evers, Program Committee

Enclosures

The assumption is that you will be using a #10 envelope (9.5" x 4"). If possible (depending on your printing capabilities), prepare an envelope for each letter. Use paper cut to size for the envelopes. The text for the return address is included in the instructions for Job 4. Check with your instructor to see if you can keep the return address in the address book on your computer for the other times you'll be needing it. (It might interfere with the work of other students.)

If you can't do envelopes at all because of printer limitations, choose the label form from Lesson 20 that works best with your printer. Then prepare labels for all of the mailings.

Agendas

You will prepare an agenda for each meeting within the week following the preceding meeting. A copy of a sample agenda is provided in Figure Sim-2. In real life, you would make a copy of the agenda for each member of the committee and mail those agendas to the committee members. For this simulation, you need to prepare only one copy of the agenda. Place a small check mark to the left of the name of Seminar Chairperson Georgia Gates to identify that copy of the agenda as hers. Then prepare an envelope to mail the agenda to Georgia at 399 Apple Valley Road, Eden, Wisconsin 53019.

Each agenda will have a copy of the budget attached. You will prepare the budget form as one of your first jobs. Each month it will be your responsibility to enter the figures provided to you by Seminar Treasurer Erv Thorson and update the budget.

Other Documents

Most of the remaining documents are one-of-a-kind documents. Many of them are forms. You may use any of the methods you have learned to create your forms. Keep in mind as you create the forms that you will probably be expected to fill in the blanks on some of those forms. Create the forms in such a way that you won't struggle later on when you are expected to complete them.

You will also be working with Merge. Letters to speakers, exhibitors, corporate sponsors, and prospective participants will be prepared using a form file and a data file. In some cases, the same data file will be merged with more than one form letter.

Saving Your Documents

You will be creating quite a number of documents in planning this seminar. If you wish to save them on your data disk, you may want to get another disk just for the simulation. If you prepare all of the documents in the simulation, they will more than fill a 1.44Mb disk.

Keep your disk from your previous training handy, because you'll be using a number of the form files created in your WordPerfect training.

You will probably wish to name the documents by job. For example, in the first job you will be creating an audiovisual checklist. On the job you would probably name it something about "audiovisual." For the simulation it would probably be easier to call it **job1**. Some jobs require the preparation of a number of documents. You can expand the document name to **job1a** or **job1b** for those jobs.

General

Your work will be divided into months. The work for each month will come from source documents given to you by other members of the committee. The source documents begin on page 539. Most work will be as a result of the committee meetings held that month. The jobs are all numbered consecutively, although some of them require the preparation of more than one document (such as the merge applications). Instructions are provided for most of the jobs, either in the preliminary materials for that month's work or on the source document for the job itself.

**Eden Chapter
P.O. Box 552
Eden, WI 53019**

AGENDA FOR OCTOBER

Spring Seminar Planning Committee

1. Approve arranged speakers—Becky

2. Approve AV checklist—Francis

3. Approve location for seminar, reserve rooms—Francis

4. Determine size of mailing; get names—Rhonda

5. Discuss the CEU (5 hours of instruction = .5 ceu)—Rhonda

6. Plan brochure—Jacob

7. Discuss budget—Erv

Attachment: Budget

Copies to:

Georgia Gates, CPS	Chairperson	555-3778
Becky Brown	Speakers	555-7812
Joanne Dahleen	Food and Flowers	555-6234
Rhonda Evers, CPS	Registration	555-3791
Francis Fiera, CPS	Facilities	555-0665
Tica Hayes	Corporate Sponsors	555-2468
Jacob Jensen, CPS	Publicity	555-2871
Erv Thorson, CPS	Seminar Treasurer	555-2276
Whitney Woo, CPS	Exhibitors and Door Prizes	555-1357

Much of the work will come to you in either rough draft or handwritten format. Be sure to study the information for each job in the monthly preliminary materials, as well as on the source document itself, before beginning the job.

Check your calendar to find out the date for the day after each of the committee meetings. It will usually be the second Wednesday of the month. Use that date for any work you prepare for that month.

You may prepare just one copy of each of the forms and documents. If you were taking the prepared documents to the committee meetings, you would make a copy for each of the committee members.

In real life, you would have plenty of other office work to keep you busy without the complications of helping to prepare for the IAAP seminar. In this simulation all you have to concentrate on is efficiently preparing documents that you would be proud to mail. Remember that you are a member of a professional group. Be professional in your work!

September

The September organizational meeting of the Eden IAAP seminar committee was a very productive meeting. The following topics were discussed and preliminary plans were made:

- The date of the seminar—April 1, (year)

- The location for the seminar—the Adams Hotel in Eden

- Possible speakers and topics for the seminar

- The way the program for the day will be arranged

- Corporate sponsors who might help defray seminar expenses

- Audiovisual and room arrangement needs of the speakers

- The budget for the seminar

Job 1. Prepare a rough draft of the audiovisual (AV) checklist to be sent to the speakers. Put it on Eden Chapter letterhead. (See the Training Manual for instructions.) Use Newspaper Columns or Balanced Newspaper Columns for the items. Turn off Columns for the last section.

Use check boxes for the major items in the checklist. Short graphics lines or underline can be used for the secondary items. Turn on Underline Tabs and use Alt+F7 for the section at the bottom so the lines end evenly at the right of the page.

Job 2. Prepare a rough draft of the budget form on plain paper. For the lines, clear all tabs. Using the Ruler Bar, set Left tabs at 5.75", 6.5", 6.75", and 7.5". Set Decimal tabs at 6.25" and 7.25". Drag the Right margin to 0.875". Use Underline Tabs and create lines from 5.75" to 6.5" and 6.75" to 7.5". Copy the first pair of lines to the Clipboard, and paste them in place for the other items.

Job 3. This is a rough draft working program. Keep it simple.

Job 4. This job has several parts. Read through all of the instructions for this job before beginning.

Part a. Key the list of recipients of the letter (the data file). Arrange the data file so that you can address the contact person (as Ms. Aronstein, for example) in the salutation. The records will look like the sample in Figure Sim-3.

You'll find one small problem in this job. Eden is a really little town. Can you find a number that HAS to be an error in the list?

FIGURE SIM-3

```
Ms. ENDFIELD
Andrea ENDFIELD
Aronstein ENDFIELD
Andrea's Auto Body ENDFIELD
35 South Main ENDFIELD
Allentown, WI ENDFIELD
53002 ENDFIELD
ENDRECORD
```

Before saving the data file, sort it by ZIP code and alphabetically by last name within the ZIP code groups.

Part b. Use the Eden Chapter letterhead and prepare the form file. The mailing address portion of the form file might look like Figure Sim-4.

Part c. Use Merge to prepare the letters. If you can, prepare envelopes to accompany the letters. The envelopes should have POSTNET bar codes. Position the bar code below the address.

Include the information in Figure Sim-5 as the return address. Change the font of the return address to Arial 10-pt.

If you can't prepare envelopes, set up a merge to prepare labels to accompany the letters.

Part d. Finally, sort the data file again so the companies are in alphabetic order and merge it with a simple form file that creates a list. Remember that in order to keep each record from printing on a separate sheet of paper you must click the Options button in the Perform Merge dialog box and deselect the option that separates the merged documents with a page break.

Arrange the list into two columns. Use Block Protect to keep any records from being broken from one column to the next.

Job 5. Open the budget sheet from Job 2. Click to position the insertion point at the Decimal tab and fill in the amounts on the dollar planner. Attach the budget to the October agenda.

October

Job 6. Revise the AV checklist according to the instructions.

Job 7. Use Merge to send confirmation letters to the speakers for the concurrent sessions. Print only the first letter for the group of speakers at 11:00 and the first letter for the group of speakers at 1:15. Attach the AV checklist, the envelope, and the format for handout layouts to each letter.

The letter to Ms. Cavness will be a two-page letter. Be sure to include the proper second-page heading (see Figure Sim-6) and the other appropriate attachments. Ms. Cavness will speak on two topics: "Thriving in a Changing World" and "Beyond the Office."

Job 8. This is a confirmation letter for the hotel. Don't forget the envelope.

Job 9. The seminar committee has decided to send the local ZIP codes to IAAP headquarters and pay IAAP for labels to mail brochures to all of the IAAP members in the immediate area. Rhonda has been in touch with IAAP, and about 200 labels will be sent by IAAP at a cost of $140.

Members of your local group have been bringing in names and addresses of non-IAAP members in the area who should be invited to the seminar. Those names and addresses are saved in the **datafile** folder as **iaap-job9a**. You need to add a few more names and addresses to the list and keep the list for the preparation of the labels next month.

FIGURE SIM-4

```
FIELD(title) FIELD(firstname) FIELD(lastname)
FIELD(company)
FIELD(street)
FIELD(city, state) FIELD(ZIP code)
```

FIGURE SIM-5

```
Eden Chapter
International Association of
Administrative Professionals
P.O. Box 552
Eden, WI 53019
```

FIGURE SIM-6

```
Ms. Cassie Cavness
Page 2
(date)
```

Job 10. This job is to produce the brochure to be mailed to prospective seminar participants. A suggested solution is illustrated and includes all the information you'll need for the brochure. This solution assumes you can use an 8-pt. font. It is set up so that the brochure can be folded into thirds, and the registration portion is on the flip side of the address portion. This setup leaves the seminar participant with all of the pertinent information about the seminar after the registration portion has been torn off and returned. (Perhaps the Make It Fit tool will be helpful in this job.)

If you can't squeeze the entire brochure onto two pages (to be printed back-to-back), you might wish to spread it out and put the registration portion on a separate half-sheet that will be inserted into the brochure for mailing. Use your imagination and your considerable design skills to create a brochure that's better looking than the suggested solution.

The *International Association of Administrative Professionals* line is **iaap-oneline.wpg**. The IAAP symbol is **IAAPColr.jpg**. Both of the trademarks are in the **datafile** folder. Perhaps you can use the symbol somewhere on each side of your brochure.

Job 11. Make this agenda like the one for October. (Can you use the September agenda and just change the month and the items in the list?)

November

Job 12. This is a letter to the corporate sponsors who have agreed to help with the seminar. You may use the same data file as the one you prepared in Job 4. You will need to delete the sponsors who are not participating and add a field listing the donation. After merging the letters, look at the paragraph where the donation is listed. You might need to edit the paragraph so it makes better sense. Prepare the envelopes (or labels) and submit one of each.

Job 13. Revise the brochure according to the instructions given. Then transmit it to the printer with Jacob's letter.

Job 14. Create a Graphics box that is 2 inches wide and 3 inches tall. Space the information for the advertisement attractively in that box. You will need to choose a small font.

Job 15. Look in your **Units 5 and 6** folder and find the form file named **ticket xxx.frm**. Open it and customize it so that you can use it to merge with the list you created in Job 9 for mailing the brochures. Be sure to save the form file with a different name than the original in Lesson 20 so that one will remain in case you need it again.

Sort the list of prospective seminar participants by ZIP code order before merging the data file with the form file. Print all of the labels.

Job 16. Prepare the agenda for the December meeting. Take a few minutes to key the numbers for the Budget into the first column. They are not likely to change. It's the Actual amounts that will change. You may write in the few that Erv has supplied.

December

Job 17. Create an invitation to join IAAP. Rhonda has done all the work for you!

Job 18. A blank of the application for CEUs is saved in the **datafile** folder. The name of it is **application-ceu**. Open the form and fill in the information by clicking on the line at the location for information, turning on Typeover, and keying the information. Key the letter to IAAP and include the biographies of the speakers. Don't forget an envelope.

Job 19. This is a simple Merge application to send letters to possible exhibitors. Use the same format for your form and data files that you've been using up to this point. Consistency will save you time.

Job 20. This is the seminar program. A suggested solution is provided for you, although you will probably be able to improve on the design. You may use the **IAAPColr.jpg** graphic that is in the **datafile** folder for the IAAP logo.

If you can print in the landscape orientation, use narrower margins and the subdivided page feature. You can even use booklet printing, if you wish. If your printer only prints in portrait orientation, set your margins so you have the same page size as the illustration but print each page on a separate sheet of paper. Then you can tape the pages together for printing purposes.

If your smallest font is too large to include all the information in the suggested solution, edit some of the text in the program to make it fit.

Job 21. This is the agenda for the January meeting.

January

Job 22. A suggested evaluation form is illustrated as a source document. Use the **IAAPColr.jpg** logo that's in the **datafile** folder somewhere at the top of the form.

Job 23. Proofread and correct the seminar program before printing the final copy to be sent to the printer.

Job 24. Jobs 24 and 25 require you to prepare tickets for the concurrent sessions and for the luncheon. They also involve preparing name tags for the seminar participants.

One of the better ways to do these jobs is to use the format with which you created tickets in Lesson 20. That format was saved as **ticket xxx.frm**. If you remember, it enabled you to create a set number of tickets with numbering on the tickets. Since a limited number of people may attend some of the sessions, it will be nice to have the tickets numbered.

Your job will be to open **ticket xxx.frm** or return to Lesson 20 and prepare it again. This time, however, you will prepare a copy of it for the luncheon and one for each of the eight concurrent sessions. When you merge each one of them, you will end up with enough tickets for each session. We'll begin with the luncheon tickets.

Open **ticket xxx.frm** and change the number in the {FORNEXT} line at the top from *23* to **120**. Delete the *IMAGE SPECIALISTS* portion of the line. Key the information to be included on the luncheon ticket. At the bottom, remove the *Ticket* portion but leave the {VARIABLE}x code. The tickets will be numbered, but no words will accompany the numbers. Save the revised form as **job24.frm**.

Use Merge to create the tickets. Remember that there is no data file. Print only one page of the tickets. To print only one page of the tickets, you must tell WordPerfect to print pages 1-8 because there are eight "pages" on one sheet of paper.

Job 25. Use **ticket xxx.frm** for the tickets to the concurrent sessions. Prepare 20 tickets each for Sessions 1 and 5. Prepare 35 tickets each for the other six sessions. Remember to set the number in the {FORNEXT} line at the top of each ticket and key the correct information for the sessions. Print the first "page" of tickets for each of the sessions.

Job 26. Now open **badge xxx.frm**. Create a name tag with a very large (bold, if you'd like) first name in a sans serif font and a smaller last name. Use a normal size font for the city, state, and ZIP code. For this job, merge the name tag form file with the list of prospective registrants you created in Job 9. You'll have about 55 name tags. Print only the first eight of them.

Job 27. Complete the agenda for the February meeting.

February

Jobs 28 through **31.** Since you did such nice work with these, all that's left is to check them over carefully for accuracy and print the final copies. If the copies you've already printed are perfect, you need not reprint them.

Job 32. This is the agenda for the March meeting.

March

Jobs 33 and **34.** Work again with the shortened list of registrants you created in Job 9. Some of these people are registered for the hands-on sessions, and some didn't get their registrations in before the sessions were filled. Letters must be sent to all four groups of registrants. In Job 34 you can add a sixth field to the records in the data file to fill in the name of the replacement sessions.

Job 35. Send the letter to Ms. Cavness. You may need to use Make It Fit to get the entire letter on one page. (It isn't long enough to justify a second page.)

Job 36. Send the letter to the speakers. You can use the same data file you used in Job 7.

Job 37. In creating the posters, use a sans serif font. This will be easier to read than a serif font. If you can't make big letters like requested, do the best you can. DO NOT clip the letters from the newspaper in ransom note fashion!! Print all eight posters.

Job 38. The function sheet needed for this job is saved in the **datafile** folder with the name **function**. You may open it, print it, and fill it out by hand for the hands-on sessions as directed. Francis has already completed the function sheets for the rest of the sessions.

Job 39. You can probably use the original list of vendors for this job. Delete those not exhibiting and add an extra field for the table number(s).

Job 40. This is the agenda for the April meeting.

April

Job 41. Open the evaluation and key the numbers that are circled near the appropriate numerals on the evaluation. Fill in only this one form. Actually, there would be a form for each of the seven sessions.

Job 42. The participant list needs to be completed, listing all 98 of the seminar participants. The participant list is saved in the **datafile** folder as **partic**. Open it and fill out only one page of the list with the information provided by Rhonda.

Job 43. Complete the Attendance Report. It is saved in the **datafile** folder with the name **attend**. You can get most of the information for the Attendance Report from the CEU application completed in Job 18. The number assigned by headquarters is WI4419.

Job 1

AUDIOVISUAL EQUIPMENT CHECKLIST

☐ 35 mm slide projector
— no. carousels needed
— remote control
— extension cord
— extra bulb

☐ screen
— wall mount
— portable
— stage screen

☐ tape recorder

☐ videocassette player and
monitor
— 3/4 inch
— 1/2 inch

☐ flip chart
— no. of pads needed
— markers

☐ easel

☐ board
— white board
— markers
— chalkboard
— chalk
— eraser

☐ pointer
☐ lectern with microphone
☐ podium with microphone
☐ lavalier microphone
— 20-foot cord
— 50-foot cord

☐ standing microphone
— number needed

☐ table microphones
— number needed

☐ overhead projector
— acetate roll needed
— blank transparencies
— water soluble markers
— extension cord
— extra bulb

☐ display panel
— extension cord

Please make a rough draft on Eden letterhead. Glad to have you on the committee! Thanks — Francis

Other: (please describe fully) ____________________________

____

Job 2

DOLLAR PLANNER

	Budget	Actual

<u>Revenue</u>

Target Number of Attendees @ $40 each
Contributions from Corporate Sponsors
Target Profit

<u>Expenses</u>

<u>Speakers</u>

Keynote — fee and transportation
Session Speakers — honorariums and transportation
Lodging and meals
Reproduction of speaker materials
   (consider who might donate this service)
Communication expenses (calls, mailings, etc.)
Complimentary registrations (actual costs)

<u>Publicity</u>

Advertising
Brochure layout, printing, and mailing
Door prizes (consider donations)

<u>Facilities</u>

Meeting room charges (check for hidden costs)
AV equipment (rental or setup costs)
Breaks
Seminar luncheon
Executive committee dinner

<u>Participant Materials</u>

Printing of handouts
Program
Folders
Name tags
Pencil & paper (may be provided by hotel)

<u>CEU Costs</u>

Certificates
$20 processing fee
Recording costs ($1.50 per person)

Job 3

Proposed Program

8:00 a.m. – 9:00 a.m.
~~8 a.m. to 9 a.m.~~

    Registration; Continental Breakfast; Office Products
    Exhibits

9:00
~~9~~ a.m. ~~to~~ 10:30 a.m.
    Keynote Speaker

10:30 a.m. ~~to~~ 11:00 a.m.
    Break; Office Products Exhibits

11:00 a.m. ~~to~~ 12:15 p.m.
    Four concurrent sessions (one hands-on)

          – 1:00
12:15 ~~to 1~~ p.m.
    Luncheon (included in cost of registration); Office
    Products Exhibits

1:15 p.m. ~~to~~ 2:30 p.m.
    Four concurrent sessions (one hands-on)

2:30 p.m. ~~to~~ 2:45 p.m.
    Break

2:45 p.m. ~~to~~ 4:00 p.m.
    Closing Session—Keynote speaker; wrap-up and evaluation;
    CEU certificates; door prizes.

Job 4

The Eden, Wisconsin, chapter of International Association of Administrative
Professionals is holding an educational seminar at the Adams Hotel in Eden on
Saturday, April 1. It is anticipated that as many as 100 secretaries and administrative
assistants from Eden and the surrounding area will attend the seminar.

As a representative of the program committee, I have been asked to contact you to see
if (company) would be willing to help with our seminar. You can help by donating
some of your products to be used as door prizes. Or your company could underwrite
the expense of bringing in some of our speakers. Our keynote speaker is from the
DePere area and a graduate of St. Norbert College. Another way you could help us
would be by making a cash donation with which we may purchase door prizes or pay
some of the costs of the seminar, such as the printing of handouts and program
brochures.

Please let me know by November 1 whether (company) would be able to contribute in
some way to our seminar. You may call me at 555-2468 between 8 a.m. and 4 p.m. on
weekdays.

Mr. Stephen Paulus
Paulus & Paulus, Inc.
3380 Apple Valley Road
Eden, WI 53019

Mrs. Phyllis Jegen
Cross Construction
76 Green Bay Avenue
Eden, WI 53019

Miss Lucia Stumpf
Lucia's Lighting
3211 Apple Valley Road
Eden, WI 53019

Mr. David Warren
Sumner Publishing Company
327 Winding Way
Oostburg, WI 53070

Mr. George Dehart
Geohart Electronic Assembly
945 N. Main Street
Waupun, WI 53963

Mr. Wendell Lokensgard
Wendell's Marina
P.O. Box 332
Fond du Lac, WI 54936

Miss Debbie Davies
Designs & Signs
113 Apple Valley Road
Eden, WI 53013

Mrs. Jan Juckem
Jan's Leather Loft
76 First Street
Lomira, WI 54048

Ms. Amy Arnold
Kettle Valley Bank
12 Main Street
Eden, WI 53019

Mr. Gaardner Gumbly
Gamble & Gumbly
437 Third Street
Eden, WI 53019

Ms. Andrea Aronstein
Andrea's Auto Body
35 South Main
Allentown, WI 53002

Mr. Charles Cook
Cook's Ceramics
548 Carver Lane
Campellsport, WI 53010

Miss Susi Stachowicz
Spartica Sports
549 Wisconsin Avenue
Kewaskum, WI 53040

Ms. Signe Nelson
Nelson's Shrub Nursery
1338 South Oregon Street
North Fond du Lac, WI 54937

Miss Carla Covioux
Custom Catering
669 California Lane
New Holstein, WI 53061

Mr. Tony Condon
Condon, Condon, and Hill
              Investment Counseling
340 North Main
Eden, WI 53019

Please send this letter to all of these businesses. Use Eden Chapter letterhead. Also, please arrange the businesses in alphabetic order (by business name) and print them in a list so we can use it at our meetings.

Oh yes – for the mailing, the businesses must be in ZIP code order. Is it easier to sort before you print?

Thanks!
Jica

Job 4 (continued)

Mr. Stevenson Sommers
Bank of Eden
42 North Main
Eden, WI 53019

Miss Francie Kraus
Speed King Mfg. Co.
3904 Apple Valley Road
Eden, WI 53019

Ms. Dinah Delwich
Delwich's Sandwiches
761 South Main
Eden, WI 53019

Mr. Joseph French
Columbia Crystal Works
1290 Oak Street
Oakfield, WI 53065

Ms. Marcy Missling
Proctor Pharmaceuticals
1408 Random Lake Lane
West Bend, WI 53095

Mrs. Jeanette Archer
Lionhart Leather Works
65 Limekiln Lane
West Bend, WI 53095

Mr. Phillip Pearson
Crockery Cookery
110 East Main Street
West Bend, WI 53095

Mrs. Jackie Jones
Moraine Pest Service
34 Third Avenue
Kewaskum, WI 53040

Dr. Donald Dudley
Dudley's Dude Ranch
446 Oakridge Road
Greenbush, WI 53026

Mrs. Paula Preston
Preston Press
568 Eighth Street
Eden, WI 53019

Miss Polly Peckham
Peckham Photography
43 Pilgrim Parkway
Plymouth, WI 53073

Ms. Georgie Gregg
Georgie's Greenhouses
667 Apple Valley Road
Eden, WI 53019

Mrs. Norma Steiner
Workers Health
3448 Shogun Road
DePere, WI 54115

Mr. Ramsey Hart
Rivermoor Paper Company
418 River Street
DePere, WI 54115

Job 5

AGENDA FOR OCTOBER
Spring Seminar Planning Committee

1. Approve arranged speakers - Becky
2. Approve AV checklist - Francis
3. Approve location for seminar; reserve rooms - Francis
4. Determine size of mailing; get names - Rhonda
5. Discuss the CEU (5 hrs. of instruction = .5 CEU) - Rhonda
6. Plan brochure - Jacob
7. Discuss budget - Erv

Please put this agenda on Eden letterhead. At the bottom, include the names, committee responsibilities, and phone numbers of the committee members.

i.e.   Georgia Gates . . . . . Chairperson 555-3778

Erv has penciled the budget numbers into your dollar planner. They are shown on the next page. Print a copy of the planner. Write in the numbers. Then make a copy to attach to each member's copy of the agenda.

Thanks,
Georgia

Attachment: Budget

Job 5 (continued)

DOLLAR PLANNER

Revenue	Budget	Actual
Target Number of Attendees @ $40 each	4000	
Contributions from Corporate Sponsors	1500	
Target Profit	1000	

Expenses		

Speakers	Budget	Actual
Keynote—fee and transportation	850	
Session Speakers—honorariums and transportation	400	
Lodging and meals	300	
Reproduction of speaker materials		
(consider who might donate this service)	25	
Communication expenses (calls, mailings, etc.)	50	
Complimentary registrations (actual costs)	50	

Publicity	Budget	Actual
Advertising	50	
Brochure layout, printing, and mailing	300	
Door prizes (consider donations)	100	

Facilities	Budget	Actual
Meeting room charges (check for hidden costs)	200	
AV equipment (rental or setup costs)	200	
Breaks	200	
Seminar luncheon	1000	
Executive committee dinner	200	

Participant Materials	Budget	Actual
Printing of handouts	50	
Program	100	
Folders	100	
Name Tags	25	
Pencil & paper (may be provided by hotel)	?	

CEU Costs	Budget	Actual
Certificates	15	15
$20 processing fee	20	20
Recording costs ($1.50 per person)	150	

Job 6

AUDIOVISUAL EQUIPMENT CHECKLIST

☐ 35 mm slide projector	☐ pointer
___ no. carousels needed	
___ remote control	☐ lectern with microphone
___ extension cord	
___ extra bulb	☐ podium with microphone
☐ screen	☐ lavalier microphone
___ wall mount	___ 20-foot cord
___ portable	___ 50-foot cord
___ stage screen	
	☐ standing microphone
☐ tape recorder	___ number needed
☐ videocassette player and monitor	☐ table microphones
___ ¾ inch	___ number needed
___ ½ inch	
	☐ overhead projector
☐ flip chart	___ acetate roll needed
___ no. of pads needed	___ blank transparencies
___ markers	___ water soluble markers
	___ extension cord
☐ easel	___ extra bulb
☐ board	☐ display panel
___ whiteboard	___ extension cord
___ markers	
___ chalkboard	
___ chalk	
___ eraser	

[handwritten: move this section to the top of Column 2]

[handwritten: make this the first section]

[handwritten: Add that statement at the bottom, please. Francis]

Other: (please describe fully) ____

____

____

[handwritten: Please draw a diagram of the preferred room layout on the back of this page.]

Job 7

Dear (speaker):

The members of the Eden Chapter of International Association of Administrative
Professionals are pleased that you have agreed to speak at the seminar to be held on Saturday,
April 1, (year), at the Adams Hotel in Eden. We expect about 100 secretaries with a wide
range of experiences, backgrounds, and years in the office. Your presentation on (name of
presentation in quotes) should be well received at this time. In the past few years, the
profession has undergone some major changes. We hope you will be able to help us meet
the challenges of these changes.

Your session will begin promptly at (time) and end at (time). As agreed upon, you will
personalize your presentation for us and will provide handouts for participants. The Eden
IAAP Chapter will gladly reproduce the handouts if photo-ready copy is sent to me by
February 15. Enclosed you will find a suggested format for the note-taking portion of your
seminar handouts. Also enclosed is the seminar information that should appear at the top of
the first page of your handouts or on a cover sheet.

Please send a vita and a brief description. Our committee of your session within the next two weeks for the
seminar brochure and program. Also, please return the enclosed AV checklist by October 31
and indicate your preferred room setup. IAAP will handle securing the equipment and
working with the hotel facilities staff.

As agreed, an honorarium of (amount) will be paid to you immediately after the seminar. On behalf of the
program committee, I would like to extend my thanks to you for agreeing to be part of our
seminar. I am looking forward to working with you. If you have any questions, please call
me at 555-7812.

Sincerely,

Becky Brown, Program Committee
Enclosures

Please send this letter to the speakers on the attached list. I've noted the time for the presentation and the amount of the honorarium for each. Oh, yes — please make the corrections shown in the copy above. Thanks, Becky

Mrs. Marcia Carlson
Mt. Calvary College   11:00 - 12:15 $50.⁰⁰
661 Third Street
Mt. Calvary, WI 53057
Presentation: "Beautiful Documents with Report Publisher"

Mr. Bret Bowers
The Humor Shoppe   11:00 - 12:15 $50.⁰⁰
7839 Silver Spring
Milwaukee, WI 53229
Presentation: "Surviving the Workday with Humor"

Dr. Terry Lawrence
UW Milwaukee $ 50.⁰⁰
1266 Downer Street   11:00 - 12:15
Milwaukee, WI 53228
Presentation: "Teamwork: Enhancing Office Productivity"

Mr. Roy St. Claire
Computer Heaven $50.⁰⁰
88 South Main Street   1:15 - 2:30
Eden, WI 53019
Presentation: "Perfect Documents with WordPerfect"

Miss Patricia K. Morin
PK Morin & Associates
12445 Bluemound Drive   1:15 - 2:30 $ 50.⁰⁰
Milwaukee, WI 53226
Presentation: "Rightsizing: How It Could Affect Your Job!"

Ms. Lucia Lewin
Eden County Social
    Services Department   1:15 - 2:30 $ 50.⁰⁰
481 Apple Valley Road
Eden, WI 53019
Presentation: "A Balancing Act: Home & Career"

Job 7 *(continued)*

Ms. Cassie Cavness
Cavness Training & Consulting
34 Casa Loma Lane
Los Carlos, CA 94337

Dear Ms. Cavness:

The members of the Eden Chapter of International Association of Administrative Professionals are pleased that you have agreed to speak at the seminar to be held on Saturday, April 1, (year), at the Adams Hotel in Eden, Wisconsin. We expect about 100 secretaries with a wide range of experiences, backgrounds, and years in the office. Your presentations "Thriving in a Changing World" and "Beyond the Office" should be well received at this time. In the past few years, the profession has undergone some major changes. We know you will be able to help us meet the challenges of these changes.

As agreed, you will speak to the entire group of seminar attendants from 9 a.m. to 10:30 and again from 2:45 to 3:45 p.m. We have also scheduled you for two 1¼-hour breakout sessions beginning at 11:00 a.m. and 1:15 p.m. where you will work with smaller groups of participants. As agreed upon, you will personalize your presentation for us and will provide handouts for participants. The Eden IAAP Chapter will gladly reproduce the handouts if photo-ready copy is sent to me by February 15. Enclosed you will find a suggested format for the note-taking portion of your seminar handouts. Also enclosed is the seminar information that should appear at the top of the first page of your handouts or on a cover sheet.

The Eden IAAP Chapter will arrange for your round-trip flight between Los Carlos and Milwaukee. Please let us know your airline preference and your wishes regarding the time of travel as soon as possible so that tickets can be purchased. Our committee will arrange for your lodging.

Please send a vita and a brief description of your session within the next two weeks for the seminar brochure and program. Also, please return the enclosed AV checklist by October 31 and indicate your preferred room setup. Our committee will handle securing the equipment and working with the hotel facilities staff.

Your fee of $500 will be paid to you immediately after the seminar. On behalf of the program committee, I welcome you to the Eden IAAP Chapter seminar as a speaker and look forward to working with you. If you have any questions, please call me at 414-555-7812.

Sincerely,

Becky Brown, Program Committee
Enclosures

To appear on the cover sheet or on the first page of your handouts:

Eden Chapter
International Association of Administrative Professionals™
P.O. Box 552
Eden, WI 53019

Include somewhere near the beginning of the handout:

TITLE OF PRESENTATION or TOPIC

Objectives:
1.
2.
3.
4.
5.

Possible format for note-taking forms:

(Statement of fact or discussion from your presentation.)

____

____

____

(Another statement of fact or discussion from your presentation.)

____

____

____

etc.

Job 8

Ms. Eve Warren, Manager
276 Wisconsin Avenue ← Adams Hotel
Eden, WI 53019

Dear Ms. Warren:

This letter is a confirmation of our discussion last week regarding the use of the convention facilities at the Adams Hotel for the International Association of Administrative Professionals seminar to be hosted by the Eden Chapter on Saturday, April 1, (year).

Our group would like the Abel and Cain Ballrooms joined and set up with round tables for our opening session at 9:00 a.m. and the closing session at 2:45 p.m. We would also like lunch to be served in that conference area.

We will need four smaller meeting rooms (approximately 30 people each) for our concurrent sessions at 11:00 a.m. and 1:15 p.m. When registrations have been received, we will complete the function sheets for those rooms.

Our plan is to have a number of exhibits set up around the sides of the ballrooms. Exhibitors will want to have their exhibits in place by 8:00 a.m. so they are ready for the registration time. Exhibits will be removed while the ballrooms are being cleared after lunch.

Committee member Joanne Dahleen will contact you in January regarding food and beverages for the breaks and for the luncheon.

On behalf of the committee, we are looking forward to working with you for our spring seminar. If you have any questions, you can reach me weekdays at 555-0665.

Sincerely,

Francis Fiera, Program Committee

Please make the corrections indicated and send this letter to Mrs. Warren. Thanks — Francis

Miss Kris Gehrke
28 W. Kamps Street
Eden, WI 53019

Mrs. Mattie Cavers
437 Henry Street
Theresa, WI 53091

Ms. Margot Christian
432 E. Forest Avenue
Oakfield, WI 53065

Mrs. Elyda Crisman
4391 Ann Street
Fond du Lac, WI 54935

Ms. Connie Erickson
4732 Henry Street
West Bend, WI 53095

Miss Nancy Thiex
4691 Apple Valley Road
Eden, WI 53019

Please add these people to the list that has already been keyed. This is for the brochure mailing.
Thanks! Rhonda

Job 10

Eden Chapter

International Association of Administrative Professionals™

presents . . .

A one-day spring educational seminar
at the Adams Hotel in Eden, Wisconsin
Saturday, April 1, (year), from 8 am to 4 pm

Registration Cost   Optional: IAAP Discount Hotel Rate $49

      Non-Members $45

      IAAP Members $40   .5 CEU for seminar attendance

      Early Registration (before Feb 15) $40   Reservations are due by March 1, (year).

Cancellation requests must be made in writing and postmarked no later than March 10 to qualify for a refund.

International Association of
Administrative Professionals™

Secretaries & Administrative Assistants

Devote one day to becoming all that you can be!
Learn to have the right attitude and to do your work better
so that you feel better about yourself.
You can also increase your chances for advancement.

You are invited to come to the seminar . . .

Eden Chapter
International Association of Administrative Professionals
P.O. Box 552
Eden, WI 53019

IAAP SPRING SEMINAR SCHEDULE

8:00 am	- 9:00 am	Registration; Continental Breakfast; Office Products Exhibits
9:00 am	- 10:30 am	Keynote Speaker - Cassie Cavness **"Thriving in a Changing World"** Listen and learn as this well-known speaker presents ten techniques for meeting the challenges of today's office. Become an innovator rather than a follower as you develop career enhancement strategies made possible by your own personal development.
10:30 am	- 11:00 am	Break; Office Products Exhibits
11:00 am	- 12:15 pm	Concurrent Sessions

#1 Hands-on Workshop A*: "Beautiful Documents with Report Publisher." Join Marcia Carlson as you learn to use Report Publisher® to enhance the appearance and readability of the documents you create every day on the job—reports, letters, memos, contracts, and tabular material. (Two people per computer. Limited to the first 20 registrants.)

#2 "Beyond the Office" by Cassie Cavness. Get more tips from the keynote speaker about enhancing your life by extending the principles learned in the morning session into your daily life.

#3 "Surviving the Workday with Humor" by Bret Bowers, humor aficionado. Learn appropriate ways to apply the positive power of humor and creativity to some of the not-so-humorous things that happen in the course of the day's work.

#4 "Teamwork: Enhancing Office Productivity" by Terry Lawrence, Professor of Supervisory Management at the University of Wisconsin, Milwaukee. In this era of changes of office management, many companies have begun organizing workers into self-directed teams. Learn how you can become a good team player without sacrificing productivity.

12:15 pm	-1:00 pm	Luncheon (Included in cost of registration); Office Products Exhibits
1:15 pm	-2:30 pm	Concurrent Sessions

#1 Hands-on Workshop B*: Perfect Documents with WordPerfect." Join Roy St. Claire as you learn to use WordPerfect® to enhance the appearance and readability of the documents you create every day on the job—reports, letters, contracts, and tabular material. (Two people per computer. Limited to the first 20 registrants.)

#2 "Beyond the Office" by Cassie Cavness. (This session is a repeat of Session #2 at 11 am.)

#3 "Rightsizing: How It Could Affect Your Job!" by Patricia K. Morin of PKMorin & Associates, Milwaukee. Ms. Morin has consulted with dozens of companies as they make changes in management style in an effort to keep costs in line with revenues. In this session you will learn how being prepared for management changes can actually give you an edge in getting the promotion for which you've been preparing.

#4 "A Balancing Act: Home & Career" by Lucia Lewin of the Eden County Social Services Department. Ms. Lewin has had extensive experience in working with families who are suffering from the problems that may be the result of mothers having to work. Learn techniques for dealing with children and/or spouse in making the home a place where everyone WANTS to return after a stressful day at work or in school.

2:30 pm	- 2:45 pm	Break
2:45 pm	- 4:00 pm	Closing Session by Cassie Cavness; Wrap-up and Evaluation; CEU Certificates; Door Prizes

*Computers and software graciously provided and set up by Computer Heaven of Eden, Wisconsin

Spring Seminar Registration
Eden Chapter—International Association of Administrative Professionals
Saturday, April 1, (year) Registration from 8 to 9 am at the Adams Hotel in Eden, Wisconsin

Name _____________________ Home Phone _____________________ IAAP Member ID Number _____________

Address _____________________________ City _________________ State _________ ZIP ___________

Social Security # (Required for CEU Credit) _____________________ Enclosed check or money order for $ ___________

Concurrent Sessions: Number your first and second choices (1 & 2) for the am sessions and the pm sessions.

Morning Concurrent Sessions

_____ #1 Report Publisher® _____ #3 Humor

_____ #2 Beyond the Office _____ #4 Teamwork

Afternoon Concurrent Sessions

_____ #1 WordPerfect® _____ #3 Rightsizing

_____ #2 Beyond the Office _____ #4 Balancing Home & Career

Mail Registration form by March 1 with check made payable to:
Eden Chapter, International Association of Administrative Professionals
% Rhonda Evers, Program Chairman
P.O. Box 552
Eden, WI 53019

Non-Member Registration Fee	$45
IAAP Member Registration Fee	$40
Non-Member Early-bird Fee	$40
(postmarked by Feb. 15)	

Job 11

AGENDA FOR NOVEMBER

1. Approve brochure (with corrections) – Jacob
2. Authorize printing of brochures – Georgia
3. Determine registration fee – Georgia
4. Discuss results from mailing to corporate sponsors – Tica
5. Review budget – Georgia

(Please prepare and distribute this agenda.
It should be done like the October agenda)
Thanks! Georgia

Our donations from corporate sponsors have been wonderful!
Workers Health is footing the entire bill for our keynote
speaker because she's a St. Norbert alumni. A supporter who
wishes to be anonymous has contributed for advertising, and
a couple of the local printing companys have donated there their
services. What's more, Francis has convinced the manger of the
Adams to provide pins and notepads for all seminar
participants. pens

I've filled in all of these figures on the attached dollar
planner and marked the donations with an asterisk to be
explained in the at the bottom of the form. Those amounts are
included with the cash donations on the Contributions line at
the top. Please key all figures into a dollar planner and
distribute it with the November agenda.

Please forgive this mess. My typewriter at home is broken and
I've lost my eraser.

Thanks!! Erv

Job 11 (continued)

DOLLAR PLANNER

Revenue	Budget	Actual
Target Number of Attendees @ $40 each	4000	
Contributions from Corporate Sponsors	1500	1485
Target Profit	1000	

Expenses

Speakers	Budget	Actual
Keynote—fee and transportation	850	850 ★
Session Speakers—honorariums and transportation	400	
Lodging and meals	300	
Reproduction of speaker materials (consider who might donate this service)	25	
Communication expenses (calls, mailings, etc.)	50	
Complimentary registrations (actual costs)	50	

Publicity	Budget	Actual
Advertising	50	50 ★
Brochure layout, printing, and mailing	300	160 ★
Door prizes (consider donations)	100	

Facilities	Budget	Actual
Meeting room charges (check for hidden costs)	200	
AV equipment (rental or setup costs)	200	
Breaks	200	
Seminar luncheon	1000	
Executive committee dinner	200	

Participant Materials	Budget	Actual
Printing of handouts	50	50 ★
Program	100	
Folders	100	
Name Tags	25	
Pencil & paper (may be provided by hotel)	?	0

CEU Costs	Budget	Actual
Certificates	15	15
$20 processing fee	20	20
Recording costs ($1.50 per person)	150	

★ Expense to be picked up by corporate sponsor

Job 12

The Eden Chapter of the International Association of Administrative Professionals
would like to extend its warmest appreciation to you and to (company name) for being a
sponsor of our spring seminar that is coming up on April 1, (year).

Your gift of (gift—you may need to adjust the sentence to fit the gift—cash, for
example) will help the IAAP chapter to provide seminar participants with something
with which to remember the seminar as well as the good day they had in Eden. In
addition, (company name) will be listed in the seminar program as a seminar sponsor.

The members of the Eden IAAP chapter are fortunate indeed to live and work in a
region where so many of the area businesses are supportive of its activities. Again,
thank you for your participation.

*Please send the letter above to the businesses on the
list below thanking them for their donations. Insert
the item donated in the blank at the beginning of
Paragraph 2.   Thanks! Whitney*

Andrea's Auto Body: a free lube and oil change
Columbia Crystal Works: a pair of crystal candle holders
Condon, Condon, and Hill Investment Counseling: $50
Cook Ceramics: 12 pots for centerpieces
Crockery Cookery: $100
Delwich's Sandwiches: two $5 gift certificates
Geohart's Greenhouses: a 25-percent discount on flowers
Jan's Leather Loft: two billfolds
Kettle Valley Bank: $25
Lionhart Leather Works: a 50-percent discount on a brief case
Paulus & Paulus, Inc.: $50
Peckham Photography: a free sitting for family portrait
Preston Press: free printing and folding of seminar brochures ($160)
Proctor Pharmaceuticals: $50
Speed King Mfg. Co.: $100
Sumner Publishing Company: free duplicating of handouts ($50)
Workers Health: your sponsorship of the keynote speaker
      (transportation and speaking fee) ($850)

Job 13

Please double-check the registration charges on the brochure. They should be $45, $40, and $40.

Also, we've decided to number the afternoon concurrent sessions as a continuation of the morning sessions. Change the afternoon sessions to #5, #6, #7, and #8 in both places on the brochure.

Thanks, Georgia

Attached is a letter to be sent along with the completed brochure to Mrs. Preston at Preston Press. Please get it out this week, if possible.

You may sign my name on the letter and put your initials beside the signature.

Thanks, Jacob

Job 13 *(continued)*

Enclosed is camera-ready copy of the brochure for the Eden IAAP spring
seminar to be held on April 1 at the Adams Hotel. As Whitney Woo, a member
of our program committee, discussed with you several weeks ago, Preston Press
has offered to print and fold our brochures at no charge as a donation to our
seminar.

We would like 300 copies of the brochure printed on light green paper. The
finished brochures should be folded in thirds so they can easily be prepared for
mailing. We would like the printed brochures delivered by January 8 so that we
can address them and have them in the mail by January 15.

As mentioned in an earlier letter, the Eden IAAP Chapter appreciates the fine
work done by your company as well as your willingness to support our efforts.
Thank You!

Job 14

Eden Daily Enquirer is donating
space for a 2" by 3" advertisement
for the seminar. Please prepare an
ad that looks kind of like this. If you
wish, you can include the IAAP
logo in the ad.

Make it attractive!

Thanks!   Jacob

Eden Chapter of
International Association of
Administrative Professionals

is sponsoring a
one-day seminar

**Thriving in a Changing
World**

Saturday, April 1, (year)
Adams Hotel, Eden

Call for information:
Jacob Jensen   555-2871
Georgia Gates   555-3778

Job 15

Please prepare the labels for the brochure mailing and bring
them to the next meeting! Thanks! Rhonda

Job 16

AGENDA FOR DECEMBER

1. Discuss flowers and/or table decorations — Joanne
2. Discuss the CEU application — Rhonda
3. Discuss the seminar printed program — Jacob
4. Discuss exhibits; list vendors to exhibit — Whitney
5. Discuss registration packets — Rhonda
6. Review budget — Georgia

Thanks! Georgia

Our dollar planner needs to be amended because we decided to buy mailing labels preprinted with the names of local IAAP members from the international headquarters of IAAP. It was expensive, but we'll make up for the extra dollars somewhere else.

Please add two lines under the Publicity section of the dollar planner and fix the line above the new lines so it looks like this:

Brochure layout and printing	300	160*
Paid to IAAP for labels		140
Postage for mailings	90	

Thanks — Erv

Job 17

INVITATION TO MEMBERSHIP IN
INTERNATIONAL ASSOCIATION OF ADMINISTRATIVE PROFESSIONALS™

Are you an executive assistant who possesses a mastery of
office skills, who demonstrates the ability to assume
responsibility without direct supervision, who exercises
initiative and judgment, and who makes decisions within the
scope of assigned authority? If so, you are eligible for
membership in International Association of Administrative
Professionals.

International Association of Administrative Professionals
(IAAP) is the world's leading organization for secretaries.
Its aim is to elevate the secretarial standards and offer
opportunities for professional and personal growth and
development to achieve that goal. You, too, can achieve your
goal by becoming associated with IAAP. Membership affords the
opportunity to become a better secretary through education and
to share companionship with secretaries who have similar
interest.

Would you like to become part of a professional association
for secretaries? Then International Association of
Administrative Professionals is the association for YOU!

We invite you to check the following items for further
information:

______ I would like information on IAAP.
______ I would like information on the Certified Professional
       Secretary (CPS) program.
______ I would like to attend a meeting of the Eden Chapter of
       IAAP. Please let me know of future meeting dates.

Name ____

Home Address ________________________________

Employer ____________________________________

Telephone No. ____________________

Please complete and leave this form on the table or mail it
to:

       Rhonda Evers, CPS
       Membership Chairman
       Eden Chapter, IAAP
       P.O. Box 552
       Eden, WI 53019

Ms. Susan Fenner, Ph.D.
Education and Professional Development *Manager*
International Association of Administrative Professionals
10502 NW Ambassador Drive
P.O. Box 20404
Kansas City, MO 64195- 0404

Dear Dr. Fenner:

Enclosed is the application for Continuing Education Units for
the participants of our spring seminar on April 1, (year). As you
can see, we are expecting about 100 secretaries and
administrative assistants to attend.

I am enclosing $15.00 for 100 blank certificates along with the
required $20.00 processing fee. Also enclosed are brief
biographical sketches on the keynote speaker as well as the six
speakers for the concurrent sessions and a copy of the seminar
brochure.

Plans are going well for our seminar. We are proud to be offering
it with IAAP endorsement since any affiliation with IAAP adds
credibility and substance to a seminar.

Sincerely,

Rhonda Evers, Program Committee

Required to be included:
Application (3 copies)
Biographical information on speaker(s)
Outline of program, topics to be covered, and time frames
$20 processing fee
Certificate cost

Please put this on Chapter letterhead, too, and make it look good. Prepare the attached forms. There is no special format for the speaker descriptions.

Rhonda

Job 18 (continued)

Speakers:

Keynote Speaker: Cassie Cavness   "Thriving in a Changing World"

Cassie Cavness is well known in the Midwest for her energetic and stimulating presentations regarding the frustrations faced by office workers in this changing world. Ms. Cavness discusses the transition from electric to electronic equipment and how it impacts everything that must be done in the office. She addresses international business and how office workers can arm themselves for the office of the future.

Ms. Cavness received her undergraduate training at St. Norbert College in DePere, Wisconsin. She has master's degrees in management and business from the University of Southern California. She is president of Cavness Consulting, Inc., in Los Carlos, California, a management consulting firm teaching leadership skills to administrative support staff.

Concurrent Sessions:

Marcia Carlson   "Beautiful Documents with Report Publisher"

An instructor in the office occupations department of Mt. Calvary College, Marcia Carlson has been teaching students how to design documents for a number of years. Her designs have won a number of national awards, and she is eager to pass on her skills to those who are in the business of document design.

Bret Bowers   "Surviving the Workday with Humor"

Bret Bowers, owner and manager of The Humor Shoppe in Milwaukee, has a number of tried and true methods of salvaging a disastrous workday with humor. His tasteful presentations have helped office workers from coast to coast. Mr. Bowers has a degree in psychology from St. Olaf College, and he worked in management for a number of large companies in the Minneapolis-St. Paul area before moving to Milwaukee.

Terry Lawrence   "Teamwork: Enhancing Office Productivity"

Dr. Terry Lawrence is a graduate of the University of Wisconsin, Milwaukee, and she earned her PhD at Stanford University in California. In addition to teaching in the Supervisory Management program at the University of Wisconsin in Milwaukee, she has lectured widely in the area of Total Quality Management and is a firm believer in the power of work teams.

Roy St. Claire   "Perfect Documents with WordPerfect"

Roy St. Claire is trainer and instructor at Computer Heaven in Eden, Wisconsin. His degree in computer science from UW—Oshkosh provided him with a head start in computers. From there he was manager of information systems for ALP Insurance, Greenbush, in their home office for five years. He moved to the document design department for a change of scenery and discovered a love for the WordPerfect program and its seemingly endless features used in the design of attractive and readable documents.

Patricia K. Morin   "Rightsizing: How It Could Affect Your Job!"

Patricia K. Morin is owner and president of PKMorin & Associates, a management consulting firm in Milwaukee. A graduate of Marquette University with a degree in management, Ms. Morin's vocation and avocation is the study of downsizing and rightsizing in corporate America. In the process of studying the management changes being made by companies of all sizes, she has developed a plan for support staff members that helps them cope with the changes in their companies.

Lucia Lewin   "A Balancing Act: Home & Career"

With degrees in sociology and psychology, Lucia Lewin's job involves working with families and helping them to function as a happy family unit. Ms. Lewin's approach is that since it's the norm for both parents to be breadwinners in today's families, adjustments must be made so that all of the family members are happy, healthy, and involved in the business of being a family. In addition to working with individual families in Eden County, Ms. Lewin has lectured nationally regarding her strategies for helping families survive.

International Association of
Administrative Professionals™

Job 18 *(continued)*

APPLICATION

Program Number
Assigned by HQ

Eden IAAP Chapter
Sponsor Name

1234
Sponsor ID
Number

0.5
CEU Requested
(based on contact hours)

100
Number of
Participants
Expected

April 1, (year)
Event Date(s)

Five
Total Number of Contact Hours

One
Number of Meeting Days

Program Site Adams Hotel
276 Wisconsin Avenue
Eden, WI 53019

Name of Instructor(s)
Fill in all seven names.

Title of Program Thriving in a Changing World.

Program Objective (to be written on certificate) To provide workers with the skills to improve their job satisfaction and their chances for advancement.

Signature of IAAP Sponsor President

Phone: Business 414-555-8213

Fax 414-555-8227

Residence 414-555-1967

Date: _______________

Signature of IAAP Program Chairperson

Phone: Business 414-555-3778

Fax 414-555-3779

Residence 414-555-1653

Date: _______________

MAIL CORRESPONDENCE TO:
Name and Address

Ms. Rhonda Evers
P.O. Box 552
Eden, WI 53019

Number of Certificates Ordered:

Customized _______________ Blank 100

FOR HEADQUARTERS USE ONLY

Applications Received _______________

Number of CEU Awarded _______________

CEU Registrar _______________   Date _______________

Submit three (3) copies of application.

Job 19

On Saturday, April 1, (year), the Eden Chapter of International Association of Administrative Professionals is hosting a spring seminar at the Adams Hotel in beautiful downtown Eden. A number of speakers and seminar presenters will share information about working in today's office with IAAP members as well as other secretaries and administrative assistants from the surrounding area. A copy of the seminar brochure is attached.

An important part of the plan for the day is for businesses like yours to be represented with an office products display in the ballroom, which will be the main meeting room. We are hoping for displays of office equipment, furniture, and supplies. While the primary purpose of the displays is not to sell products but to show seminar participants what is available, the sale of small office items will be allowed.

The seminar committee joins me in extending this invitation to you to participate in our IAAP seminar. Please call me at 555-1357 by January 15 to tell me whether you can join us.

Mr. Hoan Nguyen
Eden Business Machines
4487 Apple Valley Road
Eden, WI 53019

Mrs. Phyllis Nagel
Micro & Office Supply
347 N. Main Street
Eden, WI 53019

Miss Lou VanDyke
Office Stop 'n Shop
111 Melrose Avenue
Mt. Calvary, WI 53057

Mr. Abe Williams
Computer Heaven
8933 Apple Valley Road
Eden, WI 53019

Ms. Maralyn Hankburg
Kettle Morraine Computers
1176 Saratoga Drive
West Bend, WI 53095

Mrs. Marilyn Munroe
The "Other" Office Store
333 Dexter Avenue
Fond du Lac, WI 54935

Mr. Ollie Dreyfus
Ollie's Office Supplies
437 Olive Street
Oostburg, WI 53070

Mr. Frederick Rivera
The Computer Tutor
27 Main Street
New Holstein, WI 53061

Mr. Paul Hamilton
Grafton Office Supply
290 First Street
Grafton, WI 53024

Ms. Lucille Caulkins
Copy-Quik, Inc.
211 West Pine Street
Juneau, WI 43039

Please send the letter above to these local businesses.

Thanks,
Whitney

Job 20

About the Speakers . . .

CASSIE CAVNESS holds degrees from St. Norbert College in DePere and UCLA. She is president of Cavness Consulting, Inc., in Los Carlos, California, a management consulting firm.

MARCIA CARLSON is an instructor in the Office Occupations Department at Mt. Calvary College. She has won numerous awards for her document designs.

BRET BOWERS has a degree in psychology from St. Olaf College and has held several management positions. He is currently owner of The Humor Shoppe in Milwaukee.

TERRY LAWRENCE teaches in the Supervisory Management program at UW-Milwaukee. She earned her PhD at Stanford University and is a trainer for Total Quality Management.

ROY ST. CLAIRE is a graduate of UW-Oshkosh with a degree in computer science. Currently he is a trainer and instructor at Computer Heaven in Eden.

PATRICIA K. MORIN is owner and president of PKMorin & Associates in Milwaukee. She is a graduate of Marquette University and a student of the downsizing and rightsizing theory of management.

LUCIA LEWIN is employed by the Eden County Department of Social Services, where she works with families to help them function as real families. She has degrees in sociology and psychology.

• • •

*Thanks to the following **Corporate Sponsors:***

Andrea's Auto Body	Jan's Leather Loft
Columbia Crystal Works	Kettle Valley Bank
Condon, Condon, and Hill	Lionhart Leather Works
Investment Counseling	Paulus & Paulus, Inc.
Cook Ceramics	Peckham Photography
Crockery Cookery	Preston Press
Delwich's Sandwiches	Proctor Pharmaceuticals
Geohart Electronic Assembly	Speed King Mfg. Co.
Georgie's Greenhouses	Workers Health

Thriving in a Changing World

8:00 - 9:00 am
Registration . . . . Abel and Cain Ballrooms
Continental Breakfast, Office Products Exhibit

9:00 - 10:30 am
Cassie Cavness . . . . Abel and Cain Ballrooms
Thriving in a Changing World

10:30 - 11:00 am
Break, office Products Exhibits . . . . Ballrooms

11:00 - 12:15 pm   Concurrent Sessions   (Tickets Required)
#1 **Report Publisher®**, Marcia Carlson . . . . Room C*
#2 **Beyond the Office**, Cassie Cavness . . . . Room A
#3 **Surviving with Humor**, Bret Bowers . . . . Room D
#4 **Teamwork**, Terry Lawrence . . . . Room E

12:15 - 1:00 pm
Luncheon . . . . Abel and Cain Ballrooms

1:15 - 2:30 pm   Concurrent Sessions   (Tickets Required)
#5 **WordPerfect®**, Roy St. Claire . . . . Room C*
#6 **Beyond the Office**, Cassie Cavness . . . . Room A
#7 **Rightsizing**, Patricia K. Morin . . . . Room D
#8 **Balancing Home & Career**, Lucia Lewin . . . . Room E

2:30 - 2:45 pm
Break . . . . Abel and Cain Ballrooms

2:45 - 4:00 pm
Closing Session . . . . Abel and Cain Ballrooms
The Trip Home, Cassie Cavness
Wrap-up and Evaluation, CEU Certificates, Door Prizes

*Computers, software, and technical assistance for today's seminar graciously provided by Computer Heaven of Eden, Wisconsin.

Make the commitment *. . . to your profession*
. . . to your career . . . to yourself

Membership in a professional association is evidence of your commitment to excellence as a team member with management. Whether you're an administrative assistant, executive secretary, word processing secretary, information specialist, office manager, or executive assistant, IAAP can help you continue your career growth and assist in your personal and professional development.

By joining IAAP, you will . . .

- Benefit from numerous personal and professional development programs that provide the opportunity to build management and leadership skills.

- Gain personal visibility and recognition while strengthening the image of the profession in the community.

- Network with colleagues who are experts in a variety of fields.

- Keep "up to date" on industry news and trends through association publications such as *OfficePRO™* magazine and *IAAP Bits & Bytes* member newsletter, and through local, regional, and international conferences.

- Take advantage of reduced rates on educational materials and courses, and numerous other member benefits.

Our mission is to be the acknowledged, recognized leader of office professionals and to enhance their individual and collective value, image, competence, and influence.

The Eden Chapter . . .

The Eden IAAP chapter meets the first Tuesday of every month at the Adams Hotel. Each meeting includes dinner and a program as well as the business meeting. You are encouraged to contact Rhonda Evers, CPS, who is membership chairman. She will provide any information you'd like about the Eden chapter of IAAP or make a reservation for you for the next meeting.

Thriving in a Changing World

sponsored by

Eden Chapter

International Association of Administrative Professionals

April 1, (year)

Adams Hotel

Eden, Wisconsin

Job 21

AGENDA FOR JANUARY

1. Discuss evaluation forms - Georgia
2. Approve flowers and decorations - Joanne & Francis
3. Discuss door prizes - Whitney
4. Discuss name tags - Rhonda
5. Discuss tickets for luncheon and concurrent sessions - Rhonda
6. Revise seminar program - All
7. Assemble mailing of brochure - All
8. Review budget (There are no major changes in the budget since the last meeting.) - Erv

Job 22

Please draft an evaluation form for the seminar. A suggested format is attached.

Thanks, Georgia

Job 23

Because of registrations and room sizes, we must change the rooms of Concurrent Sessions 7 & 8. Session 7 will be in Room E and Session 8 will be in Room D. Please make these changes on the seminar program.

Thanks,
Rhonda & Francis

Job 22

PARTICIPANT EVALUATION

International Association of
Administrative Professionals™

Chapter/Division ____

Seminar Title ____

Seminar Date ____

		STRONGLY DISAGREE			NEUTRAL		STRONGLY AGREE	
PRESENTER/METHODS								
1.	The presenter stated his/her objectives clearly.	1	2	3	4	5	6	7
2.	The presenter was knowledgeable of the topic(s) covered.	1	2	3	4	5	6	7
3.	The presenter taught the material in a way that made it seem practical or easily understood.	1	2	3	4	5	6	7
4.	I am satisfied with the methods used to help me accomplish my learning objectives.	1	2	3	4	5	6	7
5.	The audio/visual aids and other methods used to enhance my learning were effective.	1	2	3	4	5	6	7
SEMINAR CONTENT								
6.	The seminar content matched the stated objectives.	1	2	3	4	5	6	7
7.	The seminar content was relevant to my present or future work or personal life.	1	2	3	4	5	6	7
8.	The content was arranged in a way that was conducive to my learning.	1	2	3	4	5	6	7
9.	The skills and/or ideas taught in this seminar are relevant.	1	2	3	4	5	6	7
10.	I can apply the skills and/or ideas I learned in this seminar.	1	2	3	4	5	6	7
PARTICIPANT BENEFITS								
11.	The seminar met my expectations	1	2	3	4	5	6	7
12.	I learned new skills and/or ideas.	1	2	3	4	5	6	7
13.	The quality of my work and/or life will be enhanced as a result of participating in this seminar.	1	2	3	4	5	6	7
14.	I will likely change my thinking and/or actions as a result of participating in this seminar.	1	2	3	4	5	6	7
15.	The workbook/handouts or other materials obtained in the seminar will be useful in my work.	1	2	3	4	5	6	7

<table>
<tr><td>SEMINAR SETTING</td><td>STRONGLY
DISAGREE</td><td>NEUTRAL</td><td>STRONGLY
AGREE</td></tr>
</table>

SEMINAR SETTING							
16. The facilities used for this seminar were satisfactory.	1	2	3	4	5	6	7
17. The materials advertising the seminar stimulated my interest in attending.	1	2	3	4	5	6	7
18. I am satisfied with the greeting and orientation I received upon arrival.	1	2	3	4	5	6	7
19. I felt comfortable (physically) throughout the seminar.	1	2	3	4	5	6	7
20. The scheduling of the seminar was convenient.	1	2	3	4	5	6	7

OVERALL

	STRONGLY DISAGREE		NEUTRAL			STRONGLY AGREE	
21. Overall, I was satisfied with the seminar.	1	2	3	4	5	6	7

Comments ____

____

____

____

Did you come to this seminar voluntarily?   Yes _______   No _______

Will there be barriers at work or home to prevent you from using what you learned in this seminar?

Yes _______   No _______   Not Applicable _______

Suggestions for speakers/topics you would like to see presented at future seminars. _________________

____

____

Please complete and give this form to a IAAP monitor at the end of the program or leave on your table.

THANK YOU FOR ATTENDING

Job 24

Please prepare 120 luncheon tickets that have the following information on them.
Thanks!
Joanne

"Thriving in a Changing World"
LUNCHEON
Saturday, April 1, 19—
12:15 - 1:00 p.m.
Adams Hotel Ballroom

1

Job 25

Please prepare 20 tickets each for Concurrent Sessions 1 & 5. Session 1 should look like this. Bold the name of the software.

Prepare 35 tickets for each of the other Concurrent sessions.
Rhonda

Beautiful Documents With **Report Publisher** ®
by
Marcia Carlson
11:00 - 12:15 in Room C

1

Job 26

Please prepare name tags with a LARGE first name, smaller last name, and an even smaller line with the city, state, and ZIP code.
Thanks,
Rhonda

RAFAEL
Zapata

Newburg, WI 53060

Job 27

AGENDA FOR FEBRUARY

1. Revise evaluation forms – Georgia
2. Approve name tags – Rhonda
3. Approve luncheon tickets – Rhonda
4. Approve concurrent session tickets – Rhonda
5. Approve seminar program – All
6. Review registrations – Rhonda
7. Review budget – Erv

Please attach the same budget as you attached in January. We'll work on the figures at the meeting.
Erv

Job 28

The evaluation forms are great. Good work!
Georgia

Job 29

The seminar program is wonderful!
The Committee

Job 30

The name tags are perfect!

Rhonda

Job 31

The luncheon and concurrent session tickets couldn't be better. Numbering them was a nice touch.

Thanks.   Rhonda

Job 32

AGENDA FOR MARCH

1. Review registrations and concurrent session requests — Rhonda
2. Double-check registrants for hands-on workshops — Rhonda
3. Review speaker AV requests — Becky
4. Determine room layouts — Francis
5. Review exhibitor requests — Whitney
6. Review budget — Erv

We're winding down. Keep up the wonderful work!

Georgia

DOLLAR PLANNER

Revenue	Budget	Actual
Target Number of Attendees @ $40 each	4000	*3970*
Contributions from Corporate Sponsors	1500	1485
Target Profit	1000	

88 @ $40 and 10 @ $45

Expenses

Speakers	Budget	Actual
Keynote—fee and transportation	850	850*
Session Speakers—honorariums and transportation	400	
Lodging and meals	300	
Reproduction of speakers materials (consider who might donate this service)	25	*0*
Communication expenses (calls, mailings, etc.)	50	*37*
Complimentary registrations (actual costs)	50	*70*

Publicity	Budget	Actual
Advertising	50	50*
Brochure layout, printing, and mailing	300	160*
Paid to IAAP for labels		140
Postage for mailings	90	*87*
Door prizes (consider donations)	100	*65*

Facilities	Budget	Actual
Meeting room charges (check for hidden costs)	200	*200*
AV equipment (rental or setup costs)	200	*175*
Breaks	200	*225*
Seminar luncheon	1000	*984*
Executive committee dinner	200	*215*

Please add the new line under Revenue, and insert the new figures! Thanks! Ev

Participant Materials	Budget	Actual
Printing of handouts	50	50*
Program	100	*50*
Folders	100	*85*
Name tags	25	*30*
Pencil & paper (may be provided by hotel)	?	0

CEU Costs	Budget	Actual
Certificates	15	15
$20 processing fee	20	20
Recording costs ($1.50 per person)	150	*147*

*Expense to be picked up by corporate sponsor

Job 33

Concurrent Session 1 - Report Publisher

Natalia Krings
Adeline Gill
Floyd Smits
Vicky Smolaric
Linda Gauldon
Carol Reichelle
Elyda Crisman

Concurrent Session 5 - WordPerfect

Rafael Zapata
Beth Gnewuch
Jean H. Julsetz
Bea Brockman
Darcy Bork
Adeline Gill
Lisang Zheng
Tammy Sue Krause

Please send a letter to each of these people, according to the session in which they have registered. Thanks, Rhonda

---

Dear (first name)

Congratulations! You were one of the 20 people who got their reservations to us in time to be included in the hands on workshop "Beautiful Documents with Report Publisher."

That workshop is scheduled from 11:00 to 12:15 at the April 1 seminar in Room C. Please be prompt.

We are looking forward to seeing you at our IAAP spring seminar. Your ticket for the workshop will be included in your registration packet.

Sincerely,

Rhonda Evers, Program Committee

Job 34

Concurrent Session 1 - Report Publisher

Cindysue Thiel   (Surviving)
Camille Yu   (Surviving)
Dawn Paterick   (Teamwork)
Sallie Wilke   (Beyond)

Concurrent Session 5 - WordPerfect

Debbie Gillmore   (Beyond)
Jessie DeSoto   (Rightsizing)
Star Zeske   (Balancing Act)
Bertie Eick   (Beyond)
Enoch Jacobchick   (Rightsizing)

These people had to be assigned to their second choice session. Please send them each a letter listing the session to which they were assigned.
Rhonda

Dear (first name)

Thank you for registering for our IAAP spring seminar. I am sorry to inform you, however, that the hands-on workshop "Beautiful Documents with Report Publisher" was filled by the time your registration arrived.

Consequently, you are being scheduled for your second choice at that time, which was (insert the full name of the second choice session). I trust that you will find this session educational and useful to you on your job.

We are looking forward to seeing you at our IAAP spring seminar. Your ticket for the workshop will be included in your registration packet.

Sincerely,

Rhonda Evers, Program Committee

Job 35

Dear Ms. Cavness:

The time for our IAAP spring seminar is rapidly approaching. Registrations are better than expected. It appears as though there will be nearly 100 seminar participants. The committee members have been working hard to assure that it will be a great seminar—one at which you will be proud to be a guest speaker.

Your room at the Adams Hotel has been reserved. The Adams is a luxury hotel with all of the comforts of home away from home—including a fully equipped exercise room, swimming pool, and whirlpool. We are certain you will enjoy your stay in Eden.

You are cordially invited to an executive committee dinner the evening before the seminar. Arrangement details will be provided to you when you check into the hotel. You may charge your breakfast to your room, and you are invited to attend the seminar luncheon at 12:15 p.m.

Your airline tickets are enclosed. As you can see from the itinerary, you will arrive in Milwaukee on United Flight #1270 at 3:10 p.m. on March 31. You will be met in the baggage claim area by Georgia Givins, who is a member of the Eden IAAP Chapter. She has promised to wear a red coat and hat so you can pick her out of the crowd. Georgia will be available throughout your visit to help you set up your AV equipment, hand out materials, answer questions, or do whatever else is needed. She will also provide transportation to the airport for your return flight on April 1.

Again, we are looking forward to meeting you on March 31. If you should have any questions, please do not hesitate to contact me at 414-555-7812.

Sincerely,

Becky Brown, Program Committee

Enclosures

Job 36

Dear (speaker):

The time for our IAAP spring seminar is rapidly approaching. Registrations are better than expected. It appears as though there will be nearly 100 seminar participants. The committee members have been working hard to assure that it will be a great seminar—one at which you will be proud to be a guest speaker.

Eve Warren, manager of the Adams Hotel where the seminar will be held, has arranged for a block of rooms for seminar participants. IAAP will arrange for your room if you wish to arrive the evening before the conference. The Adams Hotel provides free parking for hotel guests as well as a health center complete with exercise equipment, a swimming pool, and whirlpool.

Please let me know if you wish to arrive on March 31. You are cordially invited to an executive committee dinner the evening before the seminar at 7:30 p.m. Arrangement details will be provided to you when you check into the hotel. A complimentary registration to the seminar is also being arranged for you, and you are invited to attend the seminar luncheon at 12:15 p.m.

Thank you for getting your handouts to us so promptly. They are currently being processed. You can expect about 30 people in your session at (time). Again, we are looking forward to your participation in our seminar. If you have any further questions, please don't hesitate to call me at 555-7812.

Sincerely,

Becky Brown, Program Committee

Job 37

Use 8½ x 11-inch paper to prepare a "poster" for each of the concurrent sessions to put outside of the door. Use big bold letters – (one inch tall, if you can) and make them beautiful!

Francis

Room C

BEAUTIFUL DOCUMENTS
WITH
REPORT PUBLISHER®

Marcia Carlson, Speaker
11:00 - 12:15

Job 38

Please fill out the hotel function sheet for the hands-on session in Room C. Both speakers would like the room set up in classroom style.

Both speakers will use a demo computer (provided by Computer Heaven) attached to a display panel and an overhead projector. This requires extra extension cords. Make a note of that on the function sheet.

A lavalier microphone with a 20-foot cord is requested since the speakers will be moving between the lectern (better request one) and the demo computer. Also, a wall-mount screen will be best.

Water on a table outside of the room is requested. A one-time charge of $25 will be paid for room setup. No deposit is necessary.

Thanks, Francis

Job 39

I am pleased that you have agreed to represent your company at the Eden IAAP chapter's spring seminar on April 1 at the Adams Hotel in Eden.

Registration begins at 8:00 a.m. on April 1, and participants will have until 9:00 a.m. to look at the exhibits. A 10:30 to 11:00 a.m. break time and the 12:15 to 1:00 p.m. lunch time will also afford participants an opportunity to check out your merchandise.

The hotel will have the ballroom open by 7 a.m. so you will have time to set up before the registration.   You may remove your exhibits when the participants return to the concurrent sessions at 1 p.m.

You have been assigned to Table(s) (insert the table number(s)). We are looking forward to seeing you at the seminar. If you have any questions, please call me at 555-1357.

The following exhibitors will be at the seminar. I've indicated their table numbers in parentheses. Please send them this letter.

Eden Bus. Machines (1 & 2)   *The "Other" Office Store (5)*
Micro & Office Supply (3)   *Ollie's Office Supplies (6)*
Computer Heaven (4)   *The Computer Tutor (7)*
                                      Copy-Quik, Inc. (8)

Whitney

Job 40

AGENDA FOR APRIL

1. *Review seminar and make notes for next year – Georgia*
2. *Pay bills – Erv*
3. *Review the budget – Erv*
4. *Assemble information for the CEU – Rhonda*
5. *Tally the evaluations – Rhonda*
6. *Pat each other on the back for a job well done !*
        (hopefully !!)

Job 41

Program Number
Assigned by HQ

PARTICIPANT EVALUATION

Chapter/Division __Eden Chapter__

Seminar Title __Thriving in a Changing World__

Seminar Date __April 1, (year)__

PRESENTER/METHODS	STRONGLY DISAGREE			NEUTRAL		STRONGLY AGREE	
1. The presenter stated his/her objectives clearly.	1	2	3	4	5 (12)	6 (45)	7 (41)
2. The presenter was knowledgeable of the topic(s) covered.	1	2	3	4	5 (10)	6 (45)	7 (43)
3. The presenter taught the material in a way that made it seem practical or easily understood.	1	2	3	4 (2)	5 (10)	6 (30)	7 (56)
4. I am satisfied with the methods used to help me accomplish my learning objectives.	1	2	3 (1)	4	5 (7)	6 (40)	7 (50)
5. The audio/visual aids and other methods used to enhance my learning were effective.	1	2	3	4 (2)	5 (5)	6 (39)	7 (53)

SEMINAR CONTENT

6. The seminar content matched the stated objectives.	1	2	3 (5)	4	5 (17)	6 (14)	7 (62)
7. The seminar content was relevant to my present or future work or personal life.	1	2 (1)	3 (7)	4 (4)	5 (29)	6 (47)	7 (20)
8. The content was arranged in a way that was conducive to my learning.	1	2	3	4	5 (15)	6 (53)	7 (30)
9. The skills and/or ideas taught in this seminar are relevant.	1	2 (10)	3	4 (3)	5 (27)	6 (10)	7 (48)
10. I can apply the skills and/or ideas I learned in this seminar.	1	2 (8)	3 (5)	4	5 (30)	6 (37)	7 (18)

PARTICIPANT BENEFITS

11. The seminar met my expectations	1	2	3	4 (2)	5 (46)	6 (40)	7 (10)
12. I learned new skills and/or ideas.	1	2	3	4 (11)	5 (30)	6 (48)	7 (9)
13. The quality of my work and/or life will be enhanced as a result of participating in this seminar.	1 (3)	2	3 (7)	4 (14)	5 (29)	6 (21)	7 (24)
14. I will likely change my thinking and/or actions as a result of participating in this seminar.	1 (2)	2 (1)	3 (8)	4 (13)	5 (24)	6 (26)	7 (24)
15. The workbook/handouts or other materials obtained in the seminar will be useful in my work.	1 (14)	2 (2)	3 (17)	4 (10)	5 (33)	6 (10)	7 (12)

582

SEMINAR SETTING

| | STRONGLY DISAGREE | | | | NEUTRAL | | | STRONGLY AGREE |

16. The facilities used for this seminar were satisfactory.
    1 2 3 4 5 6 7
    (1) (20) (45) (32)

17. The materials advertising the seminar stimulated my interest in attending.
    1 2 3 4 5 6 7
    (5) (14) (48) (31)

18. I am satisfied with the greeting and orientation I received upon arrival.
    1 2 3 4 5 6 7
    (25) (26) (47)

19. I felt comfortable (physically) throughout the seminar.
    1 2 3 4 5 6 7
    (49) (49)

20. The scheduling of the seminar was convenient.
    1 2 3 4 5 6 7
    (10) (8) (40) (40)

OVERALL

21. Overall, I was satisfied with the seminar.
    1 2 3 4 5 6 7
    (40) (48) (10)

Comments ____

____

____

____

____

Did you come to this seminar voluntarily?   Yes __92__   No __6__

Will there be barriers at work or home to prevent you from using what you learned in this seminar?

Yes __9__   No __80__   Not Applicable __10__

Suggestions for speakers/topics you would like to see presented at future seminars. _______________

____

____

Please complete and give this form to a IAAP monitor at the end of the program or leave on your table.

THANK YOU FOR ATTENDING

Job 42

PLEASE KEY INFORMATION TO INSURE ACCURACY

Name __Judy Abdullah__

Address: Home __X__ or Work ______

Get the addresses from the mailing list!

SSN __333-44-8291__

IAAP-ID Number __4672__

Name __Delores Bartlein__

Address: Home __X__ or Work ______

SSN __443-34-5632__

IAAP-ID Number __4850__

Name __Kris Gehrke__

Address: Home __X__ or Work ______

SSN __532-76-4196__

IAAP-ID Number __4831__

Name __Kathleen Gillett__

Address: Home __X__ or Work ______

SSN __343-76-4904__

IAAP-ID Number __4673__

Name __Ricci Giordana__

Address: Home __X__ or Work ______

SSN __461-32-5196__

IAAP-ID Number __4692__

Name __Beth Gnewuch__

Address: Home __X__ or Work ______

SSN __398-72-5143__

IAAP-ID Number __4699__

(Reproduce additional sheets as necessary)

Job 43

Eden Chapter
P.O. Box 552
Eden, WI 53019

International Association of
Administrative Professionals™

ATTENDANCE REPORT

Sponsor Name

Program Number Assigned
by Headquarters

CEU Granted
Each Participant

Event Date(s)

Total Number of Contact Hours   Number of Meeting Days

Program Site ________________

Name of Instructor(s)________________________________

Title of Program ________________________________

Number of Attendees: __________ x $1.50 = Amount Submitted $ ________________

Signature of IAAP Sponsor President

Signature of IAAP Program Chairperson

Phone: Business ________________

Phone: Business ________________

Fax ________________

Fax ________________

Residence ________________

Residence ________________

Date ________________

Date ________________

Attach typed participant list and check for $1.50 per participant.

THIS IS THE SIMULATION YOU'VE BEEN LOOKING FOR

Pathways: Simulation for Word Processing: Par Fore, by Eisch and Voiers, is a generic simulation covering the work done by the pro shop staff at the Ohio River Golf Club in Cincinnati, Ohio, to maintain the Par Fore golf league throughout the season. The league plays every Tuesday afternoon for a six-month period. There are 24 two-person teams in this league.

Several times throughout the season, members participate in local area tournaments and also host one invitational tournament at their club. Sponsors help offset the costs of these tournaments with their donations of prizes. Officers of the league are elected in the fall to serve one-year terms starting the following spring. The president, secretary, and treasurer work with the pro shop staff sharing the word processing responsibilities. Sometimes committees are formed to handle special events, but the staff has authority over all communications bearing the letterhead of the club.

Activities include:

1. Maintaining a membership list
2. Handling club and league dues
3. Maintaining records of scores
4. Updating members' local course handicaps
5. Sending regular mailings to the members
6. Creating, formatting, and editing a handbook:
   - local rules
   - bylaws
   - membership list
   - schedule of events
7. Creating labels and name badges
8. Creating and editing forms
9. Arranging an event
10. Preparing invitations to special tournaments
11. Creating prize certificates
12. Maintaining the pro shop inventory
13. Creating an ad for the local yellow pages
14. Preparing an employee's time sheet

ISBN: 0-538-68767-3

For More Information or to Order from
South-Western
Join Us on the Internet

South-Western
Educational Publishing

www.swep.com">

The Hardware

If you have never had any formal training on the computer, it is important that you are comfortable with the parts of the equipment at which you will be working for the duration of this course. Even if you consider yourself "computer literate," it might be a good idea for you to look through the information in this appendix so that you can see how each part of the computer will be used in your WordPerfect training.

Turn to the Start-Up Checklist in the front of this text. Here you will see that a certain level of computer is required for your work with WordPerfect. Your instructor has made sure WordPerfect will run on your computer. You need to be familiar with the computer parts.

Now look at the computer in front of you. It consists of six major hardware components: the video display terminal (VDT or screen), the central processing unit (CPU), the keyboard, the disk drives, the mouse, and the printer. In most classrooms the printer is located in a different part of the room, but it is connected to your computer with a cable. Can you identify the parts of the hardware illustrations in Figures A-1, A-2, and A-3 as they are discussed? Find them on your own computer.

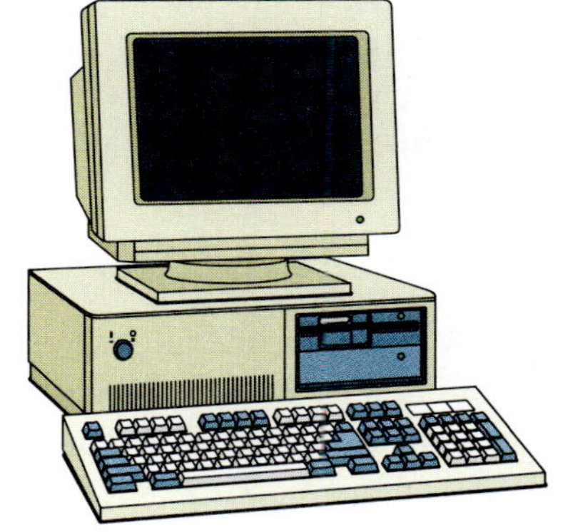

FIGURE A-1
Computer

1. **The VDT**. Starting at the top, the *video display terminal* (VDT) is used to show you what you are doing as you use the computer. Look at your VDT. Can you find a power switch and controls for brightness and contrast? You should be familiar with the features of your VDT so that you can adjust the controls for maximum eye comfort.

2. **The CPU**. The brains, or logic center, of the computer is housed in the piece of equipment called the *central processing unit* (CPU). Sometimes the CPU sits on your desk under the VDT. In other cases the CPU might be on the floor beside the desk. Inside of the CPU is a hard drive where WordPerfect has been installed if you are working on a stand-alone machine. In many cases, however, WordPerfect is installed on the file server of a network. That means your PC will be running a program stored on the CPU of a computer in a different part of the room or even in a different room.

    In addition to the hard drive of the computer, the CPU has a temporary memory area called RAM (random access memory) where your work is remembered until you save it on your disk. Find the power switch on your CPU. When the power switch is turned off, any text in RAM is lost.

3. **The Keyboard**. Look at the keyboard. In addition to the alphabetic keys, you should find a set of function keys. The function keys are labeled with *F* and a number, and they may be in a row across the top of the keyboard (there will be 12 of them) or they may be in a double row at the left.

On the right is a series of different keys. You should have a number keypad and some keys with arrows for moving the insertion point. There should also be keys with labels such as **Home**, **End**, **Page Down**, **Page Up**, and **Delete**. (The *insertion point* is the little flashing line in the window showing where you are working at any time.)

4. **The Disk Drives**. In addition to the hard drive of your computer, there are a number of possible configurations for the floppy disk drives. You might have one or two drives that hold $3^1/_2$-inch disks, or you might have a drive for a CD-ROM. If you are working in a networked environment, you might not have any drives for disks.

    Your instructor will help you determine what kind of drives your computer has and what type of disk you should use for your training. If you have never before used a computer, ask your instructor to give you special instructions regarding the handling of disks and how to insert them into the computer.

5. **The Mouse**. While it is possible to use WordPerfect without a mouse, the use of a mouse is almost imperative. Many features are available only with a mouse. In addition to accessing features with the mouse, the mouse is an efficient means of selecting text, positioning the insertion point, displaying QuickMenus, and moving through your documents. If you have never before used a mouse, specific instructions for the use of a mouse are included in Appendix D.

FIGURE A-2
Mouse

6. **The Printer**. There are literally hundreds of printers that might be connected to your classroom computer. Most printers today feed cut sheets of paper from a bin or tray. These printers are either *laser printers* or *ink jet printers*, and the printed pages look like they might have come from a copy machine.

    Some classrooms have printers where the paper is connected in one long sheet. The paper is pushed or pulled through the printer by way of sprocket wheels that fit into the holes of tear strips on the sides of the paper. These are called *dot matrix printers*, and they are noisy.

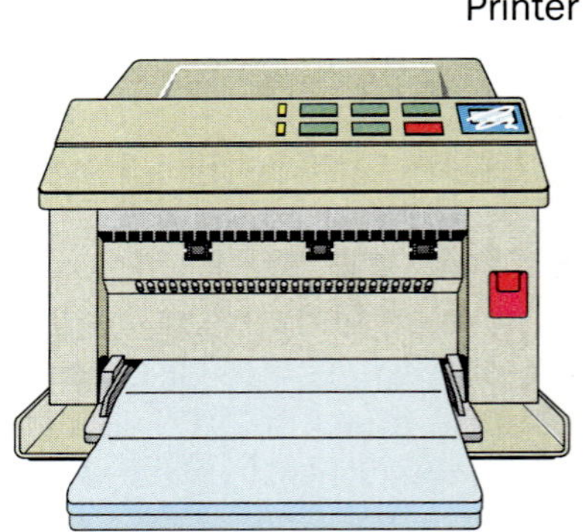

FIGURE A-3
Printer

Network

You may be using a stand-alone version of the software, or your computer might be connected to a number of other computers by way of a network. Whether or not you are using a network won't affect your training, but it may affect how you print and how you save your work. Be sure your instructor gives you the "rules" for your particular classroom so your work is properly saved in a location where you can find it when you need it.

The WordPerfect® Environment

It is important that you are comfortable with the environment in which you are working when you learn a computer program. In the case of WordPerfect 9, that includes the WordPerfect working window, as well as the Windows interface.

You must know how to start and exit from the program. You also need to know the parts of the WordPerfect window. In this appendix you will learn about all of those things and more. You will even have some practice exercises to help you learn. Follow along carefully.

Starting and Exiting WordPerfect®

Look at the Windows desktop. Do you see an icon with a picture that looks somewhat like Figure B-1? The word(s) identifying the icon might be different, but the pen in front of the globe will be the same. The arrow indicates that the icon is a shortcut to the program.

If you don't see the icon, you may start WordPerfect from the Start button. WordPerfect might be included in the list at the top of the Start pop-up menu, or you may select it from the list of programs that appears when you choose Program from the Start pop-up menu. You can also select it by clicking the pen icon if the Desktop Application Director (DAD) is displayed on your desktop.

FIGURE B-1
WordPerfect Icon

S TEP-BY-STEP ▷ B.1

1. Start WordPerfect using one of the following four methods:
   a. If the icon pictured in Figure B-1 appears on your desktop, point to it and double click to start WordPerfect.
   b. If the icon is not on the desktop, click the **Start** button and look at the short list at the top of the pop-up menu. Is *WordPerfect Office 2000* there? If so, choose it and then choose **WordPerfect 9** to start WordPerfect.
   c. If neither of the first two conditions exist, click the **Start** button and choose **Programs**. Find *WordPerfect 9* in the list of programs. Choose it to start WordPerfect.
   d. Click the pen icon on the DAD bar.

2. Look at the WordPerfect window. Find the parts that are identified in Figure B-2, including the insertion point.

(continued on next page)

3. Move your mouse around in the window. What does the mouse pointer look like? Key your first name. Note that it begins at the vertical and horizontal guidelines. Move the mouse pointer over the name. What does the pointer look like when it is over text?

4. Press **Enter** several times and watch the *Ln* indicator on the Application Bar at the bottom of the window. The Title Bar will change from *WordPerfect 9 – Document1 (unmodified)* to

WordPerfect 9 – Document1. Press the **space bar** several times and watch the *Pos* indicator change.

5. Press **Backspace** until both the *Pos* and *Ln* indicators have returned to 1".

6. Finally, open the **File** menu and choose **Exit**. WordPerfect will ask if you would like to save the document. Click **No**. You should be returned to the Windows desktop.

FIGURE B-2
The WordPerfect 9 Document Window

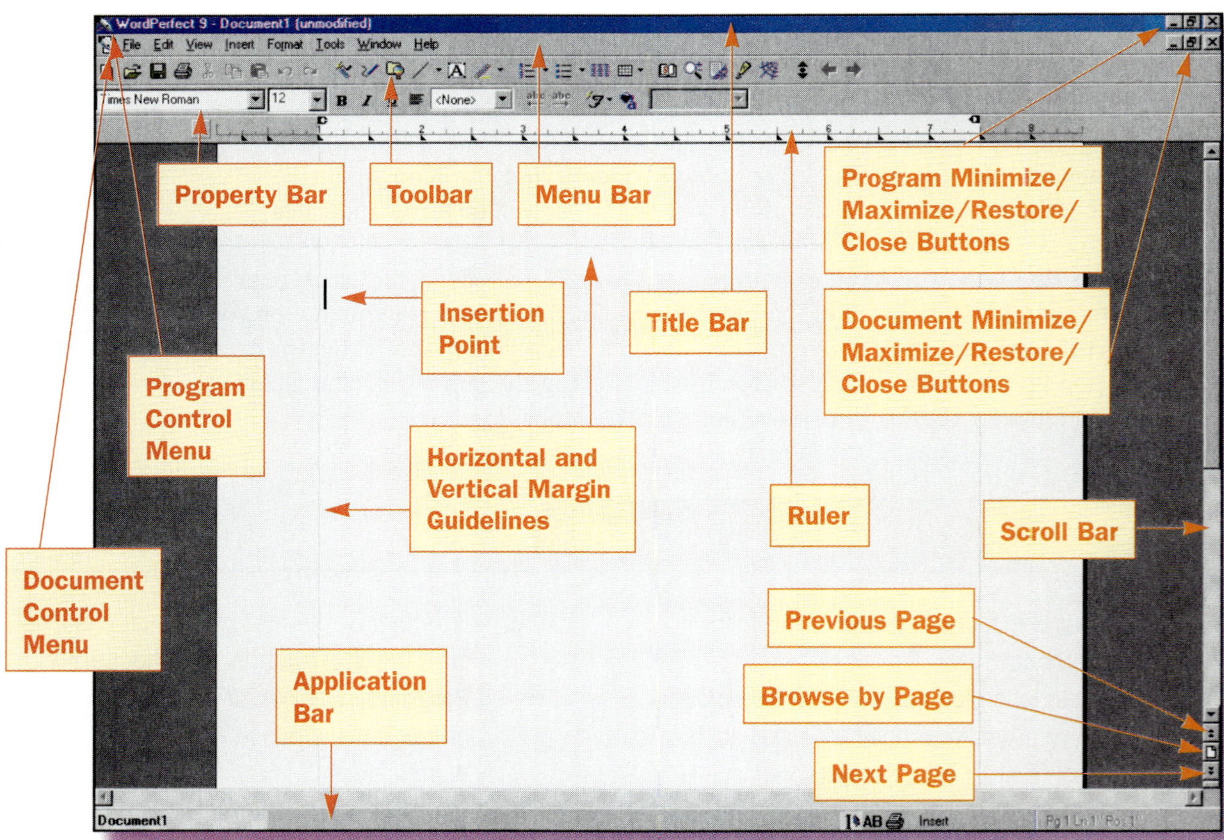

If you have never before worked in a Windows environment, the window may look strange to you and contain a number of parts that look confusing. After using the window for a short time, you'll become quite comfortable with its parts. Work to achieve that comfort zone, so you can begin using WordPerfect efficiently.

590

Giving Commands

There are two ways for you to give commands to your computer when you're working in Windows. As you've already learned, one of those ways is by making selections with the mouse.

Another way to communicate with the computer is by using the keyboard. You can move the insertion point with the arrow keys. You will enter text and numerals with the keyboard. If you prefer to keep your fingers on the keyboard, you can even use the keyboard to work through the menu system to choose many of your commands.

You can also use the function keys on the keyboard. This set of 12 keys provides access to many of the features available in the WordPerfect menus.

We'll begin to learn about all of these tools for communicating with your computer by starting WordPerfect again and creating a short text document. Then we'll look at some of the parts of the WordPerfect window.

Creating Text

To create text, simply key the information you wish to include in your document. If you make a mistake when you are keying, use the Backspace key to correct the error. Then continue keying as before. Let's practice.

S T E P - B Y - S T E P B.2

1. Using the steps in Step-by-Step exercise B.1, start WordPerfect. Key your name and press **Enter** twice.

2. Key your name again and press **Enter** two more times. The two occurrences of your name should be separated by a blank line, and the insertion point should be a double space below the second occurrence of your name.

3. Repeat Step 3 so your name appears in the window three times with the insertion point a double space below the third name.

4. Leave the text in the window as you read on.

The Application Bar

You may remember from Figure B-2 that the bar at the bottom of the working WordPerfect window is known as the *Application Bar*. This bar provides important information as you work. Look at the Application Bar in your window. A sample Application Bar is illustrated in Figure B-3. This Application Bar reports the following information:

FIGURE B-3
Sample Application Bar

| Document1 | | AB | Insert | Pg 1 Ln 1" Pos 1.04" |

- At the left side of the Application Bar, WordPerfect reports the names of open documents. In this case *Document1* is listed as the document you have open. It has not been saved, so it doesn't have a name.

- The button with the **I** and the arrow may look like it is depressed.

  - When the button is depressed, your mouse pointer looks like an arrow if positioned away from text. The arrow is followed by a Shadow Pointer that helps you locate your position. If you click in an empty portion of the window, the insertion point will be positioned wherever you click. You'll learn more about this later.

  - When the button is NOT depressed, the mouse pointer always looks like a large **I**. With the button in the "up" position, move the mouse pointer over your name. Leave the button in the "up" position, so your insertion point is always an **I**. Keep it that way as you work.

- The AB button is depressed when Caps Lock is turned on.

- The Printer button can be used to print a document.

- The Insert button tells you WordPerfect is working in Insert mode as opposed to Typeover mode, where new characters take the place of existing characters. You should work in Insert mode. (You'll learn to use Typeover in Lesson 2.)

- At the right, the Application Bar reports that the insertion point is on page 1 (*Pg 1*), it is 1" from the top of the page (*Ln 1"*), and it is 1" from the left side of the paper (*Pos 1"*).

The Application Bar can be customized so it might display different information. Compare your Application Bar with the one in Figure B-3. Is it the same? If not, what is different? Does the current date appear on your Application Bar?

You will find the information on the Application Bar to be very useful in your work—especially the part that reports the location of the insertion point in your document. Look at the Application Bar in your window. If your insertion point is below the final keying of your name, it should be somewhere around Ln 2.2". Use the arrow keys on the keyboard to move your insertion point. Does the Application Bar report the new location of your insertion point?

WordPerfect® Menus

The Menu Bar is the first gray bar at the top of your window. While all Windows programs have a Menu Bar, the menus listed on the Menu Bar vary from program to program. In WordPerfect 9, eight menus are listed. Within these menus, you should be able to find all of the tools needed to create, edit, and format documents, plus a large number of specialized tools to make your work easier.

Each menu has characteristics to help you work. Let's look at a menu and discuss what you see there.

1. Open the **Edit** menu and compare it to the menu illustrated in Figure B-4.

2. Look at the items that appear in gray. Those items are not available at this time. If you had text selected, more of the choices would be available.

3. Look at the items followed by three dots. If you choose one of these items, a dialog box will be opened. (You'll learn about dialog boxes soon.)

4. Look at the items followed by an arrow pointing to the right (▶). When you choose one of these items, another menu appears, growing from the side of the original menu.

5. Look at the information at the right of some of the menu items in Figure B-4. The menu shows that you can choose Cut, for example, by pressing Ctrl+X, or Find and Replace with Ctrl+F. Your menu may not display this information. You'll learn how to display these shortcuts at the end of this appendix.

6. Use your mouse to click **Convert Case**. Look at the little menu that appears.

FIGURE B-4
Edit Menu

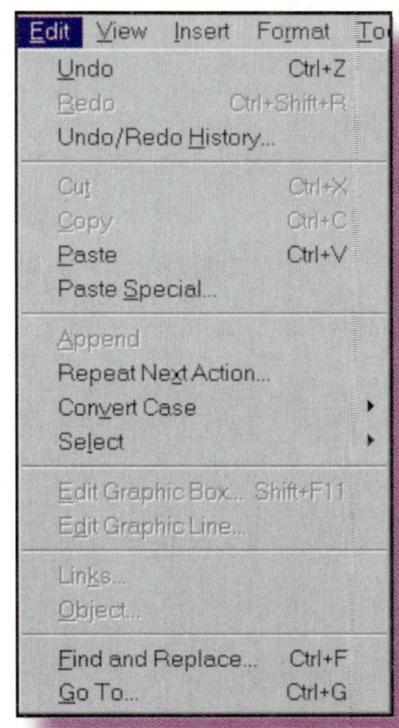

7. Use your mouse to click **Repeat Next Action**. Look at the little dialog box. Click **Cancel** to close the dialog box.

If you open a menu in error or decide you don't wish to make a selection from that menu, you can close it by clicking somewhere outside of the menu in the window. You can also close a menu by pressing the Alt key or by pressing Esc twice. If you open the wrong menu, simply open a different one. The original menu will disappear when the new one is opened.

Now that you know all about menus, let's take a look at dialog boxes and how they make your work easier.

WordPerfect® Dialog Boxes

Like menus, dialog boxes are used to group features to make them easy to find and choose. While some dialog boxes look complex because they contain many parts, most dialog boxes present choices in a logical manner. Dialog boxes usually contain information about *default* settings (preset conditions in the program). Let's explore a simple dialog box. Then we'll look at one that contains more parts.

Figure B-5 illustrates the dialog box used for setting margins. Notice that the default margins are 1" on all sides of the page. While this portion of the dialog box is used only for margins, the dialog box provides a number of options. You can:

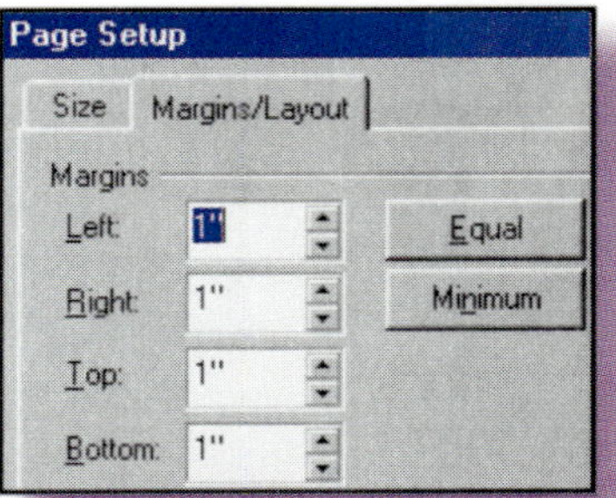

- Key the new setting over the highlighted setting in the white text box area. (It usually works well to use the Tab key to move from one text box to the next, although you can use the mouse to double click into each box, if you prefer.)

- Use the mouse to click the up or down buttons to change any of the four margins.

- Look at the illustration at the right to see how your document would look with the selected margin settings.

- Adjust the margins for binding booklets.

- Click the Help button to learn more about setting WordPerfect margins.

- Click OK to accept any setting changes you've made and return to your document

- Click the Cancel button to return to your document without making any changes.

- Choose a tab at the top to set a different aspect of a page setup.

Now it's time for you to try it.

STEP-BY-STEP ▷ B.4

SCANS

1. Open the **Format** menu and choose **Margins**.

2. Using the up or down buttons, change all four margins to **2"**.

3. Then change all four margins to **1.5"** by keying **1.5** into each text box.

4. Set the top and bottom margins at **1"** and the side margins at **1.25"**.

5. When you are comfortable with this dialog box, click **Cancel** to cancel any margin changes you made and return to your document.

Some dialog boxes contain additional parts like scroll bars, check boxes, and radio buttons. You will learn about those parts as you encounter them in your Step-by-Step exercises.

The Toolbar

Many of the choices you can make from menus have been made more readily available to you on the Toolbar, located just below the Menu Bar. The Toolbar contains a series of buttons, each with an icon to tell you what the button does. The WordPerfect 9 default Toolbar looks like Figure B-6.

When you use the mouse pointer to point at one of the buttons on the Toolbar, a small Quick Tip box will appear, identifying the function of the button. For some of the buttons keystroke equivalents will also be displayed. A variety of Toolbars comes with the program, and they automatically change to fit the feature you are currently using. You can also create your own Toolbars for your particular project needs. You will learn to do this much later in your training. Let's take a quick look at the default Toolbar.

FIGURE B-6
WordPerfect 9 Default Toolbar

S TEP-BY-STEP B.5

1. Point to the first button on the Toolbar. Do NOT click the mouse button. The Quick Tip should appear, telling you that button can be used to create a new blank document, and that you can do the same thing with Ctrl+N.

2. Point to the second button. It looks like a file folder. The Quick Tip should tell you it can be used to open a document.

3. The third button looks like a disk. What does the Quick Tip tell you? Of course, it is used for saving a document.

4. The fourth button is supposed to look like a printer. That's probably why the Quick Tip says *Print*.

5. Point to anywhere on the Toolbar and click the RIGHT mouse button. (This is called *right clicking*.)

6. Look through the list of Toolbars to get an idea of what features have their own Toolbars. Click outside of the list to close it.

Are you getting the idea of what the Toolbar can do for you? All of those choices are available in the various menus, but the Toolbar buttons enable you to choose the features more quickly. You will learn about more Toolbar buttons as you continue with your training.

The Property Bar

The Property Bar is just below the Toolbar. It includes a number of miscellaneous choices, some of which will be useful now and others that will be more useful later in your training. The default Property Bar looks like Figure B-7. Let's take a quick look at the buttons on the Property Bar.

WordPerfect 9 Default Property Bar

STEP-BY-STEP ⟹ B.6

1. Use the mouse to point to each of the buttons on the Property Bar and look at the Quick Tip descriptions to see what the button is used for.

2. Use the arrow keys to move your insertion point so it is a double space below the third keying of your name.

3. Click the **Bold** button. It has a dark uppercase *b* on it. The button will look like it is depressed. Key your name. (It should appear in bold.)

4. Click the **Bold** button again to deselect that attribute and press **Enter** twice.

5. With your insertion point a double space below your bolded name, point to the arrow beside the *12* on the Property Bar and click once.

6. When the drop-down menu of font sizes appears, choose **18 pt.** by pointing to *18* and clicking once. Key your name again. It should be quite large.

7. With the insertion point following your large name, display the font size drop-down menu again and choose **12 pt.** Press **Enter** twice. (You may need to use the scroll bar at the right to see the *12*.)

QuickMenus

Another way to make choices when you are using a mouse is by using a QuickMenu. A QuickMenu is displayed each time you point somewhere in the text part of your working window and click the right mouse button. (Remember *right clicking*? You used it in the Toolbar to display the list of available Toolbars.) The QuickMenu for the text part of a document window is illustrated in Figure B-8.

The features available in a QuickMenu depend on where the pointer is when you right click. What features are available also depends on what kind of application you are using. A right click in a WordPerfect table, for example, will display a *tables* QuickMenu. A different QuickMenu will appear if you have text blocked, or selected.

When you have right clicked to display a QuickMenu, you can choose options from the menu just like you would from any other kind of menu. If you decide you don't want any of the choices, you can close the QuickMenu by pointing anywhere outside of the QuickMenu and clicking the LEFT mouse button. You will have an opportunity to practice displaying QuickMenus in the next Step-by-Step exercise.

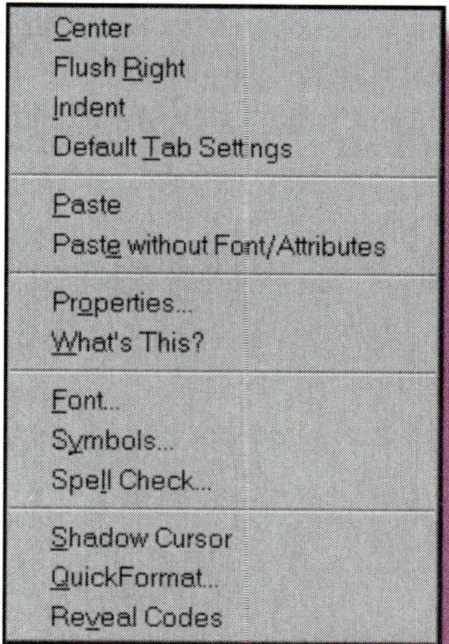
FIGURE B-8
Text QuickMenu

NOTE:

In these learning materials you will click (always with the **left** mouse button), double click (always with the **left** mouse button), and right click (using the **right** mouse button). If you remember that terminology, the mouse won't be a pest to you at all!

The Function Keys

When working with most computer applications programs, features can be chosen using the function keys—those keys across the top of the keyboard that are identified with *F* and a numeral. Word-Perfect uses the 12 function keys to give you access to nearly 70 features. This is done by combining the function key with one or more other keys, such as Alt, Ctrl, or Shift.

Earlier versions of WordPerfect came with a plastic or heavy paper strip to be placed on the keyboard near the function keys to tell you which key to use for which feature. That strip was known as a *function key template*. A function key template does not come with WordPerfect 9, but if you have an old one from WordPerfect 6.0 or 6.1 for Windows, most key assignments have not changed.

In the lessons, when a feature may be chosen with a function key combination more easily than from a menu, your instructions will include that information. The function key assignments you learn will also appear in the Command Summary at the end of each unit and in the Quick Reference at the end of the text.

Closing a Document

Normally when you close a document, you are finished with it and wish to save it on a disk. Sometimes you simply wish to throw it away. To close, open the File menu and choose Close. A dialog box that looks like the one in Figure B-9 will appear.

If you choose No, the document will be closed but not saved. If you choose Cancel, the dialog box will disappear and you will be returned to your document. If you choose Yes and it's a new document, the Save As dialog box will appear so you can name your document and tell WordPerfect where it should be saved.

FIGURE B-9
Close Dialog Box

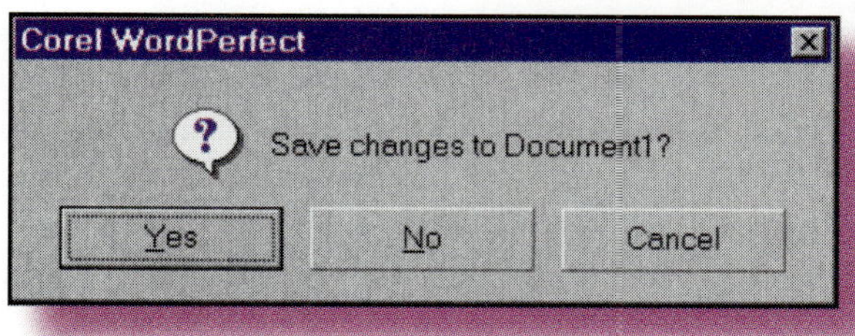

Note that the Yes button is enclosed with a heavy black line. Any time the button containing the choice you want to make is enclosed with the black line, you may simply press Enter. If you want a different choice, point to that button with the mouse pointer and click. Sometimes it's convenient to use the Tab key to move from one choice in the dialog box to another.

For this Step-by-Step exercise we will practice with QuickMenus and then close your document without saving it.

S TEP-BY-STEP ▷ B.7

1. With the insertion point a double space below the big version of your name, key **This is fun**.

2. Point to the words you just keyed and right click. Does the QuickMenu that appears look like the one in Figure B-8? Click outside the QuickMenu to close it.

3. Point to somewhere above the guideline at the top of your document (in the top margin) and right click. The QuickMenu should have to do with headers, footers, and watermarks. Close the QuickMenu.

4. Point somewhere in the left margin area (to the left of your text) and right click. The options listed have to do with selecting text and a variety of other things. Close the QuickMenu. (This is enough about QuickMenus for now. You'll be working with them later.)

5. Open the **File** menu and choose **Close**.

6. When the dialog box illustrated in Figure B-9 appears, either use the mouse to click **No** or press **Tab** to move to **No**, and press **Enter** to affirm the command.

Saving a Document

Now that you are familiar with the parts of the WordPerfect window and you know how to close a document without saving it, you will create some more text to be saved on your disk. In this Step-by-Step exercise you will be keying text in a paragraph.

When keying paragraphs on computers, it is important to remember to press Enter only at the end of the paragraph. Let text wrap to the next line when a line is filled (*Word Wrap*). This allows you to key continuously without worrying about line endings. It also makes editing your text much easier.

S TEP-BY-STEP ▷ B.8

1. Key the text paragraph in Figure B-10. Press **Tab** to indent the first line. Then key continuously, until the paragraph is complete. Don't worry about errors!

2. Press **Enter** twice at the end of the paragraph.

3. When you finish, keep the paragraph showing in your window as you read on.

Please make a note of the fact that our corporate offices are being moved to a new location at 1234 Washington Avenue. Beginning the first of next month, all of our officers will be making their business contacts in their new offices.

Before you can save your work, you must know where your instructor would like your documents saved. The Step-by-Step exercises in this book are written with the assumption that your work will be saved on a diskette in Drive A of your computer. If your instructor would like your work saved elsewhere, you will have to make the proper changes to the instructions as you work. Be sure to ask for help if you need it.

STEP-BY-STEP ▷ B.9

1. Open the **File** menu and choose **Save**, or click the third button on the Toolbar (the one that looks like a disk).

2. The Save File dialog box will open. While the dialog box may not look much like Figure B-11, it will have some of the same characteristics. The parts you will work with here don't change, no matter how the appearance of the box is altered.

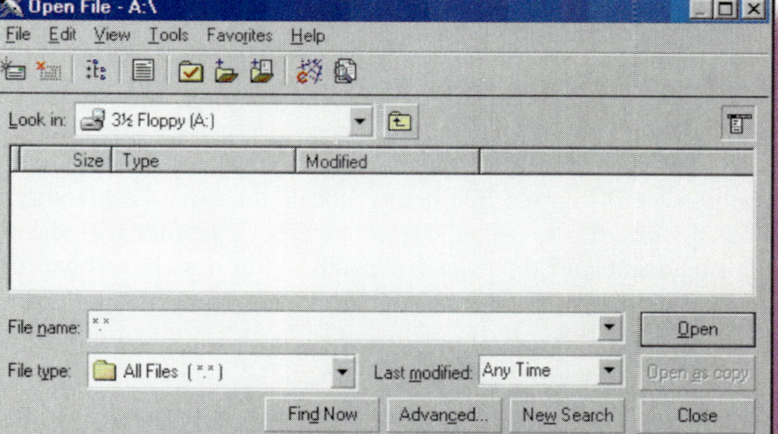

3. The insertion point will be at the bottom in the *Filename* text box. For the name of the document, key **move b-9 xxx** (with your initials taking the place of the *xxx* portion of the filename). DO NOT PRESS ENTER!

4. Near the top is the *Save in* text box. That portion of the dialog box has a small arrow beside it. Click the arrow to display the box that enables you to choose the directory or drive. Assuming you are saving your work on the disk in Drive A, use the scroll bar, if necessary, to locate *3½ Floppy (A:)*. The drop-down list should resemble Figure B-12.

5. Click to select that drive.

(continued on next page)

STEP-BY-STEP ⟹ B.9 CONTINUED

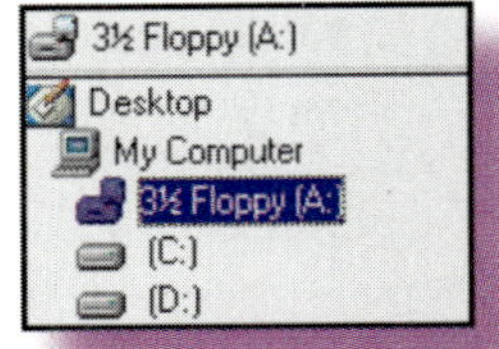

6. Press **Enter** or click **Save** to tell WordPerfect you have made your choices in the dialog box. You will see the light on Drive A as your document is saved on your disk. The document will remain in the window.

Look at the Application Bar at the bottom of the window. The name of the document should appear there. Look at the Title Bar at the top of the window. The document name and location (*filepath*) appears there.

A couple of other things need to be mentioned at this point. Pressing Enter usually closes a dialog box. If you press Enter before you have made all of the changes in the dialog box, you may get some unwanted results. For example, if you had pressed Enter after keying the name of the document in Step-by-Step exercise B.9, your document might have been saved in a strange place, and you might not have been able to find it again.

Also, had you been finished with your document, you could have chosen Close from the File menu. The same Save File dialog box would have been opened, and your procedure for saving your document would have been the same. The only difference would have been that the document would be cleared from your screen right now if you had used Close.

Opening and Resaving a Document

When a document has been saved, you can reopen it for any reason. To open a document, simply choose Open from the File menu. Locate the drive or directory where the document has been saved. Then double click to open the document. Let's practice with the paragraph you just saved. We will close the document and then open it again. After you have opened the document, you will change the document slightly and then save it with a new name using Save As. (If you save it again with the Save, the new file will be saved over the old file. When you use Save As, you'll end up with both files.)

STEP-BY-STEP ⟹ B.10

SCANS

1. Display the **File** menu and choose **Close**. Your document should disappear.

2. Now display the **File** menu again and choose **Open**.

3. If necessary, change to $3^1/_2$ *Floppy (A:)*, the way you did in Step-by-Step exercise B.9.

4. Click to position the highlight on the **move b-9 xxx** document. You may open the document in one of three ways.

- With the highlight on the desired document, press **Enter** because the **Open** button is chosen.
- With the highlight on the desired document, click **Open**.
- Point to the desired document and double click.

Choose a method and do it now. The document should appear in your window.

5. With your insertion point at the beginning of the document (that's where it is when a document is opened), key your complete name and press **Enter** twice to make some room between your name and the paragraph.

6. Choose **Save As** from the **File** menu. The Save As dialog box will appear.

7. In the *Name* text box, click to position the insertion point at the end of the word *move*. Key **2**. (The new document name is **move2 b-9 xxx**.)

8. Click **Save** to save the document. Keep the document open as you read on.

WordPerfect® Help

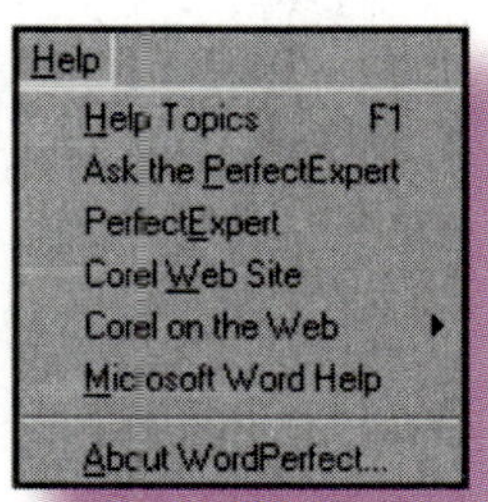

FIGURE B-13
Help Menu

In the earlier discussions of menus, one of the menus mentioned was the Help menu. A vast resource for help in using WordPerfect is available from the Help menu.

Help looks the same in most programs running under Windows. You may access Help from the Help menu or by pressing F1. The Help menu is illustrated in Figure B-13.

The first choice, *Help Topics*, brings up the Help dialog box (see Figure B-14). Note the tabs near the top of the dialog box. The first tab (*Contents*) provides a variety of ways of using Help. A wide variety of topics are available when you choose this tab. *Getting started*, for example, contains many topics of Help from which you may choose. You might wish to explore the choices in this dialog box when you have some extra time.

The second tab, *Index*, provides an extensive alphabetized list of topics, much like an encyclopedia or dictionary. To find a particular topic, begin keying the name of the feature. The more you key, the closer WordPerfect will get to the topic you're seeking. When the topic is displayed, double click to go to the Help window for that topic.

The third tab, *Find*, sets up a database of words in the Help topics so you can search for Help more efficiently—after the database has been established. You won't work with that feature in this training.

The fourth tab, *Ask the PerfectExpert*, enables you to ask WordPerfect a question. Then it will display a list of possible locations to answer your question.

FIGURE B-14
WordPerfect Help

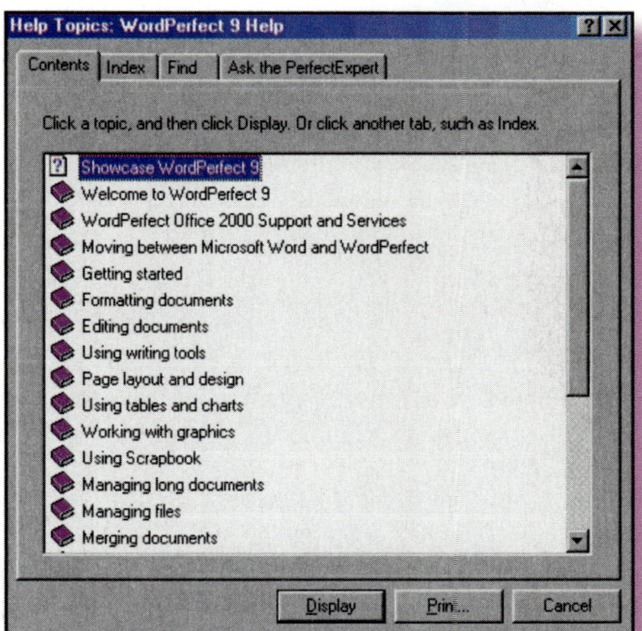

Help can also be chosen by pressing F1. The window that appears whenever you choose Help is the same one that was used last time Help was accessed. In other words, WordPerfect remembers which Help window you used last. We'll use Help to learn about QuickFinder, a powerful tool that helps you find files.

1. Open the **Help** menu and click the **Index** tab. Key **QuickFinder** and double click **QuickFinder: About**.

2. Double click the second choice. The Help window in Figure B-15 will appear. Read the QuickFinder information.

3. Point to the *To find a file by name* button at the bottom. Note that the pointer turns into a hand. Click the button.

4. Read about finding a file. Then click the **Help Topics** button at the bottom of the box to return to the list of Help topics.

5. Use the scroll bar to go to the bottom of the Help topics. What is the last major group of topics in the list? It should be a series of *zoom* choices.

FIGURE B-15
PerfectFit Dialog Box

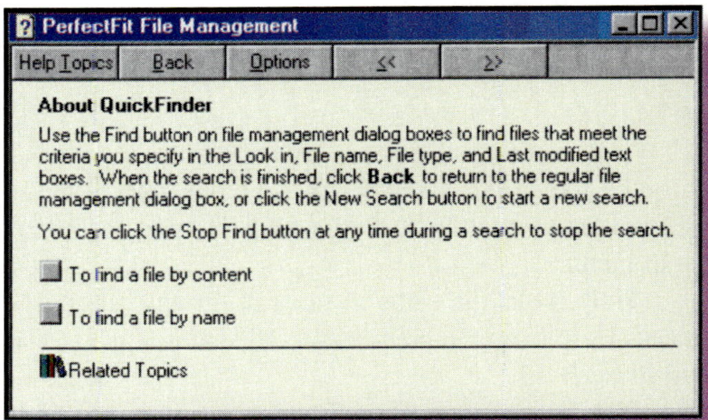

6. Click the **Cancel** button at the bottom right to close the dialog box. Click the **X** to close the PerfectFit help box.

The Help menu (refer back to Figure B-13) contains some other ways to get help. *PerfectExpert* is a feature that will lead you through several common tasks. If you have a modem and an Internet connection, *Corel on the Web* will take you to the Corel WordPerfect 9 home page.

Finally, *About WordPerfect* provides program information about your registered serial number and release numbers of the program. This information may be important when you call WordPerfect for technical help.

The Help feature is packed full of important information. What's more, it is said to be *context-sensitive;* that is, when you are using a feature and you access Help, WordPerfect will often take you to the special Help topics related to the feature with which you are working. You will want to spend some time exploring Help when you've learned a little more about WordPerfect features.

Changing Defaults

As you will learn throughout your training, WordPerfect is set for you to use. That includes many decisions made by the developers of the software regarding what is best for you when you are working. Most of the time, those decisions are fine. Occasionally you'll want to make some changes to help you learn.

In the next Step-by-Step exercise you will go to the Settings dialog box to look at where you can make some of those changes. **With your instructor's permission**, you may change a couple of settings. One is to display the keyboard shortcuts in your menus. Another is to change the number of minutes between automatic backup.

Ask your instructor if you should make any changes to WordPerfect in Step-by-Step exercise B.12. If so, go ahead and follow the steps in the exercise. If not, look at the dialog boxes in the Step-by-Step exercise, but don't make any changes. (If you are working on a network, WordPerfect may not accept any changes you make in this lesson.)

S TEP-BY-STEP ⟹ B.12

(Optional, with instructor's approval)

1. Open the **Tools** menu and choose **Settings** (at the bottom). A dialog box with icons will appear.

2. Double click to choose **Environment** and click the **Interface** tab. At the left are three items regarding what will be displayed in the menus. If *Shortcut keys* doesn't have a check mark, click to choose that option. Click **OK** to leave this dialog box.

3. In the Settings dialog box, choose **Files**. Look at the choices in the dialog box. It is here that you tell WordPerfect to save your documents with the *.wpd* extension. It is here that you can also set the time for automatic backup. The default is 10 minutes.

4. Change to 5 minutes and click **OK** to close the dialog box. Close the Settings dialog box to return to your document window.

Exiting WordPerfect®

You are about finished with the Step-by-Step exercises in this appendix. Let's practice exiting from WordPerfect. You already did it earlier without a document in the window. This time you have a document open that has already been saved. Note that the Title Bar displays the name and location of the document. The name of the document is also on the Application Bar at the bottom of the window. We'll change the document before exiting so you are asked about saving again. Follow along carefully.

1. Be sure your insertion point is a double space below your document. If it isn't, hold the **Ctrl** key while you press the **End** key (**Ctrl+End**) to move it there.

2. Key your name.

3. Open the **File** menu and choose **Close**. A dialog box will appear, asking if you would like to save the changes to the document.

4. Press **Enter** (because **Yes** is the selected response) or use your mouse to click **Yes**.

5. Open the **File** menu and choose **Exit**. You will be returned to the Windows desktop.

Summary

This appendix has given you a good introduction to using WordPerfect for creating and saving text. You learned:

- How to start and exit WordPerfect.
- A number of ways to give commands to WordPerfect.
- About the Application Bar.
- About the WordPerfect Toolbar and Property Bars.
- About WordPerfect menus and dialog boxes.
- How to use QuickMenus and function keys.
- How to close and save a document in the desired location.
- How to open a document that has been created and saved.
- How to resave a document.
- How to use WordPerfect Help.

It is important that you have a good understanding of this material before you embark on Lesson 1. If you feel you need additional help with any of the topics covered in this appendix, please ask your instructor for help.

File Management

Creating and saving documents (or files) is only part of what a good word processing program can help you do. Managing those files after you've prepared them is an important part of what YOU must do. The computer can help you, but it is your responsibility to manage your files in such a way that they can be located when needed.

Naming Files

A file name may consist of up to 255 characters, spaces, or punctuation marks. For example, both **appendix.c** or **appendix c for WordPerfect 9 text** would be acceptable for the file name of this appendix. When naming your files, you should use consistency and organization. This not only makes naming easier, but it also makes locating the files easier.

Whatever method you choose, be sure that it is indeed a method—not just a haphazard naming of files. To find a file, you need to know exactly "which drawer to open and which file folder to retrieve."

In this training you will be given the names for the files you create or edit and save. These file names will include some information about the topic of the file, the lesson and Step-by-Step exercise number of the file, and your initials (in place of *xxx*) to help you and your instructor identify your work. The suggested names make it easier for you and your instructor because they will be the same for all students. As you work with naming files, think about how you might have named the file if given a choice in the matter.

Organizing Files

Visualize an office with no organized paper filing system. When you open the file drawers, you find letters, memos, reports, and contracts piled into the drawers. The same thing can happen when you store files on disks and have no plan for what is stored on which disk or in which folder. File management is as important for computerized files as it is for paper files—maybe even more so because you can't see what's on a disk by looking at it. You must access each file, unless it is very clearly named, to see what that file is about.

Whether you save your files on diskettes or a hard disk, the issue of file management is critical. Let's look at some of the principles of file management.

Filing on Diskettes

If you save your files on diskettes, be organized about what you put on each disk. Think of your disks as file folders in the drawers of a filing cabinet. Organize your work so you can access your files as efficiently as you would be able to access a paper document from the proper file folder in the proper drawer of the filing cabinet.

Plan ahead and organize your disks. In the office you might arrange your files by client and/or matter, case, type of documents (i.e., letters, memos, reports, etc.), or by author.

Filing on a Hard Disk

In most cases with a hard drive system, both your software files and your document files are stored on the same hard disk. With everything stored on one disk, it is especially important to set up a system of organizing files so you can find them when you need them.

When you save on the hard disk, you must group the files into *folders,* as discussed in the next section. The main folder on a hard drive is usually known as **C:**. If you are working on a network, you may have a number of drives, each named with an alphabetic letter. Unless you are a network specialist, you won't mess with those drives.

Regardless of the drive name, the main folder can contain dozens of folders, and each of those folders can contain dozens of folders of their own, and so on. The same is true of diskettes. If the diskette is in Drive A, the main storage area is referred to as **A:**. You can create folders on diskettes, and those folders can contain more folders.

Using Folders

Since it isn't practical to save all files in the same location, the accepted method for separating them is into what are known as *folders*. A folder is a place where related documents are kept together. Sometimes you will create a folder to hold a special kind of work before you begin the work. Then, as the files are created, they will be saved into that folder.

Sometimes you will create the folder for related files after some of the files have been prepared and saved. At that point, you will need to move the files into the folder. In Lesson 8, you will learn to create such a folder and move or copy practice files into that folder.

Figure C-1 illustrates the folder tree structure after you complete the Step-by-Step exercises in Lesson 8. Note that you have two levels—the original main level and a set of folders on the second level. The names of the folders on each level must be unique. In other words, you can't have two **Applications** folders on the same level. You could, however, use **Applications** as a folder in the **Units 1 and 2** folder AND the **Units 3 and 4** folder, if you chose.

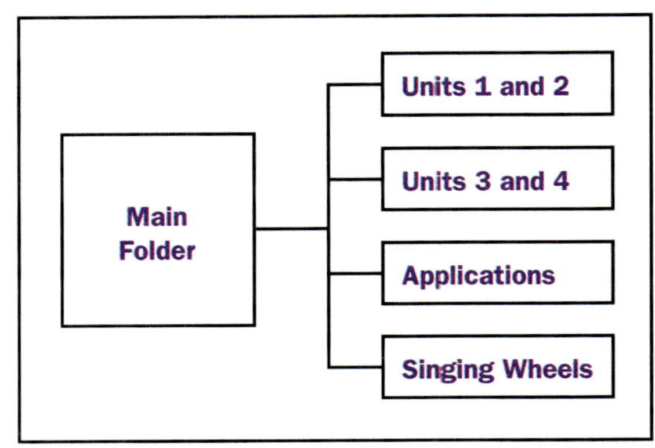

FIGURE C-1
Folders after Lesson 8

It is very important that you THINK about the arrangement of your folders so your work is stored logically. If it isn't, you are likely to have trouble finding a file when you need it.

Making Backup Files

One of the most important things you must do when you are filing documents on disk is to make backup files on a regular basis. This prevents loss of important files due to disk damage or problems with the computer. Proper backup procedures also protect your office from theft and natural disaster. Backup disks or tapes may be stored in a fireproof vault or at a different location.

Backup of your files may simply include copying all of the files created during one working day from the file disk or folder you were using that day onto another disk. This gives you two copies of everything you save.

The Disk Operating System (DOS) Copy and Backup commands may be used for making backup copies. Backups can be made from the Windows Explorer. Tape backup systems can be used to back up entire hard drives on a regular basis. This includes document files as well as program files, although most systems allow you to specify which folders are to be backed up.

The method of backup your office uses might determine how you name your files. In any case, it is important that you back up your work regularly and save your backup disks in a safe place.

Purging Files

Regular paper filing cabinets must be cleaned out regularly. A good records management program mandates the disposal of files that are old or no longer needed. Disk files need to be cleaned out on a regular basis, too. Time should be set aside each week, or preferably each day, to go through the files on your disks and "clean house." The Preview feature in the Open dialog box (discussed in Lesson 8) will help you preview files when you can't immediately remember a file name. By limiting the files stored in the main folder on your disks to those currently needed, your retrieval time for accessing files will be improved.

Some files can simply be discarded when they have no further value to you or your firm. You can do that with the Delete option when you are in the Open dialog box. Other files may have value but may be used only once every several months. Those files that are not needed on a regular basis might need to be archived.

Archiving refers to storing seldom-used files in a safe but out-of-the-way place. By copying these seldom-used files to a special disk and deleting them from your working disks, you can improve your retrieval time. In addition, your working disks or folders will have more room for your current work. You will want to have some system for archiving files so that you can find them when you need them.

Disk Capacity

Obviously, the total bytes available on a disk is limited. (A *byte* is approximately equal to a character.) The most commonly used diskette is the high-density $3^1/_2$-inch size, which holds 1,440,000 bytes (1.44 megabytes, or Mb). Be careful not to fill a diskette more than three-quarters full. The Open File dialog box reports the number of bytes in the files on a disk or in a folder and the number of bytes remaining unused. Sometimes file sizes are reported in kilobytes (Kb). Each kilobyte is 1,024 bytes.

The current capacity of hard drives is much, much greater than that of diskettes, but much of the space on today's hard drives is filled with operating system and program files. This means that you must be as careful with disk space on the hard drives as on diskettes.

In your lessons you will be asked to save some files that have no future importance. Some of the Step-by-Step exercises in the lessons involve deleting some files and moving others to related folders. Complete these Step-by-Step exercises along with the others in the lessons so you continue to have room to save your files as directed.

Selecting Files

To select a single file, display the Open File dialog box, use the mouse pointer to point to the file to be selected, and click. When a file has been selected, you may open the File menu and choose Delete, Move, Copy, Rename, or a number of other options.

To select a group of files, point to the first file to be selected with the mouse pointer and click to highlight it. Then hold the Shift key while you click the last file in the group to be selected. The first and last file will remain highlighted, and all of the files between the two will also be highlighted. If there are more files to be selected than are showing at one time in the *file name* box, continue to hold the Shift key and use the scroll bar to move the list so you can see the final file to be selected. Click that file and release the Shift key. The Status Bar at the bottom of the Open File dialog box may tell you how many files are selected and how many bytes are in the selected files. If the Status Bar doesn't show, you may choose it from the View menu in the Open File dialog box. With the files selected, you may copy, delete, or move the highlighted files.

To select scattered files, hold the Ctrl key while you click those to be selected. You may use the scroll bar (still holding Ctrl) to move through the list to find the files. When you have highlighted all of the files to be selected, open, delete, move, or copy the files as desired.

Using a Mouse

Whenever you use a computer that's working in the Windows environment, you will need a mouse to start programs, move the insertion point, select text, and choose items from menus or dialog boxes. When used properly, the mouse is a helpful little critter.

There is a lot of press these days about using a computer for extended periods of times and remaining physically healthy. One consideration is sitting properly in a good chair. Another consideration is the keyboard—whether you keep your wrists straight when your fingers are busy keying, or if you allow your wrists to rest somewhere in front of the keyboard. The third consideration, although it receives less attention, is the use of a mouse.

Hand Position

The basic guidelines for using the mouse in such a way that it doesn't cause physical problems to your hand, arm, or shoulder are listed here. Use this list to check your hand position:

- Align your thumb along one side of the mouse, with two or three fingers on the other side.
- The mouse should nestle in the palm of your hand, with two or three fingers (depending on whether you have a two-button mouse or a three-button mouse) over the mouse buttons.
- Keep your wrist straight! This means supporting at least a portion of your forearm on the surface where the mouse is positioned. With the wrist straight and the mouse in your palm, you should be able to draw a straight line from your elbow to the cord end of the mouse.
- Position the mouse so you don't have to reach for it. Right beside the keyboard would be good if you have proper arm support with it in that position.
- The mouse should be at about the same height as the keyboard.

The Mouse Buttons

On most personal computers the mouse has either two or three buttons. The button at the left is known as the *primary* mouse button. When you are told to click with the mouse button, the assumption is that you will use the left button.

The button on the right is known as the *secondary* mouse button. In some programs, using the button on the right is becoming much more common for certain tasks. In these learning materials, whenever you are to use the right mouse button, you are told to *right click*.

Sometimes a mouse will have three buttons. When you have a three-button mouse, the mouse driver can be configured to assign special tasks to the middle button. Most often, that assignment is a double click. In other words, when you need to double click, click the middle button one time.

Lefties

Left-handed people can learn to use the mouse with their right hands, if they wish. On a computer that is shared with other workers who are right-handed, this might be the better option.

If the left-handed person wishes to use the mouse with his or her left hand, a couple of options are available. One option is to learn to click the primary mouse button with the middle finger. Then the index finger is used to click the secondary mouse button. That may seem awkward because most of us move our index finger better than any of the others.

It is a simple process to exchange the left and right mouse assignments. This is done in the Windows Control Panel. If you wish to make this change on your home or office machine and you are not familiar with the Control Panel, someone who has had Windows training can help you make this change. Your instructor would probably prefer that you NOT make this change in the classroom.

In the learning materials of this text it is assumed that the primary mouse button is the left button. If you have switched your mouse buttons, keep that change in mind as you proceed.

Clicking and Dragging

When you move the mouse on its mouse pad, the mouse pointer moves in the window. The appearance of the pointer differs, depending on its location in the window. Most of the time, when it is in the document portion of the window, it is a vertical line. When the line is in the position where you want the insertion point, click the left mouse button to position it there.

When the pointer is an arrow, it helps you choose menu items or buttons from one of the many bars or dialog boxes. It also is used with the scroll bars. When the pointer is in the left margin, the fat white arrow points in the opposite direction. Following is a summary of some of the things you will do with the mouse on your computer:

- **Click** once to select an item from the Toolbar, the Property Bar, or a dialog box. You will also click once to position the insertion point in your document. You will always use the left mouse button for this.

- **Right Click** to display the QuickMenu or certain bar preferences.

- **Double Click** to select a word or start a program. In the Open File dialog box you may need to double click to change drives or folders. Many choices made in dialog boxes may involve clicking to select an item and then clicking OK to close the dialog box. If you double click the item you are selecting, the process often makes the selection and closes the dialog box automatically. Until you get used to working in dialog boxes, you may struggle with WHEN to click and when to double click.

- **Triple Click** to select a sentence. You won't use triple clicking very often.

- **Click and Hold** for some drop-down menus in dialog boxes. If you don't hold the mouse button after pointing to the button and clicking, the menu will close before you have a chance to make your choice.

- **Drag** is when you press the mouse button and hold it while you drag the mouse across the mouse pad, moving the pointer from one location to another. You might use this to select or highlight a block of text. You might also use it to drag selected text from one location to another.

Mouse Pad

It is important that you use a mouse pad under your mouse. This helps the mouse work well for you. It is very frustrating when your mouse doesn't do what you want it to do! The mouse pad provides a better surface "grip" for the ball in the mouse.

Without a mouse pad, the mouse ball picks up all kinds of dirt and needs to be cleaned more often. Also, the bottom of the mouse wears more rapidly when a mouse pad is not used.

Take good care of your mouse. Clean it regularly. With a little practice, you'll develop skill using the mouse that will serve you very well.

Codes

As you learn new formatting skills in your lessons, look at the codes in the Reveal Codes window. Then turn to this page and make a note of each code you see. Keep this list up to date so that you can use it as a reference for WordPerfect formatting.

CODE	DESCRIPTION

CODE	DESCRIPTION
	613

Working with Type

One of the joys of working with a text editing program on a computer is the capability of using a variety of typefaces and sizes to give your documents a professional appearance. Before you can work knowledgeably with type, however, you should be acquainted with the terminology.

Type Terminology

- **Typeface**. One design of type. A typeface has a name, like Arial, Times New Roman, Swiss, Courier, and Marigold.

- **Style**. A variation within a typeface. Some of the commonly used variations are bold and italic.

- **Typeface Family**. A group of all related sizes and styles derived from a master typeface.

- **Point Size**. The smallest unit of measure in typography is the point. One point equals approximately $1/72$ of a vertical inch. Another way of saying it is that 72-pt. type is approximately one inch tall.

- **Font**. A set of all characters (letters, numbers, and symbols) in a particular typeface in a particular size. When you select a font (e.g., Times New Roman 12 pt.), you are specifying typeface and size.

- **Leading** (pronounced "ledding"). The vertical space between lines of type. The term comes from the days when strips of lead separated the lines of type. In WordPerfect, leading is taken care of automatically, although if you wish to force a manual change, you can go to the Typesetting portion of the Formatting menu and choose Word/Letter Spacing.

- **Kerning**. Adjusting the space between individual pairs of letters. Adjustments to spacing can be made in the Word/Letter Spacing dialog box. Kerning is most often used when you are working with very large fonts.

- **Serif**. Type with strokes, or feet, at the ends of the main strokes of letters. Examples of typefaces with serifs include Bitstream Charter, Dutch, and Times New Roman. Serifs contribute to the readability of a typeface by helping the eye quickly differentiate between similar letters. You are reading serif type because it is used for most body text.

- **Sans Serif**. Type without serifs. The letters have no feet or strokes at the ends of the main strokes. Examples of sans serif typefaces include Swiss, Helvetica, Arial, and Univers. Sans serif typefaces are most often used for headings, headers, and any portion of the well-designed page except long passages of text. Can you find an example of sans serif type in this book?

- **Display**. Decorative and novelty typefaces. These typefaces are used for special purposes, like short announcements, but are avoided for body text. They are quite hard to read, especially in all caps. Examples of display typefaces include Script, Marigold, and Shelley Volante, as well as quite a number of other typefaces shipped with Windows and WordPerfect.

- **Monospaced**. Often called fixed-pitch type. Monospaced type requires the same amount of space on the line for each character, regardless of the size of the character. If you measure a horizontal inch in any document prepared in 12-pt. Courier, for example, you'll find that there are exactly ten characters in that inch.

- **Proportional**. Type in which characters take as much space as they need. Proportional type is characterized by the fact that wide characters like *m* and *w* take more space on the line than skinny characters like *i* and *t*. Depending on the text, you can fit one-half to one-third more information on a line with proportional type than with monospaced type, and it's usually easier to read.

As you can readily see, there is much to know about fonts. In WordPerfect you can easily choose a typeface as well as the point size for the document or portion of a document you are creating. Therefore, you can say you are choosing a font. All of the above definitions may be somewhat overwhelming to you. Let's look at some samples.

This is 24-pt. Times New Roman.

This is 16-pt. Times New Roman.

This is 12-pt. Times New Roman. This is a serif typeface. Notice the feet (ending strokes) on the letters. Notice, too, the extra space between lines to make room for the "descenders," like the bottom of the *p*. In WordPerfect that spacing is automatic. All of the characters in this paragraph are the same proportional typeface, but the letters obviously vary in size. Each size is a different font.

This is 24-pt. Arial.

This is 16-pt. Arial.

This is 12-pt. Arial. Note the lack of feet. Arial is a proportional *sans serif* typeface.

```
This is Courier 10cpi (characters per inch) and it looks much
like typewriter spacing. This is Courier 12cpi. Courier is a monospaced
font.
```

Sources of Type

Hundreds of different typefaces are available today. The illustrated typefaces make up only a small sample from which you may choose. You can supplement the built-in fonts of most printers by purchasing interchangeable font cartridges or downloadable soft fonts.

WordPerfect contains a variety of scalable fonts. Most are True Type fonts and are marked with two T's in the font list.

Introduction to Windows

Welcome to Microsoft Windows 95/98®. Both of these versions of Windows provide you with an operating system that encourages you to think of your computer as your desk. It is a working area with quick access to the tools you use daily, such as your calculator, telephone, fax, and filing cabinet. It also enables you to run applications.

The majority of this text is dedicated to helping you learn to use WordPerfect 9 which runs under Windows 95/98. This appendix will give you a brief glimpse of your operating system, the tools that come with it, and how the mouse works in the operating system. Most of the features you'll read about in this appendix are present in both versions of the operating system.

While Windows 95 and Windows 98 may look much alike, Windows 98 has been designed so that certain features resemble a Web page. A vast number of Internet tools are tightly integrated into the operating system, and many of the mouse and browsing techniques are similar to those of the Internet.

Benefits of Windows 95/98

Windows 95/98 is a popular operating system because it provides a number of important benefits. Following is a list of some of the benefits that are important to most users:

- **Consistent Interface**–All programs that you run using this operating system look the same. The window is similar, the dialog boxes are similar, and the menus are similar, along with the other window parts. This makes it easier for you to go from one program to another.

- **Multitasking**–This operating system allows you to run several tasks or applications at the same time, enabling you to better manage your time.

- **Plug and Play**–A number of drivers come with the operating system, enabling you to install software or hardware in your computer, and have your system updated automatically.

- **Internet Access**–Microsoft Network, which comes as part of Windows, makes it easy for you to access the Internet, whether you wish to use it for e-mail or research purposes. (Windows 98 has a wealth of built-in Internet features.)

- **32-Bit Processing**–In the Windows environment, your programs can process data 32 bits at a time as opposed to the 16 bits at a time standard in earlier Windows and DOS environments.

- **Long File Names**–In naming your documents in a Windows environment, file names can be up to 255 characters or spaces long, freeing you from the DOS convention limiting you to an eight-character file name with a three-character extension.

New or Improved Features in Windows 98

In Windows 98, any window that displays folders, drives, and/or hardware objects is now referred to as an *Explorer window*. You can change the look of those windows so they look like a Web page containing hyperlinked objects. Some of the additional features or enhancements in Windows 98 include the following:

- A new filing system for your hard drive that uses less space when you store files. It stores information in smaller clusters and is referred to as FAT32.

- A new disk defragmenter that reorganizes data on the hard drive for faster computing.

- A system file checker that keeps track of important files needed to operate your computer. If these files are accidentally deleted, the checker will put them back.

- A disk clean-up tool that scans the hard drive for old, unused files and deletes them.

- A Windows update tool that automatically scans your system to see what free upgrades are needed and downloads them from the Internet. It then installs them.

- A new accessibility wizard which sets up the computer for persons with hearing or sight impairments.

- A DVD (Digital Video Disk or Digital Versatile Disk) driver that increases storage capacity. This will impact games and digitized movies.

- The ability to concurrently run several monitors on a single CPU.

- A choice between working using the *classic style* (Windows 95 style) or the *Web style*.

- The TV add-in enabling users to use their PC as a full-purpose multimedia box. With this device, users can access and interact with browser-based Web TV.

- The ability to use a Web page as a background and add Web components to the desktop that are updatable.

The Desktop

All work in programs running Windows begins at the desktop. Regardless of how your system has been customized, the desktop contains some common tools. If necessary, have your instructor help you to display the Windows desktop. Then find the following tools as they are discussed:

- **Taskbar**–The wide gray bar at the bottom (usually) is known as the taskbar. Your taskbar may contain some buttons, indicating that some applications are in use.

- **Start Button**–The Start button is at the left of the taskbar.

- **Clock**–In the lower right corner is a clock, telling you the current time (assuming your computer has been set with the time and date).

- **Icons**–The icons on the desktop will vary. The two you are most likely to see are the Recycle Bin and My Computer. In addition, a variety of other icons might appear. If the icon contains a bent black arrow in the lower left corner, that icon has been put on the desktop as a shortcut to a program or tool. To start an application using an icon, point to it with the mouse pointer and double-click.

- In Windows 98, the icons may be underlined. Applications represented by underlined icons can be started with a single click.

The Taskbar

As mentioned in the previous section, the default location for the taskbar is at the bottom of the window, although it can be at either side or the top. When you open a program, document, or window, a button for it appears on the taskbar. You can use this button to switch quickly between the windows or programs you have open. The more programs or tools you have running, the smaller the buttons for those tools are so they can all be displayed at one time. If necessary, you can make the taskbar deeper to hold more buttons.

In Windows 98, the taskbar can be customized to include additional tools–either for Internet purposes or to start applications. The Windows 98 taskbar can also contain Toolbars. A Toolbar available at start-up contains four new buttons. Three of them have to do with e-mail and the Internet. The fourth one may be used to minimize all open windows so you can view the desktop.

The Start Button

The Start button opens the Start menu, from which you can choose whatever you need to do your work. Figure G-1 shows the choices in the Start menu and what you can expect from each of those choices.

The Start button always shows in the taskbar, so you can make any choices you wish, even when you have a different window open or a different application running.

Accessories

A wide variety of tools are included in the accessories that come with Windows. These tools include a calculator, two simple word processing programs, and some games. If you are using a computer in the classroom, however, the games may have been removed to help keep you on the "straight and narrow." Figure G-2 lists most of the accessories and gives you a brief description of each.

Several of the accessories, such as Fax, Dial-Up Networking, HyperTerminal, and Phone Dialer, require the use of a modem and communications capabilities. Others, such as Calculator, Notepad, Paint, and WordPad are ready for use.

FIGURE G-1
Choices in the Start Menu

- **Programs**–Used to open the Programs submenu. This gives you access to the programs you use most often. An arrow to the right of an item indicates that a submenu will appear.

- **Documents**–Displays the names of the last 15 documents you have opened. Click the document you wish to open. Windows will load the appropriate program and open the document.

- **Settings**–Enables you to access many of the Windows environment settings.

- **Find**–Used to search for files and folders on your computer or on a network.

- **Help**–Opens the Windows Help feature.

- **Run**–Used to start a program.

- **Shut Down**–Used to shut down and restart Windows safely.

- **Favorites** (Windows 98)–Used to keep track of folders you use frequently.

- **Log Off** (Windows 98)–Used to log off the network without exiting Windows.

- **Fax**–Sends and receives faxes if you have the appropriate hardware.

- **Games**–Provides miscellaneous games.

- **Internet Tools**–Contains the Internet Explorer and Internet Setup Tools.

- **Multimedia**–Provides the ability to use video and sound or other media in your work, if you have the appropriate hardware.

- **System Tools**–Includes several utilities you can use to maintain your system's performance.

- **Calculator**–Performs mathematical calculations.

- **Character Map**–Provides a utility for displaying and printing unusual characters not found on the computer keyboard.

- **Dial-Up Networking**–Allows you to connect the computer to other computers and a network by way of a modem.

- **Direct Cable Connection**–Allows you to physically connect two computers that are running Windows. The computers don't need to be networked.

- **HyperTerminal**–Allows you to transfer and receive data over telephone lines if you have the appropriate hardware.

- **Notepad**–Provides a simple word processing program for writing and reading text files.

- **Paint**–Provides a drawing program with tools for creating or editing graphics.

- **Phone Dialer**–Stores up to ten phone numbers and speed-dials your calls using a modem.

- **Tips and Tour**–Introduces Windows 95 and displays tips–each time you start the program, if you wish.

- **WordPad**–Provides a simple word processing program for creating and saving text files.

My Computer

You can use My Computer to quickly and easily see everything on your computer. Double click the My Computer icon on the desktop to display the My Computer dialog box. It will look much like Figure G-3 with differences, of course, in the type of computer and configuration. My Computer in Windows 98 contains an Address Toolbar to quickly move from one location on the computer to another.

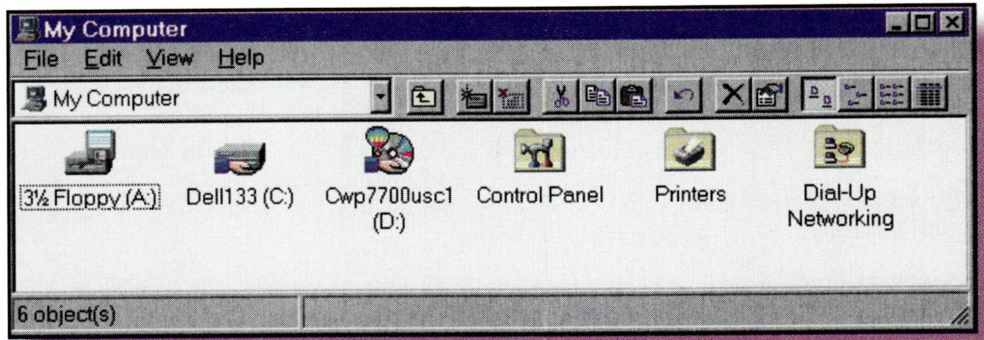

CD-ROM Drive

A very important tool in the My Computer dialog box is the CD-ROM drive. If you or your instructor has the WordPerfect Office 2000 CD and your computer has a CD-ROM drive, you can put that CD in the CD-ROM drive and install WordPerfect 9. You may have Clipart stored on a CD-ROM or additional fonts that you can access from the CD-ROM drive.

In addition, the WordPerfect Office 2000 CD contains the *Reference Center*. This is a set of on-line books containing detailed instruction for using the suite of applications. As you progress with your training in WordPerfect, your instructor may require you to use the *Reference Center* so that you become familiar with it.

Control Panel

Another important tool in the My Computer dialog box is the Control Panel. When you are using your own computer or you are in charge of the computer at your job, you may find the Control Panel useful for a wide variety of tasks. In the classroom you will probably be asked to not make any changes in the Control Panel. The items listed below are the Control Panel items you are most likely to use:

- **Printers**–Provides access to the **Printers** folder where you may install a printer, choose the default printer, assign ports, specify graphics resolution, connect to network printers, or choose paper size.

- **Keyboard**–Adjust the speed settings for repeating (typematic) keys, cursor blink rate, etc.

- **Display**–Controls the type of video display terminal attached to your system. Allows you to change visual settings.

- **Accessibility Options**–Opens a dialog box that lets you choose a variety of options to make your system easier to use if you have a visual, dexterity, or hearing impairment.

- **Add/Remove Programs**–Installs or uninstalls parts of the Windows program or installs or removes applications programs.

- **Mouse**–Tailors the way your mouse performs–double clicking and mouse speed. Also used to switch left and right mouse buttons.

File Management in Windows

My Computer can be used for file management. It is a graphical-user approach to conducting important and common file management tasks.

To **format a disk** using My Computer, follow these steps:

1. In My Computer, click once to select the icon for Drive A.

2. Open the File menu.

3. Choose Format. Follow the prompts to complete the formatting.

    To **create a folder** using My Computer, follow these steps:

1. In My Computer, double click to select Drive A.

2. Choose File and then New. Choose Folder.

3. Key the folder name and press Enter.

    To **rename a folder** using My Computer, follow these steps:

1. Point to the folder to be renamed and right click.

2. Select Rename.

3. Key the new folder name.

    To **copy and move folders** using My Computer, use these procedures:

1. To **copy** a folder to a different disk, drag the Folder icon on top of the Destination Disk icon.

2. To **copy** a folder to a different location on the same disk, hold Ctrl while you drag the Folder icon on top of the Destination Disk icon.

3. To **move** a folder to a different disk, hold Shift while you drag the Folder icon on top of the Destination Disk icon.

4. To **move** a folder to a different location on the same disk, drag it to the new location.

Creating Shortcuts

Windows has a number of ways for you to create shortcuts so that you can run the programs or start the desired applications from the desktop. One way is to do it from the Windows Explorer.

To **create a shortcut using Explorer**, be sure you can see a portion of the desktop outside of the Explorer dialog box. Then follow these easy steps:

1. Open the Explorer and locate the icon that starts the program to which you would like easier access. Click that icon to select it.

2. Open the File menu in the Explorer and choose Create Shortcut. Windows will make a copy of the icon and drop it to the bottom of the open folder. It will still be highlighted.

3. Drag that icon to the desktop. If you wish to change the text under the icon, click it once to select it. Then right click and choose Rename. Key the new name.

4. If you wish to delete a shortcut from the desktop, click once to select it. Press the Delete key on your keyboard and confirm the deletion.

Summary

This has been a quick introduction to Windows 95/98. In order to be good with this operating system, you will want to take a class or two. Windows works very well to get you in and out of WordPerfect. If WordPerfect is all you use, you don't need much Windows skill. You can use WordPerfect for most of your needs.

A

Archiving Moving important but seldom-used documents to a safe, out-of-the-way place. (p. 607)

B

Block Protect The feature that enables you to keep a block or section of text together on a page. You can adjust the size of the block to make soft page breaks fall in desirable locations. (p.167)

Bookmark A WordPerfect feature that enables you to mark a location in your document so that you can return to that location quickly. (p.179)

Boot To start a computer or program.

Border A line that extends around parts of a document or sections of text. (p. 351)

Button A rectangular section in a dialog box where you may click to accept or confirm a selection. (p. 592)

Byte The computer measurement of storage—usually representing one character, space, or command such as Tab or Hard Return. (p. 607)

C

Cascade Separate documents in separate windows displayed with parts of windows overlapping other windows. (p. 106)

Case-sensitive A feature, such as Search, where the results vary, depending on whether the letters are uppercase or lowercase. (p. 81)

Cell The intersection of a row and a column in a table or spreadsheet. A cell can hold text, a number, or a formula. (p. 199)

Click To position the mouse pointer on something and then press and quickly release the mouse button. (p. 597)

Codes The hidden commands that cause your document to be formatted. In WordPerfect you can use the Reveal Codes feature to see what codes are formatting your document and the location of those codes. (p. 22)

Concordance file A listing of the words or terms to be included in an index. When a concordance file has been prepared, WordPerfect will search through the designated text, list the occurrences of the words in the concordance file, and arrange an index, complete with page numbers. (p. 453)

Context-sensitive A feature that responds differently, depending on what you are doing when you use it. In WordPerfect the Help feature will go directly to the section on Outlining if you are working on an outline when you press F1 for Help. (p. 602)

CPU The working portion of the computer, known as the Central Processing Unit, that contains the processing and memory chips and the circuit boards that enable the computer to process your commands. (p. 587)

D

Data source (Data file) A collection of information to be merged with a form document. Often the data source contains names, addresses, telephone numbers, etc., of customers or clients. (p. 272)

Database A collection of related information, such as a collection of names and addresses of a group of people or a collection of parts in an inventory. In WordPerfect a database is referred to as a *data file*. (p. 272)

Default A setting built into a program that takes effect unless some alternative setting is specified. For example, in WordPerfect, the default margin settings are one inch on all sides of the page. (p. 593)

Delimiter A character used to mark the end of one part of a command and the beginning of another. (p. 413)

Desktop The opening window in a graphic environment, where the user may start a program by choosing an icon representing the desired program. (p. 616)

Dialog box A box that appears in the window to provide you with information or to let you select options and settings. (p. 593)

Document Any collection of information stored on a disk. You create a document when you collect graphics and/or text, give it a name, and save it. This term is used interchangeably with *file*. (p. 605)

DOS (Disk Operating System) Software that enables your computer to communicate with your disk drives and your software. (p. 607)

Double click To click the mouse button twice. Some actions can be accessed by clicking once. Others must be double clicked to be accessed. (p. 168)

Download To transfer data from a mainframe computer or network to a smaller unit, like your computer. Downloadable fonts are those fonts being downloaded from the computer hard drive to the printer. (p. 365)

Drag The act of positioning the insertion point in the window and holding the left mouse button while you move the mouse to the end of the section to be selected. (p. 86)

Drop cap A large letter dropped below the line of writing. It is used to call attention to the beginning of an article in a newsletter or magazine. (p. 391)

E

Em dash A symbol that is used to join two related phrases. It is the longest dash you can key. In WordPerfect you can key it by pressing the hyphen key three times. (p. 74)

Endnotes Endnotes are references to other works or publications. Endnotes are printed as a list on the final page of the document. (p. 152)

Extension The part of a document name following the period. DOS restricts the extension portion of a document name to a maximum of three characters. In WordPerfect it is not imperative that a document name include an extension. Exceptions are macros, style libraries, templates, form documents, data files, and graphics. (p. 616)

F

Field A single piece of information in a data file. Fields are separated by ENDFIELD codes and a hard return. (p. 273)

File Any collection of information stored on a disk. You create a file when you collect graphics and/or text, give it a name, and save it. This term is used interchangeably with *document*. (p. 605)

File name The first part of the name of a document to be saved on a disk. (p. 4)

Filepath The route to where a document is stored on a disk. A filepath includes the use of different levels of directories. For example, a document named *whale* in a folder named *mammals* that is within a main folder named *animals* on the hard drive would have the following filepath: *C:\animals\mammals\whale*. (p. 600)

Fill The background or shading that is present in some graphics or objects. (p. 351)

Find A WordPerfect feature that enables you to key a unique string of characters and then tell WordPerfect to find that text string. (p. 80)

Fixed-pitch font A font that allocates the same amount of space for every character. It is also known as a *monospaced* font. (p. 615)

Floating cell A one-cell table in a WordPerfect document that is attached to a larger table in the same document. When changes are made in the larger table, those changes are reflected in the floating cell. (p. 216)

Flush right The alignment of text at the right margin, leaving the left edges of the text ragged. (p. 127)

Font A set of all characters (letters, numbers, and symbols) in a particular typeface in a particular size. When you select a font (e.g., Times New Roman 12-pt.), you are specifying typeface and size. (p. 614)

Footer A piece of information printed at the bottom of the pages of a multiple-page document to tie the document together. Footers might include page numbers, chapter or unit titles, the title of the publication, or the date, depending on the kind of document being prepared. (p. 140)

Footnotes Footnotes are references to other publications or quotations taken from other publications. Footnotes are usually numbered and positioned at the bottom of the page on which the quoted or referenced text is mentioned. (p. 150)

Form document (Form file) The shell document or file used in a merge that contains the standard text to be merged with the data source. (p. 273)

Format (a disk) To prepare a disk to be used in the computer. When you format a disk, you are setting up the disk so that it can communicate with the computer in which you will be using it. (p. 621)

Formula An equation used to perform a calculation in a spreadsheet or a table. (p. 207)

Function keys The set of 12 *F* keys on the keyboards of IBM and IBM-compatible equipment are referred to as function keys. The function keys are used as an alternative to the menu system in choosing and executing WordPerfect features. (p. 597)

G

Global Find and Replace The ability to locate and change automatically the same word or phrase throughout a document or portion of a document. (p. 82)

GUI (Graphic User Interface) An operating system or program where the documents appear in multiple windows, complete with menus, scroll bars, and icons. Popular examples of operating systems using a graphical user interface are Windows and OS/2.

H

Handle A small box that is displayed on the perimeter of a graphic when a graphic has been selected. Handles can be dragged to size and shape a graphics image. (p. 347)

Hanging indent A paragraph format where the first line of the paragraph begins at the left margin and the remaining paragraph lines are indented to the level of the first tab stop. (p.66)

Hard copy The printed copy of a document.

Hard disk The high-capacity storage device that is usually permanently affixed inside of the CPU of the computer. Computer programs such as WordPerfect are recorded on the hard disk for easy access. (p. 588)

Hard page break A page break entered manually by the person preparing the document. Hard page breaks always stay in the same position in a document, regardless of text added or deleted. A hard page break is entered by holding Ctrl while pressing Enter. (p. 69)

Hard space A space used between two words or word parts which are not to be separated at the end of the line; e.g., between the first name and the initial in Gail M. Weber. A hard space is entered by holding Ctrl while pressing the space bar. (p. 74)

Headers Pieces of information printed at the top of the pages of a multiple-page document. Headers tie a document together and might include page numbers, chapter or unit titles, the title of the publication, or the date, depending on the kind of document being prepared. (p. 140)

HTML (Hypertext Markup Language) The commands needed to format documents for the Internet. WordPerfect will convert documents to HTML format. (p. 493)

Hyphen character A kind of hyphen used between two word parts which are not to be separated at the end of a line. Hyphen characters might be used as minus signs in formulas or between the parts of a telephone number. A hyphen character is entered by holding Ctrl while pressing the hyphen key. (p. 73)

I

Icon A miniature graphic representing a window, a document, or a program. Icons are most often used on the desktop. (p. 617)

Insertion point The place in a document where something will be added, represented by a blinking vertical bar. (p. 13)

J

Justification How text is aligned at the ends of the lines. The default in WordPerfect is Left Justification (text is aligned at the left margin). Other choices are Full Justification (both the left and the right sides are justified), Center Justification (all lines are centered), and Right Justification (meaning the left margin is ragged and the right margin is even). (p. 127)

K

Kerning Adjusting the space between individual pairs of letters to make the text more visually appealing. (p. 614)

Key A criterion for sorting order when working with WordPerfect Sort. (p. 314)

Keyboard merge To merge a form document with no data source, you key the variable information into the document as the merge progresses. A KEYBOARD code tells WordPerfect to stop for you to key the required information. (p. 284)

Kilobyte A unit of storage consisting of 1,024 bytes. (p. 607)

L

Landscape Page orientation where the long edges of the paper are at the top and bottom of the page and the short edges are at the sides. (p. 247)

Leaders Dots (periods) that direct (lead) your attention from one column of a line of text to another. (p. 35)

Leading A term used in page layout that refers to varying the amount of space between lines of type. In early years of printing, measured strips of lead were inserted between the rows of type when pages were laid out. (p. 614)

Line spacing The vertical distance between two lines of type, measured from baseline to baseline. (p. 125)

List box A box that contains a list of choices, typically in a dialog box. When a list is too long to be completely displayed, it will have a scroll bar so you can view additional choices. (p. 599)

M

Macro A collection of keystrokes that are accumulated because they are used together frequently. Macros are used to simplify and automate repeated sets of commands. (p. 252)

Macro chaining Adding the command to start one macro to the end of another macro so that when the first macro is finished, the second macro will run. (p. 259)

Masthead The large title and date section at the top of a newspaper or newsletter identifying the document, the volume or edition, and the date. Publishers use the same layout for the masthead with each edition so the reader feels comfortable with the look of the publication. (p. 512)

Megabyte A unit of computer storage consisting of 1,024 kilobytes or 1,048,576 bytes. (p. 607)

Menu A list of choices. (p. 592)

Menu Bar The list of menus across the top of the WordPerfect window from which you can choose WordPerfect features. (p. 592)

Merge code A code used to organize the text appropriately when two files are combined. Merge (sometimes called mail merge) is most useful for repetitive documents, such as in combining the names and addresses in a mailing list with a standard letter. (p. 273)

Mnemonics Related letters used to simplify commands, like *b* for *bold* or *u* for *underline*. In WordPerfect menus, choices may be made by keying the underlined mnemonic letter.

Modem A device that transmits digital information over telephone lines. Modem is short for *modulator/demodulator*. (p. 602)

Monospaced Spacing in which each character takes up the same amount of space horizontally, regardless of the size of the letter. Courier 10cpi is a monospaced font. (p. 615)

N

Named macro A macro that has a specific name. When a named macro is to be used in WordPerfect, the command to start the macro is given, and the name of the macro must be keyed. (p. 254)

Network A configuration of computers cabled together with one workstation designated as the file server. In a networked environment WordPerfect frequently is loaded on the file server only, and individual workstations access the program from the file server as needed. (p. 588)

No-print zone An area around the outside edges of a sheet of paper where the printer is incapable of printing. The size of the no-print zone varies according to the manufacturer or model of printer. (p. 130)

O

Option A choice in a dialog box. (p. 296)

Orphan The last line of a paragraph that appears by itself at the top of a page of text. (p. 146)

OS/2 An operating system utilizing the graphical user interface which allows a user to have several documents or programs available at any one time and to move easily from one to another without having to exit from a program.

P

Page break An instruction to the printer to start a new page. A *soft page break* is inserted by WordPerfect when a page is full. A *hard page break* is inserted wherever necessary by pressing Ctrl+Enter. (p. 69)

Page orientation The way a page is oriented in relation to the printing on it. When the paper is vertical, it is said to be in *portrait orientation*. When the page is horizontal, the orientation is referred to as *landscape*. (p. 247)

Paste To insert text that has been copied or cut from a different location in your document into place at the location of the insertion point. (p. 84)

Path The route or address for a file. The path includes the drive, the main folder, and any folder within the main folder. (p. 18)

Point size The vertical size of a character of type. A 72-pt. character would be approximately an inch tall. A 12-pt. character would be approximately a sixth of an inch tall. The greater the number of points, the taller the letter. (p. 614)

Pointing Using the mouse to move the pointer in the window. Normally, when you have positioned the pointer at the desired location, either the left or right mouse button is used to position the insertion point or make menu choices. (pp. 609-610)

Pop-up list A list of options that appears when a pop-up button is selected. Most pop-up buttons have double arrows or triangles on them. (p. 587)

Portrait The page orientation where the short edges of the paper are at the top and bottom of the page and the long edges are at the sides. (p. 247)

Printer driver The software file that enables a program to communicate with the printer. In WordPerfect, the printer drivers are identified by a *.prs* file extension. (p. 7)

Proportional The method of printing where each printed character takes up only the width it needs, rather than a fixed amount of space. In proportional spacing, for example, a *w* would take considerably more width than would an *I*. (p. 615)

Q

QuickCorrect This feature automatically replaces certain text with other specified text. It will also correct errors and capitalization and can be used to correct predetermined keying and spelling errors. (p. 91)

QuickMenu Context-sensitive menus that appear when you click the right mouse button. (p. 85)

QuickSelect Selecting words, sentences, or paragraphs by double, triple, or quadruple clicking text. (p. 19)

QuickWords Abbreviations set up by the user that expand into complete text. (p. 163)

R

Radio buttons The round option buttons in dialog boxes. Usually only one radio button may be selected at a time. (p. 594)

RAM (Random Access Memory) The temporary storage area or working space for the document you are creating and the program you are using. This storage area is emptied if the computer is turned off or if the electricity supplying it is interrupted. (p. 587)

Record All of the information about a particular customer, client, or product in a data file. It is the complete collection of data about that individual. Records usually are separated by an ENDRECORD code and a Hard Page code. (p. 273)

Redline A feature that enables you to mark text suggested for addition to a document. Text marked with Redline is printed with a shaded background. (p. 395)

Relative tab Tabs set in relation to the left margin; that is, if you change the left margin, the tab will not remain in the original position but will move in relationship to the new margin. (p. 131)

Resident fonts Fonts that are built into the microcircuitry of your printer so you don't have to create the fonts or download them from your hard drive. (p. 615)

S

Sans serif Type without serifs. Letters have no feet, or curves, at the ends of the main strokes. Sans serif type is contrasted with serif type. Sans serif type is best used for headlines and text to which you wish to call attention. (p. 614)

Save (a document) Transferring a document from the memory of the computer to a disk so that it is available at some future time. (p. 4)

Scanning Using a scanner to convert a document on hard copy into a digital image. (p. 364)

Scroll bar The bars on the right side or bottom of the window that provide a tool for moving vertically and/or horizontally through a document or a list. You can move by clicking on the scroll arrows or by dragging the scroll box. (p. 104)

Scrolling Moving through text or a list box using the arrow keys, the Home key together with the arrow keys, the Page Up and Page Down keys, or the scroll bar. (p. 3)

Selected In word processing, a section of text that has been blocked or highlighted. You might select text to be moved, copied, or deleted. You might also select text to add a special kind of formatting, like bold, underline, or a new font. (p. 19)

Serif The feet, or curves, at the ends of the main strokes of letters. Serif type is contrasted with sans serif type where there are no feet, or curves, on the letters. Serif type is easy to read in body text. (p. 614)

Size To change the size of an object by dragging the sizing handles that appear when an object is selected. (p. 349)

Skewing Changing the slant or angle of text or objects. (p. 215)

Soft page break A page break that is automatically inserted by WordPerfect when a page is full. (p. 37)

Spreadsheet Columns and rows forming a grid that contains data, labels, or formulas. Spreadsheets are often used for calculations and accounting purposes. (p. 199)

Strikeout A feature that enables you to mark text suggested for deletion from a document. Text marked with Strikeout is printed with a line drawn through it. (p. 395)

Style A master format for a particular kind of document or document part in WordPerfect. Styles are collections of keystrokes and menu choices to speed up the formatting of documents when the same formats are used repeatedly. (p. 438)

Subdocuments The term used when working with the Master Document feature to describe the individual documents that are to be combined to make up the master document. (p. 465)

Subscript   The term used to refer to the position of a character that is printed below the normal line of writing (the baseline). An example is the 2 in H_2O. (p. 75)

Superscript   The term used to refer to the position of a character that is printed above the normal line of writing. An example is the 2 in x^2. (p. 75)

Suppress   A feature that tells WordPerfect not to include the header, footer, or page number on a specific page of a document. (p. 145)

T

Template   A master format for a particular kind of document in WordPerfect, or a document part in other brands of word processing software. (p. 50)

Tile   To display more than one document in separate windows at the same time. (p. 106)

Toggle key   A key on the keyboard that you press once to turn on and again to turn off. Examples are the Caps Lock and Insert keys. (p. 105)

Typeface   One design of type. A typeface has a name, like Arial, Arrus, Times New Roman, and Univers. It includes all characters of all sizes in the matching design. (p. 614)

U

URL (Uniform Resource Locator)   An address code for finding hypertext or hypermedia documents on World Wide Web (WWW) servers around the world.

V

Variable-pitch font   A font that varies the amount of space used by each character. It is another name for a proportional font. (p. 615)

VDT   (Video Display Terminal) The screen or monitor of the computer. It is on the VDT that you can watch your work with the computer. (p. 587)

W

Widow   A widow is the first line of a paragraph that appears by itself at the bottom of a page. (p. 146)

Wild card   A character used to replace one character (?) or a series of characters (*) in a search string. (p. 80)

Window   The area where you key a document when using a graphical user interface. (p. 589)

Windows   An operating system utilizing the graphical user interface which allows a user to have several documents or programs available at any one time and to move easily from one to another without having to exit from a program. (p. 106)

Word Wrap   The feature that causes a word that doesn't fit at the end of one line to drop to the beginning of the next line. (p. 3)

WYSIWYG   Acronym for What You See Is What You Get. In a WYSIWYG interface the printed copy will look like what is showing in the window.

Z

Zoom   To expand or reduce the size of a document or an image in the window. (p. 6)

NOTE: Some of the terms in this Glossary are terms used when discussing computerized production of documents, but are not used in this text.

FEATURE	MENU CHOICE	KEYBOARD	LESSON
Address Book	Tools	—	18, 25
Advance	Format, Typesetting	—	11
All Justification	Format, Justification (Property Bar)	—	9
Application Bar	—	—	1, Appendix B
Balanced Newspaper Columns	Format, Columns (Toolbar)	—	14
Block Protect	Format, Keep Text Together	—	12
Bold	Format, Font (Property Bar)	Ctrl+B or F9	3
Booklet Printing	File, Print, Two-Sided Printing	Ctrl+P	24
Bookmark	Tools, Bookmark	—	12
Bulleted List	Insert, Outline/Bullets & Numbering	—	5
Bullets & Numbers	Insert	Ctrl+Shift+B	5
Caps Lock	—	Caps Lock	3
Cascade Windows	Window, Cascade	—	8
Center	Format, Line	Shift+F7	3
Center Justification	Format, Justification (Property Bar)	Ctrl+E	9
Center Page(s)	Format, Page	—	5
Chart	Insert, Graphics, Chart	—	29
Close	File	Ctrl+F4	1, Appendix B
Column Border	Format, Columns Border/Fill	—	23
Columns	Format, Columns (Toolbar)	—	14
Comment	Insert, Comment	—	12
Compare	File, Document	—	24
Condense Master	File, Document	—	28
Convert Case	Edit	Ctrl+K	3
Copy	Edit (Toolbar)	Ctrl+C	6
Copy Files	File, Open (Toolbar)	Ctrl+O	4
Create Data File	Tools, Merge, Data File	Shift+F9	17
Create Folder	File, Open	Ctrl+O	8
Create Form Document	Tools, Merge, Form	Shift+F9	17
Current Document Style	File, Document	—	11
Cut	Edit (Toolbar)	Ctrl+X	6
Dash (em dash)	—	---	5
Data Source, Create	Tools, Merge, Data Source	Shift+F9	17

FEATURE	MENU CHOICE	KEYBOARD	LESSON
Date Code		Ctrl+Shift+D	5
Date Text	Insert, Date/Time	Ctrl+D	5
Default Font	File, Document	—	11
Define Index	Tools, Reference, Index	—	27
Define T. of Auth.	Tools, Reference, T. of Auth.	—	28
Define T. of Cont.	Tools, Reference, T. of Cont.	—	27
Delay Codes	Format, Page	—	27
Delete Line	—	Ctrl+Delete	2
Delete Word	—	Ctrl+Backspace	2
Divide Page	Format, Page, Page Setup	—	15
Document Assembly	Tools, Merge, Merge	Shift+F9	18
Dot Leaders	—	Alt+F7, Alt+F7	3
Double Indent	Format, Paragraph	Ctrl+Shift+F7	5
Draft View	View, Draft	Ctrl+F5	1
Drag and Drop	—	—	6
Draw	Insert, Graphics, Draw Picture	—	29
Drop Cap	Format, Paragraph	Ctrl+Shift+C	24
Em Dash	—	---	5
ENDFIELD Code	Tools, Merge, Data Source	Alt+Enter	17
ENDFOR Code	Tools, Merge, Form	—	20
ENDIF Code	Tools, Merge, Form	—	19
Endnote	Insert, Footnote/Endnote	—	10
ENDRECORD Code	Tools, Merge, Data Source	Ctrl+Shift+Enter	17
Envelope (Merge)	Tools, Merge, Merge	—	17
Envelope (Single)	Format, Envelope	—	3
Equations	Insert, Equation	—	24
Exit	File	Alt+F4	1, Appendix B
Expand Master	File, Document	—	28
Extract	Tools, Sort	Alt+F9	19
Favorites	File, Open (Toolbar)	F4 or Ctrl+O	4
Field Names	Tools, Merge, Data Source	—	17
Fill	Format, Page or Paragraph, Border/Fill	—	23
Find	Edit, Find	F2 or Ctrl+F	6
Flush Right	Format, Line	Alt+F7	3
Font Face	Format, Font (Property Bar)	F9	3
Font Size	Format, Font (Property Bar)	F9	3

FEATURE	MENU CHOICE	KEYBOARD	LESSON
Footers	Insert, Header/Footer	—	10
Footnote	Insert, Footnote/Endnote	—	10
Form Document, Create	Tools, Merge, Form	Shift+F9	17
FORNEXT Code	Tools, Merge, Form	—	20
Full Justification	Format, Justification (Property Bar)	Ctrl+J	9
Full Page Zoom	View (Toolbar)	—	1
Generate	Tools	Ctrl+F9	27, 28
Go To	Edit	Ctrl+G	2
GO(label) Code	Tools, Merge, Form	—	20
Grammatik	Tools	Alt+Shift+F1	7
Graphics Box	Insert, Image	F11	21
Graphics Line, Custom	Insert, Line, Custom Line	—	23
Group Graphics Boxes	Quick Menu or Property Bar	—	22
Hanging Indent	Format, Paragraph	Ctrl+F7	5
Hard Page Break	Insert, New Page	Ctrl+Enter	5
Hard Space	Format, Line, Other Codes	Ctrl+Space Bar	5
Headers	Insert, Header/Footer	—	10
Help	Help, Help Topics	F1	Appendix B
Highlight	Tools (Toolbar)	—	6
Horizontal Line	Insert, Line, Horizontal Line	Ctrl+F11	23
Hypertext	Tools, Reference	—	28
Hyphen Character	Format, Line, Other Codes	Ctrl+–	5
Hyphenation	Tools, Language, Hyphenation	—	14
IFNOTBLANK Code	Tools, Merge, Form	—	18
Image Tools	(QuickMenu)	—	22
Images, Draw	Insert, Graphics, Draw Picture	—	29
Images, Edit	Insert, Graphics, Draw Picture	—	29
Indent	Format, Paragraph	F7	5
Insert	—	Insert	2
Insert File	Insert, File	—	2
Insert Image	Insert, Graphics, Clipart	—	21
Internet Publisher	File, Internet Publisher	—	26, 30
Italic	Format, Font (Property Bar)	Ctrl+I or F9	3
Justification	Format, Justification	—	9
KEYBOARD Code	Tools, Merge, Form	—	17
Keyboard Map	Tools, Settings, Customize	—	30

FEATURE	MENU CHOICE	KEYBOARD	LESSON
LABEL(label)	Tools, Merge, Form	—	20
Labels, Create	Format, Labels	—	20
Landscape Orientation	Format, Page, Page Setup	—	15
Left Justification	Format, Justification (Property Bar)	Ctrl+L	9
Line Numbering	Format, Line	—	24
Line Spacing	Format, Line (Property Bar)	—	9
Lists	Tools, Reference	—	27
Macro, Edit	Tools, Macro	—	16
Macro, Play	Tools, Macro	Alt+F10	16
Macro, Record	Tools, Macro	Ctrl+F10	16
Make It Fit	Format	—	11
Margins	Format, Margins	Ctrl+F8	9
Master Document	File, Document	—	28
Merge	Tools, Merge, Merge	Shift+F9	4, 17
Move Files	File, Open (Toolbar)	Ctrl+O	4
Name Badges	Format, Labels	—	20
New Blank Page	(Toolbar)	Ctrl+N	6
New Page Number	Format, Page, Numbering	—	10
Newspaper Columns	Format, Columns (Toolbar)	—	14
NEXTRECORD Code	Tools, Merge, Form	—	20
Open	File (Toolbar)	F4 or Ctrl+O	1, Appendix B
Open as Copy	File, Open	Ctrl+O	8
Orientation	Format, Page, Page Setup	—	15
Outline/Bullets & Numbering	Insert	—	5
Page Border	Format, Page, Border/Fill	—	23
Page Break	Insert, New Page	Ctrl+Enter	5
Page Numbering	Format, Page, Numbering	—	10
Page Size	Format, Page, Page Setup	—	15
Page View	View, Page	Alt+F5	1
Paragraph Border	Format, Paragraph, Border/Fill	—	23
Paste	Edit (Toolbar)	Ctrl+V	6
Path and Filename	Insert, Other	—	2
PerfectExpert	Help (Toolbar)	—	26
Portrait Orientation	Format, Page, Page Size	—	15
POSTNET Bar Code	Tools, Merge, Merge	Shift+F9	18
Print	File (Toolbar)	Ctrl+P	1
Print Preview	File, Print Preview	—	1

FEATURE	MENU CHOICE	KEYBOARD	LESSON
Prompt-As-You-Go	(Property Bar)	—	7
Property Bar	View	—	8, Appendix B
Proofreaders' Marks	—	—	4
QuickCorrect	Tools	—	7
QuickFinder	File, Open	Ctrl+O	12
QuickFormat	Format, QuickFormat (Toolbar)	—	11
QuickMark, Find	Tools, Bookmark	Ctrl+Q	12
QuickMark, Insert	Tools, Bookmark	Ctrl+Shift+Q	12
QuickMenu	—	—	6, Appendix B
QuickWords	Tools	—	11
Redline	Format, Font	F9	24
Redo	Edit (Toolbar)	Ctrl+Shift+Z	2
Reference	Tools	—	27
Replace	Edit, Replace	F2	6
Reveal Codes	View	Alt+F3	2
Right Justification	Format, Justification (Property Bar)	Ctrl+R	9
Ruler	View, Ruler	Alt+Shift+F3	9
Save	File	Shift+F3, Ctrl+S	1, Appendix B
Select All	Edit, Select	Ctrl+A	15
Select Records	Tools, Merge, Merge	Shift+F9	19
Select Text	Edit, Select	F8	2
Settings	Tools, Settings	—	16, Appendix B
Shadow Pointer	(Application Bar)	—	11
Shapes	Insert	—	29
Soft Hyphen	Format, Line, Other Codes	Ctrl+Shift+−	14
Soft Page Break	Automatic	—	3, 5
Sort	Tools, Sort	Alt+F9	19
Spell Check	Tools (Toolbar)	Ctrl+F1	7
Spell-As-You-Go	Tools (Property Bar)	Alt+Ctrl+F1	7
Strikeout	Format, Font	F9	24
Styles	Format, Styles	Alt+F8	26
Subscript	Format, Font	F9	5
Superscript	Format, Font	F9	5
Suppress	Format, Page	—	10
Symbols	Insert	Ctrl+W	11
Tab	—	Tab	3

FEATURE	MENU CHOICE	KEYBOARD	LESSON
Tab Set	Format, Line (Ruler)	—	9
Table, Create	Table, Create (Toolbar)	—	13
Table of Authorities	Tools, Reference, T. of Auth.	—	28
Table of Contents	Tools, Reference, T. of Cont.	—	27
Templates	File, New	Ctrl+T	26
TextArt	Insert, Graphics, TextArt	—	24
Thesaurus	Tools	Alt+F1	7
Tile Windows	Window, Tile	—	8
Toolbar	View, Toolbars	—	8, Appendix B
Two Pages View	View, Two Pages	—	1
Typeover	—	Insert	2
Underline	Format, Font (Property Bar)	Ctrl+U or F9	3
Underline Tabs	Format, Font	F9	15
Undo	Edit (Toolbar)	Ctrl+Z	3
Vertical Line	Insert, Line, Vertical Line	Ctrl+Shift+F11	23
View Page	View	Alt+F5	1
Watermark	Insert, Watermark	—	10
Web Page	File, New from Project or File, Internet Publisher	—	30
Widow/Orphan	Format, Keep Text Together	—	10
Zoom	View (Toolbar)	—	1